Portrait of Caesar, Turin, Museo Archeologico. Photo Deutsches Archäologisches Institut, Rome.

BLACKWELL COMPANIONS TO THE ANCIENT WORLD

This series provides sophisticated and authoritative overviews of periods of ancient history, genres of classical literature, and the most important themes in ancient culture. Each volume comprises between twenty-five and forty concise essays written by individual scholars within their area of specialization. The essays are written in a clear, provocative, and lively manner, designed for an international audience of scholars, students, and general readers.

ANCIENT HISTORY

A Companion to the Roman Army
Edited by Paul Erdkamp

A Companion to the Roman Republic
Edited by Nathan Rosenstein and Robert Morstein-Marx

A Companion to the Roman Empire
Edited by David S. Potter

A Companion to the Classical Greek World
Edited by Konrad H. Kinzl

A Companion to the Ancient Near East
Edited by Daniel C. Snell

A Companion to the Hellenistic World
Edited by Andrew Erskine

A Companion to Late Antiquity
Edited by Philip Rousseau

A Companion to Archaic Greece
Edited by Kurt A. Raaflaub and Hans van Wees

A Companion to Julius Caesar
Edited by Miriam Griffin

A Companion to Ancient History
Edited by Andrew Erskine

LITERATURE AND CULTURE

A Companion to Classical Receptions
Edited by Lorna Hardwick and Christopher Stray

A Companion to Greek and Roman Historiography
Edited by John Marincola

A Companion to Catullus
Edited by Marilyn B. Skinner

A Companion to Roman Religion
Edited by Jörg Rüpke

A Companion to Greek Religion
Edited by Daniel Ogden

A Companion to the Classical Tradition
Edited by Craig W. Kallendorf

A Companion to Roman Rhetoric
Edited by William Dominik and Jon Hall

A Companion to Greek Rhetoric
Edited by Ian Worthington

A Companion to Ancient Epic
Edited by John Miles Foley

A Companion to Greek Tragedy
Edited by Justina Gregory

A Companion to Latin Literature
Edited by Stephen Harrison

A Companion to Ovid
Edited by Peter E. Knox

A Companion to Greek and Roman Political Thought
Edited by Ryan K. Balot

A COMPANION TO JULIUS CAESAR

Edited by

Miriam Griffin

WILEY-BLACKWELL
A John Wiley & Sons, Ltd., Publication

This edition first published 2009

Blackwell Publishing was acquired by John Wiley & Sons in February 2007. Blackwell's publishing program has been merged with Wiley's global Scientific, Technical, and Medical business to form Wiley-Blackwell.

Registered Office
John Wiley & Sons Ltd, The Atrium, Southern Gate, Chichester, West Sussex, PO19 8SQ, United Kingdom

Editorial Offices
350 Main Street, Malden, MA 02148-5020, USA
9600 Garsington Road, Oxford, OX4 2DQ, UK
The Atrium, Southern Gate, Chichester, West Sussex, PO19 8SQ, UK

For details of our global editorial offices, for customer services, and for information about how to apply for permission to reuse the copyright material in this book please see our website at www.wiley.com/wiley-blackwell.

Library of Congress Cataloging-in-Publication Data

A companion to Julius Caesar/edited by Miriam Griffin.
p. cm. – (Blackwell companions to the ancient world)
Includes bibliographical references and index.
ISBN 978-1-4051-4923-5 (hardcover : alk. paper) 1. Caesar, Julius. 2. Generals–Rome–Biography. 3. Heads of state–Rome–Biography. 4. Rome–History–Republic, 265–30 B.C. I. Griffin, Miriam T. (Miriam Tamara)

DG261.C76 2009
937'.02092–dc22
[B]

2008046983

A catalogue record for this book is available from the British Library.

Set in 10/12.5 pt Galliard by SPi Publisher Services, Pondicherry, India
Printed in the United Kingdom

01 2009

Contents

List of Figures

Notes on Contributors

Ernst Badian, FBA, John Moors Cabot Professor of History, Emeritus, Harvard, was born in Vienna and educated in New Zealand and at University College, Oxford. He was a Professor at Leeds and at Buffalo, before his appointment to Harvard (1971–98). His publications include *Foreign Clientelae (264–70BC)*, 1958; *Studies in Greek and Roman History*, 1964; *Roman Imperialism in the Late Republic*, 1967 (revised and enlarged as *Römischer Imperialismus in der Späten Republik*, 1980); *Publicans and Sinners*, 1972 (translated into German and augmented as *Zöllner und Sünder*, 1997); *From Plataea to Potidaea*, 1993; and numerous contributions to the *Oxford Classical Dictionary* and to journals.

Timothy Barnes was educated at Balliol College, Oxford and held a Junior Research Fellowship at the Queen's College. He taught in the Department of Classics at the University of Toronto from 1970 to 2007, and was elected a Fellow of the Royal Society of Canada in 1985. He won the Conington Prize at Oxford for his first book, *Tertullian: A Historical and Literary Study* (1971) (2nd edition, with postscript, 1985). His major publications since then have been *The Sources of the Historia Augusta* (1978), *Constantine and Eusebius* (1981), *The New Empire of Diocletian and Constantine* (1982), *Athanasius and Constantius: Theology and Politics in the Constantinian Empire* (1993) and *Ammianus Marcellinus and the Representation of Historical Reality* (1998). He now lives in Edinburgh and is attached to the University of Edinburgh.

Thomas Biskup is Research Councils UK Fellow and Lecturer in Enlightenment History at the University of Hull. He gained his PhD at the University of Cambridge in 2001, and was Mary Somerville Research Fellow at the University of Oxford from 2001 to 2004. His main research interests are the cultural history of European monarchy and courts in the early modern and modern eras and natural history in eighteenth-century England and Germany. Recent publications include: 'German court and French Revolution: Émigrés in Brunswick around 1800', in *Francia*, 33 (2007); 'A University for Empire? The University of

Göttingen and the Personal Union, 1737–1837', in Brendan Simms and Torsten Riotte (eds.), *The Hanoverian Dimension in British History, 1714–1837* (Cambridge, 2007); 'Napoleon's second Sacre? Iéna and the ceremonial translation of Frederick the Great's insignia in 1807', in Alan Forrest and Peter H. Wilson (eds.), *The Bee and the Eagle: Napoleonic France and the End of the Holy Roman Empire* (Basingstoke, 2008); and (co-edited with Marc Schalenberg), *Selling Berlin: Imagebildung und Stadtmarketing von der preußischen Residenz bis zur Bundeshauptstadt* (Stuttgart, 2008).

Luciano Canfora studied at the University of Bari and at the Scuola Normale of Pisa. He is currently Professor of Classical Philology at the University of Bari. He is chief editor of the journal *Quaderni di Storia* (1975–) and of the series "La città antica" (published by Sellerio, Palermo). In 2000 he was awarded the Gold Medal of the President of the Italian Republic for cultural merits, and in 2005 he received the Golden Honour Cross of the Hellenic Republic. Among his publications are: *Conservazione e perdita dei classici* (Padua: Antenore 1974); *Cultura classica e crisi tedesca. Gli scritti politici di Wilamowitz 1914–31* (Bari: De Donato 1977); *Ideologie del classicismo* (Turin: Einaudi, 1980); *Studi di storia della storiografia romana* (Bari: Edipuglia, 1993; *Il copista come autore* (Palermo: Sellerio, 2002); *Il papiro di Dongo* (Milan: Adelphi, 2005); *Democracy in Europe: A History of an Ideology* (Oxford: Blackwell 2006); *Julius Caesar: The People's Dictator* (Edinburgh: Edinburgh University Press, 2007); *Filologia e libertà* (Milan, Mondadori, 2008); and *Exporter la liberté. Échec d'un mythe* (Paris: Desjonquères, 2008).

Carol Clark studied at Somerville College, Oxford and Westfield College, London. She then taught in London, in West Africa and at Glasgow University before being elected to Balliol College, Oxford, where she remained for many years as Fellow and Tutor in Modern Languages. She has published books and articles on Rabelais and Montaigne and translations from Baudelaire, Rostand and Proust.

Ronald Cluett holds a Ph.D. in Classics from Princeton University. From 1992 until 2004 he held a joint position in Classics and History at Pomona College in Claremont, California. He has published on ancient numismatics and Roman women as well as on the Continuators. He is currently completing his J.D. at the Georgetown University Law Center, where he has been surprised to discover numerous structural and stylistic similarities between the *Iliad* and the United States Internal Revenue Code.

Nicholas Cole is currently a Junior Research Fellow in History at St. Peter's College, Oxford. He read Ancient and Modern History at University College, Oxford, where he also completed his MPhil in Greek and Roman History and his doctorate. His particular interests are the influence of classical political thought on America's first politicians, and the search for a new 'science of politics' in post-Independence America. He has been a Visiting Fellow at the International Center for Jefferson Studies at Monticello. His book, *The Ancient World in Jefferson's America*, will be published by Oxford University Press.

Elaine Fantham took her degrees at Oxford and Liverpool and taught at St. Andrews University before emigrating in 1966. She has taught at the University of Toronto (1968–86) and Princeton University (1986–2000) and is now Giger Professor of Latin Emeritus. She has published commentaries on Seneca's *Troades*, Lucan *BC* II and Ovid

Fasti IV, and monographs including *Roman Literary Culture* (1996) and *The Roman World of Cicero's De Oratore* (2004). She is editor and contributor to the conference volume *Caesar against Liberty?* (Proceedings of the Langford Seminar, 2005), reviewing Roman perspectives on Caesar's autocracy.

Jane F. Gardner is Emeritus Professor of Ancient History, School of Humanities, University of Reading, UK. Her publications include two in the Penguin Classics series, *Caesar: The Civil War* (1967) and a revision of S. A. Handford's *Caesar: The Gallic War* (1951, rev. 1982), and three monographs on Roman legal and social history, *Women in Roman Law and Society* (1986), *Being a Roman Citizen* (1993) and *Family and* Familia *in Roman Law and Life* (1998).

Julia Griffin studied Classics and then English at Oxford and Cambridge Universities and is Associate Professor of English at Georgia Southern University. She has published on various Renaissance authors, and is particularly interested in later uses of the classical writers. Among her publications is *Selected Poems of Abraham Cowley, Edmund Waller and John Oldham* (London: Penguin Classics, 1998).

Miriam Griffin is Emeritus Fellow in Ancient History of Somerville College, Oxford. She is the author of *Seneca: a Philosopher in Politics* (Oxford: Clarendon Press, 1976; reissued with Postscript, 1992), of *Nero: the End of a Dynasty* (London: Batsford, and New Haven, CT: Yale University Press, 1984), and (with E. M. Atkins) of *Cicero: On Duties* (Cambridge: Cambridge University Press, 1991). She is currently working on a study of Seneca's *De Beneficiis.*

Erich S. Gruen is Gladys Rehard Wood Professor of History and Classics Emeritus at the University of California, Berkeley. His research has been primarily in the Roman Republic, Hellenistic history, and the Jews in the Greco-Roman world. His books include *The Last Generation of the Roman Republic* (1974), *The Hellenistic World and the Coming of Rome* (1984), *Culture and Identity in Republican Rome* (1992), *Heritage and Hellenism* (1998), and *Diaspora: Jews Amidst Greeks and Romans* (2002). His current project is a study of Greek and Roman perceptions and representations of the "Other."

Christina S. Kraus taught at New York University, University College London, and Oxford before moving to Yale. She works on Roman historiographical narrative, and has published studies on Caesar, Sallust, Livy, and Tacitus. She is currently writing a commentary, with A. J. Woodman, on Tacitus, *Agricola.*

Matthew Leigh is Professor of Classical Languages and Literature at Oxford University and a Tutorial Fellow of St. Anne's College, Oxford. He is the author of *Lucan: Spectacle and Engagement* (Oxford, 1997) and *Comedy and the Rise of Rome* (Oxford, 2004).

Barbara Levick, Emeritus Fellow and Tutor in Literae Humaniores at St. Hilda's College, Oxford, is the author of *Tiberius the Politician* (1976), *Claudius* (1990), *Vespasian* (1999), and *Julia Domna: Syrian Empress* (2007), and is co-editor with Richard Hawley of *Women in Antiquity: New Assessments* (1995). She is working on a book about Augustus.

Andrew Lintott is now retired, after teaching first Classics, then Ancient History, successively at King's College London, Aberdeen University, and Worcester College, Oxford. He has published *Violence in Republican Rome*, *Violence, Civil Strife, and Revolution in the Classical City*, *Judicial Reform and Land Reform in the Roman Republic*, *Imperium Romanum: Politics and Administration*, and *The Constitution of the Roman Republic*, and, most recently, *Cicero as Evidence: a Historian's Companion*.

Martin McLaughlin is Fiat-Serena Professor of Italian Studies and Fellow of Magdalen College, Oxford. Recent publications in the area of Renaissance studies include *Literary Imitation in the Italian Renaissance* (Oxford University Press, 1995) and chapters in *Mapping Lives: The Uses of Biography*, ed. Peter France and William St. Clair (Oxford University Press, 2002), and *The Cambridge History of Literary Criticism*, vol. II: *The Middle Ages*, ed. Alastair Minnis and Ian Johnson (Cambridge University Press, 2005). He also co-edited (with Zygmunt G. Baranski) *Italy's Three Crowns:. Reading Dante, Petrarch, and Boccaccio* (Oxford: Bodleian Library, 2007), and (with Letizia Panizza) *Petrarch in Britain: Interpreters, Imitators and Translators over 700 Years* (Oxford University Press, 2007; Proceedings of the British Academy, vol. 146).

Claude Nicolet was born in Marseilles. He studied at the École Normale Supérieure de la rue d'Ulm from 1950 to 1954, becoming Agrégé in History in 1954. He was attached to the cabinet of P. Mendès France, Minister of State, in 1956, and served as editor-in-chief of the *Cahiers de la République* in 1956–7 and 1961–3. He was Professor of Ancient History at the University of Paris (1969–96). He served as Directeur de l'École Française de Rome from 1992 to 1996 and was an advisor to J. P. Chevènement, Minister of National Education (1984), of Defence (1992), and the Interior (1996). He is Membre de l'Institut (Académie des inscriptions et Belles Lettres) and a Member of the British Academy. Among his publications are: *L'Ordre équestre à l'époque républicaine (312–43 av. J.-C.)*, De Boccard vols. I (1966) and II (1974); *The World of the Citizen in Republican Rome*, trans. by P. S. Fallu from the 1976 French edition (London: Batsford, 1980); *L'Idée Républicaine en France. Essai d'Histoire critique (1789–1924)* (Paris: Gallimard, 1982); and *Inventaire du Monde*, (Paris: Fayard, 1988).

Jeremy Paterson is Senior Lecturer in Ancient History at Newcastle University. He is a social and economic historian of the ancient world with wide interests in the political life of the Republic and Early Empire. He recently edited *Cicero the Advocate* (2004) with Jonathan Powell and discussed the creation of Roman Imperial Court society in A. J. S. Spawforth (ed.), *The Court and Court Society in Ancient Monarchies* (2007). He is currently working on a study of early Christian reactions to Roman power.

Christopher Pelling is Regius Professor of Greek at Oxford University. He has worked extensively on Greek and Roman historical writing, especially Greek accounts of Roman history, and his books include a commentary on Plutarch, *Life of Antony* (Cambridge, 1988), *Literary Texts and the Greek Historian* (Routledge, 2000), and *Plutarch and History* (Classical Press of Wales, 2002). He is currently writing a commentary on Plutarch, *Life of Caesar*.

Luke Pitcher is Lecturer in the Department of Classics and Ancient History at Durham University. His published work includes articles on ancient historiography, biography, and epic, as well as commentaries on fragmentary Greek historians. He is currently completing an introduction to history writing in the classical world.

Kurt Raaflaub is David Herlihy University Professor and Professor of Classics and History and Director of the Program in Ancient Studies at Brown University. His main interests are the social, political, and intellectual history of Archaic and Classical Greece and Republican Rome, and the Comparative History of the Ancient World. Recent publications include *The Discovery of Freedom in Ancient Greece* (2004), *Social Struggles in Archaic Rome* (ed., new expanded edn. 2005), *Origins of Democracy in Ancient Greece* (co-author, 2007), *War and Peace in the Ancient World* (ed., 2007).

John T. Ramsey (MA Oxford, PhD Harvard) is Professor of Classics at the University of Illinois at Chicago. He is the author or co-author of five books and numerous articles and reviews. His specialty is Roman history and Latin prose, and in 2003 he published a commentary on Cicero's *Philippics* I & II (Cambridge University Press). He also has an interest in ancient astronomy, being co-author with the physicist A. Lewis Licht of *The Comet of 44 BC and Caesar's Funeral Games* (Oxford, 1997). Most recently he produced *A Descriptive Catalogue of Greco-Roman Comets from 500 BC to AD 400* (2006), the first ever comprehensive collection of European reports of comet sightings in antiquity.

Nathan Rosenstein is Professor of History at the Ohio State University. He is the author of *Imperatores Victi: Military Defeat and Aristocratic Competition in the Middle and Late Republic* (1990), *Rome At War: Farms, Families, and Death in the Middle Republic* (2004), various articles, and the editor (with Kurt Raaflaub) of *War and Society in the Ancient and Medieval Worlds: Asia, The Mediterranean, Europe, and Mesoamerica* (1999) and (with Robert Morstein-Marx) of *A Companion to the Roman Republic* (2006), published by Blackwell.

Catherine Steel is Professor of Classics at the University of Glasgow. She is the author of *Cicero, Rhetoric and Empire* (Oxford, 2001), *Reading Cicero* (London, 2005) and *Roman Oratory* (Cambridge, 2006).

Almut Suerbaum is Fellow and Tutor in German at Somerville College, and University Lecturer in Medieval German, at the University of Oxford. She has published on twelfth- and thirteenth-century German narrative texts, medieval women's writing, and the relationship between Latin and vernacular culture in the Middle Ages.

Mark Toher is the Frank Bailey Professor of Classics at Union College in Schenectady, New York. He is the author of articles and essays on topics in Greek and Roman history and historiography, and along with Kurt Raaflaub he co-edited *Between Republic and Empire: Interpretations of Augustus and His Principate* (Berkeley and Los Angeles, 1990). He is presently at work on an edition of the life of Augustus by Nicolaus of Damascus.

David Wardle is Professor of Classics at the University of Cape Town. His research interests lie in the areas of Roman historiography and Roman religion. He is the author of commentaries in the Clarendon Ancient History Series, *Valerius Maximus Book I* (Oxford, 1998) and *Cicero: On Divination Book I* (Oxford, 2006), and is currently working on Suetonius' presentation of Augustus.

Maria Wyke is Chair of Latin at University College London. Her research interests include gender and Roman love poetry (*The Roman Mistress: Ancient and Modern Representations*, Oxford University Press, 2002), and the reception of ancient Rome in popular culture (*Projecting the Past: Ancient Rome, Cinema and History*, Routledge, 1997). Most recently, she has investigated the reception of Julius Caesar, resulting in her monograph *Caesar: A Life in Western Culture* (Granta, 2007) and an edited collection *Julius Caesar in Western Culture* (Blackwell, 2006). She is currently preparing a further study of Caesar's reception, *Caesar in the USA: Classical Reception, Popular Culture, American Identity* (University of California Press, forthcoming).

Paul Zanker, FBA, studied at the Universities of Munich, Freiburg im Breisgau, and Rome. He was Professor of Classical Archaeology at the Universities of Göttingen (1972–6), then Munich, where he is now Professor Emeritus. From 1996 to 2002 he served as Director of the German Archaeological Institute in Rome. He is now Professor of the History of Art at the Scuola Normale Superiore di Pisa. Among his many publications are his Jerome Lectures, *The Power of Images in the Age of Augustus* (Ann Arbor, 1988), and his Sather Lectures, *The Mask of Socrates* (Berkeley, 1995).

Preface

When the idea of editing a *Companion to Julius Caesar* was first mentioned to me some years ago, I asked myself whether or not there was a need for such a book. A little reflection showed me that there was. No recent volume had treated Julius Caesar in the round, first examining him in his historical context as politician, conqueror, writer and intellectual, then treating his writings and the work of his continuators, and finally describing his subsequent reputation, first at Rome and then in European history. All of these areas were being written about, but there was as yet nothing to accommodate a reader, who, given the growing interest in reception, might wish to study Caesar's *Nachleben*, while having to hand the ancient ingredients that went into the mix.[1]

The intention has been to produce a book that, through a series of chapters written by contributors distinguished in their own very diverse areas, would attempt to do justice to Caesar's double reputation as conqueror and author, as well as to the importance of his actions and words to the thinkers and leaders of most subsequent periods of history.

The contributors have all approached the project with enthusiasm, as was demonstrated at a meeting in July 2006 of those that could attend. Many came from overseas, and the philosophy of the volume and the division of labour were discussed. Even more important was the process of collaboration between contributors that began there and has continued. We were all grateful for the support, financial and otherwise, that was offered for that meeting by Blackwell, by Somerville College, and by the Jowett Copyright Trustees of Balliol College, Oxford.

The editor of the series Al Bertrand, who was present at the meeting to answer questions, has been encouraging and helpful throughout, showing considerable

[1] Since then there has appeared M. Wyke's *Julius Caesar: A Life in Western Culture* (2007), which treats a selection of key incidents in Caesar's life: the ancient evidence and their later reception up to the present.

flexibility when faced with a rather self-willed editor. Barbara Duke, who handled the illustrations and other practical matters, has worked with great speed and good will as has Glynis Baguley, who edited the copy. The contributors have demonstrated persistent good humour and efficiency in responding to corrections and comments. I owe debts of gratitude to my husband Jasper, who translated Paul Zanker's German, to Martin McLaughlin, who saved me from several misinterpretations in the translation of Luciano Canfora's Italian, and to Julia Griffin, who gave welcome assistance with the meeting and with the preparation of the material for publication.

Reference Works: Abbreviated Titles

AClass	*Acta Classica*
AFLM	*Annali della Facoltà di Lettere e Filosofia*
AJP	*American Journal of Philology*
Anc.Soc	*Ancient Society*
ANRW	*Aufstieg und Niedergang der römischen Welt.* Berlin, 1972–
BICS	*Bulletin of the Institute of Classical Studies*
CA	*Classical Antiquity*
CJ	*Classical Journal*
CP	*Classical Philology*
CR	*Classical Review*
CW	*Classical World*
FGrH	F. Jacoby, *Die Fragmente der griechischen Historiker.* 1923–
GRBS	*Greek, Roman and Byzantine Studies*
ILLRP	A. Degrassi, *Inscriptiones Latinae Liberae Rei Publicae*, 2 vols., 2nd edn, Florence, 1963–5
ILS	H. Dessau, *Inscriptiones Latinae Selectae*
JHS	*Journal of Hellenic Studies*
JRS	*Journal of Roman Studies*
LCM	*Liverpool Classical Monthly*

LTUR	M. Steinby (ed.), *Lexicon Topographicum Urbis Romae* I–VI, Rome, 1993–2000
Mattingly	H. Mattingly, *Coins of the Roman Empire in the British Museum*, vol. III, London, 1936
MD	*Materiali e discussioni per l'analisi dei testi classici*
MH	*Museum Helveticum*
MRR	T. R. S. Broughton, *The Magistrates of the Roman Republic*. 3 vols. Atlanta, GA: Scholars Press, 1951–2, 1986
OCD	*Oxford Classical Dictionary*, 3rd edn., Oxford, 1996
OGIS	W. Dittenberger, *Orientis Graeci Inscriptiones Selectae*, Leipzig, 1903–5.
OLD	*Oxford Latin Dictionary*
ORF	Enrica Malcovati, *Oratorum Romanorum fragmenta*. In aedibus I.B. Paraviae: Aug. Taurinorum, Mediolani, Patavii, 1976.
PACA	*Proceedings of the African Classical Association*
PBSR	*Papers of the British School at Rome*
PP	*La parola del passato*
RE	A. Pauly, G. Wissowa, and W. Kroll, *Realencyclopädie des classischen Altertumswissenschaft*. 1893–
REA	*Revue des études anciennes*
REL	*Revue des études latines*
Rh.Mus.	*Rheinisches Museum für Philologie*
RIC	H. Mattingly and E. A. Sydenham, *Roman Imperial Coinage*
RRC	M. H. Crawford, *Roman Republican Coinage*, 2 vols., Cambridge, 1974.
RS	M. H. Crawford (ed.). *Roman Statutes*, vol. 1. London: Institute of Classical Studies, 1996.
SP	*Studies in Philology*
TAPA	*Transactions and Proceedings of the American Philological Association*
TLRR	M. Alexander, *Trials in the Late Roman Republic, 149 BC to 50 B.C.* Toronto, University of Toronto Press, 1990.

CHAPTER ONE

Introduction

Miriam Griffin

In recent years the direction of scholarship in ancient history has largely shifted away from an emphasis on great rulers and generals, even from a concentration on the governing class, towards the population of the city of Rome and its subject peoples, towards the social structures and the cultural attitudes current in the Roman Empire. Yet Julius Caesar is still perceived, as he always has been, as an extraordinary individual, not just another Roman consul, proconsul, imperator, or even dictator. His name has been used in various local forms – Kaiser, Czar, Tsar – as the highest title for rulers far from Rome in place and time; his account of his campaigns has been read, not only by historians and students of literature, but by rulers and generals like the Emperor Charles V, Suleiman the Magnificent, King Louis XIV, and both Napoleons, for their own instruction (Canfora, chapter 29, p. 431; Nicolet, chapter 27, pp. 411–12; 416). Biographies, of varying degrees of seriousness, still continue to be written and published, with ever-increasing frequency.

There are individuals whose lives burn through the mists of history like the path of a comet. They have, in most cases, already impressed their contemporaries as exceptional, and they have also been fortunate enough to have that strong impression transmitted by readable contemporary authors to later writers of talent. Powerful visual images, created in the lifetime of such people by gifted artists, help to establish an enduring familiarity not only with their looks but, if the artists are skillful enough, with their personalities too: one thinks of the head, immediately recognizable, of Alexander or of Nero. Such individuals often generate mysteries and controversies connected with their motives and intentions, which contribute to their enduring fascination. Finally, a violent or premature death can enhance, if not create, a haunting historical presence.

All these factors have contributed to Caesar's posthumous fame. Another crucial ingredient is his own literary work, for Caesar did not leave his immortality to chance. He was unusual among men of action whose fame endures, in being also a brilliant writer, the author of one of the few extensive accounts by a commander of his own campaigns. Ever since they first appeared, these accounts of his campaigns in Gaul and of the civil war against Pompey have been admired, even by those who have deplored Caesar's ambition and his autocracy (Clark, chapter 24; Biskup, chapter 26). Experienced generals, like Napoleon I, have always been able to criticize his military decisions (Canfora, p. 434); scholars have discovered in his version of events some misrepresentation and even mendacity. But his style, an essential element in his glory, has remained invulnerable and immortal.

Before we explore these factors further, however, it is important to acknowledge that the setting of Caesar's life in time and place also helps to explain the vitality of his reputation. Caesar may have said, as he journeyed through a small Alpine village, "I would rather be first here than second in Rome" (Plut. *Caes.* 11), but the fact is that he was first in Rome, the most powerful nation on earth, at a time when her domains and her influence were expanding at a furious pace. Rome left her permanent mark on world history, and Caesar helped her do it, paying with his life and reaping the reward of eternal fame.

The Scheme of the Volume

Though this volume is not intended to provide a history of the Late Roman Republic, the biographical chapters, narrative in Part I and thematic in Part II, will of necessity recount some very important historical events. After all, the earliest extant biographers of Caesar, Plutarch and Suetonius, acknowledged the necessity of narrating his wars, however briefly (Plut. *Alex.* 1; Suet. *Iul.* 25), and the same was true of his legislation and of his political alliances (Pelling, chapter 18, pp. 254–5; 259). But the focus of these two Parts will be on the difference which this one individual can be seen to have made to that history.

Part III forms a bridge between Caesar's life and his afterlife, discussing his own writings and their continuations by others. In these works Caesar presented to his contemporaries, and left for later readers, not only a record of his actions but also a carefully constructed portrait of himself. As Kraus (chapter 12) and Raaflaub (chapter 13) show, his intention to produce a self-standing literary work, not a mere sketch for later historians to elaborate, and his skill in putting himself in a good light, without actually lying, are now increasingly appreciated. His continuators fill out the story of his campaigns, and also – no less importantly – bear witness to the powerful influence he exercised over his officers and his men (Cluett, chapter 14, pp. 199–202).

Part IV explores Caesar's posthumous reputation among the Romans themselves, as reflected both in literature of various genres and in visual representations. Part V explores Caesar's image at certain key points in history – of necessity, a sample only. The importance of Caesar's example, as ruler and as general, continued across Europe in the early Middle Ages when his works were little read and his reputation largely depended on the popularity of Lucan's epic poem on the civil war (Suerbaum, chapter 22). From the fifteenth century on, editions and translations proliferated, giving solidity to the fascination with him as a general: in Italy his works were used to teach geography and as guides to military strategy, tactics, and technology (McLaughlin, chapter 23, pp. 350–5). At all times, approval and disapproval of Caesar could reflect contemporary political debates, not only Republicanism vs. monarchy, but also traditional vs. enlightened or reforming monarchy (Biskup, chapter 26; Nicolet, chapter 27; Cole, chapter 28). The effect of Caesar's conquests on his provincial subjects was variously estimated by the descendants of those subjects, in Germany, France, and Britain (Suerbaum, chapter 22; Clark, chapter 24; Biskup, chapter 26). Finally, the continued use of Julius Caesar and Rome in political thought and rhetoric is exemplified by the twinned analogies of the Roman empire and Julius Caesar with the United States and the American president, analogies used both by the right as a boast and by the left as a condemnation (Wyke, chapter 30).

The Contemporary Impression and its Preservation

The way in which the impression made by Caesar in life was transmitted and received in all its vividness, by later generations, is well illustrated by a passage of the Elder Pliny, writing under the Emperor Vespasian, a century after Caesar's death. In his great encyclopedia, the *Natural History*, Pliny writes:

> The most outstanding example of innate mental vigour, in my view, was Caesar the Dictator. I am not now thinking of moral excellence or steadfastness nor of a breadth of knowledge encompassing everything under the sun, but of innate mental agility and quickness, moving like fire. We are told that he used to read or write while at the same time dictating or listening, and that he would dictate to his secretaries four letters on important matters at the same time. (*HN* 7.91)

These vignettes, like the story in Suetonius (*Iul.* 56) that he composed the two volumes of his grammatical work *On Analogy* while crossing the Alps from Italy to Gaul, emanate from eyewitnesses. Indeed, Plutarch actually ascribes to Caesar's close associate Oppius his picture of the commander dictating letters on horseback, keeping at least two scribes busy at once (*Caes.* 17). There also survives, in addition to contemporary flattery, his loyal officer Hirtius' posthumous testimony to the speed with which he wrote his *commentarii* (*BG* 8. *pref.*). Suetonius claims that Caesar himself, in his Pontic triumph , displayed the words "Veni, vidi, vici," rather than the usual names of the places he had conquered, to emphasize the speed of his victory (*Iul.* 37, cf. Plut. *Caes.* 50).

The reservations of the Elder Pliny about Caesar's scholarship reflect not only the encyclopedist's admiration of Caesar's contemporary, the great scholar Terentius Varro, but also the downside of Caesar's speed and spread of interests, remarked already by contemporaries. Thus Caesar himself admitted that his style would not bear comparison with that of Cicero, who had the time to cultivate his natural talent, while Plutarch comments that Caesar was a talented political orator but came second, not first (*Caes.* 3.2–4; Pelling, chapter 18, p. 255). His contemporary, Asinius Pollio, is said to have seen signs of carelessness and inaccuracy in the *commentarii*, born both of the failure to check reports that came in and of disingenuousness, or possibly forgetfulness, in describing his own actions, and to have believed that Caesar intended to rewrite and correct them (Suet. *Iul.* 56.4). The copious and unqualified praise in Cicero's *Brutus* (261–2) of Caesar's style of oratory and of writing, so different from Cicero's own, was perhaps inspired by the Dictator's generous tribute to Cicero as the "winner of a greater laurel wreath than that of any triumph, it being a greater thing to have advanced so far the frontiers of the Roman genius than those of the Roman Empire" (Plin. *HN* 7.117; cf. Cic. *Brutus* 254).

It is important to note that this willingness to praise was a vital ingredient of Caesar's great charm and also of his ability to make people feel liked and appreciated. If his soldiers adored him for his personal attention to their deeds and their hardships, even his social equals were disarmed by his courtesy and generosity (Paterson, chapter 10, pp. 138, 139). Thus Asinius Pollio wrote, just a year after Caesar's death, "I loved him in all duty and loyalty, because in his greatness he treated me, a recent acquaintance, as though I had been one of his oldest intimates" (Cic. *Fam.* 10.31); while Cicero, who had been pardoned by Caesar in the civil war yet was allowed to resist his request for active support as Dictator, admitted after his death that, if the Republic turned out to be doomed, he would have at least enjoyed favor with Caesar, "who was not a master to run away from" (*Att.* 15.4.3). Cassius too, a year before he joined the conspirators, said "I would rather have the old easy-going master than try a new cruel one" (Cic. *Fam.* 15.19: he meant Pompey's elder son Gnaeus). Yet Cassius stabbed Caesar, and Cicero rejoiced in the result.

The poet Catullus, who was forgiven for his insulting poems when he apologized (Suet. *Iul.* 73; Steel, chapter 9, p. 118), declared in another poem his total indifference whether Caesar was "a white man or a black" (93.2). Others were more distressed by Caesar's alarming and unfathomable nature. Pliny, as we saw, was to distinguish Caesar's remarkable qualities from his moral excellence, and Pliny's description goes on to mention – not to Caesar's credit – the number of human beings he killed in battle. Yet he balances that against Caesar's eventually self-destructive clemency, and he sets against Caesar's luxurious spending on public works and games the true generosity he showed in destroying the letters from his enemies which were captured in the civil war (*HN* 7.93–4). Like his tracing of Caesar's death to his clemency (*Att.* 14.22.1), Pliny's juxtaposition of Caesar's undoubted moral qualities with his less admirable character traits goes back to assessments by Caesar's contemporaries. Cicero, comparing his political opponents, Caesar and Mark Antony, to the advantage of the former, gives this description of the dead Caesar:

> In him there was innate ability, skill in reasoning, a good memory, literary talent, industry, intelligence, and a capacity for hard work. His deeds in war, although disastrous for the commonwealth, were nonetheless great achievements. Having for many years aimed at kingship, he achieved his goal by making great efforts and taking great risks. By his shows, buildings, largesse, and banquets, he conciliated the gullible masses; his own followers he bound to himself by rewards; his enemies, by a show of clemency. (*Phil.* 2.116)

Then again, the historian Sallust, whom Caesar had appointed governor of Africa in 46 BC, singled out as the two men of outstanding character within his own memory Caesar and his enemy Cato. The qualities he picks out in Caesar are similar to those stressed by Cicero: his generosity, accessibility, willingness to forgive, and concern for others, combined with a taste for hard work and an ambition for sweeping commands in which he could win military glory (*Cat.* 53–4). Sallust's comparison, however, casts a shadow on Caesar, for the antithetical virtues of the austere and self-controlled Cato, with his unshowy integrity, suggest at the very least that certain admirable traits were missing from Caesar's character (Toher, chapter 16, pp. 225–7).

Enduring Problems in Fathoming Caesar

The difficulty of understanding that character, which was a practical problem for many of his contemporaries, contributes to the fascination which Caesar continues to exercise as a historical figure. The mystery of his intentions, and the controversies generated by that mystery, run through the essays in this volume and give them a thematic unity. But the contributors have also taken seriously the aim of Blackwell's Companions to encourage readers to enter into the debate themselves, by making liberal use of source material and by indicating areas of contention. Readers will be exposed to some very different points of view: some old, some new.

Were Caesar's early ambitions just the ordinary ones to be expected in a Roman aristocrat and member of the governing class (Badian, chapter 2; Gruen, chapter 3)? Or was he always, as Lucan, Plutarch, and Dio tend to see him (Leigh, chapter 17; Pelling, chapter 18; Pitcher, chapter 19), determined "not to bear an equal"? If so, in which direction did his ambition point – to be the equal of Alexander as a conqueror, or to be the ruler of Rome and its empire? (See Zanker, chapter 21, pp. 289–96 on the different visual representations.) As a politician, did Caesar cultivate a consistently *popularis* image down to the Dictatorship, being anti-Sullan in constitutional matters and ideologically committed to increasing the power and amenities of the people (Badian, chapter 2; Steel, chapter 9), or was he, more pragmatically, concerned to heal the wounds of civil conflict in the eighties and to prevent discontent among the subjects of Rome (Gruen, chapter 3)?

Did his charm and warmth go with a serious commitment to his friends, or was his conception of friendship a matter of opportunistic political alliances (Steel, chapter 9)? How do his intellectual projects, his interest in language, in ethnography, and in systematization in general, fit with his ambitions (Fantham, chapter 11)? Was his clemency to his opponents in the civil war a matter of opportunistic calculation, pragmatic policy, or genuine softness of heart (Paterson, chapter 10)?

Did Caesar cross the Rubicon to defend his *dignitas* and the rights of tribunes, as he says in the *Civil Wars* (1.7), or was he genuinely afraid of prosecution, as his friend Pollio thought (Suet. *Iul.* 30: see Ramsey, chapter 4, p. 48)? How genuine were his conciliatory offers to effect a compromise? Does his legislation in his consulship, and later as Dictator, add up to a coherent vision for Rome? In particular, did he have a constitutional solution in mind, or was he "stuck," unable to devise one – or at least one that would be acceptable, as his friend Matius thought (Cic. *Att.* 14.1): "If he, with all his genius, could not find a way out, who will find it now?" Did he decide to campaign in Parthia in order to escape the vexations and frustrations of the Roman political scene, or did he hope to return with such power that there would be no more resistance to his monarchic rule? Did he have a plan for the succession? Was his acceptance of divine honors a reluctant concession to sycophantic followers, or a case of entrapment by his enemies, who counted on his hunger for glory (Zanker, chapter 21)? Or was it a way of ensuring his own posthumous deification (Wardle, chapter 8)?

The contrary judgments pronounced on Caesar's murder, and the ambiguous actions taken after his death, show how unresolved these questions about Caesar and his intentions were at the time. Cicero was clearly struggling in *De Officiis* to find a philosophical justification for the questionable act of killing a friend. Antony had the Dictatorship abolished but made sure that Caesar's promises, policies, and memory, were honored. Caesar's grand-nephew Octavian, who ultimately succeeded him as Augustus Caesar, had him deified but still expressed respect for Cicero and Cato: it is not clear what role he thought Caesar's memory should play in the ideology of the new regime (Toher, chapter 16; Levick, chapter 15). It is thus not surprising that, later on, his biographer Suetonius should decide that while, on the one hand, he was "rightly killed," because of his acceptance of excessive honors and his demonstration of contempt for the Republican constitution, yet, on the other, his murder was a crime for which his assassins were rightly punished (*Iul.* 76–9, 89).

Once the new system of the Principate was entrenched, it was easy to think that Caesar's assassins had just been vainly resisting the inevitable direction of history, which Caesar was following. But whenever a Princeps became a tyrant, veneration for Caesar's opponents would surface. Throughout later history, monarchical rulers might either claim him as a forerunner or avoid comparison with him as a potential murder victim. Opponents of rulers might see in him either an inspiring enlightened reformer, or a justly murdered demagogue, usurper, and tyrant (McLaughlin, chapter 23; Biskup, chapter 26; Cole, chapter 28).

The Historical Significance of Caesar

For serious historians, and to a lesser extent for biographers, there is also the bigger question: did Caesar kill the Republic, or was it, in any case, terminally ill? The particular events that led immediately to civil war and to the demise of the Republic were, in themselves, no more inevitable than any other events in history; but were they just a concatenation of unfortunate circumstances, or was that demise explicable: an event with intelligible long-term causes, an event, as Montesquieu thought, waiting to happen at some time? These questions may not have much bearing on Caesar's responsibility for his actions, but they do affect our assessment of his impact on history. The brilliant account by Theodor Mommsen in his youthful *History of Rome* (1854–6), which can be said to mark the beginning of modern historiography on

Caesar in Europe (except in France: Nicolet, chapter 27, p. 416), contained an authoritative answer. Mommsen held that the Republic could not bear the strains of her growing empire, so that – as Caesar saw – some kind of constitutional monarchy was necessary. Mommsen has influenced the views of many subsequent historians, even the sober and scholarly Gelzer, but not all have been convinced, and those that have, like Christian Meier, do not necessarily agree that Caesar had a plan to solve the problem.[1]

The same question, that of the viability of the Republic, affects our political assessment of Caesar's assassins. If the Republic was still vital, then their bungling after the murder can be blamed for its demise; but if it was already doomed, then their act was simply futile. Mommsen showed his contempt for their adherence to the dying Republic by omitting the murder and ending his treatment of Caesar with his program and his vision for Rome as a cosmopolitan state, with citizenship extended to the whole world: a free state ruled by a constitutional monarch. Critics, then and later, have noted the folly of regarding success as necessarily fated or deserved (Badian 1982) and have pointed out that Cato and Brutus have, through the centuries, been inspiring figures (Christ 1994: 153). These, again, are questions for historians.

Whatever one thinks about the political wisdom of the assassination, however, the moral questions about the act remain. And this question has been the leading inspiration of the dramatic tradition about Julius Caesar. Brutus may have genuinely championed republican liberty, but he also murdered his friend and benefactor (perhaps even, for some playwrights, his father). Caesar may have usurped power and become tyrannical, but he showed clemency and generosity undeserving of such cruelty (see Griffin, chapter 25). Dramatists, like Lucan and Seneca before them, explore other moral questions about Caesar too: was he driven to civil war simply by ruthless ambition? Was his regret at the murder of Pompey by the Egyptians just a pretence (Leigh, chapter 17; Griffin, chapter 25)?

The Great Man in History

We have explored the various factors that have kept the memory of Julius Caesar so vivid and so relevant. But how far was the path of his comet, as it burned its way through the mists of history, really an unusual one? How far was Caesar a man of his time and class, more energetic and more able than most, but not essentially different in aims and vision? Did he become the initiator of a new form of government at Rome, the forerunner or even the first of the Roman emperors, as Suetonius and some others have thought (see Pitcher, chapter 19; Barnes, chapter 20; Levick, chapter 15). If so, was it by accident or by design? As for Caesar as a general and governor, recent studies pinpoint, through Caesar's writings, the preconceptions which he shared with his readers about imperialism and about warfare. Nonetheless, his place in the history of Roman imperialism is as ambiguous as his place in the history of the Roman constitution, for some have thought the enormous expansion brought about by Pompey and Caesar marks them as unusual for their generation

(Eckstein 2006a). Indeed it might be argued, that Caesar, in taking Illyricum as his province, showed that he already saw the need to which Augustus would give high priority, i.e. that Pompey's eastern conquests had now made it imperative for Rome to forge a land route through the Balkans, to facilitate communication between the halves of her sprawling empire.

Ronald Syme, the great scholar of the transition from Republic to Principate, was critical of studies of Caesar that treat him in isolation from his peers. The manuscript entitled *Caesar*, found among his papers when he died, was intended to measure Caesar's career against what might be considered normal or typical in the career of a young Roman aristocrat. Brutus and Cassius, Decimus Brutus and Trebonius, were all to have had chapters in the book And yet, even Syme wanted to write a book about Caesar in particular. First, because he could not escape the fascination of Caesar's personality: he saw him as a dandy in dress, a pedant about language, and a rigorous purist, and remarked, "such persons may be intolerably despotic; he was an expert on religious ritual and loved ceremony – a kind of ancient 'Anglo-Catholic'."[2] But he was also fascinated by Caesar's situation, seeing in him a child of his time who was bewildered and dismayed by the political change he had unwittingly precipitated. Far from having an early ambition to achieve the position of absolute power, which he finally did achieve, Syme believed that Caesar relished the game of Republican politics – at which he excelled – until, by one rash move, he "wrecked the playground" and destroyed all that he most valued. Far from having a grand plan for a new kind of government, he found himself in a position which he deplored and which he decided to escape by fighting a war in the East. Syme's Caesar is a tragic figure, almost looking for assassination.[3]

As Cicero said in 46 BC, addressing the Dictator himself, "Among those yet unborn there will arise, as there has arisen among us, a sharp division of opinion. Some shall laud your achievements to the skies, others will find something missing in them" (*Marcell.* 29). This volume can pose, but it cannot answer, the questions about his place in history: it does not decide between the Mommsen and the Syme approaches to Julius Caesar. Still less does it pass moral judgment, on Caesar or on his opponents. Yet these essays should provide readers with the ancient evidence and the historical context for his life and opinions. It should also acquaint them with the many interpretations that have been placed on them, in history and literature, in art and music, through the more than two thousand years that have elapsed since the Ides of March.

NOTES

1 Strasburger was unusual among German scholars in questioning both the extraordinariness of Caesar and his adherence to any sort of program (see, in particular, Strasburger 1953). But see Yavetz 1971 on the inadequacy of classifying views concerning Julius Caesar on national lines.

2 The manuscript is among the Syme papers deposited by Wolfson college in the Bodleian Library: a table of contents shows that there were to be seventeen chapters, four of them biographical.

3 These ideas had already been aired in Syme 1985 (1988).

PART I

Biography: Narrative

CHAPTER TWO

From the Iulii to Caesar

Ernst Badian

The origin of the Iulii was shrouded in myth deriving their ancestry from Aeneas and Venus long before the age of Caesar. Dionysius of Halicarnassus 1.45 ff. collected what he found in the first century BC, in writers of much earlier periods. By about 200, the outline of their "history" had emerged. It was agreed that Ascanius, son of Aeneas, founded and ruled over Alba Longa, where the "Trojan" families settled and which was the *metropolis* of Rome. The myth is alluded to on the coins of Sex. Iulius Caesar, dated by Crawford, *CRR* no. 258, to 129, and of L. Iulius Caesar (no. 320), dated to 103. (The coin of Sex. Iulius Caesar is illustrated in figure 2.1.) Alba Longa was destroyed by the Roman king Tullus Hostilius, who transferred the "Trojan" families to Rome, where they became part of the small circle of Patrician families. There was a further refinement: Ascanius won the name of Iulus in battle and became the ancestor of the Iulii. (For some earlier versions on Ascanius, before the myth had become established, see Dion. Hal. 1.65.1, 72.1, and on "Iulus" 1.70.3; and see below.)

The Patricians were the oldest Roman aristocracy. All of them, with the exception of the Sabine Claudii, could trace their ancestry to the time of the kings. As the name shows, the original Patricians were men who had "fathers" (*patres*), not in the merely physical sense, but in the Roman legal sense of heads and originally almost owners of their families. They had to be married by the sacred ceremony of *confarreatio*, in the presence of ten witnesses and the highest priests, to women whose fathers were also *patres*. The *patres* were alone eligible to be enrolled (*conscripti*) by the king in his body of (ultimately) 300 advisors, the Senate. The Patrician families contrasted with the "Plebs," the "Fillers," the majority of citizens, needed for the defense of the city, but given few legal rights. Relying on that need, the Plebeians in due course acquired full personal and most public rights (some remained reserved for Patricians), until, by the first century BC, the tribunes they annually elected had *de facto* power superior to that of the magistrates (even the consuls) elected by the whole community. At some time in the fourth century it was laid down that one of the two consuls had to be a Plebeian (in due course both of them increasingly often were). Thus was founded a

Figure 2.1 BMCRR Rome 1140; RRC 258, Plate XXXVII, no. 23. Obv. head of Roma; rev. Venus driving a Chariot with Cupid behind.

new aristocracy, one of consular families, the "nobility." By the end of the second century, both the censors, quinquennial magistrates with considerable power over the public and private lives of citizens, could be Plebeians. (The first instance, in 131, was specially noted in the public record: see *MRR* 1.500.) But even after this, down to the end of the free Republic, the Patrician families retained unequalled social prestige and, much of the time, superior political power.[1]

In the fifth and fourth centuries the Iulii were by no means distinguished among the Patrician families. They did occasionally reach the highest offices: the consulship, the consular tribunate when it took the place of the consulship, and in 451, a year when ten supreme magistrates were elected, with the power to compile a law code, one of those decemvirates, for which in 451 only Patricians were eligible. According to our records, which for the earliest period of the Republic are by no means reliable, a Iulius held one of the highest offices between fifteen and twenty times; and since some did so more than once, the number of men attaining those offices is even smaller. About that total was reached by one family of the Fabii (the Vibulani), and among the Valerii it was far surpassed by the intertwined families of the Poplicolae, the Potiti, and the Volusi. The record is respectable, but by no means distinguished, even if we add a dictatorship (352), a tenure of the censorship (393), and a turn as *magister equitum* to a dictator (431). With one exception (C. Iulius Mento, consul 431, on whom see further below), the Iulii of this period all, or persons we know, bear the *cognomen* Iullus. It seems to be an original personal name, from which the *gentile* Iulius was formed (cf., for example, Marcus/Marcius, Quintus/Quin(c)tius.) The chances are that Mento also belonged to these Iulli and tried to found a family of his own. His name does not recur.

None of these early Iulii shows any attachment to Aeneas or to Venus. The only dedication recorded for any of them is an underhand one (for the story see Livy 4.29.7) to Apollo, by Mento – recognized as valid by the Senate, presumably because of the known connection of the Iulii with Apollo (see further below). The story of the descent of the Iulii from Venus and Aeneas does not appear in developed form before the second century BC. The first possible trace of it seems to be in the fragments of Cato's *Origines*: it seems that he knew the myth in some form (F 9–11 Peter). He tells the story of Ascanius' founding of Alba Longa after killing Mezentius, and he records that the name Iulus was conferred on Ascanius because he performed the deed when he was just old enough to be sprouting the first down of his beard (Greek *ioulos*). But in Cato Ascanius then dies childless, and his name is taken on by his half-brother, the son of Aeneas and Lavinia, at birth named Silvius. The surviving fragments do not tell us whether the name Iulus went with it. We may probably assume that it did, for there would be no point (in the myth) in bestowing the name Ascanius on Silvius by itself. It was probably done, whether by Cato himself (who is not known to have had any contact with the Iulii) or earlier, in order to give the Iulii the ancestor they needed, since the original Ascanius was not available. However, the duplication merely created confusion, and by the time of Livy, at least, the Iulii insisted on deriving their family from the original ("Trojan") Ascanius, presumably a superior heritage. (On this and on the confusion see Livy 1.3.2–3, with the resigned comment: "For who could assert an event of so long ago as certain?" For the total confusion on the mythical "prehistory" of Rome, and attempts to sort it out, see for example *RE* 12 s.v. Lavinia. It seems to have taken a long time for the myth to settle into the shape in which we find it, for example, in Vergil.)

What we are entitled to conclude is that by the time Cato wrote (perhaps the 170s BC: see *HRR* 1. CXXX f.), the claim of the Iulii to descent from Venus, via Aeneas and Ascanius, was well known among the upper class. It was about this time that, after long obscurity, a family of the Iulii was rising to modest prominence. The only Iulius known in the third century until near its end is a consul of 267, L. Iulius L.f. L.n. Libo, who shared a triumph over the Sallentini with his colleague M. Atilius Regulus after their joint capture of Brundisium (see *MRR* 1.200). Nothing else is known about him – neither his earlier career nor later any participation in the First Punic War, when he was probably still alive. But his grandfather, a L. Iulius, deserves scrutiny, even though he did not reach high office. Let us go one generation further back. C. Iulius (his *cognomen* is not recorded) was appointed dictator in 352 (Livy 7.21.9). His *cognomen* was surely Iullus, since no other family of Iulii is known at this time and for some time before and after as holding high office. He should therefore be a descendant of an attested Iulius Iullus. Several men are possible: L. Iulius Iullus, military tribune with consular power 403; another L. Iulius Iullus, who held the same office twice, in 401 and 397; a third who held those offices in 388 and 379; and a C. Iulius Iullus, censor in 393. The dictator must have been a son of one of these men and in each case would be the offspring of a long line of Iulli in the highest offices (see *MRR* 2.575). It is an attractive (perhaps an almost inevitable) hypothesis that L. Iulius Libo, consul 267, was a great-grandson of the dictator of 352 and would provide a bridge between the Iulii Iulli and the Iulii Caesares – a connection that the Caesares were to claim. Even if we inevitably discount the claimed descent from Venus, the real line thus goes back to the beginning of the Republic in the highest offices.

This at last brings us to the Caesares. Which Iulius at what time chose to adopt what had been a *praenomen* (see *Auct. de praenom.* 3) as a *cognomen*, we cannot tell. (Ancient etymologies and explanations of the name are best ignored.) The first Caesar on our record, at any rate, is an undistinguished praetor of 208, assigned the most undistinguished command, over the soldiers who had escaped from the battle of Cannae and who had been sent to serve in Sicily on humiliating terms (Livy 27.22.9). His son's more fully attested nomenclature (Sex.f. L.n.) shows that the praetor was the son of a Lucius who can confidently be conjectured to be the son of L. Iulius Libo, who left no descendants bearing his *cognomen*, and who, as we have seen, takes the descent of the Caesares back to the Iulli.

The praetor's homonymous son in fact had a distinguished career. After service as a military tribune (181) and an important embassy to Greece (170), he was one of the curule aediles of 165, under whom Terence tried to produce his first play. Finally, in 157, he brought the consulship back to his *gens*, for the first time since his great-grandfather L. Iulius Libo, 110 years before (see *MRR* 1 under the dates). But the glory turned out to be fleeting. Down to the end of the second century, no other Iulius reached the consulship, although several Iulii rose to a praetorship: L. Iulii in 183 and 165, both presumably Caesares descended from L. Libo, and a Sex. Caesar, *praetor urbanus* in 123, who must be the son of the consul of 157. No *cognomen* other than Caesar appears in Iulii of the Roman upper class from the rise of the Caesares down to the end of the Republic.

It is near the end of the century, with no recent consulship to show and several ambitious young men embarking on their careers (see *MRR* 2, Index, pp. 574–5, and 3.109–10), that it becomes important for the Iulii to display their mythical heritage. We have noted the moneyers of 129 and 103. There is also, for the first time, surviving monumental evidence for their claim. An altar dedicated to Vediovis at Bovillae, a town connected by various legends with Alba Longa (its inhabitants later claimed the succession to that city and called themselves Albani Longani Bovillenses), bears an inscription stressing that connection and claiming it for the Iulii: *Vediovei patrei/ genteiles Iuliei./ Vedi[ov]ei aara leege Albana dicata* (*ILLRP* 270). The attempt at archaizing spelling and the (inconsistent) doubling of vowels to denote length give us an approximate date: the orthographic fancies introduced by the poet and grammarian L. Accius, which did not have a long life.[2] The work and the form of its dedication must be due to the Caesares (see above). We do not know of any connection of the Iulii with Vediovis (they do not appear in conjunction anywhere else). But Vediovis was usually identified with Apollo, the old family god of the Iulii (so it seems). (For the identification see Gell. 5.12.11–12.) He was the death-dealing Apollo, marked by his arrows and a goat, an animal connected with the underworld (see Wissowa 1902:236 ff.).

The altar has had a disastrous effect in modern scholarship, reinforced by the family propaganda of Augustus and Tiberius (see below). It has led to the identification of Bovillae as the place of origin of the Iulii (thus *Der Neue Pauly*, 2.759 s.v. "Bovillae": "Stammort der *gens Iulia*") or, with further elaboration of fiction, *OCD* 258: "Here [at Bovillae] survivors from destroyed Alba Longa allegedly found refuge [so indeed one of the legends]: they included the *gens* Iulia which thereafter always maintained close associations with Bovillae." Wissowa (1902: 296), in an excess of fancy, has made the cult of Vediovis the family cult of the Iulii, through which they were led to the worship of Apollo.

A dose of reality clearly needs to be injected. We have already noted that there is no conjunction between the Iulii and Vediovis outside this text. And we must not be misled by the appellation of *pater*. This, as Wissowa well knew, was a title commonly applied to the ancient Italic gods: see Lucil. 19–22 Marx (making fun of it: cf. Marx's *Commentary*, 2.11).

As to the close associations with Bovillae, it needs to be pointed out that there is no record of any contact between the Iulii and Bovillae before this inscription, and indeed no record, literary or epigraphic, after it down to Augustus (see below). The *gens*, of course, had had many centuries in which to show an interest in Bovillae, but apart from this text and monument, no such interest appears – not even by Caesar, who proudly proclaimed his ancestry on suitable occasions (see below). We must look for a different explanation, bearing directly on this text.

In fact, as has already been indicated, it is due to the attempt of the Iulii to find their way back into the political mainstream, as a basis for the careers of the younger Caesares. The sudden emphasis on the family legend tracing their descent to Alba Longa and ultimately to Venus, serves as a political manifesto. Vediovis presumably had no structure dedicated to him at Bovillae (unlike Rome, where several had long existed), but there was probably an *area* sacred to him, which gave the Iulii their opportunity. An altar could be used as the vehicle for a suitable inscription: it was much cheaper than a temple and seems not to have needed public authorization.

By the time the Iulii were firmly established among leading families, with consulships in 91 and 90 (*MRR* 2.20, 25), they had no further need of Bovillae. Interest was resumed only by Augustus, under whom *ludi* at Bovillae were founded, and by Tiberius, who built a *sacrarium* to the *gens Iulia* there and had a statue of Augustus set up, no doubt in it.[3] (Augustus and Tiberius, of course, had a special interest in "proving" their Julian descent.)

We must now concentrate on the family of Iulii that leads to Caesar the Dictator (henceforth "Caesar" for short). Nothing is known about the career of Caesar's grandfather (*RE* Iulius no. 129). He may well have reached a praetorship, since few names of praetors are known in his generation. But he clearly had an eye for talent. Married to a Patrician Marcia, of the house of the Reges (a marriage no doubt arranged by his father), he chose an Aurelia (*RE* Aurelius no. 248) of the family of the Cottae, among the oldest Plebeian nobility (a consul in 252 and 248), as a wife for his son (*RE* Iulius no. 130), but for his daughter he chose a Plebeian of no known family – an ambitious man, who had been an active tribune of the Plebs (*MRR* 1.526) and had recently returned from a successful proconsulate in Spain (*MRR* 1.534–5, 3.139–40): Gaius Marius. The connection with Marius was kept up by his son, Caesar's father, who served on a commission to distribute land in 103 (not 100, as *MRR* 1.577: see 3.109). He was joined on this commission by C. Caesar Strabo (*RE* Iulius no. 135), of another branch of the Caesares, who had stressed his heritage by adding the old Julian *praenomen* Vopiscus (see the *cos.* 473, *MRR* 1.29) to his name as a *cognomen*.[4] Much of the land was to go to Marius' veterans.

Caesar's father went on to be praetor, then proconsul of Asia for at least two years (see *MRR* 3.104–5). Since we have no record of his interacting with any person who can be at least approximately dated, we do not know the precise dates of his tenure. (For discussion of conjectures on the dates of proconsuls of Asia at this time see *MRR* 3.128, on L. Lucilius.) He is not mentioned in connection with the Mithridatic War, hence must have left Asia before its outbreak (89). We know nothing about him after this, except that he died at Pisa in 85 (see *RE* 10.185–6). He had obviously had no stomach for the troubles in Rome in the early 80s and did not seek a consulship (this would certainly have been noted by our Caesar sources), which he might well have got (Caesares were consuls in 91 and 90: see above), but chose to retire to a peaceful part of Italy. What his son thought of this decision is not recorded.

Caesar, to whom we can now turn, was born on 12 July 100. The year is unanimously attested by our sources: see Groebe, *RE* 10.2 (1919) 187, in an article still worth reading (186–259). Mommsen tried to impose 102, Carcopino suggested 101, but these attempts to abandon the sources, based on the *leges annales*, may be ignored. (There are other ways of explaining the discrepancy: see already Zumpt 1874; later explanations abound.)

The date has been debated, and a mistaken date now prevails in (especially German) scholarship. The true date is assured by a precise quotation (though in indirect speech) by Macr. *Sat.* 1.12.34, of a law passed by the consul M. Antonius (i.e. in 44), changing the name of the month Quintilis to Iulius, "because in that month, on the fourth day before the Ides (i.e. the 12th), Iulius was born" (*quod hoc mense a.d. quartum idus Quintiles Iulius procreatus sit*: the numeral is written out in full and there are no textual variants). All our other sources agree on the date (see the full list in Degrassi 1963: 13.2, 189, 208, 481–2), down to John the Lydian in the sixth century AD, with the sole exception of Dio Cassius, in the third century, who gives 13 July, adding the tale that the date was officially changed to the 12th by a law of "the Triumvirs." (He cites no source.) There should be no doubt that this cannot stand against the law of M. Antonius.

Caesar's first public appearance was in his seventeenth year (see Suet. *Iul.* 1.1), when the consul L. Cinna designated him flamen Dialis (priest of Jupiter), one of the most venerable of Roman priesthoods, the holder of which had to be married to a Patrician wife. Caesar therefore broke his engagement to a wealthy woman of equestrian family, arranged when he was still a child, and married Cinna's daughter Cornelia. (Plut. *Caes.* 5.3, implies that Caesar had actually married Cossutia, but a divorced man could not be flamen Dialis.) The priesthood thus conferred on the young man (there is no doubt that he was actually appointed: see Suet. *Iul.* 1.2) gave him immense distinction, but its taboos would debar a conscientious holder from a political career. (See *RE*, 6.2486–91 (Ernst Samter, 1909) s.v. Flamen Dialis, still one of the best treatments.) In view of the relative obscurity of that branch of the Caesares Cinna no doubt did not foresee a chance of a major career for the young man and tried to compensate by giving him the highest non-political honor.

When Sulla assumed the dictatorship after defeating the *Cinnani* (82), he annulled all the *acta* of Cinna, including Caesar's appointment, and ordered him to divorce Cinna's daughter. But Caesar refused, probably on the ground that the flamen Dialis was not allowed to divorce his wife. By thus in fact denying the legitimacy of Sulla's annulment of his appointment, hence by implication of all of Cinna's *acta*, Caesar was showing extraordinary courage. Sulla was practically forced to put him on his proscription list. Escaping from Rome, Caesar spent a short time in hiding, bribing his pursuers, so the Caesar myth alleges. (This is an example of how the myth pervades our accounts and makes it difficult to get at the facts. It cannot be true, since confiscation of his fortune went with his proscription, and he cannot have had the hefty sum such bribery would need with him on his flight.)

Meanwhile some relatives of his among the highest nobility (Suet. *Iul.* 1.2 found only two names) persuaded Sulla to relent. They were supported by the Vestal Virgins, no doubt in contact with Caesar through his priesthood. A compromise was reached: he agreed to resign his priesthood, which would in any case have made an official career impossible, but was allowed to keep his wife and no doubt to regain his possessions. Sulla's reported remark, that there were many Mariuses in the young man, is clearly part of the myth. Sulla in fact never executed a fellow Patrician: the most striking example is L. Scipio Asiagenus, who actually broke a treaty with Sulla, but was allowed to retire into comfortable exile at Massilia.

Although perhaps pleased to be freed of his priesthood, he had suffered a major blow to his *dignitas*, for which he never forgave Sulla and the *Sullani*. For the moment, he left their uncongenial predominance and went to Asia, to serve in the *contubernium* of M. Minucius Thermus, proconsul of Asia, who had been praetor in 81, but had no close personal connection with Sulla.

The institution of *contubernium* here deserves some comment, since it is rarely noted. I must in part repeat what I wrote about it in *Gnomon* 62(1990), 28, where I called it "the cement of the *res publica*." By Caesar's day the requirement that *equites*, including sons of senators, must serve ten years in the cavalry before they gained full equestrian privileges and were eligible to stand for office had been abandoned, but some service seems still to have been required (or was at least an advantage). Cicero (we happen to know) served for two years in the Social War, and the censors, on the rare occasions when there were censors in the late Republic, still asked the ritual question whether *equites* who appeared before them had done the required service (see Plut. *Pomp.* 22.8). The answer was probably a ritual "Yes." However, young *equites* interested in a political career, including sons of senators, now did their military service as *contubernales* (lit. "tent-mates") in close attachment to a commander. There sons of senators mingled with sons of *equites*, and bonds were formed that might shape a career. An aristocracy, in order to survive, must set up a procedure for replenishment from below. That was one major purpose of *contubernium*. The long survival of the senatorial aristocracy was largely due to its continuous acceptance of an influx of *equites* into its ranks, and *contubernium* was the process that made it possible, combining the formation of contacts between young *equites* and senators with the advantage of the *res publica*. The single surviving list of a commander's suite (*ILLRP* 515) shows us that, by not having more, we are prevented from a full understanding of the history of the Roman upper class in the late Republic.

Caesar was now a member of the proconsul's suite, but the cautious commander preferred to use the inexperienced young man on a diplomatic mission. He was sent to Nicomedes IV of Bithynia, whom Sulla had restored to his throne, to collect a fleet. The young Caesar was impressed by his first experience of an Oriental court. He became Nicomedes' *hospes* and, so it was rumored, his Ganymede. The rumor was never to leave Caesar (see Paterson, chapter 10, p. 135).

After his successful completion of the mission he was given military employment, which enabled him to discover and display his ability as a soldier. At the capture of Mytilene, which had been holding out ever since it joined Mithridates at the beginning of his war with Rome, he won the outstanding distinction of a *corona ciuica*, which was awarded to one who had saved a Roman's (perhaps also an ally's) life by killing the enemy attacking him. It conferred extraordinary privileges: thus, the Senate was supposed to stand up when one so decorated entered the Curia; and he was allowed to wear his *corona* on all public occasions (see Gell. 5.6.11 ff.). It was Caesar's first taste of outstanding honors, a foretaste of things to come. As usual, we do not know who were his *contubernales*, but in 49 a Q. Minucius Thermus, probably a nephew of Caesar's old proconsul, evacuated Iguvium, which he was supposed to defend, without resistance at the approach of Caesar's forces (Caes. *BC* 1.12; Caesar gives him little credit for it).

With the fall of Mytilene that campaign was concluded, and Caesar, not wanting to return to Rome while Sulla was alive even though no longer in power, took service under P. Servilius Vatia in Cilicia. When he heard of Sulla's death in 78, he hurriedly left for Rome. There he found M. Lepidus' bid for power on an anti-Sullan platform in progress (see *MRR* 2.85, 89). But seeing little support for Lepidus and doubting his ability as a leader (Suet. *Iul.* 3), he kept out of the conflict, waiting for better times.

He next tested his skill as an orator, while demonstrating his hatred for *Sullani*, by prosecuting Cn. Cornelius P.f. Dolabella, hand-picked for a consulship of 81 and then for three years proconsul of Macedonia, where he earned a triumph and the hatred of some of the Greek cities (Suet. *Iul.* 4.1, Plut. *Caes.* 4.14 – but Plutarch's timetable of events is confused throughout; further references *MRR* 2.89). However, in 77/6 the *Sullani* were too firmly entrenched in power for Caesar to succeed. (It happens to be from this, his first public speech, that we have the first fragment of his oratory: Gell. 4.16.8.) Hoping he would do better against smaller fry, he next attacked C. Antonius, a major profiteer of the proscriptions (and later Cicero's colleague as *consul* 63), who had been a prefect of cavalry in Greece while Sulla was in the East; when the praetor M. Varro Lucullus ruled against Antonius in the preliminary stages, Antonius appealed to the tribunes and secured his acquittal by this unprecedented maneuver (Asc. 84C: in 70 he was expelled from the Senate by the censors, i.a. *quod iudicium recusarit*). Caesar's two speeches were later much admired, but at the time Caesar naturally concluded that he needed more training in rhetoric. He therefore left Rome, to study under the most eminent teacher of the day, Apollonius Molon, then residing in Rhodes. (Cicero had received instruction from him earlier: see *Brutus* 307, 313, and elsewhere.) On his way to Rhodes he was captured by pirates, who treated him very well, but demanded a ransom of fifty talents (see Suet. *Iul.* 4, further embroidered Plut. *Caes.* 1–2). The money was raised by Greek cities and he was freed; he then at once raised more money, manned a fleet, and succeeded in capturing most of the pirates. He put them in prison and asked the proconsul M. Iunius Iuncus (see *MRR* 3.113) to execute them. For reasons not very plausibly given in the sources, Iunius postponed action. Thereupon Caesar, although he had no official standing, had their throats cut before having them crucified – an act that Suet. *Iul.* 74.1 cites as an example of his merciful disposition (*et in ulciscendo natura lenissimus*). In fact it is the first example of his callous ruthlessness that was to reach its climax in the Gallic War.

His study in Rhodes was soon interrupted by the incursion of an advance guard of Mithridates into Asia, which began the Third Mithridatic War (75/4). Caesar is said to have collected *auxilia* (for which the Greek cities no doubt again had to pay) and "by expelling the king's prefect from the province secured the loyalty of the cities that had been wavering" (*Iul.* 4.2). This is a striking example of the Caesar myth. That a scratch force collected by a man with minimal, if any, experience of commanding a military force, and no doubt collected from different cities, could achieve such a splendid success would be difficult to believe – even if we did not actually know that several cities joined Mithridates. At most we can assume a minor success by Caesar's miscellaneous force against a small advance detachment of Mithridates. But the story of Caesar's achievement casts a terrifying light on the helplessness of the cities of Asia against Roman demands. They had now had to pay for Caesar three times: first to free him from the pirates; then to give him a force to defeat the pirates; and now for a force to enable him to fight against Mithridates' advance guard. Yet Caesar, although no doubt known to them as the son of a recent proconsul, was a young man with no official standing and no authority to make demands on them. We begin to understand why some of the cities were glad to escape from Roman demands and to embrace a hope of better treatment under Mithridates.

To return to Caesar: in 73 he was coopted in his absence to succeed his relative C. Cotta as pontifex (Vell. 2.43.1). It was customary for a relative to succeed a pontifex who had died, but election in his absence was a special distinction. (Since at the time most of the members of the priesthood were Plebeians, it did not matter that a Patrician now succeeded a Plebeian. For a list see *MRR* 2.114.) With his honor thus fully restored, Caesar felt able to return to Rome. Possibly at once in 73, but more probably in 72 for 71, he was elected *tribunus militum* of one of the first four legions. (He cannot be the C. Iulius who served as a legate under M. Antonius (Creticus) in Greece in 73 (see *MRR* 2.113 and 115–6 n. 6, 3.105, accepting the identification). The numerous later writers dealing with Caesar's military career could not have missed such a *legatio*.)

The twenty-four military tribunes elected for the first four legions (election was never extended to the other legions, in which the posts went by appointment) seem by now to have been removed from their nominal service. We do not hear of Caesar's performing any military tasks, even though at that very time the war against Spartacus required service by several officers in Italy (see *MRR* 2.119, 125) and Caesar had earlier shown eagerness to engage in war. What we hear of is political agitation. Suet. *Iul.* 5 writes of "most eager support" for removing the restrictions on the tribunate of the Plebs imposed by Sulla[5] and also (*etiam*) for the law of an unidentifiable tribune Plautius (presumably with the support of the Senate, for members of aristocratic families were involved) to allow the return with a full pardon of the adherents of M. Lepidus who had fled to join Sertorius in Spain after Lepidus' death. (Suetonius, who seems to have read a *contio* on this by Caesar (*Iul.* 5), actually makes Plautius Caesar's agent – a further example of the Caesar myth.) All this is assigned by Suetonius (l.c.) to Caesar's military tribunate, which securely dates Plautius' tribunate to 71 (see *MRR* 2.130 n. 4 for discussion of different dates proposed). The *contio* refers to Caesar's duty to his brother-in-law L. Cinna, who was among those pardoned. It must have touched on Cinna's father and so on Sulla. This is what links it with the efforts to restore the powers of the tribunes, as in Suetonius.

In 70 the efforts to overturn the central provisions of Sulla's settlement at last fully succeeded. The consuls Cn. Pompeius and M. Crassus, old *Sullani*, secured the repeal of Sulla's curbs on the tribunate, only one of which (the prohibition on holding higher offices) had so far been removed, as it happened by a relative of Caesar's, the consul C. Aurelius Cotta (75), whom Caesar later succeeded as pontifex. In the later seventies a series of tribunes had mounted increasing attacks on those restrictions (see *MRR* 2.93, 97, 103, 110, 122). We are told that Caesar, in his military tribunate, eagerly supported those attacks. However, unlike the case of the *lex Plautia*, where we hear of an actual speech apparently seen by Suetonius (a fragment of it is quoted Gell. 13.3.5), there is no record of a speech supporting the restoration of the tribunes' powers. This may of course just be accident. But at least no speech survived, to be read by later scholars, and it is possible that his support for this cause was less eager, and that he delivered no major speech on this topic, whether because as a Patrician he felt it was not for him to be prominent in support, or perhaps because he had some doubts about the issue as such. He could not, of course, refuse actual support for a measure dismantling a mainstay of Sulla's system.

In 70, in the middle of the political turmoil, he was elected quaestor for 69, to take up office in December 70. Under Sulla's reform, this part of which no one wanted to overturn, Caesar would become a member of the Senate for life. He was allotted to serve in Hispania Ulterior, under Antistius Vetus, a member of one of the oldest politically active Plebeian *gentes.* (The *cognomen* Vetus no doubt claimed that this family was the oldest in the *gens.*) There had been a consular tribune in 379, but since then no Antistius before Caesar's commander is known to have risen as high as the praetorship (see the index, *MRR* 2.530).

Before Caesar could leave for his province (see *MRR* 2.136 n. 7, with a reference to Taylor) his fortune dealt him two personal losses, which he was quick to turn to political advantage. First his aunt Iulia, the widow of C. Marius, died, and soon after Cornelia, his wife, who had borne him what would turn out to be his only legitimate child, his daughter Iulia. Suetonius (*Iul.* 6.1) reports that he pronounced their funeral *laudationes e more pro rostris.* Plutarch distinguishes (*Caes.* 5.2): it was an ancestral custom to deliver funeral eulogies over older women, but Caesar's eulogy of his wife was the first over a young woman. Both accounts oversimplify, Suetonius' grossly. Funeral eulogies over women were by no means an ancient custom. We are told by Cicero (*De or.* 2.44) that the eulogy delivered by Q. Catulus (consul 102) over his mother Popillia was the first. (Cicero must have known of the very early precedent we find in Livy 5.50.7: a special privilege granted to the women who had contributed their ornaments to raise money for the ransom demanded by the Gauls occupying Rome; he no doubt regarded it, as we do, as legendary.) If the custom had been kept up after Catulus (which it probably had), it went back only a generation. Nor are we told where Catulus delivered his oration: whether *pro rostris* or, like later orations over less prominent women, in a more private setting, even if, like for example the *laudatio Turiae*, they were later published and perhaps intended for publication (see Horsfall 1983: 85 ff.). Caesar will not have had many precedents, during one generation, on how to speak in honor of a distinguished matron, and he may have made politically motivated innovations (see below). As for the eulogy of Cornelia, there had not been much time, in about thirty or forty years since Catulus' eulogy, for many aristocratic women to die in their early thirties and be given a public funeral. Plutarch's statement that Caesar's eulogy of Cornelia was the first instance may well be correct.

We do not know what arrangements had been made for the funerals of aristocratic women before Caesar. Caesar, at any rate, modeled his arrangements on the full ceremonial for aristocratic men: no doubt actors wearing masks represented Iulia's distinguished ancestors. (For a full description of the ceremony for men in the middle of the second century see Polybius 6.53.) In the new custom of *laudationes* for aristocratic women, their husbands (if dead) must have been similarly represented by masked men. Caesar used the occasion for a powerful political proclamation. Following custom (so he might claim), he introduced the *imago* of Iulia's husband, C. Marius, into the procession. Marius had been condemned by Sulla not only to death, but (it appears) to oblivion: to what was later called *damnatio memoriae*; and Sulla's law, in this respect, had so far been fully observed. It may not have suited high aristocratic families to revive memories of Marius. Given the Romans' love of pictorial representations, we can easily imagine the man wearing Marius' mask as not only dressed in the triumphal toga, which Marius had twice earned, but carrying actual pictures of some of his achievements and certainly a tablet showing Marius' *honores*. The display, whatever its details, aroused popular enthusiasm (Plut. *Caes.* 6.2), as no doubt planned by Caesar. It laid the foundation of Caesar's career as a champion of the People.

We fortunately have the opening section of his *elogium* (quoted by Suet. *Iul.* 6.1): his aunt was descended on her mother's side (the Marcii Reges) from King Ancus Marcius – this was introduced first, deliberately taking precedence over her father's side. It was followed, with striking effect, by her paternal descent – from Venus, as was by now the accepted claim of the Iulii. Caesar's rhetorical education was producing its effect. (See Kierdorf 1980, especially pp. 112 ff..) He proceeds to stress the application to himself: *cuius gentis* (the Iulii) *familia est nostra*. The speech in its setting is rightly described by Kierdorf as "well-aimed political propaganda" (p. 135).

We do not hear much about the eulogy for Cornelia: only that, according to Plutarch, it showed Caesar to be "warm-hearted." He must have refrained from using it for political effect, perhaps because the memory of Cinna was unlikely to arouse enthusiasm anywhere; and in any case, there would be no application to himself (*familia nostra*). Yet the banned *imago* of L. Cinna, Caesar's early promoter (whose family, of course, was much more distinguished than Marius'), must also have been considerable, even if he could in no way match the glory and popularity of Marius. Caesar could leave for Spain well satisfied with the way he had turned personal misfortune to good political effect, and the way he had used what generations of Iulii had made possible.

NOTES

1 See the summary of the evidence for consulships in my article (Badian 1990a, esp. 412). In the last generation of the free Republic one third of consulships held for the first time were held by Patricians. I know of no relevant statistics, but it seems clear that Patrician men will not have been nearly one third of the upper class.

2 *ei* for *ī* is reasonably common at all times. However, the gemination of long vowels due to Accius never quite caught on and was never consistently practiced. The Bovillae text of the Iulii is among the most consistent. For a list of texts printed in *ILLRP* that show it, see the index, 2.502. Most of the instances are isolated.

3 That the games were founded in honor of a *domus regnatrix* is clear from the context (Tac. *Ann.* 15.23.2). Since Tiberius is not mentioned in connection with them, it is most likely that they were founded under Augustus. But Tiberius cannot be excluded. To say that Tiberius "restored" a *sacrarium* of the *gens Iulia* there indicates failure to read the text: *sacrarium genti Iuliae effigiesque diuo Augusto apud Bouillas dicantur* (*Ann.* 2.41.1). To translate *sacrarium* as Gedenkstätte (thus *Der Neue Pauly*: 2.759) shows inadequate understanding of Latin. I doubt whether a statue of Augustus, whenever set up, needed restoring in 16.

4 C. Caesar Strabo was a son of L. Iulius Sex.f. Caesar and of Popillia, who by an earlier marriage was the mother of Q. Lutatius Catulus, who set the precedent of pronouncing a funeral eulogy over her. Catulus had reached his consulship (102) after three failures, with the help of Marius, who also aided him in his campaign against the Cimbri and chose to share his triumph with him (see Badian 1957: 322 ff.). Hence this branch of the Caesares had their own connection with Marius through his friendship (at that time) with their brother Catulus.

5 We have few precise details on the restrictions imposed on the tribunes by Sulla, except that he debarred them from higher office (a restriction removed by C. Cotta; see p. 20) and that he restricted (perhaps removed) their right to propose laws. Livy's epitomator (*Per.* 89) states that he abolished it, but the epitomator is known to be unreliable and, when unsupported, cannot be believed. The question is too complicated to be discussed here.

6 I wish to thank Professor John T. Ramsey for looking at an early draft of this chapter and correcting some errors. Any that remain are not his fault.

CHAPTER THREE

Caesar as a Politician

Erich S. Gruen

In the year 63 BC Julius Caesar achieved an astounding political victory. He was a mere thirty-seven years old, not yet even of praetorian rank. But he gained election, purportedly by an overwhelming margin, to the post of Pontifex Maximus, defeating in the process two considerably older and more eminent candidates, P. Servilius Isauricus, consul 79, and Q. Lutatius Catulus, consul 78.

The outcome is quite stunning. And it must have seemed so to contemporaries. Seventeen of Rome's thirty-five voting tribes, selected by lot, constituted the electors. Ancient commentators postulated lavish bribery that plunged Caesar into heavy debt, giving rise to the famous anecdote according to which Caesar declared to his mother on the eve of election that he would either return to her as Pontifex Maximus or flee into exile (Plut. *Caes.* 7.1–3; Suet. *Iul.* 13; cf. Dio 37.37.1–3).[1] Whether or not cash changed hands in substantial quantity, Caesar's victory thrust him dramatically into the spotlight, suggesting a political rise of extraordinary speed and success. As "chief priest" he was now titular head of the college of pontiffs. Although this did not mean that he ran Rome's religious establishment (it was far too diverse and fragmented a system for one-person control), the office, normally reserved for senior members of Rome's aristocratic families, afforded immense prestige and distinction (Beard 1990: 17–48). To underscore the point, Caesar promptly moved his residence from the unfashionable Subura district to the official residence of the priests in the Forum itself, near the Temple of Vesta and the Regia (Suet. *Iul.* 46). It is tempting to see in this audacious accomplishment (as many have) a sign that Caesar cared little for Republican convention and set his path firmly on a precedent-shattering career.

Or did he? Matters are more complex. How unorthodox a political course had Caesar hitherto followed in fact? It is worth noting (what few have observed) that Caesar was not the first underdog to win election to the chief pontificate over older and more seasoned contenders. As long ago as 212 P. Crassus, who had not yet attained even an aedileship, defeated two rivals who had held consulships twice and censorship once, a striking success (Livy 25.4.2–4). And in 180 M. Lepidus obtained a majority of votes over a plethora of distinguished candidates (Livy 40.42.12). Caesar could not therefore be accused (and was not accused) of breaking precedent to advance unparalleled ambitions. Nonetheless, the feat had few antecedents, and it attests to remarkable political influence garnered by one still at an early stage of his career. This surprising achievement can serve as centerpiece for exploring the background of Caesar's rise to eminence and the qualities and associations that brought him unusual authority. It also raises a critical question about the significance of his political path: how far did it represent conventional politics, shrewdly and adroitly played, and how far did it constitute a dramatic turn for the Republic that presaged radical change?

Personal charisma doubtless played a role in Caesar's swift emergence to fame. But this success story required more than charm and flash. Connections of an unusual variety, quality, and effectiveness, sedulously cultivated, and positions taken that appealed across a broad spectrum must be included in the reckoning.

Caesar followed no formulaic line that would place him consistently in one political camp or another. Nor does it help to apply labels such as *popularis*, "anti-Sullan," or indeed "outsider" (as Meier 1995: 130–2, 149–50; Baltrusch 2004: 44–8, 51). His family had not, to be sure, wielded authority of a high order in recent generations. But Caesar claimed a proud heritage: royal stock through his mother's line and a paternal lineage that he traced back to Venus (Suet. *Iul.* 6). To what degree that fanciful genealogy boosted his political advancement may be questioned. Powerful connections counted for more. And Caesar had them. His aunt Julia had been wife of Marius, Rome's most successful general of the previous generation and seven times consul (Vell. Pat. 2.41.2; Plut. *Caes.* 1.1). The young Caesar was himself wed to the daughter of L. Cinna, staunch ally of Marius and himself four times consul in the 80s, a woman whom he refused to divorce, even at the insistence of Sulla the dictator (Vell. Pat. 2.41.2; Suet. *Iul.* 1.1–2; Plut. *Caes.* 1.1). That he got away with this carries important implications. The tradition ascribes it to heavy bribery, a recurring motif in his story, doubtless alleged by his enemies later (Suet. *Iul.* 1.2). In fact, Caesar had important affiliations with the circle of Sulla that protected him from the wrath of the dictator. His mother Aurelia came from the prominent family of the Cottae, allies of Sulla, with two consulships in the mid-70s and one in the 60s (Suet. *Iul.* 1.2, 74.2; Plut. *Caes.* 9.2). Such associations help to account for his political advancements in the 70s, a military tribunate, cooptation into the college of pontiffs filled with Sullan supporters, and election to the quaestorship which gave him a permanent place in the Roman senate (see above).

This was not a man identified with the "Marian party" (if such a term had meaning at all). Caesar's contacts reached across political lines, and his successes defy partisan identification. To be sure, when Caesar as quaestor took the occasion of his aunt's funeral in 69 not only to deliver a eulogy but to display the *imagines* of Marius for the first time since Sulla had repressed the Marians, this provoked some loud objections (that were themselves shouted down). And he followed it with yet another funeral oration, this one for his wife Cornelia, daughter of Cinna, an unusual ceremony, for young women rarely received such laudation (Plut. *Caes.* 5.1–2). But Caesar was not here announcing his political alignment. The fact that he shortly thereafter married the granddaughter of Sulla makes that abundantly clear (Suet. *Iul.* 6.2; Plut. *Caes.* 5.3). Rather, he celebrated the exploits of a great military hero and enhanced the profile of his own family by reminding the public of his illustrious heritage (Suet. *Iul.* 6.1; cf. Goldsworthy 2006: 98–100). Caesar underscored the point during his aedileship of 65. He restored the trophies that Marius had earned for his victories over Jugurtha, the Cimbri, and the Teutones, and that had been dismantled or destroyed by the regime of Sulla. And he added images of Marius himself, to the consternation of some like Catulus, but to enthusiastic response from most senators and the populace (Plut. *Caes.* 6; Suet. *Iul.* 11; Vell. Pat. 2.43.4). This too should not be interpreted as a partisan act (contra: Badian, chapter 2, p. 21). Caesar revived the triumphal tokens of a man whose exploits had rescued the state from its foreign foes – and, of course, he enhanced his own family's image in the process.

Caesar also knew where real power lay. He moved gingerly to associate himself with Rome's most formidable figure, Pompeius Magnus. Indications of this may be discerned already in the late 70s when Caesar very energetically supported those who advocated the restoration of tribunician powers that Sulla had curtailed (Suet. *Iul.* 5). It is probably not coincidental that Pompey took that same line publicly in these years and then implemented the change as consul in 70 (Sall. *Hist.* 3.48.23 Maur. = 3.34 McGushin; Cic. *Verr.* 1.45; *MRR* 2.126). Certainly in 67, when the tribune A. Gabinius proposed sweeping powers for Pompey to deal with pirates all over the Mediterranean, Caesar spoke up most conspicuously in favor of that controversial measure. Report had it even that he was the only senator to support the bill, an exaggeration no doubt, but a sign of his vociferous advocacy (Plut. *Pomp.* 25.4). He took a similar stance in the following year, prominent among those who argued for transference to Pompey of the coveted command against Mithridates of Pontus, Rome's chief enemy in the East (Dio 36.43.2–4).[2] How much weight the opinion of Caesar, a mere *quaestorius*, may have had on these proceedings is questionable. But the energetic promotion of such moves can have done him no harm with Pompey. He carried more clout in 63 when he backed a bill by two tribunes, supporters of Pompey, proposing extraordinary honors for the great general's victories in the East (Dio 37.21.1–4; cf. Vell. Pat. 2.40.4). In that same eventful year, as we have seen, Caesar gained his remarkable elevation to the post of Pontifex Maximus, a lifetime appointment. It causes no surprise to learn that this stunning victory came at the expense of the eminent Q. Catulus, a staunch opponent of Pompey's eastern commands until his objections were overborne (Cic. *Imp. Pomp.* 51, 59–61; Vell. Pat. 2.32.1–2; Dio 36.36a). The influence of Pompey and his friends was surely not irrelevant in Caesar's success.

But Caesar's rise to eminence involved more than just alliances and alignments. He took strong public stands on a number of controversial issues involving the interests of the state and its citizens from the early years of his career. The aftermath of the Sullan era left a residue of matters that required redress. Caesar's urging (already noted) that tribunician powers be restored falls into that category. So does his backing in 63 of a measure proposed by the tribune T. Labienus (also a supporter of Pompey) that priests be elected rather than coopted. Such had been the case for a quarter-century until Sulla removed that privilege from the electorate. The promulgation of

Labienus' bill, with Caesar's help, restored the earlier procedure. Not a radical move, but the reinstatement of voting rights previously enjoyed by the citizenry.[3]

Caesar, however, went beyond institutional change in seeking to reverse some of the effects of Sulla's dictatorship. He delivered a speech in 70 supporting a measure to recall from exile those who had been part of Lepidus' uprising in 78 and had fled to Sertorius in Spain, the leaders of resistance to the Sullan regime (Suet. *Iul.* 5; Dio 44.47.4; Gell. 13.3.5). The fact that Caesar's brother-in-law L. Cinna was among the exiles was an added bonus. But the proposal had broader significance: amnesty and reconciliation a decade after the wounds inflicted by Sulla on the body politic. Atonement for those wounds remained of central importance for Caesar. In the mid-60s he took an active part, whether as accuser or as presiding judge, in the prosecution of men who had carried out executions or had profited financially from them during the Sullan dictatorship.[4] And he pursued his championship of rehabilitation for the victims of Sulla in these same years, promoting the reinstatement of rights for children of those proscribed by Sulla (Vell. Pat. 2.43.4; Cic. *Pis.* 4, *Leg. agr.* 2.10; cf. Dio 37.25.3). Success in this effort would have to wait a few years. But Caesar delivered a clear message: it was high time that Romans put the violence and divisiveness of the Sullan years behind them.

Caesar projected himself further as advancing Roman generosity in yet a different sphere. In 68, upon returning from his proquaestorship in Spain, he tarried in Transpadane Gaul (Italy north of the Po) where he encouraged the Latin colonies in that region in their quest for full citizenship (Suet. *Iul.* 8). The franchise had been granted to all Italians up to the Po at the end of the Social War in 90 and 89. Inhabitants of the Latin colonies just to the north, well integrated into Roman ways, had good reason to claim similar treatment. Caesar's support for their claims – hardly, as Suetonius suggests, an incitement to rebellion – was sound and proper policy, though still premature in the political atmosphere of Rome in the 60s. Caesar reinforced this posture in indirect fashion in 63 when he prosecuted C. Piso for extortion. During the proceedings he made a point of denouncing Piso for his willful execution of a Transpadane Gaul (Sall. *Cat.* 49.2). Caesar here called attention once more to the injustice of withholding citizen privileges from those dwelling across the Po.

The promotion of civic causes acquired a more dramatic flair in 63. Caesar played a prominent role in the colorful trial (more like a spectacle) of C. Rabirius, an aged and largely inconsequential figure. Thirty-seven years earlier Rabirius, a minor member of the senate, had been instrumental (so it was alleged) in the murder of the popular tribune Saturninus. The deed took place under cover of the *senatus consultum ultimum*, the senate's emergency decree that authorized magistrates to take whatever steps were necessary, however drastic, to protect the safety of the state. The particular offense, obscured by the passage of time, counted for little, and Rabirius himself was insignificant. Prosecutors indeed resurrected antique and obsolete procedures to conduct the trial, Caesar serving as one of two appointed judges to deliver a verdict in a judicial setting that had not been employed for centuries. The proceedings ended without issue, more as farce than as serious judgment. The purpose was demonstration, not justice. Only the principle mattered: a warning about abuse of power by the senate and an indirect challenge to the *scu* itself (Gruen 1974: 277–9; Gesche 1976: 33–5; Tyrell 1978; Goldsworthy 2006: 121–4).

The issue arose again later in the year, not perhaps altogether coincidentally. The notorious "conspiracy of Catiline," ostensibly an effort at a political coup through internal sabotage and external rebellion, had been unmasked, largely through the efforts of the consul Cicero. A number of accused plotters were now in custody, and the senate debated their fate, while others were still at large and fomenting upheaval. The debate proved to be vigorous and memorable. The *patres* leaned heavily toward the death penalty as proposed by the consul-designate D. Junius Silanus, until Caesar, only a praetor-designate, rose to resist that proposal. His speech left a potent impact, often recalled by later sources (Suet. *Iul.* 14; Plut. *Caes.* 7–8, *Cic.* 21.2–4, *Cato* 22.4–5; Dio 37.36.1–2; App. *B Civ.* 2.6). Caesar's *ipsissima verba* no longer survive, but the historian Sallust, a near contemporary of the events, puts a potent and plausible oration in his mouth (Sall. *Cat.* 51). Caesar, himself the object of unsubstantiated rumors regarding collaboration with the conspirators, denounced their aims and actions in no uncertain terms. But he counseled caution and restraint in punishing the plotters, urging a dispassionate decision on the model of Rome's forefathers. Among other things, Caesar pointed to the excesses of the Sullan years when too many Romans suffered unjust executions and confiscations of property, a path to be shunned. He had associated himself with that motif more than once in the past. If the senate is to run roughshod over established procedures, however justified that might be in this case, it would set perilous precedents for the future (Sall. *Cat.* 51.32–6). He makes reference here explicitly to the dangers of military action by magistrates against Roman citizens on the basis of a senatorial decree (Sall. *Cat.* 51.36). Caesar himself, paradoxically, recommended an unprecedented remedy, namely the confinement of the prisoners in Italian municipalities for an indefinite period and the confiscation of their property (Sall. *Cat.* 51.43; Cic. *Cat.* 4.7–8; Ungern-Sternberg 1970: 92–111; Drummond 1995: 23–50). The proposal, initially welcomed, failed to carry the senate after a powerful speech for summary execution by Cato the Younger (Drummond 1995: 51–77). But Caesar, while not explicitly renouncing the institution of the *senatus consultum ultimum*, had once more put on record his opposition to unrestrained exercise of that measure in violation of the traditional rights of Roman citizens. To punctuate the point, Caesar conspicuously harassed Cicero who as consul carried out the execution of the conspirators (Plut. *Cic.* 23.1–2). He made sure that his championship of citizen privileges in the face of government power would have public exposure.

All this allows for a deeper understanding of Caesar's remarkable ascension to the position of Pontifex Maximus. One does not have to endorse the aspersions of his enemies that he bribed his way into the office. Nor should much weight be placed upon another sort of bribery, namely the lavish public spectacles that Caesar organized as curule aedile in 65 (Goldsworthy 2006: 105–8). He put on the major festivals of the year, the *Ludi Romani* and the *Ludi Megalenses*; he sponsored theatrical performances, public banquets, and showy processions; he mounted colonnades to display his own art collection; and he staged expensive funeral games in honor of his father (long since dead), featuring gladiatorial contests that included no fewer than

320 pairs of gladiators. The ceremonies plainly made a splash. Caesar's fellow curule aedile, M. Bibulus, who had joint responsibility for many of the events, complained that Caesar took all the credit for them (Suet. *Iul.* 10; Plut. *Caes.* 5.5; Dio 37.8). But it would be wise not to make too much of this as a principal boost for Caesar's career. All curule aediles were expected to sponsor games as part of their official duties. Yet they catapulted few to prominent political positions. The effects of aedilician generosity and public relations upon later electoral success have been much exaggerated (Gruen 1992: 188–93). Caesar's shows may have been more lavish than most. But how much impact would they have had two years later upon the electors from seventeen tribes chosen by lot to select the Pontifex Maximus?

Caesar's political assets by the time he attained that office were broad and varied. He had strong links across the spectrum of Rome's political society. He enjoyed kinship relations with the families of Marius and Cinna and resisted pressures to break them in the Sullan years. And he had equally tight ties with powerful elements in the Sullan establishment itself that helped to assure advancement in the period when that group held sway. Moreover, Caesar placed himself within the circle of Pompey, collaborated with the great man's friends, and spoke up prominently for his appointment to major commands. The connections with influential figures and families were instrumental and indispensable in the political arena.

But the network of affiliations does not tell the whole story – or the most important part of it. Caesar repeatedly took positions on matters of significance for the civic well-being of the polity. He argued conspicuously for reviving institutions that had been weakened in the Sullan years and restoring privileges that had been stripped from the victims of Sulla. This was no mere championing of "Marians" against "Sullans." Caesar eludes simplistic political labels. Nor is it to be interpreted as advocacy of the "popular" against the "senatorial" line. That form of reductionism is unhelpful. The need to bind up the wounds left by civil war in the 80s was paramount. And comparable motives account for Caesar's arguments to extend civic privileges for peoples across the Po: it would further the task of reconciliation with Italians that followed the Social War. Similarly, Caesar's criticisms of misuse of the *senatus consultum ultimum* reminded Romans of the dangers that institution carried for the traditional rights of Roman citizens. It diminishes this public activity to characterize it as "popular" posturing. Larger goals may have struck responsive chords in a society looking for concord and healing after the divisiveness of civil strife.

None of this activity, however, involved breaking with conventional modes of political behavior. Caesar stood for each office of the magisterial ladder in proper sequence and at the time when he became eligible. The cultivation of aristocratic allies and collaboration with persons of prominence and influence constituted standard behavior for the ambitious. And none will question Caesar's ambition. Indeed the adoption of controversial stands and outspoken opinions on matters of public concern hardly signal a break with customary practices in Rome. Nothing here presaged revolutionary change. But the combination of elements worked to Caesar's advantage. And his strongest suit may have been a more generous vision of society that resonated with a citizenry hoping to erase an era of turmoil.

The motifs that surfaced in Caesar's career to that point received reprises in subsequent years. He gained election to the praetorship for 62, *suo anno*, i.e. in the earliest year of his eligibility – no premature candidacy, but also a clear demonstration that there would be no delay. He continued to foster political connections in different sectors of the aristocracy. He made certain to advertise his association with Pompey, now on the brink of returning from his grandiose victories in the Near East. And he retained a commitment to advance an agenda of reform in various parts of the civic arena.

Caesar employed his praetorship in part to promote the interests of Pompey, and in part to settle some scores. The venerable senior statesman Q. Catulus, defeated by Caesar in the pontifical elections, had helped to thwart Caesar in the debate over the Catilinarian conspirators (Cic. *Att.* 12.21.1; Plut. *Caes.* 8.1, *Cic.* 21.3), and had even sought to implicate him in the conspiracy itself (Sall. *Cat.* 49.1–2; Plut. *Caes.* 7.3). Caesar lost no time in retaliating. On the first day of his praetorship, he demanded at a public meeting that Catulus render an account of why he had failed to complete the job of rebuilding the Temple of Jupiter Capitolinus. The task, he suggested, should be transferred to a more competent person, namely Pompeius Magnus (Cic. *Att.* 2.24.3; Suet. *Iul.* 15; Dio 37.44.1). Catulus' influential friends fended off that effort, but Caesar had succeeded in embarrassing the elder statesman and also in reaffirming his own allegiance to Pompey. He took the latter purpose a step further in backing the motion of Pompey's vigorous ally, the tribune Q. Metellus Nepos, to have the general commissioned to stamp out the remnants of the Catilinarian uprising. This led to heated wrangling and even a violent fracas between Nepos and Cato, with the result that Caesar was nearly stripped of his praetorship (Plut. *Cato* 26–9; Dio 37.43.1–4). He may have gone too far in his zeal to show fidelity to Pompey. But prudent backtracking and an orchestrated demonstration assured his reinstatement by the senate itself (Suet. *Iul.* 16). How far this whole bizarre affair may have been stage-managed is impossible to tell. But Caesar made sure that his praetorship would be memorable.

Pompey was not the only powerful personality whose friendship Caesar cultivated. M. Licinius Crassus, probably the wealthiest man in Rome (at least before Pompey's eastern spoils), victor over Spartacus and the slave rebellion, consul in 70 and censor in 65, a man to whom many senators were in debt financially or politically, one whose favors were sought and whose influence was feared, had reason to promote the political fortunes of promising younger men (Marshall 1976; Ward 1977; Gruen 1977: 117–28). How close a connection Caesar formed with him in the 60s is difficult to say. The first occasion on which we hear of Crassus' financial backing of Caesar comes in 61, when he stood surety for part of Caesar's heavy debts (Plut. *Crass.* 7.6, *Caes.* 11.1; cf. App. *B Civ.* 2.8; Suet. *Iul.* 18.1). Nothing suggests that he had supported Caesar's prior electoral campaigns, financed his expenditures as aedile, or bankrolled his candidacy for the chief pontificate.

Rumors and reports, none of them substantiated by direct contemporary sources, linked Crassus and Caesar in various schemes and intrigues of the 60s. One tale had them lurking in the background of a nefarious plot at the end of 66 to murder the consuls and other senators, a consequence of which would be the elevation of Crassus to dictator and Caesar as his deputy to master of the horse. The allegation, however, came from sources hostile to Caesar and was spread in the following decade (Suet. *Iul.* 9; Gesche 1976: 24–8). As censor in 65 Crassus advocated extension of Roman citizenship to those dwelling beyond the Po, a policy which Caesar had endorsed earlier and would certainly sympathize with, though he is not explicitly mentioned (Dio 37.9.3). In that same year Crassus argued for exacting tribute from Egypt and evidently even for tactics of intimidation and the threat of military force (Plut. *Crass.* 13; Schol. Bob. 92–3, Stangl). Caesar, aedile in the year of Crassus' censorship, allegedly attempted to persuade some tribunes to have him appointed as military commander to seize control of Egypt (Suet. *Iul.* 11). No source connects the two endeavors, and the likelihood that Caesar could expect such a potent and prestigious post as a mere aedile is remote in the extreme. But retrospective rumors continued to fly. One of them claimed that Crassus and Caesar backed the campaign of Catiline and his fellow candidate Antonius for the consulship of 63 in order to prevent the election of Cicero, a report based on later and dubious testimony (Asc. 83, Clark). Indeed each of them was accused in 63 of actually aiding and abetting the rebellion fomented by Catiline. The charges were flimsy, promoted by political foes, and swiftly dismissed (Sall. *Cat.* 48.5–49.4; Plut. *Cic.* 20.3–4, *Caes.* 7.3–4, 8.1–2; App. *B Civ.*, 2.6; cf. Suet. *Iul.* 17). Little of substance attaches to any of these innuendoes, retailed by enemies or subsequent reconstructions (Strasburger 1938: 109–17). But even if no fire produced all that smoke, the repeated conjoining of Crassus and Caesar suggests the plausibility of political collaboration, at least in the public perception. Crassus' cash and patronage were welcome to the younger man. And the talented and popular Caesar could be a valuable ally in the ranks of the senate. For Caesar, expanding the breadth of his political connections was altogether characteristic.

A proconsulship in Spain in 61 and 60 allowed Caesar to hone his military skills and earn some notable successes against the Lusitanians. The victories gave him a claim on a triumph, a coveted honor that all Roman aristocrats sought as emblematic of military prowess and accomplished leadership (*MRR* 2.180, 184–5). But the consular elections of 60 loomed, and Caesar aimed to capture that office, the top of the *cursus honorum*, also in his first year of eligibility. The impressive course of his career inevitably stirred envy and resentment among rivals and adversaries. The senate could not deny him the triumph that his accomplishments in Spain had earned. His opponents, however, set up a roadblock should he wish to be both *triumphator* and consul. The date of the consular elections approached, and the law required that candidates be in Rome in order to stand for the office. Insufficient time remained to await the triumph and then cross the *pomerium*, Rome's sacred boundary, to stand for office. Caesar asked for an exemption, so as to offer his candidacy *in absentia*, but his detractors stood in the way, Cato talked out the proposal with a filibuster, and Caesar had to forgo his triumph (Suet. *Iul.* 18.2; App. *B Civ.* 2.8; Plut. *Caes.* 13.1, *Cato* 31.2–3; Dio 37.54.1–2).

He would not, however, be denied his consulship *suo anno*. Caesar's long-standing nourishment of linkages with the powerful came to the fore here. He conducted his canvass in conjunction with the wealthy L. Lucceius who would later show himself a close advisor to Pompey the Great. And the intermediary who effected this joint candidature was Q. Arrius, a known partisan of M. Crassus (Cic. *Att.* 1.17.11; Suet. *Iul.* 19.1). The combination clicked for Caesar – though not for Lucceius who lost the election to M. Bibulus, a bitterly hostile foe of Caesar. The backing of both Pompey and Crassus, no friends of one another, exhibited the remarkable success of Caesar's courting of the mighty to his own benefit (Meier 1995: 184–8).

The event presaged formation of what moderns have labeled "the first triumvirate," an informal pooling of resources and an understanding to cooperate politically by Pompey, Crassus, and Caesar, to collective advantage. Caesar took the lead in reconciling the two old foes. The task may not have been accomplished by the time of the elections. Caesar had the backing of both men individually. Intermediaries suggested that he was still at work on placating the other two in December of 60 (Cic. *Att.* 2.3.3). The coalition probably came into effect after Caesar's consulship opened in 59 (Gesche 1976: 42–5). It was largely his handiwork. Pompey had much to gain. His military triumphs abroad had not been matched by comparable success at home. The great general had expected the extensive changes he had implemented among Roman provinces and client states in the East to be ratified by formal senatorial approval. And he pressed for measures to provide land grants for the veterans who had served with him and anticipated rewards from his patronage. But Pompey found his wishes repeatedly thwarted by opponents in the senate who were only too pleased to embarrass the commander and to demonstrate that his exploits on the battlefield did not translate automatically to dominance on the home front. Although Pompey had loyal supporters in the consulships of both 61 and 60, they proved ineffectual in the face of fierce opposition led by Cato and his political allies. Efforts on behalf of Pompey's veterans and his eastern settlement languished. The general could certainly use an energetic and popular man in the consulship of 59. Caesar, of course, fit the bill. What Crassus had to gain is less obvious. He had been among those who resisted Pompey's claims and sought to make life uncomfortable for him since his return from the East. But he had had his own differences with Cato over a request to renegotiate the contract of a Roman tax-farming company for the lucrative revenues of Asia, newly secured by Pompey's victories. That petty deal apart, Crassus had more long-range ends in view. He could look ahead to the opportunities for expanded patronage (always a central objective for Crassus) that distribution of extensive land grants would bring. A linkage with the formidable general and the over-achieving Caesar held the promise of giving Crassus a position of preeminent influence over the political scene (cf. Dio 38.1.7; Vell. Pat. 2.44.2; Florus 2.13.10–11).

For C. Julius Caesar, the backing of men who carried so much weight and authority, possessing widespread connections within the senatorial class and esteem among the populace, was incalculably valuable. Not just for securing the consulship. His election occurred before the cementing of the "triumvirate." Caesar's determined efforts to bring Pompey and Crassus together (and even to add Cicero to the coalition) had broader objectives: implementation of a serious program of social and civic changes advantageous to the body politic as a whole. The trio carried substantial collective clout. But it was Caesar who had the agenda – and who drove the engine.

The measures carried in that memorable year of 59 held a significance that set them apart from mere personal ambition and political battles (though there were plenty of those as well). Caesar's first act as consul (rarely noted or discussed in modern treatments) had the daily deliberations of the senate and the official proceedings of the people's assemblies recorded and published (Suet. *Iul.* 20.1). This opening of transactions to public scrutiny and to permanent record sent a significant signal: political leaders and their actions were to be regularly held accountable by their constituencies – at least in principle. It supplied an emblematic beginning for the consulship.

Caesar moved directly to a bill of broad significance for Roman society: a sweeping measure for the distribution of land. Pompey had endeavored for two years to obtain agrarian allocations for his veterans, but had been stymied by the resistance of his opponents. Caesar's proposal, however, went well beyond rewards for returned soldiers. It would provide more broadly for settlement of the urban poor on the land (Dio 38.1.2–3, 38.5.2; cf. Cic. *Att.* 2.3.4; Plut. *Pomp.* 47.3, *Caes.* 14.1, *Cato,* 31.4; App. *B Civ.* 2.10). Caesar had carefully crafted the bill to avoid the impression of radical reform. The state would purchase property for the purpose, but only from landowners who were willing to sell. There would be no confiscations or devious appropriation through fabricated land titles. Prices would be fixed in accord with previous assessment, thus to short-circuit debates over property values. The bill wisely exempted from its provisions the state-owned property in Campania which was leased out to farmers and brought in a handsome return for the treasury. Distribution would be in the hands of twenty men, a commission from which Caesar explicitly excluded himself, thereby avoiding charges of personal profiteering. And money to finance the operation would come from the new taxes and other revenues accruing to the state from the recent eastern acquisitions (Dio 38.1.4–7; cf. Cic. *Att.* 2.6.2, 2.7.3, *Fam.* 13.4.2, *Dom.* 23). The measure was sober, comprehensive, and intelligent, a major step toward social and economic equity on the land. Further, Caesar did not desire to ram the bill through in unconventional fashion. He made sure to bring it before the senate for full discussion and expressed willingness to alter any objectionable provisions (Dio 38.2.1). It is noteworthy that no one uttered an objection. The bill's drafters had anticipated every potential challenge. Yet obstructionism came anyway. The detractors feared the popularity and influence that Caesar might gain from this *lex agraria.* Cato and others resisted simply on the professed grounds that the current system sufficed and no change was necessary (Dio 38.2.2–3.1). Only then did Caesar present the bill to the assembly and overbear the opposition of his fellow consul Bibulus and of Cato by summoning the open support of Pompey and Crassus (Dio 38.3.2–5.5; Plut. *Caes.* 14.2–3, *Pomp.* 47.4–5; App. *B Civ.* 2.10). Caesar would brook no further impediments to a measure that could not be faulted and, despite some well-orchestrated agitation and disorder, the assembly passed the bill into law (Dio 38.6.1–4; Suet. *Iul.* 20.1; App. *B Civ.* 2.11; Plut. *Cato* 32.1–3).[5]

The available land under the *lex agraria* proved to be inadequate for the numbers who needed it. Hence Caesar sponsored a supplemental measure later in the year that would parcel out the rich and hitherto inviolable Campanian land. This drew the inevitable complaints and dissent, transparently demonstration rather than serious resistance (Cic. *Att.* 2.16.1–2, 2.17.1; Suet. *Iul.* 20.3–4; Plut. *Cic.* 26.3, *Cato* 33.1–2; Dio 38.7.3; Vell. Pat. 2.44.4; App. *B Civ.* 2.10). The necessity for the new law gained wide recognition, and the parceling out of land generated no known resistance. The sound and sensible character of both the agrarian enactments redounds to the credit of Caesar.

Comparable credit goes to Caesar for his *lex repetundarum*, designed to expand protection for provincials against the depredations of Roman magistrates abroad. Previous enactments against extortionate activities by Roman provincial governors stood on the books, but none so comprehensive, detailed, and thorough as this one. The Caesarian law contained over one hundred clauses, specifying every imaginable infraction for which Roman promagistrates, legates, and envoys could be held accountable. Its enduring character cannot be gainsaid. Contemporaries heaped praise upon it (Cic. *Rab. Post.* 8, *Sest.* 135, *Pis.* 37). And jurists continued to cite it well into the era of the Roman Empire (e.g. *Dig.* 1.9.2, 22.5.13, 48.11; Paul. *Sent.* 5.28; cf. Cic. *Fam.* 8.8.3, *Att.* 5.10.2, 5.16.3, 5.21.5, *Pis.* 50, 61, 90). This was plainly not petty politics. The labors expended on the measure preclude that interpretation. Caesar's interest in the relationship between Rome and her provincial subjects was a serious one. The *lex repetundarum* generated no dissent. And it enjoyed enduring impact.

In this connection, two other minor pieces of legislation on judicial matters sponsored by associates of Caesar in the year 59 warrant mention. One instituted certain changes in the procedure for challenging jurors, the other discouraged bribery of jurors by having the votes of the individual groups that sat on a case tabulated separately (Cic. *Vat.* 27; Dio 38.8.1). The bills themselves were not of earthshaking consequence. But their very existence indicates that Caesar's consulship directed itself at more than short-term political advantage. That he and his confederates took the time to shape complex measures on social, judicial, and administrative reform reflects tellingly on the consul's long-range commitments.

Not that they eschewed political advantage. Of course, the "triumvirs" looked to their own interests and advancement. The ratification of Pompey's arrangements in the East, stalled until Caesar took office, now passed through the assembly without difficulty (Dio 38.7.5; Plut. *Pomp.* 48.3; Vell. Pat. 2.44.2; App. *B Civ.* 2.13). That act was long overdue, a matter of state interest to make permanent the temporary arrangements for Rome's stake in the Near East. Reduction of the tax-farmers' Asian contract, urged by Crassus, gained approval by the assembly – accompanied, however, by a pointed warning from Caesar that they restrain themselves from reckless bidding in the future (Cic. *Att.* 2.16.2, *Planc.* 35; Suet. *Iul.* 20.3; Dio 38.7.4; App. *B Civ.* 2.13). The commission to distribute land under the *lex agraria* included both Pompey and Crassus (Dio 38.1.7). And Caesar arranged for himself an extended military command. The tribune, P. Vatinius, a loyal supporter, sponsored a *lex* to assign to Caesar the provinces of Cisalpine Gaul and Illyricum for a five-year period (Suet. *Iul.* 22.1; Dio 38.8.5; Cic. *Prov. cons.* 36–7). The specified period of time and the fact that the popular assembly made the assignment were unusual but by no means unprecedented – or even controversial (cf. Gruen 1974: 534–43). The desire to govern Cisalpine Gaul may reflect Caesar's long-standing interest in expanding the civic privileges of Italians living across the Po. It was not an appointment that normally added greatly to the governor's stature on the political scene. Illyricum might have afforded an opportunity for military laurels in the northern Balkans. But the province on which Caesar was to build his remarkable military reputation was Gallia Transalpina, and this he gained as an afterthought. The province was vacant since the death of Q. Metellus Celer to whom it had been assigned. And Caesar received it by senatorial decree under customary procedure, subject to annual renewal (*Prov. cons.* 36, *Att.* 8.3.3; Suet. *Iul.* 22.1; Dio 38.8.5). Few senators could have anticipated what success Caesar would have in that part of the world. The advancement of the "triumvirs'" personal aims did not entail revolutionary change.

But a question arises. Did not the joint exercise of so much authority by a small coterie constitute a sharp and irremediable break with the past? They cowed and intimidated opponents, resorting occasionally to strong-arm tactics as they pushed through their legislation (Meier 1995: 204–23). And they succeeded further in having their choice of candidates elected to key offices for the following year, thus to continue their ascendancy: the consuls L. Piso, Caesar's father-in-law, and A. Gabinius, a loyal henchman of Pompey; and the energetic tribune P. Clodius, who gained eligibility for that office (closed to patricians like Clodius) by a phony adoption engineered by Caesar and Pompey (Tatum 1999: 95–108). The historian Asinius Pollio, reflecting later upon the situation, began his history with the year 60, when Caesar gained election to the consulship, evidently as a milestone in the dissolution of the Republic (Horace *Carm.* 2.1). And later writers pinned blame on the three dynasts for their seizure of the state (Livy *Per.* 103; Florus 2.13.10–11; Vell. Pat. 2.445.1; Lucan 1.84–6). It was the "three-headed monster" (App. *B Civ.* 2.9). No wonder that some view the triumvirate as a long-term scheme for dominance by Caesar or as a definite caesura in Rome's political history (e.g. Baltrusch 2004: 52–3; Canfora 2007: 66–70).

But facts on the ground, as we have seen, were not so dire. The enactments sponsored by Caesar and backed by his compatriots had legitimate ends in view: stability in the East, an equitable distribution of land, the protection of provincials from the excesses of governors, and adjustments to the administration of justice. As for bullying or bludgeoning their political foes, many of the encounters were orchestrated or sham, a stage on which opponents could claim coercion with an eye to subsequent challenge and overturning of the trio's accomplishments (Meier 1966: 282–5; Gruen 1974: 91–2; Burckhardt 1988: 195–201; de Libero 1992: 72–80). The famous jibe, "consulship of Julius and Caesar" was part of that mock propaganda (Suet. *Iul.* 20.2). In fact, cooperation among the "triumvirs" themselves was shaky almost from the start. The tactics of Cato, Bibulus, and others, feigning victimization and denouncing the tyranny of the dynasts, and the attacks leveled even by their supposed protégé Clodius proved to be quite effective. Those attacks created dissension among the dynasts already in 59, bringing embarrassment particularly to Pompey and widespread hostility to all three. The coalition thus ran into serious difficulty in the very year of its formation, thereby rendering suspect any notion of a stranglehold on Roman politics or a prelude to the Republic's ruin (Gruen 1974: 90–102; Goldsworthy 2006: 170–81; contra: Baltrusch 2004: 54–5). The legislation of 59 had far greater endurance than the fragile political union. That testifies to the broader civic concerns of C. Julius Caesar.

We return now to the question with which this essay began. Did the early stages of Caesar's career, featured most strikingly by his election as Pontifex Maximus and the dramatic events of his consulship, represent a shattering of convention that illustrated the failings of the Republic and presaged the great man's future dictatorship? Not many contemporaries could have forecast the events that would occur a decade and more later. Caesar's career through 59 had observed the normal conventions and pursued the customary goals of ambitious aristocrats, but with an astuteness and deliberation that put most of his contemporaries in the shade. He had moved through the ladder of offices at the proper pace (always, to be sure, in the first year of eligibility), he had amassed an assemblage of kinship relations and influential connections that crossed the political spectrum and defied party labeling, and he had taken up causes that could remedy some of the ills of the Sullan years, speak to social and economic needs in the city and the countryside, protect the civil liberties of Rome's citizenry, expand privileges to Italians, and enforce proper governance of the provinces. None of this entailed drastic or revolutionary change. Even the strong-arm tactics of the "triumvirs" in Caesar's consulship arose from posturing and political theatre rather than representing a challenge to Republican institutions. Caesar operated largely within traditional modes of political behavior. And he promoted policies and principles that others too had embraced. He was simply better at it than anyone else.

FURTHER READING

Caesar has never been short of biographers. Mommsen's admiring interpretation of Caesar (1904) as the one man who saw clearly the ills of the Republic and aimed throughout to substitute a new system still has its followers. The classic biography remains that of Gelzer, first published in German in 1921, then revised through six editions until 1960, and made available in English in 1968. It is a thorough and judicious political study, well documented, and an indispensable starting point. Meier's extensive treatment (1995), which appeared first in German in 1982, offers a strongly personal and stimulating view of Caesar and is well worth reading, but lacks footnotes or bibliography. Among the newest works, that of Goldsworthy (2006) is the most comprehensive, readable, and reliable. It is directed to a broader readership than Gelzer, and its references to modern scholarship are highly selective. Canfora (2007) presents an idiosyncratic portrait, often lively and provocative, but short on argumentation and peculiar in its organization. A most serviceable and annotated assemblage of modern scholarship on Caesar, up to the date of its publication, can be found in Gesche (1976). On the early stages of Caesar's career, Strasburger (1938) is relentlessly critical and questioning of the sources, and, although he may err on the side of skepticism, he supplies an invaluable check on speculation. The politics of the 60s and the consulship of Caesar are aptly summarized by Wiseman (1994) and explored through the perspective of other major figures, Crassus, Pompey, and Cicero, by Ward (1977), Seager (1979), and Mitchell (1979, 1991). Among studies of the late Republic more generally, Meier's notion (1966) of a "crisis without an alternative" has given rise to much discussion and argument, but the book is no easy read. On the workings of late-Republican politics, Taylor (1949), Gruen (1974), and Brunt (1988) give a good sense of the major controversies, and suggest very different answers.

NOTES

1 Extensive borrowing and the dispensing of cash are still emphasized in the most recent studies: Goldsworthy 2006: 125–6; Kamm 2006: 44–5.
2 It is conceivable that Caesar spoke up for just one of those measures, each of our sources assigning his appearance to a different occasion; so Strasburger 1938: 100–1.
3 Dio 37.37.1–2. Dio wrongly concludes that this change enabled Caesar to win the post of Pontifex Maximus in that year. In fact, the chief priest, by contrast with the other pontiffs, was already subject to election; Cic. *De Leg. Agrar.* 2.18. See the discussion, with bibliography, by Gesche (1976): 35–8.
4 Suet. *Iul.* 11, suggests that he was judge. Cic. *Pro Lig.* 12, Schol. Gronov. 293 Stangl, and Dio 37.10.1–2 have him as accuser. See Strasburger 1938: 117–19.
5 On the agitation, more show than substance, see Gelzer 1968: 72–4; Meier 1995: 207–13; Goldsworthy 2006: 168–9.

CHAPTER FOUR

The Proconsular Years: Politics at a Distance

John T. Ramsey

Coalition of Caesar, Pompey, and Crassus Put to the Test (58, 57 BC)

Since the consuls in 58, L. Piso and A. Gabinius, were political allies of the dynasts, it fell to two praetors, L. Domitius Ahenobarbus (consul 54) and C. Memmius, to launch an attack challenging the validity of Caesar's consular acts on the ground that they had been passed contrary to the auspices (Suet. *Iul.* 23.1; Cic. *Sest.* 40, *Vat.* 15, cf. *Pis.* 79). Caesar submitted to an examination by the senate (Cic. *Vat.* 15, with *Schol. Bob.* 146St), and the inconclusive debate lasted for three days, after which he crossed the sacred boundary of the city (*pomerium*) to take up his command, thereby gaining immunity from prosecution (Suet. *Iul.* 23). In his defense, Caesar published three no-longer extant speeches *In C. Memmium et L. Domitium* (*Schol. Bob.* 146St).

The attack in the senate by the two praetors against Caesar and against the measures he had passed as consul for the benefit of his political allies Pompey and Crassus played into the hands of the tribune P. Clodius, whose support the dynasts could ill afford to alienate (Cic. *Sest.* 40) because Clodius enjoyed an enormous popular following.[1] Clodius claimed that the three potentates were on his side in his attack on his political enemy Cicero, and that he could even rely upon the backing of Caesar's army (Cic. *Sest.* 39–40, *Hars.* 47). The deafening silence of the Big Three spoke volumes (Cic. *Sest.* 140). The orator himself (*Pis.* 79) more or less confesses that Caesar feared his opposition when Caesar's consular *acta* were challenged in January. Hence Caesar took no active part in trying to block Clodius from driving his hated enemy Cicero into exile (Nisbet 1961: x). And yet in the previous year Caesar appears to have been willing to shield Cicero from Clodius' vendetta by offering Cicero a legateship on his staff (Cic. *Att.* 2.18.3, 19.4 of June, July 59; cf. *Prov. cons.* 41). Such an appointment would have conferred on Cicero immunity from prosecution, and he could even have remained in Rome. It was only necessary for Cicero to swallow his pride and put aside his political principles. He would have to agree to join Caesar and his political allies, something that the orator eventually did in May 56 and came to regret not doing earlier (Cic. *Fam.* 14.3.2). We know that Caesar remained just outside Rome until Cicero was driven into exile (Cic. *Red. sen.* 32, *Sest.* 41; Plut. *Caes.* 14). His departure must have taken place c. 20 March, since Caesar covered the distance between Rome and Geneva on the Rhône within eight days (Plut. *Caes.* 17.5) when he learned that the Helvetians were to gather on 28 March, preparatory to their intended march through Transalpina (*BG* 1.6.4).

The danger posed to the Big Three, should they lose the good will of the tribune P. Clodius, was no trivial matter. Later in the year, Clodius openly flouted Pompey by freeing from custody a hostage taken by Pompey from Armenia, the son of the Armenian king Tigranes (Asc. 47C.12–26; Plut. *Pomp.* 48.6; Dio 38.30.1–2), and Clodius interfered with Pompey's Eastern settlement when he stripped from a local king, Deiotarus, some of the privileges conferred by Pompey (*MRR* 2.195–6). Most likely Clodius resolved to take this anti-Pompeian stance when he sensed that Pompey was sympathetic to the movement to overturn Clodius' bill of exile against Cicero and recall the orator (Cic. *Att.* 3.3.8, 9.2). By his acts against Pompey, Clodius intended to send a warning message and also, no doubt, to win favor with Pompey's (and Caesar's) political enemies, the ultra-conservative element in the senate. That faction may well have felt resentment at the exile of Cicero and were doubtless offended by Clodius' use of violence in early 58 to quash the prosecution of Caesar's former ally, the ex-tribune P. Vatinius (Tatum 1999: 168). And probably for this same reason, by the summer Clodius began attacking the validity of Caesar's *acta* in 59 (Cic. *Dom.* 40, *Har. resp.* 48, *Prov. cons.* 43), although in the spring the two men had been on such good terms that Caesar wrote to Clodius from Gaul to congratulate him on passing legislation that temporarily removed from Rome the arch-conservative M. Cato (Cic. *Dom.* 22). Eventually, by August, Clodius succeeded, through violence in the streets and by hints at assassination, in causing Caesar's political ally Pompey to withdraw entirely from the public scene and seek safety in his home for the remainder of the year (Plut. *Pomp.* 48.5, 49.2). The rift between Clodius and the dynasts, Pompey and Caesar, will explain why Caesar backed the candidacy of P. Cornelius Lentulus (*BC* 1.22.4), a devoted adherent of Pompey (Cic. *Att.* 3.22.2) and a known sympathizer with the movement to work for Cicero's recall from exile.[2]

In August, Pompey was awaiting a letter from Caesar concerning his support for a reversal of Cicero's exile (Cic. *Att.* 3.18.1). Years later (in 49) Pompey claimed that he had been barred by Caesar from protecting Cicero when Clodius passed his bill in March 58 to drive Cicero into exile (Cic. *Att.* 10.4.3). Caesar's precise attitude in this period is difficult to ascertain. In November 58, the tribune-designate P. Sestius visited Caesar at his winter quarters in Cisalpina with the aim of securing the proconsul's blessing for Cicero's recall (Cic. *Sest.* 71). A passage in Cicero's *In Pisonem* of 55 (§80) suggests, however, that Caesar's eventual support was not granted until the spring of 57. Furthermore, the terms worked out for Caesar's backing are likely to have included a demand for certain guarantees that Cicero's brother Quintus is said to have given Pompey, assuring him that the orator would not work against the interests of the dynasts (Cic. *Fam.* 1.9.9, 12).

Before he embarked on his military campaigns in 57, Caesar recruited two new legions in Cisalpina (*BG* 2.2.1), thereby further increasing the size of his army. In the previous year, his forces had grown from an original strength of four legions – one in Transalpina and three in Cisalpina/Illyricum (Dio 38.8.5) – to six, by the recruitment of two new legions before the campaign against the Helvetians in 58 (*BG* 1.10.3). Caesar relied upon the political backing of his partners Pompey and Crassus to take this bold step of doubling the size of his army in the space of slightly less than twelve months (Suet. *Iul.* 24.2). However, for the time being he had to shoulder the not inconsiderable burden of finding pay for these additional troops out of his own coffers (roughly four million sesterces per legion, per annum: Shatzman 1972: 33 n. 26). The senate did not authorize a subsidy for these four new legions until May 56 (Cic. *Fam.* 1.7.10). With this augmented force, Caesar went on to conduct two highly successful campaigns in northwest France and Belgium: against the Belgae in May–June (*BG* 2.3–15) and against the Nervii in late July (*BG* 2.16–28).

Events in Rome during the first half of 57 centered around efforts to bring about the recall of Cicero, and with this in view, two friendly tribunes, T. Milo and P. Sestius, began countering violence carried on by gangs of P. Clodius, whose term of office ended on December 9, 58. Milo recruited professional street fighters, and finally, on August 4 Cicero's return from exile was authorized by a bill passed in the centuriate assembly (Cic. *Att.* 4.1.4), where voting was weighted in favor of the well-to-do and citizens from the Italian countryside, whose support for Cicero's cause tended to be strong. One month later, on September 4, Cicero entered Rome (ibid. §5), and immediately began again to take an active role in politics. One of his first acts was to propose for Pompey a special commission to organize the grain supply since the weeks leading up to and following Cicero's return were characterized by a shortage of grain and food riots in Rome.[3] What was needed was a massive overhaul, and the senate in due course authorized a law granting Pompey a commission for five years with fifteen legates to superintend the grain supply (ibid. §7). Not long afterwards (about October), a dispatch (*litterae*) arrived in Rome from Caesar making the overly optimistic claim that all Gaul had been pacified (*omni Gallia pacata*, *BG* 2.35.1). In response, the senate decreed in Caesar's honor a Thanksgiving (*supplicatio*) of 15 days (*BG* 2.35.4; Cic. *Pis.* 45, 59; Dio 39.5.1; Plut. *Caes.* 21.1), triple the number of days normally accorded to such celebrations.

Towards the close of the year 57, about mid-December, Caesar's consular legislation was challenged once again, this time when one of the new tribunes for 56, P. Rutilius Lupus, advocated suspending the settlements in Campania that were authorized by Caesar's second *lex agraria* of 59 (Cic. *Q Fr.* 2.1.1). No doubt the need for cash to address the food crisis was a factor. The disruption of agriculture in Campania and the loss of revenue from rents on public land that was being parceled out to settlers under Caesar's law must have placed a severe drain on the treasury (cf. Cic. *Q Fr.* 2.6.2 of April 56). At the same time, the raising of this topic in December suggests that there may have been disharmony within the coalition since the issue of suspending Caesar's law was introduced by a tribune who one month later, in January 56, is found acting as a partisan of Pompey, when Lupus lobbied for Pompey to assume the coveted assignment of restoring King Ptolemy Auletes to the Egyptian throne (Cic. *Fam.* 1.1.3, 2.2). Other signs point as well to the conclusion that the coalition was encountering difficulties. In the elections for 56, the supporters of the dynasts had not fared well, whereas their opponents met with success. Two of the tribunes of 59 who had sided with Caesar's fellow consul Bibulus in his attempted obstruction of Caesar's legislation were elected praetors for 56: Q. Ancharius and Cn. Domitius Calvinus (Cic. *Sest.* 113, *Vat.* 16, 38 with *Schol. Bob.* 135, 146, 151St; Dio 38.6.1). By contrast, two Caesarian tribunes of 59 were defeated: C. Alfius for a praetorship in 56 (Cic. *Sest.* 114; *Schol. Bob.* 135, 151St; Broughton 1991: 35) and P. Vatinius for an aedileship (Broughton 1991: 43).

Coalition Renewed (56, 55 BC)

In the winter of 57–56, Caesar paid one of his rare visits to Illyricum (*BG* 3.7.1), which shared a border with Cisalpine Gaul at the head of the Adriatic and had been assigned to Caesar at the same time, for a term of five years. At his headquarters at Aquileia, Caesar is said to have reviewed the setbacks in the elections for 56 (Cic. *Vat.* 38). Neither of the men elected to the consulship of 56 can have been to the liking of the dynasts. One of them, Cn. Cornelius Lentulus Marcellinus, to Cicero's delight, successfully blocked in March several of the tribunes from proposing measures designed to benefit Caesar (called *monstra* in *Qfr.* 2.5.3). Later, in early July, shortly before the consular elections, Marcellinus took a position diametrically opposed to Caesar when he appears to have been in favor of making Cisalpine Gaul consular for 54, meaning that it would be assigned to one of the consuls of 55, who would thereby oust Caesar from his command after 1 March 54 (Cic. *Prov. cons.* 39). And finally, throughout the latter part of the year 56, Marcellinus strenuously opposed the election of Caesar's two partners, Crassus and Pompey, to the consulship of 55 (Dio 39.27.3; Plut. *Crass.* 15.1, *Pomp.* 51.5). Marcellinus' consular colleague, L. Marcius Philippus, was no less troublesome to the dynasts. Although Philippus later became the stepfather of the future adopted son of Caesar, the emperor Augustus, in 56 Philippus appears to have been allied with his son-in-law, the arch-conservative M. Cato (Plut. *Cato Min.* 25.1). In July, Philippus, like his colleague Marcellinus, opposed the pro-Caesarian stance adopted by Cicero in his speech *De provinciis consularibus*, which argues that Caesar's command in Gaul should not be cut short (*Prov. cons.* 18, 21). Later, Philippus opposed the election of Pompey and Crassus to the consulship of 55 (Dio 39.27.3).

As the year unfolded, it became clear that Caesar's enemies hoped to cut short his command. Although Caesar's tenure in Cisalpine Gaul was guaranteed by the *lex Vatinia* of 59 until March 1, 54 (Cic. *Prov. cons.* 37), his control of Transalpine Gaul, the springboard from which he had launched his conquests, was potentially subject to annual review. Transalpina had been granted to Caesar by the senate in 59 (Suet. *Iul.* 22.1; Dio 38.8.5), through the influence of Pompey and Crassus (Cic. *Att.* 8.8.3; Plut. *Crass.* 14.3), and Caesar could be removed as early as 55, if the senate chose to reassign the province to an outgoing praetor of 56. Still, a certain degree of protection against such a precipitous reassignment was afforded to Caesar by the fact that he could employ a friendly tribune to veto the senate's action, a means of obstruction that was not possible if the senate chose, instead, to assign Transalpine Gaul to one of the consuls of 55. Under the terms of the *lex Sempronia* of 123 BC, which was still in force in 56, the senate was obliged to name two provinces for the consuls of the following year in advance of their election, and this act was not subject to a tribune's veto. It was possible to argue that the whole of Gaul was now thoroughly subdued, a claim made by Caesar himself in describing the outcome of the campaign of 57 (*BG* 3.7.1). Among Caesar's enemies, one of the most threatening was L. Domitius Ahenobarbus, who had earlier as praetor challenged Caesar's consular *acta* in January 58 (see above, p. 37). Domitius was a determined nobleman whose wealth, ancestry, and political connections all but guaranteed his election to the consulship of 55 under normal circumstances (Cic. *Att.* 4.8a.2). For the past two generations, Domitius' family had taken a prominent role in Rome's conquest and organization of Transalpine Gaul, and Domitius let it be known in the spring of 56 that he fully intended to oust Caesar from his command (Suet. *Iul.* 24.1, cf. *Ner.* 2.2).

Moreover, in 56 Caesar came under pressure from his political enemies both in the courts and in the senate. Legal difficulties were posed when a tribune, L. Antistius (most likely Antistius Vetus, tr. pl in 56, Cic. *Q Fr.* 2.1.5), tried unsuccessfully to prosecute Caesar (Suet. *Iul.* 23.1: *TLRR* no. 257, assigned to 58; but the proper context seems to be 56, *MRR* 3.17). The case was bound to fail because Caesar's proconsular *imperium* shielded him from any immediate need to answer a summons (Suet. *Iul.* 23.1), but it served to put him on notice that he could expect a legal battle in due course. Another and more immediate threat was posed by the possible repeal, or suspension, of the second of Caesar's agrarian laws. This issue had already been tentatively raised in December 57 (see above, p. 39). Now the matter resurfaced, and when on 5 April the senate voted the substantial sum of 40 million sesterces to Pompey to meet the expenses of his grain commission, it also resolved to take up in due course the question of whether a halt should be called to the settlements on public land in Campania that continued to be made under Caesar's consular law (Cic. *Q Fr.* 2.6.1). In writing to P. Lentulus in December 54, Cicero even claimed to have been the sponsor of the motion setting a date in May 56 for the senate to consider the possible suspension of Caesar's law (*Fam.* 1.9.8). It is unclear to what extent Pompey was in favor of this attempt to erode Caesar's consular legislation, but certainly when Pompey dined with Cicero on the eve of April 8, he gave no indication that he was displeased with Cicero's role in the senate on the 5th (*Qfr.* 2.6.1).

News of this latest mood in the senate appears to have reached Caesar via his political ally M. Crassus, who around April 8–13 joined Caesar in Cisalpine Gaul, at his headquarters in Ravenna on the Adriatic coast (Cic. *Fam.* 1.9.9). Crassus criticized Cicero both for his motion to take up the Campanian question and also, perhaps, for attacks Cicero had ventured to make against Caesar in his speech against Vatinius in March (Cic. *Fam.* 1.9.7). Meanwhile Pompey, who was planning to leave Rome for Sardinia on April 11 in order to carry out the duties of his grain commission (Cic. *Q Fr.* 2.6.3), made a detour, and about April 17 he met with Caesar (and Crassus?) at Luca (modern Lucca), a town on the southwest boundary of Caesar's province. Some 200 senators and 120 lictors, attendants of proconsuls and praetors, are said to have been present at Luca (App. *B Civ.* 2.17; Plut. *Pomp.* 51.3, *Caes.* 21.2) – doubtless an exaggeration. We are surely not to suppose that a throng of that magnitude assembled on a single occasion. The story does, however, demonstrate the influence the dynasts were regarded as being able to exert. Two ex-magistrates of 57 are known to have visited Caesar on their way to govern provinces in the spring of 56. Appius Claudius (pr. 57; governor of Sardinia in 56) paid a call in March (Cic. *Q Fr.* 2.5.4), so presumably at Ravenna. Plutarch (*Caes.* 21.2), however, puts the meeting at Luca, where he also has Metellus Nepos (consul 57; governor of Nearer Spain) consult with Caesar. Possibly the purpose of Appius' visit was to request Caesar's backing in a future bid for the consulship (of 54) and to lobby for Caesar's support in advancing the career of Appius' younger brother, the ex-tribune P. Clodius, who was aedile in 56. Clodius' following among the urban proletariat would not alone suffice to carry him to the praetorship.[4]

The plans made by the Big Three at the meeting in Luca included a second consulship for Pompey and Crassus (in 55, to block the threat of L. Domitius), provinces for Pompey and Crassus to be held for five years on the model of Caesar's command in the two Gauls, and additionally an extension of Caesar's command for a further five years. Once these matters had been settled among the dynasts, Caesar had to dash off to the scene of warfare against the Veneti and other Gallic tribes on the Atlantic coast. An uprising had broken out in that maritime region against Caesar's legate P. Crassus early in 56 (*BG* 3.7–8; Oros. 6.8.6–8), and according to one tradition (Strabo 194C fin.), the rebellion had been sparked, in part, by a desire on the part of the natives to maintain their monopoly on trade with Britain by thwarting Caesar's suspected ambition of wanting to extend his conquests across the English Channel. If this is true, and Caesar had already begun to think about launching an expedition against Britain (carried out in 55 and 54), it will help to explain his desire not to be limited, as he was under the terms of the *lex Vatinia* of 59, to the one further season of military action (in 55) after the current year. The need to fight the naval war against the coastal tribes and to complete the conquest of Aquitania in the southwest of Gaul, bordering the Pyrenees (*BG* 3.20–7; Dio 39.46; Oros. 6.8.19–22), must have convinced Caesar that he needed an extension of his command (Stevens 1953: 16–18).

As a consequence of the decisions taken by the dynasts at Luca in April, and in response to a request made by Pompey through Cicero's brother Quintus, reinforced by a message delivered to Cicero from Pompey via his trusted agent L. Vibullius Rufus (Cic. *Fam.* 1.9.9–10), Cicero dropped his intention to participate in the debate on the Campanian question on 15 May. He stayed away entirely from that meeting of the senate (Cic. *Q Fr.* 2.7.1–2). Soon afterwards, Cicero supported (Cic. *Prov. cons.* 28), perhaps even as the sponsor (Cic. *Balb.* 61), a decree to give Caesar pay for his four new legions and the right to appoint ten legates instead of the normal three, which greatly enhanced Caesar's patronage. In a letter of June to Atticus, Cicero announces his intention to turn from relying upon the *nobiles* to looking instead to the three dynasts for backing (Cic. *Att.* 4.5.2–3). Shortly thereafter (on July 1–9,

Kaster 2006: 405 n. 42) Cicero delivered his speech *De provinciis consularibus*, in which he successfully argued against the proposal of Caesar's political adversaries to cut short his command by assigning one or the other of the two Gauls to a future consul of 55. Then in about September Cicero embarked upon what was to be the first of many cases that he undertook to please his new political allies, his defense of the Spaniard L. Cornelius Balbus (Gruen 1974: 312–13). Balbus had recently served in Gaul as Caesar's aide-de-camp (*praefectus fabrum*) and owed to Pompey his Roman citizenship, which was being challenged in this case (*TLRR* no. 276). Balbus, therefore, had close ties to two of the three dynasts, and Cicero, who was joined in the defense by both Pompey and Crassus, does not hesitate to characterize the prosecution as having been undertaken to strike a blow at Balbus' powerful patrons (*Balb.* 59).

A little later in the year 56, Cicero clearly exaggerates the control exercised by the dynasts over the course of politics when he asserts rather gloomily in November that Pompey doubtless has a long list of future consuls who are to be elected with the backing of the coalition (Cic. *Att.* 4.8b.2). Even Pompey and Crassus were apparently not powerful enough to derail the candidacy of L. Domitius in a straightforward manner. Instead, they concealed their intention to stand for the consulships of 55, delaying the announcement of their candidacies until the deadline for such official notification had already passed. Significantly, there is no hint in Cicero's speech *De Provinciis consularibus* of early July that Pompey and Crassus had any intention of standing for the consulships of 55; and they were still not formally reckoned as candidates as late as about November 15 (Cic. *Att.* 4.8a.2). Instead, they blocked the holding of the elections by employing the veto of a friendly tribune, C. Cato, who had switched sides after Luca (*MRR* 2.209). Pompey and Crassus resorted to obstruction because the consul Marcellinus refused to recognize their candidacy, and there was stout opposition in the senate as well (Plut. *Crass.* 15.1–2, *Pomp.* 51.5; Dio. 39.30.1–2). Therefore, they stood a much better chance of being successful at an election conducted in January 55 by an *interrex*, the official who temporarily assumed consular power when there were no consuls in place at the beginning of a new year. After Marcellinus ceased to hold office, the opposition to the dynasts would lack strong leadership with power to act. Postponement of the election to January also made it possible for Caesar to send troops on furlough from Gaul to sway the vote by their physical presence and to employ violence (Dio 39.31.2; Plut. *Pomp.* 51.4, *Crass.* 14.6), which ultimately drove off the persistent rival candidate L. Domitius (Plut. *Crass.* 15.4, *Cato Min.* 41.2–42.1).

After Pompey and Crassus had gained the consulship, they proceeded to preside over the elections to fill the remaining curule magistracies, rewarding their backers with political office, which they secured by means of lavish bribery and violence when necessary. Praetorships were conferred on two of the tribunes in 56 who had aided Pompey and Crassus by blocking their enemy Marcellinus from holding the consular elections: C. Porcius Cato (*MRR* 3.170) and M. Nonius Sufenas (*MRR* 3.148). To thwart the election of M. Cato to a praetorship, for which he seemed destined to be chosen when he carried the votes of the first unit called upon, Pompey dissolved the assembly by announcing that he had heard thunder, an unfavorable omen.

Subsequently, Pompey employed bribery and violence to defeat Cato and secure the office for the Caesarian tribune of 59, P. Vatinius (Plut. *Cato Min.* 42.1–4; Dio 39.32.1–2).

Next, in keeping with the understandings reached at Luca, the tribune C. Trebonius proposed a bill to give Pompey and Crassus five-year commands over important provinces and armies after their consulships. Opponents of the coalition put up stiff resistance and were met with violence (*MRR* 2.217). By April 27, the date of *Att.* 4.9.1, the *lex Trebonia* must have been passed, but the provinces not yet assigned by the drawing of lots (Plut. *Crass.* 15.5), since Cicero names Syria and Spain without specifying which consul was to receive which. No doubt by prior agreement, Pompey eventually took both Nearer and Farther Spain, which he chose to administer through legates while he remained in Italy. Crassus received Syria, from which he planned to launch a grand war of conquest against the Parthian Empire in the Middle East. Although the *lex Trebonia* itself apparently granted no formal authorization for initiating this war, Crassus' partner Caesar is said to have sent a letter from Gaul in which he endorsed Crassus' intention (Plut. *Crass.* 16.3).

Possibly on the same day that the *lex Trebonia* was adopted (Dio 39.36.2), but certainly not earlier (Plut. *Cato Min.* 43.5), Pompey and Crassus enacted a bill that added five years to Caesar's tenure in Gaul. In describing the effect of the *lex Pompeia Licinia,* the Latin sources invariably use the verb *prorogare*, which means to "extend, or prolong (a term of office)" (Cic. *Att.* 7.6.2, *Phil.* 2.24; Vell. 2.46.2; Suet. *Iul.* 24.1). Hence the five-year term awarded in 55 is not to be viewed as commencing afresh with that year, but instead it lengthened by five years Caesar's term under the *Lex Vatinia* of 59. This interpretation of the effect of the *Lex Pompeia Licinia* is confirmed by Cicero's statement in December 50 (Cic. *Att.* 7.7.6, cf. 9.4) that Caesar had enjoyed a command lasting ten years (*annorum decem imperium*) which had been legally conferred, although Cicero himself did not approve of the legislation. Furthermore, since it clearly emerges from *Prov. cons.* 37 that under the *lex Vatinia* of 59 Caesar's tenure of Cisalpine Gaul was to expire on March 1, 54 (*pace* Seager 2002: 191–2), the effect of the *lex Pompeia Licinia* was to put at Caesar's disposal five further campaign seasons (*aestiva*), those of 54, 53, 52, 51, and 50. Such a view finds support in Hirtius' statement that in the summer of 51 the Gauls realized that only one further summer of campaigning (that in 50) remained at Caesar's disposal (*BG* 8.39.5, *reliquam esse unam aestatem*; see Holmes 1923: 2.303–4 for the correct interpretation of that key passage).

On two separate occasions in February 55, Cicero remarked to his correspondents that the dynasts were firmly in control of affairs for the foreseeable future (*Fam.* 1.8.1, *Qfr.* 2.8.3), but the coalition continued to face opposition and occasionally suffered setbacks. Two tribunes of the plebs, P. Aquillius Gallus and C. Ateius Capito, remained consistently hostile to the consuls and opposed their every move (*MRR* 2.216). Also, despite the fact that Caesar's political ally Pompey presided over the elections for 54, it proved impossible for the dynasts to block for a second time the election of their enemy L. Domitius to a consulship and of their foe M. Cato to a praetorship. Caesar's political stock remained high, however. Late in the year, news of Caesar's daring crossing of the Rhine, which he spanned with a bridge in a mere ten days (*BG* 4.18.1), and his even more astounding feat of crossing the English Channel caused such a sensation that the senate decreed a Thanksgiving of 20 days, five days more than on the previous occasion, two years earlier (*BG* 4.38.4; Dio 39.53.2). At the same time, however, Caesar's political enemy M. Cato took the occasion afforded by Caesar's report of his activities in 55 to propose that Caesar himself be handed over to the Germans in expiation for a massacre carried out against two German tribes during a declared truce (Plut. *Cato Min.* 51.1–4; cf. *Caes.* 22.3, *Comp. Nic. Crass.* 4.3; Suet. *Iul.* 24.3; App. *Celt.* 18). Caesar's justification for his annihilation of the Germans is given in *BG* 4.7–15. No action, of course, was taken by the senate,[5] but the incident served to put Caesar on notice that a day would come when his political enemies would seek to take their revenge, and in the meantime groundwork was being laid for future prosecution.

Coalition under Pressure (54, 53, 52 BC)

In 54, the ties between Caesar and Cicero grew much closer thanks to the appointment of Cicero's brother Quintus as a legate of Caesar in the spring of that year (serving in 53 and 52 as well). Writing to Quintus in July, Cicero remarks that he is confident of the backing of Pompey and Caesar, and he reminds Quintus of one of his brother's chief goals in becoming an officer in Caesar's army, namely the accumulation of enough wealth to settle his considerable debts (*Qfr.* 2.15.2–3). In a letter of the same period to his friend Atticus, Cicero pairs his own name with that of Caesar's agent Oppius and describes the two of them as "friends of Caesar" (*Caesaris amici*, Cic. *Att.* 4.16.8). Cicero goes on to relate their joint activity on behalf of Caesar, who in this year was embarking upon an ambitious building program in Rome.[6] Cicero states that he and Oppius have expended, with Caesar's authorization, 60 million sesterces to purchase land in the heart of Rome that was to become Caesar's new Forum Iulium, extending to the north of the old Roman Forum. This outlay was clearly an enormous sum when we bear in mind that 40 million sesterces was the annual tribute later imposed upon the whole of the new province organized from Caesar's conquests (Suet. *Iul.* 25.1). The purchase of this land reveals the size of the vast financial resources at Caesar's disposal, and it is, in fact, but one part of the whole picture. In the same letter, Cicero describes another building project in which he was also assisting as Caesar's agent, namely the construction of a marble enclosure (Saepta) in the Campus Martius for the voting assemblies.

In 54, Cicero exploited his friendship with Caesar to help advance the careers of young men in his orbit. In April of this year Cicero sent his friend, the up-and-coming jurist C. Trebatius Testa, to join Caesar, and in a surviving letter of introduction addressed to Caesar himself (*Fam.* 7.5) Cicero reveals (§2) both that he had already been in touch with Caesar to press for an appointment on behalf of another young friend, and that Caesar had written to his agent in Rome, the ever-efficient and trusted Balbus, to encourage Cicero to send him more protégés who wanted to seek fame and fortune in Gaul. Both from letters to Cicero's brother (e.g. *Qfr.* 2.14.3) and from letters to Trebatius after he arrived in Gaul (*Fam.* 7.6–18, spanning May 54 to June 53), we can form a vivid impression of the challenges facing young city folk who joined Caesar on campaign with the hope of snatching quick riches and returning to the civilized world of Roman society.

In August 54, one of the bonds that had joined Caesar and Pompey was suddenly and unexpectedly severed by the tragic death of Pompey's young wife Julia, the daughter of Caesar. She died in giving birth to a daughter, who herself died a few days later. Pompey's plans to bury his wife on his country estate at Alba were overridden by the Roman populace, which forced the body to be cremated and buried in the Campus Martius, and this show of popular affection provides a stunning indication of Caesar's standing with the common man in this period (Liv. *Per.* 106; Val. Max. 4.6.4; Vell. 3.47.2; Plut. *Pomp.* 53.4–5, *Caes.* 23.4; Flor. 2.13.13; App. *B Civ.* 2.10; Dio 39.64; cf. *Fam.* 7.9.1, *Qfr.* 3.1.7, 8.3). At that time, Caesar had not yet returned from his second invasion of Britain, and hopes of vast riches from that enterprise were still high, though they were soon to be dashed. Despite the fact that Pompey declined Caesar's later offer to form another marriage connection (Suet. *Iul.* 27), their political alliance showed no signs of strain for the next several years.

As proof that the dynasts continued to be all-powerful, Cicero (*Qfr.* 3.4.1) points to the influence that Pompey had been able to exert in rescuing his old follower A. Gabinius, the ex-consul of 58, from certain conviction on a charge of *maiestas* (treason) in October (*TLRR* no. 296). Although Cicero had little to do with that trial (apart from appearing as a hostile witness), despite his undying hatred for Gabinius because of the aid he had given Clodius in bringing about Cicero's exile, Cicero found himself increasingly pressed into service on behalf of clients who were forced on him by the dynasts. One of these was Caesar's man P. Vatinius, the ex-tribune of 59, whom Cicero defended successfully in August 54 on charges arising out of Vatinius' campaign for the praetorship of 55 (*TLRR* no. 292). Another was the odious Gabinius himself, whom Cicero was compelled to defend at a second trial, when Gabinius was charged with extortion (*TLRR* no. 303). By the time of that trial in November–December, Caesar had returned from his expedition to Britain (*BG* 5.23) but was prevented by an uprising in Gaul from returning south of the Alps in keeping with his usual custom. Therefore, he sent a letter in support of Gabinius, which Pompey read at an assembly of the people (Dio 39.63.4), yet despite the best efforts of the two dynasts and Cicero's defense speech, Gabinius was convicted and went into exile. This setback for the coalition was compounded by the failure of Pompey and Caesar to elect their slate of consuls for 53. In fact, because of a scandal that arose from a bribery scheme that burst out into the open in September of 54 (Cic. *Att.* 4.17.2), the year ended in chaos, without elections having been held. This state of affairs generated a persistent rumor that Pompey was angling to have himself named dictator (Cic. *Q Fr.* 3.6.4, 7.3), and it was not until the summer of 53 that consuls and praetors were finally elected.

Throughout 53, Caesar was occupied with stiff fighting in Gaul, and at the beginning of the year he even had to borrow from Pompey a legion that Pompey had raised in Cisalpine Gaul during his consulship in 55 (*BG* 6.1.2, 8.54.2; Plut. *Cato Min.* 45.3). Caesar acquired these reinforcements from his political ally and enrolled two new legions of his own (*BG* 6.1) to compensate for the loss of 15 cohorts (the equivalent of a legion and a half) that were destroyed in the uprising of the Eburones in late 54 (*BG* 5.26–37). In the late summer of 53, Caesar sent his young officer Mark Antony to Rome to stand for the quaestorship, and Caesar wrote to Cicero, asking him to patch up his previous differences with Antony and support his candidacy (Cic. *Phil.* 2.49). Caesar's letter to Cicero must have been typical of many that he wrote from Gaul to influence the course of Roman politics from afar. In the early months of 53, Caesar also sent a squadron of 1,000 Gallic horse, under the command of his young legate P. Crassus, to join the ill-fated Parthian expedition of the dynast Marcus Crassus (Plut. *Crass.* 17.4). The defeat of Crassus at the Battle of Carrhae on June 9 and his subsequent death (*MRR* 2.230) left Pompey and Caesar as the sole surviving members of the three-way alliance. Meanwhile, in Rome, violence reigned, caused by rivalry between the gang leaders Milo, whom Cicero backed for the consulship of 52, and Cicero's old archenemy P. Clodius, who was a candidate for the praetorship. Finally, the year ended, as had the previous one, without it being possible to elect magistrates for the new year.

In the winter of 53–2, after an absence of two whole campaign seasons (in 54 and 53), Caesar found himself once more in his customary winter quarters south of the Alps (*BG* 6.44.3). Cicero (as Pompey's emissary?) paid Caesar a visit at Ravenna, where he was asked to use his influence with the tribune M. Caelius to secure one of Caesar's political goals in 52 (Cic. *Att.* 7.1.4). At the beginning of that year, there occurred a serious breakdown in law and order in Rome. The crisis in the city was precipitated by riots sparked by the murder of the demagogue P. Clodius, who was killed on January 18 in a brawl with followers of Milo. As yet no consuls or praetors or quaestors had been elected for 52; there were those who proposed that Pompey and his partner Caesar be named consuls to restore order (Suet. *Iul.* 26.1). However, whereas Pompey was on the scene and available for this assignment, Caesar was faced with the necessity of hastening to Transalpine Gaul to combat a serious and widespread rebellion that broke out in the recently conquered territories under the leadership of the charismatic chieftain Vercingetorix (*BG* 7.1–5).

Ultimately, absolute power was placed in Pompey's hands when the senate adopted the highly unusual expedient of recommending the election of Pompey as consul without a colleague (*MRR* 2.234). This was done on the motion of M. Cato's son-in-law M. Bibulus, Caesar's ex-consular colleague and long-time political opponent (Asc. 36C). The aim was to avoid resurrecting the office of dictator, the normal means of arming a single magistrate to cope with a serious crisis, but an office in bad odor because of the murderous tyranny of the dictator Sulla (82–79 BC). To compensate Caesar for the loss in sharing power with Pompey as his consular colleague, Pompey supported passage of a bill granting Caesar the right to stand for a future consulship *in absentia* (Cic. *Att.* 7.3.4, 8.3.3; Flor. 2.13.16; App. *B Civ.* 2.25). The law conferring this privilege on Caesar was passed with the backing of all ten tribunes (Caes. *BC* 1.9.2; Liv. *Per.* 107; Suet. *Iul.* 26.1; Dio 40.50.3–4), despite stout opposition from Cato (Caes. *BC* 1.32.3; Liv. *Per.* 107; Plut. *Pomp.* 56.3). And later in the year, when Pompey passed his law *de iure magistratuum* reaffirming the requirement that candidates canvass in person for public office in Rome, he specifically upheld Caesar's exemption (*Cic. Att.* 8.3.3).[7]

It must have become increasingly evident to Caesar that his political enemies, led by Cato, intended to take revenge on him by haling him into court as soon as he ceased to enjoy immunity from prosecution by virtue of holding *imperium*. This threat is what Caesar claimed, after his victory at the Battle of Pharsalia in 48, had forced him to go to war for the sake of self-preservation (Suet. *Iul.* 30.4, on the authority of Asinius Pollio, who was present at the battle). Doubts raised by Shackleton Bailey (1965: 39), who challenged the plausibility of that ascribed motive, have recently been restated at length by Morstein-Marx (2007), but given the attempt by the tribune Antistius to prosecute Caesar in 56 and the demand by Cato in 55 that Caesar be handed over to the Germans, the threat of prosecution was certainly to be reckoned with (Brunt 1986: 18). Hence the Law of the Ten Tribunes in 52, granting Caesar an exemption from the requirement of canvassing in person for his second consulship, represented for Caesar an asset of considerable value. Because of it, he could stand for office without having to return from his province and without having to surrender his *imperium* (and immunity from prosecution) as a consequence of being forced to cross the *pomerium*, as he had been compelled to do at the time of his first candidacy for the consulship in 60 (Suet. *Iul.* 18.2).

While it is true that no specific year for Caesar's future candidacy was most likely specified in the tribunician legislation of 52 (so Gruen 1974: 476), the extension of five campaign seasons granted by the *lex Pompeia Licinia* of 55 (those of 54, 53, 52, 51, and 50) made it logical for Caesar to stand in 49 for the consulship of 48 – the first for which he would be eligible under Sulla's requirement that ten years had to elapse before the consulship was repeated.[8] It was for a candidacy in 49 that Caesar began laying the groundwork in the summer of 50, when he canvassed the voters in support of Mark Antony's election to an augurate (Hirt. *BG* 8.50.4). Caesar himself later claimed that the Law of the Ten Tribunes specifically had in view a candidacy in the year 49 (*BC* 1.9.2). And he also complained in the same passage that by demanding his return from Gaul in January 49, his enemies were depriving him of half a year of his governorship because the dispensation granted to him by Law of the Ten Tribunes should have permitted him to remain in Gaul for another six months and sue for the consulship of 48 *in absentia*.

When Caesar set out in early March of 52 for Transalpine Gaul to crush the revolt of Vercingetorix, Caesar expressed himself as well satisfied with the steps that Pompey was taking in Rome to restore order (*BG* 7.6.1). It is against this background of trust between the two dynasts that we are to judge the legislation sponsored by Pompey in his third consulship. Among a whole host of reforms enacted by Pompey in 52, the one that had the most far-reaching consequences for Caesar's command was Pompey's *lex de provinciis*, which introduced a five-year gap between holding office in Rome and governing a province abroad (Dio 40.56.1, cf. 30.1, 46.2; Caes. *BC* 1.85.9). The new regulations had dire consequences for Caesar's security, which hinged upon his ability to retain his command in Gaul up to the beginning of his prospective second consulship (in 48). Previously, under the procedure prescribed by the Sempronian law, the senate had to designate consular provinces in advance of the consular elections, and so, because the *lex Pompeia Licinia* of 55 appears to have barred the senate from considering the assignment of the Gauls prior to March 1, 50 (unless Caesar completed the pacification of Gaul before that date), the earliest that Caesar could have been succeeded was 49 BC, by one of the consuls elected in 50 for 49. The clearest indication that the law of 55 contained such a restriction on the reassignment of the Gauls is provided by the statement attributed to Pompey in October 51 that before March 1, 50 no decision could be taken concerning Caesar's provinces *sine iniuria* – i.e. it would be illegitimate to do so (Cael. *Fam.* 8.8.9, cf. 9.5). However, since under Pompey's *lex de provinciis* of 52 succession could take place without any appreciable gap between the senate's decision and the assumption of power by the new governor, Caesar became potentially exposed to replacement any time after March1, 50. Still, the senate was not entirely free to do as it pleased because Pompey's law, unlike the Sempronian, did not ban the use of a tribune's veto to block action by the senate. Therefore, Caesar's strategy during the last few years of his command was always to have on his side the services of one or more loyal tribunes. The names and activities of four of these pro-Caesarian tribunes are well documented in 51 (*MRR* 2.241). In 50, the chief role of defending Caesar's interests was played by the tribune C. Scribonius Curio (*MRR* 2.249). And after Curio laid down his office on December 9, 50, the torch was passed to the tribunes Mark Antony, who had served with Caesar in Gaul since late 54, and to Q. Cassius Longinus (not to be confused with C. Cassius, the future assassin of Caesar, also tr. pl. in 49).

Of course, extended commands like Caesar's and Pompey's lay outside the normal practice, which envisaged the replacement of governors every year or two. Since Pompey's five-year term as governor of the two Spains, granted by the *lex Trebonia* of 55, was due to run out at the end of the following year, Pompey took the step of having his command extended for five years (Dio 40.44.2, 56.2; App. *B Civ.* 2.24; incorrectly stated as a four-year extension by Plut. *Pomp.* 55.7, *Caes.* 28.5). Although this maneuver was later viewed as a grab for power at the expense of his partner Caesar, who was locked in a desperate struggle against the insurgent leader Vercingetorix, the strengthening of Pompey's position was, on the contrary, potentially useful to Caesar in his bid for a future consulship (of 48). It posed no threat to him, so long as the two dynasts remained on friendly terms, as they most certainly did in 52 and the year following.

In these and other respects, then, the power of Caesar and Pompey was well secured by the legislation of 52. Furthermore, their archenemy M. Cato was defeated for the consulship of 51 (Plut. *Cato Min.* 49.2; Dio 40.58.1–3; Liv. *Per.* 108; cf. Caes. *BC* 1.4.1), and Caesar's success in crushing the revolt of Vercingetorix was celebrated with the decree of a Thanksgiving lasting 20 days (*BG* 7.90.8; Suet. *Iul.* 24). On the other hand, one of the two consuls elected for 51, M. Claudius Marcellus, was an avowed enemy of Caesar (Plut. *Caes.* 29.1), and in December 52, or early 51, the dynasts were powerless, despite Pompey's best efforts, to avert the conviction of the ex-tribune T. Munatius Plancus when he ceased to hold office after December 9, 52 (*TLRR* no. 327). Plancus succumbed to a prosecution launched by Cicero for Plancus' role in the violence sparked by Clodius' murder (*Fam.* 7.2.2), and the convicted defendant sought refuge at Ravenna, in Caesar's province, where his needs were well provided for (Cael. *Fam.* 8.1.4). Caesar, however, chose to remain north of the Alps, both in the winter of 52–1 (at Bibracte, *BG* 7.90.8) and in the one following. For this reason, his accessibility to politicians in Rome was restricted to correspondence and intermediaries, as opposed to face-to-face consultations in Cisalpina.

Coalition Dissolves (51, 50 BC)

In 51, the chief opponent of Caesar was the consul M. Claudius Marcellus. Early in the year, Marcellus called upon the senate to annul the citizen rights of the colonists settled by Caesar at Novum Comum, a town at the foot of the Alps, in Transpadane Gaul, the region of Cisalpina north of the Po River (Suet. *Iul.* 28.3). Marcellus asserted that Caesar had exceeded the authority granted to him under the *lex Vatinia* of 59, but action by the senate was apparently blocked by the veto of a pro-Caesarian tribune (Cic. *Att.* 5.2.3). The issue was a volatile one because residents of native communities north of the Po, unlike their citizen counterparts in Cisalpina to the south, lacked full voting privileges in Roman assemblies and could not hold political office in Rome. Instead, the Transpadanes enjoyed a status known as Latin rights (*ius Latii*), a half-way house to Roman citizenship, and as early as around 68 (see *MRR* 3.106) Caesar had supported the aspirations of the Transpadanes to gain full Roman citizenship (Suet. *Iul.* 8). In May 51, there were even rumors, which proved false, that Caesar was going to encourage the Transpadanes to lay claim to this status illegally (Cic. *Att.* 5.2.3; Cael. *Fam.* 8.1.2).[9] To keep up pressure, in June Marcellus took the bold step of seizing a citizen of Comum and ordering this visitor to Rome to be flogged, a punishment that was not legally permitted against a Roman citizen (Cic. *Att.* 5.11.2). Marcellus did so, apparently, on the grounds that in his view Caesar's citizen colony was illegal and so its members were entitled only to Latin status. This will explain why Cicero in his letter raises the issue of the status of Marcellus' victim as a possible ex-magistrate since magistrates of a Latin community gained by virtue of their office full Roman citizenship.[10] Cicero judged the matter an "ugly" affair (*foede*) in either case, one that was bound to offend both Caesar and Pompey.[11]

Meanwhile the consul M. Marcellus kept demanding that Caesar give up his provinces and dismiss his army on the grounds that there was no longer any need for such a large military force (ten legions) after the fall of the rebel stronghold Alesia in the autumn of 52.[12] Caesar's decision to spend the winter of 52–51 north of the Alps demonstrated, however, the need for vigilance and for further action against potential trouble spots. Indeed, in May 51 there was briefly a rumor, which proved to be false, that Caesar was once again in difficulty and under siege by a rebel uprising that had resulted in the loss of his cavalry (Cael. *Fam.* 8.1.4). Marcellus' agitation to have Caesar recalled was blocked by his consular colleague, Ser. Sulpicius Rufus (Suet. *Iul.* 28.2; App. *B Civ.* 2.26; Dio 40.59.1; Liv. *Per.* 108; cf. *Fam.* 4.4.3), but Marcellus kept pressing his case. As part of the strategy of Caesar's enemies to undermine his strength and detach Pompey from his political alliance with Caesar, Pompey was urged at a meeting of the senate on 22 July to set a date for the recall of the legion that he had loaned to Caesar in January 53 (see above, p. 46). Pompey refused to commit himself to a specific date, but he did agree to reclaim the troops, and thus reduce the size of Caesar's army, at some future date (Cael. *Fam.* 8.4.4). Later, by early September, Pompey let it be known that he was adamantly opposed to any decision being taken in 51 concerning Caesar's succession (Cael. *Fam.* 8.9.5), but at the same time Pompey's father-in-law, Metellus Scipio (sending a signal on Pompey's behalf?), sponsored a motion calling upon the senate to give priority to a decision on the Gallic provinces on March 1, 50 BC (ibid.). This motion caused Caesar's agent Balbus to remonstrate with Scipio (ibid.), but on September 29 a compromise was struck. The senate decreed that on and after March 1, 50 priority should be given to a decision on *all* consular provinces (*de consularibus provinciis*), not just Caesar's provinces of Gaul (Cael. *Fam.* 8.8.5). However, at the same meeting on September 29, three tribunes friendly to Caesar blocked an attempt by Caesar's enemies to make the future debate not subject to a tribune's veto. And so, when the time came, Caesar could, and did, ward off any decision unfavorable to his interests by having action by the senate vetoed.

In July of 51, the elections did not produce results favorable to Caesar. One of the new consuls, C. Marcellus (a cousin of the consul of 51), was the husband of Caesar's grand-niece Octavia (sister of the future emperor Augustus) but not a Caesarian (Suet. *Iul.* 29.1; Dio 40.59.4; App. *B Civ.* 2.26). Marcellus' colleague, L. Aemilius Paullus (brother of the future Triumvir M. Lepidus), had no fondness for Caesar, but his great need for cash to carry out his lavish rebuilding of the Basilica Aemilia (Paulli) on the north side of the Forum, just to the east of the senate-house, made it possible for Caesar to purchase his loyalty in exchange for Gallic gold: 1,500 talents (= 36 million sesterces) according to Plut. *Caes.* 29.3 and App. *B Civ.* 2.26. The elections in 51 also elevated to the tribunate an inveterate enemy of Caesar, C. Scribonius Curio (Cael. *Fam.* 8.4.2). Curio's political leanings at the time of his election, and as late as October 51 (Cael. *Fam.* 8.8.10), were judged to be decidedly anti-Caesarian, as they had been throughout the decade. It was even said that Caesar had shown his contempt for Curio by not attempting to purchase his support (Cael. *Fam.* 8.4.2). To everyone's surprise, however, Curio did a sudden about-face in the spring of 50 (Cic. *Att.* 6.3.4) and turned into Caesar's staunchest supporter. The tradition in later sources is that Caesar won Curio to his side by settling his enormous debts.[13]

When the senate took up the consular provinces in March 50, Curio used his veto to prevent any decision to name Caesar's replacement, and he opposed Pompey's proposal in April that Caesar leave his province on the Ides (13th) of November (Cael. *Fam.* 8.11.3). If, as argued previously, the *lex Pompeia Licinia* of 55 envisaged granting Caesar five further military campaign seasons (those of 54, 53, 52, 51, and 50), it is quite easy to see how Pompey could have represented the Ides of November as a fair and reasonable terminal date (*aequum*), one in keeping with the spirit of the extension of Caesar's command in 55. The Ides of November was a time of year by which it would have been normal to disperse legions to winter quarters and for warfare to be suspended.[14] On the other hand, it could, of course, be objected by

Caesar and his supporters that he was being deprived of his command approximately one year ahead of the schedule that had been projected in 55, when succession by one of the consuls of 49, in late 49, would have been anticipated (see above, pp. 48–9).

About May 50, alarm was raised over the possibility of a Parthian invasion on the eastern frontier, and the senate decreed that Pompey and Caesar should each contribute one legion to bolster forces in Syria. Pompey, who had been pressed by Caesar's enemies to do so earlier (see above, p. 51), now demanded back from Caesar the legion that he had loaned to his partner in January 53, and Pompey offered it in fulfillment of the requirement that he furnish a legion.[15] The result of this action, therefore, was to subtract not merely one but two legions from Caesar's available forces since, in addition to sending back Pompey's legion, Caesar had to contribute one of his own (*BG* 8.54.3; Plut. *Caes.* 29.3, *Pomp.* 56.3; App. *B Civ.* 2.29; Dio 40.65). The two legions were sent to Capua for trans-shipment to the Middle East, but when the threat of danger from the Parthians evaporated (Cic. *Fam.* 2.17.5) the troops remained stationed in Italy to serve as a defense in case Caesar invaded from the north.

Clearly this maneuver of Pompey in May, which deprived Caesar of two legions, coupled with Pompey's proposal in April that Caesar be required to hand over his army and province on the Ides of November, signaled a serious rift in relations between the two former partners. By early August, Pompey was said to have made up his mind not to allow Caesar to be elected consul, unless he first surrendered his army and provinces, whereas Caesar was equally convinced that he could not escape destruction by his political enemies unless he retained his army (Cael. *Fam.* 8.14.2). Cicero's correspondent M. Caelius (aed. 50) was certain that Caesar would call up his army and come to the defense of his tribune Curio, if Caesar's political enemies presumed to ride roughshod over Curio's veto (Cael. *Fam.* 8.11.3).

There was one brief moment, however, in the late spring of 50 (May–June) when fate nearly took a hand to prevent Pompey and Caesar from coming to blows. On a visit to Naples, Pompey fell seriously ill, and for a time it appeared that he was likely to die. The glorious rejoicing and public sacrifices of thanksgiving throughout Italy that celebrated his miraculous recovery doubtless served to give Pompey a false sense of invincibility and of devotion on the part of the Roman people (Vell. 2.48.2; Plut. *Pomp.* 57.1; Dio 41.6.3–4). Something of Pompey's puffed-up state of mind is revealed by the boast that he is said to have made at that time when he asserted that merely by stamping his foot on the ground he could raise vast armies in Italy (Plut. *Pomp.* 57.5). Later, when in the first few months of 49 Caesar's rapid advance from the north forced Pompey to carry out a strategic retreat from Rome and Italy because he lacked seasoned troops, Pompey had these words cast back at him by his impatient senatorial backers (Plut. *Pomp.* 60.4).

At about this same time (May?) Caesar sent his quaestor of 51, Mark Antony, to Rome to stand for a vacancy in the augurate and for a tribunate in 49. Antony was successful in both elections, and his defeat of Caesar's inveterate enemy L. Domitius (consul 54) for the augurate must have given Caesar great pleasure. We are told that the proconsul wrote to the citizen communities in Cisalpine Gaul south of the Po to solicit support for Antony's candidacy. Caesar even returned to Cisalpina (probably in July) for the first time since the winter of 53–52 (Hirt. *BG* 8.51.2) in order to canvass on Antony's behalf, but before he could use his influence, he learned the successful outcome of Antony's candidacy (Hirt. *BG* 8.50.3). Quite a different outcome, however, greeted Caesar's candidate for the consulship of 49, his former legate Ser. Sulpicius Galba. At the elections of 50, Galba failed to gain office despite a strong showing at the polls,[16] and the two consuls chosen for 49 were bitter, irreconcilable enemies of Caesar: C. Claudius Marcellus, brother of Caesar's implacable foe M. Marcellus (consul 51), and L. Cornelius Lentulus Crus. There was briefly a rumor that Caesar had been able to win Lentulus Crus to his side (Cic. *Att.* 6.8.2 of Oct. 50), but in the end Caesar's chief allies among the magistrates of 49 were restricted to three praetors (ibid.), one of them M. Lepidus, the future Triumvir, and the two tribunes Mark Antony and Q. Cassius.

As the year 50 drew to a close, it became increasingly evident that the vast majority in the senate wanted to avoid open conflict. On December 1, Curio proposed a motion calling upon both Caesar and Pompey to dismiss their armies, and it drew support from 370 senators against a mere 22 naysayers (App. *B Civ.* 2.30; Plut. *Pomp.* 58.3–5, *Caes.* 30.1–2), but the consul C. Marcellus dismissed the senate before any formal resolution could be certified (Hirt. *BG* 8.52.5). On the next day, Marcellus tried to pass a motion summoning to Rome as a defense force the two legions that had been withdrawn from Caesar and stationed at Capua. When that proposal was vetoed by Curio, Marcellus, on his own authority, presented Pompey with a sword and urged him to take command of the two existing legions and enroll additional troops (Dio 40.64.4; Plut. *Pomp.* 58.6; App. *B Civ.* 2.31). After his last day as tribune on December 9, Curio hastened off to join Caesar at Ravenna (App. *B Civ.* 2.31; Dio 40.66.5), by which time Caesar had already summoned two of his eight legions in Transalpina (the 8th and the 12th) to join him south of the Alps, where he had at his disposal one legion, the 13th (Hirt. *BG* 8.54.3). See Carter 1991: 165–6.

From December 10 onwards, the chief role in defending Caesar's interests fell to the daring tribune Mark Antony, who on December 21 delivered at a public meeting a blistering invective against Pompey (Cic. *Att.* 7.8.5). By the end of the first week of January 49, the attempt to reach a compromise in the senate had broken down. On the night of January 7–8, perceived threats against their safety caused the tribunes Antony and Q. Cassius to flee from Rome in disguise and join Caesar in Cisalpine Gaul (*BC* 1.5.5), where he was poised to launch a blitzkrieg against his woefully unprepared enemies in Rome. Four days later, on the night of January 11–12 (*BC* 1.8.1), Caesar crossed the tiny river Rubicon, which served as a boundary between his province and Italy on the Adriatic coast. He thereby set in motion a civil war that was to rage intermittently for two decades, until an end was finally marked in August 29 BC by the triple triumph of his grand-nephew Octavian Caesar, the future emperor Augustus. It was a desperate act, in a desperate situation, aptly encapsulated in the famous remark that is attributed to Caesar: "Let the die be cast."[17]

FURTHER READING

Still the best and most scholarly biography of Julius Caesar in English is the one by Matthias Gelzer, *Caesar: Politician and Statesman* (1968). A detailed account of Caesar's proconsulship is found in chapter 4 (pp. 102–94). For a good treatment of the politics in the decade of the 50s, see T. P. Wiseman, "Caesar, Pompey and Rome, 59–50 B.C.," *CAH*, vol. 9, 2nd edn. (1994). Of the other major figures in this period, the best recent biographies are those by Thomas Mitchell for Cicero (1991), by W. Jeffrey Tatum for Clodius (1999), and by Robin Seager for Pompey (2002). Erich Gruen, in his *Last Generation of the Roman Republic* (1974), provides in chapter 11 (pp. 449–97) a careful analysis of the years leading up to the outbreak of the civil war in 49. One will find there a good summary of scholarly opinion on the vexed question of Caesar's "right" to retain his provinces, the so-called *Rechtsfrage*, and in Robert Morstein-Marx's 2007 *Historia* article there is a thorough review of the considerations that may have driven Caesar to embark upon the civil war. The many criminal prosecutions in this period that often had political implications for the dynasts and their enemies are treated in chapters 7 and 8 of Gruen's *Last Generation*. Particularly enlightening for the years 58 to 56 is Robert Kaster's translation of and commentary on Cicero's *Pro Sestio* (2006). Appendix I, "Ciceronian Chronology, 58–56 BCE" (pp. 393–408) provides a detailed ephemeris for politics in Rome during those crucial years, and the supporting evidence for conclusions drawn in the table is presented in lavish footnotes. For Caesar's activities and movements in Gaul during the period of his proconsulship, there is, alas, no comparable ephemeris in English, but for those who read German, the appendix in Wolfgang Will's *Julius Caesar: Eine Bilanz* (Stuttgart, 1992), "Chronologie des Krieges in Gallien," (pp. 105–14), can be most heartily recommended. And finally, for a good discussion, with bibliography, of the supposed musings of Caesar before crossing the Rubicon and the famous utterance "Let the die be cast," see the appendix of Robert Morstein-Marx's paper "*Dignitas* and *res publica*: Caesar and Republican legitimacy," in K.-J. Hölkeskamp (ed.), *Eine politische Kultur (in) der Krise? Die "letzte Generation" der römischen Republik* (Munich, Oldenbourg 2008). That same paper tries to show that Caesar's public actions and his public explanation of them at the outbreak of the civil war were consistent with widely shared, traditional views about how the Republic was supposed to work. And so, Caesar's position was probably seen by many, especially outside the senate, as in better accord with Republican traditions than that of Pompey and the diehards in the senate.

ACKNOWLEDGMENT

My work on this chapter was supported by a Fellowship from the National Endowment for the Humanities. I thank E. Badian and R. Morstein-Marx for reading and commenting on an earlier draft.

NOTES

1 Early in January 58, Clodius had passed a rapid succession of laws that ingratiated him with the urban mob (*MRR* 2.196). Among these laws was a bill providing for the distribution of free grain to Roman citizens and another that overturned the senate's ban on *collegia* (trade guilds or mutual-aid societies), which had been suppressed in 64 to

prevent their use to influence the vote in assemblies or to promote violence for the disruption of assemblies and courts (Asc. 7C).

2 At the time of the elections (14 or 18 July, see Kaster 2006: 398) Caesar was in a lull between his two major campaigns in 58 and so able to turn his attention to affairs in Rome, the Helvetians having been defeated at Bibracte in late June (*BG* 1.23–6; Dio 38.33.3–5), while the victory over Ariovistus fell sometime in September, before the 25th (*BG* 1.50–3; Dio 38.4–50).

3 Ibid. §6. The trouble is to be explained, no doubt, as having been caused, in part, by Clodius' grain law of 58 (see above, n. 1), which placed a severe strain upon the treasury, as well as on the infrastructure for the transport, storage, and distribution of grain.

4 Such a set of understandings between Appius and Caesar will help to explain the dramatic switch in allegiance on the part of Clodius. After he reconciled his differences with Pompey (Cic. *Mil.* 21, 79; *Schol. Bob.* 170St), Clodius began to praise Pompey (Cic. *Har. resp.* 50–2) and aid his bid for the consulship of 55 (Dio 39.29), while helping block the rival candidacy of L. Domitius (Cic. *Att.* 4.8a.2). Part of the basis for the good relations between Clodius and Pompey may lie in the marriage of Clodius' niece, the daughter of App. Claudius, to Pompey's son Gnaeus, if that marriage occurred in 56, as Tatum (1991) argues.

5 Suet. (*Iul.* 24.3) alone claims that the senate sent out *legati* (a commission) to investigate the charges, apparently confusing with a special commission the senate's authorization of Caesar's ten legates in the spring of 56 (see above, p. 42). Dio (39.25.1) likewise mistakenly connects these ten *legati* of Caesar with the senate's usual practice of sending a commission of ten to regulate affairs after the conquest of new territory. Stanton (2003: 88) accepts the commission of inquiry as fact.

6 Caesar's aim, of course, was to win popular acclaim by rivaling the magnificence of Pompey's recently completed stone theatre in the Campus Martius (dedicated 55 BC).

7 The tradition that Pompey out of forgetfulness (*per oblivionem*) failed at first to recognize Caesar's recently won privilege, only to restore it by the dubious means of adding a codicil to his law after it had already been inscribed and filed in the Record Office (Suet. *Iul.* 28.3; Dio 40.56.3), almost certainly rests on anti-Pompeian propaganda. The fact that Pompey's bill is not known to have met with resistance from any of the tribunes, as it surely would have if it had been perceived as canceling Caesar's privilege outright, is proof that Pompey bore in mind the interests of his political partner Caesar (Balsdon 1962: 141).

8 App. *B Civ.* 1.100; cf. Caes. *BC* 1.32.2. However, when pressure grew in the senate for Caesar to hand over his provinces at the earliest possible date, there was speculation in October 51 that he might stand at the elections in 50 for the consulship of 49 (Cael. *Fam.* 8.8.9). To do so would have required a dispensation from Sulla's ten-year rule, but the third consulship of Pompey in 52, a mere two years after his second consulship in 55, demonstrates how easily such a statute could be waived.

9 The stakes were high because to have earned the credit for extending the Roman franchise to the region north of the Po would have added enormously to Caesar's *clientela* and greatly enhanced his clout in Roman voting assemblies. His enemies in the senate could not stand still for this.

10 The later sources show some confusion over the status of Marcellus' victim, Plutarch (*Caes.* 29. 2) making him a member of the town council, while Appian (*B Civ.* 2.26) identifies him as an ex-magistrate. Appian (ibid.) is surely mistaken in asserting that Caesar founded a Latin, not a citizen, colony at Novum Comum. The *lex Vatinia* of 59 had

clearly empowered Caesar to confer full Roman citizenship on his new colonists (Suet. *Iul.* 28.3; Strabo 213C, with Cic. *Fam.* 13.35.1).

11 Pompey's interests were affected because his father, Pompey Strabo (consul 89), had founded a colony at Comum in the previous generation (Strabo 213C) and had conferred Latin rights on the whole Transpadane region by a law passed in his consulship (Asc. 3C). Possibly, too, some of Caesar's colonists were drawn from Pompey's veterans (How 1926: 244).

12 Marcellus' demand appears to have been made as early as the beginning of March 51 (Cic. *Att.* 8.3.3); see Giovannini 1983: 139–41 for the correct interpretation of that passage.

13 Said to have ranged anywhere from a few million (Schol. Lucan 4.820; Serv. *Aen.* 6.621) to as high as ten (Vell. 2.48.3–4) or even 60 million sesterces (Val. Max. 9.1.6). No contemporary source, however, reports such a cash transaction, and it is tempting to follow Lacey (1961: 324–9) in viewing Curio as changing sides out of political considerations, much as Cicero's friend M. Caelius did in December 50 (Cic. *Att.* 7.3.6).

14 Balsdon 1939: 67 points out that the Ides November may have been the traditional date for consuls to set out from Rome to assume command of their provinces.

15 This was not done without some justification since pay for that legion had continued to be drawn from Pompey's account even while it was serving under Caesar in Gaul (Cael. *Fam.* 8.4.4).

16 The language in Hirtius (*BG* 8.50.4) suggests that undue influence was used by Caesar's enemies to block Galba: see Girardet 2000: 704.

17 Said to have been uttered in Greek (Plut. *Pomp.* 60.2, cf. *Caes.* 32.6), it being a well-attested proverb, not confined to Menander (fr. 59, ed. Körte). I thank E. Badian for spurring me to ponder why Asinius Pollio, Caesar's companion at the crossing of the Rubicon and clearly the origin of "let the die be cast" tradition, caused this colorful detail to be added to the story of Caesar's invasion of Italy, while Caesar himself gives it no place in *BC* 1.8. It seems that the aim in Caesar's account was to portray the conqueror of Gaul as the victim of circumstances, forced to go to war as the only alternative to surrendering to his enemies. Pollio, by contrast, chose to introduce an element of anguished hesitation and dramatic hand-wringing on the part of Caesar before he took such a momentous and irrevocable step. In that context, the proverbial expression "let the die be cast" provides ideal closure.

CHAPTER FIVE

The Dictator

Jane F. Gardner

Caesar's constitutional powers during the period 49–44 BC were derived partly from the consulship, to which he was elected four times (48, 46–44) and partly from the dictatorship, to which he was first appointed, irregularly, in 49. A dictator was not elected, but nominated directly by a consul. Caesar's most urgent need in 49 BC was immediate election to the consulship for 48, but since both consuls had already fled from Italy early in 49, the consular elections for 48 could not be held. An enabling law allowed the praetor M. Lepidus to nominate a dictator (Cic. *Att.* 9.9.3, 9.15.2; Caes. *BC* 2.21.5), and he duly nominated Caesar, while the latter was still at Massilia (mid-49 BC).

Dictators had been appointed only rarely under the Republic, to meet a variety of immediate needs, and the powers of the office seem never to have been precisely defined in law. Despite some traditions to the contrary, these powers do not seem in practice to have been regarded as absolute, nor as overriding those of other magistrates (Lintott 1999a: 109–13). The two tribunes, Caesetius and Marullus, to whose provocative, and increasingly disruptive, behavior Caesar had reacted with impatience in 44 BC (Plut. *Caes.* 61.10; Suet. *Iul.* 79.1), were deposed from office early in that year, not directly by the dictator himself, but on the proposal of a fellow tribune, C. Helvius Cinna (Dio 44.10.3; 46.49.2). Caesar's personal dominance during these years rested not so much on any office as on his military power and the loyalty (so far as it could be relied upon) of those who had gained, or hoped to gain, something from him.

Traditionally, the dictatorship had been a short-term magistracy, to carry out any duties, military or civil, for which the consuls were unavailable. It had the advantage that, unlike a consul, the dictator had a deputy, his "master of horse" (*magister equitum*), who was not an equal colleague, but personally appointed by him and responsible directly and solely to him. While Caesar was engaged, as he was for much of the remainder of his life, away from Rome, his master of horse could act at Rome with the authority of the dictator. However, as events soon showed, this did not mean that Caesar was able closely to monitor, let alone control, the activities of his subordinates.

The terms of reference of dictators were often unspecific; the official description was *rei gerundae causa* (roughly "to take necessary action"). This was a general term, which might cover appointment both for military command (the most common case mentioned in the sources) and for civil duties in general, although appointments had sometimes been made for specific administrative tasks, such as holding elections, or organizing the Latin Festival.

A dictator (and perhaps also his master of horse) could convene assemblies. Whether he could also put legislation directly to them is unclear. Neither Sulla nor Caesar, Rome's last two dictators, can provide a clear answer to this historical question, nor is one strictly necessary. Sulla, the first dictator for over 120 years, was exceptionally given unlimited powers "to enact such laws as he thought best, and to regulate the constitution," and without time limit (though he abdicated after about a year); Appian called this "absolute tyranny" (App. *B Civ.* 1.98–100; *MRR* 2.66–7, 3.74–5).

Caesar, it must be remembered, was not only appointed dictator several times, but during the same few years also had four consulships. Besides, as he himself emphasizes (*BC* 3.2), laws could be enacted on his behalf by other magistrates. The sources attribute many measures to Caesar, without always specifying whether they were actually carried through by him personally, or by others on his behalf, or which of several possible methods – e.g. enactment through assembly, plebiscite, senatorial decree, edict – was used.

Caesar's first dictatorship, in 49 BC, was of brief duration, and by his own account (*BC* 3.1–2) was primarily administrative. He spent 11 days in Rome, late in the year, before abdicating and going to Brundisium in pursuit of Pompey. He conducted the essential routine business of holding elections of magistrates (including his own consulship for 48 BC), assigning magistrates to the provinces, and celebrating the Latin Festival; he appointed no master of horse.

How explicitly, if at all, the terms of reference of Caesar's subsequent dictatorships were laid down is unknown. He spent much of the time away from Rome, and when he returned from Spain in 45, after defeating the remnants of Pompeian opposition, he was already planning further prolonged absence, for campaigning against Parthia. The long-disputed, though often now accepted, view that these dictatorships should be described, not as *rei gerundae causa*, but, like Sulla's, as *rei publicae constituendae* ("for the reconstitution of the state") rests on very slender evidence (*MRR* 3.107–8), and is less important than what was actually done.

The precise dates of appointment, and duration, of the dictatorships, and their relation to his consulships, cannot be established. For the evidence, and its problems, see *MRR* 2, under the years 49–44 BC, especially 284–5 n. 1, and see also 3.106–8. The sources are generally imprecise. Moreover, any dates given are difficult to calibrate precisely with any ancient or modern calendar, since the introduction of the Julian calendar (see Wardle, chapter 8, Fantham, chapter 11, and Raaflaub, chapter 13 in this volume), though necessary, itself introduced further complications

(Bickerman 1980: 40–51; Michels 1967: 22, 33 n. 3). As a necessary preliminary, 46 BC was extended by intercalations to 445 days, in order to realign the beginning of the astronomical and calendar years with each other and with the start of the new Julian calendar in 45 BC. Much dating is therefore approximate; moreover, we are often dependent on much later sources, such as Cassius Dio, or on indirect evidence, such as the presence or absence of relevant titles (e.g. serially numbered consulships or dictatorships) from coins or inscriptions.

Consul in 48 BC, Caesar was nominated dictator for the second time by his fellow consul in Rome, P. Servilius Isauricus, after news of Pharsalus arrived (October 48?), and by December Mark Antony was apparently behaving as his master of horse at Rome (Cic. *Att.* 11.7.2). According to Plutarch *Caes.* 51.1 and Dio 42.20.3, Caesar held this dictatorship for a full year (the traditional limit had been six months), returning to Rome from the East at the end of it (late September 47?) for a brief period, before leaving again for Africa. There appears to have been a gap between the end of the second dictatorship, and the start of the third, several months into 46 BC.

The third dictatorship was to be for ten years, initially renewed annually (*Bell. Hisp.* 2.1; Dio 43.14.3), then held continuously. This step was probably taken in the interests of some continuity of authority, because Roman government was already in danger of becoming unworkable under the demands of a civil war involving not only Italy but also much of Rome's recently acquired territories elsewhere. At home the strains were already showing in 47. No consuls had been elected for the current year, Caesar's veterans awaiting discharge in Campania were mutinous, and, at Rome, there was dissension among the tribunes, threatening to undermine Caesar's measures for debt relief, and leading to serious civil disturbance. When he left for Campania, Mark Antony took the unprecedented step, for a master of horse (Dio 42.30.1), of appointing a city prefect (*praefectus urbi*); this was his uncle (and a remote cousin of Caesar) the elderly Lucius Caesar, who proved ineffectual. Mark Antony himself failed to restore order, and meanwhile he and others had abused their position by taking over Pompeian properties without payment.

All this Caesar had to deal with during his brief stay in Rome towards the end of 47 BC before departing for Africa, and only then, late in the year, were the consuls for 47 BC elected. They were Caesar's legates Q. Fufius Calenus and P. Vatinius, who had been campaigning on his behalf in Greece and Illyricum. Caesar himself was elected, irregularly, consul for 46 BC, along with M. Aemilius Lepidus, who had been proconsul in Nearer Spain for two years.

After his return from Africa in 46, Caesar celebrated a quadruple triumph, before leaving for his final campaign in Spain. Unsurprisingly, when nominated dictator for the third time he chose as his master of horse not Mark Antony, but his fellow consul Lepidus. Lepidus continued also as master of horse during Caesar's fourth dictatorship in 45 BC, and into the spring of 44. Caesar was elected as sole consul for 45 BC. Meanwhile Lepidus looked after affairs in the city in his absence with the aid of numerous city prefects. This again was a temporary stop-gap measure, no curule magistrates apparently having been appointed for 45 until after Caesar's return from Spain (Suet. *Iul.* 76.2; Dio 43.48.1–4).

Caesar abdicated the consulship at the start of October 45. The suffect consuls, who had returned with him from Spain, were Q. Fabius Maximus and C. Trebonius. On these two, and the ill-received replacement of the deceased Maximus by C. Caninius Rebilus for the last few hours of the year, see Lintott, chapter 6, p. 76. Mark Antony (apparently restored to favor) and Caesar were to be consuls for 44, with Lepidus as master of horse until his departure in the spring of 44 to be proconsul of Narbonese Gaul and Nearer Spain, by Caesar's appointment. His designated successor as master of horse for 43 was another Caesarian commander, Cn. Domitius Calvinus, with the young C. Octavius, Caesar's great-nephew, to fill the period between. Early in 44 BC (before February 15), his dictatorship was made perpetual – an apparent misjudgment which, as shown in chapter 6, is likely to have precipitated his assassination.

The picture that emerges of the years 48–44 is one of haste and improvisation in times of crisis, rather than the execution of some long-premeditated plan, attributed to him by Cicero, to make himself autocratic sole ruler over Rome and its empire. Cicero, in a now lost letter, allegedly (Suet. *Iul.* 9.2) characterized Caesar's consulship of 59 BC as *regnum* (despotism), claiming that Caesar had already had this in mind as early as his aedileship, and alludes to him as *rex* in correspondence of 45 BC (*Att.* 13.37.2; cf. *Fam.* 6.19.2, *munerum regiorum*, "the royal games"). These remarks, however, reflect Cicero's own reaction to Caesar's behavior, rather than Caesar's actual intentions. Nor are Suetonius and Dio convincing, especially the latter, when they assert that Caesar was eventually seduced into despotism by the honors and powers heaped upon him by an adulatory Senate.

To fill governmental, military, and civil posts, he had hitherto made use, of necessity, of people on whom he thought he could rely, not only his own former officers and supporters, but latterly also some former Pompeians, beneficiaries of his *clementia*. One purpose of this well-publicized clemency, it has been suggested (Rawson 1994: 440), was to acquire better subordinates. Caesar was inevitably in a position to dispense patronage, but his own pressing practical concern, especially in view of his impending departure for Parthia, was to ensure the continued working of the machinery of government in his absence. The rules for appointments to office laid down in Sulla's *lex annalis* of 81 BC had increasingly been disregarded, not least in Caesar's own repeated consulships.

He eventually, in 45, accepted the powers offered him of nominating half the magistrates for the next three years (Suet. *Iul.* 41; Dio 43.14, 51); however, there is no evidence that he intended this to become a permanent arrangement, whether or not the eastern campaign was over by then. It has, rather, the feel of an interim arrangement, a cessation, at least temporary, of destructive political competition, and enforceable by his own continuance as dictator, albeit far away, with a large army at his command. With major magistracies and provincial commands bestowed in advance on loyal supporters or former Pompeians, it afforded a breathing space, a chance for things to settle down and the situation to become clearer "in one way or another" (so Syme 1939: 53).

Caesar's Legislation

Such evidence as there is for Caesar's legislation as dictator gives little clue to his future intentions. Sulla as dictator had altered the constitution by measures designed to strengthen the authority of the Senate. These included weakening the influence of the tribunes, and imposing controls upon individual advancement through magistracies and provincial commands. The restrictions on the tribunate were removed within a few years of his abdication. The rules for the career structure of office (*cursus honorum*) and the length of provincial commands remained in force. However, they had from time to time been set aside, both by the Senate itself, for the institution of extraordinary commands, and by individuals able to command the armed force and political support to enforce their will. We have no evidence that Caesar intended any profound or lasting changes to the Republican constitution, or indeed that he had as yet formulated any long-lasting plans. What we have is only what he managed to carry out in the short period before his assassination (or imminent departure for Parthia), much of it a response to immediate needs. Though some, naturally, evoked contemporary indignation, there is little that could be called unprecedented or novel, let alone revolutionary.

Yavetz (1983) attempts a detailed, but necessarily tentative, list of numerous measures attributed in the sources to Caesar, and carried out by him or at his instance, as well as many allegedly planned or projected. There is almost no contemporary evidence for Caesar's measures in the period 49–44. We are mainly dependent on later literary sources, which are less concerned with the problems, both immediate and of long standing, which had to be addressed, than with Caesar's supposed personal ambitions. Much modern writing has tended to perpetuate this hostile tradition and interpret the evidence accordingly; Caesar and his work should, rather, be considered in their historical context.

Measures such as the increase in the numbers of magistracies, the replenishment of the depleted Senate (and Sulla had done both), and the creation of new patricians afforded plentiful opportunities for patronage, and the reward of supporters. It should not, however, be too readily assumed that their sole, or main, purpose was to shore up Caesar's own personal dominance. There was also increased practical need. The patriciate was now of social rather than political importance, and for some religious offices patrician status was still a requirement. Caesar, by a *lex Cassia*, and later Augustus, by a *lex Saenia*, created new patricians (Tac. *Ann.* 11.25; Suet. *Iul.* 41.1; *Res Gestae* 8.1), to compensate for the losses in civil war. We may also see this as connected with their religious reforms (Wardle, chapter 8 in this volume; Suet. *Aug.* 31), and as intended to contribute to the restoration of stability and order.

As well as the losses in the civil war, changes in Italy and the Empire had to be taken into account. To cope with the increased demands of home and provincial government, more magistrates were needed. (Suet. *Iul.* 41.1). In particular, Rome's territorial expansion since Sulla's time had almost doubled the number of provincial governorships required. To fill these posts, and to provide, as Sulla had tried to do, for annual change of governors, more praetors were needed, and also more quaestors (financial officers, often also serving as governors' deputies: Lintott 1999a: 133–7). Caesar raised the number of praetors in stages to ten then to 14 and finally 16, and doubled the number of quaestors to 40 (Dio 43.49.1, 43.51.3). As ex-quaestors, since Sulla, entered the Senate immediately on vacating office, this automatically doubled the annual intake of senators. Caesar also, as dictator, revised the roll of the Senate three times, in 47, 46, and 45 (Dio 42.51.5, 43.27.2, 43.47.3). The final figure of 900 claimed by Dio is unlikely to have been exact or permanent – losses in war and natural deaths had to be accounted for.

Caesar's new senators, particularly those of provincial and Italic birth, are scorned in the ancient sources as of "ignoble and disgusting origin" (Syme 1979: 99), as soldiers, centurions, scribes, sons of freedmen and even newly enfranchised aliens ("semibarbarian, trousered Gauls": Suet. *Iul.* 76.3, 80.1). Syme 1938b, 1939: 79–96 long ago subjected such allegations to critical scrutiny and advised caution and skepticism. It cannot be assumed, Syme points out, that these were necessarily first-generation Roman citizens, or even of non-Roman descent (see also Syme 1999: 3–126; Wiseman 1971).

Caesar's grants of citizenship to individuals and to groups had precedents, and should be seen in the context of historical developments in the last century of the Republic and into the early Principate. Thus the Cisalpine Gauls north of the Po received citizenship from Caesar in 49 BC, but this had been preceded by decades of gradual "Romanization" of the area. By the end of the Social War, virtually the whole of Italy, including Cisalpine Gaul up to the river Po, had received Roman citizenship. The *lex Julia* carried by L. Caesar, consul 90 BC, enfranchising all Latins and Italians who had remained loyal in the Social War, also authorized other commanders, in consultation with their *consilium*, to make further grants. Such a grant was made in 89 BC by Pompey's father, Cn. Pompeius Strabo (consul 89 BC), to a squadron of Spanish cavalry (ILS 8888; Cic. *Balb.* 19).

Also in 89, Strabo gave the *Transpadani*, allied communities in Cisalpine Gaul north of the Po, the "Latin right," meaning that, like the inhabitants of traditional Latin colonies, those who had held magistracies in their own communities could obtain full Roman citizenship (Asc. *in Pis.* 3C). Much of Cisalpine Gaul had long been under Roman control and there was already a substantial Roman presence there, especially south of the Po. By 90 BC there were several long-established colonies, four or five Roman and four to six Latin (Brunt 1971: 166–203). Since these latter will also have received full citizenship in 90 BC, the local opportunities for marriage between Romans were substantially increased. The Roman content of the population of this area is therefore likely to have grown markedly in the intervening years.

We have inscriptional evidence from Spain in the Flavian period of non-Roman communities given Latin status, and with their local government organized by a Flavian municipal law along the lines of Roman *municipia* (González 1986; Lintott 1993: 140–5). There, the grant of citizenship applied not only to the local ex-magistrates but also to their parents, wives, children and sons' children (*lex Irnitana* ch. 21). We cannot assume that the grant already extended so widely among the families of the *Transpadani*; after all, the Latins themselves had only recently become citizens. Nevertheless, Caesar's enfranchisement of Cisalpine Gaul in 49 BC (Dio 41.36.3) appears much less dramatic and revolutionary than sometimes represented.

Caesar awarded Roman citizenship to the people of the Spanish town Gades in the same year (Liv. *Per.* 110; Dio 41.24.1.), but this in itself tells us little about his attitude to any large-scale extension of Roman citizenship beyond Italy. Brunt goes only so far as to say (1971: 239), "It is agreed that Caesar was much more ready than Republican statesmen had been to enfranchise provincials," and he cites the *Transpadani*, Gades, and "conceivably some other provincial towns." In the East, no Greek cities received either citizenship or Latin rights, though several prominent Greeks and others received individual grants (Cic. *Fam.* 13.36, *Phil.* 13.33; Plut. *Cic.* 24). So did teachers of the liberal arts and doctors, many of whom will have been Greeks, settling in Rome (Suet. *Iul.* 42.1). Caesar obviously valued the contribution practitioners of these professions made to the city, as did Augustus, who expelled "all foreigners, except doctors and teachers" from Rome in the famine of AD 6–7 (Suet. *Aug.* 42.3). The Greeks of southern Italy had already received the franchise in 89 BC; Caesar granted those in Sicily only the Latin right. Antony's claim, after Caesar's death, that his own law giving them citizenship was in fulfillment of Caesar's intentions was received with skepticism (Cic. *Att.* 14.12.1) and seems never to have been implemented. Augustus allowed only gradual extension of citizenship to Sicilian communities, together with some colonization.

It is difficult to discern any coherent policy towards the empire and the provinces. In both West and East, Caesar rewarded certain areas or towns (for instance, Gades, Ilium, Mytilene, Pergamum, and Judaea), and punished others (for instance, Massilia and Megara). After Pharsalus, the cities of Asia were given some limited relief from the extortions of the *publicani* (tax-farmers), which Caesar blamed chiefly on the rapacity of Pompey's father-in-law Metellus Scipio, governor of Syria (Caes. *BC* 3.31–2). One-third of the direct taxes were remitted and their collection taken out of the hands of the *publicani* and handed over to the communities themselves; indirect taxes, however, continued to be raised by the *publicani* (App. *B Civ.* 2.92, 5.4; Dio 42.6.3). Caesar himself may also have exempted the island of Crete from indirect taxes (*vectigalia*). However, Cicero exposes the falsity of Antony's claim that Caesar had also intended to free Crete from provincial status after the expiry of Brutus' proconsulship there (Cic. *Phil.* 2.97); Brutus was not assigned the post until months after Caesar's death.

There was also some attempt to control provincial governors by a law limiting their term of office, propraetors to one year, proconsuls to a maximum of two consecutive years (Cic. *Phil.* 1.19; Dio 43.25.3). Sulla had likewise tried to provide for annual governorships, but the extraordinary commands needed for the large-scale and distant campaigns of the intervening decades had made the Sullan ideal unsustainable. Caesar's motive seems to have been not so much to curb the rapacity of governors as to prevent their acquiring too much personal power and threatening the stability of the Republic; Cicero, with Antony in mind (*Phil.* 8.28), heartily approved.

One important development between 48 BC and AD 14 was a striking increase in the numbers of Romans in the provinces, only partly attributable to grants of citizenship to provincials and to independent emigration from Italy to the provinces.

A major source was a massive program of colonization under Caesar and, later, Augustus. Though many colonies were established, those initiated by Caesar himself cannot easily be distinguished from other "Julian" foundations originating with his "adopted" son, who took his name (Brunt 1971: 244–61, 589–601). The most notable overseas colonies were those at Carthage and Corinth, according to Plutarch (*Caes.* 57), who apparently regarded these places as having special symbolic importance. He remarks that both had in the past been captured at the same time (146 BC), and were now both restored together. There were others in the Greek East, for instance at Lampsacus and Sinope, but the great majority were in the Western provinces.

The most pressing requirement was provision for the veterans. After the mutiny of 47 BC, some were allocated lands in Italy (Suet. *Iul.* 38.1; App. *B Civ.* 2.94; Dio 42.54.1), to be provided, Caesar said, not by confiscation, but from his own property and purchased land, as well as public land. In Italy itself, however, little unallocated public land was now available. Suetonius (*Iul.* 42.1) said that Caesar sent 80,000 "citizens" to overseas colonies, though to which colonists this figure relates is unclear. Among the overseas colonists there were, in addition to veterans, civilians (including freedmen, who were allowed to hold office in some colonies), not only urban proletarians but probably also Italian peasants, people for whom, without such state-organized assistance, emigration would hitherto have been unattractive or impractical (Brunt 1971: 159–65, 256–7). These colonies, therefore, helped to relieve some of the social and economic pressures on Rome and Italy. Many colonies planned by Caesar, such as Urso in Spain, were formally established only later, by others.

Italy itself received only a few colonies, and they, like Caesar's Western foundations and *municipia* (enfranchised provincial communities), apparently received constitutions based on the municipal system of local government which had been evolving in Italy since the Social War. The reorganization of Italy itself is poorly documented. Our knowledge is supplemented by later epigraphic evidence, mainly from the West, especially the surviving portion of the foundation law, *lex coloniae Genetivae* (*RS* no. 25), of Caesar's colony at Urso in Spain, and the later Flavian municipal law (Gonzáles 1986) for Spanish *municipia* with Latin rights, mentioned above. The key epigraphic texts have been re-edited and assembled in Crawford 1996 (= *RS*), with full translation, commentaries, and bibliographies. Lintott (1993: 129–45) provides an accessible summary and analysis of the relevant material.

There is little evidence for Caesar's own contribution to the municipalization of Italy. Some sort of municipal law was in preparation during 45 BC (Cic. *Fam.* 6.18.1, cf. 13.11.3). At least part of it may be preserved in the curious patchwork document, the Table of Heraclea, *Tabula Heracleensis* (*RS* no. 24). The *Tabula* itself, however, is certainly not, as it was once thought to be, an actual text of a *lex Julia municipalis*; for discussion and bibliography, see Crawford 1996 on *RS* no. 24, specially pp. 355–62, and commentary on the text. It looks more like a collection of existing regulations, some meant for the city of Rome itself (lines 1–82), others applicable to Roman communities outside Rome, assembled, possibly on local initiative, no later than 43 BC, in preparation for drafting a new constitution for Heraclea.

The parts originally designed for Rome relate to the making of certain declarations, *professiones*, and their use in connection with the corn distributions (lines 1–19), and to the maintenance and use of roads and public spaces in Rome (lines 20–82). The latter part of the document contains regulations for municipal government, particularly concerning qualifications for being a local magistrate or member of the *decuriones*, the local senate (lines 83–141), and also regulations for taking censuses locally in Italy and sending the results to Rome.

None of the contents of the *Tabula* can be definitely proved to be a Caesarian innovation; the most likely is the admission of former, but no longer practicing, *praecones* (criers or auctioneers), ushers, and undertakers to local office and the local senate (lines 94–5, 104–5). In answer to a query from Cicero, Balbus had confirmed (Cic. *Fam.* 6.18.1) that Caesar's new rules would allow *praecones* to be *decuriones.*

The arrangements for the corn-distributions at Rome described in the Heraclea Table (lines 13–19) are generally thought to pre-date Caesar. He himself as dictator created in 44 BC two new aediles, the *aediles cereales*, with special responsibility for Rome's corn supply (Dio 43.51.3), and reduced the number of recipients of the free corn dole from 320,000 to 150,000 by revising the list and removing fraudulent claimants (Suet. *Iul.* 41.3; Dio 43.21). These, like many of the actual or allegedly intended measures of Caesar summarized in Suet. *Iul.* 41–4, can be seen as meant to address some of the pressing social and economic problems of Rome and Italy, and to restore stability and order to society; most of the more ambitious projects, however, specially those for land reclamation and improvements of land and sea communications (Suet. *Iul.* 44) were either not carried out at all, or carried out only long after his death.

Plans for the Future

In all this, however, there is nothing to indicate that Caesar had formulated any definite plans either for his own future in the government of Rome, or for changes to the Republican constitution itself. His imminent departure for the East seems a possible context for the alleged remark about Sulla being a dunce for having abdicated the dictatorship (Suet. *Iul.* 77). If Caesar ever said anything of the sort, he may simply have meant that Sulla should have kept power at least long enough to ensure having effectively restored order to the Republic – not that he himself wished or intended to hold on indefinitely to supreme power.

This, however, has been the inference often drawn from his change, earlier in 44, to a "perpetual" dictatorship, that is, one with no fixed terminal date. In context, however, with the civil war barely concluded, and given the problems he had previously experienced with retaining the protection afforded him by a fixed-term *imperium* in Gaul, it may have been intended simply as a measure of self-preservation. Sulla's appointment had had no time limit, but he had abdicated quite quickly. Whether Caesar, given more time, would eventually have found what he considered a better constitutional solution to Rome's political turmoil, and whether he would then himself have abdicated the dictatorship, we do not know. His assassins clearly did not think so.

In these final months, honors, some quasi-religious, some quasi-regal, were heaped on him by senatorial decree (see Lintott, chapter 6, pp. 76, 78, 80). Most he accepted. Though they conferred no real political power, Dio, who gives the fullest account (43.44–6, 44.3–8), points out (44.3) that Caesar was liable to be put in an invidious position, whether he accepted or rejected them, and hints (44.3.1) that this may have been the intention of their proposers.

What Caesar thought about being represented as divine is ultimately unknowable (see Wardle, chapter 8, pp. 105–7). The claim that he wanted to make himself a king, or even a Hellenistic-type king worshiped with divine honors, was first put about by his opponents and detractors, and has been unduly perpetuated in later historiography. In the weeks before his assassination, there were several, probably stage-managed, incidents, and rumors of plans to have the title of king conferred on him (Suet. *Iul.* 79; Plut. *Caes.* 61; App. *B Civ.* 2.108–9; Dio 44.9–11).

Caesar was well aware of the odium attaching at Rome to the status of king (App. *B Civ.* 2.107). Though he tried at least once to deflect it good-humouredly, saying to those hailing him as king (*rex*) that his name was not Rex but Caesar (Suet. *Iul.* 79.2; Dio 44.10.1), he did react with public irritation to the demonstratively discourteous behaviour of a tribune, Pontius Aquila (Suet. *Iul.* 78.2). The severe action he had the Senate take against the tribunes Caesetius and Marullus is all the more understandable since, even in the hostile account of Dio (44.9.2–10.3), their persistence does appear not merely officious but deliberately provocative. If the incident of the offering and refusal of the crown at the festival of the *Luperci* (see Lintott, chapter 6, p. 77) had Caesar's foreknowledge and approval (and this we do not know), it may have been intended as a demonstration to the people that he did not want to be king. At any rate, he used it as such; he ordered the offer, and his refusal, to be recorded in the Fasti (Cic. *Phil.* 2.87).

Caesar's office as *dictator perpetuus* would lapse with his own lifetime, at latest. He had taken no action to make such an office, whether under the title of "king" or any other, a permanent part of the Roman constitution. Antony, then consul, was quick to obtain Caesar's papers after the assassination, and to represent himself as executing his plans and intentions. Caesar himself, however, had done nothing to single out and build up any one of his senior commanders and associates as inevitable successor to his political power (even supposing that were possible), let alone to establish a hereditary dynasty.

That he did either is a myth created and sustained by the opportunism and eventual success (but only after further civil wars) of his great-nephew C. Octavius, born 63 BC, whose maternal grandmother had been Julia, younger sister of the dictator; Caesar had no male siblings. Octavius, son of Julia's daughter Atia and a "new man" from Velitrae, C. Octavius (praetor 61 BC, died 59 BC), was therefore one of Caesar's closest male relatives. As he was orphaned at the age of four, it is hardly surprising that, once he assumed the *toga virilis* (that is, became officially adult), his great-uncle Caesar helped to introduce him into public life. However, such favors as this unusually influential relative showed him are mostly unexceptional; they scarcely amount, even in the hagiographic account of Nicolaus of Damascus, to enough to support the belief that Caesar had as yet entertained the idea of training Octavius as his eventual political successor. The two apparent exceptions, neither mentioned in Suetonius, are the appointment as (probably) *praefectus urbi* during the absence of the consuls Q. Fufius Calenus and P. Vatinius for the Latin Festival of 47 BC (Nic.Dam. V.13; *MRR* 2.292), and designation as master of horse to succeed Lepidus in 44 (*MRR* 2.319). On closer examination, however, both are somewhat less impressive.

The *praefectura urbis feriarum Latinarum (causa)*, to give the office the full title attested under the principate (ILS 1051), was essentially an honorific post, lasting only for the few days of the magistrates' absence from Rome, given to young men of rank not yet of senatorial age. The holder was not expected to conduct major business (Tac. *Ann.* 4.36; Suet. *Nero* 7; Gell. 14.8). Designation of someone so young as master of horse is perhaps more surprising. Caesar had also wished, however, to designate P. Cornelius Dolabella (then barely 25 years old) as *consul suffectus* to take over whenever he himself should depart for his eastern campaign (*MRR* 2.315, 317). His most senior and (he thought) trustworthy men were needed for other key positions. Octavius was to take over as master of horse only when Aemilius Lepidus should depart for his province, and to be succeeded by Cn. Domitius Calvinus. Meanwhile Mark Antony was consul for 44, and Caesar's date of departure uncertain. Octavius' tenure of the post would have been fairly brief and circumscribed.

Despite its subsequent exploitation by Octavian for both purposes, Caesar's will is not evidence for any intention to designate a successor to his political power, still less to establish some form of hereditary dynasty. Testamentary heirs were, in effect, merely the executors of an estate, responsible for settling debts, paying out legacies and honouring other bequests, in proportions corresponding to their individual fractions of the estate. It was customary, and prudent, to name in the will grades of heirs, the lower coming in if the higher declined; among other heirs nominated (though not eventually succeeding) to a lower grade was one of the assassins, Decimus Brutus.

Caesar's will (Liv. *Epit.* 116; Suet. *Iul.* 83) was entirely conventional. His main heirs and beneficiaries were family and friends (the latter inevitably including some political associates). For the first half of the 50s, until the death of Julia and her infant child in 54 BC, Pompey, as his son-in-law, was both, and continued to be regularly named as an heir in Caesar's wills until the outbreak of civil war. Caesar's heirs in the first grade were any posthumous child of his own (whose specific inclusion or exclusion was a legal requirement for a valid will: Gaius *Inst.* 2.130–2), and C. Octavius, his great-nephew, each to receive half. In the end, Caesar died childless. Two heirs in the next grade (Suet. *Iul.* 83), L. Pinarius and Q. Pedius, grandsons of Caesar's older sister, shared one-quarter of the estate, half of what had been due to a posthumous heir, while Octavius received the other quarter.

It was a condition of Octavius' inheritance that he take Caesar's name; he seized the opportunity of making political capital out of the name, by representing himself as "adopted" by the will. This "condition of taking the name" (*condicio nominis ferendi*) appears to have been not uncommon among the Roman elite as a way of preserving a family name. As elite Romans will have known, it did not amount to legal adoption (Champlin 1991: 144–6); women, who could not adopt, could make such a condition, and the designated person might not even be a major beneficiary. Cicero, in a letter of December 50 BC, has some pragmatic comments (*Att.* 7.8.3) on the desirability or otherwise of Dolabella's accepting the condition, for the sake of a one-ninth share in the estate, of unknown value, of a certain Livia.

The persistent belief among some modern scholars in the legal reality of "testamentary adoption" rests entirely upon the subsequent action by Octavius, now calling himself C. Julius Caesar Octavianus (Suet. *Aug.* 7.2; Dio 46.47.5). Some supporters followed suit; his stepfather, however, continued to call him Octavius as, initially, did Cicero (Cic. *Att.* 14.12.2), though the latter within a few weeks prudently began to refer to him as "Octavian" and later "Caesar Octavianus" or "Caesar" (for instance, *Att.* 15.12.2, *ad Brut.* 1.3, *Fam.* 12.23).

The legal facts about the *condicio nominis ferendi* would certainly be known to upper-class Romans. However, many other Romans would be less well informed, and it was presumably for their benefit that Octavius arranged a "posthumous adoption" (App. *B Civ.* 3.94, Dio 45.5.3), or rather *adrogatio* (adoption of an orphan). In imitation of the procedure used for such genuine adoptions, he had a *lex curiata* passed by the *comitia curiata*, an assembly of the Roman people, by this period represented merely by thirty lictors.

Appian and Dio both struggle to provide an explanation. According to Dio, in order to allow Octavius to "meddle with the property," that is, to claim his inheritance (the Roman legal term was *bonis se immiscere*: Gaius *Inst.* 2.163), he had to be made Caesar's son according to law. There was no such need; a simple declaration of compliance with the condition, and use of the name, would have been enough, and Octavius had already seen to that formality immediately on his arrival in Rome by making such a declaration to the praetor C. Antonius, Mark Antony's brother (App. *B Civ.* 3.14). Appian says he was adopted "again" by the *comitia curiata*, in order to obtain patronal rights over Caesar's rich freedmen (that is, over their estates). These rights were otherwise available only to a patron's own children and sons' children, not to extraneous heirs (Gaius *Inst.* 3.40, 45). As a principal motive, especially in the current sensitive political situation, this strains credulity. Thus, both Appian and Dio implicitly acknowledge that the "adoption" in the will was not a real legal adoption (as indeed it was not).

The ceremony arranged for Octavius had no legal validity; *adrogatio* (adoption of orphans), like ordinary adoption, could in classical law be performed only *inter vivos*, during the lifetime, and with the active participation, of the adopter as well as the adoptee. The *comitia curiata*, under the title of *comitia calata*, met twice a year for adrogations. In early Rome, it had also been used for the making of a primitive form of will by instituting an heir to a man's property (Gell. 15.27.3; Gaius *Inst.* 2.101–3). Almost nothing is known, however, about the "comitial" will, which fell into disuse before the last century of the Republic, and was superseded by the more convenient mancipatory will *per aes et libram* ("by bronze and scale"), which was the form in use in classical law.

Although some modern legal historians believed the comitial will to have been originally a form of adrogation, taking effect only at the testator's death (bibliography and discussion in Kaser 1971: 105–6), there is no evidence for this "rather attractive view" (Watson 1975: 65 n. 36). Moreover, since Octavian's "adoption" is the only known instance of such a posthumous procedure after a mancipatory will, arguments for its validity in classical law, then or later, are likely to be circular.

The adoption was in fact a mere charade. It was intended to give a semblance of "legitimacy" to Octavius' self-presentation as the *filius* of Caesar, and so to consolidate his immediate claim to succeed to Caesar's political influence; the propaganda value of the name was, for the time being, enormous. Being *Divi filius*, once his late "father" had been deified, was even better.

In what Julius Caesar the dictator actually did, as opposed to what has been surmised or alleged at the time or since, it is hard to find C. Julius Caesar, the determinedly ambitious autocrat and would-be sole ruler. The latter description fits much better Imperator Caesar *Divi filius* Augustus, who besides having the good fortune to win the ensuing civil wars, had the shrewdness and ruthlessness to exploit his opportunities, and to build up a powerful propaganda machine.

As suggested in chapter 6, the imminence of Caesar's intended departure for the East merely increased resentment of his continued control of affairs, among both Caesarians and former opponents, and precipitated his assassination. He had not yet secured a lasting end to Rome's political turmoil – but, as Caesar's old friend C. Matius remarked to Cicero some time after the assassination (*Att.* 14.1.1), who could? "If he, with such genius, was not finding any way out, who is going do so now?" In 46 BC, Cicero delivered a speech in the Senate, thanking Caesar for agreeing to the recall of M. Claudius Marcellus (consul 51 BC). Amid the fulsome praise of Caesar, and reminders of his clemency, there is an implicit appeal to all the assembled senators to make true what Cicero asserts to be already the case. They should put old enmities aside, accept the necessity of Caesar's leadership, and cooperate with him and with each other in restoring peace and good order to the Republic (*Marcell.*, esp. 22–4, 31–2). However, the immediate jockeying for political power, and renewal of civil conflict, after Caesar's death suggest that the general will to do so was still lacking. Caesar himself is said to have forecast this as the likely outcome of his own death (Suet. *Iul.* 86.2)

In the speech (whether as originally given, or only in the published version, we do not know) Cicero outlined for Caesar a programme for healing the wounds of civil war and promoting Rome's social, economic, and moral recovery (*Marcell.* 23). It corresponds closely to legislation elsewhere attributed to Caesar: reorganization of the lawcourts (Suet. *Iul.* 41.2; Dio 43.25.1), re-establishing of credit (a lengthy and ongoing process: Yavetz 1983:133–7), promotion of the birth rate (by financial rewards: Dio 43.25.2) and, if Cicero's *comprimendae libidines* (restraining of desires) may be so interpreted, a sumptuary law (Suet. *Iul.* 43.2; Dio 43.25.2; Yavetz 1983:154–7).

Cicero also urges Caesar himself to restore the constitution (*Marcell.* 27: *rem publicam constituas*) and to give priority to that, rather than to the pursuit of further glory through conquests far from Rome. He seems to have taken a similar line in a letter of political advice to Caesar which he began to draft, with much literary agonizing, in May 45 BC. He sent it for approval to Caesar's confidential agents Oppius and Balbus, who rejected it and suggested extensive rewriting (*Att.* 13.27). What little detail we know of its contents comes mainly from another letter about this to Atticus (*Att.* 13.31.3). "What they say he [Caesar] writes, that he will not go against the Parthians until matters are settled here (*nisi constitutis rebus*) is just what I recommended in that letter." However, *constitutis rebus* is a vague phrase, especially as relayed second-hand through others. Caesar probably had in mind, not the immediate restoration of the *res publica* urged by Cicero, but the enforcement of his own laws. A week or two later, in June 45 (*Att.* 13.7), Caesar was thinking of staying in Rome after all, to ensure that these laws were not disregarded in his absence, as was already happening with the sumptuary law. To enforce the latter, spot checks for sumptuary violations were made, Suetonius says (*Iul.* 43.2), in markets and even in private houses.

Nevertheless, the Parthian project was not abandoned. Why did Caesar decide to go himself, rather than entrusting the command to one of his senior generals? Was it, as some have suggested, simply a way of shelving the unsolved problem of the *res publica*, and also of escaping the increasingly overt manifestations of ill-will and opposition, and rumors of plots (Cic. *Marcell.* 21), which beset him? These advantages (from his point of view) may have occurred to him, but the main explanation for his decision may be quite simple. Rome's experience over the last 50 or 60 years had demonstrated again and again the danger presented by a commander abroad with a large and loyal army at his back. For Caesar's own protection, as well as Rome's, he may have thought, that commander had better be himself. Unfortunately, all his plans for the future, whatever they may have been, were abruptly forestalled by his assassination.

FURTHER READING

A. Lintott, *The Constitution of the Roman Republic* (Oxford: Clarendon Press, 1999) discusses the nature, powers, and historical development of the magistracies and political institutions of Republican Rome, with an extensive modern bibliography.

A. K. Michels, *The Calendar of the Roman Republic* (Princeton, NJ: Princeton University Press, 1967) is fundamental for understanding the pre-Julian Roman calendar and its significance in Roman religious, political, and business life. Ancient literary sources are set out (untranslated), and technical terms explained in detail.

On Caesar's legislation as dictator, in many ways the most helpful analysis is that of Z. Yavetz, *Julius Caesar and his Political Image* (London: Thames and Hudson, 1983). Measures attributed to Caesar in the sources are arranged in three categories (chs. II–IV), political, administrative and, thirdly, economic and social. Ancient sources, historical context, possible legislative methods, and key modern discussions are examined in detail. Caution is advisable, however, in regard to Yavetz's claims about Caesar's motivation. Useful for basic reference are the lists chronologically and by Latin title of Roman laws (with source references and brief descriptive text in Italian) in G. Rotondi, *Leges Publicae Populi Romani* (repr. Hildesheim: Georg Olms Verlagsbuchhandlung, 1966).

Modern books about Roman private law are generally written by and for academic lawyers. For historians, useful introductions to Republican lawmaking and legal procedure are W. Kunkel (trans. J. M. Kelly), *An Introduction to Roman Legal and Constitutional History* (2nd edn, Oxford: Clarendon Press, 1973), and A. Watson, *Law Making in the Later Roman Republic* (Oxford: Clarendon Press, 1974). A comprehensive and readable account of Roman private law and civil procedure, which takes into account much recent work on Roman social history, is A. Borkowski and P. du Plessis, *Textbook on Roman Law* (3rd edition, Oxford: Oxford University Press, 2005). On Caesar's will and the alleged 'testamentary adoption' of Octavius, there is, unsurprisingly, nothing in ancient legal sources. This, and various matters relating to adoption, adrogation, wills, and inheritance generally, are discussed in J. F. Gardner, *Family and* Familia *in Roman Law and Life* (Oxford: Clarendon Press, 1998) (use index).

CHAPTER SIX

The Assassination

Andrew Lintott

Most of the main accounts of Caesar's assassination, as of his reforms and projects, were composed at least 150 years after the event by people for whom the rule of the emperors was inevitable and the best government possible, the murdered dictator being the hero-founder of that form of government. The exception is found in the fragments of the biography of Augustus written by his contemporary Nicolaus of Damascus, a client of the Julian dynasty. Comparison of Nicolaus with later writers suggests that, in spite of some discrepancies between them in detail and in attitude to the conspirators, by the time Nicolaus wrote, a vulgate had already been established. In this the underlying causes of the plot were a mixture of personal resentment and true or bogus republican sentiment, provoked by both Caesar's current behavior and fears over his future plans. "Nevertheless the rest of his actions and words are of preponderant importance to the extent that he can be thought to have abused his domination and to have been justly killed" (Suet. *Iul.* 76). Among the immediate causes of the conspiracy listed were fears that his eastern expedition would lead to a relocation of Rome's capital to the East, his excessive honors, his manipulation of the elections, his failure to rise to meet a deputation of senators, his deposition of the two tribunes who imprisoned the man who crowned his statue with a diadem, the incident of the diadem offered by Mark Antony at the Lupercalia, and the rumor that it would be proposed in the senate that he should have the title of king on his Parthian expedition. Thus the story is one of an arrogant claim to supremacy, leading to the tragic fall of an otherwise good man. Unlike Agamemnon who walked on the purple carpet, Caesar actually refused a diadem, but the combination of other words and actions suggested that he was not at heart reluctant to have one.

Nicolaus and his successors, writing, as most of them did, in Greek, were not only conscious of tragic parallels, but of stories of similar episodes in Greek historians. Nicolaus' digression begins with an echo of Herodotus' phraseology: "From this point the story (*logos*) inquires further how the assassins formed the conspiracy ...." The reader is led to expect an account of the downfall of some eastern potentate.

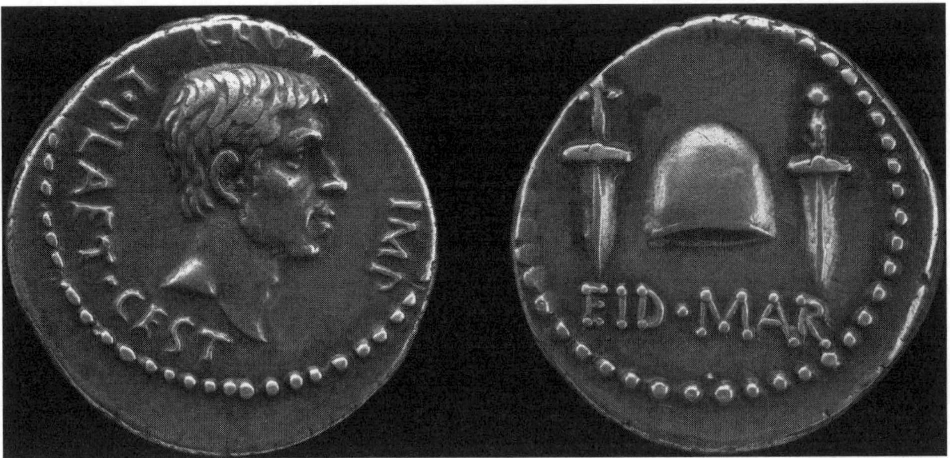

Figure 6.1 BMCRR East 68 = Crawford, Roman Republican Coinage 508/3. Denarius of 43–2 BC. Obv. Head of Brutus. Rev. Cap of Liberty with two daggers and EID(VS) MAR(TIAE).

However, within a few lines the explanation of causation is Thucydidean. " Some formed the conspiracy with some sort of hope that, if they put him (Caesar) out of the way, they themselves would be leaders in place of him; others were embittered through indignation over what they suffered in the war because of the death of their kin or the loss of money or high office in the city, and, concealing their indignation, they claimed as a specious pretext that they resented the rule of one man and sought republican government" (Nic. Dam. *FGrH* 90 F130, *Life of Caesar* 19.60). Thucydides did of course provide a model narrative for a plot against Greek tyrants, one well known to the Romans, that against Hippias and Hipparchus of Athens. A statue of one of Hipparchus' assassins, Aristogiton, has been found under the southern slope of the Capitol – evidence for a statue-group probably from the late-Republican period celebrating that event – and a complete group forms part of the Farnese collection (Coarelli 1969). Dio Cassius (44.19.3), remarking on how the conspirators were able to gather round Caesar, echoes a parenthesis of Thucydides about Hippias: "for he was especially easy to approach and affable." The reminiscence is more than superficial in that, like Pisistratus and his sons, Caesar was generally understood to have been an intelligent and merciful ruler.

It would be helpful if we could contrast these accounts with an appreciation of the situation from Cicero's correspondence and oratory. However, although his letters provide useful evidence up to the beginning of January 44, there is then a gap until after the murder. There are a few references in his subsequent writing to what actually happened on the Ides of March and the next few days, especially the conduct of Mark Antony, but nothing on the genesis of the plot.

The causes of the assassination can, however, be traced back far beyond the last months of Caesar's life. Roman tradition held that, in spite of the achievements of the kings who were its founding fathers, the institution of monarchy was proved intolerable by the actions of Tarquin the Proud. "Later, when the command of kings, which initially had been for the preservation of liberty and the promotion of the common interest (*res publica*), turned into arrogance and domination, they changed their practice and created for themselves annual commands and two commanders." So Sallust described the creation of the republic (*Cat.* 6.7). According to the annalists, the new regime was terrified of the reimposition of monarchic rule, whether from outside through the deposed dynasty or another Etruscan chief such as Lars Porsenna, or from inside through the aspirations of the aristocratic leaders who had deposed the Tarquins. Hence Lucius Iunius Brutus executed his two sons for treason against the republic, while Valerius Poplicola not only moved his house from the summit of the Velia to counter accusations that he was being tyrannical but enacted a law declaring *sacer* (that is in this context "open to seizure and destruction") the person and property of anyone who should have plotted to seize a monarchy (Livy 2.7.12, 8.2). Monarchy (*regnum*) was held equivalent to tyranny or despotism.

There were also stories in the annals of early Rome about men who were thought to be aspiring to a tyranny. "Was it for this reason that Lucius Tarquinius was expelled, while Spurius Cassius, Spurius Maelius, Marcus Manlius were killed, that many centuries afterwards a king should be set up at Rome, contrary to law, by Marcus Antonius?" Thus wrote Cicero, denouncing Mark Antony's behavior at the Lupercalia (*Phil.* 2.87). The moral of these stories was that such men should be killed on suspicion, with or without normal judicial process, before they could make a decisive step towards tyranny. Unlike Caesar, they did not have soldiers under their command at the time of their deaths, but they were held to be dangers to the constitution through demagogic cultivation of the poor. Hence Cicero could use their deaths as examples justifying the treatment of more recent demagogues such as the Gracchi, Saturninus, Catiline, and Clodius. Caesar had begun his political career as a "popular" politician and many of his actions as dictator were in the same vein.

In the last century this Roman tradition had been reinforced for the intellectual elite by Greek philosophers who, following Plato, treated tyrants as undeserving of the respect normally accorded to fellow human beings. Marcus Brutus was an adherent of Plato's Academy and this must have influenced his conduct once he was convinced that Caesar had become a tyrant (Sedley, 1997). Cicero discussed Greek views of tyranny in his work *On the Commonwealth* (*Rep.* 2.47–51), which appeared in 51, and returned to this subject in later works *On Friendship* (*Amic.* 52–5) and *On Duties*, written in 44 after Caesar's murder: "Surely then, anyone who kills a tyrant, although he is a close friend, has committed himself to crime? But it does not seem so to the Roman people, which deems that deed the fairest of all splendid deeds. Did the beneficial, therefore, overcome honourableness? No indeed; for honourableness followed upon what benefited" (*Off.* 3.19, tr. Atkins). There were also the examples of tyrannicide in Greek history, illustrated at Rome by the sculptures of Aristogiton and Harmodius we have mentioned earlier.

At the time of his death Caesar had the office of "perpetual dictator" – in effect, if not by name, a monarch. However, it must be stressed that the dictatorship was in origin a republican magistracy, devised to give temporary authority to one man in various sorts of special circumstances. Traditionally this concession to monarchy was brief, lasting less than a normal annual magistracy. It had fallen into disuse in the second century BC but had been revived by Sulla as an instrument for setting in order the republic after the civil wars. Sulla had resigned it; Caesar, a hostile historian alleged, remarked that Sulla's resignation of the dictatorship showed that he was politically illiterate (Suet. *Iul.* 77).

As early as Caesar's consulship of 59 BC Cicero had talked of politics as a *regnum* or tyranny owing to the dominance of Caesar, Pompey, and Crassus – a dominance that had been initially manifested in the use of violence in order to facilitate the passage of legislation through an assembly. However, at this time it was Pompey who was generally regarded as the chief tyrant and Cicero gave him nicknames in his letters to Atticus which implied that he was an oriental monarch (e.g. *Att.* 2.3.1, 9.1, 14.1, 16.2, 17.3): Pompey had indeed granted or taken away kingdoms in the East. When civil war threatened in 50, Cicero anticipated that it was bound to end in the tyranny of either Pompey or Caesar (*Att.* 7.5.4, 7.7). Once it became clear that Pompey's strategy was to retire to the East, Cicero compared him to Sulla (*Att.* 8.11.2, 9.10.2, 6, 10.7.1); as for Caesar, he called him Pisistratus, one of the prime examples of a demagogic Greek tyrant (*Att.* 7.20.2, 8.16.2).

Caesar's intention of imposing his will on territory under the control of his army was already patent after his successful invasion of Italy in 49. This and his personal affection for Pompey led Cicero to join the Pompeians in Greece. However, after Pharsalus, like a number of other Pompeians including Brutus and Cassius, Cicero took the view that it was better to accept Caesar's victory than prolong civil war. Exhaustion, horror over the blood shed by fellow Romans, and Caesar's carefully cultivated reputation for sparing the lives of opponents, all contributed to this attitude. In his speech on behalf of Marcellus in 46 Cicero praised this clemency and expressed hopes about Caesar's restoration of the *res publica*. Nevertheless in the same year he dropped a heavy hint at the end of his *Brutus* (331) – a work on oratory dedicated to Marcus Brutus – that the latter should aspire to imitate his ancestors L. Brutus, who had expelled the kings, and Servilius Ahala, who had killed Maelius.

Cicero cooperated with the regime but disliked it. He told Servius Sulpicius that the best thing about it was Caesar himself (*Fam.* 4.4.5). To Papirius Paetus he summed up his feelings as follows: "Regarding the man in whose power is all power I see nothing to fear, except that everything is uncertain, once the rule of law (*ius*) has been abandoned, nor can the future nature of anything be guaranteed which depends on another's will, not to say whim" (*Fam.* 9.16.3). The loss of *ius*, which means the loss of republican government, entailed that all magistrates were no longer subject to a higher authority. At the beginning of 45, with Caesar's last campaign against Pompey's sons in prospect, the later conspirator Cassius wrote to Cicero: "Damned if I am not worried and prefer to have an old and clement master than try a new and cruel one. You know what an idiot Gnaeus (Pompey's elder son) is; you know how he thinks cruelty a virtue, you know how he thinks we all have despised him. I am afraid that he may want like a peasant to take reprisals with a sword" (*Fam.* 15.19.4). For Cassius too, though he prefers Caesar to the young Pompey, only the appearance of republican government remained. During Caesar's absence in Spain the most important power was not exercised by the magistrates but by Caesar's friends, men like Oppius and Balbus. It was probably the latter, who, according to Cicero, while Caesar was still at Rome, forged decrees of the senate which had been allegedly proposed by Cicero and whose accuracy he was stated to have certified when they were drafted (*Fam.* 9.15.4).

There may have been hopes that normal republican government would resume after Caesar's return from Spain about the end of August 45, now that the civil wars were apparently over. Shortly before this Atticus reported a remark of Marcus Brutus that Caesar was going over to the "good men," that is, the conservative republicans. In reply Cicero commented, "Where will he find them unless perchance he hangs himself?" and went on to refer to the stemma Atticus had constructed for Brutus displaying his descent from L. Brutus and Ahala (*Att.* 13.40.1). Brutus had in fact left to meet Caesar on his journey home. However, the extravagant honors proposed for Caesar after the victory at Munda in the spring of 45 were a poor omen. When Cicero heard that a statue to Caesar as the Unconquered God was to be erected in the temple of Quirinus, the ancient deity identified with the divinized Romulus, he wrote that he preferred Caesar to share a temple with Quirinus (there was a tradition that Romulus had been murdered by senators) than with Salus (Safety) (*Att.* 12.45.2). Caesar was expected also to share a temple with Clemency (they were represented on coins greeting one another), a statue of his was placed among those of the kings in the temple of Jupiter Capitolinus, and an ivory image of him was carried in the procession of divinities through the Circus – probably first at the games to Apollo in July 45 (*Att.* 13.44.1).

Cicero was later to allege that Mark Antony had conspired with Trebonius to murder Caesar at the time when they were both at Narbonne (*Phil.* 2.34), but it is doubtful how far we should trust this. Nevertheless, Caesar's behavior after his return seems to be rightly regarded by our sources as a turning point. Cicero's defense speech for king Deiotarus of Galatia, delivered before Caesar, includes a decidedly ambiguous concluding passage on the Roman attitude to the name of king (*Deiot.* 40–3). This was a speech that Dolabella, otherwise a loyal Caesarian, was eager to read. Cicero later entertained Caesar and his massive traveling entourage of staff and soldiers at Puteoli during the Saturnalia festival in December. "Not a guest to whom you would say, 'Please look in on me again on your way back.' Once is enough. No talk about politics, much about literature" (*Att.* 13.52.2). The lack of political conversation between Rome's chief magistrate and a leading ex-consul and senator shows the nature of the regime. So too did the notorious episode on December 31, when on the death of the consul Fabius Maximus, Caesar had Caninius Rebilus elected in his place for the rest of the day and night. "In the consulship of Caninius no one had lunch. Nothing bad was done. For he was so vigilant that he saw no sleep throughout his consulship" (*Fam.* 7.30.1).

In the secondary sources the background to the plot is Caesar's overweening behavior, the honors voted to him, and disturbing rumors, such as that he intended to become a monarch in Alexandria with Cleopatra and Caesarion. There are suggestions that the honors were deliberately piled on him by his enemies in order to make him unpopular (apart from sympathy with Caesar, the imperial sources may be casting Caesar in a tragic mold, where the honors are a trap like Clytemnestra's carpet for Agamemnon). The assassination is precipitated by a number of dramatic incidents that illustrate Caesar's arrogance and ambition. When supervising the construction of his forum, he failed to rise to greet a deputation from the senate. When two tribunes, Caesetius and Marullus, removed a diadem from his statue and imprisoned the man who had put it there, he treated this as an incident manufactured by them to make him appear a tyrant and dismissed them from office, in spite of the fact that tribunes were sacrosanct. Finally, when watching the festival of the Wolfmen (*Luperci*) on February 15, he was crowned with a diadem by Mark Antony but set the crown aside. In Nicolaus of Damascus (F130, 21.71–3) this is the climax of a scene, in which first a certain Licinius attempts to crown Caesar, then Cassius and Casca put the crown on his knees, while the crowd calls on Lepidus to crown him, and finally Antony responds to the crowd's request. Caesar's arrogance is also betrayed by his refusal to be moved by his wife's dream and the unfavorable omens in the sacrificial victims, in spite of their authoritative interpretation by the Etruscan diviner Spurinna.

It was evident that Caesar was not intending to resign his supreme position when he moved in the first weeks of 44 from being dictator for the fourth time to dictator in perpetuity (before February 15). Moreover he was planning to leave to campaign first by the Danube and then in the East against the Parthians. In preparation for this he held special elections to appoint magistrates for the two years following 44. According to Suetonius (*Iul.* 80.4), this was the occasion first selected by the conspirators for their action, but later abandoned in favor of the senate meeting. The conspiracy was initiated by a small group which later allegedly expanded to more than 60 (Nic. Dam. F130, 19.59). Caesar's wounds are said by Nicolaus of Damascus to have numbered 35 (ibid. 24.90); later authors say 23 (Suet. *Iul.* 82.2, Plut. *Caes.* 66.14; App. *B Civ.* 2.117.493), but it is not clear that even 23 conspirators were able to strike Caesar in the mêlée surrounding him. The figure of over 60 perhaps reflects the number of those later accused under the Pedian law, passed after Caesar's adopted son had seized the consulship in August 43 BC; this provided for the prosecution of those involved in the plot – thus overruling the amnesty agreed on March 17, 44 (see below).

Our sources are unanimous in placing Gaius Cassius Longinus and Marcus Iunius Brutus at the centre of the conspiracy. Decimus Iunius Brutus Albinus is closely associated with them by Nicolaus (F130, 19.59), Appian (*B.Civ.* 2.111.464), and Dio (44. 14.3–4). The first two were pardoned Pompeians; the last was a trusted former lieutenant of Caesar's, as were Gaius Trebonius and Servius Sulpicius Galba. Other known conspirators are L. Tillius Cimber, C. and P. Servilius Casca, L. Minucius Basilus, Q. Ligarius, M. Spurius, P. Sextius Naso, L. Pontius Aquila, Pacuvius Antistius Labeo, D. Turullius, C. Cassius Parmensis, Petronius, Rubrius Ruga, Caecilius and his brother (Caecilius) Bucolianus (Drumann and Groebe 1906, though they omit Rubrius Ruga, App. *B Civ.* 2.113.474). We also hear of sympathizers who were not directly involved in the murder. Among them was Lucius Cornelius Cinna, the son of the former Marian dynast and a former brother-in-law of Caesar, who had been allowed to return to politics through Caesar's victory. He had sought to reinstate the tribunes Caesetius and Marullus and on Caesar's murder he removed his magistrate's toga on the ground that he had received it from a tyrant (Nic. Dam. F130, 22.76; App. *B Civ.* 2.121.509). A Stoic follower of Cato, Favonius, and the Epicurean Statilius allegedly refused an invitation to participate, the one because civil war was worse than tyranny, the other because involvement would threaten his philosophical tranquility without appropriate justification (Plut. *Brutus* 12.2–3). However, Favonius is said to have joined the conspirators after the murder, as did Lentulus Spinther, Staius Murcus, M. Aquinus, a certain Patiscus, and even Dolabella (App. *B Civ.* 2.119. 500) – not to mention Cicero himself, though he refused to act as the conspirators' envoy to Antonius (*Phil.* 2.89).

The primacy assigned by the secondary sources to Marcus Brutus and Cassius is confirmed by their high profile after the assassination. The two were related by marriage and Cicero describes a family conference at Antium in June 44, presided over by Brutus' mother Servilia and attended by their wives (*Att.* 15.11). Apart from his descent from L. Brutus and Ahala, Brutus was married to the daughter of Cato, who in death remained the epitome of the Republic. Decimus Brutus was clearly also very important. It was he who undertook the dangerous task of ensuring that Caesar did attend the meeting of the senate on March 15, and whom Hirtius approached as an intermediary after the murder. Marcus Brutus is portrayed as being induced to embark on the plot by remarks from his friends, especially Cassius, calls from passers-by, and graffiti both on the statue of his ancestor L. Brutus and on his praetor's tribunal in the forum, reminding him of his family's hostility to tyranny (e.g., Plut. *Brut.* 9.5–10). It is perhaps best to assume that the graffiti on Brutus' tribunal occurred, when he first became praetor in January 44, some time before the assassination, and that the passage of time had dispelled the suspicions of Brutus that these must have inevitably inspired.

According to Nicolaus the plot was concerted by a number of small-scale meetings in private houses, without the conspirators ever meeting as a group (F130, 23.81). That is plausible in view of the secrecy that was maintained. The actual time and place of the assassination must have been decided at short notice. Nicolaus also relates that they originally considered alternative plans to attack him on the Sacred Way, at elections in the Campus Martius, or at a gladiatorial show (cf. Suet. *Iul.* 80.4). Caesar had convened the senate to discuss the constitutional crisis created by Mark Antony's refusal to declare Dolabella as his elected colleague in place of Caesar (Cic. *Phil.* 2.88); he was due to leave Rome in three or four days. It was perhaps the last chance before Caesar was surrounded by loyal troops – he had dismissed his Spanish bodyguard some time before (Suet. *Iul.* 86.1; Nic. Dam.F130, 22.80). One tradition, which is found as a rumor in Cicero's contemporary work *On Divination* (2.110; cf. App *B.Civ.* 2.110.460–1), claims that it was to be proposed at a meeting in the senate that Caesar should be given the title of king, at least in the provinces, because of a prophecy found in the Sibylline books that the Parthians could only be conquered by a king: Suetonius (*Iul.* 80.1) suggests that the conspiracy was hastened because men like Brutus and Cassius would have had to either endorse this motion or show their disloyalty. This must be treated with caution. For Cicero the story is only a rumor, and the conspirators had paid lip service to extravagant honors to Caesar before. In any case, if this had been actually planned for March 15, it would have been cited in our sources as a compelling reason for Caesar to attend the senate that day.

The sources give various explanations for the choice of the senate as the location: Nicolaus that Caesar would be isolated from likely support (F130, 23.81); Appian that senators not in the plot could be expected to join in (*B.Civ.* 2.114.476); Dio that senators would not defend Caesar, because they were unarmed (44.16.1). Of these the third seems most plausible. Dio adds that the weapons could be brought into the senate-chamber in the boxes usually used for writing-tablets. The majority of the senate were in fact loyal Caesarians. Some conspirators had special tasks: Decimus Brutus to encourage Caesar to come to the senate, Trebonius to distract Mark Antony (so Cicero, *Phil.* 2.34 and the majority of secondary sources; Plutarch, *Caes.* 66.4, assigns the task to Decimus Brutus); Tillius Cimber to obstruct Caesar with a petition, and the two Cascas to begin the attack.

In spite of the planning there were two questions that created uncertainty about its success, which are highlighted in our ancient narratives: would Caesar come to the senate, and would the plot be betrayed? The conspirators might have been frustrated, if Caesar had paid any attention to the unfavorable omens he received beforehand. Caesar, however, believed in his own fortune and had never run away from danger. In Cicero's work *On Divination* (1.119) it is argued that though true, the omens could not deflect the course of history. Decimus Brutus was able to argue persuasively that Caesar could not insult the senate by his absence, exploiting the fact that the dictator had been previously accused of insulting that body. As they waited for Caesar, Brutus and Cassius were given good wishes by someone outside the plot, Popilius Laenas, as if he was in the know, and then had to watch him deliberately converse with Caesar on the latter's arrival outside the theatre (App. *B Civ.* 2.115.484; 116.486). However, Caesar, as one can judge from his surprised protest, "This really is violence!" when he was first manhandled by Tillius Cimber (Suet. *Iul.* 82.1), suspected nothing until the last moment. The actual assassination was a clumsy and inefficient business: a physician claimed that only the second wound in the breast was lethal (Suet. *Iul.* 82.3). The story that Caesar reproached Marcus Brutus in Greek, addressing him as "my child" (Suet. *Iul.* 82.2; Dio 44.19.5), was not found in all accounts and must be subject to doubt, especially as Caesar's relationship with Brutus' mother Servilia probably commenced after Brutus' birth.

There were no doubt personal grievances at work and, for some, Pompeian sentiment (the final location of the assassination in the precinct of Pompey's theatre and before Pompey's statue was surely no coincidence), but it is also clear that there were Caesarians who believed that Caesar's course should be stopped. Their objection may not have been only to his manipulation of the ostensibly republican government, but also to his policies, in particular towards land division for the benefit of legionaries and other supporters. Caesar had ordered the confiscation of Pompeian estates, including some belonging to those whom he had pardoned, and appointed Mark Antony to supervise this. His land-commissioners seem also to have been exploiting any land that could be claimed as public. This had the potential to dispossess occupiers whose families had been in possession for some time. Such a policy was resumed by the land commission set up by Mark Antony in June 44 and was to be taken even further by the triumvirs.

An argument that the conspiracy was an attack not just on Caesar but Caesarism may be found in the tradition about Mark Antony. Cicero was to complain regularly after the event about the "leftovers": it was illogical to kill a tyrant and leave behind his heir. We find in secondary sources the story that some conspirators argued that Mark Antony should be included in their target, but Brutus vetoed this, because it would make the act seem one of political faction not of liberation from tyranny (App. *B Civ.* 2.114.478; Plut. *Brut.* 18.3–4). This shows that it was thought correctly that Mark Antony was likely to continue Caesar's plans and methods. Hostility to the regime in principle may also explain why they hastened to kill Caesar when his presence was not going to be felt in Rome for some time. For the answer must be that in some ways Caesar's monarchy would become more disagreeable when he was absent than when he was present. Instructions would have arrived from the dictator – not necessarily sent to the magistrates but to Oppius, Balbus, and their kind – and these would have been put into effect, whether in a constitutionally proper fashion or not. As Cicero had remarked to Servius Sulpicius, the best thing about the Caesarian regime was Caesar himself.

The conspirators seem to have hoped that leading Caesarians would cooperate with them to restore true republican government, once Caesar was slain. They were quickly disillusioned. After the initial shock and panic were over, Lepidus (who was the dead dictator's master of horse) transported troops from the Tiber island to the Campus Martius and kept them at the disposal of Mark Antony, who, as consul, was now Rome's chief magistrate. The hostility of the plebs led to the conspirators being besieged on the Capitol. We possess a desperate letter written, probably on March 16, by Decimus Brutus to Marcus Brutus and Cassius. Decimus refers to the "most untrustworthy" attitude of Antony, suggesting that some conspirators now expected his help, and points out that the conspirators had no secure base, short of taking refuge with one of the two remaining Pompeian rebels, Sextus Pompeius in Spain and Caecilius Bassus in Syria (*Fam.* 11.1).

In the senate meeting on March 17, where Antony and Lepidus had bodyguards of veteran soldiers, an amnesty was voted to the conspirators on Cicero's proposal, but in the same session the senate also voted to ratify Caesar's appointments to office and all his other measures, whether enacted or merely planned. Hostility to the conspirators was exacerbated by the reading of Caesar's will (with its generous gifts to the people of Rome) and by Antony's "tear-jerking oration" on the day of the funeral (*Att.* 14.10.1). It should be noted, however, that, according to Suetonius (*Iul.* 84.2), this oration was a very brief pendant to a recitation by a herald of the decree, in which the senators had voted Caesar all divine and human honors at one stroke, and of the oath by which they had all bound themselves to preserve his life. In the face of popular fury Cassius and Marcus Brutus, though they were the praetors in charge of civil jurisdiction, found it impossible to remain in the city to carry out the duties of their office. By contrast, Decimus Brutus, Trebonius, and Tillius Cimber were allowed within about a month to leave for the provinces they were due to hold under Caesar's last arrangements.

Caesar's friend C. Matius, whom Cicero visited in early April, was both grieved and dismayed at his death: "If he with all his genius did not find a solution, who will find it now?" He actually took pleasure at the grim prospects for Rome and expected an uprising in Gaul both of the Gauls themselves and of Caesar's soldiers there (*Att.* 14.1.1). For the less rational there were the portents of doom in the heavens.

It is likely that already in April there were atmospheric disturbances resulting from the eruption of Etna. Later, in July, the appearance of a comet during games for Caesar was to be interpreted as a sign of Caesar's deification. In his work *On Divination* (1.119, 2.23) Cicero plays with the idea that Caesar's murder was an outcome of divine providence (the portents before his death were to forewarn him, not to enable him to evade his fate). However, the notion of providence was not so comforting, when he looked at the result of the assassination. He consoled himself for the present humiliation of Cassius and Brutus and the increasing dominance of Mark Antony by recalling the assassination itself. However, "it was less dangerous to speak against that nefarious party when the tyrant was alive than when he is dead" (*Att.* 14.17.6). "That deed was done with the courage of men but the strategy of children. Who did not realize this: an heir had been left to the monarchy?" (ibid. 14.21.3). Cicero means here Mark Antony, but by early May Octavian had arrived to claim his inheritance and Cleopatra was still at Rome with her son. At the end of May, learning of Antony's plans to strip Decimus Brutus of his province and army, Cicero had revised his views further: "I get no joy from the Ides of March. For he (Caesar) would never have returned, fear would never have driven us to ratify his measures" (ibid. 15.4.3). He had earlier written to Cassius, "After the king has been killed, we are putting into effect every royal nod .... Enactments are being posted, immunities are being given, vast sums of money are being disbursed, exiles are being allowed home, forged decrees of the senate are being put on record ..." (*Fam.* 12.1.1–2). Cicero expected the conspirators to do something more, but it was not clear what they could do, short of beginning another civil bloodbath.

As Brutus and Cassius prepared to leave Italy for the East they declared in an open letter to Mark Antony, "Our policy is that we desire you to be a great and renowned man in a free community (*res publica*). We challenge you to no feud, but we value our liberty more than your friendship" (*Fam.* 11.3.4). That in effect was their attitude to

Figure 6.2 BMCRR Africa 32 = Crawford, Roman Republican Coinage 540/1. 36 BC Obv. Head of Octavian; Rev. Temple with star in pediment, DIVO IVL(IO) on architrave, and lighted altar to left. (See Zanker, chap. 21, p. 298.)

Caesar also. By contrast, Matius, when he defended himself to Cicero for his past allegiance to the dead dictator and his support for Caesar's heir Octavianus, placed the claims of friendship first: "They criticize me for my grief and outrage at the death of a man close to me and whom I have loved. For, they say, I should have put my fatherland before friendship, assuming that they have proved that his death was in the public interest." Matius claimed that he had followed Caesar as a friend, had been against civil war, and had worked for clemency towards Caesar's defeated opponents. This clemency had not been extended to Caesar himself by his opponents. "What unheard of arrogance that some should take pride in a crime, others should not be allowed to grieve with impunity! This has always been free for slaves, to fear, rejoice or grieve at their own rather than another's discretion. This is what those self-styled authors of liberty are trying to wrench from our grasp by threats" (*Fam.* 11.28.2–3). In the struggles that followed, the cry of liberty soon became devalued. Caesar Octavianus' loyalty to his dead parent became a banner which led him to a greater power than Caesar's and was ultimately celebrated in the temple to Mars the Avenger in the Forum of Augustus.

FURTHER READING

The main narratives of the assassination, the events leading up to it, and those immediately following are to be found in: Nicolaus of Damascus' *Life of Caesar* (F. Jacoby, *Die Fragmente der griechischen Historiker* IIA, no. 90, frr. 125–30), esp. paragraphs 58–106; Appian, *Civil Wars* 2.106.440–147.614; Cassius Dio, Book 44; Suetonius, *Deified Julius* 76–85; Plutarch, *Caesar* 60–8, and *Brutus* 1–20. Modern narratives are provided by M. Gelzer, *Caesar: Politician and Statesman* (Oxford: Blackwell, 1968), pp. 322–9, E. Rawson in *Cambridge Ancient History*, 2nd edn (Cambridge: Cambridge University Press, 1994), vol. IX, pp. 464–73, and R. Syme, *The Roman Revolution* (Oxford: Oxford University Press, 1939), pp. 95–104. On tyrannicide see A. Lintott, *Violence in Republican Rome*, 2nd edn (Oxford: Oxford University Press, 1999), pp. 53–8. The monument to Harmodius and Aristogeiton on the Capitol is discussed by F. Coarelli, "Le 'Tyrannoctone' du Capitole et la mort de Tiberius Gracchus," *Mélanges d'Archéologie et d'Histoire* 81 (1969), 137–60. The best treatment of the philosophical background to the assassination is David Sedley, "The Ethics of Brutus and Cassius" *Journal of Roman Studies* 87 (1997), 41–53. The attitude of Cicero to Caesar and the assassination is discussed in A. Lintott, *Cicero as Evidence: A Historian's Companion* (Oxford: Oxford University Press Oxford, 2008), chs. 17–18.

The fullest account of the membership of the conspiracy is in W. Drumann and P. Groebe, *Geschichte Roms in seinem Übergange von der republikanischen zur monarchischen Verfassung*, 2nd edn (Leipzig: Borntraeger, 1906), vol. 3, pp. 627–43. On the astronomical phenomena after the murder see J. T. Ramsey and A. Licht, *The Comet of 44 B.C. and Caesar's Funeral Games*, American Classical Studies 39 (Atlanta, GA: pub, 1997).

PART II

Biography: Themes

CHAPTER SEVEN

General and Imperialist

Nathan Rosenstein

The Evidence

Any attempt to analyze Caesar's generalship and diplomacy must at the outset face up to the fundamental problem of the evidence. Nearly everything we know about Caesar in these roles we know from Caesar himself. The *Bellum Gallicum* and the *Bellum Civile* are classics in the literature of military history and unique documents for the study of ancient warfare – the only first-hand accounts that we possess of military campaigns and conquests by the general who conducted them. However, Caesar was also central to the political struggles of the late Republic, particularly during and after his consulship, and instigated a civil war that ended in the Republic's overthrow. Therefore the *Bellum Gallicum* and especially the *Bellum Civile* are scarcely objective accounts of the events they describe. The broader implications of these facts other chapters (chapter 12, Christina S. Kraus, and chapter 13, Kurt Raaflaub) will explore; here the point that needs underscoring is that we cannot know in most cases to what degree Caesar's political (or even artistic) concerns affected the way he told the story of his military achievements and how he presented himself in the role of general and imperialist. Undoubtedly they did, but only rarely can we know when and how. So, for example, after Pompey inflicted a serious defeat upon Caesar at Dyracchium in 48, Caesar portrays himself as calmly and decisively electing to withdraw his forces and blaming his soldiers for their defeat (*BC* 3.73). We learn from Plutarch, though, that Caesar spent a troubled and sleepless night reproaching himself for bad generalship before finally resolving upon what he must do next (*Caes.* 39.6–7). What Caesar presents to us in his writing, in other words, is a construct, an image of himself that is certainly not the plain, unvarnished account of his actions that it purports to be, yet not cut from whole cloth either.

Still, what gives confidence that such an enterprise is not wholly without validity is the knowledge that Caesar was not writing in a vacuum but for an audience of Roman readers who had very clear notions of what generals should do and how they should comport themselves on campaign and in dealing with other peoples. Indeed, the men who led the Republic's armies were themselves as much a product of their culture and its expectations of military commanders as anyone else. It is a fair surmise, then, that they tried to the best of their ability to live up to those expectations. However undemocratic the Republican political system was in practice, public opinion mattered. The performance of Rome's military leaders therefore cannot have been completely divorced from Roman citizens' expectations of them – expectations that are reflected in the literary portraits of them, even if we cannot take those portraits as unadulterated reflections of reality.

Becoming a General

When Caesar reached Gaul in March of 58, he was not unpracticed in the arts of war, but it is important to understand the nature and extent of his preparation to lead a Roman army. Prior to the age of Caesar, military glory paved the way for a young aristocrat seeking to make his mark at Rome (Rosenstein 2006a, 2007). Although a relatively small group of noble families (and a few outsiders) dominated the Republic's highest offices, entry into the ruling elite was not strictly speaking hereditary. Rather, the members of each family's new generation had to validate their claims to the offices and honors their ancestors had held by measuring up to the standards the latter had set. Foremost among these was adherence to an aristocratic ethos that stressed an intense dedication to the welfare of the *res publica* and the relentless pursuit of honor in its service. During the third and second centuries, this meant striving to win a reputation for bravery and valorous deeds on the field of battle. The *gloria* and *fama* that accrued were universally judged to demonstrate the superior *virtus* that was the aristocracy's hallmark and that fit a man to lead his fellow citizens and conduct the Republic's weightiest affairs. Ten years of military service were required before young aristocrats could stand for public office, and this period not only provided ample scope for them to demonstrate their prowess at war but also an opportunity at least to observe how campaigns were organized and military operations conducted. During this period, young aristocrats served in the cavalry and typically won election once or twice to the post of military tribune where, as junior officers of the legions, they undertook a number of important responsibilities. Success during this military service in time led to success in future competition to win election to public offices, including those that would entail leading Roman armies to war – the consulate and at least occasionally the praetorship.

By the early first century, when Caesar was coming of age, this system had changed. Roman citizens no longer formed the Republic's cavalry, and ten years of military service no longer constituted a prerequisite to public office. These developments had their roots in the practicalities of Roman warfare but stemmed also from alterations in the aristocratic ethos itself (McCall 2002). However, the cachet of military glory remained strong, and young aristocrats still sought it even though they now spent less time at war than their forebears. Since they no longer served as cavalrymen, and infantry service would have been beneath their dignity, they were attached to an army's commander as "tentmates" (*contubernales*) where they might function as quasi-staff officers and where proximity enabled them to observe closely how a general went about his business (Badian, chapter 2, p. 17). This sort of learning by close observation was very much in keeping with Roman traditions of education.

Caesar's early career falls very much into this pattern. In 81, at the age of 19, he became the "tentmate" of the praetor M. Minucius Thermus, who was at that time besieging Mytilene in Asia Minor. Thermus dispatched him to bring a naval contingent from Rome's ally Nicomedes, the king of Bithynia, to assist in the siege. The following year when Roman forces at last stormed the city Caesar took part in the attack, in the course of which he won the "civic crown" (*corona civica*) (Suet. *Iul.* 2). The decoration was not trivial. A wreath of oak leaves, it was awarded to a Roman citizen for saving the life of a fellow citizen in battle with exceptional gallantry: the recipient had to have stood his ground without retreating by as much as a step and killed the enemy threatening the citizen being rescued (Gell. *NA* 5.6.13). Caesar's feat is our earliest indication of the extraordinary personal bravery he was later to display time and again in command. We next catch sight of him two years later, again in the East, when he served briefly under P. Servilius Vatia in the campaign against the Cilician pirates (Suet. *Iul.* 3). Pirates perhaps also figured in his next military assignment, for he may have served as a senior staff officer (*legatus*) for M. Antonius who in 73 was battling sea robbers in Crete (*Syll.* 748.22: see chapter 2, p. 19). Finally, in 71 Caesar won election to the military tribunate, although we do not know where or under whom he served, or whether he saw combat (Suet. *Iul.* 5; Plut. *Caes.* 5.1). In all, Caesar spent perhaps a little over six years learning to wage war, assuming he remained with the armies in the East during 79 and 72. During this time (and perhaps subsequently) he may also have been reading military treatises by Greek and Roman authors and imbibing their precepts (Lendon 1999).

Of equal or perhaps greater note are two further episodes abroad. One was the sequel to his capture by pirates in 75. After he was ransomed and released and despite being a civilian and a comparatively young man by Roman standards, he quickly raised a naval force from Roman allies in the region and with it attacked and captured his former captors, whom he put to death (Suet. *Iul.* 4.1–2; Plut. *Caes.* 1.4–2.4). In the following year while Caesar was studying rhetoric on the island of Rhodes, King Mithridates of Pontis invaded the Roman province of Asia Minor, which encompassed Rhodes. In response, Caesar organized local forces, once again on his own initiative, and drove off the contingent of Mithridates' army threatening the region (Suet. *Iul.* 4.2; see chapter 2, p. 19). Both episodes reveal that Caesar had absorbed important lessons about the organization and conduct of campaigns during his apprenticeships with Thermus, Vatia, and Antonius and perhaps from his reading. More importantly, they are our earliest evidence of the boldness and speed that were to be the hallmarks of Caesar's conduct of military operations in Gaul and elsewhere.

However, it was not his military laurels that brought Caesar his first command but politics. The key to becoming a general at Rome lay in election to high public office, and to win required far more than a good or even an outstanding service record. As noted above, the ways in which aristocrats defined themselves and won renown were changing in the later second and first centuries, and martial *virtus*, while always respected, no longer trumped other claims to preferment. Sallust in his famous description of Caesar prior to his election to the consulate conspicuously omits any mention of his military achievements (*Cat.* 53.6–54.5). Throughout his twenties, when he was not at war Caesar was laying the non-military foundations of future political success. He honed his skill as a public speaker, undertook high-profile prosecutions, lavished money and favors, and in a variety of other ways made himself conspicuous and won favor with the great many people, both powerful and humble, on whose support his hopes for election to the praetorship and ultimately the consulate depended (see Gruen, chapter 3 of this volume).

Empire Builder

Caesar's intentions in his proconsulate were anything but pacific. As Sallust puts it in the description of Caesar noted above and set a few years before his consulship, "He longed for a great military command, an army, and a new war where his *virtus* could shine" (*Cat.* 54.4). That new war, however, Caesar initially expected to wage in Illyria. The *lex Vatinia* of 59 that gave Caesar his proconsular command seems originally to have encompassed only that province along with Cisalpine Gaul. Gallia Transalpina was added only following the death of its governor (see chapter 3, p. 34). Illyria had been a praetorian province shortly before 59 while early in 58 we find three veteran legions encamped at Aquileia, in the far northeastern corner of Italy. The area to the east was clearly not pacified, for in 53 and 52 raids on Italy originated there (Brennan 2000: 425). So Caesar may at first have seen his best opportunity for conquest in the Balkans; Transalpine Gaul had been quiet in recent years. Only when the migration of the Helvetii drew his attention to the west and offered prospects of a quick victory does he seem to have changed his plans.

This shift was fully in accord with the principles governing generals' pursuit of the senate's foreign policy goals. Generals had always enjoyed wide latitude in their diplomatic and military operations (Eckstein 1987). Rarely were the senate's instructions to one of its commanders very specific. The slowness of communications simply did not permit it to exercise close supervision of a general's conduct in his province, for the situation in the field could change rapidly and render his original instructions irrelevant. Rather, generals were given a broad mandate to protect the majesty of the Roman people and pursue the best interests of the Republic as they saw fit. A few laws imposed restrictions, such as the prohibition against a governor leaving his province. But Caesar's abandoning operations in Illyria to campaign in Gaul was completely in keeping with this mandate to protect Rome's interests, as he is at pains to stress in the early chapters of the *Bellum Gallicum*.

Still, many scholars have judged, not without reason, that his pursuit and destruction of the migrating Helvetii were nothing less than a brazen effort to provoke a war on the flimsiest of pretexts in order to reap the glory that victory would bring. But the Romans' world was very different from our own, and Caesar very much a product of it. Most readers of the *Bellum Gallicum* would have seen nothing morally objectionable about his aggressive pursuit of conquests in Gaul, as Caesar's plainspoken account of them amply demonstrates, and his justifications of them are highly revealing of the mindset, not only of the man who undertook them, but of Roman attitudes towards war and empire. Caesar advances several reasons for his various campaigns. Often, they sprang from the imperative to defend the Republic's friends. Soon after the defeat of the Helvetii in 58, for example, Caesar learned that the Aedui, a Gallic tribe long friendly to Rome, were being oppressed by a large German war-band led by their king, Ariovistus, and accordingly he marched against them. Also important in his judgment was fear that these Germans, if not checked, would not only overrun all of Gaul but break into Italy itself, as the Cimbri and Teutones had done half a century earlier (*BG* 1.33). This claim that conquest was in fact a defensive act appears elsewhere. In the following year reports reached Caesar that the Belgae, a group of powerful tribes in northeastern Gaul, were gathering their forces against him, which impelled him to strike first. Moreover, the Belgae if left unconquered would have constituted a source of military manpower that dissident Gallic chiefs might use to resist Roman rule or further their political ambitions within their tribes (*BG* 2.1). Again and again Caesar claims that his conquests required further military action in order to protect the gains he had already won. So he justified his bridging of the Rhine and foray into Germany in 56 by the need to deter German tribes from intervening in Gallic affairs, either on their own initiative or at the invitation of Gauls seeking to enlist their aid in resisting Roman rule (*BG* 4.16). Similarly his expedition to Britain in the same year arose from a need to cut off a source of support for Gallic resistance to Roman rule. (*BG* 4.20) And finally, for Caesar it went without saying that any act of rebellion on the part of Gallic tribes once they had submitted had to be vigorously suppressed (*BG* 3.10).

All of these explanations are very much in keeping with the logic of their empire as the Romans saw it. The international scene in antiquity, as Eckstein has aptly described it, was an anarchy, a world without laws or authority capable of preventing war between states (Eckstein 2006b). He stresses that the threat of aggression was unrelenting, and the consequences of defeat could be truly terrible: wholesale slaughter, rape, torture, mutilation, or sale into slavery. This harsh reality forced every state to prepare for war, to maximize its military potential, and to attack rather than risk being caught unawares. The Roman Republic had been born into this harsh, Darwinian world and had had little choice but to fight for its survival. It responded by building up its military strength in two ways. Culturally, a strong ethos of service to the Republic developed, particularly among the aristocracy, as noted above, that manifested itself in a thirst for military glory. In addition, soldiers and their officers understood that with victory could come substantial material rewards for themselves as well as the Republic (Harris 1979: 9–53). So there were real incentives to go to war (as well as some significant deterrents). But in this the Romans differed little from other ancient peoples. Where they were exceptional was in their success at both increasing the size of their citizenry and in creating a hegemonic system of alliances. Both gave Rome enormous reserves of military manpower. Yet having allies – those with treaties as well as informal "friends" of Rome – also entailed frequent obligations to deploy that military power, for with hegemony came the need to protect those subject to it. Any lack of resolution on Rome's part, any failure to respond to provocation or refusal to avenge swiftly and fully injuries done to itself or its friends would have been taken as signs of weakness, not only by those across the frontiers but by Rome's subjects. And weakness invited either aggression or revolt. The logic of empire therefore made it incumbent on Rome to project an image of strength, although the Romans themselves would not have put it in quite those terms. They would have couched matters in the language of morality and honor – upholding the majesty of Rome, punishing arrogance, humbling the proud, protecting the weak, and defending the Republic's friends (Rosenstein 2006b).

Caesar's dealings with the Gallic and German tribes he encountered are in complete accord with these principles. Ariovistus' oppression of the Aedui, for example, Caesar felt to be "a terrible disgrace to himself and to the Republic, considering the magnitude of its empire" (*BG* 1.33). It mattered not at all in his appraisal of the situation that he was injecting himself into what was simply a power struggle among two important Gallic tribes and Ariovistus. Indeed, Ariovistus, in Caesar's telling, offers what often strikes modern readers as a rather strong defense of his actions and a reasonable demand that Caesar mind his own business (*BG* 1.44). But the logic of empire in an anarchic world meant that there could be no compromise for Caesar and Rome: once the Aedui had appealed to Caesar, if he did not defend them, if he did not prove that Rome had the power to make its orders obeyed and show its promises of protection to be credible, he would only have been inviting further aggression by Ariovistus or someone else against the Republic's friends and ultimately against Rome itself. Nor, of course, had Caesar's thirst for glory and booty been slaked by his destruction of the Helvetii. His aggressive stance towards Ariovistus sprang as much from his enormous personal ambition as from the dictates of imperial policy. The two marched in step. But it does allow us to see Caesar's policy in Gaul as something more than simply a smash-and-grab operation on a gigantic scale.[1]

Rome's friends were more than simply a pretext for aggression, however. They were vital to Caesar's ability to wage war. He expected and received substantial assistance from his Gallic allies in his campaigns. They were the source of grain and other supplies for his army. They were a depot for stockpiles of equipment and food as well as a stronghold where Caesar could intern the many hostages he took to secure the loyalty of those who submitted to him and the enormous sums of money and loot his victories yielded. His soldiers, too, cached their heavy baggage and booty in friendly towns (*BG* 5.47). And Gallic troops, especially aristocratic cavalry, constituted a crucial component of Caesar's strike force. To secure their cooperation therefore Caesar supported friendly tribes like the Aedui, placing others under their jurisdiction and increasing their honor (*BG* 4.13). Equally important, Caesar built up particular aristocrats within these tribes to ensure their loyalty and thus increase his ability to conquer and hold Gaul. Gallic society was sharply divided between commoners and the elite, of whom the former counted for little and were attached as dependents to the latter. Securing the allegiance of a tribe, therefore, in practice meant winning the allegiance of the men in it who counted, and this Caesar did assiduously, rewarding them handsomely with wealth and honors and seeing to it that their political rivals were suppressed or in some cases destroyed (e.g. *BG* 7.32). Creating an empire in Gaul involved Caesar not simply in managing the diplomatic relations among the tribes but in creating advantageous political conditions within them.

Strategist

From the moment he entered his province, Caesar was on the march – every summer and at times in winter as well. In part, this practice simply reflects his thirst for glory, which he could not win by waiting for some enemy to come to him. He needed victories to secure his position at the top of the Republic's political hierarchy, and to get them he would have to find enemies to conquer. But in doing so, he was also acting in accord with a broad strategic consensus at Rome. Throughout the Republic strategic doctrine tended to be quite simple. Large-scale operations involving the coordination of multiple armies and generals were very unusual, and Roman armies only rarely stood on the defensive when combat was in prospect. Rather, campaigns typically were waged by a single commander operating with a few legions. Generals were expected to cross the frontier, locate the enemy's forces, meet them in a pitched battle, and by defeating them secure the surrender not only of the army but of the people or state that it had been defending. Often, the simple appearance of Roman forces in an enemy's territory would be enough to bring out their army to oppose it. If not, or if the enemy refused to surrender after being beaten in the open field, the legions would devastate the enemy's croplands and pillage its territory. And either in conjunction with these activities or as an alternative to them, a Roman general would besiege the enemy's strongholds and fortified cities and by reducing them compel the inhabitants to capitulate or face slaughter. A strategic doctrine founded on the offensive grew out of the imperatives of empire. To ensure the quiescence of its subjects, to deter attacks from neighbors, and to cow those over whom Rome might intend to extend its dominion, the Republic needed to cultivate an image of irresistible strength against which resistance was futile. Regular conquests filled the bill. In pursuing the Helvetii, in marching against Ariovistus, in invading the territory of the Belgae, and in undertaking his other campaigns, Caesar was simply following the strategy expected of any Roman general.

Caesar's success in implementing an aggressive strategy was greatly facilitated by the diplomatic situation in Gaul in the mid-first century BC, which provided ample opportunities for anyone looking for enemies to conquer. As Caesar has one of the Gallic leaders explain in 58, the two principal Gallic tribes had for some years contended for primacy. When one summoned Ariovistus and a powerful force of Germans from across the Rhine, they tipped the balance of power in its favor. However, Ariovistus soon grew more powerful than his erstwhile Gallic allies and brought them into subjugation as well (*BG* 1.31). Once Caesar had demonstrated his army's power by defeating the Helvetii and revealed his own readiness to use it to intervene in Gallic affairs outside the Roman province, the Gauls saw in him a new force in the region that they could mobilize for their own ends. And that is precisely what the Gallic tribes under the thumb of Ariovistus now sought to do by seeking Caesar's protection against the wrongs they alleged they were suffering at Ariovistus' hands. Caesar, eager for victories and operating under a strategic doctrine that supported the aggressive deployment of Roman military power, was happy to comply with their wishes. He was able to conquer Gaul because it was divided, and from that perspective his campaigns during his early years in Gaul can be viewed as simply a continuation of the long-standing internecine warfare endemic to the region. For Gauls were only too ready to cooperate in helping Caesar conquer not only Ariovistus' Germans but other Gauls as well. Thus in the following year Caesar enlisted the aid of the friendly Aedui. They were to mount an attack against one of the Belgic tribes in order to divert their forces while Caesar marched against the rest (*BG* 2.5). Throughout his years in Gaul, Caesar regularly availed himself of the aid of contingents of Gallic troops from friendly tribes as he subdued their neighbors. This strategy only failed when, after several years of Roman occupation, awareness spread among the Gauls that the Romans had come to stay. This realization led most of them, at last, to unite against Caesar in a desperate bid to regain their freedom.

Caesar pursued his conquests with remarkable boldness and speed. The rapidity (*celeritas*) with which Caesar formulated his plans of campaign and put them into execution is evident from the very beginning of the Gallic wars. Upon learning of the impending migration of the Helvetii, Caesar rushed from Rome to Gaul to meet this threat, and by covering about 90 miles a day he reached the province in eight days (*BG* 1.7; Plut. *Caes.* 17.4). Within the space of about two weeks he had broken down the bridge over the Rhone and constructed a wall across the valley, blocking the Helvetii's attempt to march through the Roman province. Thereupon he raced back to Italy, gathered his three legions, enrolled two more, then hurried back to Gaul to confront the enemy (*BG* 1.10). Similarly, when he set out against Ariovistus later that same year, he did so by forced marches, moving day and night, until he had secured a stronghold threatened by the German warleader (*BG* 1.38). Caesar highlights the swiftness with which he and his army acted over and over throughout the *Bellum Gallicum* and not just in crises like that in early 53, when all of Gaul had risen in revolt and Caesar had to travel north to his army once again, by forced marches day and night, in order to forestall any attempt on his life (*BG* 7.9). Hirtus, his continuator in the eighth book of the *Bellum Gallicum* is equally emphatic on this point (e.g. *BG* 8.3), and it emerges even more strikingly in the early stages of the civil war, when Cicero found the speed of Caesar's advance through Italy "unbelievable" (Cic. *Att.* 8.22 [SB 146].1). Indeed, by that point "Caesarian swiftness" had become all but proverbial (e.g. Cic. *Att.* 16.10 [SB 422].1, cf. Vell. Pat. 2.41.1, 51.2).

Caesar placed this rapidity of action at the service of a willingness to take substantial risks in order to achieve his strategic aims. Again, this characteristic appears at the very beginning of Caesar's command in Gaul. During his first two years there, he not only attacked the Helvetii who, if Caesar is to be believed, greatly outnumbered his own forces, but then picked a fight with the most powerful figure in central Gaul, Ariovistus, and in the following year marched against an even more potent foe, the Belgic confederation. His defeat of the Belgae induced many of the remaining tribes in Gaul to surrender; those that did not he mopped up piecemeal, so that by the end of 57 Caesar could claim that "all of Gaul had been pacified," an achievement given official recognition at Rome by the senate's decree of an unprecedented 15 days of thanksgiving (*BG* 2.35–6). In Caesar's telling, the campaigns of 58–57 were all forced upon him: the new homeland the Helvetii intended to occupy threatened Roman territory; he could not refuse the Gauls' plea for succor against the Germans without dishonor to himself and Rome; and the Belgae were already gathering their forces to attack Caesar, leaving him no choice but to defend himself. Yet it is not difficult to see here a bold but very shrewd strategic gamble by Caesar, in which he staked all his hopes of conquering Gaul on swiftly overcoming the two most important centers of opposition, reckoning that everything else would fall into place once these campaigns had been won. This sort of strategic risk-taking is evident throughout the remainder of Caesar's military career, not only in Gaul but in the civil war that followed, when in January of 49 Caesar gambled that he could overcome his opponents if he struck swiftly with only limited forces before they had time to gather strength.

While Caesar owed much of his success in war to this combination of speed and boldness, at times these qualities could put him in a tight spot. Once Pompey had foiled Caesar's attempt to end the civil war almost before it began by trapping his opponents in Italy in 49, Caesar swiftly turned west, intending to deal with the threat posed by Pompey's forces in Spain to his position in Gaul, the source of much of the money and cavalry he needed to wage this war. It was a bold stroke, typical of Caesar's style of campaigning. He reached that province in June, before the grain harvest was in, and established a camp near the Pompeian forces. However, when a sudden storm turned the Segre River into an impassable torrent and broke down the bridges his troops had previously constructed across it, Caesar found himself unable to bring in the supplies coming from Italy or to gather enough grain from the countryside round about to feed his troops. His enemies quickly took advantage of the situation to further isolate Caesar by attacking his supply train. News of his predicament reached Rome, where Caesar's destruction was confidently expected. Only his ability to improvise boats to transport his legions across the river, which enabled him to bring his supply train into camp, rescued his army from starvation (*BC* 1.48–55). In the following year Caesar transported his army from Italy to Greece, where Pompey was gathering his forces. Seeking to force a decisive battle quickly, Caesar attempted to cut Pompey's army off from its supply base at Dyrrachium. When Pompey countered by moving to protect the city, the conflict developed into a positional struggle, with Caesar attempting to cut Pompey off by building fortifications around his encampment and Pompey countering with fortifications of his own. But Caesar had acted precipitously. Once again, he had moved before grain was ripe in the area, making it difficult for him to collect food for his army. Pompey controlled the sea, so that he and his men had what they needed despite Caesar's blockade while Caesar's troops went hungry. A difficult situation became untenable when Pompey launched a surprise attack on a weak point in Caesar's fortifications, and he was forced to retreat south hoping to find food and regroup. Pompey and his army followed in hot pursuit, expecting to finish Caesar off in short order (*BC* 3.41–99).

In evaluating Caesar as a strategist, it is instructive to compare his performance to Pompey's in their struggle against one another. The Gallic campaigns did not require Caesar to do much more than find the enemy's forces and defeat them, but in waging war against Pompey Caesar found himself contending against a veteran commander with wide experience and, apart from himself, the most successful general of his day. And indeed Pompey comes off very well in this contest. Knowing that his strength lay in the East, Pompey managed a strategic withdrawal from Italy in the face of Caesar's determined onslaught, embarking his forces despite Caesar's effort to trap him in Brundesium. And Pompey prevented Caesar from following for almost a year, thus enabling himself to gather an army to meet the one Caesar already had in being. So round one must go to Pompey. It is true, he lost his Spanish legions to Caesar, but they were mere pawns in the larger game; the war would be won or lost in Greece. When Caesar attempted to besiege Pompey at Dyrrachium, Pompey was able not only to resist but to break the siege by a well-timed attack at precisely Caesar's weakest point. Caesar here had clearly been out-generaled, as he himself recognized (Plut. *Caes.* 39.6–7). Furthermore, Pompey continued to press his advantage as he pursued Caesar in his retreat. Round two therefore also ought to be scored for Pompey. And even in the final contest, Pompey clearly held the dominant position, since he was able to choose the time and place for battle. In his struggle against Pompey, Caesar was pursuing the only strategy he could, seeking by speed and boldness to overcome Pompey's superiority in manpower and money. But Pompey proved himself the better strategist, able to check Caesar at every turn until they faced one another at Pharsalus. Yet Caesar possessed one great strength as a general that won him not only this battle but nearly every one he would ever fight.

Tactician

Battle was where Caesar most clearly demonstrated his particular brand of military genius. He was a master tactician. If his strategic thinking was largely conventional – albeit boldly and swiftly executed – once combat was in the offing Caesar could display an inventiveness and extraordinary sureness of touch that set him apart from his peers. Pharsalus can stand as one striking example among many. In August of 47 after several times declining Caesar's offers of battle, Pompey at last decided that it was time to move in for the kill. He commanded 11 legions to Caesar's eight, but since his troops would be no match for Caesar's veteran legionaries, he placed his chief hope for victory in his far more numerous cavalry, 6,400 to Caesar's 1,000. Massing them on his left flank and supporting them with light infantry, Pompey intended their charge to drive off Caesar's horse. Pompey's cavalry would then swing around behind Caesar's line of infantry and attack them from the rear while his own infantry held Caesar's legions in place until the trap could be sprung. This plan of attack had venerable roots stretching back to Hannibal's victory at Cannae and even earlier to the battles of Alexander the Great against Persia. It ought to have worked, and against a lesser general it would have. But Caesar's tactical abilities were more than equal to this challenge. As the two sides deployed and Caesar watched Pompey's cavalry mass against his own, he understood immediately the threat they posed not only to his cavalry but to his infantry. To meet it, Caesar improvised. A Roman legion in this period was organized in ten cohorts of about 500 men each. In combat, each legion's cohorts were usually marshaled in three lines of three or four cohorts each, one behind the other, and the legions in this formation lined up next to each another. Caesar therefore ordered one cohort from the third line of each of his eight legions to fall out, march to the right flank, and form a fourth line behind and at an oblique angle to the Tenth Legion, which held the end of the right wing. Thus prepared, he gave the signal to advance. Everything fell out as Caesar had foreseen. Pompey's cavalry drove off Caesar's horsemen and then attacked the legions on Caesar's right. At that point, Caesar ordered his fourth line, held in reserve until then, to attack Pompey's cavalry. They charged so vigorously that they put them to headlong flight. With the protection of their cavalry gone, Pompey's light infantry were no match for Caesar's heavily armed legionaries, and they were slaughtered. That accomplished, Caesar's fourth line was free to attack Pompey's legions in the flank and rear. The result was a rout: Pompey's legions fled, along with Pompey himself and the rest of his officers (*BC* 3.88–99).

It is worth dwelling on this battle at some length because it strikingly illustrates just what sets Caesar so much apart from other generals: his ability not simply to grasp what the enemy intended but to improvise a brilliant counter-stroke to meet it. Pompey's tactic at Pharsalus is often termed "hammer and anvil," in that the infantry, the "anvil," holds the enemy infantry in place, while the "hammer," the cavalry, swings around the rear and strikes it from behind. It had never, to our knowledge, been effectively countered – until Pharsalus. And Caesar's achievement in doing so is all the more impressive because it went against the grain of almost the entire history of Roman tactical doctrine to that point. One of the keys to Rome's unparalleled record of battlefield successes had always been the independent maneuverability of the cohorts and earlier the maniples of which their legions had been composed. This feature had allowed generals to move maniples and cohorts back from direct contact with the enemy as they became exhausted or overwhelmed and to move fresh units forward to take their places. But almost never do we find generals going beyond this in open field battles to exploit the vastly greater range of tactical options that the ability of these units to maneuver independently allowed. At Pharsalus Caesar did, and it won him the day.

However, Caesar's genius at tactical improvisation would have gone for naught without superbly trained soldiers to execute his orders. It is worth stressing that Caesar's orders for cohorts to fall out of the third line and march to the right required them to carry out a highly unusual maneuver, and just the sort of unexpected change in long-standing tactical practice that could lead to confusion and disaster, especially at a moment as fraught with tension as that just before a battle began. That the maneuver did not fail but was carried out smoothly and rapidly is testament to the exceptionally high state of training and discipline among the men Caesar commanded. For if Caesar was a virtuoso on the battlefield, the instrument he performed on was one fully capable of meeting his standard of performance. In part Caesar's success at Pharsalus can be chalked up to the fact that centuries of warfare had brought the Roman army to the apogee of its development.

Roman soldiers in this period were not, as sometimes claimed, professionals. They were citizen-soldiers, conscripted from Italy's small farms. The men served for ten years or more before they returned to the land to marry and begin families. The lengthy periods that Roman legionaries could be kept at war – all year round for years at a time – allowed them to develop a skill at soldiering, a degree of discipline and a depth of experience, and a familiarity and trust in one another that could sustain them through the rigors of long, difficult campaigns as well as in the crucible of combat (Rosenstein 2004: 29–31). Ten years' fighting in Gaul had brought Caesar's legions to a point where they could not only execute flawlessly a new and unexpected maneuver, but even direct themselves in battle. When Caesar gave the order to charge at Pharsalus, his men began to advance rapidly, ready to hurl their *pila*. But when they saw Pompey's legions remaining in place, as Pompey had ordered, to await their charge, they feared that they would reach their opponents exhausted and disordered. Caesar's legions then of their own accord halted, dressed their lines, and resumed their advance. Only when they came within missile range did they hurl their *pila* and charge (*BC* 3.92–3). Faced with the furious onslaught of these highly trained, disciplined, and battle-hardened troops, Pompey's forces did not stand a chance, even had Caesar's fourth line not attacked them from the rear.

Caesar's battlefield virtuosity developed over long years and many campaigns.[2] His first battles against the Helvetii reveal clearly how far he was from tactical mastery at that point. At Bibractae, where he faced the main body of their forces, he elected to await their charge at the top of a hill, only pursuing when the enemy's ranks had been broken, much as his great-uncle Marius had done half a century earlier at Aquae Sextiae. Yet his army nearly came to grief when they were surprised in their pursuit by the sudden arrival of the Helvetian rearguard behind the Romans. At their appearance Caesar found himself trapped between two enemies. While his third line of cohorts faced about to confront this new threat, the first and second continued the attack against the main body of the enemy, who, given fresh heart by the reinforcements, renewed the fight with great vigor. The battle raged long and hard, and although the Romans ultimately triumphed, their losses were heavy. Caesar had to spend three days tending to the wounded and burying his dead (*BG* 1.23–6). Caesar had surrendered the tactical initiative by allowing the enemy's actions to dictate how the battle unfolded, and in so doing he had come very close to defeat. He would never make the same mistake again. Against Ariovistus a few months later, Caesar seized the initiative, forcing battle on his terms despite the Germans' initial reluctance to come out and fight (*BG* 1.50–1).

More important is the fact that Caesar soon after this began to embrace what might be termed a tactical template developed initially by Sulla and refined subsequently by two of Sulla's lieutenants, Lucullus and Pompey. This template entailed taking control of the field of battle by altering its contours through fortifications, fortified camps, and entrenchments. In 57, at his initial encounter with the Belgae, Caesar used well-defended earthworks and a fortified camp to neutralize his opponents' superiority in numbers (*BG* 2.9). Caesar and his subordinates repeatedly altered the military topography in order to gain a tactical advantage in their conquest of Gaul and in the battles during the civil war that followed. His most masterful employment of this technique was unquestionably at Alesia, the climactic battle of the Gallic revolt. Here Caesar surrounded the Gallic stronghold with a highly elaborate and very strong double-walled fortification and presented its defenders with a stark choice between attacking those fortifications and starvation. Thereby he forced not only the besieged, but the relief force sent to break the siege, to fight on his terms, enabling his outnumbered legionaries nonetheless to prevail (*BG* 7.60–89).

At Alesia, too, another ingredient in Caesar's battlefield generalship emerges forcefully. He possessed enormous personal courage, and repeatedly displayed a readiness to share the dangers of combat with his men, especially in crises (cf. Suet. *Iul.* 62; Plut. *Caes.* 17.2). His appearance spurred his men to fight even more fiercely until they prevailed, and in ancient battles that sort of determination and ferocity often made the critical difference between victory and defeat. At the climax of the battle at Alesia, when an attack by the Gallic relief forces was on the verge of capturing a key fort, threatening to compromise fatally Caesar's defenses and break the siege, Caesar sent in his reserves and then went himself to the scene of the action with more troops. Both sides recognized him. His men redoubled their efforts and finally put the enemy to flight (*BG* 7.87–8). More than once, his soldiers' awareness that the eyes of their commander were upon them steadied them, increased their resolve, and fired their ardor. By far the most striking instance came in 57, at the Sambre River, where the Belgae's ambush surprised the legions at the end of their day's march as they were making camp. The legionaries struggled to arm themselves and form ranks, aided by their experience and training and the presence of their officers. However, on the right, Caesar noticed that the men of the Twelfth Legion were bunched together. Most of the centurions had been killed or wounded, and the whole formation was in danger of collapse. Caesar seized a shield from one of the men in the rear ranks and then, as he writes, "he [Caesar] advanced into the front ranks, and calling on the centurions by name and encouraging the rest of the soldiers, he ordered them to advance and open up their ranks so that they could use their swords more easily. His arrival brought hope and renewed their courage since each soldier strives to do his best in the sight of his commander no matter how desperate his situation" (*BG* 2.25).

In part, Caesar's willingness to expose himself to danger was conventional. Roman generals were expected to display bravery and steadfast determination, especially when defeat loomed, precisely because any general's presence incited their men to do their utmost (Rosenstein 1990: 114–52). And generals needed to be close to the action in order to control the movements of their forces as the battle progressed (Goldsworthy 1998: 206–10). However, as we have seen, Caesar's personal courage is evident at the very outset of his military career in his winning of the *corona civica* for exceptional bravery in battle. His readiness to enter the thick of the fray when necessary was simply one aspect of his unwillingness to spare himself or to observe any limits in the pursuit of the goals he had set himself. The same ambition that drove him to do anything and everything for the friends whose help he hoped would be the foundation of his political success (Sall. *Cat.* 54.4) also impelled him to endure unflinchingly whatever hardships presented themselves on campaign. This willingness to share their toils endeared him to his men and forged a powerful bond between the soldiers and their general that was another of the keys to Caesar's military success (Suet. *Iul.* 57; Plut. *Caes.* 17.1–3). That bond Caesar strengthened through the lavish rewards he bestowed upon his men following their victories and at times a permissiveness that struck traditionalists as un-Roman and corrosive of their fighting spirit: Caesar was wont to boast that his soldiers could fight well even drenched with perfume (*BG* 2.33; Suet. *Iul.* 67.1–2). Yet he expected instant obedience to his orders and iron discipline when necessary, and he got both time and again (Suet. *Iul.* 65). He was devoted to his men, and they responded in kind (Suet. *Iul.* 67.1–70). The steadfast loyalty of his legions and their determination not to fall short in his estimation placed in Caesar's hands as formidable a military instrument as any Roman general – or any other general for that matter – ever wielded.

Conclusion

As a military commander, Caesar was both conventional and unique. Roman generals were diplomats and empire-builders as well as leaders of armies. In the former roles Caesar's actions were entirely in keeping with the ethos of conquest and the need to project an image of strength, protect the Republic's friends, and punish those who injured its majesty – all required for the preservation of Rome's empire. The strategy he pursued, while remarkable in the rapidity and boldness of its execution, was not unusual in its aggressiveness or its reliance on the offensive. His use of fortifications to control the field of battle and to force the enemy to fight on his terms had its origins in the innovations of a group of commanders a generation earlier. Without question, however, Caesar was a brilliant battlefield commander and a charismatic leader of men. But it must be remembered that Caesar also enjoyed an extraordinarily long tenure in command. Most promagistrates in the late Republic only spent a year or two in their provinces, and the majority never saw military action. Even a century or more earlier, republican generals' tenures at the head of armies were similarly brief. Caesar's eight years in Gaul, doing battle every year, gave him an opportunity to hone his skills as a commander that few of his contemporaries enjoyed. It would have been much more surprising if Caesar's driving ambition had not enabled his exceptional natural gifts to manifest themselves, given that amount of time, in an extraordinary ability to lead armies. Certainly, if victories and conquest are the measure of a great general, Caesar richly deserves that epithet, for few of his contemporaries – and few subsequently – could equal him on that score.

FURTHER READING

The best accounts of Caesar's wars are of course his own, but modern biographies with extensive discussion of his military activities are not lacking: Goldsworthy 2006, Meier 1982,

Gelzer 1968, and Holmes 1911, 1923, and 1936. The latter author in particular offers blow-by-blow accounts, albeit in some respects dated, of all of Caesar's campaigns. Very useful on aspects of war making in this period are Goldsworthy 1996 on battles, Erdkamp 1998 on the logistics of food supply, and Austin and Rankov 1995 on military intelligence. The case for distortion in Caesar's *Commentaries* is most forcefully made by Rambaud 1966; see now however the essays in Welch and Powell 1998 for a more nuanced assessment. Riggsby 2006 offers a very provocative recent study of the portrayal of warfare in the *Bellum Gallicum*.

NOTES

1 On the scale of Caesar's looting of Gaul, see Badian 1968: 89–91 and cf. Suet. *Iul.* 54.2.
2 See, on what follows, David Potter, "Caesar and the Helvetians" (forthcoming).

CHAPTER EIGHT

Caesar and Religion

David Wardle

Weinstock begins the conclusion to *Divus Julius* by summing up Caesar "as an imaginative and daring religious reformer, who planned and created new cults, accepted extraordinary honours and died when he was about to become a divine ruler – a reformer who did not want to appear as an innovator . . . but to be guided by tradition; and yet one who in the end radically broke with it" (1971: 411). These words encapsulate well the apparent contradictions that arise in considering Caesar and religion. An extraordinary career, which began with Caesar slated to become Jupiter's representative on earth and ended with his assumption of divine status, naturally receives wildly differing assessments. One feature in writing about Caesar and religion is the natural tendency to work backwards from the dictatorships, which saw major innovations in many aspects of Roman religion, and ascribe to Caesar from the outset a mission to either reform or restore the traditional religious practices of the Roman state (e.g. Warde Fowler 1916: 69). Preferable is a Caesar whose aspirations changed over time, as the opportunities available to him increased.

A second apparent contradiction emerges if we attribute to Caesar either cynicism or scepticism regarding the religious system of which he was the senior official for much of his life. This is, however, primarily created by modern scholars, as they import into the Roman world "christianising assumptions" (cf. Beard, North, & Price 1998: 42–3). In the Roman polytheistic system, where correct observance of rites rather than personal belief was crucial, what mattered most was what Caesar *did* and whether it was compatible with what his contemporaries considered ancestral practice (*mos maiorum*). It is also easy and dangerous to slip into talking about Caesar's "thoughts": Ida Paladino, for example, suggests that Caesar in some way continued to think of himself as Jupiter's earthly representative throughout his career (1994: 191).

Beyond the theoretical problems of the place of belief, there are basic questions about evidence. First, "How do we know what Caesar 'believed,' if he doesn't tell us?" When, for example, Caesar claimed that Venus had given him the bloom of youth (Suet. *Iul.* 49.3; Dio 43.43.3; Weinstock 1971: 18, 23–6), it is unclear what significance should be attributed to his proclamation of a supernatural benefit from one of the gods, for claims to such were part of the rhetoric of the Roman elite, a kind of one-upmanship endemic in the competitive political environment of the Late Republic. They were not necessarily evidence of an individual's "belief" in his own destiny but rather indications of his intention to use every means at his disposal.

Then, "How reliable are our surviving sources?" Different types of evidence have differing usefulness. Caesar's own words in his *commentarii* are fundamental, but reveal little directly. In fact, Caesar's Caesar gives the least prominence of any extant Roman historian to Roman religion (see pp. 107–8). The other ancient sources, literary, epigraphic, and numismatic, from which we assemble our Caesars, provide far more material, but often at a remove of more than a century from Caesar's day and viewed through the eyes of those inured to imperial rule.

Religious Offices and Actions in Caesar's Career

I shall start with Caesar's public career, concentrating on his role in the Roman state religion and attempting to isolate what he did (or permitted to be done to or for him) before discussing his own treatment of religion in his works, and our sources' representation of Caesar attitudes towards religion.

Because the opening chapters of the biographies of both Suetonius and Plutarch are lost, the earliest incident relevant to this study is Cinna's designation of the young patrician Caesar as flamen Dialis and husband to his daughter Cornelia. The flamen Dialis was a senior priesthood dedicated to Jupiter and open only to patricians born of parents married by the form of marriage known as *confarreatio*; its holder was bound by a wide range of sacral restrictions and ritual rules which made some elements of a typical career for an ambitious member of the Roman elite difficult. A straightforward reading of Velleius Paterculus, who credits both Marius and Cinna with the initiative, places the designation in 86 when Caesar was only 13 or 14. Suetonius' version, which fixes the designation to the consular year after the death of Caesar's father, requires 84 (Last 1944: 15–17). At that stage Caesar would have assumed the *toga virilis*, but still have merited the ancient descriptions of his youth. The appointment was intended by Cinna as an honor to the young Caesar, not as an obstacle to a military or political career for him (Meier 1995: 86), nor as a means of avoiding the solemn curses against Cinna and his supporters by the last flamen Dialis, Cornelius Merula, who had sacrilegiously committed suicide to avoid death at the hands of Cinna (*pace* Liou-Gille 1999: 439–42). The discrepant terminology of Suetonius (*destinatus*) and Velleius (*creatus*) can best be reconciled with the formal terminology (*nominatus*, *captus*, and *inauguratus*) by holding that Caesar was nominated as one of the three candidates, probably by the *pontifices*, and was *captus* (i.e. specifically chosen, perhaps symbolized by "taking by the hand"; cf. Aul. Gell. 1.12.13–16) by the Pontifex Maximus, but was not finally inaugurated (Linderski 1995: 554–5, 2007: 636–7). It is not, however, clear who was responsible, or what were the grounds, for the disqualification of Caesar. If, for example, the Pontifex Maximus Q. Mucius Scaevola objected on the grounds that Caesar's parents had not been married by *confarreatio* or that his mother was a plebeian, that involves him in an apparent inconsistency, as he must already have given his approval to Caesar in the *captio* (cf. Simón 1996: 207–12). The civil conflict doubtless played a part. After his seizure of power in November 82, Sulla declared all the enactments of the Cinnan period invalid, perhaps on the grounds that the consuls had been appointed without the approbation of the auspices. But Suetonius seems to view the loss of the flaminate as a consequence of Caesar's refusal of Sulla's demand that he divorce Cornelia. Presumably, on this view, the instruction to divorce was motivated by hatred of Sulla's political enemy Cinna, although one might consider that Sulla believed, on the basis of historical precedent, that the flaminate belonged most appropriately to the Cornelii and not to the Iulii (see Vanggaard 1988: 75–6). For his part, Caesar may have refused to divorce Cornelia on the grounds that the flamen Dialis was not permitted to divorce, but that would also have served as a blatant protest that Sulla's *acta* were invalid (cf. Badian, chapter 2, pp. 16–17), demonstrating Caesar's loyalty to his Marian political heritage. Yet, if the former motive was prominent, we have early evidence of a Caesar who displayed a remarkable intransigence in respect of ancestral practice (Zecchini 2001: 36).

While absent in the East in 73, Caesar was coopted as one of the fifteen *pontifices* to take the place of his mother's plebeian cousin C. Aurelius Cotta (Vell. Pat. 2.43.1). Such an appointment was impossible without the support of some aristocratic members of the college. Hence Gelzer (1968: 25) conjectures that Mamercus Aemilius Lepidus Livianus proposed the appointment, while Weinstock (1971: 30–1) attributes it to the efforts of his mother Aurelia and "her political friends." Evidently the majority of members of the college considered the young Caesar no threat. Indeed, no evidence has survived of any activity engaged upon by Caesar in his capacity as pontifex before his appointment as Pontifex Maximus.

In 69 or 68, Caesar delivered the funeral oration for his aunt Julia, the widow of Marius, in which he made much of the descent of the Iulii from Venus (Suet. *Iul.* 6.1). While this has been used to indicate a particular belief by Caesar in his divine past (cf. the claim that he had received the bloom of Venus), several other families were making similar claims during the Late Republic (Wiseman 1974: 153–64) and the context of gentilician rivalry must be at least as important here as personal conviction (Lincoln 1993: 387–91). Nonetheless, the way that Caesar clearly employed his divine ancestry to boost his own career seemed remarkable to his biographers (Ramage 2006: 46–8). A second funeral oration, this time for his wife Cornelia, was noteworthy because she did not possess exceptional merits or prominence (cf. Plut. *Caes.* 5.4–5). Caesar's celebration of her is better explained by the desire to advertise his *popularis* connections than by any putative attachment to the archaic marriage rite of *confarreatio* (*pace* Zecchini 2001: 38).

As Gruen argues (chapter 3 in this volume), Caesar's election as Pontifex Maximus in 63 to replace Q. Caecilius Metellus Pius was a striking achievement by a young man who had not yet held even the praetorship. His defeat of the distinguished consulars and Optimates Q. Lutatius Catulus and P. Servilius Vatia Isauricus was overwhelming, in that he secured more votes in their tribes than were cast for them in all the 17 tribes which had been selected by lot for the electoral procedure (Suet. *Iul.* 13). Earlier in the year Caesar had given prominent support to a tribunician proposal by Titus Labienus that canceled Sulla's change and restored to the popular vote the election of the *pontifices*. He doubtless benefited from that and his other *popularis* activities (cf. Taylor 1949: 92–3).

On December 5, 63, in the senatorial debate on the fate of the Catilinarian conspirators, Caesar spoke in his capacity as *praetor urbanus* elect. As he had polled most votes in the praetorian elections, he held the senior post. There are no grounds to link Caesar's rejection of a capital sentence for the conspirators with his role as Pontifex Maximus (*contra* Zecchini 2001: 39–40) rather than with his *popularis* sympathies and ideological defence of the *lex Porcia* and *lex Sempronia*, which forbade the putting to death of Roman citizens without popular trial.[1]

In December 62, Pompeia, Caesar's wife, hosted the celebration of the rites of the Bona Dea in his private residence. Clodius' infiltration of these rites was referred by the Senate to the pontifical college, over which Caesar presided as Pontifex Maximus, and was judged by the pontiffs to be sacrilege. Caesar spoke to this in the Senate (Schol. Bob. Cic. *Clod.* fr. 28 St.) and divorced Pompeia, maintaining that "I thought my wife ought not even to be under suspicion" (Plut. *Caes.* 10.6). In taking this line, he was exhibiting not merely wounded pride but concern for his office.

Caesar's consulship of 59 was marked by a highly politicized use of the divinatory techniques of the Roman state religion by his colleague Bibulus to thwart Caesar's legislative program. Although *obnuntiatio* was a legitimate tactic, Caesar was able, by physically preventing Bibulus from presenting in person his report of inauspicious signs, to ignore the reports without contravening augural law, to carry through his legislative program and to hold the elections of 59 (Linderski 1995: 73–4, 480, 634). Combined with his tacit support for Clodius' legislation in 58 which restricted the use of *obnuntiatio*, Caesar's attitude may seem to have struck at the heart of the Roman state religion, at least as Cicero represented it (cf. *Vat.* 18), but Caesar's manipulation of the system was little different from Bibulus' (cf. Beard, North, & Price 1998: 126–8). Again, his influence was probable in the nomination of his cousin Sex. Julius Caesar as flamen Quirinalis in 58, but was unexceptional in the context of the Late Republic.

During his campaigns as proconsul, Caesar's plundering of Gallic temples (Suet. *Iul.* 54.2) and premeditated violation of treaties (Plut. *Caes.* 22.3, *Cat. Min.* 51.2–3) were no more than allegations by political opponents, if his correct behavior towards shrines during the Civil War is any guide (e.g. *BC* 1.6.8, 2.21.3; Dio 42.48.2). His lengthy absence in Gaul for most of the 50s, however, severely restricted his opportunity to fulfill the ceremonial duties of the Pontifex Maximus and to introduce the necessary intercalary months to keep the civil calendar in line with the seasons. If no suggestion emerges at this stage of a man with a far-reaching plan to reform or restore Roman religion, or of a man with a consistent preference for the archaic, significant changes occurred during the Civil War, as Caesar made great play on his coinage with religious imagery and with the office of Pontifex Maximus in particular (cf. Stepper 2003: 34–5). The first military issue of *denarii* minted by Caesar represented pontifical emblems

(*RCC* 1.443 no. 1): as he was effectively in revolt against the state, his best claim to legitimacy was his pontifical office. From his campaigns in 48 and 47 a *quinarius*, one of the five types minted, has a *culullus* (beaker) and a Salian shield (*RCC* 1.452 no. 3); in 47 the eastern mint produced *aurei* alluding to his acquisition of the augurate (*RCC* 1.456 no. 1) and in 46–5, while in Spain, one of two types of his *denarii* featured the augural *lituus* (staff) (*RCC* 1.468 no. 2). In 44 several types of *denarii* feature the *lituus* or the *cullulus*, or both, while a prominent innovation is the appearance of the legend PM (Pontifex Maximus) on a coin of L. Aemilius Buca (*RCC* 1.480 no. 4). This imagery suggests that Caesar's religious offices were not unimportant. Yet it is far less prominent than images of victory, for example, and should not be exaggerated.

Even from the years of Caesarian dictatorship it is difficult to argue that Caesar himself accorded any priority to religious matters or that he had an overriding vision of Roman religion. In any case, his frequent extended absences from Rome meant that there was little time to concentrate on implementing his ideas, and even his last sojourn was an extended preparation for a lengthy absence in the East. Caesar's legislative activities during his dictatorships in relation to Roman religion are wide-ranging, but not unprecedented: (1) reform of the calendar, (2) reform of the priestly colleges by a *lex Iulia de sacerdotiis*, (3) the creation of a third group of Luperci, the *Iulii* or *Iuliani*, (4) the formal introduction of the cult of Liber Pater, and (5) the extension of privileges to the Jews.

In 46 Caesar first remedied the consequence of pontifical delinquency in omitting four intercalations, by the insertion of 90 intercalary days.[2] He then undertook a radical reform of the Roman calendar. This was traditionally the responsibility of the *pontifices* (Suet. *Iul.* 40; Plut. *Caes.* 59), but the use of an edict to promulgate his reforms (Macr. *Sat.* 1.14.13) suggests that it was in his capacity as dictator that Caesar acted (Malitz 1987: 116). He abandoned the existing pseudo-solar calendar for a truly solar calendar of 365 days per year, thus enabling the celebration of rites and sacrifices at the correct time; the addition of extra days to March, May, Quinctilis and October was done so as not to disturb the traditional relationship of festivals to the Nones and Ides (Macr. *Sat.* 1.14.8). All in all a highly conservative end was achieved by revolutionary means, through the employment of foreign expertise (Plin. *NH* 18.212) and at the cost of the freedom of the *pontifices* henceforth to manipulate the calendar. Dio's account reveals subsequent senatorial decrees to record his birthday (45 BC; Dio 44.4.4) and victories in the calendar, and to rename the month Quinctilis Iulius (44 BC; Dio 44.5.2; Macr. *Sat.* 1.12.34). Whether these were his initiative, and thus evidence of a striking plan to celebrate himself in the Roman calendar as Liberator, after the example of Demetrius Poliorcetes (cf. Weinstock 1971: 152–6), or to insert himself into a reconstructed matrix of the Roman past as Augustus was to do, is unclear (see Tarver 1996; Feeney 2007).

Secondly, in 47 he added one member to the three most important priestly colleges, the *pontifices*, *augures*, and *Quindecimviri sacris faciundis* (Dio 43.51.4), primarily to make room for his supporters in colleges traditionally dominated by Optimates and to permit his own acquisition of an augurate on top of his pontificate (Yavetz 1983: 110–11). Hitherto the simultaneous tenure of more than one senior priesthood was alien to the competitive spirit of the Republican elite. In 44 Dio records that a new sodality, the *Iulii* or *Iuliani*, was added to the existing *luperci Quinctiales* and *Fabiani* (44.6.2; see Weinstock 1971: 332–3). A brief comment by Servius (*Ecl.* 5.29) preserves the information that Caesar was the first to transfer to Rome the *sacra* of Liber Pater (traditional Italian name of Bacchus). While the interpretation of this is not uncontroversial, it seems that Caesar removed the ban on the celebration of the rites of Bacchus first imposed in 186, perhaps after his victorious return from the East, and that the rites were celebrated in connection with the quadruple triumph of 46 (Dio 43.22.1; cf. Pailler 1988: 728–43). A link with Dionysus (to give the god's most common Greek name) would be useful in the context of his eastern campaign planned for 44 (cf. Turcan 1977: 323–5).

Josephus preserves a series of *senatus consulta* which purport to record Caesarian initiatives during his dictatorships to restore to the Jews jurisdiction over issues relating to their own law, the rights of high priests and priests, and permission to observe the Sabbath and perform other rites, and exemption from military service (Jos. *AJ* 14.195, 208, 241–2). Eilers (2003: 191–213; cf. Rajak 1984: esp. 112–13) makes a strong case for not attributing these *senatus consulta* to the Caesarian period. But even if they belong here, the concessions were typical of Roman grants to defeated peoples who had subsequently demonstrated loyalty and do not indicate a particular affinity for Judaism (cf. Pucci Ben Zeev 1998). At the beginning of the Civil War Caesar saw that the Jews, who loathed Pompey for his capture of Jerusalem, his violation of the temple, and his disaggregation of the Jewish state, could serve as a useful threat to Pompey's rear, so he established strong personal links with Hyrcanus and Antipater. For their assistance during the Alexandrian war the two were rewarded personally. It is often argued (e.g. Firpo 2000: 135–41), on the basis of another document in Josephus (*AJ* 14. 213–16), that Caesar felt the need to do more and freed Jews from the constraints imposed on their worship by Roman legislation against *collegia*, thus restoring to them the position they had enjoyed before 63. However, Caesar's exclusion of the Jews from his measures against *thiasoi* belongs best during his praetorship (Eilers 2003). Caesar's actions towards the Jews throughout his career were not governed by some special regard for Judaism or by a more general concern for religious freedom, but by pragmatic concerns: the need for Jewish support against Pompey and then later for a peaceful Judaea in his rear as he dealt with Parthia.

Caesar and Ruler Cult

The most controversial aspect of Caesar's religious activities is the role he played in the institution of "ruler cult" in Roman public life. Whereas intermittent traces or reflections of cult offered to prominent Romans in the East and even in Rome can be found before Caesar's dictatorships, that period of four years saw an enormous increase in both the frequency and the level of cult manifestations, as the magnitude and probable permanence of Caesar's dominion became clear. Caesar's responsibility for this response to his growing power, and his intentions, are the key questions in an area that has attracted great scholarly interest – was there a program?

Dio's account, which must form the basis of any study as the most detailed of all extant sources, reveals three stages in the public honors voted to Caesar by the Senate. While Dio plausibly records that the senators intermingled secular and religious honors without clear distinction in their attempts to respond to Caesar's unique position, I isolate here the latter. After his victory at Thapsus in 46 he received a statue, erected on the Capitol, which took the form of his figure in some way surmounting the world, and bore an inscription which stated that he was *hemitheos* (43.14.6: ἡμίθεος; see Fishwick 1975: 624–8; Rizzo 2002: 613–20). Although it is generally argued that Dio's Greek effectively conceals the Latin of the original, the testimony of Servius [Auctus] may suggest that the Senate used the Greek term (*Ecl.* 9.46: *eique in Capitolio statuam ... inscriptum in basi fuit "Caesari emitheo"*), although Caesar himself later had the term chiseled from the inscription (Dio 43.14.6). After Munda in 45 a statue of him was to be placed in the *cella* of the temple of Quirinus with an inscription calling him "unconquered god" (43.45.3), and his statue was carried in a procession to the Circus next to that of Quirinus (Cic. *Att.* 13.28.3). As in the former case, the honors stop short of unambiguously attributing divinity to Caesar, but deliberately leave open the question of his status. Thirdly, in the last weeks of his life, a law, rather than just a senatorial decree (probably the *lex Rufrena*; *CIL* 1.626), proclaimed him a state deity, who was to be worshiped by the cult name *Divus Iulius* and to be given a flamen, M. Antonius, a state temple to himself and his Clemency, and a *pulvinar* for his image (44.6.3–4; cf. App. *B Civ.* 2.106, Suet. *Iul.* 76.1, 84.2).

The contemporary testimony of Cicero, who was hostile to the cult innovations (*Phil.* 2.110), is crucial in establishing the historicity of the formal deification, cult honors and the title assumed by the new divinity:

> quem is honorem maiorem consecutus erat, quam ut haberet pulvinar, simulacrum, fastigium, flaminem? Est ergo flamen, ut Iovi, ut Marti, ut Quirino, sic Divo Iulio M. Antonius.
>
> What greater honor had he secured than that he should have a couch, a cult-image, a pediment, and a flamen? So, as Jupiter, as Mars, as Quirinus have a flamen, so Divus Iulius has M. Antonius.

The cult title of Divus Iulius was deliberately chosen, for the archaic sound of Divus lent to what was in the Roman context a revolutionary maneuver of deifying a living human being something of the sanctity of tradition, and it was particularly appropriate to the legal context, here underlining the legally conferred status that Caesar enjoyed (Wardle 2002: 190–1). Oaths were sworn by Caesar, as by a god. Balbus' oath, recorded by Cicero (*Att.* 9.7B.3) in March 49, was informal, but Dio asserts that there was also an official oath by Caesar's *genius* (tutelary spirit) and *salus* (well-being) (44.6.1, 50.1). While Dio may be guilty of anachronism or have misunderstood the significance of unofficial oaths sworn by senators by Caesar's *genius*, certainly in the immediate aftermath of his assassination such oaths were common in the forum-based cult around the column on which Caesar was honored as *parens patriae* (Suet. *Iul.* 85; cf. Beare 1979: 469–73).

What I see emerging from the study of the moves towards Caesar's eventual deification is a tentative, uncertain groping by the Senate for appropriate forms of honors by which to celebrate the achievements of Caesar, rather than a carefully planned or thought-out progression towards a politically inspired deification, skillfully orchestrated by Caesar himself (cf. Stevenson 1998: 263–6). The sources, Dio in particular, conceal the master's hand. Zecchini argues plausibly (2001: 59–62) that Caesar was opposed to deification during his lifetime and that he signaled this deliberately in his rudeness to the senatorial delegation that presented him with the decree. Indeed, he did nothing as Pontifex Maximus to realize the elements of the decree – M. Antonius was not inaugurated as flamen – nor did he celebrate on the coinage any aspect of his deification. Although the right to place his image on the coinage during his lifetime (Dio 44.4.4) was radical, it did not signal divine status (cf. Weinstock 1971: 274–5). Caesar's aim was for a posthumous deification, for which good Roman precedent existed in Romulus and exemplary Greek precedent in Hercules. Caesar, while conscious of Roman sensibilities and tradition, was effecting, nevertheless, a revolutionary change – the most lasting changes are often achieved under the guise of tradition, as Augustus was to demonstrate.

Caesar and the Observance of Religious Practices

Simply to consider Caesar's legislative activities as Pontifex Maximus gives a restricted picture of his religious actions: as a commander he regularly carried out the ceremony of *lustratio* important for the definition and dedication of the army (*Caes. BG* 8.52, *Alex.* 56, *Afr.* 75; Plut. *Caes.* 43.2), and, although no trace of this appears in his own *commentarii*, he took the traditional auspices before battle and consulted a *haruspex* for sacrificing (cf. Plut. *Caes.* 43.2). Indeed, going beyond the regularly observed proprieties, Caesar permitted the standards of his legions to bear the device of a bull, which has been interpreted as the constellation of Taurus, the sign under which Venus was ascendant (Domaszewski 1909: 5–6; *pace* Weinstock 1971: 119) and he made use of his relationship with Venus, taking Venus Victrix as his password at Pharsalus (App. *B Civ.* 2.76). In his dealings with his troops, he took care not only not to appear impious, but also used their superstitions to his advantage, as an effective commander would. Caesar was also responsible for a unique act of public piety: on the day of his Gallic triumph in 46, to avert an ill omen, he ascended the Capitol on his knees (Dio 43.21.2).

Religion in Caesar's Own Works

Caesar is often claimed as a cynic or a rationalist (e.g. Lateiner 2005: 49), but the full picture from our ancient sources is different. Regarding his attitudes to religion there is a significant difference of emphasis between what the man himself reveals in his own words and what the other ancient sources say, but a coherent overall picture is discernible. His *commentarii* reveal very little (cf. Le Bohec 2003: 543–8), although there is an interesting progression between the *Bellum Gallicum* and the *Bellum Civile*. The former reveals Caesar as an effective student of the religious practices of his enemies: his description of the Druids and the gods worshiped by the Gauls (*BG* 6.13–18) is an informative piece of ethnographic writing;[3] the standard-bearer of the Tenth Legion prayed before committing himself to the waters of the English Channel (4.25), and religious celebrations were a part of the general celebration of his final victory (8.51); and he used intelligently information received about German divinatory prophecies (1.51). On only two occasions does Caesar himself mention the gods – and then only in speeches to the Helvetii (1.15) and to his own troops (5.52); nor does he indisputably attribute success or failure to divine intervention (1.12). In the *Bellum Civile*, Caesar describes the religious fervor of the Massiliotes under siege (2.5) and draws a stark contrast between the Pompeians' disregard for the sanctity of temples and their treasures and his own scrupulous preservation and restoration of them (1.6, 2.21, 3.36, 72, 105); he gives a psychologically shrewd speech to soldiers unsettled by setbacks, which plays heavily on the theme of fortune (3.73). Caesar argues for the illegitimacy of the Republican government on the grounds that the consuls had not made their vows properly, and, as a consequence, the Feriae Latinae had been celebrated incorrectly (1.6–7; Stewart 1997: 178). As a total surprise comes a lengthy paragraph (3.105) enumerating the portents experienced across the eastern Mediterranean, from Elis to Ptolemais, by which Caesar's victory at Pharsalus was announced. This must be considered an interpolation, on the grounds of both non-Caesarian language and content (Reggi 2002: 216–26). So, while he does not indulge in the traditional historiographical taste for the supernatural, in the *Bellum Civile* Caesar carefully presents himself as a defender of traditional attitudes towards the gods, learning from the charges that were leveled against him for his desecration of Gallic temples (cf. Suet. *Iul.* 54.2).

His continuators in the *Bellum Alexandrinum* include generalizations on the fickleness of fate (25) and the kindness of the gods who intervene in all the circumstances of war, especially those in which rational calculation is impossible (75). In the *Bellum Africanum* we are told that the gods were clearly indicating victory (82) and that Caesar took the auspices before holding a *contio* and dismissing his troops (86). This last passage, which reveals that Caesar observed the traditional practice, is a reasonable basis for assuming that this was Caesar's regular practice, rather than a unique example (cf. Plut. *Caes.* 43.2); indeed, any failure to follow custom would certainly have caused comment. As a military commander in the field, conscious of the superstitions of the soldiery, Caesar was not openly dismissive or skeptical of the most Roman of the public divinatory practices, augury, or of haruspical activity.

Ancient Sources' Picture of Caesar and Religious Observance

The overwhelming impression of Caesar from the other literary sources is of a man who not only carried out his religious duties, but also was receptive to divine communication through various types of divinatory practice. With the benefit of hindsight Suetonius seems to have constructed a Caesar who was divinely destined for power and conscious of his destiny. While Caesar's career before his quaestorship seems marked only by an extraordinary ambition to succeed rather than by special, supernatural guidance or affirmation,[4] his decision to embark on radical *popularis* policies was a direct consequence (*ergo*) of the dream promising world rule that he received at Gades during a probable incubation at the temple of Hercules (*Iul.* 7–8; Fear 2005: 326). His Caesar accepts a divine epiphany at the Rubicon (32; Marinoni 2002: 278) and apparently gives credence to a haruspical prophecy that the owner of an extraordinary horse born on his estate would rule the world (61). Plutarch's Caesar respects a dedication by the Arverni (26.4), performs the ceremony of *lustratio* before Pharsalus, and interacts with seers on favorable signs in sacrificial entrails (43.2). Appian's Caesar sacrifices before (and after) Pharsalus, makes a vow, and interprets a portent in his own favor (*B Civ.* 2.68, 88), and prays ostentatiously before Munda (2.104). Dio's Caesar uses religious language and ideas in a speech (38.40.1), outdoes Pompey in erecting an altar on the Pyrenees (41.24.3), strips the Capitol of all its offerings, but is encouraged by the interpretation given to the portent of a bull escaping sacrifice (41.39.1–3), plunders the temple of Hercules at Gades (43.39.4), accepts the portent of a shooting palm tree as relating to his own successes (43.41.1–3), and is ostentatiously devoted to Venus (43.43.3).

The ancient sources emphasize that he received a series of warnings on his last day: his own and Calpurnia's dreams (Suet. *Iul.* 81.3), doors opening ominously, and the arms of Mars rattled (Dio 44.17.2), inauspicious auspices and sacrificial victims at home on the morning of the Ides and at the door of the senate-house (Nic. Dam. 84, 86; App. *B Civ.* 2.115–16). But these same sources also show that Caesar did not dismiss the warnings out of hand; indeed, he had the *haruspex* repeat the sacrifices, but yielded finally to severe pressure from Decimus Brutus and others. In short, even as they spell out the disastrous consequences of Caesar's actions, the ancients do not characterize him as a Flaminius, deliberately ignoring divine warnings and thereby bringing disaster on himself and the state.

Within the rubric on his military excellence Suetonius comments that Caesar was never delayed or deterred by any religious scruple from an enterprise that he had begun (59) and illustrates this with three examples from the African campaign. The sacrificial victim escaped as he sacrificed at the beginning of the campaign; he slipped as he disembarked, but immediately saved the situation by crying out "I have hold of you, Africa" (cf. Dio 42.58.2–3; Front. *Strat.* 1.12.2), and he successfully nullified the prophecies that seemed to indicate victory for his opponent Metellus Scipio on the basis of his name by adding to his own staff an ignoble Scipio (cf. Plut. *Caes.* 52.2; Dio 42.57.5–58.1). None of these instances marks out Caesar as a general "despiser of portents" (cf. App. *B Civ.* 2.152: σημείων ὑπερόπτης). Rather, Suetonius presents Caesar as a skillful employer of the freedom that was fundamental to Roman religion, in which there was no place for determinism (e.g. Lateiner 2005: 56).

Caesar seems to ignore divine warnings inappropriately only in one area of the Etruscan discipline, namely when they were mediated to him via members of the Order of LX *haruspices* (Zecchini 2001: 65–76; cf. Montero 2000: esp. 236–44).

This body, the expertise of which in respect to portents the Senate recognized, was comprised of members of the Etruscan elite (e.g. Cic. *Div.* 1.92). Lower-level *haruspices*, such as assisted at sacrifices on campaign, attracted no criticism from Caesar (Dio 41.39.2; Plut. *Caes.* 43.2; Polyaen. 8.32–3). But Cicero records (*Div.* 2.52) that the *summus haruspex* (possibly identical with Spurinna) personally warned Caesar against embarking on his African campaign in late 47, and was ignored. In February 44, when no heart could be found in the sacrificial victim Caesar had offered, Spurinna explained this as indicating danger to Caesar's life; on the next day, when no caudate lobe (*caput*) could be found on a new victim (Cic. *Div.* 1.119), Spurinna appears to have set a time limit for Caesar to beware the danger (Suet. *Iul.* 81.2; Plut. *Caes.* 63.3) which he notoriously mocked on the Ides (Val. Max. 8.11.2). It seems that the elite from southern Etruria had followed Pompey and that Spurinna's latter warning was a direct challenge to Caesar's assumption of the perpetual dictatorship (cf. Rawson 1978: 132–46; Aigner-Foresti 2000: esp. 11–18). Caesar's fraught relations with the Order of LX *haruspices*, then, derive from his anger at their political bias during and after the Civil War, rather than from derision of their divinatory science *per se*.

Great debate surrounds the notion of Caesar's Fortune – did he "believe" that his successes emanated from his being a favorite of the goddess? The evidence of his own works is not conclusive, but it seems plausible that, while the idea was common currency (cf. Cic. *Fam.* 1.9.7), the major military reverses Caesar suffered in Gaul from 54 ensured that he treated the notion cautiously. In his *Bellum Gallicum* chance/fortune is predominantly the unforeseeable element in warfare that can sometimes be influential (e.g. 2.21, 5.44, 6.30, 34–5, 42) rather than a quality given to a general (cf. *BG* 4.26), although that is present (Cupaiuolo 1984: 9–14; Champeaux 1987: 259–67). His special fortune was a part of Caesar's propaganda from the start of the Civil War (cf. Cic. *Att.* 7.11.1) and after his victory (Cic. *Deiot.* 19, 21) was celebrated on the coinage of 44 (*RIC* i. 480 no. 25).

Conclusion

Caesar, then, emerges as one who took seriously his responsibilities with regard to the Roman state religion, as a political and religious office-holder and as a military commander. He exploited the possibilities of self-promotion offered by the religious system and latterly by his position of supreme power, setting new boundaries only in his plans for posthumous deification. Being neither superstitious nor inappropriately skeptical of traditional forms of cult, Caesar closely approximated to the Roman paradigm.

FURTHER READING

Central to any study of Caesar's religion is S. Weinstock's *Divus Iulius* (Oxford, 1971), a highly detailed study of innovations introduced during Caesar's dictatorship, but the critiques of

J. North, *JRS* 65 (1975), 171–7, and A. Alföldi, *Gnomon* 47 (1975), 154–79, are important, as is I. Gradel, *Emperor Worship and Roman Religion* (Oxford, 2002), pp. 54–72. For readers of Italian and French concise accounts appear in G. Zecchini, *Cesar e il mos maiorum* (Stuttgart, 2001), chapters 2 and 3, and Y. Le Bohec, "César et la religion," in C. Alonso del Real et al. (eds.), *Urbs aeterna. Actas y colaboraciones del coloquio internacional "Roma entre la litteratura y la historia." Homenaje a la profesora Carmen Castillo* (Pamplona, 2003), 543–51. On the Lupercalia and Caesar's new Luperci Iuliani, see now J.A. North, 'Caesar at the Lupercalia', *JRS* 98 (2008), 144–60.

NOTES

1 Words in the speech attributed to Caesar by Sallust (*BC* 51.20) are sometimes interpreted as a presentation of the Epicurean view that death is not a punishment, but an end to suffering. The rhetorical requirements of Caesar's case made this typically Epicurean idea valuable, but do not represent either a position appropriate to the Pontifex Maximus or Caesar's own views, in so far as we can determine them from anything else in his own writings or in the ancient sources. Nor is it necessary to think that the words are a specifically Epicurean doctrine (see Mulgan 1979: 337–9; *contra* Rambaud 1968: 411–35 and Bourne 1977: 417–32).

2 Brind'Amour's calculations (1983) show that in 63 the civil and solar calendars were in alignment; the omission of the usual intercalary months during the 50s created chaos by 46. Blame was to be shared by Caesar with other members of the pontifical college (cf. Malitz 1987: esp. 107–9).

3 Picard 1977: 232–3, rightly emphasizes the quality of Caesar's information and the tendency of his description to exculpate the Druids from responsibility for the revolt of 54 and to minimize their "barbarian" aspects. Zecchini (2001: 42–4) argues that Caesar's description of Gallic religion is partially motivated by a concern to refute slanders of his impious treatment of its shrines and that, influenced and advised by Diviciacus, it reveals his desire to hasten integration between Romans and Gauls. The counterfactual aspect of these arguments, i.e. Caesar never took any steps to assimilate or incorporate Gallic religion, need not detract from the basically positive picture of Druidism. Caesar's interest seems better explained by the concern of a good general to know his enemy.

4 The lost beginning of the *Life* certainly contained portents before and at his birth indicating his future greatness (cf. Weinstock 1971: 19–22).

CHAPTER NINE

Friends, Associates, and Wives

Catherine Steel

> Flattery, which is the accomplice of vicious behavior, should be removed to a distant place: it is unworthy of a free man, let alone a friend. Living with a tyrant is one thing, living with a friend quite another.

So Cicero in his treatise on friendship (89) which, despite its dramatic setting in 129 BC, cannot escape its compositional date of 44 BC in the period after Caesar's death. Throughout the work, Cicero's reflections return to power, autocracy, and the strains placed on friendship by political disagreement and ambition. It is hard to separate these anxieties from Rome's recent, and potentially continuing, exposure to tyranny: many of his ideas can be traced back to Hellenistic writers, but it was precisely the changing nature of politics at Rome which made these aspects of friendship troubling, and urgent.

Yet we should be cautious about using Caesar's position as dictator as the framework for understanding his friendships throughout his public career. There is a series of stages in the pattern of Caesar's relationships, and only in the final one does his practice pose a fundamental challenge to the norms of aristocratic behavior. Earlier in his life, we can trace an adroit, often contentious, but fundamentally traditional handling of the possibilities of a variety of relationships.

Roman politics relied for its working on the relationships between individual men – and, to a limited extent, women (Spielvogel 1993: 5–19). In the absence of the organizational and ideological structures of formal political parties, those involved in public life had to use personal connections to promote themselves. Both the processes of establishing a distinctive and attractive identity to the electorate, and the means to accomplish anything once elected, involved cooperation with others as the necessary and unavoidable concomitant of the intense competition within the political arena. The kind of relationships thus engendered might seem to have little in common with an understanding of friendship as a personal and emotionally significant bond with another. But the Romans used the language of friendship to describe such political alliances. At the same time, friendship – *amicitia* – was also, as Cicero clearly demonstrates, a concept with a strong emotional charge. To describe someone as one's *amicus*, "friend," can therefore cover a very wide range of links, from a lasting and emotionally resonant relationship to surface courtesy concealing distrust and even dislike, as well as acquaintanceships of a relatively slight nature. Moreover, *amicitia* brings with it obligations to support one's friends in a variety of ways as the situation demands and talents allow: the loan of money, support at elections, defense advocacy or the giving of supportive witness statements in criminal trials. These ethical considerations, as well as the potential for emotional engagement, are present in every relationship which is described as a "friendship," however much, in practice, they may be evaded or remain unfulfilled. As the Republic collapsed into civil war in 49 BC, those faced with having to make a choice between the two sides had to consider their obligations towards their friends as well as a judgment of the rightness of each cause and an assessment of the likely victor.

Moreover, *amicitia* was not confined to those of similar status; it could exist between two men despite substantial differences of position and age. Patron–client relationships were often described by the language of friendship, precisely to avoid the offense caused by openly asserting a disparity of status and power. And the conventions of political apprenticeship established relationships between older and younger men which created the expectation of lasting obligation of the younger: so, for example, the relationship between a provincial governor and his quaestor and other members of his entourage.

It is clear, then, that if we seek to understand the detailed workings of political life at Rome, the relationships between individual politicians must be an element in how we do so (Gruen 1974: 47–50). The precise role that *amicitia* plays, however, has been the subject of intense debate among modern historians. In the earlier part of the twentieth century, an influential model of how Roman politics should be understood involved heavy emphasis on family connections and friendships in order to construct political groupings which controlled the Republic (Gelzer 1912; Münzer 1920; Syme 1939; Taylor 1949); on this view, Republican government was essentially oligarchic, despite the formal role of the citizen body, since the dominant group at any one time was capable of exerting sufficient pressure on voters to ensure their continuing power. Consequently, assertions of friendship, among politicians, need be no more than assertions of political cooperation: as Sallust puts it, in a speech of the *popularis* tribune Memmius, "this kind of behaviour is called friendship when it occurs among good men and faction among bad" (*BJ* 31.15). More recently, the importance of the democratic element in the Roman constitution has been emphasized as well as the unpredictability of voting patterns and the attention paid by politicians to courting the people, challenging the assumption that such personal connections are sufficient to *explain* Roman politics (Millar 1998; Morstein-Marx 2004). At the same time, the breadth of the concept of friendship has been asserted more strongly (Brunt 1988; Konstan 1997), alongside the corollary that there is no simple correlation between an assertion of friendship – let alone the existence of a relationship by blood or marriage – and similarity of political purpose at any one time. Nonetheless, it is indisputable that friendships are a key element in articulating and implementing political action, even if they do not always determine it.

Personal relationships at Rome should not be seen as behavior governed by a set of rigid rules but, instead, as a range of opportunities and choices. Any politician's operation in this field will be governed by the complex interplay of a number of factors, including his temperament and willingness to transgress convention as well as the social and economic advantages he can offer to others. It is important, therefore, not to assume that everyone approached the matter in the same spirit or with the same aims; and this is particularly important given that so much of our evidence is provided by Cicero. His status as a "new man" meant that his political success depended particularly heavily on his capacity to attract and retain supporters; and temperamentally he seems – on the evidence of his correspondence, especially with Atticus – to have had a heavy emotional dependence on his close friends. His practice and theory demonstrate a commitment both to acquiring and cultivating useful contacts and to an ideal model of friendship as "nothing other than agreement about all matters divine and human combined with goodwill and affection" (Cic. *Amic.* 20). Caesar's situation was, of course, rather different; even if his family's recent obscurity meant that he could not be regarded as one of those destined to the consulship from his cradle (Cic. *Leg. agr.* 2.100), he nonetheless could rely on a wide range of inherited connections with the choices and possibilities that they brought with them.

Caesar's own place and positioning within the unstable period immediately following the Social War first become apparent in his marriage to Cornelia. Little can be said about his engagement (or marriage) previously to a woman called Cossutia; her family was equestrian and wealthy (Suet. *Iul.* 1; Rawson 1975), and the latter fact presumably explains the alliance. Members of the senatorial elite not infrequently married outside the senatorial class and financial motives were important when this happened (Wiseman 1971: 53–64; Treggiari 1991: 93–5). However, the relationship was brief; he was still in his teens when he married Cornelia. She was the daughter of Cinna, and establishing a connection with the dominant political figure at Rome in the mid-80s is enough to explain Caesar's motivation; less clear is why he was an attractive prospect as a son-in-law, and there Caesar's connection, through his aunt Julia, with Cinna's ally Marius (now dead), may be vital (see Badian, chapter 2, p. 16).

Divorce followed by immediate remarriage is sometimes a sign of a change of political allegiances, though we should be careful about assuming that marriages invariably reflect political groupings: there are plenty of counter-examples. More striking as an indication of political stance is Caesar's refusal to divorce Cornelia after the collapse of the Cinnan regime and the return to Rome of Sulla. As a result, Caesar was briefly an outlaw, though his friends and family managed eventually to restore his position. Caesar's initial connection, not of his own making, with some of the leading *popularis* politicians of the 80s, was turned into a statement of his own position by a series of choices he made; on its own, his aunt's marriage to Marius would not constitute a marker of stance or allegiance. Here one can compare Cicero, who was also connected to Marius by marriage but whose early career decisions place him firmly in the Sullan camp. At any rate, Caesar's marriage to Cornelia strengthened an existing connection; but it also represents a choice on his part to espouse *popularis* ideology and tactics, in which he is consistent up to his consulship. This attitude may also explain his decision to deliver a funeral speech for Cornelia, an innovation, it seems, and one which brought him a great deal of public sympathy (Plut. *Caes.* 5). Nonetheless, this stance did not preclude his marrying the granddaughter of Sulla after Cornelia's death: this was the ill-fated Pompeia whom he divorced after the Bona Dea scandal on the grounds that "Caesar's wife must be above suspicion" (Plut. *Caes.* 10.6). And he was sufficiently acceptable to senior figures to be coopted into the college of pontiffs in 73 BC (Gelzer 1968: 25; Wardle, chapter 8, p. 102).

Lasting friendships are less easy to trace in Caesar's career before 60. His support in the late 70s for amendments to Sulla's constitutional legislation led to speeches in favor of tribunician legislation, but no secure alliances; more significant, perhaps, is his apparent emphasis on the importance of family relationships, and specifically his duty towards his brother-in-law L. Cinna, when he spoke for Plautius' law recalling Lepidan exiles (Gell. *NA* 13.3.5). There appear to have been no immediate outcomes from his junior military appointments, initially as a member of the entourages of Minucius Thermus, the governor of Asia, and Servilius Isauricus in Cilicia and then, in the late 70s, with Marcus Antonius Creticus in Greece (cf. Badian, chapter 2, p. 19). Creticus died before returning to Rome, which will have hampered the usefulness of the connection, though his son was later one of Caesar's most prominent adherents. Caesar also became friendly with Nicomedes of Bithynia at this time: he described the relationship with him as one of *hospitium* (Gell. 5.13), and the rumor that it was sexual proved long-lasting (Suet. *Iul.* 49).

As quaestor, Caesar was assigned to the province of Further Spain under the governor Antistius Vetus; similarly, no close connection was formed, though Vetus' son – as well as Servilius Isauricus' – ended up on the Caesarian side in the Civil War (Syme 1939: 64). A more significant result of Caesar's quaestorship was the connections he established with the province, which were further strengthened by his period as governor of Further Spain following his praetorship. Spain was an area where Pompeius already had strong ties from the campaigns against Sertorius in the 70s, and during the Civil War the personal connections between Spaniards and Romans on both sides were an important factor, as elsewhere within Rome's empire, in determining tactics and outcomes.

At Rome, Caesar engaged in some high-profile *popularis* activities (see Gruen, chapter 3, pp. 25–6), including prominent support for Pompeius' commands against the pirates and then Mithridates. He also established links with some associates of Pompeius. In 63 the tribune Labienus, a protégé of Pompeius, prosecuted Gaius Rabirius for his part in the death of Saturninus in 100; Caesar was one of the two presidents of the court and was regarded as a supporter of Labienus' actions (Syme 1938a). And Caesar chose as his *praefectus fabri*, as governor of Further Spain, L. Cornelius Balbus, who was a leading figure in his home community of Gades and had received the Roman citizenship in 72 BC as a favor from Pompeius. But Caesar also established links now – if not earlier – with Crassus, borrowing heavily from him to fund his aedileship and other gestures designed to win the support of the people; and his marriage to Sulla's granddaughter is from this period. Finesse and flexibility are most strikingly demonstrated in his relations with Catilina. He was accused of involvement in the conspiracy directly (Sall. *Cat.* 49), but by his contribution to the debate on the punishment of the conspirators on December 5, 63 he ensured that he was clearly separated from the conspirators while not forfeiting any popular good will. We can contrast Gaius Antonius, Cicero's colleague as consul, who appears to have lost popular support by taking command of the army which destroyed Catilina's forces (Cic. *Flac.* 95).

More apparent, indeed, are the enmities which he acquired for himself. He engaged in prosecutions for extortion against Cn. Cornelius Dolabella, presumably soon after the latter's return from Macedonia, C. Antonius, for his depredations in Achaea, M. Iuncus, a former governor of Asia, and C. Piso (consul 67). His bad relations with Bibulus, later to be his colleague in the consulship, are traced by his biographers back to their tenure together as curule aediles in 65 BC, during which Caesar managed to attract all the credit for the games put on jointly. Bibulus is supposed to have said that he was Pollux to Caesar's Castor: just as the temple dedicated to the pair was known just as the temple of Castor, so the generosity shown by him and Caesar was regarded as Caesar's only (Suet. *Iul.* 10). And his relations with Catulus were bad, at least from the time of Caesar's defeat of him in elections for the position of Pontifex Maximus in 63; Catulus was one of the two (the other being Piso) who accused Caesar of involvement with Catilina, and Caesar returned the favor early in 62, on taking office as praetor, when he attempted to relieve Catulus of his responsibility for restoring the temple of Capitoline Jupiter, suggesting as he did that Catulus had been embezzling funds (Suet. *Iul.* 15). Catulus and Bibulus could trace marriage connections through their links with the younger Cato, but it would be overly simplistic to see any consistency in Caesar's activity; he was accumulating men with a grievance against him through the exercise of ambition and a lack of care about causing offense. And while he and Cato found themselves, prominently, on opposing sides in the debate on the execution of the Catilinarians, they had been united, for a time, in pursuing Sullan profiteers the previous year (Suet. *Iul.* 11).

In the period before his first consulship Caesar appears to have used his connections in a flexible and opportunistic manner, but without becoming part of a consistent or permanent group. He formed no lasting alliances, nor any documented close friendships, at least not with other men. Anecdotes survive of remarks by Caesar indicative of his ambition: in one, he comments while traveling through a small Alpine village that he would prefer to be the leading man there than hold second position in Rome; and reading a history of Alexander he sighs as he reflects that Alexander had conquered the world by the time he had reached Caesar's age (Plut. *Caes.* 11.3; in another version, gazing upon a statue of Alexander the Great at Gades is the trigger [Suet. *Iul.* 7]). In these stories, the audience is a group of anonymous "friends"; the biographical tradition does not know of a single named confidant. And it is important not to read any consistent political line into such alliances as we can trace; he used and developed the popularity with the people which his connection with Marius supplied without abandoning the advantages which his birth gave him.

Nonetheless, as he planned his bid for the consulship, his methods shifted and he entered into a more substantial political compact.

The political background and significance of the so-called "First Triumvirate" are dealt with in chapter 3 in this volume. In terms of the workings of political friendship, this compact is an excellent example of useful *amicitia*, men coming together in order, by pooling their resources, to secure specific ends, with a political alliance leading to familial connections rather than the opposite. And the reverberations of the political compact were substantial:

> Caesar was trying to tie himself even more closely to Pompeius' power. He had a daughter, Julia, who was betrothed to Servilius Caepio; he now betrothed her to Pompeius, and said that he would give Pompeius' daughter to Servilius, even though she too was already betrothed, having been promised to Faustus, Sulla's son. A little later Caesar married Calpurnia the daughter of Piso, and got Piso made consul for the following year. Cato violently protested at this, claiming that it was intolerable for positions of power to be procured by marriages and men to get positions and armies and powers through the exchange of women. (Plut. *Caes.* 14.4)

What is notable in this episode is not simply the sealing of an alliance through a marriage; there is also the perturbation of existing plans. This set of marriages was an open demonstration that the new dynamic within political life would disrupt arrangements already in place; this may have been as important as the marriages themselves. (The marriage between Pompeia and Faustus Sulla appears eventually to have taken place.) Cato's response suggests that the scale of the marriage network thus created was unusual, as well as implying that the situation was an affront because electoral success and subsequent political and military power appeared to follow directly from marriage. Cato had no reason to underplay his outrage, but the line he takes suggests that the way in which Caesar and Pompeius openly demonstrated their unity could be presented as a dangerous innovation in political life. In addition to marriage connections, the compact led to some sharing of existing friendships. We have already considered Balbus' relationship with Caesar; and T. Labienus spends the entirety of Caesar's proconsular campaigns in Gaul on his staff.

In addition, this period contains more evidence on Caesar's handling of his political enemies. Perhaps the most striking episode is his abandonment of Cicero by allowing Clodius' adoption, in response to Cicero's attack on the triumvirate in his defense of Gaius Antonius. But implacable hostility is not his only policy. Dio comments on this aspect of Caesar's behavior in the context of his first consulship:

> For these reasons he exacted vengeance unobtrusively and where least expected: both to preserve his reputation for not being prone to anger and to stop anyone from realizing his intentions and taking steps to protect himself or attacking Caesar before being a victim himself. Caesar was not concerned with what had already happened; he wanted to prevent things from happening. As a result he would forgive many people, even those who had caused him considerable harm, or take only limited steps against them, believing that they would cause no further trouble. But concerned about his own safety he responded to others even more vigorously than was appropriate. (38.11.5–6; cf. Suet. *Iul.* 74–5)

Willingness to pursue enemies beyond what is considered fitting is also striking; conventions of aristocratic behavior can be overcome by practical considerations.

Dio's comments here may be influenced by the importance later of mercy in Caesar's dictatorship, but both aspects of Caesar's behavior, as Dio describes it, are visible in his dealings with Catullus. Two of the poems in the Catullan collection (57, 93) attack Caesar directly by name and a number of others have Caesar's associate Mamurra as their target, under his own name or an easily comprehensible pseudonym. The poet is incensed by Mamurra's profiteering in Gaul and Britain, in which he implies that Caesar is complicit: "Was it for this, supreme general, that you went to the furthest island of the west, that that fucking tool of yours might gobble up twenty or thirty million?" (Cat. 27.11–14; translation, Lee 1990). In poem 57 he accuses both men of being the penetrated partner in homosexual relationships, and of bankruptcy; and 93 is a two-line epigram expressing complete contempt for Caesar. One could add, too, poem 11, where the "monuments of great Caesar" provide a bathetic backdrop to the imagined wanderings of Lesbia, with Furius and Aurelius in pursuit. These poems can be interpreted as moves within the vigorous invective culture of the late Republic (Corbeill 1996; Booth 2007). But Catullus' urbanity was not, it seems, met by comparable urbanity from Caesar. Suetonius (*Iul.* 72) records that Caesar acknowledged that the poems harmed his reputation, and that he accepted an apology from Catullus and marked this by dining immediately with Catullus' father. Catullus' father was an inhabitant of Cisalpine Gaul, in which province Caesar was, at that time, holding *imperium*, and linked to Caesar by ties of guest-friendship; in such circumstances, a demand from Caesar for an apology would be difficult to ignore. Moreover, the existence of Suetonius' anecdote suggests a carefully orchestrated and public demonstration that Catullus' offense had been repented, and magnanimously pardoned. The damage done by the poems was clearly, as far as Caesar was concerned, significant.

The eventual length of Caesar's campaigns in Gaul gave him an exceptional position from which to accumulate a loyal coterie of supporters. Here the comparison with Pompeius becomes difficult to avoid; Pompeius had used his influence at Rome to ensure the election to high office of his close associates, not always with the desired results. Caesar had ten legates under the terms of the *lex Vatinia* and he, not the Senate, appointed them; he had therefore an enormous store of patronage at his disposal, in addition to informal arrangements with younger and less experienced men. (Caes. *BG* 1.39, a description of panic early in the campaign, gives an impression that this group was substantial.) In some cases, the identity of his legates can be explained by pre-existing links: Quintus Pedius was Caesar's nephew, and P. Licinius Crassus the younger son of Crassus; Vatinius had supported Pompeius, Crassus, and Caesar in 59 while holding the tribunate. Cicero's brother Quintus spends three seasons (54–52) with Caesar, sandwiched between service for Pompeius in Sardinia and for Cicero in Cilicia. In other cases, too little is known about the earlier careers of Caesar's legates to speculate on or explain how they ended up with him, though the breadth of background is noticeable (Gruen 1974: 112–19).The effects of service with Caesar on subsequent careers are obvious. Q. Fufius Calenus, C. Trebonius, and C. Caninius Rebilus all held the consulship between the Civil War and Caesar's death, and Hirtius in 43, and T. Sextius, L.Munatius Plancus and L. Minucius Basilus were praetors in 45; Roscius Fabatus was praetor in 49 and P. Sulpicius Rufus in 48; he subsequently campaigned for Caesar in Illyricum and in Pontus and Bithynia. M. Antonius was not one of Caesar's legates, but was chosen by him as his quaestor when elected to that office in 52; Antonius' mother was a Julia, though not a close relative of Caesar, and there was a connection from the time when Caesar had served with Antonius' father in Cilicia. But Caesar's choice of Antonius is as likely to be explained by Antonius' military competence, already demonstrated as a cavalry commander in Gabinius' army in Syria – and Gabinius was an adherent of Pompeius. Most of Caesar's legates remained loyal to him in 49; the striking exception was Labienus, whose return to Pompeius was regarded by Cicero at least as highly significant: "He [Caesar] has received a huge blow because T. Labienus – his most senior officer – is not willing to be a party to his crime; he has left Caesar and joined our side, and many are said to be about to do the same" (Cic. *Fam.* 16.12.4; cf. *Att.* 7.12.5).

In addition to this group of associates, who were themselves pursuing a political career, Caesar had close links with men who were not themselves politically active. We have already come across Balbus; he presumably played a key part in the negotiations setting up the compact with Pompeius and Crassus, and it was Balbus who attempted, unsuccessfully, to persuade Cicero to join the three (Cic. *Att.* 2.3.3), promising him close intimacy with Pompeius, and with Caesar if Cicero wants it, as well as popularity with the people, reconciliation with his enemies, and a peaceful old age. At this point Cicero describes Balbus as the "associate of Caesar" – not of Pompeius. Throughout the 50s he is working for Caesar, at first in Gaul and then in Rome; his importance is probably demonstrated by his being prosecuted for illegal assumption of the citizenship in 56 BC. Cicero defended him, relying largely on arguments from his position within a network of relationships, chief among which are those with Pompeius and Caesar (Steel 2001: 98–110). Other close associates of Caesar included Mamurra, his prefect of engineers whose alleged profit from service in Gaul aroused Catullus' rage (29, 41, 43, 57, 94, 105, 114, 115). Mamurra may have had an earlier connection with Pompeius (but see McDermott 1983). Oppius emerges in 54 BC as an agent of Caesar, organizing the post between Gaul and Rome and negotiating between Pompeius and Caesar (Cic. *Q Fr.* 3.1). Oppius and Mamurra were both Roman knights, as was Gaius Trebatius Testa, who was seeking his fortune in Gaul as an unofficial camp follower in 54 and 53; Cicero wrote a letter of recommendation on his behalf to Caesar (Cic. *Fam.* 7.5). Another associate of Caesar whose background resembles more closely Balbus' was Pompeius Trogus, who worked in Caesar's campaign bureaucracy. He too had a connection with Pompeius: his father had obtained the Roman citizenship from Pompeius during the war against Sertorius (Just. *Epit.* 43.11–12). Hall (1998: 25–6) points out that Caesar's group of associates, of this kind, is distinctive in comparison with his contemporaries because it contains so few men from a Greek cultural background, and because many of them, too, were writers, in Latin. A conscious cultural move may, as he suggests, be involved here. But it is also noticeable that many of those who emerge as close associates in the 50s have an earlier connection with Pompeius. Caesar proved rather effective at headhunting the talent which Pompeius had accumulated over two decades as Rome's leading military commander.

Although Caesar was able to construct a power base in Gaul, his political success depended also on having competent associates in Rome. Initially he relied on Pompeius and Crassus; the importance to all three men of cooperation is underscored by their successful negotiations in 56 at Luca. But after Crassus' death and as Pompeius began to waver he looked for other agents. Balbus and Oppius were clearly active in this regard, but others holding office were also required. Four of the tribunes of the people in 51 vetoed senatorial measures aimed at Caesar; two (C. Caelius and P. Cornelius) are otherwise unknown but Vibius Pansa remained a loyal and prominent supporter of Caesar, and Vinicius resurfaced from obscurity as suffect consul in 33. It seems likely that their support owed something to money; Caesar's campaigns were proving extremely lucrative. We know he lent money to Cicero at this period; and an enormous bribe was suspected in 50 when the tribune Curio publicly, and surprisingly, switched allegiance from Pompeius to Caesar. Caelius informed Cicero: "What I've just written about Curio being a no-show – well, he's hotting up and being pulled apart pretty harshly. He's jumped over to the popular side just like that, because he didn't get his way over the intercalary month, and started to speak on Caesar's behalf ..." (Cic. *Fam.* 8.6.5). Caesar also ensured the neutrality of L. Aemilius Paullus, consul in 50, through bribery (which helped to fund the construction of the basilica Paulli in the forum: Wiseman 1993: 187–9; App. *B Civ.* 2.26), and courted Lentulus Crus, consul in 49, in a similar manner, though unsuccessfully.

In the period before the Civil War, Caesar's friendships do not, in themselves, challenge the norms of aristocratic society. But the differences are striking between his relationships, in so far as they can be determined, and, say, the sentimental economy assumed by Cicero as the basis for understanding and theorizing friendship. There is no single individual whose name is linked with Caesar in this way: no Favonius to his Cato or Atticus to his Cicero. But, just as striking, there is in this period no consistent faction or grouping which Caesar strives to maintain. The improvisatory and opportunistic nature of his political activity is reflected in his provisional and temporary approach to political alliance making. We could say that Caesar does politics without long-term stable alliances; or, to put it another way, his approach to dealing with his peers is a much better example of utilitarian manipulation of friendship than Cicero's emotional understanding of the relationship.

Caesar's own account of the outbreak of civil war acknowledges the role that personal relationships have played in creating political catastrophe. But there is no straightforward justification of men's actions on these grounds. The opposition to peace negotiations has, on Caesar's account, three principal leaders: Lentulus, Scipio, and Cato (Caes. *BC* 1.4.1).

> Old grievances against Caesar, and the grief caused by electoral failure, stir up Cato. Lentulus' motives are the size of his debts, hope of a province and military command and the profits to be derived from installing kings in power. He boasts to his circle that he will be a second Sulla, to whom supreme power will return. The same hope of provinces and armies drives on Scipio, who thinks that he will share them with Pompeius because of

their marriage connection, and at the same time fear of prosecution, the flattery and showing off of his friends and of the powerful, who at that time were dominant in the state and courts. Pompeius himself, urged on by Caesar's enemies, and because he was not willing for anyone to match him in prestige, broke off his friendship with Caesar entirely. He returned to a state of good relations with their shared enemies, the majority of whom Pompeius had inflicted on Caesar at the time when they were linked by marriage. He was also disturbed by the scandal of the two legions which he had diverted from their journeys to Asia and Syria to form part of his own resources and power, and was keen to bring things to open warfare."

Ties of friendship here take their place in sordid lists of self-interest which prevent these men from attending to the interests of the *res publica*. Caesar, by contrast, although he acknowledges that "his standing has always been his first concern and more valuable than his life," continues, in his negotiations with Pompeius, by acknowledging that "he is willing to stoop to any measures and put up with anything for the sake of the state" (Caes. *BC* 1.9; Ruebel 1996).

Once war had broken out, Caesar naturally had less control over the identity of his followers. And the choices of those who took sides were not dictated simply by pre-existing friendships and connections: principle and advantage also took a part (though ancient theorizing about these two motors of decision making acknowledged that friendship could play a role in assessing both; Powell 1995). Cicero's process of decision-making as war loomed is apparent in great detail in his correspondence, though in essence he does not shift from the position he articulates to Atticus in December 50 (Cic. *Att.* 7.3). In this letter, as he considers what he should do, he agrees with Atticus that Caesar has not been as generous to him, Cicero, as he should have been. But he goes on to say, "But if things were different, and he had given me everything he could have, nonetheless, that figure whom you mention, the guardian of the city, would force me to remember my fine dedication and would not allow me to do the same as Vulcatius and Servius (whose actions you approve of) but would want me to feel something worthy of myself, and to act upon it. And if it were possible, I would be doing this in a different way from the course which is now necessary." Even if there were stronger bonds of obligation between the two men, Cicero could not pursue a course of action which he regarded as morally wrong. And though he did consider neutrality (which was the line taken by other ex-consuls, including Volcatius Tullus and Servius Sulpicius Rufus), particularly as it became apparent that Pompeius was going to abandon Italy, both what he regarded as right and his friendship with Pompeius pushed him towards Caesar's opponents (Cic. *Att.* 7.12.3, 7.20.2, 7.21.3, 7.22.2, 7.23.3, 7.26.2–3, 8.1.4, 8.3 *passim*, 8.16.2) (Brunt 1986). Cicero's letters also document the efforts that a number of individuals made on Caesar's behalf at least to ensure his neutrality (Cic. *Att.* 7.17, 7.21, 8.2, 8.9a, 8.11, 8.15a) and we should assume that this network was engaged on similar efforts with other senior figures.

Others seem to have given different factors more weight. M. Caelius Rufus was expecting conflict and assessing each side in the autumn of 50, writing to Cicero: "I don't think you're unaware that men ought to follow the more honorable party, when internal disagreements arise, for as long as the conflict isn't armed; but when it comes to war and fighting, to follow the stronger, and judge the better party to be the safer. In this dissension, I see that Gnaeus Pompeius will have the Senate with him and those who sit on juries, and everyone who lives in fear and despair will go to Caesar. But there's no comparison between their forces" (Cic. *Fam.* 8.14.3). Caelius followed his own advice and assessment of Caesar's strength; but personal factors may have played a part too. He quarreled with Appius Claudius Pulcher in the autumn of 50, and assumed that anything Appius could achieve against him would be welcome to Pompeius (Cic. *Fam.* 8.12.1); and later, when praetor in 48, he writes in despairing tones of the situation and blames his involvement on Curio, "whose friendship has dumped me in this impossible situation!" (Cic. *Fam.* 8.17.1). Personal considerations had a role in Caelius' choices, but these do not, it seems, include any direct link with Caesar himself.

Caesar's victory in the Civil War meant that offices at Rome were held by his supporters. We have already seen that many of the most senior figures had connections with Caesar which went back to the campaigns in Gaul. The prominence of others can be explained by their birth and status; given that the vast majority of senior figures in the senatorial class supported Pompeius, those who chose the other side were correspondingly valuable. M. Aemilius Lepidus seems initially to have owed his prominence among Caesar's followers to his holding the praetorship in 49, ensuring the appointment of Caesar as dictator in the autumn of 49 (a move for which there was precedent, though Cicero regarded it as illegal [Cic. *Att.* 9.15.1]). Support from Servilius Isauricus, consul with Caesar in 48, marks a decisive shift in his political affiliations: as praetor in 54 he had cooperated with the younger Cato and permitted the prosecution of one of Caesar's legates. In his case, marriage may be part of the shift, though it is unclear whether as cause or consequence; his wife was one of the daughters of Servilia: another daughter was Lepidus' wife (the third was married to Cassius Longinus, another Caesarian). Also in this category of associates is Cornelius Dolabella, who had been nominated by Caesar to take over his consulship in 44. Syme (1939: 68–70) identifies these men within a wider group of patricians who chose to support Caesar (Servilius was plebeian, but his family claimed patrician status originally).

Caesar's victory was followed by a much wider accommodation among the elite with the new political landscape. Caesar, moreover, was keen to ensure that his rule was distinguished from what happened after earlier bouts of civil conflict by the public practice of *clementia*, mercy, pardoning his enemies and permitting them to return to political life. The most striking example of this was his support for M. Iunius Brutus, who fought on the Pompeian side during the Civil War but was rapidly rehabilitated and promoted within Caesar's government; in this case, the influence of his mother Servilia, Caesar's friend and lover, was crucial. Caesar decisively resisted the more violent extremes of factionalism in his handling of the peace and was alert to opportunities to publicize this; hence in part, surely, the apparent vehemence of his *Anti-Cato*, when faced with Cato the Younger's transformation, through his suicide at Utica, into a symbol of resistance to tyranny. An uneasy mix of personal and ideological motives is also apparent among the group who killed Caesar; whatever unified the liberators, it was not simple hatred of Caesar (see Lintott, chapter 6 in this volume). Nonetheless, Cicero at least appears to have sensed a shift in what could and could not be said during the dictatorship, with his *Cato*, indeed, perhaps being the catalyst. In discussing that work with Atticus, he appears to accept without much anxiety that it will cause offense to Caesar (*Att.* 12.4.2; Griffin 1994: 696). A year later, as he plans and drafts a letter of advice to Caesar (which was apparently never sent), he writes to Atticus (*Att.* 13.27.1):

> As for the letter to Caesar, I've always and for very good reasons been in favor of those men [Balbus and Oppius] reading it beforehand. To do otherwise would have been disobliging to *them* and almost dangerous for me, if I did offend him. They've behaved straightforwardly and I'm grateful to them for not concealing their views; and indeed the best thing is, they want so much to be changed that there is no point in my starting it again from scratch.

Free expression is no longer safe; and Caesar's transformation of social relations amongst the elite is, for Cicero, one aspect of his rule becoming a tyranny.

A concluding example of how friendship with Caesar could be understood is given by an exchange of letters between Matius and Cicero after the assassination (Cic. *Fam.* 11.27–8; Griffin 1997; Hall 2005). Matius was another equestrian adherent of Caesar; Cicero remarks that he was instrumental in strengthening the relationship between Caesar and Cicero in the mid-50s, and he was putting Caesar's case in the early months of the Civil War (Cic. *Att.* 9.11.2). The context for the exchange of letters appears to be that Matius had heard of Cicero's making critical remarks about his, Matius', behavior; and Trebatius reported Matius' complaint to Cicero. Cicero wrote a self-exculpatory and self-justifying letter, to which Matius then replied. The first part of Cicero's letter emphasizes the friendship between them and Matius' role in protecting Cicero and his family during the Civil War and re-establishing good relations between Cicero and Caesar: "After Caesar's return what was of greater concern to you than that I should be as closely attached to him as possible? And you achieved this" (Cic. *Fam.* 11.27.5). He proceeds to deny the specific causes of Matius' complaint; but he then sets up a philosophical analysis of Matius' friendship with Caesar: "As a learned man you are well aware that if – as I believe – Caesar was a king, one can put both sides of the case concerning your obligations. The side, which I put, is that the loyalty and human feeling which you display in loving your friend even after his death are commendable. The other side, which not a few put, is that one should put the freedom of one's fatherland before the life of a friend" (Cic. *Fam.* 11.27.8). Cicero is politely acknowledging that Matius' behavior can be justified; but with the loaded term *rex* he is also reminding him that Caesar's assassination has good philosophical justification, as well as being in harmony with Roman sentiments. Matius' response is robust:

> I'm well aware of what people have said about me in the aftermath of Caesar's death. They regard it as a fault that I grieve deeply at the death of a close friend and am upset that a man whom I loved has died; they say that country comes before friendship, as though they have already made their case that his death is beneficial to the state. But I'm not going to debate with cleverness; I confess that I haven't got to that stage of wisdom.

> I didn't follow 'Caesar' in the political conflict, I followed a friend and I didn't desert him even though I found the situation distasteful and I never approved of civil war, or even of the grounds for conflict, and did everything I could to put it out even as it was starting. (Cic. *Fam.* 11.28.2)

And later in the letter he points out the inconsistency of Caesar's assassins, who claim freedom as their justification but now deny others freedom of thought (Cic. *Fam.* 11.28.3).

Cicero's description of his feelings in relation to Caesar and his supporters can easily be contrasted with what he says elsewhere, and can be described as hypocrisy or politeness according to one's interpretative framework. But the exchange also shows that fundamental disagreement about the place of friendship within politics was possible among members of the Roman elite. Matius' language suggests that he regarded his friendship with Caesar as a matter of sentiment and emotion, not advantage; indeed, he points out that he has suffered materially from Caesar's legislation (Cic. *Fam.* 11.28.2). And, as far as he is concerned, that relationship of friendship is sufficient to explain and justify his political conduct.

Matius articulates his loyalty to Caesar more clearly than other associates but there is nothing to suggest that his feelings were exceptional. Indeed, the biographical tradition attests to Caesar's personal charm (Plut. *Caes.* 4.2; cf. Paterson, chapter 10, pp. 136,139) and to his consideration for his friends (Suet. *Iul.* 72), and Cicero attests to the former, most notably in a letter to Atticus describing having the dictator to dinner (*Att.* 13.52). At the same time, we should be careful about excessive sentimentality in assessing Caesar's friendships, or, indeed, too faithful an acceptance of the tropes of biography. Many of the relationships discussed in this chapter were not lasting, and their basis in mutual advantage means that they are better understood as political alliances than as friendships. In other cases, "friendship" is a label for loyal service, rewarded as such.

In assessing the identity and significance of Caesar's friends and associates, we can distinguish a pattern of behavior which appears to be entirely normal for the late Republic: relationships, described as friendships, are built up as a man climbs the ladder until he has reached a position – in Caesar's case, his proconsulship in Gaul – which enables him to reward his friends and acquire new ones. Caesar brought to the task of a career in public life a specific set of advantages and disadvantages which limited but did not determine the choices he had, including whom he associated with. Thus, we can describe his friendships within the political sphere as improvisatory and flexible; other men behaved differently, but Caesar's choices in this field are not exceptional.

FURTHER READING

David Konstan's *Friendship in the Classical World* (Cambridge, 1997) provides a lucid introduction to the nature and role of friendship in classical antiquity. There are a variety of insights into different aspects of friendship, some specifically relevant to the late Republic, in the collections of essays edited by John Fitzgerald (*Greco-Roman Perspectives on Friendship,*

Atlanta, 1996) and by Michael Peachin (*Aspects of Friendship in the Graeco-Roman World*, Portsmouth, 2001). Current debates on friendship in the Roman Republic are still dominated by the issues raised initially by Peter Brunt in his 1969 article on friendship which was published in revised form in the collection of papers *The Fall of the Roman Republic* (Oxford, 1988). Key works in the development of a prosopographical approach to Roman history are Gelzer's *Die Nobilität der römischen Republik* and Münzer's *Römische Adelsparteien und Adelsfamilien*; both are available in English translation, the former by R. Seager (Oxford, 1969), the latter by T. Ridley (Baltimore, 1999). Gruen's *Last Generation of the Roman Republic* (Berkeley, CA, 1974) offers a comprehensive account of the period from this perspective, including detailed analysis of Caesar's network of associates up to the outbreak of the Civil War. Syme's *The Roman Revolution* remains fundamental for the period during and after the Civil War. There is a commentary on Cicero's *de amicitia* (together with a translation) in the Aris and Phillips series by J. G. F. Powell (Warminster, 1990), who also edited the Oxford Classical Text of this work (Oxford, 2006).

CHAPTER TEN

Caesar the Man

Jeremy Paterson

The sorts of material on which modern biographers thrive are rarely available for people in the classical world. Yet, even with the gap of so many centuries, the prospects for understanding the character and personality of Julius Caesar seem at first sight rather good. We have some of his writings. Casual remarks by Caesar in letters are reported by Cicero, a contemporary, who in his own letters and writings also provides a commentary on a man he was both infuriated and charmed by. We have collections of Caesar's reported sayings. For the psychoanalyst some of his dreams, or what are claimed to have been his dreams, are recorded. We have a contemporary bust, and the coinage issued towards the end of his life is the first in Rome to seek to depict a living person. Above all we have the biographies by Plutarch and Suetonius, who clearly drew upon a wide range of sources no longer directly available to us. However, much of what we may seek to use comes preselected for us by the ancient biographers, who naturally record or give credence to anecdotes and stories which fit with their own theories of character and their own assessments of Caesar. Far more significant is the fact that so much of even the most innocent-seeming material available to Suetonius and Plutarch had already passed through the distorting lens of the political rhetoric of the Late Republic, in which casual remarks, physical defects, personal traits, dress, and revelations from the bedroom became the stuff of political attack in ways that even modern tabloid journalists might envy.

Appearance

Suetonius (*Iul.* 45) offers a vivid pen portrait of Julius Caesar. He was tall (*excelsa statura*), well built (*teretibus membris*), with a fair complexion (*colore candido*). He had a rather overlarge mouth (*ore paulo pleniore*), and lively dark eyes (*nigris vegetisque oculis*). Plutarch (*Caes.* 17) confirms the "fair and soft skin," but describes

Caesar's general appearance as "spare" or "lean." It is difficult to know where the biographers got this information from. Plutarch, though not Suetonius, makes frequent references to statues when trying to describe the character of his subjects (Wardman 1967). However, Suetonius prefaces his account with the word *traditur* ("it is said that"), which suggests he is drawing from a written account, perhaps the memoirs of one of Caesar's contemporaries, such as Gaius Oppius. The desire to preserve a memory of a person's appearance may owe something to the popularity since Aristotle of the pseudoscience of physiognomy (Evans 1935, 1941). It is interesting to note that Suetonius also wrote a work, now lost, *de vitiis corporalibus* ("On physical defects"). To some extent the biographers' descriptions of Julius Caesar are confirmed by the one bust which may be contemporary and by the portraiture on the coins issued in Caesar's last years and soon after his death (Toynbee 1957). The bust from Tusculum has a high, furrowed forehead, a prominent nose, pinched cheeks, and the broad mouth which Suetonius had noted. All these features are found again on the coinage, which also emphasizes a very prominent Adam's apple (Fig. 10.1). Further, the portraiture amply confirms the most commented-upon aspect of Caesar's appearance, his thinning hair. Suetonius said that "he took very badly the disfigurement of his baldness (*calvitii* ... *deformitatem*) because in his experience it was often the subject of jokes by his detractors."

Caesar's sensitivity about his baldness was not unusual among Roman men. In the fourth century AD Synesius wrote a short encomium on baldness as a response to an earlier sophistic exercise by Dio Chrysostom in praise of hair. Synesius (*Encomium on Baldness* 1 and 2) expresses in mock-heroic style the sense of shame and shock at the "disaster" of his hair loss. The Roman elite frequently envisioned their "manliness" (*virtus*) in terms of Homeric heroes, who were usually represented with ample, flowing locks (the *Achilleae comae* of Martial 12.82.10). Caligula was extremely touchy about his bald patch (Suet. *Cal.* 50, see also 35.2). The emperor Otho sought

Figure 10.1 BMCRR Rome 4155; RRC 480/7b, Plate LVII, no. 4. Obverse of a denarius of 44BC showing head of Caesar with DICT PERPETUO behind.

to disguise his loss of hair by wearing a toupee (*galericulum*) (Suet. *Otho* 12). Domitian shared Caesar's unhappiness at gibes about his baldness, although he was sufficiently able to see the joke to publish what has been represented as a mock *consolatio* on his hair loss (Suet. *Dom.* 18; Morgan 1997). When his troops chorused at Caesar's Gallic Triumph, "Men of Rome, lock up your wives, we are bringing home the bald adulterer (*moechum calvum*)," they were alluding to the common association of baldness with being oversexed. This idea originated with Aristotle (*gen. anim.* 783b25ff.), who drew an analogy with the loss of leaves from trees with the onset of the cold of autumn. The head was already thought of as the coldest part of the body, and Aristotle argued that it was cooled further when heat drained away in intercourse, so that "those who are naturally prone to intercourse go bald." Finally there was an additional ironic factor specific to Julius Caesar; one of the suggested derivations of the *cognomen* "Caesar" was from *caesaries* ("hairiness").

It was a normal part of political rhetoric of the Late Republic to seize on any perceived failing, so in this case, critics were ready to argue that the real reason why Julius Caesar was delighted by the honorific decree to permit him to wear the laurel wreath of a triumphing general was that he was able to hide his baldness in public (Suet. *Iul.* 45). Like many men throughout the ages, Caesar's response to all this was to make the most of what he had; "he used to comb his failing hair forward from the crown of his head" (Suet. *Iul.* 45). But this created in its turn a new opening for the critics, because being over-fussy about one's hair could be construed as a sign of effeminacy. So Cicero is reported as claiming sardonically, "When I look at the way Caesar's hair is arranged with such nicety and see him scratching his head with one finger, I cannot think that this fellow would ever conceive of such a great crime as the overthrow of the Roman state" (Plut. *Caes.* 4). The reference to "scratching one's head with a single finger" is somewhat unclear. However, it was something of a commonplace. It was used in abuse against Pompey: Clodius chanted it before a crowd in attacking Pompey (Plut. *Pomp.* 48.7), and we have two lines from an epigram of the contemporary poet Licinius Calvus (quoted by Seneca *Contr.* 3.19), which include it and to which the later historian Ammianus Marcellinus (17.11.4) alludes, taking it to be a sign of a dissolute man (*dissolutum*). A range of sources includes it as a sign of someone who is unchaste (*impudicus*) and effeminate (Seneca *Ep.* 52.12; Lucian *The Teacher of Orators* 11; Juvenal 9.130). Some have seen the scratching of the head with one finger as a secret "gay" sign; but much more probable is that it refers to being too fussy and careful to avoid disrupting well-groomed hair (Williams 1999: 222–3).

Suetonius (*Iul.* 45) also claims that Caesar had his hair not only trimmed and shaved but also plucked out. This was also a source of criticism, because it was thought that he was being more fastidious than he should have been about the care of his person (*circa corporis curam morosior*). The adjective suggests that there was a scale in such matters. Keeping hair and the beard trimmed, even removing underarm hair, was expected; but removing body and leg hair could be construed as steps too far. True Roman men exhibited a certain hairy masculinity (Williams 1999: 130; Gleason 1995: 74). As Cicero, a contemporary of Caesar, pointed out, "we must present an appearance of neatness (*munditia*), which is neither disagreeable nor too refined, just enough to escape the charge of boorish and uncivilized lack of care (*agrestem et inhumanam neglegentiam*)" (*Off.* 1.130). Cicero went on to say that the same principle applied to matters of dress, namely moderation in all things. Clothing as a reflection of character provided useful ammunition for rhetorical invective (Dyck 2001; Heskel 1994). But it was recognized that people cannot always fly in the face of fashion – the fault may be more with the times than with the person; increased prosperity brought with it luxury and the first indicator of luxury was people paying closer attention to their bodies (*cultus primum corporum esse diligentior incipit*, Seneca *Ep.* 114.9).

"Beware the badly belted boy," Sulla is supposed to have warned about Caesar (Suet. *Iul.* 45, Dio 43.43.2, and Macr. *Sat.* 2.3.9). According to Suetonius, Caesar always used to wear a belt over a senatorial tunic with its broad stripe, which in his case had fringed sleeves which reached down to his wrists. Cicero produced another bitter joke about the way Caesar wore his toga. Asked why he, Cicero, had picked the wrong side in the civil war of 49 BC, the orator replied that he had been fooled by the way Caesar wore his toga (*praecinctura me decepit*, Macr. *Sat.* 2.3.9, presumably taken from the collection of Cicero's *bons mots* made by his secretary, Tiro (Quintilian, *Inst.* 6.3.5)). These remarks plunge us into the world of Roman high fashion. Here, as in so many other aspects, Roman society was coming under the influence of Greece. The traditional senatorial tunic was sleeveless or had short sleeves (as in the bronze statue of the Etruscan magistrate, the so-called "Arringatore," of about 100 BC). However, increasingly the Greek fashion for long sleeves (*tunica chirodota*), derided by traditionalists as only usual in women's dress, was being adopted. Indeed, it had already become a part of political invective in the second century BC, when Scipio Aemilianus, as censor in 142 BC, attacked P. Sulpicius Galus for his long sleeves and effeminacy. It became a staple for Cicero, whose political enemies are constantly represented in this way (e.g. Catiline's supporters as the sort of men who dressed in long-sleeved and ankle-length tunics, Cic. *Cat.* 2.22). Caesar also invariably wore a belt over the tunic. Belts, simply knotted rather than with a buckle, were normal with ordinary tunics, but not with the senatorial tunic with the broad stripe. Further, Suetonius talks of a *fluxiore cinctura* ("a loose binding"), which probably suggests that Caesar created the effect of a blouse, which again is characteristic of women's tunics. However, there is just the possibility of an entirely different explanation for Sulla's remark. It was a characteristic of sayings and witticisms that they were frequently wrenched out of context and could then be imbued with completely new significance when repeated (Laurence & Paterson 1999: 189–94). In the mid-80s BC the young Julius Caesar was nominated for the priesthood of flamen Dialis (Ridley 2000: 213–18). Plutarch (*Caes.* 1) and Suetonius (*Iul.* 1), though they both give garbled accounts, make it clear that Caesar was never inaugurated, and that in some way Sulla was responsible for bringing about the eventual rejection of Caesar for the priesthood. One of the key characteristics of the flamen Dialis was that the holder was surrounded by an extraordinary number of taboos (Gell. *NA* 10.15) – one of which was that the flamen could not have a knot in his headdress, his belt, or any other part of his clothing. Perhaps Sulla's reference to Caesar being "belted in the wrong way" was to one of the technical grounds he cited for rescinding Caesar's nomination.

Cicero's sneer at the way Caesar wore his toga was interpreted as an attack on his habit of "trailing the fringe of the toga on the ground (*trahendo laciniam*) like an effeminate." Again fashion was changing. The traditional toga came down to between calf and ankle, but by the first century BC fashion textbooks were recommending that the toga should go down to the heels, like the Greek cloak, the *himation* or *pallium* (Quintilian *Inst.* 11.3.143, quoting the work of the first century BC rhetoricians, Plotius Gallus and Nigidius Figulus). Even Cicero was supposed to have adopted the fashion in order to hide his varicose veins! The problem was that hems which swept the floor were normal only in female dress; hence it is easy to construct a charge of *mollitia* (effeminacy) (on Roman dress see Sebesta and Bonfante 1994).

Caesar clearly was something of a man of fashion, but he was not unusual in this, and the charges leveled against him in this regard were used against many of his contemporaries. It was no accident that one of his leading political opponents, Cato the Younger, went out of his way to represent himself as the rough, hairy Roman of tradition with his short toga (*exigua toga* in Horace *Ep.* 1.19.13), which he wore in the old-fashioned way without a tunic underneath (Plut. *Cato Minor* 6.3).

Health

Caesar's biographers have slightly different takes on the question of his health, despite the fact that they are using essentially the same material (possibly from the memoir of Caesar's friend, C. Oppius; Townend 1987). While Suetonius (*Iul.* 45) considers Caesar's health as generally good, apart from the fact that towards the end of his life he suffered sudden fits and nightmares, Plutarch (*Caes.* 17) has him battling against a delicate constitution, headaches, and epileptic fits – but not making an excuse of them, rather using the rigors of campaign life to increase his strength and energy. For purposes of his own Shakespeare made Caesar deaf in his left ear ("Come on my right hand, for this ear is deaf"; *Julius Caesar* I.ii.209), but there is no classical source which mentions this. It is possible that Shakespeare was making neat use of Alexander the Great's practice of covering his ear when listening to an accusation in order to hear only the defense (Plut. *Alex.* 42; Velz 1971). Suetonius (*Iul.* 1) is the only source for the claim that Caesar suffered from a regular recurrent fever, that is malaria, while in hiding from Sulla (see Ridley 2000: 225 for speculation about the longer-term psychological effects of this).

There can be no denying the restless energy which drove Caesar throughout his life. He was an excellent horseman; as a boy he learned to gallop with his arms crossed behind his back (Plut. *Caes.* 17). He was a strong swimmer; during the Alexandrian campaign in the chaos of a failed attack he was forced to throw himself into the sea and swim for safety carrying important documents in one hand above the water (Plut. *Caes.* 49).

Suetonius knew of only two epileptic attacks while Caesar was engaged in public affairs (*inter res agendas*). He does not specify them. One of the incidents which Suetonius had in mind was alleged in some sources to have happened in the African campaign against the Pompeians in 46 BC at the battle of Thapsus. Plutarch (*Caes.* 53) in his narrative has Caesar at the head of his army in the attack, as does the author of the *African War* 83 who has Caesar leading the charge. But Plutarch then goes on to cite a different tradition, in which Caesar was overcome by an epileptic fit just as he was drawing up his troops and had to be carried to a nearby tower where he rested. This alternative narrative smacks of a convenient "political" illness, either feigned by Caesar himself or concocted by his supporters afterwards, because in the battle the Caesarian troops got out of hand and went on the rampage, slaughtering Pompeians without let-up and even turning on their own officers in a way that shocked Caesar. It would have been convenient for Caesar and his reputation to have had a reason for not presiding over this shambles.

The second occasion Suetonius may have had in mind was a fit which Plutarch briefly mentions as having taken place at Corduba in Spain (*Caes.* 17). Historians have attempted to date this to any of the occasions on which Caesar was in Spain (69, 61, 49, 45 BC). However, if it happened, then it surely belongs to the campaign against the sons of Pompey in Spain in 45 BC, and was the "illness" which Dio (43.32.6) says overcame Caesar as he was besieging Corduba. Again, there is a hint in Dio of the illness being used as an excuse for Caesar's failure to press home the siege and his retirement in the face of Pompeian reinforcements.

Plutarch has one further possible attack. Among the long list of resentments felt by his opponents at Caesar's monarchical behavior after the civil war was the occasion when Caesar allegedly failed to stand up at the approach of the senate led by the consuls and praetors (Dio 44.8). It appears that Caesar and his supporters went out of their way to seek to explain his behavior away by alleging an illness, which Dio took to be diarrhea, but which Plutarch (*Caes.* 60) says was one of his fainting fits. Suetonius finally suggests that Caesar hesitated about attending the senate on the Ides of March because of his poor health – possibly another reference to a "political" use of epilepsy (Suet. *Iul.* 81.4).

All these incidents are surrounded with doubt; but, even if they are instances of a "convenient illness," they become more plausible if it was known that Julius Caesar in reality suffered from epilepsy. They were sufficient to enroll Caesar among the lists compiled in the Renaissance of great men with epilepsy, which included Hercules, Socrates, Plato, Muhammad, Petrarch, Emperor Charles V, and Torquato Tasso (Temkin 1971: 163–4). The linking of genius with epilepsy and melancholia was made in antiquity (the Aristotelian *Problems* 30.1, quoted by Cicero in *Tusc.* 1.73). As Suetonius noted, the incidents all occurred towards the end of Caesar's life, a fact indirectly confirmed by Appian (*B Civ.* 2.110), who suggested that Caesar's epilepsy and convulsions came upon him when he was not active, and contributed to the reason why Caesar sought new challenges by planning the invasion of Parthia at the end of his life. Ancient medicine was not very precise about epilepsy and included all manner of fits. It is possible that Caesar suffered from late-onset epilepsy. Recently, however, medical scholars have linked the nightmares, possible personality changes, and the fits of later years, and suggested the possibility of a brain tumor (Gomez, Kotler, & Long 1995). Diagnosis, of course, must be a very tentative business over such a distance in time.

The recording of dreams was an important aspect of ancient biography. The "science" of the interpretation of dreams was well developed in the classical world and interest in dreams was widespread. However, before Caesar's dreams are used as clues to his personality, it needs to be recognized that in the ancient world dreams were seen principally as externally generated prophecies, ways of divining the future, and only secondarily, if at all, as internally generated reflections of the dreamer's personality or state of mind. As Simon Price has pointed out, the work on dreams of the second-century AD scholar Artemidorus, whom Freud admired as a distinguished predecessor, clearly made a distinction between *oneiroi*, dreams which had a predictive or oracular character, and *enhypnia*, dreams which reflected the dreamer's current state of mind; but Artemidorus goes on to dismiss *enhypnia* as trivial and of little interest, while *oneiroi* were all-important (Price 1986). Chris Pelling (1997) has argued that the distinction may not be so clear-cut in the ancient historians and biographers. Cicero (*Rep.* 6.10), for example, sees dreams as often arising from thoughts and conversations in waking hours; but the fact remains that ancient sources did not primarily see dreams as windows on the minds of their subjects. So we should pause before leaping gleefully to a Freudian interpretation of the claim that Caesar had a dream of committing incest with his mother. Such stories often came from collections of dreams, in which the accounts have often been separated from their historical context. In any case, according to Herodotus 6.107, the Athenian tyrant Hippias had had a similar dream before the battle of Marathon. So Plutarch (*Caes.* 32) has Caesar dreaming of incest with his mother on the night before he crossed the Rubicon, but offers no interpretation, though he does describe the dream as "unlawful." Suetonius (*Iul.* 7) and Dio (37.52.2), on the other hand, put the dream during Caesar's quaestorship in Spain in 69 BC. This is, in itself, a curious context because his wife, Cornelia, had died just before he set out for his province. But neither Suetonius nor Dio hesitates in interpreting the dream as a prophetic sign of future greatness. According to Suetonius, interpreters of the dream claimed that he was destined for world power because the mother he had dreamed of dominating was mother earth, the parent of all mankind. This was precisely the interpretation recorded later by Artemidorus (*On.* 1.79) when he describes the dream as a good one for politicians, because "the mother signifies one's native country and, just as a man who follows the guidance of Aphrodite when he makes love, takes complete control of the body of his obedient and willing partner, so the dreamer will control all the affairs of the city."

Food and Drink

A person's eating and drinking preferences were staple elements of ancient biography. The omnipresence of wine in classical society made it a key social indicator. It helped to define Graeco-Roman culture, gender roles, status, and private and public *mores.* What one ate and drank were opportune topics for the orator, particularly one intent on emphasizing the *incontinentia* (unrestrained behavior) and *luxuria* (luxurious living) of an opponent. Further, there was the idea of "wine in, truth out," as Mrs. Nickleby has it. Plato (*Laws* 649) saw plying his potential Guardians with drink as an inexpensive and relatively harmless means of revealing character, which fitted in with the biographer's idea that a man's psyche can be revealed in his minor, unpremeditated actions (Plut. *Alex.* 1.2). Against this background, at first sight, Julius Caesar's apparent unconcern about what he ate and drank seems unexceptional. Plutarch (*Caes.* 17) talks of his "simple diet" and, although the connection is never explicitly made in the sources, it may be significant that in ancient medicine one of the main treatments for epilepsy was dieting. When Suetonius (*Iul.* 53) describes his "indifference" towards food, and Plutarch talks of him being "easily satisfied," what they had in mind was the story preserved by a contemporary of Caesar, C. Oppius, and cited by both biographers, which recorded an occasion when Caesar was served with asparagus topped with myrrh (a medicinal compound!) rather than fresh olive oil, which he ate without comment to avoid embarrassing his host. "That he drank wine most sparingly not even his enemies denied," claimed Suetonius (*Iul.* 53) most significantly, since being a drunkard was a standard charge in the political rhetoric of the period – all of Cicero's leading enemies and opponents are charged with drunkenness at one time or another. But this seems to be the one thing that Caesar could not be accused of. So in his attack on Cato the Younger after his suicide, Caesar must have felt he was on personal strong ground in repeating the stories about Cato's drunkenness in public from breakfast-time onwards that had been circulating since at least Cato's praetorship in 54 BC (Pliny *Ep.* 3.12; Plut. *Cat.Min.* 6, 44). Cato's supporters, however, defended him by pointing out that even in his cups Cato remained an all-round good fellow, and by reviving a quip of Cato himself that "Caesar was the only man to overthrow the Republic sober" (Suet. *Iul.* 53). We might also note that the Emperor Domitian, admittedly after a large lunch, was given to restricting his dinner to a Matian apple and a glass of water (Suet. *Dom.* 21). It is the mark of a tyrant to ignore social norms and conventions.

Caesar and Sex

From his teenage years Caesar was surrounded by a household of women. His mother, Aurelia, who lived down to 54 BC, was included in the list of model Roman mothers along with Cornelia, mother of the Gracchi, and Augustus' mother, Atia (Tac. *Dial.* 28). Mothers are frequently credited with playing an important part in the early education of aristocratic young men, particularly in families, such as Caesar's, where the father dies early in the son's life. Caesar's married life seems unexceptional by the standards of the times (Pompey had five wives). Marriages among the Roman Republican elite were motivated by the same mixture of dynastic, political, and personal considerations as in all aristocratic societies. His breaking off of his betrothal to Cossutia may have been in part motivated by the religious taboos associated with the post of flamen Dialis. His marriage to Cornelia was marked by Caesar's stubborn refusal to divorce her, when Sulla demanded it, and by what

Plutarch suggests was the wholly unprecedented funeral oration Caesar delivered when she died in 69 BC (Plut. *Caes.* 5), which may be indications of a relationship which was personal rather than political. His divorce of his next wife, Pompeia, was the occasion for his comment, "I consider that members of my family ought to be free from suspicion as well as accusation" (Suet. *Iul.* 74). But the context for the remark was the trial of Publius Clodius for his possible involvement in the defiling of the *Bona Dea* ceremony. Caesar had refused to give evidence in the trial (the ceremony had taken place in his own house, but, of course, he was not present). The prosecution then argued that his divorce of Pompeia was itself evidence that he believed the story of a liaison between Pompeia and Clodius. Caesar's response is meant to declare that he did not believe the story, but as Pontifex Maximus he needed to be above scandal. The subsequent marriage to Calpurnia must have been affected by the fact that Caesar was apart from her for so much of the time; but according to Plutarch (*Caes.* 53.4), on the night before his murder he was sharing his bed with her, "as he usually did."

Caesar's marriage relationships are not the end of the story. In Rome confining sexual activity to the marriage bed was sufficiently unusual to be worthy of comment (Val. Max. 4.3.3) and was clearly not expected as the norm for husbands. But there were limits. As the Elder C. Scribonius Curio comprehensively summed it up in a speech, Caesar was "every woman's man and every man's woman" (Suet. *Iul.* 52.3). Curio was hardly a dispassionate commentator. He was a fierce and vocal opponent of Caesar before and during the consulship of 59 BC and is cited by Suetonius as the source of other abuse of Caesar, much of it for his alleged sexual misbehavior (*Iul.* 9.2–3, 49.1, 50.1; the sources were probably Curio's speeches rather than a pamphlet he wrote later in the 50s in which, according to Cicero (*Brut.* 218), he railed at length against Caesar (*multis verbis cum inveheretur in Caesarem*)). But it is the nature of the charge which is somewhat startling to modern sensibilities. Roman society drew the boundaries of what was acceptable in sexual behavior in a distinctive way. Caesar is accused of being both a passive homosexual and a womanizer. The two charges were often linked (see below on Catullus 57), and Craig Williams (1999) has shown clearly that the distinction between "homosexual" and "heterosexual" plays little or no role in Roman males' construction of themselves and their sexual behavior. The essence of the Roman conception of "manliness" was that the man was an active penetrator, whether what he penetrated was male or female. So, first of all, Caesar was seen as offending against this norm by allowing himself as an adult to be penetrated. This was not acceptable in the Roman view of sexual probity (*pudicitia*). However, it was also recognized that many features of what was thought of as effeminacy, such as excessive interest in clothing, appearance, and depilation, could also make a man attractive to women. The successful pursuit of women might be seen as laudable machismo, but it also had its limits of acceptability. What lies behind Curio's accusation was that Caesar's affairs were with married women. As his troops shouted at his triumph, he was "the bald-headed adulterer." Adultery in Caesar's day was dealt with mainly within the family. However, it was possible for the head of the household to bring a charge of *iniuria* (injury) against the man involved, in effect to sue him for the damage done to the family reputation.

As so often, the accusation of this sort of behavior carried over into political rhetoric because the flagrant ignoring of social norms and of the obligations of friendship towards one's peers by seducing their wives was a characteristic of the tyrant. So, for example, later, an important part of the construction of the bad reputation of the Emperor Nero was his relations with his entourage's wives.

The two strands to Curio's charge are taken up by Suetonius. In *Iul.* 50 he introduces the long list of Caesar's alleged affairs with women as illustrations of the view that Caesar was eager and extravagant in his love affairs (*pronum et sumptuosum in libidines*), and in *Iul.* 49 he cites Caesar's alleged sexual submission to Nicomedes IV, the King of Bithynia.

In 81 BC the young Caesar went to serve as a junior officer in Asia, where the governor, M. Minucius Thermus, sent him on a diplomatic mission to the aging King of Bithynia Nicomedes. Caesar was a natural choice for such a job. His name would have been known to Nicomedes, because Caesar's father had governed Asia earlier. For some reason Caesar stayed longer than expected at the court and, indeed, returned soon after to Bithynia to arrange the settlement of a debt (Suet. *Iul.* 2). A connection was to remain between Caesar and Nicomedes; he was later to speak in the senate in defense of Nicomedes' daughter, Nysa, and was ready to list the favors shown to him by Nicomedes. The original gossip about what attracted Caesar to Bithynia circulated among Roman traders in the province, who had been present at one of the banquets thrown by Nicomedes (Suet. *Iul.* 49 – evidence, such as it is, which was exploited much later by Gaius Memmius, a fierce critic of Caesar). At that dinner Caesar is alleged to have acted as cupbearer to the king, which in the Roman mind would have immediately conjured up the picture of Ganymede, Jupiter's beloved cupbearer. Others added further details of Caesar lying on his couch dressed in purple, and of him being escorted to meet the king in his bedchamber. It was an easy step, and perhaps in the atmosphere of Rome an inevitable one, to turn all this into a story of Caesar being seduced by Nicomedes, a much older man, and submitting to him. The story is very largely the creation of the Roman mentality which was perennially suspicious of the social mores of the Greek world and of the seductive attractions of the courts of the Hellenistic rulers. However, it was a gift to critics throughout Caesar's career; even Suetonius is startled by the length of the list of references to it, which he was able to collect (*Iul.* 49). Every major opponent of Caesar – Licinius Calvus, the Elder Curio, C. Memmius, M. Brutus, and Cicero in both speeches and private correspondence – alludes to it. During the fierce exchanges between Caesar and his fellow consul, M. Bibulus in 59 BC, Bibulus referred to Caesar in his official edicts as "Queen of Bithynia." Clearly the accusation deeply irritated Caesar. In the cut and thrust of debate in the senate he could laugh it off with a joke of his own devising (Suet. *Iul.* 22.2).

Again, Caesar did not hide the fact that he was offended by the poems of Catullus that attacked his character in a similar way; but the reconciliation after an apology was not that difficult, given the fact that Caesar had been on close and friendly terms with the poet's father (Suet. *Iul.* 73) (see Steel, chapter 9, p. 118). The offending poem was certainly Catullus 57 (Suetonius describes it as "inflicting a lasting stain (*perpetua stigmata*) on Caesar's name," which picks up the references to "stains" (*maculae*) in the poem itself):

> They get on well together those wretched poofs (*cinaedi*), those effeminates, Mamurra and Caesar. No wonder. Equal stains, one from the city and one from Formiae, deeply permeate them both and will not be washed out. Diseased alike, these twin brothers, both on one sofa, dilettantes both, one as greedy in adultery as the other, partners and rivals in the pursuit of young girls. They get on well together those wretched poofs.

These are the same familiar attacks on Caesar's personal behavior. It was probably no accident that Catullus was a friend of Gaius Licinius Calvus, whose verses also offended Caesar. Such poems belong to the powerful tradition of literary lampooning, often in iambic verse (see Catullus 54: "my iambics"), which goes back particularly to Archilochus. It is often thought that such verses have no real political import. But the boundaries are not clear. Catullus 29, an attack on both Pompey and Caesar, is composed of phrases taken directly from the political debates of the time (Pompey and Caesar are said to have "ruined everything" (*perdidistis omnia*) – the exact phrase used in a contemporary letter of Cicero (*Att.* 2.21.1)) (Minyard 1971: 176–8). Equally Bibulus' attacks on Caesar in his consular declarations could be described by Cicero as "Archilochean" (*Archilochea edicta*). Catullus' personal abuse of Caesar was in a broad sense "political" and hence was taken seriously by Caesar.

That the personal attacks hit home is shown late in his life with Caesar's petulant response to the chants of his own troops at his Gallic triumph ("Caesar conquered Gaul, Nicomedes conquered Caesar"). He went to the serious lengths of swearing an oath that the story of his liaison with Nicomedes was not true. However, as so many victims of tabloid journalism in more recent times have also found, the promptness of his response only fueled the suspicions further (Dio 43.20.4).

Caesar's alleged affairs with foreign queens share many of the suspicious features of the Nicomedes story. Bogud, king of Mauretania, provided troops for Caesar's campaigns in Spain and Africa. Caesar is supposed to have had an affair with his wife, Eunoe. But the evidence was simply the many lavish gifts which Caesar gave Bogud and Eunoe – hardly surprising in view of Bogud's aid to him (Suet. *Iul.* 52). In any case, the source of the story of an affair was M. Actorius Naso, author of at least one other anti-Caesarian tale (Suet. *Iul.* 9.3).

It is the act of a true spoilsport to seek to cast doubt on Caesar's affair with Cleopatra VII of Egypt; but it may need to be done. Like his sojourn with Nicomedes, Caesar's stay in Egypt of up to nine months between October 48 and the summer of 47 BC was seen as unusually long. There were lavish feasts. There was a royal progress up the Nile (Suet. *Iul.* 52). In short, there were all the sorts of thing which made the Greek East such a morally treacherous place in the eyes of some Romans, but which in reality were no more than the usual diplomatic exchanges between Roman leaders and Hellenistic rulers. Caesar had to deal with a complex and fraught situation, once he had taken the decision to back Cleopatra's claim to the throne of Egypt. That took time to sort out. Back in Rome, people, such as Cicero (*Att.* 11.18.1, 11.25.2), were anxious to know of Caesar's movements and when he would be likely to be back in Rome. Then some time later Cleopatra herself arrives in Rome with her husband. This event must surely be associated with Caesar's celebration of his triumphs in September and October 46 BC. The purpose of the visit was to provide luster for Caesar's celebrations and it was also diplomatic. Cleopatra and her husband were declared "friends and allies of the Roman people" (Dio 43.27.3). Suspicious minds pointed out these honors and the lavish gifts which accompanied them (Suet. *Iul.* 52). There was also the fact that a gold statue of Cleopatra was placed in the Temple of Venus in Julius Caesar's new forum (Dio 51.22.3). However, this was only one of a range of paintings, statues, and *objets d'art* which were placed within the temple. The true purpose of the collection is revealed by the fact that one of the dedications by Caesar was a corselet made up of small British pearls with an inscription which made clear where the pearls had come from (Pliny *HN.* 9.116). The collection, or at least some of it, was designed to be a reminder of Caesar's achievement. So the statue was not the curious dedication of a besotted lover, but a reminder of Caesar's accomplishments and of his association with the great monarchs of the Hellenistic East.

For some, then as now, the proof of the liaison was the young boy, Ptolemy Caesar, called by the Alexandrians "Caesarion," who Cleopatra and others claimed was Caesar's son. However, nothing is heard of this child until after Caesar's murder. The likelihood is that he was not even born until after the Ides. Plutarch (*Caes.* 49) ends his account of Caesar's stay in Egypt in 47 BC with: "a little later she had a son by him whom the Alexandrians call Caesarion." However, in his life of Antony (*Ant.* 54.3) he states that the boy "was thought to be the son of Caesar who had left Cleopatra pregnant," possibly implying that the child was born after Caesar's death. The first definite mention of the child is in a letter of Cicero (*Att.* 14.20.2) of May 11, 44 BC, where he briefly remarks, "I hope it is true about the queen and that Caesar of hers too." In 43 BC the boy appears in an inscription as "Ptolemy Caesar" (*OGIS* 194.1). The existence of a natural child of Caesar was a serious threat to Octavian and a gift to his opponents. So the truth, even if recoverable, soon disappeared in a flood of propaganda from both sides. While Antony was prepared to claim in the senate that Caesar's close friends knew the child was his, C. Oppius, one of those friends and supporters, produced a work to refute the case (Suet. *Iul.* 50.2).

Never-ending gossip (*constans opinio*) added an impressive list of the wives of close associates within the elite to Caesar's conquests (Suet. *Iul.* 50): Postumia, wife of the legal expert Servius Sulpicius Rufus; Lollia, wife of Pompey's close political supporter Aulus Gabinius; Crassus' wife Tertulla; and one of Pompey's wives, Mucia. The main "evidence" in the case of Mucia, for instance, was the fact that Pompey divorced her. Yet Pompey never gave a reason in public for his action and it was left to one of the usual suspects, the Elder Curio, again to exploit the gossip in an attempt to split Pompey from Caesar in 59 BC. The most notorious of these alleged liaisons was supposed to have been with Servilia, mother of Marcus Brutus, which raised the possibility that the assassin of Caesar was in fact his son. This in turn added savor to the stories of Caesar's last words to Brutus ("And the same to you, son!"; Suet. *Iul.* 82.2) and that Brutus' own blow was aimed at Caesar's groin (Plut. *Caes.* 66.6). But again the evidence for the liaison consists of a costly gift from Caesar to Servilia, a salacious witticism of Cicero, a mysterious exchange between Caesar and Cato in the debate on the fate of the Catilinarians on December 5, 63 BC, and suspicions that Caesar went out of his way to save Brutus' life at Pharsalus (Suet. *Iul.* 50.2; Macrob. *Sat.* 2.2.5, Plut. *Brut.* 5; App. *B Civ.* 2.112). If, as seems likely, Brutus was born in 85 BC, the paternity of Caesar seems deeply improbable (Cic. *Brut.* 324; see also Syme 1980b).

In all this there is a strong inclination to suggest that there is no smoke without fire. This attitude is precisely what the debased popular press of our own era thrives upon. It becomes the historian at least to emphasize the fragility of the evidence and the way that evidence was embedded within the political rhetoric of the period.

Extravagance, Expenditure, and Connoisseurship

Caesar shared with his contemporaries a desire to own works of art, particularly Greek works. Every rich Roman had villas of increasing lavishness in this period. There was intense competition among the wealthy. But alongside that there was increasing complaint at the escalating costs associated with connoisseurship, which often took the form of a critical, moralizing lament about a decline in values, the expenses of public life, and the dangers of debt. This is the background against which to set reports that Caesar spent 80 talents on two paintings by Timomachus, that he was an enthusiastic collector of antique gems, carvings, statues, and pictures, that he had immediately torn down the villa at Nemi which he had had built, because it did not meet his exacting specifications (Pliny *HN.* 7.126; Suet. *Caes.* 46, 47). In all this Caesar was unexceptional in the Late Republic.

Character

There is no reason to doubt Caesar's personal bravery, or his ability to command the respect of both officers and men in his service and to lead troops in battle. It is true that passages such as Plutarch *Caes.* 15–18 and Suetonius *Iul.* 57–70 are derived almost certainly from favorable sources, such as G. Oppius (Townend 1987), and to a great extent they conform, as do the *Commentaries*, to the presentation of Caesar as the standard model general. But there is enough incidental detail to back up the claims. His bravery and willingness to lead from the front in the most hazardous of circumstances were shown by the early award of the *corona civica* (Suet. *Iul.* 2), and by the battle on the Sambre against the Nervii, where at a critical point Caesar seized a shield and pushed himself into the front line, cheering his men on (Caes. *BG* 2.25). (Compare also later in the Africa campaign his seizing of a fleeing standard bearer and turning him round with the words, "The enemy is over there!" (Plut. *Caes.* 52).) His presence inspired sometimes foolhardy acts of daring in others (Plut. *Caes.* 16).

Pliny (*HN.* 7.91) praises Caesar's remarkable vigor and swiftness of thought. Suetonius (*Iul.* 60) notes Caesar's ability to think on the move and to react instantaneously to changing circumstances, and his readiness to commit forces to take advantage of any opportunity without long planning. There can be no doubt about Caesar's restless energy. He was a serious multi-tasker. Pliny notes that he could read, write, and dictate simultaneously – not just that, he could dictate four letters at once to his secretaries! (Pliny's source was certainly C. Oppius again (Plut. *Caes.* 17.4).) This outdid the achievement of the orator Servius Sulpicius Galba, who in preparing a case used to dictate to two secretaries turn and turn about (Cic. *Brut.* 87). He frequently dictated on the move, invariably having a secretary seated next to him in his carriage, or sometimes he dictated on horseback (Plut. *Caes.* 17.3). All public figures in Rome relied on dictation to secretaries, but Caesar's practice was exceptional (Horsfall 1995). Even back in Rome, Caesar used to communicate with colleagues by notes, because he had no time to see them personally (Plut. *Caes.* 17.4). At the shows Caesar used to sit in his box reading and answering letters and petitions; but this led to abuse from the crowd who felt he should be joining in their enjoyment of the spectacle. It was a public relations mistake, which Augustus was subsequently careful to avoid (Suet. *Aug.* 45). At the dinner party on the last night of his life, he reclined at table signing letters while the conversation flowed around him (Plut. *Caes.* 63.4). All this required the prodigious memory for which he was famed. "I know what a memory that man has," remarked Cicero to a correspondent (*Fam.* 13.29.6), and, appearing in a case before Caesar, he used that reputation to flattering effect: "Your usual practice is to forget nothing except slights" (*Lig.* 35).

Caesar was charismatic, charming, and witty. Plutarch (*Caes.* 4) remarks on his *bonhomie* and cheerful character. This is confirmed by the way Caesar spiced up his formal correspondence with Cicero. In Gaul Caesar must have been inundated with tiresome formal letters of commendation which recommended young men for his staff. Cicero (*Fam.* 7.5.2) quotes Caesar's response to one of his requests, "You have recommended the son of M. Curtius to me. I will make him king of Gaul, or, if you like, dispatch him to Quintus Lepta. Send me someone else I can honor." Cicero replied by recommending Trebatius, a young lawyer. Back came another witty and affable thank-you note (*persalse et humaniter*): "Just what I need. Among the vast number of people out here there is no one who is competent to draw up a bail-bond (*vadimonium*)" (Cic. *Q Fr.* 2.14.3).

There was, inevitably, a hard side to Caesar. Cicero records the visit at the beginning of the civil war of the younger Curio, who told Cicero frankly that Caesar was out for Pompey's blood and that "it was not by desire or nature that Caesar was not cruel but because he thought clemency was a popular policy. If he lost popularity, then he would be cruel" (*Att.* 10.4.8). The crucified pirates and a million dead Gauls testified to Caesar's toughness.

Caesar faced the possibility of death on numerous occasions throughout his life. At the dinner party given by M. Lepidus for Caesar on the night before he was murdered, a philosophical topic would be proposed for discussion after dinner. Someone (it would be fascinating to know who) proposed the subject of death and Caesar was asked what sort of death he would prefer. "An unexpected one," was his response

(Plut. *Caes.* 63.4). What it seems he hoped to avoid was the slow lingering death from old age which he had read about in Xenophon's *Cyropaedia* (Suet. *Caes.* 87). Fear of debilitating disease was considered a possible justification of suicide (Pliny *Ep.* 1.12). But there may also have been the recognition that great men frequently met violent ends. Alexander the Great, Demosthenes, Pompey, Cicero, and Caesar himself made up the list which a later emperor, Alexander Severus, cited in explaining his happiness at hearing a prophecy that he would meet a violent end (SHA *Alex. Sev.* 62). Alexander Severus was also showing that he set death at naught (*contempsisse … mortem*), which was in line with a tradition which went back to Plato's *Phaedo* and was endorsed in various ways by Cynics, Stoics, and Epicureans.

There are bound to be many different Caesars. Perhaps every generation has to create its own. We can at least seek to attempt to rescue him from the fog of innuendo, distortion, and salacious gossip which enveloped him in his own day.

FURTHER READING

Of the many biographies of Julius Caesar, A. Goldsworthy, *Caesar: The Life of a Colossus* (London, 2006) gives the greatest attention to issues of Caesar's personality and behavior, although he belongs to the "no smoke without fire" camp. On the various assessments of Caesar's public standing see Z. Yavetz, *Julius Caesar and his Public Image* (London, 1983). On the background of the moral debate in Rome see C. Edwards, *The Politics of Immorality in Ancient Rome* (Cambridge, 1993), and on issues of Caesar's sexual behavior the excellent study by C. A. Williams, *Roman Homosexuality: Ideologies of Masculinity in Classical Antiquity* (Oxford, 1999). For the exploitation of character in rhetoric and the evidence used by orators for character see J. May, *Trials of Character: The Eloquence of Ciceronian Ethos* (Chapel Hill, NC, 1988), A. Riggsby, "The Rhetoric of Character in the Roman Courts" in J. Powell, and J. Paterson, eds., *Cicero the Advocate* (Oxford, 2004), pp. 165–85, and C. Craig, "Audience Expectations, Invective, and Proof" in the same volume, pp. 187–213. On Caesar's representation on statues and coins see J. M. C. Toynbee, "Portraits of Julius Caesar," *Greece and Rome*, 2nd ser., 4.1, 1957, 2–9. On issues of Roman male dress see J. L. Sebesta and L. Bonfante, eds., *The World of Roman Costume* (Madison, WI, 1994).

CHAPTER ELEVEN

Caesar as an Intellectual

Elaine Fantham

Let me begin by questioning this title. Does it make sense to speak of anyone in the ancient world as "an intellectual" rather than talk about his intellectual achievements? And should we distinguish between the activities of an intellectual and a scholar? The normal connotation of an intellectual is surely someone who discusses the relationship between ideas and systems (in, say, ethics or politics), like a Greek philosopher or a modern French *savant,* product of a highly theoreticized education.

Late-republican society recognized this kind of achievement in Greek culture but discouraged its imitation both overtly and more indirectly. For the Roman elite, being an intellectual was not a career option. Both duty and ambition directed the sons of senatorial families to political or military careers which would leave no time for serious pursuit of academic disciplines. After a schooling in *grammatike* (language and the interpretation of the Greek and later the Roman poets) and rhetoric, some more privileged young men might spend a year or so studying ethics or political philosophy, but most would press on to nominal military service or advocacy in the courts and candidacy for one of the 20 junior magistracies. Scholarship that focused on recovering national institutions was an acceptable diversion, but most Romans had little time and few resources for study. Apart from leisured discussions at their villas when senate and lawcourts were on vacation, few members of the elite would have time to research or write until their late forties, when they would usually give preference to personal memoirs or an apologetic version of recent history.

There were of course a host of other disciplines: medicine, architecture, mathematics and geometry (surveying), music, and "natural philosophy," including cosmology and astronomy, but such technical disciplines were practiced by Greeks, freeborn or even enslaved, and so shunned as illiberal by most elite Romans. When Cicero incorporates other intellectual activities into his record of the development of oratory at Rome, allusions to interests other than Roman history, law, and cultural history are limited to Pompey's uncle, Sextus Pompeius, who was devoted to geometry (*Brut.* 175): compare the exceptional interest of Sulpicius Gallus in astronomy (*de Re P.* 1.21–2). Even literary studies are represented by the equestrian (i.e. non-senatorial) Aelius Stilo and his son-in-law Ser. Clodius (*Brut.* 205–6; Suet. *Gram.* 3; on their scholarship, "needed to facilitate the intellectual advance of the late Republic," see Goldberg 2005: 60–2, 84–5), or by Latins like the brothers Soranus (*Brut.* 169).

Cicero himself, Rome's most prolific intellectual, might not have turned to adapting Greek philosophy and theology, if he had not been shut out of politics, first by the junta of Crassus, Pompey, and Caesar from 56–51, then under the domination of Caesar. But there was one major Roman scholar still living (and so excluded from discussion when Cicero wrote *Brutus*), a man some 16 years older than Caesar. It may be a useful index of the limits of intellectual life in the later Roman republic if we take this man, Terentius Varro, and compare his scholarly interests and achievements with those of the leading Greek intellectual Posidonius, who was born some 20 years before Varro and seems to have lived into the late 50s BC. Posidonius, educated in the Stoic tradition, came to the republic of Rhodes from Apamea in Asia Minor, and held high office, both as Prytanis and as envoy from Rhodes to Rome. Posidonius composed over 50 volumes of history, continuing from where Polybius left off just before the Gracchan crisis – history, that is, of the eastern Mediterranean world, including the prolonged wars between Rome and Mithridates; he also wrote on cultural anthropology (the development of early civilization) and moral duties, and composed works of travel and natural geography. Posidonius became the friend of Pompey (who even attended at least one lecture) and more casually of Cicero.

As it happens, Caesar spent some time as a young man studying in Rhodes, without, as far as we know, showing any interest in Posidonius' lectures; we will turn in a moment to the actual purpose of his visit, but first we should acknowledge that there is no evidence that the young Caesar took any interest in philosophy.

Now contrast the career and researches of Varro. Varro had a successful public career as far as the praetorship (in 73) and won distinction and a naval crown as one of Pompey's admirals in his pirate command. By then he was approaching 50, and for over 30 years would devote himself to scholarship – antiquarian research into the details of Roman cultural history: distinguishing the authentic plays of Plautus and recording public performances of Roman drama, researching and classifying Roman religious and secular institutions (his *Antiquitates Rerum Humanarum et Divinarum*), and composing a largely etymological study of the Latin language (six books survive), some imaginative verse satires and prose dialogues (*Logistorici*), and in old age three books of agriculture. All these works aimed to (re)construct Roman culture so as to provide a patriotic record matching the claims of Greek civilization – but what is preserved does not suggest that Varro went beyond recording and classifying, except perhaps in his approach to theology.

Caesar, as we said, does not seem to have given much attention to philosophy. He is sometimes called an Epicurean, but this is chiefly because his skeptical approach to the gods and the afterlife coincided with the Epicurean denial that the gods concerned themselves with human prayers or behavior, and with the materialist conviction that there was no life after death. This was convenient for his argument in the Catilinarian debate (discussed below), but we find him actually referring twice to the immortal gods in the first book of the Gallic War, again where it was rhetorically convenient; first to point out to his readers that whether by chance or divine planning, he had caught and defeated the Tigurini, the very clan of the Helvetii which had once inflicted defeat on the Roman commander Cassius, and secondly to warn the Helvetian envoys that the gods often gave short-term successes to those whom they wished to ruin so as to make their downfall more painful. We might add that although Caesar was a pontifex (priest of the state cult) from an early age, and Pontifex Maximus for almost 20 years, there is no evidence that he actually believed in the state gods or was personally committed to their worship. Divine power was an illusion, and Caesar was above all a pragmatist: gossip reported that he used to quote the tyrant Eteocles from Euripides' *Phoenissae*, to the effect that power was the only thing important enough to warrant behaving unjustly.

And yet, Elizabeth Rawson, in the fullest and most encyclopedic treatment of intellectual life at Rome in Caesar's own time, has constant occasion to connect Caesar with Greek intellectuals and educational activities, and rounds off the first part of her study with a vignette of Caesar's cultural interests, including literary and linguistic studies, rhetoric, ethnography, meteorology, and chronography (Rawson 1985: 109–14). Shortly before his death, when Caesar visited Cicero's Campanian villa for a quiet dinner, Cicero would report to Atticus that their conversation had been surprisingly easy, with no serious (that is, political) matters but many literary topics (*spoudaion ouden, philologa multa*, *Att.* 13.52). Caesar's intellectual interests were determined by his practical concerns, whether in government or in the effective use of language.

Caesar's Education

Let us start with what is known of his education. Elite boys of his generation were tutored at home, at best by serious Greek teachers, many of whom came to Rome from Asia Minor or Athens either voluntarily or as captives in Sulla's Eastern campaigns. They would be taught first the reading of literature, above all Homeric epic but also perhaps the early Latin epic poets, and simple exercises in basic composition, such as telling a fable in their own words. Around puberty the subject matter and methods would change, although they did not necessarily change instructor from a *Grammaticus* to a *Rhetor*, and they would begin to study rhetoric for the lawcourts, learning the precepts of Greek manuals (or manuals adapted from Greek models, such as the anonymous *Rhetoric* composed for Herennius in the mid-80s when Caesar was a teenager), and exercising by arguing imaginary cases. Pleading in the lawcourts was an adult activity expected of most young men, even those from outside the city of Rome, or families of middle rank. Only the more privileged would have occasion to take part in political debate and make a name by deliberative rhetoric. So we might fairly compare education in rhetoric for an advocate's career with the modern all-purpose MBA. This was a practical training, which would focus on particulars rather than issues of principle.

What we know of Caesar is that he studied at home with M. Antonius Gnipho, a man of mysterious origin, but undoubted learning. Gnipho had been born free in Gaul and reared as a fosterchild; without having been a slave he nonetheless earned his Latin name Antonius by manumission, presumably from a M. Antonius, who had him educated, perhaps even briefly at Alexandria, the center of Greek learning and grammatical studies (Suet. *Gramm.* 7; Kaster 1995). Could this have been the orator Antonius, consul of 99 BC, who was murdered in the Marian terror of 88? One of his sons, the father of the triumvir Mark Antony, married a Julia, suggesting connections between the families. Gnipho was not just a good teacher of grammar: he was equally learned in the study of both Greek and Latin language and literature and his rhetorical teaching was sophisticated enough for Cicero, even as an experienced speaker and senior magistrate, to frequent Gnipho's home for coaching in 66 BC. Soon after this Gnipho died, aged 50. But Caesar did not forget his linguistic principles, as we shall see.

Caesar also shared with Cicero some later years of study with the Rhodian teacher of rhetoric, Apollonius Molon, whom they had met when he came to Rome as his city's ambassador once or perhaps twice during the 80s. It was not usual for the sons of elite families to continue their education after reaching the age of military service, but the political conflicts in the decade after 88 BC interfered with the free function of the courts and may even have made it unsafe for Caesar, and for the less prominent young Cicero, to stay in Rome. As it was, both young men tried their fortunes in the courts before breaking off to leave Rome on a study tour. Cicero successfully defended Roscius of America in 80 against two dishonest kinsmen, backed by Sulla's rich freedman Chrysogonus, but left soon after for two years as a student, first in Athens then in mainland Asia Minor, where Molon had grown up, and finally with Molon himself in Rhodes (Cic. *Brut.* 305, 307). Suetonius (*Iul.* 4) tells us that Caesar too left for Asia to study with Molon after appearing in a couple of cases in 77–76. Molon taught Cicero a more disciplined style and the voice control to go with it. Caesar seems always to have disciplined his own style. Its hallmarks, as all critics agree, were vigor (*vis*) and pared-down, fastidious use of language – *purus sermo, castissimus sermo, elegantia*.

The slogan of pure speech forms another strange link between Caesar and Cicero; according to Suetonius, both Caesar and Cicero composed an epigram on the poet Terence, praising him for his pure diction but regretting his lack of comic energy. Was this perhaps a competitive exercise assigned by Gnipho to his pupils? The two men were pupils some years apart; but it is difficult to imagine them producing such epigrams as adults at a symposium, especially Caesar:

Tu quoque, tu in summis, O dimidiate Menander
Poneris, et merito, puri sermonis amator.
Lenibus atque utinam scriptis adiuncta foret vis,
Comica ut aequato virtus polleret honore.

But there is still dispute over the syntax of lines 3–4; do we understand *vis comica* with enjambement, and *virtus* alone as the subject of *polleret*, or simply *vis*, treating *virtus comica* as the subject of *polleret*? I believe the enjambed *vis comica* offers the better sense: "You too, my half-Menander, are counted among the best, and rightly, as a lover of pure speech. If only comic vitality were added to your gentle writings, so that your excellence would wield its power with due honor."

Caesar as an Orator

Caesar's first appearance in the courts when he was in his 23rd year left a strong and lasting impression of his quality, but, for a figure dominant in politics, the record of evidence for and quotations from his speeches is scanty and somewhat unusual. The Roman public man might expect to plead many cases in court and make other, shorter, speeches either to express his opinion in the senate or, as a magistrate, to explain legislation and persuade the informal assembly (*contio*) to vote in its support. As a commander he would also have to motivate his soldiers with a rousing speech before battles. Roman public life offered little occasion for ceremonial oratory, but Caesar attracted special attention precisely because he extended the practice of uttering a public eulogy at a close kinsman's funeral to the funerals of women; he did so twice during his quaestorship in 69; first for his aunt, the widow of the now discredited Marius, and in the same year for his wife Cornelia. His aunt's eulogy he turned into an occasion to celebrate his family's noble origin, and Suetonius seems to have preserved his own words:

> Amitae meae Iuliae maternum genus ab regibus ortum, paternum cum dis immortalibus coniunctum est. nam ab Anco Marcio sunt Marcii Reges, quo nomine fuit mater, a Venere Iulii, cuius gentis familia est nostra. Est ergo in genere et sanctitas regum, qui plurimum inter homines pollent, et caerimonia deorum, quorum ipsi in potestate sunt reges. (Suet. *Iul.* 6)
>
> My aunt Julia's family on her mother's side was descended from kings, and her father's family was linked with the immortal gods. For the Marcii Reges, her mother's family name, come from Ancus Martius, and the Iulii, the clan from which our family comes, descend from Venus. So in our clan there is both the holiness of kings, who have the most power among men, and the reverence due to the gods, in whose power kings themselves are held.

Caesar was not the originator of the family pride of the Iulii Caesares, which was already celebrated by L.Caesar's *Origin of the Roman Race* (*Origo Gentis Romanae* 15.4, 18.5), but, like many of his early actions, this shows him vindicating his family and declaring its association with Marius.

If we turn back to Caesar's first appearances in the courts, he does in some ways conform to the pattern reported by Cicero, in which only young men and outsiders prosecuted; once a careerist was launched with a junior magistracy he would shun the risks of feuds resulting from prosecution and appear only for the defense. First, then, Caesar prosecuted the ex-consul and triumphator of 81 Cn. Dolabella, for provincial extortion during his years governing Macedonia. Dolabella was defended by the two leading orators of the days, Cotta and Hortensius, and acquittals on such charges were becoming the norm as senatorial jurors imagined themselves in the defendant's shoes (Cicero would denounce the senatorial juries in the Verrines for their habitual acquittals), so it is not surprising that Dolabella was acquitted. Even so there was competition to prosecute this man, and we know Caesar had to plead his claim to prosecute against a rival; this preliminary *divinatio* and his two speeches from the two sessions *(actiones)* of the trial were still read and admired almost two centuries later in the time of Quintilian and Suetonius. If Velleius (2.43.3) calls the speech celebrated and speaks of popular favor, some of the glamor may have accrued in the years since Caesar's successor won the principate. But the surviving fragment (Gell. 4.16.8) suggests a popular appeal to envy by contrasting the stolen wealth of such magistrates with "the men of old in whose homes and shrines works of art were a source of both honour and beauty" (*isti, quorum in aedibus fanisque posita et honori erant et ornatu*).

Caesar's second prosecution, probably a private case, was directed against C. Antonius Hybrida, charging him with armed robbery from Greek provincials when a military prefect in Macedonia, and was aborted when Hybrida appealed to the tribunes for protection. One legacy from Caesar's first visit to Asia Minor and stay with King Nicomedes will have been his plea for the inheritance of Nicomedes' daughter, but this was probably only an intervention in the senate. Another was his defense speech for the Bithynians, which should probably be dated to 74 soon after his return from study with Molon. An excerpt shows the powerful simplicity of his appeal to duty and justice:

> Vel pro hospitio regis Nicomedis vel pro horum necessitate quorum res agitur, refugere hoc munus, M.Iunce, non potui. Nam neque hominum morte memoria deleri debet quin a proximis retineatur neque clientes sine summa infamia deseri possunt, quibus etiam a propinquis nostris opem ferre instituimus. (Gell. 5.13.6)
>
> I could not shun this duty, M. Iuncus, either as a return for King Nicomedes' hospitality or for my bond with these men, whose business is at issue. For neither should memory be obliterated from the hearts of close kin by human death nor can clients be abandoned without extreme disgrace, since we have made it our custom to bring them aid even against our own family.

We should note that prosecutions for provincial extortion were themselves, or could be represented as, generous acts in defense of clients and dependents, but it is characteristic of Caesar's fragmentary speeches and his own reports of speeches made to soldiers and envoys in Gaul that he stresses his obligations and justifies his actions by the wrongness of deserting or letting down a dependent community. He shows a similar concern with doing his public duty in a fragment from his speech supporting the Plautian law to restore the Lepidan exiles (Gell. 13.3.5). A last case from this period is Caesar's defense of Decius the Samnite, no longer read in Tacitus' youth (*Dial.* 21.6), made apparently on behalf of an Italian who had been proscribed by Sulla (*Clu.* 161); we can guess that Caesar was trying to have the man's property and/or civil rights restored.

What about Caesar's political speeches? By far the most famous is the one for which we have ostensibly the most evidence, but also strong reasons to doubt that evidence: this is Caesar's proposed amendment (in modern terms) to the motion for executing the Catilinarian conspirators in the senatorial debate of December 5, 63 BC. Caesar had seen this coming earlier in 63 and given a warning by his sponsorship of the show trial of old Rabirius for the supposed killing of Saturninus. This clearly indicated to the senate and consuls of the year that he would challenge the senate's right to declare an emergency and suspend the people's prerogative of trial on capital charges. Both the careful diplomacy of Cicero's report as presiding officer on Caesar's contribution to the debate on executing the conspirators (*Cat.* 4.7–8) and the uninhibited artistic re-creation by Sallust (*Cat.* 51) show that Caesar's speech included two main points: first the quasi-philosophical argument that death was not as severe a penalty for extreme guilt as imprisonment (and a guilty conscience); secondly and more significantly, the constitutional argument that this decision violated the Porcian laws against the flogging of citizens, giving them a right of appeal to the people against summary punishment, together with Gaius Gracchus's Sempronian law, prohibiting any form of trial not authorized by the people. He adds to this political statement the perhaps ironic warning that this would be a bad precedent, easily perverted by less scrupulous magistrates.

Some details, such as Caesar's invocation of Cato the Censor's speech advocating mercy to the Rhodians – a pointed allusion for his adversary the younger Cato – and his citation of the 30 Athenian tyrants and Sulla as tyrannical precedents for unauthorized slaughter, may well have been part of his speech; others, such as the false praise of his adversary's skilled eloquence (*composite loqui*), are probably Sallust's own embroidery. Cato too (*Cat.* 52.9), and Marius (Sall. *Jug.* 85.26, 31), implicitly question the sincerity of their adversaries by praising their professional techniques.

This was a time of great danger for Caesar, and he clearly made at least one speech to the people when he published a bill to initiate an inquiry into Catulus' handling of the restoration of the Capitol, at the beginning of his praetorship in January 62. But the Senate reacted with strong condemnation and he was forced to protect himself by obeying the senate's decree and withdrawing from his praetorian jurisdiction (*Iul.* 15–16). The fact is that, both in 62 and as consul in 59, Caesar must have spoken up for his desired legislation in the senate and at public meetings, but no specific occasions are recorded. The only evidence cited in Malcovati for speeches during his consulship refers to a defense of his Campanian land bill before he left for Gaul in 58 (*ORF*^{2} C. Julius Caesar no. 40, p. 394). It seems that he also brought the charges of illegality and violating the auspices made by Memmius and Domitius to the senate for formal discussion, but these charges failed for lack of support (Suet. *Iul.* 23).

Cicero makes Brutus declare in 46 BC that he had had no opportunity to hear Caesar speak, and it is likely that from 58 onwards Caesar was more often engaged in exhorting his forces; the *Gallic War* contains more than one commander's speech. It was routine to rally soldiers before battle (e.g. *BG* 2.21.2–3), but in *BG* 1.40 Caesar sets out in some detail the powerful speech with which he rallied and shamed his men when they were panicking before battle with the Helvetii. To the military council, including all his centurions, he declared that if they were afraid to follow him into battle he would go on with the Tenth Legion alone and this would be his praetorian cohort. Caesar clearly sees this as a more formal speech than usual, and continues his narrative with "when he had made this speech . . . ." Even in 49 he is known to have quelled a mutiny at Placentia by treating his soldiers as mere civilians, and two versions survived of speeches which he was supposed to have delivered to the soldiers in Africa. Again Suetonius quotes from one of these a more continuous excerpt that bears witness to his techniques.

> Scitote paucissimis his diebus regem adfuturum cum decem legionibus, equitum triginta, levis armaturae centum milibus, elephantis trecentis. Proinde desinant quidam quaerere ultra aut opinari, mihique, qui compertum habeo, credant, aut quidem vetustissima nave impositos quocumque vento in quascunque terras iubebo avehi. (Suet. *Iul.* 66.)
>
> Know that in the next few days the King will be here with ten legions, thirty thousand cavalry and a hundred thousand light infantry, as well as three hundred elephants. So let certain people stop asking questions and voicing views, and believe me, since I have the knowledge, or I shall order them to be loaded on a decrepit ship and carried by random winds to random quarters of the earth.

From 49 indeed Caesar's power was not openly challenged at Rome, and he will have contented himself with bare statements of his consent – to the senate, for example granting the restoration of Marcellus, and the pardoning of Ligarius, leaving to others such as Cicero the burden of devising an appropriate rhetoric.

Caesar's first consulship had taught him that political rhetoric wasted time that could be saved by the use of force, with the support of Pompey's veterans in that case, and this may have been why he turned to more productive uses of language, providing his own record of his Gallic campaigns and, in his leisure, entering the purely objective and dispassionate debate over the regularization of Latin *sermo*. Since the *commentarii* on the Gallic and Civil Wars are discussed in their own right by Kraus and Raaflaub, chapters 12 and 13 in this volume, I shall focus now on Caesar's views about language itself.

Caesar as a Theorist of Language

Although I said that the negative treatment of emotional political rhetoric by "Caesar" in Sallust's *Catiline* probably reflects Sallust's own attitude, it is highly likely that Caesar's own approach to oratory was anti-rhetorical. He was famed for his force (comparable to Demosthenes' celebrated shock and awe – *deinotes*). To obtain this forceful impact he avoided elaboration, using clarity and simplicity as tools in practice, and we can infer that he did so on principle. These two elements, combined with linguistic correctness and precision, were recommended by Theophrastus as prerequisites of formal eloquence, but they were also recognized as necessary to good *sermo*, that is informal talk.

Cicero, whose ideal of eloquence was *copia,* an abundance of rich and flowing speech, had discussed the criteria for successful rhetoric at length in his major treatise

De Oratore of 55 BC, and spoken in passing of correctness (*Latinitas* = Theophrastus' virtue of *Hellenismos*) and clarity as elementary virtues (*De Or.* 3 43). This may have been the provocation for the two-volume treatise on language composed by Caesar in his moments of leisure during the next years and dedicated to Cicero (Hendrickson 1906). Caesar's title *De Analogia* ("On analogical formation" or "consistency") needs some explaining. The critics and editors of Alexandria, such as Aristarchus, had elaborated a theory of language which built on the existing similarities of word derivation and inflexion in Greek to argue for adopting forms and inflexions of similar words according to predominant patterns. According to their theory we ought to say and write such forms (e.g. *mouses* by analogy with *houses*). The other predominant school of grammar, based on Pergamum, and introduced to Rome by the scholar Crates, argued that language depended on general usage, and on forms sanctioned by the authority of past and present writers. At Rome Caesar's teacher Gnipho was an "analogist." He is quoted by later critics as arguing that men should write *ebura* and *marmura* (not *ebora* and *marmora*) as plurals of *ebur* and *marmur*, and Caesar seems now to have argued for similar choices.

In his dedication of this treatise to Cicero, quoted proudly at *Brutus* 253, Caesar speaks in terms which Cicero received as a compliment.

> ac si ut cogitata praeclare eloqui possent, non nulli studio et usu elaboraverunt cuius te paene principem copiae atque inventorem bene de nomine ac dignitate populi Romani meritum esse existimare debemus; hunc facilem et cotidianum novisse sermonem num pro relicto est habendum? (Caesar *De Analogia fr.1 Funaioli*)
>
> If quite a few have toiled with devotion and expertise in order to utter their thoughts in a splendid form, an abundant eloquence of which you are virtual master and originator, so that we should honor you for having deserved so well of the reputation and prestige of the Roman people in giving Latin a rhetorical power to match or surpass the Greeks, does this mean we should leave aside the knowledge of this easy everyday language?

Copia is Cicero's ideal, but contrary to Caesar's own admiration for spare eloquence, and so implicit criticism; there is a further key to criticism in Caesar's last question. Should easy everyday speech be taken for granted as a skill already surpassed? (So Cicero had implied in *de Oratore* 3.38.) John Dugan's recent subtle analysis of the interaction between these two brilliant men has brought out the matching ambiguity of Cicero's praise of Caesar's Gallic *commentarii* ("for they are bare, straight and beautiful, (like statues) with all the adornments of eloquence stripped like garments," *nudi enim sunt, recti et venusti, omni ornatu orationis tamquam veste detracta*; *Brut.* 262; see Dugan 2005: 175–89). From Pliny's address to Cicero at *Natural History* 7.117 we have a further compliment by Caesar to Cicero which clearly comes from the same dedicatory context: he hails Cicero as "father of eloquence and Latin writing, and as much greater than the laurel of every triumph, as it is more important to have extended so far the boundaries of the Roman intellect than of the Roman empire" (*facundiae Latinarumque litterarum parens atque omnium triumphorum laurea maior, quanto plus est ingenii Romani terminos in tantum promovisse quam imperii*). This is not just a well-turned compliment; it is highly apposite to two recent works of Cicero: his dialogue *De oratore,* requiring a far wider range of intellectual training for the aspiring statesman, and his speech *De provinciis consularibus*, on the consular provinces to be assigned in 55, with its enthusiastic encomium for Caesar's expansion of the boundaries of Roman empire in Gaul from the Alps to the Ocean. And 16 centuries later J. J. Scaliger would use the same trope to praise the Julian calendar (see below) as "a victory in the realm of culture more lasting than any Roman victory on land or sea" (quoted by Feeney 2007: 193 and n.116).

But how was Caesar's praise of Cicero's rich language to be reconciled with the prescriptive attitude of the "analogists"? Caesar also said with equal emphasis in this proem that one should avoid an unfamiliar word as sailors shun a reef (Gell. 1.10.4), and it is clear from Caesar's own writings that he did avoid archaic or recondite vocabulary and even unusual case inflexions. Although we might expect any regularizing innovations to be lost from the manuscript tradition of the Gallic War *commentarii* which Caesar was engaged on at this time, Oldfather and Bloom (1927) investigated the manuscripts of the *Bellum Gallicum* for traces of such forms, and found no support for the idea that Caesar actually followed his own principles. (For example, Caesar recommended that one should write the dative of fourth declension nouns like *exercitus* in *–u*, not *ui,* and the genitive of fifth declension nouns like *dies* in *–e* not *–ei*, but Gellius (4.16.8, 9.14.25) notes only one or two rare examples in Caesar's writings. But it is fairly clear that there were very few word forms argued for by the theorists that had not been in actual use; even the most purist grammarians were in fact relying to some extent on the familiarity of past usage, in poets like Lucilius. According to another discussion reported by Gellius (6.9.15), both Caesar and Cicero actually used forms of reduplicated perfect constructed by analogy with the Greek perfect, writing *memordi, pepugi, spepondi.*

The inflexion of Greek names was another problem: this was not just a matter of using Greek or Latin case endings, but stem formation. Quintilian notes that Caesar recommended the Latinizing form *Calypsonem* as accusative of Calypso. But was this not perhaps under the influence of Rome's oldest schoolbook, the third-century *Odysseia* of Livius Andronicus, who wrote *apud nympham Atlantis filiam Calypsonem*? As in any language, poetry and poetic tags in common speech preserved or revived archaic forms, and could make purely invented forms acceptable. So when the whole topic was taken up and argued on both sides by Varro ten years later in the eighth and ninth books of *De Lingua Latina* (also dedicated to Cicero), Varro concluded that orators could not be expected to introduce regularization with analogical forms that went against the usage of the common people; only poets had that license, and it would be the task of poets to make new analogically formed words acceptable.

Any writer finds himself called upon to make decisions based on his own concept of what is correct and desirable in language. Even while recognizing that both casual speech and written texts of the younger generation increasingly resort to new turns of phrase the writer may judge them to be careless or crude. He has the option of reshaping his thought so as to avoid forms he does not approve of without inflicting obvious pedantries on his readers. While Oxford and Cambridge University Presses disagree on how to write the possessive form of Brutus (*Brutus'* or *Brutus's*?) we can usually substitute "of Brutus." This is, I think, how Caesar handled his own linguistic principles.

A more significant aspect of Caesar's language use in the *commentarii* is his preference for choosing and using one word from a group of synonyms, such as *flumen* rather than *fluvius* or *amnis* for "river", and sticking to it even at the cost of repetition. In his detailed study of Caesar's diction Eden (1962) suggests that Caesar began his work as a sort of logbook, indifferent to stylistic refinement. This is borne out by the monotonous reuse of certain adverbial phrases and legalistic repetitions of an antecedent noun in subordinate relative clauses.

Was Caesar's deliberate limitation of vocabulary intended to make his work easier for an ordinary Roman to understand when it was read or recited? Peter Wiseman has argued (in Powell and Welch 1998) that rather than composing his accounts as official dispatches to the Senate, Caesar wanted to write and circulate the reports of his achievements so that they would be accessible to people in the Roman street. This would also, perhaps, explain his constant concern to give the motives for his military initiatives, justifying what his enemies might represent as unwarranted aggression. It might also explain an increasing resort to imaginative reported speeches by Caesar's adversaries or by common soldiers, which climaxes in book 7. Most memorable, and rhetorically effective, are the speeches of self-sacrifice by the centurion Petronius (7.50), and the extraordinary advocacy of carrying resistance to Rome to the point of cannibalism (7.77.12) by Critognatus of the Arverni, an extremist not mentioned elsewhere. The *commentarii* had begun as records, but they were soon infused with Caesar's own command of rhetoric and loaded argument.

Ethnography

How interested was Caesar in ethnography? As Harmand (1973) showed in his discussion of Caesar's knowledge of Gaul and its peoples, the *commentarii* contain a wide range of such material: this can be broken down into eleven categories of which the military practices of the diverse tribes constitute 31%, their political life, such as the role played by noble leaders and their clients,14.5%; next come comments on their economy and technology, 9%, and then roughly equal concern with natural landscape (8.5%) and its use by the Gauls as habitat (8.5.%). Caesar could have used Posidonius' ethnographic study of southern Gaul, but this was probably limited to the regions accessible up the Rhone from Massilia; there are also a number of places where he seems to be writing not so much post-Posidonius as anti-Posidonius. There is a series of ethnographic excursuses, from *BG* 2.15–16 on the warlike lifestyle of the Nervii, to 3.22 on *soldurii,* to his account of the rotation of agricultural and military duties among the Suebi, and their reliance on hunting (4.1f), before we come to his major excursus (6.11–24) on the customs of the Gauls – including precious information on the training and privileges of the Druids – which he contrasts with those of the Germans, described in the following four chapters (6.25–8). Caesar makes it clear that he used both native spies and foreign merchants to obtain information, and distinguishes between tribes which welcomed merchants and those that excluded them. While the Suebi welcome merchants so that they can sell their spoils, he notes on other occasions that warlike tribes exclude merchants and prohibit import of wine (Nervii, Suebi). Alongside sharp observation on, for example, mixed use of (imported) coin and bullion as currency in Britain, because of the shortage of local metal ores, or the British taboo on eating hares, ducks, and geese, which they actually reared as pets (*BG* 5.12 *haec tamen alunt animi voluptatisque causa*), Caesar includes more hackneyed assumptions implying the limited judgment of barbarians: that the Gauls are eager for political change (*res novae*), easily deceived by lying informers, excitable primitive people precipitate to foment conflict, but lacking endurance or courage in the face of danger (3.8, 3.18.6, 19.6; 4.5).

Alongside the physical landscape of hills and rivers, lakes and woods, Caesar shows a real interest both in the outer Ocean, whose tides require ships with less draft and sturdier materials like tough oak and sails of skin, and in topics we might class under meteorology: the relationship of Ocean tides to the full moon (*BG* 4.29.1) and the equinox (4.36.2, 5.23.5), and the length of northern winter nights, according to "some writers" and his own unsuccessful inquiries. Indeed some scholars have commented on Caesar's concern to make enquiries; he went to Illyria because he wanted to visit those tribes too and know their habitats (*eas quoque nationes adire et regiones cognoscere volebat*, 3.7), but this seems to be pragmatic; in 4.20 he explains that he thought it would be most advantageous to him to visit the island of Britain and see for himself the nature of the inhabitants, getting to know the sites, harbors, and points of access, all of which were virtually unknown to the Gauls. He mentions as problems that the traders he had consulted did not know the size of the island, the number of tribes or their mode of warfare or customs, or even which harbors were suitable for accommodating a large fleet. These questions are clearly focused on prospective invasion and conquest.

This leads us to a more indirect tradition, concerning Caesar's curiosity about Egypt, most explicit in Lucan's imaginative account of Caesar's conversation at Cleopatra's banquet. Before reading this as a genuine reflection of Caesar's own intellectual interests we must make allowances both for the epic tradition itself, and for Lucan's delight in displaying his own erudition. Meeting the priest Acoreus, Caesar asks him about the origins of the Pharian race (Egyptians rather than Ptolemaic Macedonians), "the lie of the land and customs of the common people, the rituals and appearances of their gods, and the inscriptions on ancient shrines, since the gods wish to be made known" (*terrarumque situs vulgique edissere mores/ et ritus formasque deum quodcunque vetustis/ insculptum est adytis, profer, noscique volentes/ prode deos*, Lucan 10.178–81). In a reference that we shall follow up, Lucan's Caesar adds somewhat prematurely that even in the thick of battle he has always found leisure to contemplate the regions of the stars and heaven, and "my year will not be surpassed by the calendar of Eudoxus." Stressing his great love of the truth (*amor veri)* Lucan's Caesar declares that there is nothing he would rather discover (*noscere* again) than the causes of the great river that has so long kept hidden and its unknown source; if he could but see the sources of the Nile he would abandon civil war. Ironically, of course, both the poet Lucan and the author Caesar did break off their

"Civil War" narratives very soon after this point. Some of Lucan's portrait may be a fair representation. Surely if he had had the time, the author of the Gallic War would have wanted to write even more about the lands and peoples of Egypt and their customs than we have seen him reporting about the Gauls? But there was only minimal time. Caesar supposedly traveled up the Nile with the Queen, and certainly brought back from Egypt the refinements that enabled him to legislate an accurate solar calendar for Rome.

Caesar's Calendar

So we have come to the last and most lasting of Caesar's scientific achievements – his calendar. In a sense it was not his at all. He recognized the astronomical superiority of the Egyptian calendar, originally of twelve 30-day months plus five end-of-year days, to the confusing and by now retarded Roman calendar. This had followed a pattern of years 355 days long based on more or less accurate lunar months, brought into line with the sun by the priestly insertion every three years of an additional "intercalary" month of 22 days: this was inserted at the end of the religious calendar after the last feast day in February. But for some years now the college of pontiffs (of whom Caesar was the senior man, but absent in Gaul) had refused to insert the extra days from political motives, and the Roman calendar was now three months ahead of the real solar year. Caesar must have already experienced the frustrations of this situation and he brought the Egyptian astronomer Sosigenes to Rome to help him implement a new calendar – the calendar we still observe. This involved two steps: the calculation of the number of supplementary days needed to bring the calendar date into coincidence with the winter solstice, and the adjustment of the number of days in the year. First then he inserted an intercalary month after February 24, 46 BC, plus two intercalary months after the end of November, to make this a year of 445 days (Macr. *Sat.* 1.14.3). Starting in January 45, Caesar extended the year from 355 to 365 days by distributing ten extra days over seven of the old Roman months. Apart from February these seven months had been of either 29 or 30 days (see Feeney 2007: 152–3).

What Caesar did makes sound sense if we take into account respect for the old calendar, and, I would suggest, the desire to equalize the four seasons. The days he added to the old calendar were inserted after the last festival of the month, and so did not affect the old religious calendar. But by adding two days to the 29 days of January, August, and December, and one each to the 30 days of April, June, September, and November (and inserting a leap day every four years), Caesar achieved as nearly as possible a year of 365(+¼) days containing four equal seasons: January, February, and March make a winter of $31+28+31 = 90$ days (91 days in leap years), April to June a spring of $30+31+30 = 91$ days, July to September a summer of $31+31+30 = 92$ days, and October through December an autumn of $31 + 30 + 31 = 92$ days. This would also keep as close as possible to the orbit of the moon, which takes between 29 and 30 days to complete each cycle. And we must not forget leap year, with the extra day which Caesar intended to be added every four years to cover the six extra hours of the sun's orbit.

After Caesar's murder the leap day was mistakenly inserted every three years and had to be adjusted by his heir Augustus in AD 8. Cicero might joke that on January 5, 45 the constellation Lyre was rising "by Caesar's decree," but it did take a decree to impose the new calendar, and a good deal of scholarly explanation to relate it to the old Roman calendar and the expected risings and settings of constellations. Sosigenes, according to Pliny the Elder (*Nat. Hist.* 18.211), wrote three books of *Commentationes* to explain his calendar. But what was Caesar's *De astris* ("On the constellations")?

As Feeney shows, this work of Caesar's affected the way both Varro and Pliny the Elder indicated the significant days in their agricultural calendars (Varro *On Agriculture* 1; Pliny *Nat. Hist.* 18.211–end): Varro can now give stable calendar dates for his stars rising and setting, and Pliny quotes Caesar for a number of synchronizations between his astronomical data and the civil calendar. Starting at 18.234 he lists Caesarian synchronisms for December 30, for February 16 and 22, for the "deadly" Ides of March, for March 18, and for other days from the winter solstice to the coming of the warm south wind (*a bruma in favonium*), the first of Varro's eight divisions of the farmer's year. Caesar must have depended on the collaboration of Sosigenes, but Macrobius, more oddly, claims (*Sat.* 1.14.2) that Caesar had the support of a scribe, M. Flavius, "who brought the individual days written out to Caesar in such a way that their order could easily be found and once it was found the fixed system (*certus status*) would persist." I think we can make sense of this if we assume Sosigenes and Caesar harmonized the new months with the celestial calendar (which would have to be adjusted from the sky at Alexandria, quoted by Pliny at e.g. *Nat. Hist.* 18, 246, 270 to the sky at Rome). Then Flavius applied this to the civil calendar as modified by Caesar, providing celestial data for each civil day.

Where does Caesar come into this? Suetonius describes the calendar (*Iul.* 40) but does not include any volume on this topic in his list of Caesar's published works. Was it simply ascribed to Caesar because he had decreed the calendar? Scholars like Le Boeuffle (1972, in Le Bonniec's edition of *N.H.* 18) and Domenicucci (1990) rightly consider a middle possibility: that Caesar did not make all the calculations in the detailed calendar listing of the volume, but authorized its issue, and, I would suggest, composed the introduction in the form of his actual public decree; that is, *De astris* was in two parts: the preamble Caesar had composed for his decree, and its implementation in the form of a *parapegma*, or representation of the traditional calendar board with its movable wooden pegs, now in fact no longer needed, because the new calendar would ensure that constellations rose and set on the same day each succeeding year. It would be this latter part which Sosigenes and Flavius assembled for Caesar. If this is right, Caesar had actually carried his enthusiasm to the point of promulgating a work reconciling the civil and astronomical calendars.

One more general idea may emerge from the range of Caesar's investigations. According to Varro (*De Lingua Latina* 9.24, written for Cicero but in the time of Caesar's dictatorship), analogists justified their imposition of regularized forms on Latin nouns by analogy with the regularity of the tides and of the seasons. We know that Posidonius wrote about the tides of the Ocean, so that this topic was at the center of scientific theorizing when Caesar wrote his *Gallic Wars*. But rather than see Caesar's comments as a reaction for or against Posidonius, I would suggest that the three topics are linked in Varro's comment because they all reflect rudimentary systems, and that Caesar commented on these topics because he was naturally attracted to systematization. Most recently, Feeney (2007: 197) rightly diagnoses "the same Caesarian regularizing and ordering urge at work in the reform of the calendar as in his grammatical work on Analogy."

Epilogue

It is possible that Caesar embarked on a more ambitious attempt to extend and control knowledge not only of time but of place. There is plausible evidence (cited in the *cosmographia* attributed to Julius Honorius and the mysterious Pseudo-Aethicus: see Nicolet 1991: 95–8; Wiseman 1992) that Caesar had initiated a geographical investigation of the *oikoumene*, sending out four learned Greeks to explore and measure the four quarters of the civilized world a generation before a similar plan was implemented by Agrippa. It is most unlikely that Caesar's project was implemented as or when claimed by Honorius, but Wiseman is surely right to attribute it to a time earlier than Honorius' date of 44 BC and to link it with Caesar's designs in 54 BC for a new portico to enclose the voting Saepta (which became the new Saepta Iulia of the 20s BC, at a time when elections were increasingly pointless and ineffectual).

How many other achievements of Augustus and Agrippa were actually conceived and even begun by Caesar? At least two more intellectual projects are reported as among his intentions. We are told by Suetonius that Caesar had wanted to systematize the civil law, something which Cicero too saw was necessary, and which their contemporary Servius Sulpicius planned to take up: Caesar may well have encouraged Sulpicius, but Sulpicius died in 43, and this task would prove too complex for their generation. We might add that Caesar's plan to establish a public library collection and his offer of responsibility for this task to the polymath Varro could be seen as an attempt to put Roman literature "on the map," giving it status as a counterpart to Greek literature (see Goldberg 2005: 193–6) and constructing a canon in each representative category. In that respect it might not be unfair to say that Caesar as an intellectual was as conceptually sophisticated as he was pragmatic and scientific.

FURTHER READING

There are some difficulties in knowing what to recommend under the rubric of Caesar as an intellectual: clearly his intellectual interests included a number of areas – religion, historiography, ethnography, and political theory and ideology (such as his invention of the weapon of clemency) – discussed in other chapters of this companion. I took for my portion Caesar's knowledge and theories of grammar, his skill in public rhetoric, his interest in geography and natural phenomena, from rivers and tides to the supposedly geocentric astronomical calendar, as well as his perception of other societies. The following three monographs have an importance beyond Caesar.

E. D. Rawson's *Intellectual Life in the Late Roman Republic* (London/Baltimore, 1985) gives prominence to Caesar among Roman intellectuals and the Greeks whom they patronized, and discusses in its second part each of the nine disciplines recognized in Caesar's time (*grammatike* is divided between a chapter on grammar/language and another on the critical study of poetic texts). Claude Nicolet's *Space, Geography and Politics in the Early Roman Empire* (Ann Arbor, MI, 1991) is rooted in the age of Augustus but incorporates important insights into Caesar's interests and cultural achievements. Most recently Denis Feeney's *Caesar's Calendar: Ancient Time and the Beginnings of History* (Berkeley, CA, 2007) re-creates the historiographical and political background to Caesar's own achievement.

Apart from the excellent introduction to R. A. Kaster's edition of Suetonius *de grammaticis* (Oxford, 1995), I do not know of any recent scholarship on Caesar's grammatical interests. But I do warmly recommend Claude Moatti's *La Raison de Rome: Naissance de l'esprit critique à la fin de la république* (Paris, 1997; unfortunately not yet translated into English), which discusses his *de analogia*, and other cultural interests: Caesar is ubiquitous in her highly sophisticated analysis of intellectual development. In particular ch. 2, "L'Ouverture au monde; naissance de la curiosité," puts his geography and ethnography into context. *Caesar's Civil War* (Oxford, 2006) by William Batstone and Cynthia Damon is a fine complement to the papers collected by K. Welch and A. Powell, *Julius Caesar as Artful Reporter* (London/Swansea, 1998).

The following primary texts were used for this chapter: Caesar: *Commentarii De Bello Gallico I–VII*, Oxford Classical Texts 1900, and *Commentarii De Bello Civili I–III*, Oxford Classical Texts; *Rhetorical fragments* in E. Malcovati, *Oratorum Romanorum Fragmenta*; *Grammatical fragments* in Funaioli, *Fragmenta Grammaticorum Latinorum*;

Posidonius: *Posidonius*, ed. L. Edelstein and Ian Kidd, Cambridge 1977–98.

PART III

Caesar's Extant Writings

CHAPTER TWELVE

Bellum Gallicum

Christina S. Kraus

Caesar's seven-book history of the events in and around Gaul between 58 and 52 BC has variously proved a stumbling block for centuries of readers. They have been unable to agree on its intent, deeming it both propagandistic and innocent; on the nature of its dissemination, deeming it to have been distributed either year by year as a Roman magistrate's (necessarily) incomplete record of his deeds, or all at once, as a finished product designed to make a particular argument; or even on its authorship. Though by now long accepted as the work of Julius Caesar – it was not always so (V. Brown 1979: 113–16) – questions remain about the integrity of its composition and about its sources. There is not even agreement about the basic characteristics of its genre. Perhaps no other ancient work has provoked such radical disagreement. Safest, perhaps, to keep the *Bellum Gallicum* in the schoolroom, where the correctness of its Latin and its exciting fighting scenes can introduce young readers to the glamor and grit that was Rome on its frontiers. In this chapter, I propose to investigate some of these trouble spots, concentrating on (1) genre, narrative voice, and style; and (2) on the *BG*'s place in the traditions of ancient military narrative.

Form, Voice, and Style

The *BG* was read (or misread) within Caesar's lifetime as a work that might serve as the basis for more ornate histories (Cic. *Brut.* 262); the Dictator was scarcely cold before its temporal parameters were regarded as inadequate. The narrative was continued in an eighth book to what Caesar's lieutenant Hirtius regarded as the (other?) end of the Gallic war (see Cluett, chapter 14, p. 197). Its year-by-year narrative – each *volumen* corresponding to a consular year (cf. 1.6.4, 7.6.1) – invites comparison with annalistic historiography, while its style has suggested to some readers the dispatches sent to the Senate by generals in the field, especially at the close of a campaign. The mention of such letters at strategic endpoints in the text encourages such a comparison (2.35.4, 4.38.5, 7.90.8). Inconsistencies between books may suggest not only serial composition while on campaign – an attractive idea, given the picture that others give us of a Caesar capable of writing "as the weapons were flying" (Fron. *Parth.* 9; cf. Plut. *Caes.* 17.7) – but also serial dissemination, in the manner of such dispatches (Wiseman 1998). It has been argued, too, that the *BG* was composed and disseminated in installments (books 1–2, 3–6, and 7: Radin 1918). Yet there are also clear and cogent indications that Caesar shaped these seven *commentarii* as a unit, with a tangible narrative arc and a marked beginning, complex middle, and fully closural end. Unlike the *Bellum civile*, whose book divisions are unclear and whose narrative is plainly unfinished (see Raaflaub, chapter 13, p. 181), Caesar's books on the Gallic war, however they were written, were, I believe, finished off as a unitary narrative.

The Gallic *commentarii* were certainly available to readers by the time of the composition of Cicero's *Brutus* in 46 BC, and probably well before (Radin 1918: 283 n. 2). They provided Livy with a model for his battle descriptions (Walsh 1961: 203; Oakley 1997: I.138–9) and have continued to influence the terms and tone of military history to the present (Keegan 1991 [1976]: 62–78). No manuscript of the *BG* written earlier than the ninth century survives, though one branch has colophons naming late-antique readers or correctors (Winterbottom 1983: 35–6).[1] The original title remains uncertain.

Caesar's own *commentarii*, plus those of his continuators, amount to 14 *volumina*. They are the only surviving examples of the historiographical, or narrative, *commentarius.* In assessing the nature of the genre, therefore, scholars have traditionally turned to other types of *commentarius* (a convenient list is at Riggsby 2006: 134). It is now the *communis opinio* that these show us little of the kind of thing which we see in Caesar. Recently, however, a persuasive case has been made that the Caesarian *commentarius* is a "fairly typical" representative of a kind of writing, very variable in nature, that can broadly be described as "notes" with a simple, paratactic structure, and which might even have included direct speech as Caesar uses it, not to provide analysis – as speeches in history generally do – but as "epigrams that cap anecdotes of isolated examples of heroism or the like" (Riggsby 2006: 142; also 137–8 (parataxis), 140 (notes)). And if Riggsby is right to argue that there is no clear evidence that the Romans recognized subtypes of the *commentarius* form, then we have no real purchase on this form as a genre. This is itself an important piece of information, especially in a literary system in which generic expectations were an important constituent of meaning and interpretation. If the designation "*commentarius*" could accommodate anything from philosophical treatises to lists of rhetorical commonplaces to catalogues of stratagems, and perhaps even memoirs such as Sulla's, then each one must have in some way set its own rules. In the period in which Caesar was writing, generic experimentation was rife; his audience would have been teased, misled, surprised, and cajoled into accepting these texts as something that shared in, but also stretched the boundaries of, the *commentarius.* Whatever the case, Cicero's own coyness about the adornment in his own *commentarius* (*Att.* 2.1.1) shows that the pose that Cicero, Hirtius, and subsequent readers have attributed to Caesar, that he wrote these texts to provide others with a basis from which to write a fuller, more "literary" history, is just that, a pose – not unlike the "unaccustomed as I am to public speaking" gesture that Cicero (of all people!) makes at the beginning of the *Pro Archia* (see further Raaflaub, chapter 13, pp. 179–80).

The Caesarian *commentarii de bello Gallico* do suggest parallels with other types of military report. First, the "military communiqué," or the *litterae* that generals sent from the front. We have a few surviving examples of these in Cicero's letters from Cilicia (*Att.* 5.20, *Fam.* 15.4; Fraenkel 1956). The short, declarative sentences and piling up of ablatives absolute, in particular – parodied as an element of a military manner (e.g. Plaut. *Pers.* 753–4) – are favorite Caesarian devices that are sometimes linked to such a chancery or administrative style (Odelman 1972: 130–4). Related are generals' inscriptions, which liberally employ the *primus*- and *solus*-language appropriate to praise (the major ones are collected in Riggsby 2006: Appendix B). There are a number of lavish examples of these from the Republic; under the Principate, this language became an expected part of imperial discourse, as in the *Res Gestae*. Though Caesar pulls back from self-puffery, choosing instead the remarkable device of a distancing, third-person narration, he emphasizes the singularity of his achievements, minimizing the contributions of his officers but enhancing that of his army (Welch 1998). He thus combines the traditional habit in strategocentric military narrative of letting the singular subject represent the general and his troops (Keegan 1991 [1976]: 22, 24, 47) with a remarkable portrayal of the army as the strong arm of the Roman people, controlled and disciplined by the path-breaking ideal general. So 7.8.1–4:

> Having made these preparations ... he set out (*proficiscitur*) for the Helvii. Though the Cevennes ... blocked the way with very deep (*altissima*) snow at this, the hardest (*durissimo*) time of the year, still, by tossing aside the snow to a depth of six feet and thereby opening up the way, by means of the greatest labor on the part of the soldiers (***summo militum labore***) he arrived (*pervenit*) at Arvernian territory. They were caught unawares, for they believed that they were protected by the Cevennes as by a defensive wall, and at that time of year the passes had never been open even to a man on his own/ an extraordinary individual (*ac ne singulari quidem umquam homini*). He ordered (*imperat*) the cavalry to wander as widely as possible and to bring as much terror as possible to the enemy (*quam latissime* ***possint***, ***vagentur*** *et quam maximum hostibus terrorem* ***inferant***).

Though the soldiers take no direct initiative in this brief passage, they are present (boldface) as the counterpart in action to his orders. His is the forward movement (underscored) and the preparation before it; his too the epiphany. That, however, is neatly shared, as in Caesar's formulation the general is both the *singularis homo* and the one who surpasses even that alleged impossibility, by bringing his whole army with him over the mountain wall. The deadpan language will not keep readers from noting the double meaning of *singularis* ("one" or "one and only": *OLD s.v.* 2b/ 4b) and the *primus* motif in *ne ... umquam*, reinforced by the superlatives *durissimo* and *altissima*. Once over the mountain, the soldiers share in the panegyric motifs, bringing the most terror possible to the widest possible area (*quam latissime ... quam maximum*). As Marincola notes (1997: 212), Caesar "is surrounded by a sea of '*nostri*,'" a Roman convention that "fosters a sense not only of intimacy but also of common achievement."

In this polymorphously perverse text, the authorial voice is not the least puzzling aspect. Until the late first century BC, the writing of Roman history was overwhelmingly done by those who helped make it: Fabius Pictor, Cato, Piso Frugi, Sallust. And most of these writers of *res gestae* seem to have used the first person, of themselves, at some point or other in their narrative, to describe historical actions in which they were themselves participants. Certainly none of them (as far as we can tell from the extant remains) refers to himself in the third person (Marincola 1997: 193–7). Caesar, famously, is different.

The narrator does use the first-person pronoun. Those instances of "I" or "we" are confined with one exception (I do not think that 5.13.4 is analogous) to remarks in which he speaks explicitly as the writer of the text rather than as an actor in it, i.e. in cross-references or in antiquarian or ethnographical contexts. The single exception is telling (7.25):

> There was fighting everywhere ... and the enemy's hope of victory was continually renewed ... fresh troops constantly relieved the exhausted, and they believed that the whole salvation of Gaul lay in that one moment of time. There happened, as <u>we</u> watched, something which seemed historically memorable and which we did not think should be passed over (*accidit <u>inspectantibus nobis</u> quod dignum memoria visum praetereundum non <u>existimavimus</u>*). Before the town gate, opposite our tower, a Gaul who was throwing into the fire lumps of pitch and tallow ... was pierced by a dart in the right side and fell dead. Stepping across him as he lay there, one of the Gauls closest by performed the same task; when that second man was killed in the same way ... a third succeeded him, and a fourth the third, nor was that position abandoned by the defenders before ... the fighting ended.

It is possible that the watching "we" (underscored) may designate the Romans; but the immediately following evaluative "we," normally associated in this text with the narrator, suggests that here the narrator and the character-on-the-spot are, in fact, one – or at the least, are separated only by literary function. At this crisis point of the battle – a moment Tacitus might see as evocative of the good old days of Roman history (*Ann.* 4.32.1 "huge wars, sacks of cities, kings routed and captured") – the complementary processes of witnessing (*inspectantibus*), evaluating (*dignum*), and memorializing (*memoria*) are shown at work together. In letting his mask slip, the narrator gains authority for his own autopsy and heightens the emotional punch, in good rhetorical style.

This separation of "Caesar" the actor/character from the anonymous narrator (who is known, but not declared, to be Caesar) has been read in different ways. It has been seen as an indicator of "epistemic objectivity" (Riggsby 2006: 152; the author does not share the point of view or desires of the actor). Conversely, it has been understood as a device masking the text's partiality: the author does share these things with the actor but, by separating the two, reassures us – perhaps speciously – that the author is self-critical. Or, as a means of self-aggrandizement (akin to the "royal we" or "one"); and, finally, as a way to give the division between author and character a meta-literary function, inviting us to question the nature of the relationship between them (Kraus 2007). The *BG*'s affinity with triumphal inscriptions suggests that self-aggrandizement is an appropriate mode for this kind of record; but its affinity with historiography and antiquarian texts may incline us to see the separated narrator as marking a scholarly, rather more distanced perspective.

One of the more interesting ways in which readers try to compensate for the absence of an explicitly identified authorial voice is to provide the *BG* with the preface it seems to lack. One way of doing that is to find in the famous opening paragraph a preface *malgré soi*: so, for example, Rüpke (1992) has detected in it kinship with the prefaces of geographical *commentarii*. That further helps the genre question, by suggesting a programmatic affiliation with an externally attested type of writing. A second option, illustrated here (figure 12.1) from an entry-level reader, tries to provide the work with the larger context it "must have had" in the historical author's mind.

This edition of *BG* 1–29 opens with Caesar wondering how he will replenish his coffers. Gaul, he knows, is wealthy – but he does not know enough about it, so summons a native informant to tell him about the land of projected conquest. The imagined scenario is worth considering not only for its comic aspects. By putting the first sentences of *BG* 1 into a Druid's mouth, the editor authenticates the

Figure 12.1 *BG* 1.1.1. From *Caesaris Bellum Helveticum*, ed. K.-H. Graf von Rothenburg with illustrations by Walter Schmid (Lincolnwood, IL, 1996). Reproduced with permission of the McGraw-Hill Companies.

geographical and ethnographical expertise put so prominently on show as we open the first *commentarius*. The map completes the illusion, but also suggests the growing Roman habit of thinking with maps as the empire expands. Caesar's standard-shaped map pin solves the problem of his purpose in Gaul (see Ramsey, chapter 4, and Rosenstein, chapter 7 in this volume) and establishes him as the chief actor in this story. This has the added benefit of collapsing Caesar and "Caesar," effectively defusing the third-person problem. In a single page, the editor has naturalized – and deproblematized – this text, which then proceeds as a "typical" narrative of conquest.

When Caesarian scholars turn to his language and use of literary devices, preoccupations with genre continue. Stimulated by the suggestions of Hirtius and Cicero that these *commentarii* had all the ornament they needed, scholars have scrutinized their diction and *figurae*, discovering elements that seem to belong more to the kind of elaborated and explicitly rhetoricized narrative written by Livy or Tacitus. And there are many such elements to be found: in Caesar's hands, stylistic nudity is indeed a costume.

Though scholars have identified a distinct trend from Book 1 to Book 7 toward increasing deployment and variety of literary *ornatus*, the style of the *BG* is neither neatly plottable nor uniform. To various extents one finds throughout the seven books traits more usually associated with full-scale historiography. Among them is (1) speech, both direct and indirect, including pre-battle *hortationes*; *oratio obliqua* predominates, with *oratio recta* first occurring in Book 4. There are many (2) spectacular scenes of single combat and the *urbs capta*, together with a pronounced emphasis on fear and pity in the battle narratives; and several (3) ethnographical digressions (see Fantham, chapter 11, pp. 151–3). Other elements found in many forms of "high" historiographical narrative include (4) intertextuality. This is much understudied in Caesar, but there are prominent quotations at least from Thucydides (1.1.1 ~ Thuc. 3.92.2, Lowell Edmunds *per litteras*) and Lucretius (5.33.2 ~ *DRN* 1.43, Németh 1984). The very decision to write a seven-book third-person narrative about adventures in a foreign land must be to some extent itself an intertextual gesture, aligning Caesar's text with Xenophon's *Anabasis* and even, by extension, with Xenophon's continuation of Thucydides, the *Hellenika*. Caesar's own implicit invitation to be continued must be considered as a possible Xenophontic turn, as well (for Xenophon and Caesar see Lendon 1999: e.g. 295; Costantini 1993). Also found is (5) bilingual word play (e.g. 7.17.3 "the slender weakness of the Boioi," a Celtic word connected in antiquity with *bos*; cf. Horsfall on Verg. *Aen.* 7.740 *maliferae*). We see (6) strong structural markers such as ring composition (Torrigian 1998: 56–9) and (7) the deployment of declamatory topics, most notably in the speech of Critognatus, with which one can compare Quint. *Decl. Maior* 12, on cannibalism. Finally there is (8) the "simple" style, the art of choice and clarity: Caesar's famous *elegantia* (Hirt. *BG* 8 *Praef.* 4). It may appear to be an absence of adornment, but it is as carefully crafted as any Asiatic effusion (Cairns 1979: 5–6, 28, 34), and was recognized as such, both in the contemporary battles over appropriate language – in which Caesar was an active participant (Fantham, chapter 11, pp. 148–151) – and in laudatory evaluations of Caesar's own style (e.g. Hirt. *BG* 8 *Praef.* 6 *emendate*). As a historiographical idiom, Caesar's language and style make a complex point about the value and use of decorum, and about the relationship of language to the events it describes.

War Narratives

> What emerged ... was a myth – not because it was false necessarily but because it located an ... event within routine structures of understanding.
>
> (Biel 1996: 24)

There are many possible approaches to the *BG* as a piece of military narrative. I concentrate here on Caesar's mythmaking: the ways in which he accommodates unfamiliar, unique experience in a distant land to patterns of speech and thought already understood and accepted by a Roman audience. Such an organization of experience into familiar, schematized categories of description and explanation does not necessarily imply that a narrative is fictionalized. It is relatively clear that Caesar did not systematically alter or propagandize events; especially where it can be confirmed by archaeology (e.g. Alesia: Le Gall 1999), the hard core of his narrative – topographical details aside – seems reliable. Nor do I intend, by this approach, to understand Caesar's narrative technique as a means of tendentiously deforming events (as does Rambaud 1966), or even as a way of simplifying the strange for an audience who would have little idea about the geography of Gallia (Pelling 1981). Instead, I want to explore how Caesar's decision to reduce the potentially infinite confusion and multiplied engagements of war to a few highlighted episodes harnesses a pre-existing grammar of military narrative to create a coherent, plausible literary representation of experience. In battle narratives, in particular, this grammar and its rhetoric are "not merely a machine to convert experience into words, but the very armature upon which that experience is organized and made sense of" (Lendon 1999: 274).

Hostes, milites, cives

Conventional military narrative divides its focus between the enemy and us, even when (e.g. in civil war narratives), in Pogo's words, "he is us." Caesar had a rich tradition of Gallic ethnography available: though our best attestations of it come from later texts, the stereotype of the fierce, loud, but ultimately unenduring Gaul can be glimpsed in the fragments of Cato the Elder and Posidonius, both of whom almost certainly served as sources for Caesar (Fantham, chapter 11, p. 151). He, in turn, combined autopsy – often filtered through the tall tales of soldiers (Aili 1995; Horsfall 1999) – with literary ethnography in creating his picture of the enemy. Remarkably, however (and despite the potential for creating fear and loathing in his readers), Caesar did not pull out all the stops in creating either his Gauls or his Germans. The opposition is factious, to be sure: this is one of the typical characteristics of barbarian nations, especially of the Gauls. It is emphasized in the *BG* by the ironic repetition of the phrase *omni Gallia pacata* (and variants), a universalizing, closural statement that never in fact seems to stay closed, thanks to the endless splitting of Gallic resistance into new combinations. There is, in fact, no "Gaul in its entirety", much less a pacified one: the opening of *BG* 1 already encodes division, both of the people and of their description, as Caesar's interwoven *Gallia omnis* and *est divisa* iconically demonstrates the impossibility of unification. Though the Gauls themselves deploy the *omnis/tota Gallia* rhetoric, notably when flattering the Romans (1.30.1), it is abundantly clear from the complexity of the various conflicts contained even in the brief *BG* 1 – the struggle with Orgetorix, the consequent *bellum Helvetiorum*, and the ensuing conflict with Ariovistus the German – that any hope of "ruling all Gaul" (*totius Galliae imperio potiri* 1.2.2) is as much a mirage for the Romans as it is for Orgetorix, Vercingetorix, and other chieftains. But it is also the force that drives the story: each unification leads to a further fragmentation of Gallia, which in turn requires further Roman intervention.

The seemingly endless tension between a unified Gaul and its component parts, then, becomes both a structuring and a thematic device. In other areas, too, Caesar avoids the unmotivated use of barbarian stereotypes. His northerners are not boastful, excessively ornamented, or comically oversized; the Germans at 1.39.1, "with huge-sized bodies," also have "unbelievable courage (*virtus*)." Though the Gauls give their famous war-cry (5.37.3, 7.80.4), it is not made part of their formal ethnographic description; and both Gallic and Germanic leaders speak with near-Roman clarity and political savvy. What is more, on several occasions the enemy almost bests Caesar, who finds his army in tearful panic at the thought of the Germans (1.39), nearly routed by the Nervii (2.18–27), close to ignominious retreat from Britain (5.8–17), massacred in the forests (5.27–37), and, finally, trounced at Gergovia and surrounded at the climactic siege of Alesia (7.36–51, 81–8). Far from being all savage show and no reliable power, like the huge Gallic Goliath to Manlius' tough little David (Claud. Quadr. 10b Peter), Caesar's Gauls are a match even for his toughened soldiers. Most significantly, Caesar "refuses numerous self-created opportunities to draw a sharp distinction between Roman self and alien other" (Riggsby 2006: 126). Mingling criticism of Roman self with praise of the alien other, the *BG* blurs any easy categorization, suggesting that in this imperialistic text, the way is already open for assimilation of the Gallic nation to the Roman state (and Caesar would soon extend citizen status to Gallia Cisalpina).

When it comes to "us" (*nos* and *nostri*) in ancient military narrative, the higher up the pecking order, the more text-time one gets. So the general, *ipse*, is the subject of most of the third-person verbs, acting representatively for the whole community of soldiers. Legates and – especially in Caesar – centurions are named, and occasionally given snippets of speech or writing; the Tenth Legion, Caesar's most trusted (1.42.5), is once or twice allowed a voice, even to make a joke (1.42.6); the mass of soldiers, unindividuated, supplies the big picture action (e.g. 2.27.1 "our men ... renewed the battle"; 3.6.2 "the Romans drove the terrified remainder into flight") and crowd noises (1.39.4 "hidden away in their tents ... they bemoaned their fate; 5.32.1 "from the nighttime brouhaha the enemy perceived their departure").

Though this literary arrangement misrepresents the very restricted perceptions available to any given actor in the mêlée of war and distorts the relative importance on the field of these various groups, it economically maintains a close, heroizing focus on the "best of the Romans." This in turn fits the Roman conception of significant historical action as exemplary deeds done by men who are *spectatissimi*, both "most visible" and "most viewed."

If the Gauls are presented as fickle and mobile, the Romans in *BG* are ordered and – even more important – capable of being restored to order if need be. Individuals are clearly separated into wrong (Sabinus, the over-trusting legate who leads his troops into disaster in Book 5; Welch 1998: 95–6) and right (Labienus, a tactful treatment throughout), easily frightened (Considius, despite his experience, at 1.21–2) and brave (only centurions and junior officers; Welch 1998: 89). The degree of Caesar's literary shaping can be judged not only by his schematization of character but by his selectivity in narrating events: he presents with concision a limited number of type scenes (e.g., battles, council scenes, river crossings, sieges: see further below) in which individuals are singled out only rarely.

Because he restricts the number of his building blocks, Caesar can make textual links correspondingly more clear by emphasis and careful deployment. Selectively elaborated scenes not only draw attention to themselves but respond one to the other across books, constructing a large-scale architecture and inviting readerly comparison and judgment (both *desiderata* of history: Cic. *De or.* 2.63). Roman actors play an important role in this elaboration. So, for instance, two good centurions fight an exemplary double combat against long odds, saving each other's lives in the process (5.44). They are put in counterpoise with two disobedient centurions – one of whom manages to compensate for the foolishness of both, again, by saving Roman *milites* with his life (7.50). Pullo and Vorenus (Book 5) serve as contrast and as model for Fabius and Petronius, in a complex structure that challenges our first impression of these scenes as episodic, self-contained vignettes.

The last Roman character in the *BG* is the *populus Romanus* (see also Cluett, chapter 14, pp. 202, 204), effectively the group whose preconceptions and expectations serve as the ideal receivers of this text. Caesar orients us to the campaigns in Gaul via a mention of what the Gauls are called in "our" language, and contrasts the far-off Belgae with the *cultus atque humanitas* of the Provincia (~ modern Provence; cf. 1.1.3 with 1.2.4, the Helvetii divided from *provincia nostra*). Linguistic, geographic, and cultural differences are established (Schadee 2008b: 159–60). Those distinctions between Romans and barbarians begin to blur, however, when Gallic "friends of the Roman people" are introduced (1.3.4). Caesar is playing a complicated game involving physical, mental, and cultural distance. These foreigners have a past with Rome, a past that has the effect of collapsing the differences between them. Henceforth, numerous possible configurations arise: hostile Gauls and Germans may be *amici populi Romani* (cf. Ariovistus at 1.43.4); allied Gauls may (and do) revolt. And indeed, the future for most of these Gauls – those who are not massacred, that is – is to become part of Rome, even, eventually, Roman citizens (Riggsby 2006: 126–32; see also above, p. 166).

Negotiating these complexities is "Caesar" as the representative of the Roman people, a relationship neatly set up in the *BG*'s first narrated conflict. Bracketing his initial encounter with the Helvetii, Caesar evokes the memory of earlier strife between this nation and the Romans. At the start he refuses their petition: "because he remembered (*memoria tenebat*) that the consul L. Cassius had been killed and his army sent under the yoke by the Helvetii, he did not think he should yield" (1.7.4). That *memoria*, we will learn, is not only Caesar's, but also belongs to *patres nostri*; conversely, the avenging of Cassius' death and his army's humiliation is not only a public act but one that punishes Caesar's private injuries (1.12.3–7):

> Caesar killed a great portion of them; the rest fled and hid in the nearest forests. This ***pagus*** is called **Tigurinus**; for the whole **Helvetian state** is divided into four ***pagi***. This one ***pagus***, after leaving its homeland, <u>in the memory of our fathers (*patrum nostrorum memoria*) had **killed** the consul L. **Cassius** and sent his army under the yoke</u>. Thus, whether by chance or the plan of the immortal gods, *the part* of the **Helvetian state** *that* had inflicted a famous disaster on the Roman people was the first to pay the penalty. And in this matter Caesar avenged *not only* public wrongs, *but also* his private ones, since the **Tigurini** had **killed** his father-in-law L. **Piso's** grandfather, the legate L. **Piso**, *in the same battle with* **Cassius**.

The underscored sentence makes an explicit ring with Caesar's own *memoria* of this same event (1.7.4, quoted above), marking the episode off as a textual unity with strong links to a past event. The post-battle wrap-up, normally devoted to casualty figures (e.g. 1.53.2–4, 7.28.5), here instead reverts to the past: the significant Roman dead are those killed, not in 58 BC, but in 107, Piso's grandfather and the consul Cassius. The repetitions punctuating the paragraph (boldface), the prominent use of correlatives (italics), the precision of Piso's naming, the double evocation of historical precedent, and an extremely rare mention of the gods (Fantham, chapter 11, pp. 142–3) highlight this firm statement of Caesar's right to act for the Roman people, whose historically validated interests work in tandem with his own. Named multiple times in every book, but most often by far in *BG* 1, the *populus Romanus* is the backdrop against which this action is played. Rome, too, is the end to which it all tends. So we read at 7.90.8 (the last sentence): "when the events of his year became known *at Rome*, a 20-day thanksgiving was decreed in return."

The generals

Caesar gave his cognomen to two millennia of autocrats; his personal image may be unique in its projection of solitary genius. But his self-presentation in the *BG* is of a commander who works within the system. I have discussed his use of the third person and his relationship with his troops above; this section will consider other aspects of Caesar the character ("Caesar").

Perhaps the first thing to notice about "Caesar" is that he is not the first person we meet in the *BG*. That honor is reserved for Orgetorix, whose story (1.2.1–4.4) serves as a prequel not only for the narrative as a whole but most particularly for Vercingetorix, Caesar's most formidable enemy, whom we will not meet until the last *commentarius* (cf. the ring structure 1.7.1 ~ 7.6.1). "Caesar" responds (1.7.1). He enters the narrative not in the nominative but in the dative case, in answer to a request for help against encroaching enemies. That sets a pattern for his behavior throughout most of the story, and has presented his contemporaries (and later scholars) with the nice question of how much his war-making in Gallia – and beyond – was a response to real threats, and how much was imperialistic in intent from the start (Ramsey, chapter 4, and Rosenstein, chapter 7 in this volume). As it progresses, the *BG* spins an ever-growing web of *pax Romana*: defense of an ally creates new territory taken from the enemy; that territory is in turn threatened – and the *imperium* goes on. In this sense, the message sent by the *BG* is fully in step with expected Roman performance. "The central aspect of Roman strategy was image," especially the inspiring of deterrent fear and the real possibility of vengeance, and the maintenance of dignity (*laus*) and effectiveness (*utilitas*) (Mattern 1999: 81–122, quotation from 122).

Being responsive to the needs of allies makes "Caesar" a good proconsul; winning battles against frightening foes and being able to speak persuasively to allies, soldiers, and enemy leaders alike show that he is good both at fighting and at speaking, the two primary virtues of a hero since the *Iliad*. The carefully constructed opening books bring "Caesar" gradually into the thick of things in a crescendo of action that puts all his virtues on show (see especially Schadee 2008b: 161–5). First to face him, the Helvetii are presented in the initial geo-ethnography as "outdoing the rest of the Gauls in *virtus*" because they fight almost daily battles with the Germans. Their story, from Orgetorix to the decisive battle at the Arar, is a microcosm of the narrative to come. Once they have been defeated – first in part (1.12–13), then in whole (1.24–9) – the Romans encounter the Germans themselves, rumors of whom terrify even the most experienced soldiers (1.39.1). At the beginning of *BG* 2, the next foes "Caesar" meets are the Belgae, introduced as *fortissimi* of all the Gauls because farthest from the Provincia (1.1.3). Thus the text in quick succession pits "Caesar" against the strongest of all the northern barbarians. On the way, he negotiates (1.7, 2.4–5), unmasks conspiracy (1.17–20), calms and exhorts his troops (1.40), and faces off rhetorically with the Helvetii (1.13–14) and with the fearsome Ariovistus (43–5). This testing in words and deeds establishes "Caesar" as exemplary in both *virtus* and responsive intelligence.

Both of those qualities are fully in evidence as "Caesar" moves to the natural extremities of *Gallia*, where lie huge rivers and mysterious seas. Topography plays various roles in this text. To begin with, in a way familiar from Herodotus on, its description, especially its names, validates the historian's authority, using "the linear progression of troops criss-crossing the landscape to map out a geographic space whose ... purpose is to convince us of the narrative's ... accuracy" (Cobley 1993: 45). Space itself can be presented as a synthetic vision of the whole of a region, as in the opening paragraph ("geographic space"), as a network of lines along which "Caesar" and the army move – the course of a march ("strategic space") – and, in the setting for a battle alongside a mountain, marsh, or forest, as a precisely represented, three-dimensional space with boundaries and relief ("tactical space": Rambaud 1974). Each kind of space presents particular difficulties, all of which are met by "Caesar's" forethought; here, as in every area of the *BG*, "Roman rationality prevails" (Hall 1998: 22).

This is an understated text: no Alps to break down with Herculean efforts, no quicksand-like mud to drown men in, no epic-scale storms to grapple with. Each of these motifs features in surviving Roman historiography; my examples come from, respectively, Livy 21.34–7, Tac. *Ann.* 1.63–5, and ibid. 2.23–4. Though each performs a complex variety of functions, at bottom is, perhaps, their important role in affirming the grand style of historical narrative and characterizing its participants accordingly. Ever expedient, Caesar prefers to sketch in the possibility of such scenes. Lists of towns and tribes suggest epic catalogue (e.g. 7.4.6), but precise terrain, and the troop movements thereon, are extensively simplified (Pelling 1981). Mountains, forest swamps, and bodies of water are natural defensive boundaries that articulate and enhance the topography of Caesarian battle and march; they also become backdrops against which to display the bravery, strength, and endurance of general and men alike. The Cevennes mountains provide a chance to surprise the enemy with a heroic show of speed (p. 161 above); marshes (*paludes*) repeatedly threaten deployment and lives (e.g. 7.19); deep forests threaten winter camps (5); the crossing of a vast river astounds the local inhabitants (1.13.1–2); and the expedition to Britain founders after a storm that destroys the boats, leaving the Romans exposed on the beaches were it not for Caesarian ingenuity (5.10.2). Above all, the deeds done here and the *virtus* demonstrated are remembered by this text; Caesarian written space "takes on a memorial function" (Lendon 1999: 315).

Throughout this Gallic space, we see "Caesar" in the distance and in close-up, as it were (for the cinematic metaphor, see Lendon 1999: 317). His speed, strategic knowledge, and endurance show him to be an "ideal general." His praiseworthy skills are seen also in vignette: energy, military knowledge, and competence in his famous gerundive-laden administrative *aristeia* at the battle *ad Sabim* (2.20); care for his soldiers in his several speeches before and after battles (especially 5.52); management of his troops' emotions (especially fear: Lendon 1999); strategic ability in his deployment of troops and, most eventfully, of himself ("Caesar" in color: 7.88.1). One key attribute of the ideal general is his ability to awe by merely appearing on the scene; the intensity of "Caesar's" presence is demonstrated even in his absence, when Labienus can conjure him up *in absentia* to act as judge and as exhortation to the soldiers fighting on the Seine (7.62.2).

But a key element of Caesar's self-presentation in the *BG* is that he is not, in fact, alone. Two other leaders share his stage: the German Ariovistus (*BG* 1) and the Arvernian Vercingetorix (*BG* 7). We see less of Ariovistus; but his big meeting with "Caesar" is instrumental both in introducing Caesar's use of significant landscape and in giving voice to barbarian *libertas* (Griffin 2008). It seems as if the colloquy will be evenly balanced between the Roman and the German commanders: they meet in a central space equidistant from each camp and from their escorts, who are themselves matched in number and rank – though "Caesar" has to provide his infantry with cavalry props in order to maintain the balance (1.42.4–6). Despite this preparation, however, their speeches are not balanced: Ariovistus' is by far the longer ("Caesar" is summarized: 1.45) and the arguments he makes are precisely those, one imagines, that Caesar himself would make were he in the same position. Ariovistus, then, can match, even outdo, "Caesar" in speaking (Christ 1974); unfortunately, despite the advance billing, he and his Germans are not a match for the Romans in fighting. His escape, in a little boat (1.53.3 *navicula*), has an element of the miraculous about it, presaging Jugurtha's solo escape from the killing fields at Sall. *BJ* 101.9. It miniaturizes this great German, whose death Caesar ignores: his unnarrated demise is, by 5.29.3, a past matter of "great grief" to the Germans alone.

Vercingetorix has a more elaborated history. He is, indeed, the best-defined of all the Gallo-Germanic characters, "the most Caesarian of all Caesar's antagonists" (Adcock 1956: 54). Unlike Ariovistus, he is definitely a military match for "Caesar" – a match that is brought out spatially in the first half of *BG* 7, as the two generals track each other along first the Loire, then the Allier (for the campaigns see Wiseman 1994: 408–12). He has "Caesar's" ability to speak persuasively (7.4, 7.20), and his speed (7.4.6, 29.5, 64.1), and is nearly his equal in commanding loyalty (7.30.1). He receives similar narrative treatment, as well: the wide sweep and the close-up vignette, especially with his army (7.20–21.1). Among other things, this parallelism with "Caesar" establishes the climax of the narrative, with the worst opponent positioned, and elaborated, last: in a familiar move, Caesar raises the enemy to the level of the Romans, enhancing his victory. That victory, like those in 57 and 55, was celebrated with a thanksgiving of unprecedented length (cf. 2.35.4, the last words of the book: *quod ante id tempus accidit nulli*). It effectively caps Caesar's portrayal of this war as one that, above all, brought the Roman people where no Roman had gone before.

The work of war

Ancient military narrative, both poetry and prose, had well-established conventions of image (the gleam of weapons, the piles of corpses), character (the loyal sidekick, the gifted opponent), and scene (the flight of frightened rustics, the *cohortatio*, noncombatants on the walls). Caesar's narratives repeatedly appeal, through their privileging of information gathered through first-hand knowledge, to the autoptic authority of the historian/commentator (cf. 1.22.4, a scout "had reported as seen something he had not seen"). Yet, as is well known, Caesar describes with a wealth of circumstantial detail events he did not see (e.g. the battles in *BG* 5) and those he could not possibly have seen (e.g. the council inside Alesia in 7). It is easy to posit – though this still does not account for the precision of detail – that in those cases he was working from notes given him by his legates, or from information garnered later (cf. *BC* 3.57). Recent analyses, however, show that, like his portrayal of character (above), his often precise descriptions of military activities are shaped also by the literary conventions of war narrative, which tends toward type scenes. Since these are drawn from Roman readers' narrative experience, Caesar can vary his treatment of a given type without significantly compromising the narrative's impact. He can prune a march plus attack, for example, down to a single sentence: so 4.4.6 "having finished this whole march with the cavalry in a single night they overwhelmed the Menapii." Or, he can give it a more leisurely treatment (5.28, the march to the Thames and defeat of Cassivellaunus), even a full-blown narrative with speeches, as he does at 7.57–62, describing Labienus' march to and battle near the Seine. Again, the literary technique tends to distort the real action on the field; but it serves the wider purpose of presenting that confusion in patterns which allow readers to understand and interpret the represented experience. In what follows I briefly consider the siege and capture of cities, the pitched battle, and the engineering *opus*.

The *urbs capta* is familiar both from epic and from rhetorical theory: it is one of Quintilian's primary examples of an embellished description that can make an orator's speech emotionally persuasive. His account claims, moreover, that even the single word *eversio* can summon up in imagination a picture of the details attendant in literary descriptions of the event. Like other narrative elements, sieges and city-captures in the *BG* run the gamut from a one-word mention (1.5.4) to a brief narrative (2.12.2) to a full-scale description, as in the sieges of Gergovia and Alesia.

Quintilian identifies a package of elements found in the typical *urbs capta* description, including flames running through homes and temples, the crash of falling buildings, a sound made up of many shouts, people embracing their loved ones, the wailing of women and children, looting and pillaging, bound prisoners, and mothers defending their children (8.1.68–9). At Gergovia, for example, Caesar includes the shouting (7.47.4), women and children begging for mercy (7.47.5), the plundering enemy (7.47.7), mothers holding their children (7.48.3). The narrative is not, ultimately, pathetic (because these are Gauls, not Romans?), but the *urbs capt(and)a* scene is unmistakable.

Once again, the literary convention need not mean that the description is fiction: sieges are formulaic by nature, and their descriptions will be so as well (Roth 2006). But that Caesar deploys such scenes for more than purposes either of "simply" recording what happened or of "propaganda" is manifest from his inclusion of not one but two sieges in which the Romans are effectively beaten: the Gallic massacre of Sabinus and Cotta in Book 5, and the Roman attack on Gergovia, an extensively narrated siege from which "Caesar" has to withdraw, being driven almost to defeat by his own troops' disobedience. Both are elaborated beyond what is even probable, and include details of the characters' feelings that would have been inaccessible to Caesar. And though one can read these stories in ways that show "Caesar" to advantage (e.g., Rambaud 1966: 220–1), he was under no obligation even to include them (Pelling 1981: 741–2). Literarily, however, these episodes build tension and suspense; show the Romans, as represented by their commanders and centurions, at their most stubborn and strong-willed; and contribute to the overall structure of the grand narrative's trajectory from victory to defeat and back to victory. All of these effects are economically illuminated by the delay that a siege necessarily introduces into a narrative. Further, the static setting of a besieged camp or town offers a place to stage significant events, from a *teichoskopia* to a fight before the gates, from the pathetic display of non-combatants to the *virtus* of Romans and enemy alike.

Pitched battles offer less chance for spatial concentration. The action can range over a potentially vast area, especially if one includes the pursuit of the routed, and can incorporate large spatial features, especially rivers and forests. That potential spread is typically played off against snapshots of individual action, such as a commander's *aristeia*. Despite its multiplicity of parts and capacity to cover terrain, however, a battle "must obey the dramatic unities of time, place, and action" (Keegan 1991 [1976]: 16). Caesar achieves this by wrapping a battle narrative around a central, "Homeric" hero – usually "Caesar" – who focuses the action and imposes control on it (R. D. Brown 1999: 339). He can exploit the dramatic device of a *peripeteia* (e.g. 1.52, 5.48); or he may track separate contingents until they turn and, by constituting a physical center of action, bring the narrative to a climax (e.g. 6.34–40).

The last element to discuss here is Caesar's war works: the descriptions of war engines, walls, camps, and bridges that punctuate the narrative. They are remarkable for their detail and frequency – no other Latin historian includes so many. The wealth and precision of detail in the descriptions has led many to try to reconstruct the objects. The bridge over the Rhine (4.17) has been the most popular, with simulations and actual reconstructions ongoing: I single out here the BBC program, "Secrets of the Ancients," which in November 1999 tried, and failed, to reproduce Caesar's feat. But attempts even to draw structures such as the tower at Massilia (*BC* 2.9) or the Gallic wall (7.23) have met with mixed results (Holmes 1911: 711–24, 746–8). One specialized study concludes: "there is substantial evidence that throughout the *Commentaries* the sections on engineering are not accurate and complete descriptions of the structures" (Dodington 1980: 5). As objects in the narrative, however, these *opera* serve a variety of functions. In one remarkable passage, describing the fieldworks at Alesia, Caesar employs bits of the *sermo castrensis*, explaining for his non-soldierly audience the names of his defensive structures (7.73). Like the occasional moments in Homer where we hear the language of the gods (e.g. *Il.* 14.291), these instances of "soldier talk" emphasize our separation from the world of the *BG* at the moment of connecting us closer to it. The other *opera*, too, offer tantalizing glimpses of physical objectivity that turn out, on closer inspection, to be less useful as mimetic descriptions than they at first appear. But they do a tremendous job of representing physically the superiority of the Romans. In addition, like centerpieces, their ecphrastic detail highlights the writer's *ars* (Scarola 1987). They raise questions of narrative and historiographical authority (Kraus 2007). Finally, like other triumphal narratives (cf. Plin. *Ep.* 8.4 on the *bellum Dacicum*), they offer future writers material for panegyric.

FURTHER READING

The best commentary on the whole of the *BG* remains Kraner, Dittenberger, and Meusel 1960; Holmes 1911 has extensive treatment of the war narratives and technical points. Hammond 1996 is an excellent translation with helpful introduction and notes. Recent work on the *BG*, especially in dissertations not yet published, has stretched the boundaries of Caesarian study, and deserves close attention: I single out here Jervis 2001, on the representation of barbarians, with Williams 2001 and Woolf 1998 on Romanization, Barlow 1998 on noble Gauls, and Krebs 2006 on the German ethnography; Erickson 2002 explores Caesar's creative use of ethnography. Melchior 2004 is a fine treatment of Caesar's battle descriptions and the representation of wounds; on his battles see especially R. D. Brown 1999 and 2004; for the ideal general see Woodman 1977: 284 (index) and Goldsworthy 1998; for Caesar's speed see Stadter 1993, and for his use of *exploratores* Ezov 1996. Finally, Nousek 2004 examines the *BG* as crafted literary response to Cicero's *De oratore*; see also the excellent, detailed treatments of aspects of Caesar's style and language in Spilman 1932, Eden 1962, Rasmussen 1963, Hall 1998, and Oldsjö 2001. Riggsby 2006 is the most thoughtful recent treatment on the nature of the narrative voice. Pelling 2006 (and elsewhere) discusses Caesar's boundary-leaping nature, Henderson 1996 his expedience, and Batstone and Damon 2006 his literary formation of character (concentrating on the *BC*, but relevant for both histories). Specialized treatments of dramatic structures (Rowe 1967), epic conventions (Miniconi 1951) and their role in historiography (Keitel 1987, Rossi 2003), the *urbs capta* (Paul 1982), and *sermo castrensis* (Mosci Sassi 1983) are helpful. On broader issues of genre see Barchiesi 2001 and, on historiography in particular, Marincola 2007; for the Roman concept of conquered space see Nicolet 1991; and for exemplarity in Roman thought see Chaplin 2000 and Roller 2004.

NOTE

1 Unsurprisingly, most of the preservation of the *BG* is owed to French copyists – a French interest in the history of Gaul that continues (V. Brown 1979: 106). For the reception of the *BG* in France, see Wyke 2007: 41–65, 261–3.

CHAPTER THIRTEEN

Bellum Civile

Kurt Raaflaub

The Civil War

The year 49 BC began in an atmosphere of massive popular agitation and fear of civil war. Caesar initially, in a letter read to the senate on January 1, repeated earlier demands, perhaps along the lines of a proposal made a month earlier by Curio, that both Pompey and Caesar should yield their provincial commands. But he then made major concessions, yielding provinces and legions with minimal exceptions (Illyricum and one legion) if only his privilege of running for consul *in absentia* were preserved. Although the senate leaders and Pompey, from his headquarters outside the city, pressured the senate to force Caesar by ultimatum to step down by a specific date, these negotiations, supported by Cicero, almost succeeded. Pompey was ready to agree, but apparently Cato and his closest friends refused. Threatened by senatorial rebuke and action, Antonius and Cassius, plebeian tribunes defending Caesar's cause, abandoned their veto, left Rome, and joined Caesar. As soon as he heard in Ravenna of the outcome, he ordered the one legion he had at his disposal to cross the Rubicon and invade Italy. The civil war had begun (Raaflaub 1974a: 56–79 and pt. 2; Ramsey, chapter 4 in this volume).

Caesar's own *Bellum civile* (*BC*) is our main source for the events of the ensuing war of 49/8, from the senate debates in early January 49 to Caesar's victory at Pharsalus in the summer of 48, Pompey's death by treachery in Egypt, and the very beginning of the Alexandrian War. The continuation of Caesar's wars, from Alexandria to Munda, is described in works that were clearly not produced by Caesar himself (Cluett, chapter 14 in this volume). Further information on the events of 49/8 (one of the best-documented periods in all of ancient history) is provided by Cicero's letters, written almost daily to Atticus and a host of friends and acquaintances, and the "Caesarian speeches" of 46/5 (esp. *Pro Marcello*, *Pro Ligario*). Among later historians, Appian and Cassius Dio offer the only completely preserved narratives. The biographies of Plutarch and Suetonius add much detail. Finally, even the Neronian poet Lucan's civil war epic *Pharsalia* and a smattering of later sources provide valuable information (Leigh, Pelling, Pitcher, and Barnes, chapters 17–20 in this volume). We are thus in an exceptionally good position both to complement Caesar's report and to evaluate its accuracy and tendentiousness.

The *BC* provides primary evidence for one of the most consequential events in world history; after all, this civil war led in an uninterrupted chain of events to Augustus' principate. Still, it has received much less attention in scholarship than the *Bellum Gallicum* (*BG*; Richter 1977: 166–8).

The *Bellum Civile*

The end of Hirtius' Book 8 of the *BG* (50–5; Kraus, chapter 12, p. 159) connects Caesar's Gallic campaigns with the civil war. It mentions actions on the part of his enemies in the years 51 and 50 that Caesar interpreted as deliberate provocations and injustices (*BC* 1.2.3, 9.4, 32.6). Although this "made it perfectly plain what was planned against Caesar, he nevertheless thought that he should put up with everything, so long as some hope remained of reaching a just settlement rather than resorting to war" (*BG* 8.55.2). With the word *contendit* ("he hurried" – to Ravenna?) the text breaks off. This ending, clearly incomplete, corresponds to the first sentence in the *BC* that mentions Caesar directly (1.5.5): when Antonius and Cassius fled from Rome, "he was at Ravenna, awaiting a reply to his very moderate demands and hoping that some human sense of justice might make a peaceful settlement possible."

The *BC* begins abruptly: "When Caesar's letter had been handed over to the consuls, the plebeian tribunes succeeded only with difficulty and the greatest efforts in ensuring that it was read in the senate" (1.1.1). Probably at least a minimal introduction (perhaps filling the first page of a codex or sharing one with the lost end of the *BG*) preceded, detailing the letter's content and naming Curio as its carrier (Carter 1991: 153–4; Raaflaub 1974b). Of the preserved beginning, the first six chapters, dense and emotional, paint a devastating picture of extremely partisan proceedings in the senate (1.1–3, 5–6), interrupted by a summary of the motives of Caesar's leading opponents (4, below). The pressure exerted by these, enhanced by Pompey's troops and intervention, deprives Caesar's supporters and the moderate majority of senators of any chance to be heard, let alone prevail. The climax is an emergency decree (*senatus consultum ultimum* [*scu*]), in Caesar's view unprecedented in its application and thus illegitimate, that forces the plebeian tribunes, Antonius and Cassius, to abandon their cause (5), which in turn enables the senate, meeting outside the city in the presence of Pompey, to make the necessary arrangements for the now inevitable war (6).

As soon as news from Rome arrives, Caesar addresses his soldiers (1.7, below). Assured of their support, he leads his legion to Ariminum (the first town in Italy) where he meets the tribunes (8.1) and two other persons with a private message from Pompey. Through these messengers, Caesar conveys to Pompey peace proposals which ultimately fail to resolve the conflict (8.2–11). He begins his rapid march through central Italy (11.4–13), prompting Pompey and the senate leadership to evacuate Rome (14). Caesar's progress (15–16) is stopped at Corfinium, which his archenemy Domitius Ahenobarbus defends, against Pompey's explicit orders. A mutiny among Domitius' soldiers causes the town's capitulation; proving prevailing fears wrong, Caesar lets the captured senators and equestrians go and incorporates the soldiers into his own army (17–23). Pompey withdraws to Brundisium (24.1–3) and sends half his army across the Adriatic, hotly pursued by Caesar who makes another effort to establish contact and restart peace negotiations (24.4–25.3). Despite Caesar's fierce efforts to block the harbor, Pompey succeeds at the last possible moment in evacuating the rest of his army (24.4–28). Of the 21 chapters covering the Italian campaign, more than four are thus devoted to peace efforts, more than five to Pompeian retreats and flights, and almost twelve to the military highlights, the sieges of Corfinium and Brundisium.

Lacking ships to pursue Pompey, Caesar orders the occupation of Sardinia and Sicily (1.29–31), returns to Rome, a futile meeting with the remaining senators, and a highly charged confrontation with a tribune who tries to prevent his access to state funds (32–3), and immediately departs to Spain to eliminate strong Pompeian forces posted there. Initially detained by the resistance of Massilia (34–6), he leaves behind a force to besiege the city and conducts a rapid, dramatic, and brilliant campaign around Ilerda. Despite major obstacles and natural disasters, he forces the Pompeian troops to submit without a major battle (37–55, 59–87) and again treats them with exemplary clemency. After a violent siege and various sea battles Massilia too capitulates (56–8; 2.1–16), as does the governor of Farther Spain (2.17–22). The remainder of Book 2 describes Curio's concomitant attempt to occupy the province of Africa and his defeat and death at the hands of the Pompeian governor Varus and the treacherous Numidian king Juba (23–44). Again, the section devoted to politics is minimal (little more than five chapters): the military actions dominate the report, which skillfully highlights the decisive phases of the Spanish, Massilian, and African campaigns.

Book 3 returns to Caesar, now (in January 48) consul and thus legitimate head of the Roman government. After emergency measures in Rome he departs to Brundisium and his army (3.1–2). Meanwhile Pompey has amassed a huge army and navy in the Greek East and is prepared to prevent Caesar's crossing (3–5). Yet Caesar, daring to tempt the wintry seas, succeeds in landing with seven legions in Epirus and in establishing a base in Apollonia (6–12). Several attempts to resume peace negotiations fail, while the two armies confront each other in fortified camps near Dyrrachium (13–19), Pompey's admirals blockade Antonius with Caesar's remaining troops in Brundisium, and one of Caesar's assistants, the praetor Caelius Rufus, causes major problems in Rome (20–2). Toward the end of the winter, Antonius finally crosses the Aegean and unites his troops with Caesar's (23–30). Meanwhile Metellus Scipio, governor of Syria, has arrived in Macedonia (31–8). An extended trench warfare ensues, when Caesar is able to encircle Pompey's positions near Dyrrachium. Pompey, however, uses his superior naval forces to supply his troops, while Caesar's soldiers starve. Eventually, profiting from general confusion caused by fighting in complicated fortifications, Pompey is able to break out, causing serious losses among Caesar's troops (41–71). In forced marches, Caesar separates himself from Pompey, restores the morale of his soldiers, and moves into Thessaly, hoping to compel Pompey to risk a decisive battle (72–81). Pompey's victory at Dyrrachium results in the hubristic self-confidence of his officers and senatorial entourage. Against his better judgment, Pompey yields to pressure and accepts Caesar's offer of battle (82–7). At Pharsalus, in the early summer of 48, despite superior numbers and optimistic prognoses, his army suffers a crushing defeat (88–99). Pompey himself barely escapes (96.3–4), reaches the coast, and puts to sea with a few ships. Seeking refuge in Egypt, he is killed treacherously by the current boy-king's advisors (102–4). Caesar arrives in Egypt with few troops and punishes Pompey's murderers, but gets himself embroiled in Egyptian internal conflicts – the beginning of the Alexandrian War (105–12; on the end, see below). Although the action in this final book is driven swiftly by intricate military maneuvers, two events dominate, occupying almost half of it: the trench-war at Dyrrachium and the battle of Pharsalus.

In general, then, Caesar gives an overview of the entire war but focuses skillfully on the dramatic highlights of every campaign.

Ancient Comments

Three important comments by Caesar's contemporaries survive. Hirtius writes in his preface to *BG* Book 8, addressed to Balbus, another long-standing supporter of Caesar,

> Under constant pressure from you, Balbus, ... I have undertaken this task – a very difficult one. I have written a continuation of our friend Caesar's commentaries on his achievements in Gaul, since his earlier writings do not link up with the later. His latest work, which leaves off at the events in Alexandria, I have completed up to the end of Caesar's life, though not to the end of civil dissension, for no end of that is in sight. ... It is an accepted fact that all the most strenuous literary efforts of others are surpassed by the elegance of these commentaries. They were published to provide writers with information about such important events, but they have received such general approbation that future writers appear to have been forestalled rather than provided with an opportunity. Yet we may feel greater admiration than all others, for they know how well and faultlessly he wrote, while we also know with what ease and speed he completed the work. Caesar not only had the gift of writing with consummate elegance, but also knew how most exactly to convey what his intentions were (*BG* 8 *praef.* 1–6; trans. Handford and Gardner, Caesar 1982).

Cicero says in his *Brutus* about Caesar's *Commentaries*:

> Admirable, indeed! ... They are nude, straight and beautiful; stripped of all ornament of style as if they had laid aside a garment. His aim was to furnish others with material for writing history, and perhaps he has succeeded in gratifying the inept, who may wish to

> apply their curling irons to his material; but men of sound judgement he has deterred from writing, since in history there is nothing more pleasing than brevity clear and correct. (262; trans. Hendrickson 1971)

Suetonius, who quotes these two assessments, adds another:

> Asinius Pollio believes that the memoirs show signs of carelessness and inaccuracy: Caesar, he holds, did not always check the truth of the reports that came in, and was either disingenuous or forgetful in describing his own actions. Pollio believes that Caesar would have been intending to rewrite and correct. (*Divus Iulius* 56.4; trans. Graves 1957, modified; see Lossmann 1957: 55–8)

These comments provide information and raise questions about three issues: the nature of a *commentarius*, the incomplete state and publication of Caesar's works, and his contemporaries' opinion of their style and accuracy.

The Genre of the *Commentarius* and Caesar's *Commentarii*

In *Brutus*, written in 46 and thus probably referring only to the *BG* (below), Cicero emphasizes its straightforward narrative, beautiful simplicity, and lack of rhetorical ornamentation. He takes it for granted that Caesar wrote it to provide material for histories to be written by others; yet in fact it already is a history – so much so that others wisely refrain from attempting to improve on it. Hirtius makes the same assumption. Do they reflect Caesar's intention?

In 55, Cicero had expressed the same view of a *commentarius* in a letter to the historian Lucceius (*Fam.* 5.12) whom he wished to write a history of his own consulship in 63. If Lucceius agreed, Cicero promised to provide *commentarii* on all aspects (10). When Lucceius declined, as others had earlier, Cicero himself wrote a Greek *commentarius* on his consulship (*Att.* 1.19). Atticus had also written one; Cicero considered it slightly rough and unkempt but charming precisely because of its lack of ornament – quite unlike Cicero's own which was richly ornamented:

> Posidonius has already written to me ... that when he read this *hypomnēma* of mine, which I had sent him with the idea that he might compose something more elaborate on the same theme, so far from being stimulated to composition he was effectively frightened away. The fact is, I have dumbfounded the whole Greek community. ... If you like the book, please see that it is made available at Athens and the other Greek towns. I think it may add some lustre to my achievements. (*Att.* 2.1.1–2; trans. Shackleton Bailey 1978a)

Apparently, this was a fully elaborated historical work, adorned with a plethora of stylistic effects and ready for publication. Hence a *commentarius* did not need to be merely a collection of material assembled and sketched out for elaboration by others.

Yet Cicero thought so, despite the efforts he invested in his work. How can we reconcile his conflicting statements and actions? Most importantly, what was a *commentarius* in Roman tradition and perceptions (Klotz 1910; Bömer 1953; Rüpke 1992; Riggsby 2006: 133–55)?

Varro wrote for Pompey a *commentarius eisagōgikos*, an introduction to senate procedures (Gell. *NA* 14.7.1–2); a *commentariolum petitionis*, a guide to campaigning for office, is attributed to Quintus Cicero. Heads of households kept records of contracts and rituals; priestly colleges and magistrates held *acta*, *tabulae*, or *commentarii* as records of actions and transactions, serving both as aide-memoire and as documentation for later use. Similarly, the collection of records that Caesar handed over to the consul Antonius before his planned Parthian campaign was called *acta* or *commentarii* (e.g., Cic. *Phil.* 2.95; 5.10–11; Vell. Pat. 2.60.4). Memoirs or autobiographical writings of eminent persons (such as M. Aemilius Scaurus, Q. Lutatius Catulus, Sulla, or Augustus) were *acta*, *res gestae*, *de vita sua* or *commentarii* (*hypomnēmata*); despite the variety of terms, they had one purpose: to preserve and describe the author's achievements from his own perspective, to justify and glorify them, and to correct misperceptions.

None of the references to such writings offer the slightest hint that they were intended to provide material for historians. How Cicero and Hirtius arrived at their different view is unclear but it is unlikely to have been shared by Caesar himself. Rather, he may have picked up another tradition of *commentarii*: traditional Roman historiography, interchangeably called *annales* or *commentarii* and written in a simple, forthright style (Eden 1962: 75–94). It is thus possible that Caesar's choice of genre entailed a conscious rejection of the Greek-style *historia*, preferred by Cicero, in favor of traditional Roman historical records. At any rate, Caesar's *commentarii* should be understood as his own presentation of his deeds and views, written in an appropriately elevated but modest style, and intended to be published and to persuade the readers. They were based on his dispatches (*litterae*) to the senate, those of his officers to himself, and probably a collection of materials (notes and records) that formed his personal archive, his own (preliminary) *commentarii* on the events he was involved in.

Composition and Publication of the *BC*

The mode and date of composition and the date of publication of both *commentarii* have been much debated. The preface to *BG* 8 (p. 178 above) suggests that Hirtius produced after Caesar's death an edition which contained both *commentarii* in a more extended form than what Caesar had left, continuing them even to Caesar's death. While the extant *Bellum Alexandrinum* probably is Hirtius' work, the *Bellum Africum* and *Bellum Hispaniense* certainly are not (Cluett, chapter 14, pp. 193–4), and we wonder why the extant *Corpus Caesarianum* shows no trace of Hirtius' supposed continuation beyond the end of the *Bellum Alexandrinum*. Suetonius' uncertainty about the author of the *bella minora* (*Iul.* 56.1) indicates that he did not know Hirtius' comprehensive edition. The text available to him probably was already the mixed bag we have. All these uncertainties suggest that perhaps Hirtius only intended or began to complete the work (*confeci*) in the shape he indicates in the preface to *BG* 8 but did not have time to realize his intention. Balbus himself may then have published the materials he found in Hirtius' papers, although the descriptions of the later wars were originally not intended for this purpose (Rüpke 1992: 220–2). However this may be, it does not help us answer the question of the initial composition and publication of the *BC*.

Although some scholars contest this (e.g. Barwick 1951: 86–93; Boatwright 1988: 36–7), the *BC* seems not only unfinished but incomplete (Batstone and Damon 2006: 29–32). Hirtius points this out (*imperfectum*). The final book breaks off at an unexpected point: not with the battle of Pharsalus, not with Pompey's assassination, but with the causes of the Alexandrian War. It lacks the polish of the *BG;* gaps, omissions, and contradictions are obvious (listed by Klotz 1950: ix–xiv). According to Suetonius (above), Pollio noticed errors, superficial treatment, and lack of diligence in the *commentarii* (presumably both) that he thinks would have been corrected – if Caesar had wanted or had had the time to do so. Cicero never explicitly refers to the *BC*; allusions in his "Caesarian speeches" to arguments and catchwords used by Caesar during the civil war need not refer to the *BC*: they are amply attested in independent sources and at the time of the events.

All this has prompted many scholars, led by the doyen of Caesar studies, Alfred Klotz (1910), to conclude that Caesar did not publish this work and that Hirtius' posthumous edition was the first ever. By contrast, Klaus Barwick (1951) and others proffered linguistic, political, and historical reasons suggesting that the work was written and published with a strong propagandistic purpose during the war, Books 1–2 at the end of 49, Book 3 a year or so later.

As John Collins (1959: 115) points out, however, Barwick's "strongest arguments indicate only that the *BC* was *written* during the progress of the war, or directly after Pharsalus, and prove nothing regarding the time of publication." Collins himself, considering the tone and "political program" of the work in its historical context, finds that the pervasive effort the author undertakes to place himself into the framework of republican traditions and to stress his determination to respect and preserve these traditions, while his opponents played havoc with them, is incompatible with the autocratic Caesar who emerged gradually after his victory at Thapsus in 47. Hence he concludes that "Barwick is correct in fixing an early date of composition, and ... Klotz ... in fixing a posthumous date of publication" (ibid. 116–25). Why, then, did Caesar compose but not publish the work? This Collins explains by the transformation of Caesar's political outlook under the deep impressions he received in Alexandria (the "enchantress" Cleopatra, the tomb of Alexander, Egyptian monarchy, and the efficient Ptolemaic administration). When he finally returned to Rome, he was no longer interested in preserving republican traditions, and the *BC* was forgotten in Caesar's archive until Hirtius discovered it in 44 (ibid. 125–30). Jörg Rüpke adds that perhaps the forms and narrative techniques Caesar had developed in the *BG* and used in the *BC* as well eventually proved incompatible with a content that required much more complex justification (1992: 212).

The thesis of Caesar's profound political transformation in Egypt is the weakest link in Collins's otherwise plausible argument. Cicero's *Pro Marcello* demonstrates that the "new Caesar" was not yet alarmingly visible even in September 46 (Gotoff 1993: xxx–xxxii), after Thapsus and Caesar's triple triumph. Hope for reconciliation and an appeal for the restoration of the *res publica* were still possible, despite the accumulation of honors mentioned by later authors. Subsequent scholarship has refined and strengthened the view of the *BC*'s early composition. For example, Mary Boatwright draws attention to the emphasis Caesar places on the legal restrictions observed in waiting for the "right" year (48) to assume his second consulship and on the way he met his obligations as the rightful consul and representative of the Roman state. Such emphasis points to "the first years of the civil war, when there was still a chance of reconciliation and Caesar was appealing to the moderate Senatorial majority" (1988: 32–40).

Observing a striking and obviously deliberate change in the terminology Caesar uses to designate his opponents, from *inimici* (personal enemies) to *adversarii* (opponents) and especially *hostes* (public enemies, occurring no less than 65 times), a change that coincides with the failure of Caesar's political strategy at the beginning of the war (in the first 33 chapters, below), R. T. Macfarlane (1996) concludes that the first section of the *BC* was written during or right after the events.

Martin Jehne (2000) emphasizes the profound crisis Caesar faced when returning from the East in the summer of 47: Italy was shaken by financial turmoil, riots, and revolts, the legions in Campania were in full mutiny, and in North Africa his opponents again posed a serious threat. Hence Caesar needed to enhance his public image: he emphasized his republican convictions, the justice of his cause, and his conscientious care for the Roman state and citizens throughout the war. This need to display ostentatious republicanism disappeared only after the victory at Thapsus. Hence, Jehne concludes, the *BC* must have been published at the time of Caesar's return to Rome from the East, intended, despite inaccuracies and imperfections, to convince the undecided majority of elite Romans who needed arguments to justify their passiveness and their hope for improved conditions after Caesar's victory.

We certainly need to distinguish between composition and publication. "Publication" at the time could be achieved by producing a few copies and sending them to carefully chosen addressees. Given Caesar's efforts, even after Thapsus in 47, to achieve reconciliation with opponents (Mitchell 1991: 267), we would expect Cicero to have been among the recipients. Between Caesar's return from Egypt and the fall of 46, Cicero had ample opportunity to mention the *BC*. His urgent appeal to the dictator in *Pro Marcello,* to restore the traditional republic, could have been enhanced significantly by reference to the republican convictions expressed in that *commentarius.* That he does not mention the *BC* at all is a powerful argument from silence. Combining this with other indications mentioned above, I consider it most likely that the *BC,* though written during the war, probably in segments close to the events, was neither fully completed nor published by Caesar.

The Text and Manuscript Tradition, Modern Editions

Over a hundred printed editions of the *BC* have been produced. The *editio princeps* was published by Giovanni Andrea Bussi in Rome in 1469. It established the precedent of incorporating all the war commentaries in one edition; accordingly, separate editions of the *BC* were extremely rare until the end of the nineteenth century (V. Brown 1972: 1–2). In 1737 Franz van Oudendorp created the first text based on the comparison of many codices, in 1847 Karl Nipperdey the first critical edition worthy of this name and the first stemma based on a systematic, though still limited, classification of codices (ibid. 6–7). Addition of authoritative manuscripts by Heinrich Meusel (1885), Alfred Holder (1898), and Pierre Fabre (1936) brought the number to eight. The editors of the best texts available today, Alfred Klotz (2nd edn. 1950) and Fabre (1936), unfortunately did not personally examine all eight codices. Virginia Brown, who did so, never realized her intention of producing a full new text (1972: preface, 9–10). Demonstrating that of the eight MSS two are derived from one other, all produced in the same French *scriptorium*, and one more can be eliminated as a copy of another, Brown reduces the number of authoritative MSS to five and postulates an archetype produced in a French school that "could have been written in any of the pre-Caroline scripts used in France or even in Caroline minuscules" (ibid. ch. 3, esp. 38–9; see also Hering 1963, critically discussed by Brown). The authoritative German commentary, written initially in the mid-nineteenth century, was repeatedly revised and updated (Kraner, Hofmann, & Meusel 1963); in the 1990s, John Carter produced a historical commentary (1991, 1993). Cynthia Damon, Gregory Bucher, and Kurt Raaflaub are currently working on a new edition and historical-philological commentary.

Little is known about the history of the text of the *BC* between Suetonius and the production of the pre-Carolingian archetype. Jean Andrieu (1949) has demonstrated that the work originally appeared in the three books of the modern editions, thus obviating alternative theses such as that of Klotz (1950: vi) or Will Richter (1977: 172–4), postulating an original two-book format, or that of M. Chênerie (1974), that the work was initially planned with an annalistic structure (against which see Boatwright 1988: 37 with n. 25).

Style and Narrative

Caesar was one of the celebrated orators of his time. He was thus thoroughly aware of the close connections between style of writing, technique of composition, and effect on the reader. His essay *De analogia* laid out the principles of transforming simple, everyday language into an effective style. Hirtius recalls how rapidly and easily Caesar wrote his *commentarii*, while Cicero praises them as "cleanly, directly, and gracefully composed, and divested of all rhetorical trappings" (*Brut.* 262, quoted above).

Indeed, of "Caesar's individual traits as a writer, the most obvious and unmistakeable are his brevity and his clarity: he seems to have been incapable of wasting words or of becoming obscure" (Eden 1962: 101). Yet graceful simplicity does not mean lack of effectiveness in serving specific ends.

This is not the place to analyze Caesar's style in detail (see, e.g., Eden 1962; Gotoff 1984; Carter 1991: 22–3; Batstone & Damon 2006). Eden suggests that Caesar's choice of genre entailed a deliberate effort to fit himself into the long tradition of Roman annalistic historiography which also adopted a simple style without much ornamentation (Cic. *De or.* 2.52–3). Correspondences with the style of the annalists are noticeable, but they should not be exaggerated; Caesar shares certain features as well with Livy and even Cicero (Gotoff 1984: 12). Moreover, Caesar's style developed over time (Adcock 1956: ch. 4). The "rise in emotional temperature," visible already in *BG* Book 7 with Caesar's heroic effort to overcome "the Gauls' last concerted effort for national freedom," increased further in the *BC*, "where his sense of engagement and involvement was inevitably paramount" (Eden 1962: 94). Such emotional involvement expressed itself in a looser and more flexible style. But this too should not be exaggerated. Gotoff shows that "a good deal of complexity and much intricacy of composition" are visible in the *BG* long before Book 7. He sees Caesar "displaying more idiosyncrasy than [he] has ever been credited with." Close reading of Caesar's text, he concludes, can still yield much more insight. Whether or not "Caesar is still to be identified with the *genus humile*," his composition "can be periodic, complex, and capable of great expressiveness through the use of varied and often subtle technique" (1984: 17–18).

Comparison between Caesar's version of an episode and that of another historian who gives the same episode "full-dress treatment" is illuminating. Batstone and Damon (2006: 27–9) do this for Pompey's death in Egypt (*BC* 3.104), demonstrating that Caesar's leaner treatment is effective in its own way, serving his specific purpose. Several scholars have examined Caesar's style with specific regard to his propaganda, some subtly (Mutschler 1975), some less so (Rambaud 1966). It is in the sphere of narrative intensity, arrangement, and drama, however, that Caesar rises most clearly above the humble style, whatever his models and predecessors (Rowe 1967; Batstone & Damon 2006). I mention as examples the siege and capitulation of Corfinium (1.16–23), the narrow escape of Pompey from Brundisium (1.25–8), the final stages of the Spanish campaign (1.54–85), and the battle of Pharsalus (3.80–99).

Tendentiousness and Reliability

The *BC*, we saw, was written to present the principal actor's perspective on the events, actions, and motives that determined the outbreak, course, and outcome of the civil war of 49/8. We should thus a priori expect a less than objective narrative, even if it is told in the third rather than the first person. Caesar clearly had an agenda and wanted the reader to hear his side of the story – especially since, as Cicero's correspondence demonstrates impressively, other sides of the story were circulated widely through a steady stream of messengers, letters, and probably pamphlets, not only by Caesar's opponents but also by his own supporters.

For example, during the Italian campaign Caesar made a huge effort to combat the widespread fear that his victory would result in a bloodbath surpassing even Sulla's proscriptions. The policy of *clementia* he implemented for the first time at Corfinium (below) was designed to prove the contrary; Caesar's agents spread the news that produced a massive swing in popular opinion (Gelzer 1968: 200–2). Yet there was also a flood of contrasting information. "You will see from the enclosed paper what sort of horrors we are reading every day," Cicero wrote to Atticus (9.13.7). After Caesar's confrontation in Rome with the tribune Metellus (p. 177 above), Cicero talked with Curio, one of Caesar's closest aides:

> Horrible! You know what he is like. He kept nothing back. ... From [Spain] Caesar and his army would go wherever Pompey was. Pompey's death would constitute his goal. ... He added that Caesar had been quite carried away with rage against the Tribune Metellus and had wanted to have him killed; in which case there would have been a great massacre. There were any number of people urging him that way, and as for Caesar himself, it was not by inclination or nature that he was not cruel but because he reckoned that clemency was the popular line. If he lost favour with the public he would be cruel. (*Att.* 10.4.8; cf. 7.19)

Not surprisingly, Caesar's characterization of his most ardent opponents is utterly negative (below); it suffices to read his bitter and sarcastic description of their oppressive manipulation of the senate (1.1–6) or his ironic comments on the utter failure of the Pompeian officers during the Italian campaign to secure the loyalty of their troops (1.12–20). Naturally, Caesar himself speaks of the letter he wanted to be read in the senate on January 1, 49 (1.1.1) as *lenissima postulata* (most moderate demands, 1.5.5), while Cicero talks of *minaces et acerbae litterae* (a threatening and harsh letter, *Fam.* 16.11.2; Raaflaub 1974a: 59–64).

The question is rather whether Caesar's partisan political perspective influenced his narrative of events as well. Following, for example, the great Eduard Meyer (1922: 293 n. 1–2), Klaus Barwick (1951) and Michel Rambaud (1966) thought so, using detailed examination of Caesar's text to accuse him of systematic and deliberate distortion. By contrast, John Collins (1972: 942–63) found that the vast amount of contemporaneous material absorbed by the extant writings on the period permits only an "almost vanishingly small" amount of factual correction. He concludes that the *BC* "does not contain gross falsification, and sources do not exist to check its misleading tone with a confrontation of facts" (943). Indeed, it is the tone rather than the facts that betray Caesar's tendentiousness.

To be sure, Caesar arranges his narrative into units, as every historian does, for greater effect and economy, and he certainly uses such arrangement to serve his interests. For example, Caesar reports the events in Rome (1.1–6), then moves to Ravenna and his decision to occupy Ariminum (1.7–8.1). The message he receives there from Pompey (1.8.2–4) prompts him to describe in one block the ensuing peace negotiations (1.9–11.3) and only then to narrate his advance beyond

Ariminum (11.4–13), news of which causes the abrupt evacuation of Rome (1.14). Chronological accuracy and precise causality seem here sacrificed at least to narrative stringency, perhaps also to the needs of self-justification.

Thus Caesar claims to have informed his soldiers of the events in Rome (including the measures reported in 1.6) while he was still in Ravenna and then to have led them to Ariminum, where he met the tribunes; at that point, he gave marching orders to his other legions, which were wintering in Transalpine Gaul (1.7–8.2). Ariminum was the first city outside his province, in Italy, but Caesar avoids mentioning that he crossed the provincial boundary (the famous Rubicon). According to later sources (at least partly based on Asinius Pollio, an eyewitness and historian of the civil war period himself), Caesar sent his army ahead, concealed his own departure from Ravenna, and addressed his soldiers when the tribunes joined them in Ariminum. This tradition, however, does not gain credibility by progressively dramatizing the crossing of the Rubicon (Gelzer 1968: 193 n. 3), and it is a priori likely that Caesar addressed his troops both before he led them into Italy *and* when he could present to them the tribunes, victims of his opponents' oppression. Calculation of dates makes clear that Caesar reacted immediately after he heard of the *scu* and before he received notice of the events reported in 1.6 (Carter 1991: 163) – which is implied by the fact that he was already in Ariminum when the tribunes arrived. The latter part of Caesar's statement is clearly wrong: information he provides about the dates when the legions from Gaul joined him in Italy indicates that he must have given orders weeks earlier, when adverse events in Rome (Raaflaub 1974a: 33–55) made an armed conflict much more likely (Carter 1991: 165–6; Ottmer 1979: ch. 1). He mentions this late (1.8.1), thus avoiding a contradiction with the emphasis he places on his extreme patience and hope for reconciliation (1.5.5) – but he mentions it, although he could easily have omitted it altogether.

Again, the connection the word "therefore" (*itaque*) establishes between the failure of negotiations and Caesar's advance beyond Ariminum (1.11.4) is clearly disproved by Cicero's correspondence. Yet it is so obviously wrong that Caesar could hardly have wanted his readers to take this literally. According to Klaus Oppermann (1933: 21–2), *itaque* here does not establish a chronological sequence but draws the consequence from political failure: war, after all, *was* inevitable. But the point was sensitive: Cicero complains bitterly about Caesar's refusal to stop his advance while negotiations were going on (*Att.* 7.17.2, 18.2) – although, typically, he was in full agreement with continuing preparations by the Pompeians – and so Caesar might have been tempted to hide or obscure this fact.

Even if he did so this is about the worst degree of distortion we find in the *BC*, and there are not many other cases that, at least on the surface, seem to attest to deliberate falsification. At any rate, it is not such "lies" or errors that illuminate Caesar's propaganda and tendentiousness. As Collins points out, "In the 'Bellum Gallicum' Caesar's purpose was perfectly served by a straightforward statement of the facts. . . . In the 'Bellum Civile' . . . he was concerned throughout to show not that he was successful, but that he was in the right, that his adversaries were stupid, un-Roman, and criminal, and that his victory was the victory of the better cause" (1972: 946).

We now turn to the portrait Caesar draws of his opponents. Here he did not need to falsify: it was easy to base a starkly propagandistic narrative on truth, but Caesar enhanced the effect by selection, omission, emphasis, and word choice.

Portraits of Personalities

Four persons dominate Caesar's narrative of the fateful events in Rome in early January 49 (1.1–6): the consul L. Cornelius Lentulus Crus, Pompey's father-in-law Q. Caecilius Metellus Pius Scipio Nasica, Cato the Younger, and Pompey himself. They bring it about that the senate majority, "forced by the consul's words, by the fear inspired by an army on the doorstep, and by the threats of Pompey's friends, vote unwillingly and under duress" for Scipio's motion against Caesar (2.6) and are deprived of their ability to decide freely (3.5). They are responsible for causing decisions to be made in haste and confusion and without proper notification of Caesar (5.1), for initiating harsh decrees concerning Caesar and the most eminent officials, the tribunes (5.5), and for taking measures that "overturned (or mixed up) all human and divine laws" (6.8).

Lentulus uses threats in urging the senate to take a determined stance against Caesar; otherwise, he will disobey the senate's will and rethink his options, including joining "the goodwill and friendship of Caesar" (1.2–3). He attacks and abuses those who offer more moderate proposals and refuses to allow a vote on them (2.4–5). His motives are despicable: huge debts, vast ambition, and a sick desire to become a second Sulla (4.2). In sharp contrast, we later see him fleeing in panic from Rome, even leaving the treasury open (1.14.1), occupying an extravagantly equipped tent in Pompey's camp at Pharsalus (3.96.1), and dying an inglorious death in Egypt (3.104.3).

Scipio, no more than Pompey's mouthpiece, also uses threats to influence the senate against Caesar (1.4–2.1). He is motivated by ambition for power, exploitation of his kinship with Pompey, fear of prosecution, love of self-display, and hunger for adulation by powerful men (4.3). Appointed governor of Syria, he claims the title *imperator* after actually sustaining military setbacks, brutally extorts money and supplies, abandons his still endangered province, and even plans to steal the treasures of Diana's temple in Ephesus (3.31–3). As an army commander, he is reckless and cowardly, causing unnecessary losses (3.36–8). Having joined Pompey's camp, he quarrels with others prematurely about the distribution of Caesar's offices and the punishment of neutrals or lukewarm supporters (3.82–3).

Cato, perhaps Caesar's most determined enemy, opposed a compromise in early January and agreed to seek peace only when the war had already broken out (Cic. *Att.* 7.15.2). Caesar mentions old enmities and resentment about an election defeat as his motives (1.4.1) and recalls Cato's attempt in 52 to block the bill that allowed Caesar to run *in absentia* (1.32.3). In the spring of 49, as governor of Sicily,

> Cato was displaying great energy in getting old ships repaired and ordering the towns to supply new ones. He had his lieutenants out in Lucania and Bruttium, enlisting Roman

> citizens, and was trying to raise a certain number of cavalry and infantry from the Sicilian towns. When these preparations were nearly complete he heard of the approach of Curio [whom Caesar had sent to take over Sicily] and complained in a public speech that he had been abandoned and betrayed by Pompey. Pompey had undertaken an unnecessary war when everything was in a state of total unreadiness and, when questioned by himself and others in the Senate, he had declared that he was fully prepared and ready for war. Having made his protest, Cato fled from the province. (1.30.4–5)

Although many have interpreted this passage as an attempt to ridicule Cato, Caesar in fact characterizes his actions positively (see also App. *B Civ.* 2.40); unlike most of Pompey's officers in Italy, Cato accomplishes much, and his preparations are almost complete when he is overtaken by military events. According to Appian (*B Civ.* 2.40), Cato decided not to risk a fight in order to spare the lives of those under his command. Overall, compared with others, Caesar describes Cato with deliberate restraint, using him, and the speech he attributes to him, to cast a devastating light on Pompey (David Yates, "The role of Cato the Younger in Caesar's *Bellum civile*," in preparation).

Pompey, indeed, receives Caesar's sharpest criticism. Applying military power and ruthless intimidation, he directs the oppression of the senate majority (1.1–3). His motives are listed in most detail (1.4.4–5): he is incapable of standing in another's shadow; manipulated himself by Caesar's enemies, he has betrayed his friendship with Caesar, used illegitimate military means to advance his own power and supremacy (*potentia dominatusque*), and is eager to force a decision by war. He misleads the senate in describing the strength and morale of the two armies (1.6.1–2). He is good at moralizing (1.8.3–4) but a failure in seeking peace (1.10–11, 26.2–5; 3.18, 57), imposing discipline on his subcommanders (1.19.4), and maintaining popularity in Italy (12–13, 15–16, 18, 28.1). At Dyrrachium he is boastful (3.45.6) but unable to grasp victory when it is in his reach (3.70.1; Gelzer 1968: 235). Before the final battle he succumbs to manipulation by others, tolerates their infighting (3.82–3), and absurdly predicts certain victory (86–7), but chooses poor tactics (92) and leaves the battlefield prematurely (94), sitting despondently in his tent and escaping in the last moment in disguise with only a few friends (96). Fittingly, this shadow of the former "great" Pompey dies in a little boat off the coast of Egypt, betrayed and alone (103–4). Obviously, Caesar was deeply angered by the betrayal of his former ally and son-in-law. Cato had at least been consistent.

These are the leaders. Smaller figures such as Labienus, also a traitor, who needs to legitimize himself by cruelty (3.19, 71), Afranius and Petreius, failures as commanders of Pompey's Spanish legions (1.41–87), and Varro, a weathervane as governor of Farther Spain (2.17–21), are treated with equal contempt and sarcasm. Generally, as Collins shows with many examples (1972: 946–56), the Pompeians are cowards and weaklings, cruel, greedy, vainglorious, and incompetent. The positive examples are all on Caesar's own side, ranging from brave centurions like Scaeva and Crastinus (3.53, 91, 99), to subcommanders like Curio, who demonstrates loyalty and bravery even in military failure (2.23–44), to Caesar himself, a model as a leader (Rosenstein, chapter 7 in this volume), always decisive and active, seeking victory even in adversity, commanding the absolute loyalty of his men because he respects them, cares for them, and shares their dangers, concerned about the safety of all Roman citizens, whether on his or the other side, and always trying to restore peace for the greater good of the *res publica*. This portrait of Caesar the general and statesman is intimately tied to his political strategy, to which we finally turn.

Political Strategy

Given the *BC*'s purpose, it offers most valuable insight into Caesar's view of politics, particularly those underlying the civil war, and the political strategies he pursued. Five aspects stressed by Caesar in varying ways seem particularly important: personal enmity (*inimicitiae*), status and reputation (*dignitas*), liberty (*libertas*), peace (*pax*), and generosity or clemency (*lenitas*).

In his description of the prelude to the civil war, Hirtius highlights some of these issues: the repeated attempts of a small group (*pauci*) of Caesar's enemies (*inimici*) to deprive him of command, power, honor, and *dignitas* (*BG* 8.50.4, 52.3), block initiatives designed to eliminate the fear of war and secure the liberty and sovereignty of the state (52.4–5), and create circumstances that would force the senate to approve what they themselves had decided (53.1–2). But Caesar refuses to act, believing that his cause will easily prevail if the senators are able to decide freely (52.4). Although the enemies' actions "made it perfectly clear what was planned against Caesar, he nevertheless thought that he should put up with everything," as long as there remained hope for a peaceful settlement (55.2).

Caesar himself emphasizes the same aspects in describing the events in Rome (*BC* 1.1–6), in speaking to his troops (7), in writing to Pompey (9), and in addressing a senator (22.5), the "rump-senate" in Rome (32), and the two armies after the capitulation of the Pompeians in Spain (85): a small faction (*factio paucorum*) of his personal enemies (*inimici*) has been conspiring to diminish his *dignitas* and honor, by treating him unjustly and insultingly in various ways (*iniuriae*, *contumeliae*), depriving him of his people-given right to run for consul *in absentia*, and preparing his personal destruction (*pernicies*, 9.4, 85) both politically and militarily; in all this, they have ignored the will of senate majority and people, depriving both of their power to decide freely (3.5, 9.5), and turning divine and human rights upside down (6.8). Caesar's language in these chapters is polemical and inflammatory, abounding in generalizations and superlatives, and throwing the worst possible light on the actions of his enemies. As a result, he, Caesar, although demanding nothing that was not perfectly legitimate (32.2–3), showing almost superhuman patience (9.3, 5), and trying his very best to preserve peace, was eventually forced to appeal to his troops in order to defend his *dignitas*, the rights of the tribunes who had suffered on his behalf, and the liberty of the Roman people (7, 22.5; Raaflaub 1974a). Independent confirmation is not lacking: for example, in the very first days of the war, Cicero wrote: "Is it a Roman general or Hannibal we are talking of? Deluded wretch, with never in his life a glimpse of even the shadow of Good! And he says he is doing all this for the sake of his *dignitas*! Where is *dignitas* without moral good (*honestas*)?" (*Att.* 7.11.1). Quintilian even characterized this conflict as a *dignitatis contentio* between Caesar and Pompey (*Inst.* 11.1.80).

Mixed into these polemics, we find arguments borrowed from a long-standing populist (*popularis*) agenda that was used in the 70s by Pompey in undermining Sulla's system and in the 60s by Caesar himself against the conservative leaders of the senate (*optimates*): the defense of tribunician power and inviolability, attacks on the illegitimate use of the *scu*, and the protection of the people's liberty (1.5.1–3, 7.2–6, 22.5; see also 1.6.5, 85.9). In fact, if we read the *BC* carefully, it becomes clear that Caesar was trying, not for the first time in his career, to forge against the small group of his opponents a "grand coalition" that comprised senate majority, equestrians, people of Rome, Roman citizens in Italy and the provinces, and the citizens who served in the armies (Raaflaub forthcoming).

Caesar's use of *libertas* is particularly interesting (Raaflaub 2003, 2007). His opponents used this catchword against him consistently since his consulship in 59 and continued to do so throughout the civil war. Caesar initially countered with his own slogan of liberty (above), contending that he was fighting for the liberty of the senate, the Roman people, and the state; coins minted early in the civil war by Caesar's supporters confirm this. After Corfinium, where he again emphasized this motive (1.22.5), *libertas* disappears from his argument in the *BC*; it appears neither in contemporaneous evidence on Caesar's statements nor in the rich coin output of Caesar and his supporters. Corfinium was also the first event in which Caesar demonstrated his principle of clemency (*lenitas*) on a grand scale (1.23). A few days later he wrote to his political agents: "I am indeed glad that you express ... such hearty approval of the proceedings at Corfinium. ... I had of my own accord decided to show all possible clemency and to do my best to reconcile Pompey. Let us try whether by this means we can win back the good will of all and enjoy a lasting victory. ... Let this be the new style of conquest, to make mercy and generosity our shield" (*Att.* 9.7C). The principle of clemency (*lenitas*; Caesar himself did not use *clementia*; Weinstock 1971: 233–43) was based on Caesar's specific interpretation of the conflict underlying the civil war, and this understanding determined his political strategy.

Since Caesar claimed to be defending himself against the hostile actions of a small group of personal enemies who were determined to destroy him, in his own presentation this was essentially a private conflict, a disagreement among citizens (*civilis dissensio*, Raaflaub 1974a: 232–9). Caesar thus fought against neither the senate nor the *res publica*. By contrast, his opponents, having secured the support of the senate, proclaimed the *scu* and declared Caesar a public enemy (*hostis publicus*), emphasizing that they represented senate and state against a rebellious governor and outcast. These divergent claims had far-reaching consequences. First, Caesar was able to exclude from the conflict all those who were not directly involved and wanted to remain neutral, as long as they abstained from fighting him. His opponents took the opposite position: a fight for the survival of the *res publica* did not tolerate neutrality. Hence Cicero said in 46: "We often heard you [Caesar] say that we treated all as our enemies unless they were on our side, while you considered all yours who were not against you" (*Pro Lig.* 11.35; cf. *BC* 1.33.1–2; Suet. *Iul.* 75.1). Second, Caesar could afford to be generous toward those he captured, as long as they did not resume fighting against him (1.23.3, 85.11–12; 3.98.2). His opponents, dealing with enemies of the state (*hostes*), used terror and cruelty as deterrents (2.44.2; 3.8.3, 28.4, 71.4; cf. Raaflaub 1974a: 293–307). Third, Caesar, fighting only those who opposed his legitimate political aspirations (recognition of his great merits for the state, a second consulship, and appropriate status, *dignitas*), was able to seek peace at every turn, as long as these minimal conditions were met. Fighting a rebel, his opponents, after the failure of a first round, neither made political concessions nor agreed to peace talks, because these would concede to Caesar the legitimacy they denied him (1.32.8–9; Raaflaub 1974a: 262–93).

Hence peace, and generosity or leniency, became Caesar's main catchwords, and in the *BC* he continually repeats his efforts on behalf of both. Placing so much emphasis on the personal nature of the conflict, though, Caesar had to drop *libertas*: whether of the senate, the people, or the state, liberty was a political value which no longer fit his political strategy. Posthumous coins accordingly celebrated him as *parens patriae* and showed a temple of *clementia*. Both these qualities are highlighted in his decision, against his soldiers' will, not to fight a decisive battle at the end of the Spanish campaign of 49 but to use other means to force the enemy to capitulate: "Why should he sacrifice some of his men, even for a victory? Why should he allow the troops who had done him such excellent service to be wounded? ... Besides, he was stirred by pity for the citizens whom he saw must be killed; he would rather gain his ends without any harm befalling them" (1.72.2–3; cf. 3.98). He was soon gloriously vindicated. His response to the enemy commander's humble request for pity (1.84–8) offered both an answer to the political problems that began the war and a proclamation of the principles that could help overcome civic division and civil war and "restore order and good government for Rome" (Batstone & Damon 2006: 34; Raaflaub forthcoming).

FURTHER READING

Caesar's *Civil War* (*Bellum civile*) is easily accessible in the Penguin translation (Gardner 1967); Carter 1991, 1993 offer translation and historical commentary. Batstone and Damon 2006 is now indispensable as a literary and narratological, but also political and ideological, analysis of the work. Caesar's career and the prehistory of the civil war of 49/8 BC, as well as the history of Caesar's last years, are discussed in part I of this volume; see also Gelzer 1968 and Meier 1995. Recent discussions of the crisis and fall of the republic and the role of the civil war of 49/8 in this process include Morstein-Marx and Rosenstein 2006, Tatum 2006, and especially Osgood 2006. On Caesar as a general and strategist, see Rosenstein, chapter 7 in this volume. Collins 1972 remains the most balanced discussion of Caesar as a propagandist. For Caesar's political strategy in the civil war, see Raaflaub 1974a (essential aspects are summarized in Raaflaub 2003: esp. 59–61) and forthcoming. Although focusing on the *Gallic War*, Riggsby 2006 offers valuable insights as well on many aspects that concern the *Civil War*.

CHAPTER FOURTEEN

The Continuators: Soldiering On

Ronald Cluett

The Pseudo-Caesars

Caesar's Continuators were those men in Caesar's army who took it upon themselves to complete Caesar's campaign narratives of the Gallic and Civil Wars, thereby bequeathing posterity unique contemporary accounts of the transitional years of 51–50 BC, as well as of the Alexandrian, African, and Spanish Wars of 48–45 BC. They knew that Caesar was a hard act to follow, in literary skill no less than political and military prowess. In a culture in which Cicero was able to assert (not without considerable self-interest, of course) that eloquence should rank higher than military victory in contributing to the greatness of the Roman people (*Brutus* 255–66), Caesar excelled at both. Even among his contemporaries, his elegant and lucid prose had already won him both praise and renown. Cicero describes the virtues and the effects of Caesar's commentaries (*Brutus* 262):

> [Brutus]: [A]tque etiam commentarios quosdam scripsit rerum suarum.
> [Cicero]: Valde quidem, inquam, probandos; nudi enim sunt, recti et venusti, omni ornatu orationis tamquam veste detracta. sed dum voluit alios habere parata, unde sumerent qui vellent scribere historiam, ineptis gratum fortasse fecit, qui volent illa calamistris inurere: sanos quidem homines a scribendo deterruit; nihil est enim in historia pura et inlustri brevitate dulcius.
>
> [Brutus]: He has even written some commentaries of his accomplishments.
> [Cicero]: And such, I say, as are worthy of high praise: for they are plain, correct, and elegant, and stripped as if undressed of all the ornaments of rhetoric. But while he wished only to furnish raw materials to others, which those who wish to write history might draw upon, he may, perhaps, have gratified the vanity of a few who would like to brand those materials with clumsy and excessive ornamentation. However, he has prevented all sensible men from writing. For there is nothing in history sweeter than pure and graceful economy of expression.

Such an assessment was not unique to Cicero, as Suetonius' approving quotation of Cicero's comments in his biography of Caesar attests (*Iul.* 56). Indeed, at least some of the Continuators were aware of the precedential burden Caesar's literary abilities imposed on their undertaking. Aulus Hirtius, legate of Caesar in Gaul and consul in the year after Caesar's assassination, composed Book 8 of the *Gallic War* and may also be the author of the *Alexandrian War* (debate over his authorship continues to this day). The letter from Hirtius to his fellow Caesarian Cornelius Balbus that opens Book 8 contains the following deferential preface:

> Coactus assiduis tuis vocibus, Balbe, cum cotidiana mea recusatio non difficultatis excusationem, sed inertiae videretur deprecationem habere, rem difficillimam suscepi. Caesaris nostri commentarios rerum gestarum Galliae, non comparantibus superioribus atque insequentibus eius scriptis, contexui novissimumque imperfectum ab rebus gestis Alexandriae confeci usque ad exitum non quidem civilis dissensionis, cuius finem nullum videmus, sed vitae Caesaris. Quos utinam qui legent scire possint quam invitus susceperim scribendos, qua facilius caream stultitiae atque arrogantiae crimine, qui me mediis interposuerim Caesaris scriptis. Constat enim inter omnes nihil tam operose ab aliis esse perfectum, quod non horum elegantia commentariorum superetur: qui sunt editi, ne scientia tantarum rerum scriptoribus deesset, adeoque probantur omnium iudicio ut praerepta, non praebita, facultas scriptoribus videatur. Cuius tamen rei maior nostra quam reliquorum est admiratio: ceteri enim, quam bene atque emendate, nos etiam, quam facile atque celeriter eos perfecerit scimus. Erat autem in Caesare cum facultas atque elegantia summa scribendi, tum verissima scientia suorum consiliorum explicandorum. Mihi ne illud quidem accidit, ut Alexandrino atque Africano bello interessem; quae bella quamquam ex parte nobis Caesaris sermone sunt nota, tamen aliter audimus ea, quae rerum novitate aut admiratione nos capiunt, aliter, quae pro testimonio sumus dicturi. Sed ego nimirum, dum omnes excusationis causas colligo ne cum Caesare conferar, hoc ipsum crimen arrogantiae subeo, quod me iudicio cuiusquam existimem posse cum Caesare comparari. Vale.
>
> Prevailed on by your persistent appeals, Balbus, I have undertaken a most difficult task, since my daily refusals appear to possess the excuse of laziness, not inability. I have compiled a continuation of our Caesar's accomplishments in Gaul, not to be compared to his own writings, which precede or follow them; and recently, I have completed what he left incomplete after the events in Alexandria – not to the end of civil unrest, of which we see no end, but of Caesar's life. If only those who read them might know how unwillingly I undertook the task of writing them, so that I might more easily escape the charge of stupidity and arrogance, in interposing myself in Caesar's writings. For it is universally agreed, that nothing was ever completed with such great care, that it is not exceeded in elegance by these commentaries, which were published so that later writers would not lack knowledge of such accomplishments; and they are so approved by all, that later writers seem deprived of rather than furnished with material. Our admiration of this fact is greater than that of other men; for others know how well and how flawlessly he composed them, while we know how quickly and easily. For Caesar possessed both ability and the greatest elegance in writing, and also a thorough knowledge of the means of conveying his ideas. It did not befall me to participate in the Alexandrian or African wars; and although these are partly known to me from conversation with Caesar himself, yet we listen differently to those things which strike us with admiration at their novelty, and those which we intend to record for posterity. But, in truth, while I urge every apology,

> that I may not be compared to Caesar, I submit to the charge of vanity, by thinking that I can be compared with Caesar in anyone's judgment. Farewell.

Hirtius' preface offers more than a diplomatic disclaimer of any ability or intent to rival Caesar as prose stylist. For one thing, Hirtius' confessed inferiority to Caesar seeks – quite unsuccessfully, as we shall see – to pre-empt unflattering comparisons between his own and Caesar's literary efforts. Moreover, at the same time as it attempts to distance and distinguish Hirtius' literary accomplishment from that of Caesar, Hirtius' preface also serves to bind himself and his work more closely to Caesar. In part, the association with Caesar is literary: however stylistically divergent (and inferior) Hirtius' efforts, they nonetheless provide continuity and completion to the otherwise disconnected and incomplete accounts Caesar himself wrote. In part, the association is political: Hirtius reminds the reader not only of the obvious fact that he was a follower of Caesar, but also of his proximity and access to Caesar himself. This intimacy with Caesar can compensate for Hirtius' absence from some of the battles he seeks to recount. Finally, Hirtius suggests a larger historical connection between his own and Caesar's campaign narratives: both address but do not conclude the story of civil unrest at Rome, which has outlasted Caesar's campaigns, Caesar's life, and Hirtius' self-defined mandate, and now stretches endlessly into the future.

In one of the many ironies of the Continuators' work, Hirtius did not complete his own attempt to complete Caesar's commentaries. Outright skepticism about his authorship of the *African* and *Spanish Wars* has accompanied uncertainty about his authorship of the *Alexandrian War* since antiquity. While insufficient evidence exists to attribute either the *African* or the *Spanish Wars* to a specific person, the consensus of current opinion both excludes Hirtius from the list of candidates and posits separate authorship for the two works. The Caesarian corpus therefore contains the works of at least four authors, and five if Hirtius did not write the *Alexandrian War*. As a result, the preface to Book 8 of the *Gallic War*, in stating Hirtius' position and intentions, does not offer a detailed roadmap of everything the Continuators wrote. It does, however, offer a robust analytical framework for understanding the Continuators' relationship with Caesar, both individually and collectively. As suggested above, that relationship was simultaneously literary, political, and historical – categories which we must consider in turn even as they insist on collapsing in upon one another.

The Discontinuators

If one of the Continuators' literary goals was to flatter Caesar by comparison, they succeeded brilliantly. Indeed, few works of Latin literature have come in for as much sustained criticism – on their own literary merits and by contrast with Caesar's – as those of the Continuators. Even Hirtius, whose Latin prose is by far the best of the group and who wrote a draft of Caesar's *Anti-Cato* cited approvingly by Cicero (*Att.* 12.40, 12.41), is not exempt. Critics have described Book 8 of the *Gallic War* as "arguably the most boring book in the Caesarian corpus" for its constant emphasis on legionary maneuvers (Welch 1998), and have accused Hirtius of "crudeness" and of replacing Caesar's "subtle thought and narration" with "unrefined judgment and representation" in his exaggerated portrayals of anti-Roman leaders (Barlow 1998: 155, 157). Both the repetitious style of the *African War* and its failure to offer a full or satisfying treatment of the battle of Thapsus – a vital victory in which Caesar defeated Scipio and Pompey's remaining Senatorial supporters – have provoked even more unflattering critical assessments. One passage in particular, which strings multiple imperfect verbs after a single subordinating conjunction, suggests the challenges that reading the *African War* presents to the rhetorically sophisticated reader (*African War* 5):

> Postquam una nocte et die ad oppidum consumpta neque responsum ullum a Considio dabatur, neque et reliquae copiae succurrebant neque equitatu abundabat et ad oppidum oppugnandum non satis copiarum habebat et eas tironum neque primo adventu convulnerari exercitum volebat, et oppidi egregia munitio et difficilis ad oppugnandum erat ascenus et nuntiabatur auxilia magna equitatus oppidanis suppetias venire, non est visa ratio ad oppugnandum oppidum commorandi, ne, dum in ea re est Caesar occupatus, circumventus a tergo ab equitatu hostium laboraret.
>
> After a night and day spent [outside] the town with no response from Considius, and [after] the remainder of Caesar's forces had not come relieve him, and [after] he had neither an abundance of cavalry nor sufficient forces to attack the town – and those he did have were new recruits – and [after] he did not wish his army to suffer wounds right after their arrival – and the approach for attacking the town was difficult and the town well fortified – and [after] it was announced that large forces of cavalry were arriving to aid the townspeople, there did not seem to be a reason for waiting around to attack the town lest, while occupied with that task, Caesar end up in a difficult situation, surrounded from behind by the cavalry of the enemy.

To call such prose "ungainly" and "marked by a definite poverty of expression" seems generous (Way 1955).

Nothing, however, can compare with the critical venom directed at the *Spanish War*, which has been variously described as the "worst book in Latin literature" (Holmes 1967 [1923]), the "worst piece of Latin literature" (Storch 1977: 201) and "the most illiterate and exasperating book in classical literature" (Van Hooff 1974: 123). Part of that exasperation results from grammar that would receive a failing grade in introductory Latin. Use of the subjunctive where the indicative is called for is particularly jarring (*Spanish War* 22):

> Qui cum ad oppidum venissent, nostri, qui fuissent equites Romani et senatores, non sunt ausi introire in oppidum, praeter quam qui eius civitatis fuissent.
>
> When they reached the town, our men, who had been Roman knights and senators, did not dare to enter the town, other than those who were part of the community.

No less exasperating are numerous passages of thoughtless disorganization. Seek in vain to identify, let alone appreciate, the narrative logic of the following (*Spanish War* 10):

> Insequenti luce Arguetius ex Italia cum equitatu venit. Is signa Saguntinorum rettulit quinque, quae ab oppidanis cepit. Suo loco praeteritum est quod equites ex Italia cum Asprenate ad Caesarem venissent. Ea nocte Pompeius castra sua incendit et ad Cordubam versus iter facere coepit. Rex nomine Indo, qui cum equitatu suas copias adduxerat, dum cupidius agmen adversariorum insequitur, a vernaculis legionariis exceptus est et interfectus.
>
> The next day Arguetius came with his cavalry from Italy. He brought five standards of the people of Saguntia, which he seized from its residents. I overlooked putting in its proper place that the cavalry who came to Caesar from Italy with Asprenas had arrived. That night Pompey burned his camp and set out on the journey to Corduba. A king by the name of Indo, who had led his own forces alongside the cavalry, was intercepted and killed by the local legions while pursuing the enemy column a bit too eagerly.

Great Latin prose that sure ain't.

The first impression the Continuators therefore make on many readers – in Latin, certainly, but also in English translation – is that they have been misnamed. They are not Continuators at all, but Discontinuators. This impression is not wholly justified. In part, it reflects the poor state of the manuscript tradition for much of this portion of the Caesarian corpus. Book 8 of the *Gallic War* is included with the manuscripts of Books 1 through 7, which are more reliable and less riddled with gaps and corrupt passages than the manuscripts of the *Civil War*. As a result, Hirtius' work, while still qualitatively different from Caesar's, appears coherent and whole. The manuscripts of the *Alexandrian*, *African*, and *Spanish Wars*, on the other hand, are included with the much weaker and less reliable manuscripts of the *Civil War*. They contain more gaps, sentence fragments, and passages of uncertain meaning, and offer fewer opportunities for cross-checking and correction, than do the Gallic War narratives. The *Spanish War* is particularly problematic in this regard. It begins with a sentence fragment and has more than five hundred corrupt passages in its 42 paragraphs. Such a compromised textual tradition would disrupt and distort even the smoothest and most polished prose; its effect on the Continuators is to render uninspired writing often unintelligible.

Moreover, some of the apparent discontinuity between the Continuators and Caesar's own writing also reflects the nature of the Continuators' literary undertaking. Caesar himself was (or so he claimed) writing commentaries, which "do not pretend to be other than documentary drafts" preparatory to "the elaborated synthesis of a historically finished text" (Henderson 1996: 269–70. See Kraus, chapter 12, pp. 159–61; Raaflaub, chapter 13, pp. 179–80). The Continuators, and the authors of the *African* and *Spanish Wars* in particular, were providing the drafts of those drafts. In other words, they were offering unredacted, unpolished, often day-by-day accounts of life on the front lines which could form the raw material for later, more sophisticated narratives – particularly since, as he himself admits, Hirtius was not an eyewitness to each battle he intends to recount. Many of the weaknesses of both style and substance in the Continuators' writing can be explained with reference to this status as rough draft, including the repetition of set phrases to establish a scene or advance the narrative, the focus on trivial detail at the expense of the broader strategic picture, and the failure to distinguish or emphasize the engagements (Thapsus in particular) of such obvious importance even in the hindsight of contemporaries. Indeed, the authors of the *Alexandrian*, *African*, and *Spanish Wars* may not have had literary goals at all, because they knew that they were offering not the finished product but the raw materials with which others would work. We should therefore not hold them to account for failing to achieve a literary goal they themselves would have disclaimed.

It is even possible to find merit in the stylistic discontinuity between the Continuators and Caesar. Certainly, as will be discussed below, there is much of sociological and political interest. Ironically, this is particularly true of the Continuators other than Hirtius, about whose career we possess some detailed knowledge. In the case of the *African* and *Spanish Wars*, and to a lesser extent the *Alexandrian War*, literary style serves as an early indication and persistent reminder that the various authors are not simply loyal to Caesar but clearly and unequivocally his subordinates, whose literary talents and ambitions are as modest as their military station. As a result, their prose can provide important evidence about contemporary colloquial Latin usage – including, in the case of the author of the *Spanish War*, a fondness for quoting the early Roman playwright Ennius – which Caesar himself would not employ. Even Cicero's more informal and personal correspondence, reflecting as it does both his literary ability and his social station, is not comparable. This is just one of the ways in which the Continuators offer a unique contemporary voice, the value of which has often been summarily and unfairly dismissed on the basis of aesthetic criteria alone. Not all discontinuity is regrettable.

However we choose to explain it and whatever interest we are able to find in it, the fact remains that the transition from Caesar to Hirtius, and between Hirtius and the subsequent Continuators, is jarring. Moreover, it is not only stylistic, but structural. In some cases, the Continuators seek to impose continuity on discontinuous events. Book 8 of the *Gallic War* begins with the admission that Caesar has already conquered all of Gaul and therefore the implication that what follows will be at best an afterword to what has preceded. As a result, as one critic has noted, Hirtius commits an "unwitting disruption of his friend's design" in violating the "closure" effected by the defeat of Vercingetorix in Book 7 (Torrigan 1998: 59). The *Alexandrian War* does seek to complete the narrative of the Alexandrian campaign which begins at the end of Caesar's *Civil War* – but the very effort at structural continuity only serves to highlight the shift in authorship. The *African War* begins abruptly and without explanation with Caesar's arrival in Lilybaeum in Sicily prior to sailing to Africa, utterly disconnected from his return to Italy at the conclusion of the *Alexandrian War*. Perhaps ironically, given the opprobrium it has otherwise suffered, the *Spanish War* does begin with a succinct summary of the previous two campaigns, "with Pharnaces defeated and Africa reduced." Of course, these inconsistent transitions reflect the unfinished nature of the individual texts and of the collection as a whole, discussed above. Nonetheless, their effect in their current form is to highlight the shifting authorial voices and the status of the individual texts as discrete narrative units rather than to emphasize any deeper continuity or coherence in Caesar's many separate campaigns and victories during the years in question.

This combination of stylistic and structural discontinuity has consequences for more than our ease and aesthetic pleasure as readers. For one thing, it serves to periodize our understanding of the events the Continuators recount. That is, in offering a series of self-contained, structurally and stylistically discontinuous narratives, the Continuators lead us to consider each campaign primarily as an independent, distinct event or sequence of events rather than as part of a larger whole. (This is true even of Book 8 of the *Gallic War*, which presents 51 BC as a distinct "transitional year" between the conclusion of hostilities in Gaul and the outbreak of hostilities in Italy as much as it offers a "completion" of the Gallic campaign.) Moreover, because of the progressive decline in literary quality from Caesar to Hirtius to the authors of the *African War* and, in particular, the *Spanish War*, this periodization further suggests a relative importance for the events in question, with Caesar's own writings dealing with the most important events and the Continuators merely tying up successively less important loose ends after him. In other words, the Continuators don't just produce second-rate writing; they write about second-rate events.

Periodization is a useful and probably inevitable tool of historical analysis, offering as it does a convenient and chronologically precise means of ordering complex chains of events. Nevertheless, we are justified in asking at least two questions about periodization in the Continuators. Is it historically accurate, or at least justifiable? Do the Continuators' accounts contain any other qualities or perspectives which work to counteract the perception of discontinuity their individual works convey?

The first question can be addressed from multiple perspectives. First, the divisions between the Continuators' works, and between their works and Caesar's, reflect a natural ordering of Caesar's campaigns of the late 50s and 40s BC. Each of the wars the Continuators recount took place in a geographically distinct area, at a chronologically distinct time, against individually distinct Roman and foreign enemies. Even the discontinuity of Book 8 of the *Gallic War* represents a distinct and final phase of the Gallic campaign, when the major foes were defeated and only residual operations remained. Moreover, to the extent that the Continuators leave the impression that the battles they deal with are secondary in importance to the ones Caesar himself narrates, that impression is justified by the identity of the enemies Caesar faces: Vercingetorix and Pompey in Caesar's own works, versus scattered Gallic holdouts and surviving Pompeian loyalists in the Continuators. The defeats of Vercingetorix and of Pompey were not merely symbolic; they were substantive as well, virtually eliminating the opposition to Caesar in one case and arguably fatally weakening it in the other.

On the other hand, the Continuators' works might reflect more accurately the importance of the events they describe were they more inclusive or more judicious in their selection of material. Book 8 of the *Gallic War*, while setting the stage for the outbreak of civil war in 49 BC, does little to explain the relationship between Caesar's victory in Gaul, his future political ambitions, and the reaction they provoked at Rome. The *Alexandrian War* is entirely silent about Caesar's relationship with

Cleopatra, thereby preserving the reticence initiated by Caesar in Book 3 of the *Civil War* but also effacing one of the most significant and memorable players in both Caesar's life and the course of events in Egypt. The *African War* expresses the expected outrage at Scipio's subordination to Juba's non-Roman leadership and concomitant betrayal of his illustrious ancestry, but provides more details about comparatively trivial events, such as an order of battle for a battle that never takes place, than it does about the battle of Thapsus, where Caesar ultimately defeated Scipio. Similarly, the *Spanish War* devotes considerable attention to trivial details while failing entirely to convey any sense of the symbolic importance of the defeat of Pompey's sons Gnaeus and Sextus at Munda in 45 BC, or even simply the non-trivial fact that Caesar's victory there completed his final military campaign of the civil war.

In other words, many events are more significant than the treatment (or lack of treatment) they receive from the Continuators might suggest. Indeed, even if we acknowledge the generic limitations of campaign narratives, which are primarily expository rather than analytical, the years 51–50 and 47–45 BC have a military importance which the Continuators convey imperfectly at best. A pacified Gaul ensured not only that Caesar's own attention would not be diverted from his political ambitions at Rome, but that his army would be available to support him if needed. After Pharsalus, the continuing resistance to Caesar was serious, substantial, and well organized. More generally – and most importantly – a civil war was being waged. Hirtius had no illusions about the nature of the conflict, as his declaration of despair at the endlessness of civil discord indicates (*Gallic War* 8). However, as we shall see, overt reference to civil war is virtually absent from the Continuators. It is the brutal truth their discrete, discreet narratives avoid, the underlying continuity their discontinuities obscure. It is a truth, moreover, that the Continuators were not alone in avoiding – indeed, their silence on the subject is not only one component of their loyalty to Caesar but also a key to the important insights the Continuators offer into the relationship between civil war and imperial conquest at Rome.

Following Caesar: Continuators after All

Criticism of the Continuators extends beyond their infelicities of style to include the lack of nuance, subtlety and originality in their portrayal of Caesar's leadership and his cause. In this analysis, the authors of the *African* and *Spanish Wars*, who give no indication that they possess any access to Caesar's inner councils or any high military rank, come off as little more than "adjutant acolytes in the secretariat" (Henderson 1996: 274). Even Hirtius, who served as praetor in 46 BC, governor of Transalpine Gaul in 45 BC, and had been Caesar's envoy to Pompey in 50 BC, completes the *Gallic War* as part of his "mimetic project" in his role as "Caesar's lieutenant and amanuensis" (Henderson 1996: 271–2). Such assessments correctly emphasize both the Continuators' place in the hierarchy of Caesar's command and their unwavering conviction in both his generalship and the legitimacy of the values he claimed to be fighting to defend. However, they fail to appreciate the importance of the foundation of the Continuators' loyalty to Caesar, and its consequences for understanding the ways in which the Continuators seek to affirm and promote Caesar's message. Ultimately, the political relationship between the Continuators and Caesar is more complex than the simple and obvious assertion that they were followers of Caesar might suggest.

The Continuators were soldiers. Although he eventually serves Caesar in many capacities, both political and military, Hirtius first appears as Caesar's legate in Gaul in 54 BC. The other Continuators never indicate that they performed any role or held any office other than giving loyal service in Caesar's army. Indeed, if their emphasis on the long service to Caesar of their fellow soldiers is any indication, they spent many years under Caesar's command (*African War* 45). The Continuators were therefore products of the unique culture of the Roman legion on long service abroad, which one Roman historian has referred to as a distinct "society" with its own customs (MacMullen 1984). These include detachment from the daily life and politics of Rome, and strong if not total identification with both their military commander and the minutiae of camp life. In the case of the Continuators, this meant repeated exposure to Caesar's rhetoric justifying his campaigns and his cause without any corresponding or counterbalancing exposure to the self-presentation of Caesar's adversaries. Indeed, the unilateral stream of defections to Caesar from his enemies suggests that while the appeal of Caesar's cause and message extend beyond his own army, that of his opponents enjoys no wider purchase. The Continuators' isolation from any larger rhetorical context thus combines with the daily exigencies of life on campaign to produce a unique window onto Caesar's reception by his subordinates, and how they not only convey but refashion his message.

That reception was not wholly positive, in spite of the image of the Continuators as unthinking sycophants that many commentators have transmitted. The Continuators record a number of occasions on which Caesar's troops call into question not only his tactical judgment, but also his strategic foresight and his ability to meet his troops' needs (*Alexandrian War* 7, *African War* 3, 16, 24). At other times, Caesar is unable to restrain his troops' zeal, and yields to their thirst for battle, thus suggesting that he does not always retain full control of his army (*Alexandrian War* 22, *African War* 54). These episodes demonstrate that Caesar's troops possess powers of critical judgment independent of their commander, and also show the raw power of their numbers to which Caesar must on occasion cede, particularly when their immediate needs are pressing. Similarly, Hirtius places more emphasis on legates in Book 8 than occurs throughout the rest of the *Gallic War* (other than Book 3), thereby reminding the reader that behind Caesar's brilliant command stand numerous loyal functionaries. The overall effect of such passages does not ultimately detract from Caesar's talents as a general. If anything, it emphasizes Caesar's unique role as the indispensable visionary of the sometimes fractious and short-sighted troops under his command, as well as his tolerance and empathy as a leader. It does so, however, in a way that retains for the Continuators and their peers a role in Caesar's campaigns that Caesar cannot take for granted.

More often, of course, the Continuators have nothing but praise for Caesar's genius and legitimacy as a leader. They articulate this praise on multiple narrative levels. First, their interest in the daily details of campaigning provides an ideal canvas on which to portray Caesar's tactical genius, and his omniscience and swiftness as a decision-maker in particular. This focus on the mundane also showcases the intimacy and rapport Caesar has with his army – not a distant, remote leader, but one who can address his troops' fears by abandoning his role as general and training them *ut lanista tirones gladiatores condocofacere* (*African War* 71). At the same time, the Continuators' immersion in the rhetoric of Caesar's camp and their uncritical acceptance of his cause result in stark juxtapositions between the legitimacy of Caesar's fight on behalf of the dignity of the Roman people and the Roman state and the behavior of his opponents, who are either despicable barbarians, or Romans such as Scipio and Gnaeus Pompey all the more despicable for acting like barbarians and thereby betraying their proud Roman heritage (Cluett 2003: 123–4). In addition, the Continuators even manage to praise Caesar for qualities about which he himself remains restrained or silent, such as his *clementia*, his *felicitas*, and his performance of his religious duties (Weinstock 1971: 26). In so doing, they not only replay but amplify important aspects of Caesar's self-presentation, providing in the process further evidence of their independent perspectives.

On other occasions, the Continuators elect to share Caesar's silence on certain sensitive topics. Most famously, the *Alexandrian War* makes no mention of Caesar's relationship with Cleopatra, or of the birth of Caesarion, thus preserving the silence Caesar initiated in Book 3 of the *Civil War*. In this regard at least, it genuinely represents a continuation of Caesar's own narrative. More broadly, however, the Continuators never use the term *bellum civile* ('civil war') to refer either to a given battle or to the overall campaign in which Caesar is engaged. Indeed, even the use of the terms 'Caesarians' and 'Pompeians' to refer to Caesar's and Pompey's followers is confined to descriptions of the campaign against Pompey's sons in Spain. This silence about the real nature of the war being fought both comports with Caesar's own preferred claim that he was fighting on behalf of his rights and for the Roman state and its people against a faction in the Senate, and reflects a deep-seated Roman discomfort about civil war that extends beyond Caesar's partisan perspective and the Continuators' judicious reticence. It is nonetheless striking, given both the presence of Roman opponents at every turn and the references throughout the Continuators to the continued unsettled conditions at Rome and in the empire at large (Cluett 2003: 127). However parochial and mundane the central concerns of their narratives may be, the Continuators do make clear that they were not ignorant of the larger political context of the years 48–45 BC.

Just as silence about civil war suggests an underlying literary continuity between the Continuators' work and that of Caesar, so that silence provides the key to understanding the Continuators' political relationship with Caesar. That relationship was predicated upon physical, psychological, and temporal distance from Rome, combined with long-term exposure to Caesar's command and Caesar's rhetoric in the insular culture of an army on campaign abroad. Such conditions enabled the Continuators to present each individual campaign as one more campaign of imperial conquest undertaken by Caesar on behalf of the Roman people, just as Caesar himself would ultimately celebrate individual triumphs over Egypt, Africa, and Spain. They also enabled the Continuators to associate Caesar's person with the Roman people for whom he claimed to be fighting, without any countervailing institutional constraints such as the Senate or a legitimate political opposition. Moreover, they allowed the Continuators to demonize their Roman military opponents, equating them morally and politically with the numerous foreign foes they faced in each provincial setting. Such demonization only further idealized Caesar, whose gentleness and clemency represented real, as opposed to barbarized, Roman values. The result is a portrait of Caesar grounded in a combination of propaganda and direct experience, in which the rupture of civil war is effaced and the continuity of imperial conquest upheld, even as the reality of civil war insists on asserting itself every time Roman faces Roman on the battlefield. In providing such an account, the Continuators demonstrated their loyalty to Caesar and their understanding of his preferred interpretation of events; but they also reflected and refracted the conditions under which they lived and fought. To the extent that they may be justly accused of parroting Caesar's propaganda, their mimesis must be understood within the context of their lives. The political and social value of the Continuators' work is therefore considerable; whether their portrayal of events has any historical merit is another question entirely.

Civil War, Province, and Empire

Hirtius makes clear in his preface to Book 8 of the *Gallic War* that he recognizes that his effort to complete the narrative of Caesar's campaigns from the conclusion of the Gallic Wars through Caesar's assassination represents only a portion of the larger narrative of the civil wars, to which he sees no end. This admission is both judicious and modest. It distances Caesar from ultimate responsibility for the course of the civil wars – the focus is on Caesar as the victim rather than the perpetrator of the conflict – and disclaims for Hirtius and the other Continuators any ambition to write a complete or thorough account of those violent and troubled years. As we have seen, such modesty is not wholly misplaced. The Continuators' work is not only fragmented, uneven, and episodic, but literally and figuratively provincial. Its ideological simplicity and lack of sustained interest in any larger political context reflect the authors' physical and psychological distance from Rome, and their social distance from the decision-making elite. (Even an emissary of some stature such as Hirtius was not a power in his own right.) At the same time, however, Hirtius for once is being far too modest. The Continuators' provincialism is their strength, not their weakness. They have provided us with dispatches from the front, in which all of the paradoxes and tensions of civil war at Rome are thrown into high relief. The Continuators are not distant or removed from the central issues of civil war – they are right in the center of them.

Civil war drew Romans into the provinces in multiple ways. Prior military service as a commander resulted in important bases of political support in the provinces, which offered a source of both manpower and leverage against one's domestic opponents. Indeed, this is exactly the role that Caesar hoped his Gallic victory would play in his conflict with Pompey. At the same time, of course, any lasting victory at Rome required overcoming one's opponents' parallel sources of provincial support. Juba's support of Pompey in Africa is a prime example. The very existence of these bases of support also made the provinces an attractive refuge and center of resistance for Romans fleeing the capital, where they hoped to rely on friendly local rulers, as well as resident Romans and veterans of Roman military service, to bolster their resistance. (Pompey's fatal reception in Egypt suggests some of the hazards of such reliance.) Finally, the larger context of civil war provided an opportunity for new conquest, as Caesar's campaign to subjugate Egypt indicates. The author of the Alexandrian war makes clear that the Egyptians themselves well understood this: they fear that if Caesar is not defeated, Egypt will become a Roman province (*Alexandrian War* 3). In response, civil war also provides an opportunity for new assertions of local resistance to Roman rule, as the guerrilla warfare against Caesar in Spain as well as the war in Alexandria attests.

At the same time as it drew Romans into the provinces for a variety of political and military motives, so civil war drew the provinces deeper and deeper into the internal politics of a divided Rome. Neutrality was not an option when your territory was a potential theatre of war, your loyalty potentially so valuable to both sides. Nor was it necessarily desirable – while prior service to and patronage from a given general undoubtedly determined many of the provincial loyalties in the civil wars, unsentimental calculation of the likely ultimate victor also played a role. The cold reception Pompey got as he sought refuge throughout the formerly loyal East in the wake of his defeat at Pharsalus is particularly striking and telling in this regard. No one – Roman or foreign – wanted to be associated with the losing side, however much antagonists like Caesar might celebrate their clemency to their defeated foes. Many of the provincial players involved, such as Juba, had been around for a long time and understood the Roman political game well. But even where the players themselves were new, as in Egypt, the issue of resistance versus subjugation to Roman rule was not.

The provinces understood what the Romans involved could not explicitly admit: that while civil war was being fought over political questions at Rome – Caesar's right to stand for the consulship, the authority of the Senate and of Pompey's leadership of it to block that ambition – the ultimate prize was actually the Roman empire itself. Caesar certainly understood this, as his celebration of triumphs over not only Gaul, but Egypt, Africa, and Spain indicated. Indeed, he suggests as much indirectly, when he states that his goal is to leave the provinces and regions he visits free from internal discord, subject to the rule of law, and without fear of external aggression – in other words, loyal subjects of Rome (*Alexandrian War* 65). Moreover, the Continuators were complicit in this agenda, not only in their silence on the issue of civil war but by seeking to create a seamless continuum of campaigns from Gaul through Spain. It is also worth remembering in this context that Caesar's next planned campaign after Spain was Parthia, which would have bracketed the civil war campaigns of 48–45 BC between the two major and openly imperial projects of conquering Gaul and Parthia. As the Egyptians' anxiety about being made another province of the Roman empire suggests, the provinces well understood this underlying imperial agenda.

This interplay of civil war and imperial ambition offered the various antagonists multiple ideological and rhetorical opportunities. It allowed someone like Caesar to position himself as the true defender of the Roman people against the designs of his enemies and adversaries. In so doing, it allowed him to cloak his own imperial ambitions – whether he wanted to be an emperor or not, he certainly wanted to command an empire – in the guise of the defense and the expansion of the power and dignity of the Roman state. The presence of so many foreign foes and the fact that the main theatres of battle lay far outside Italy further allowed Caesar to demonize his Roman opponents by associating their actions and their cause with those of the barbarian enemy, rather than confront the less palatable truth of the fact that he was fighting barbarian enemies only because of the presence of his Roman foes in the provinces – or, in the case of Egypt, only because he sought to add its territory to the *imperium romanum*. Of course, Caesar's opponents had similar if not identical rhetorical opportunities and exploited them as vigorously as he did; but in the echo chamber of Caesar's camp such voices would have been heard rarely and easily dismissed.

The Continuators are on the front lines of these imperial and rhetorical battles. They are, of course, literally on the front lines of battle – out in the provinces in question and also in roles that offered them few protections from the dangers of the battlefield. But they are also on the front lines of these ideological tensions and self-serving rationalizations. They are the Romans being asked to identify their commander with the Roman state as a whole – no longer its duly appointed servant, but its defender and aspiring conqueror. Such an identification of commander and cause was hardly novel, of course, but the Continuators knew that the Rome on whose behalf Caesar claimed to be fighting was a center that no longer held, as their anxious references to continuing unrest there attest. Most strikingly, however, the Continuators are also the Romans being asked to see their fellow Romans as foreigners, barbarians, savages – not as the fellow citizens with whom they would celebrate their citizenship and unified civic pride in less troubled times. Their success or failure in that conceptual struggle would go a long way in determining the ultimate success or failure of the military battles in which they were engaged.

Even as they throw these tensions into high relief, the stark language of the Continuators' narratives suggests that they had surprisingly little difficulty assimilating and internalizing such viewpoints. The reasons could be many: Caesar's undoubted persuasive powers; the continuators' geographical isolation and the corresponding absence of alternative viewpoints (which would only have been of Caesar's opponents making essentially the same claims for themselves, in any case); the well-established dehumanization of the enemy that takes place during any war, civil or other; or even total cynicism about the relationship between rhetoric and reality in war, which at least some of the Continuators' more demoralized peers must have felt. (To revisit one last time the dim view of the Continuators' abilities held by many critics, it could even be the result of an incapacity to do anything more than parrot what they heard.) Certainly, the contrast between rhetoric and reality is particularly stark in the Continuators, whose narratives often privilege battlefield minutiae but who also regularly juxtapose Caesar's Roman virtues and the barbarian vices of both his foreign and his Roman enemies.

The Continuators, then, are not the marginal figures many have so mercilessly pilloried. They may be living and fighting at the peripheries of empire, far removed from the power politics of the senatorial elite – or, in the case of Hirtius, closer to that elite but operating entirely under the aegis of Caesar's patronage. And they may be writing of often unimportant and mundane details of campaign life, and doing so in Latin prose that reflects their humble station and modest literary abilities. But in the fractured politics of Rome under civil war, those peripheries became the terrain on which dominance at Rome itself was contested. It had always been so, of course – the link between military success in the provinces and political power at Rome was hardly novel by the Continuators' time. But the prize was no longer the opportunity to further advance one's career through even more illustrious service to Rome; it was, instead, the power to make Rome do one's bidding, to make Rome accept the terms on which one justified one's power. The foot soldiers in that contest were the men willing to kill their fellow Romans in that fight, and to accept – if only because of expedience and a lack of any alternative – the rationales they were given for doing so. The Continuators are our field guides and scouts to this brave new world. Their dispatches from the front are rarely elegant and often frustrating. The contrast between their clumsy narratives and Caesar's subtlety and sophistication of expression is striking. But Caesar's Continuators they nonetheless are, because they took his battles to the place where they would ultimately be won or lost – the front lines of empire, and of the transformation of empire Caesar sought to impose. As Hirtius recognized, the stories they had to tell, like the civil wars themselves, long outlasted Caesar's own life. Read them and weep.

FURTHER READING

Material in English on the Continuators is sparse even for the specialist; generalist treatments are nonexistent. The *Penguin Classics* edition of Caesar's *Civil War* (Gardner 1967) also includes translations of the *Alexandrian*, *African*, and *Spanish Wars* and offers a useful introduction. The introduction to the Loeb Classical Library volume containing the *Alexandrian, African, and Spanish Wars* is less helpful, but does contain excellent summaries of the various campaigns. Worthwhile treatments of Hirtius and his relationship with Caesar may be found in K. Welch and A. Powell (eds.), *Julius Caesar as Artful Reporter: The War Commentaries as Political Instruments* (London, 1998), which is available in most university libraries. One recent attempt to place the Continuators' work in its historical and political context is R. Cluett, "In Caesar's Wake: The Ideology of the Continuators," in F. Cairns and E. Fantham (eds.), *Caesar against Liberty: Perspectives on his Autocracy* (Cambridge, 2003), 118–31.

PART IV

Caesar's Reputation at Rome

CHAPTER FIFTEEN

Caesar's Political and Military Legacy to the Roman Emperors

Barbara Levick

Caesar's legacy to his successors in power came in two forms. At first they were closely interrelated. Caesar's own acts and plans, and later conceptions of them, were things that could be consciously adopted. Then there was his name itself, which was a matter of eager choice for his immediate heir; once C. Octavius had become C. Caesar it was inherited and hardly a matter of choice at all, becoming one again only after the downfall of the Julio-Claudians. These two themes and how they developed will be dealt with in order.

Caesar Augustus, more grandly Augustus Caesar, who was born in 63 BC and held supreme power from 30 BC until his death in AD 14, was the emperor closest in time and kinship to Julius Caesar. He was also a man whose ambiguity and deviousness continue to engage modern scholars. About Caesar he may genuinely have been in two minds and may reasonably have changed his attitude over the years. There has been vigorous controversy over Augustus' attitude towards his predecessor: did he push him into the background, even renounce him, or rather put him on display? In these general terms the debate is fruitless. It is always in particular areas and over individual issues that the attitude of Augustus and his successors can be made out; and the mere passing of time and with it changes of perspective will have had more effect than it has sometimes been allowed. In any case, there were items that could not be abolished. The games celebrating the *Victoria Caesaris* may have been distasteful to some early Augustan senators – for more than a decade of vicissitudes and killing, not to say natural mortality, would have thinned the ranks of old "Caesarians" in the House – but eleven days of games could not be cut out of the people's menu, and they are attested (with Claudius' victory added) in the reign of Trajan (*CIL* 6.37834; *Inscr. Ital.* 13.2.368, 372).

As to the interrelationship of the two themes, C. Octavius took the name C. Julius Caesar on entering upon his inheritance under his great-uncle's will, which, besides bequeathing him three-quarters of the estate, offered "adoption" at the foot of the page (Suet. *Iul.* 83.2). The young Octavian, as scholars conventionally call him for the period that began with the opening of the will in March 44 until he became Augustus at the beginning of 27, "owed everything to his name" (Cic. *Phil.* 13.11.24), and to his relationship with Caesar. If his maternal grandmother had not been Caesar's sister he could have expected, as the son of a man who had died an ex-praetor, the first of his branch of the clan to enter the Senate, only a mediocre career. It was with the backing of his name alone, says Velleius Paterculus (2.80.4), that he was able in 36 BC, after the defeat of Sextus Pompeius, to enter the camp of Lepidus in Sicily and win over his fellow Triumvir's legions.

But the name and the property were not enough for Octavian. The will seems, according to Roman practice, to have made him the main heir on condition that he took the name of the testator. But he wanted to be recognized as the legally adopted son of Caesar. Then the inheritance would give him membership of his new father's tribe and establish firm claims on his father's clients formal and informal; it would ensure the loyalty of Caesar's legions, of the people of Rome, and of many of Caesar's Italian sympathizers, especially veterans whom he had settled in colonies. But Octavian's father was dead, and that made him independent (*sui iuris*). As such, he could be adopted only by the method called *adrogatio*. This form of adoption, used in AD 4 for Augustus' stepson Tiberius and his orphan grandson Agrippa Postumus, required a presiding magistrate, priests, lictors representing the thirty *curiae* (divisions of the Roman People), above all the *rogator* (proposer) himself, impossible in the case of the dead Julius, to guarantee the propriety of the move, which extinguished the family rites (*sacra*) of the person adopted.

Nonetheless, in August 43, despite the understandable opposition of M. Antonius, consul in 44, who himself had a good claim to be Caesar's political heir, Octavian, now established in his first consulship, went through a ceremony that followed that of a formal adoption. On this basis Octavian claimed to be the legal son of Caesar and, when he had brought about his deification in 42, it was the justification for the designation "Son of the Deified" (*Divi filius*). In 36 Octavian duly demonstrated his devotion by issuing gold and silver coinage bearing his own name, Imperator Caesar Divi filius, and titles, all in the nominative case, on the obverse and running over on to the reverse, and showing there a temple with the legend "To the deified Julius" in its architrave (*RRC* 540.1 = p. 81, fig. 6.2). The relationship between obverse and reverse leaves no doubt of the unity of the two designs, however hazardous it may be to interpret conjunctions on later issues as uniting or disjoining the pair. By 32 the question who was Caesar's true political heir, vital in the struggle for leadership in 44–3, had been superseded by others, though one of them, the status of Cleopatra's son Caesarion, claimed by Antony as Caesar's true son by blood, not a mere adoptee, was related to the old dispute (Suet. *Iul.* 52.2). Caesar himself was ancient history, except perhaps in his colonies, and no longer the sole guarantee of legitimacy.

Caesar and his Acts

Any heir of Caesar would have a problem: he had been assassinated as a tyrant. Hence the difficulty of Caesar's role in the Principate. It was the monarchical power he

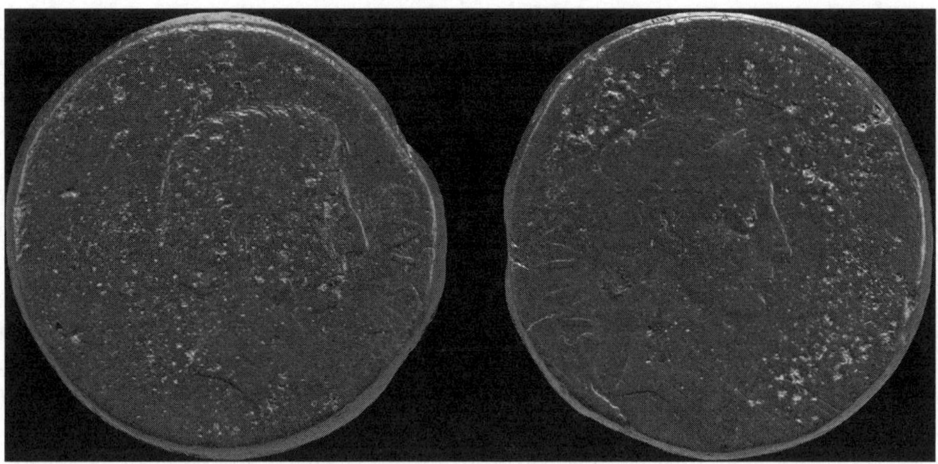

Figure 15.1 BMCRR Gaul 105; RCC 535/1Plate LXIII, no. 22 = p. 299, fig. 21.4. Obv. Head of Octavian as DIVI F; Rev. Head of Caesar as DIVOS IULIUS (see Zanker, chapter 21, p. 298).

wielded that Octavian/Augustus and his successors were after, but the better emperors knew that they should be restrained in their use of it. In the aftermath of the assassination Octavian was poised between assuaging Republican fears and outbidding Antony as the true successor. Caution did not prevent Octavian from openly swearing in late November 44 that he was entitled to aspire to the offices held by his father (Cic. *Att.* 16.15.3). When he finally joined the Caesarians Antony and M. Lepidus in the Second Triumvirate in November 43 there was no need to hold back. The swings of these years make it hard to accept the interpretation of coins showing Caesar with his wreath and full titulature on one side and Octavian bareheaded with the consulship and priestly title on the other as in any sense a renunciation of Caesarism (*RRC* 490.2; Ramage 1985). The "Liberators" were destroyed at Philippi in 42 and the relationship was an ace to play for all it was worth. In 38 C. Julius Caesar became Imperator Caesar (Syme 1958a), stressing the military merit that he had conspicuously failed to display at the battles of Philippi.

With Octavian's victories over Sex. Pompeius, his campaigns in Illyricum and then his successes at Actium and Alexandria over Antony and Cleopatra, that pressure eased. Augustus was his own man. It may have been in these post-Actian years that stories circulated of dreams experienced by the resolute defender of senatorial government Q. Lutatius Catulus and by Cicero when Octavian was just a boy (Catulus died in 60 BC) which showed him as the ruler of the Roman world selected by Jupiter (Suet. *Aug.* 94.8–9; Plut. *Cic.* 44.2–6) – but one who would be very different from the Dictator Caesar. The destined audience for the story was probably the apprehensive population of the country towns of Italy; not all senators would find the idea of a god-sent ruler acceptable. Something of the same feeling is conveyed by Vitruvius, writing in the 20s, when he speaks of Caesar's *imperium* (legally conferred power to command) being transferred to Augustus' *potestas* (legally conferred ability to act) (Vitr. *Arch.* Pr. 2).

The settlement of 28–27 BC, culminating in the conferment of the designation Augustus on the former Triumvir, marked a further decisive change: Caesar's moves towards a monarchical position in the state demonstrated to his astute son how *not* to go about reforming the Roman constitution. Syme's forthright remark in *The Roman Revolution* (1939: 317) that "Caesar's heir forswore the memory of Caesar" is at its most convincing here. The office of "Dictator" had been abolished after the assassination. Now Augustus developed the emollient title "Princeps" ("leading citizen"), which in itself carried no power and no lictors and above all was not exclusive. Certainly some of the Princeps' measures, vaunted in Augustus' *Res Gestae* or praised by later writers, may be seen as explicit renunciations of "Caesarian" behavior in vital matters, as they were of Triumviral behavior. It is a difficulty in stressing the distance that Octavian/Augustus kept between himself and Caesar, that some of the changes he made in 28–27 were also renunciations of Triumviral practice. Most obviously a repudiation of Caesar's approach was Augustus' refusal of the Dictatorship and *cura legum et morum*, both recorded in the *Res Gestae* (5f.); the latter, in its resemblance to a censorship with plenary powers and without a colleague (*summa potestate solus*) was close to Caesar's *praefectura morum*. In particular there was his handling of the State Treasury, making donations to it, as he insists, instead of rifling it as Caesar had scandalously done in 49 BC (*Res Gestae* 17.1). Then there was the matter of elections, which Caesar had arranged to be held three years beforehand to provide for the period he expected to be away fighting Parthia. He had divided elections between himself and the assemblies, so that half the candidates were nominated to office by him; and on top of that he made a mockery of electoral procedure by seeing that a protégé succeeded to a consulship that fell vacant for the last hours of 46 BC (Suet. *Iul.* 76 lists offences). By contrast Augustus explicitly restored the original procedures, which had also been disturbed by the Triumvirs, and went round canvassing in traditional style, until in AD 8 he was prevented by old age (Suet. *Aug.* 40.2, 56.1; Dio 55.34.2). Membership of the Senate was altogether a sore point in Caesar's regime. He exercised formal control, taking on the post of supervisor of manners (*praefectura morum*), and enlarged the Senate to 900 men, admitting supporters from the provinces, which caused outrage, for all their descent from Italian émigré families. Augustus himself held formal re-enrollments using consular or censorial power, and two were conducted by the senators themselves (A. H. M. Jones 1960: 19–26). As to the adlection of men from the provinces, Augustus was cautious: it was now that the country towns of Italy sent their notables to sit in the House, as the Emperor Claudius admitted, although he would have been glad of precedents for his own proposed admission of Gauls from Comata (*ILS* 212). Syme's verdict may be too sweeping, but these items show how careful Augustus was. Besides, everything he achieved provided a new precedent, his own, entailing the decline of Caesar's importance as a model. It would be too neat to claim that Augustus' agreement with the Parthians (20 BC) marked the end of his "obligations" to Caesar, but it did mark another stage in his emancipation. Sumptuary laws and attempts to increase the birth rate were traditional concerns of both Caesar and Augustus, but nothing is heard of the social reforms projected by Caesar (Suet. *Iul.* 43; Cic. *Marcell.* 23) in connection with those of Augustus, pushed through in 18–17 BC.

In lesser points of etiquette Caesar was certainly a model to avoid. In 9 BC fire damaged the Temple of Jupiter on the Capitol. Restoring it, Augustus made a point of keeping his own name off the building, as Caesar had failed to do when after his own repairs he allowed his name to replace that of Q. Lutatius Catulus (Dio 55.1.1; *RG* 20.1). Perhaps the assiduous attender Augustus knew that Caesar's blatant boredom with shows was unpopular (Suet. *Aug.* 45.1). Claudius was very willing to attend shows, but had noted another point: he rose when senators approached, and surely knew the story of Caesar's failure to do so, and how it had to be explained away (Suet. *Iul.* 78.1).

As Princeps, Augustus is known to have invoked Caesar the live statesman as a precedent only when the Senate was recalcitrant, over the funding of the new Military Treasury in AD 6–7 (Dio 55.24.9–25.6). That was a notable incident, which G. Herbert-Brown has explained (1994: 121) by the suggestion that Augustus was currently suffering from comparison with Caesar. In the later and harsher years of his Principate, when famine coincided with the Pannonian revolt and there was no military success elsewhere to report, that is possible; but if it was so, Augustus may well have been cruelly playing on such comparisons by putting forward an unwelcome "Caesarian" proposal.

Caesar has more mentions than anyone else in Augustan poetry. But signs of distancing had begun in Virgil, who omitted Caesar's figure from the shield made for Aeneas and put blame for the civil war on Caesar; most significant perhaps was his taking advantage of the ambiguity in the nomenclature to present the "Caesar" who was the culmination of the "whole progeny of Iulus" as Augustus (*Aen.* 6.789–90). Later in the Augustan Principate Livy was notoriously to praise Pompey – and to have that noticed by the Princeps (Tac. *Ann.* 4.34.3). The work of Ovid has been analyzed by Herbert-Brown (1994: 109–29). In the *Metamorphoses* (15.750, 850f.), Julius' main achievement is "fathering" Augustus (a wonderful reversal of authority of the two figures as it had been at Octavian's debut), and Caesar is glad to be surpassed (15.850f.). The *Fasti*, also written during the last decade of Augustus' Principate, does allow his achievements to appear – in the "bathos" of calendar reform (3.155–60). Of six Caesarian *Feriae* (birthday, military victories), Ovid's six-month *Fasti* celebrates one, employing an old veteran to introduce the material; the story leaves out Thapsus and Munda.

Caesar's final Augustan appearance, in Augustus' ultimate presentation of himself, the *Res Gestae,* is as the initiator of building schemes left incomplete for Augustus' attention, as a victim slaughtered by men that young Octavian had brought to justice, and as the occupant of a temple (*RG* 19–21; cf. Ovid *Fasti* 3.703f.). Not too much should be made of that. In the lost *Autobiography* of the mid-20s, the first of the 13 books must have been devoted to Octavian's early distinctions, owed to the Dictator, and, written with whatever finesse, it must have shed a favorable light on him. But the focus of the *Res Gestae* right from the start is on Augustus' achievements as an adult player in public life; his juniors in the dynasty are brought on labeled with their specific relationship to him, and as to his "father," he is simply dead before the curtain goes up.

But there was no reason why the safely dead and deified Dictator should disappear from official ideology in his capacity as a consecrated predecessor. The Principate of Augustus was replete with formal celebrations and commemorations. In 29, three days after Octavian's triple triumph, Caesar's temple was consecrated with celebratory games where his body had been cremated near the Regia (Dio 51.22.3), between two triumphal arches of the Princeps himself, to dominate the south side of the Forum Romanum; the podium of the temple was used at the funerals of Octavia in 11 BC and of Augustus himself by one of the speakers who delivered the *elogia*. Even after the constitutional changes of 28–27 BC he features, with the star that signaled his consecration, on the reverses of *denarii* from Spain (19 or 18 BC) and on obverses of 17 BC connected with the celebration of the Secular Games (the features are thought to show a close resemblance to those of Augustus); and on those of 12 (*RIC* 1^2 44, nos. 37ab and 38ab; 48 no. 102. 17: 66 no. 337–42; 74 no. 415 [See p. 300, fig. 21.6]; Pollini 1990: 352f.). The designations "Divi filius" and, for all Augustus' adopted sons, "Divi nepos" continued on inscriptions, and economies of design may account for its absence when it does not figure on coinage. Pliny the Younger, remarking that emperors, except Trajan, deified their predecessors to glorify themselves (*Pan.* 11.1), does not list Augustus, the founder, but that may be due to prudent respect.

Augustan architectural schemes in Rome (which contributed beneficially to the earnings of free workmen) were inspired in part by Caesar's plans, the Curia and Basilica Julia their realization: the Julian name, with all its dynastic implications, was to be imprinted on the city. Beside the Temple of the Deified Julius there was the Temple of Apollo attached to the Theatre of Marcellus, which had first been dedicated by Cn. Iulius, consul in 431 BC, and the Forum Augustum, first vowed in 42 BC, where, on the pediment of the Temple of Mars Ultor the ancestral Venus stood next to the dedicatee (buildings: Ramage 1985: 241–5). The deity ensconced in his temple naturally had no place in the line of great Romans who adorned the left flank of the Augustan Forum, nor in the parade of dead heroes (including Pompey) who played a role in Augustus' funeral procession. But it is also worth noticing projected buildings that were never constructed: the temples of Clementia Caesaris (dedicated 45 BC, but see Weinstock 1971: 309), Libertas, and the outrageous Concordia Nova.

The generous exposure of Caesar on the Augustan coinage did not continue after AD 14, and that was symptomatic of a change ushered in by the accession of Tiberius. The development of Divus Augustus himself as a paradigm helped to eclipse the memory of the Dictator. This is illustrated under Tiberius by the series of obverses in bronze displaying *DIVVS AVGVSTVS PATER*, sometimes with a star, and similar, though less copious, issues of Gaius and Claudius, with a strong revival during the civil wars of 68–9 struck in Spain and probably Gaul (*dupondii* and *asses*, 14–37: *RIC* 1^2 98f., no. 70–83; Gaius: 108–13; Claudius: 128 no. 101; Civil Wars: 197; 199f.; 210–12 no. 81–117; Galba: 234 no. 33). As Pliny the Younger said in his *Panegyric on Trajan* (88.10), the very title "Augustus" reminded him and his audience of the first to bear the name. Some emperors made explicit reference to Augustus in their accession speeches; others, like Vespasian, recalled him in their political language and gesture. Paradoxically, however, the deification of Augustus, a foregone conclusion in AD 14, enhanced Caesar's formal position. Caesar now became sacrosanct because of his role as Augustus' predecessor: Octavian's debt finally was repaid. Even the "Augustan" coins of the civil wars, 68–9, piquantly included a revival of the old Augustan reverse with a reference to *DIVVS IVLIVS*, with his star (*RIC* 1^2 211, no. 92). The status of Caesar had become a pendant to that of Augustus and was protected by the same law of *maiestas*, as the story of Cremutius Cordus and his writings, damned under Tiberius, seems to show, for all the defendant's implicit denial (Tac. *Ann.* 4.34f.; Dio 57.24.3).

Augustus himself was not necessarily a perfect model for a constitutionally minded Princeps, as Tiberius obliquely made clear in his colloquy with the Senate at his accession in AD 14 when he implied that the Augustan regime was an autocracy: incrustations of autocratic power due to *auctoritas* and custom were to be modified. Tacitus also makes it clear, reporting diverse summings-up of the reign (*Ann.* 1.9f.). Nonetheless, Tiberius uses Augustus as Augustus had never to our knowledge used Caesar, not as a precedent but as a trump card to play when his own ideas met opposition or disapproval. As Augustus too receded Caesar became available again as an alternative, at any rate for specific items and especially for such a ruler as Claudius, who came to power in AD 41 with the help of the Praetorian Guard while the Senate debated the restoration of the Republic and other candidates for the Principate. For the first time the Caesarian model comes to the surface: Claudius paid lip service to the example of Augustus, but seems to have felt a particular affinity with Caesar, and took up other ideas of his than the obvious one of the invasion of Britain: the draining of the Fucine Lake, the harbor at Ostia, more generally cultivation of the Roman *plebs* and generosity with the citizenship, although some of this may be no more than a shared reaction to hostility from the Senate. But there was no place for Caesar in the early years of Nero's reign, with their strong reaction against the previous regime and their repudiation of Claudian arbitrariness. His treatment in Lucan's *Pharsalia* presents him not as an imperial precedent but as a mere counterpart to Pompey.

Even Caesar's place in the conventional roll of "Emperors" is insecure. True, Suetonius starts his *Lives* with Caesar, and Appian (Praef. 6), by speaking of "Gaius Caesar," seems to present him as the creator of the Principate (but see Bucher 2000: 416 n. 18); certainly for Cassius Dio (53.17.1) Augustus' reign is the turning point between Republic and Empire. The abolition of the Dictatorship, the triumviral gap, and Augustus' performance in handing over affairs in 27 BC to the arbitrament of Senate and People made a break that was hard to bridge. Plutarch, while describing Augustus in his life of Numa as "the second to rule" (*Numa* 19.6), places Caesar unequivocally in his list of paired Greek and Republican heroes, as the counterpart of Alexander. But, as we shall see, Suetonius, favorite reading in Late Antiquity, proved influential in the highest quarters, the minds of emperors.

There was a more imposing criterion than literary choice for including Caesar in the canon, and at first sight decisive: he was the first "Divus." Yet he seems not to have been first in the line of Divi as construed in state cult under the Empire. His cult was "self-contained," like that of Cybele, who was confined to her temple on the Palatine. Uneasiness was felt about these cults, so they were isolated (Gradel 2002: 265): only Caesar's priest (a flamen; there were no *sodales*) and personnel were involved in the cult at his temple in the Forum. The Arval Brothers never sacrificed to him: their list of Divi began with Augustus (Scheid 1998). There seems to have been something unacceptable about Caesar even in his deification, which had gone further in state cult even before his death than Augustus was prepared to allow for himself: Caesar as Divus prevented Augustus and later emperors, such as Nero in 66, being deified in Rome before his death, as he had been, with a fatal outcome (Tac. *Ann.* 15.75.3). On the other hand Divus Julius, a title that avoided the ambiguous "Caesar," was included in the ritual of the third century *Feriale Duranum*, a calendar of festivals that originated under Augustus: Caesar was celebrated in the army without interruption. Here as in the minds of emperors and their subjects he was relegated to a gallery of military heroes. It is an attractive view that a shift came in perceptions of Caesar under Tiberius, when his military virtues could be celebrated without shaming the Princeps, and that the shift may be seen in the work of Valerius Maximus (Wardle 1997: 344).

For there were some essential duties of the Emperor, precisely those of the *imperator*, that Caesar had carried out impeccably: imperial conquest, demanding all of them, provided an unshakable basis for his status. He either completed a brilliant and alluring project (Gaul) or unavoidably left it uncompleted (Germany, Britain, Parthia) for his successors to carry out, excuse themselves for giving up, or claim to have dealt with by other means. So famous were Caesar's powers of leadership that Tacitus makes Germanicus Caesar, confronted by mutiny in AD 14, tell the troops how he had reduced an uprising by deriding them as "Quirites" ("citizens") (*Ann.* 1.42.3). So he would be looked back to as a soldier by Claudius and particularly by Trajan and Julian. Indeed, there was one strain in the tradition about Caesar that made him particularly attractive to certain emperors: his ambition of emulating Alexander. This was indicated by Plutarch's coupling in the *Lives* and by the story of his regretful comparison, made in Spain at the age of 31, of his own achievements with those of Alexander (Suet. *Iul.* 7.1). It was under Trajan that the reverse occurs on a "restored" coin of Caesar showing the goddess of retribution, Nemesis (Kienast 2001: 24, on *RIC* 2, 311 no. 815f.). At the time of his death he was preparing an attack on Parthia. Antony needed to take up Caesar's plan, but Augustus adroitly set it aside by scoring his diplomatic victory of 20 BC. Trajan resumed it with his war against the Parthians, 113–17 – and said how fortunate Alexander had been, so Dio reports (68.29.1). The Emperor Julian (361–3) also wished to emulate Alexander, as he admits in his own work, the *Caesars*. Already in preparation for his campaigns in Gaul Julian was studying Caesar's *Commentaries*, which he took with him into the field along with other edifying works, such as Plutarch's *Lives*, provided by the Empress herself (Julian, *Eusebia* 123D–124D) In the *Caesars* he brings Caesar on first of the Emperors, and makes him seem ready to contend with Zeus himself for dominion; his later speech parades his military successes and compares himself favorably with Alexander – who makes an indignant reply (308D; 319D–325). It is surprising that Julian included Augustus in his list of the three greatest warriors (317B); but there could be no questioning his choice of Caesar or Trajan. Later on Julian makes Augustus recall that when he sent his grandson Gaius to the East he offered him Caesar as a model for courage, alongside Pompey for cleverness, and Augustus himself for good fortune (332D). Courage is again the theme that is presented by a later source, the *Historia Augusta*, in relating the context of the assassination of Alexander Severus in 235 (*HA Sev. Alex.* 62). Severus was told by an astrologer that he would die by the sword of a barbarian; he joyfully misunderstood what was meant, taking it to refer to death in battle, and embarked on a long disquisition on eminent men who died by violence: Alexander the Great, Pompey, Caesar, Demosthenes, and Cicero. The theme, however, is not his but the late fourth-century author's; the unreliability of this biography is notorious.

Trajan's political relationship with the Dictator was weaker than that of Claudius: Caesar's political significance had faded, leaving the military aspect prime. For one thing, his post-Domitianic Senate was a very different one from what Claudius had had to contend with nearly sixty years before. A powerful military man whose position was secure, Trajan had come to power in 97–8 in the wake of an attempted Praetorian coup against Nerva. While avoiding tyranny, he ostentatiously played the military card. But it would be reading too much into this to insist on some sudden change taking place in the imperial attitude to Caesar during this reign. Long before Caesar is unequivocally presented as the first of the Emperors in Suetonius' series, he is taken as such by Josephus (*AJ* 18.32f., 224), and Valerius Maximus in his Preface makes Tiberius the third. But discussions of the practice of writers are not helpful, since each had his own agenda on each occasion he set pen to paper; one gross example is Pliny's cautious omission of Augustus from the list of Emperors who deified their predecessors for interested motives, while Tacitus includes Caesar in his assessment of the oratorical gifts of Rome's rulers; their political character is irrelevant to his survey. Equally the judgments of emperors depended on the purposes of the moment. It would have been out of the question for Flavians to include Caesarian precedents in their "Lex de Imperio" (*ILS* 244); even those of the undeified Tiberius were more relevant under the developed Principate than anything that Caesar had done. The rationale of the oaths taken to the *acta* of current and past emperors is the same: Caesar is never included, for his *acta*, though preserved, were hardly relevant after the gap of the triumviral period. Tacitus' version of the speech that Cossutianus Capito made to Nero in 66 against Thrasea Paetus makes a point of his failure to take the annual oath to observe the *acta* of Augustus and Caesar (Tac. *Ann.* 16.22.3, with Koestermann *ad loc.*). It is dangerous to claim that Tacitus' phrase is anachronistic, Caesar having been brought in by the time the last book of the *Annals* was being written, and to use this in turn to support an assumption that a change took place in short order during the reign of Trajan and even at the behest of the Emperor (so Geiger 1975). The shift in relative perceptions of Caesar and Augustus came gradually, as the issues that divided them receded and as the military qualities of emperors came to the fore. As to Tacitus' accuracy (or his source's), this was not a public speech and may well not represent Capito's words; but even if it did, there was a rhetorical point in bringing in Caesar: the feud between Thrasea and Nero has just been compared with that between Caesar and Cato.

Like Caesar, and unlike Augustus and Claudius, Trajan, who rode bareheaded in combat dress at the siege of Hatra (Dio 68.31.3), was a born soldier as well as a successful expansionist, at least north of the Danube. Thanks to the *Commentaries* on his campaigns against the Gauls (58–50) and his opponents in the civil wars (49–45), detailed memory of Caesar's military achievements survived in the liveliest form. Trajan too wrote four or five books of commentaries, the *Dacica*, on his conquests of 101–6. Perhaps he imitated Caesar's plain style, but he did not imitate Caesar's misleadingly detached use of the third person in reference to himself: he adopted the first person plural, striking a more comradely note by identifying himself with his army.

Continued indications of Caesar's position as it changed in imperial thinking after the civil wars of 68–70 were given by his appearance on the Roman imperial coinage, when his own issues appeared on "restored" coinage. Emperors struck series presenting types taken from the issues of their predecessors. Even here the results for Caesar are ambiguous. He was not included in the *aes* series struck by Titus, Domitian, and Nerva, nor in that of the *antoniniani* of Trajan Decius (250–1), but he was admitted to that of the first Trajan's "restoration" coins, perhaps of AD 107, when there was a melting down of old coinage (*BM Coins, Rom. Emp.* 3, lxxxvi, 132–8; 141 nos. 30, 31; 142 nos. 696–8; 144 no.1; *RIC* 2, 302–4, 309, nos. 800f.; 806f.; 311 no. 815f.). Bearing Trajan's titles and the legend "REST(ITVIT)" ("He restored"), they celebrate Republican heroes and their victories and civil achievements in silver *denarii,* and reputable emperors in *aurei,* and it was the view of H. Mattingly and E. A. Sydenham (*RIC* 2, 302–4) that Trajan was emphasizing the glory of Rome by placing together a series of types illustrative of her development. This interpretation is attractive, although Sextus Pompeius the "pirate" seems out of place, and is preferable to the view of Geiger (1975) that the issues are a celebration ("Jubiläum") of the 150th year since Caesar's assassination; he is in any case only one in the series. Komnick (2001: 110ff.) notes that Caesar appears as the earliest of Trajan's *aurei*, followed by Sextus Pompeius, Augustus, and other emperors. But he also appears on the *denarii*. Since the antithesis of Republic and Empire seems to be signaled on these coins by the antithesis of *denarii* and *aurei*, Caesar's presence among the *denarii*, along with Sextus Pompeius and Augustus, would mean that he is seen like them as a transitional figure, if that is the right way to interpret the metallurgy. The coinage does not establish him as an "Emperor"; his status in that canon remains ambiguous. Evidently Trajan and his mint-masters saw Republican history and the transition to the Empire in a perspective that made it possible for them to show prominent figures with equanimity, whatever their ideological position. Even that may be going too far; it would be tempting to ask if what was being brought to mind was not political history and achievements, but the power of the numismatic record to establish history, and the current emperor's contribution to that.

The Name of Caesar

At the same time, regardless of ideology, another development in the dynastic regime of Augustus and his successors was claiming Caesar a fossilized place in history – and dimming awareness of his personal contribution. Specific acts of a historical figure such as Genghis Khan may be forgotten while his name remains familiar as that of a formidable individual. But in Caesar's case there was a particular factor to be taken into account: the increasingly emblematic and resonant use of the family name by the ruler and his kin.

Every man of the imperial *gens* down to the extinction of the male line of Augustus was a Caesar: this was their *cognomen* by birth or adoption. The clan name "Julius," implied by "Caesar," had belonged to members of other branches of the clan and dropped out of use in the family, except for Augustus' female descendants; it was also passed on to enfranchised provincials and freed slaves. By contrast a woman could not be a Caesar, for the *cognomen* was not available to women, even in modified form (contrasting for example with that of the Caecilii Metelli). In addition, Julius Caesar had been the outstanding member of the family in his generation, with no brother and only a cousin, Lucius, reaching the consulship (64 BC). He speaks of himself in the *Commentaries* as Caesar and is so mentioned in Cicero's *Letters*, with the *praenomen* Gaius added only when the occasion was formal (*Fam.* 1.9.7). The name brought an individual to mind and on the basis of the terms of his will the 18-year-old Octavius likewise became "the excellent boy, Caesar" (*Fam.* 10.28.3). When Cicero and his friends found grounds for mistrusting him they denied him the name that justified his turning on Caesar's assassins (Cic. *Brut.* 1.16.5).

As one of the Triumvirs established to reconstitute Republican institutions Octavian needed military pomp to offset that of his colleague Mark Antony. He began to use Caesar as a pseudo-*nomen*, with the military salutation "Imperator" doing service as a *praenomen*: he became Imperator Caesar (Syme 1958a). Eleven years later Romans were able to greet their leader with his final designation, Imperator Caesar Augustus. The new honorific *cognomen* now firmly assigned "Caesar" to the position of a family name, *gentilicium*. However, it still remained available as a conventional *cognomen* in its original position for Augustus' first sons by adoption, Gaius and Lucius Caesar, as it did later for Tiberius and Agrippa Postumus. Left in sole power in AD 14, Tiberius eschewed "Imperator" and tried to remain "Tiberius Caesar." Towards "Augustus," pressed on him by the Senate, he remained equivocal. Outsiders took it that he would bear the same designation as his predecessor, coins and official and unofficial inscriptions assigned it to him. But the ambiguity of "Augustus," so much the property of his predecessor, and Tiberius' own scruples made it inevitable that "Caesar" could still conventionally and courteously be used in addressing and referring to the Emperor, as it had been under Augustus: a gold coin of 16 BC shows a veiled priest sacrificing on behalf of the Roman People "for the good health of Caesar" (*RIC* 1^2 69, no. 369). The text of Tacitus' *Annals* offers ample illustration; it shows that "Caesar" was what Tiberius was routinely called (cf. Dio 57.8.1f.). He made no protest when the equivalent honorific "Augusta" was conferred on his mother Livia at the command of the late Princeps; Augustus "adopted" her in his will so that she might also become a Julia.

But down the family with Tiberius' sons, respectively by adoption and natural, Germanicus and Drusus, and with their sons, the earlier pattern for Gaius and Lucius naturally continued. The fact that the *cognomen* could be borne only by males, along with the comparative scarcity of males in the imperial agnatic family, helped to make the designation distinctive: it indicated a member of the family who was a potential Augustus, or who already was one, and this distinctiveness was opening the way to its emergence as a title: the senatorial decree of AD 20 passed in the aftermath of the trial of Cn. Piso (l. 165) mentions "the name of Caesar, which brings health to this city and to the Empire of the Roman People."

When Caligula was killed in AD 41 his uncle and successor Ti. Claudius Nero had no claim to the name – but took it anyway, and with no sign of an enactment (Romans were relatively untrammeled in their choice of names). He could claim to be acting from respect for his brother Germanicus and (more relevantly) to keep the great name alive. For him, "Augustus" denoted his position as Princeps, while "Caesar" carried his entitlement to it and is omitted from only two of the 58 inscriptions alluding to Claudius that are recorded in H. Dessau's *Inscriptiones Latinae Selectae*. Claudius helped to develop the *cognomen* into a title, but it still functioned in the old way when he adopted L. Domitius Ahenobarbus as Nero Claudius Caesar Drusus Germanicus.

It was open to the successors of the Julio-Claudians after Nero's death in 68 to take the name or not, though they did not have the claim of kinship that Claudius could deploy through his grandmother Octavia. The pull of habitual and resonant use in the dynasty from the incumbent emperor downwards was very strong. The designation was accepted by Galba and in 69 perhaps by his adopted heir of a few days, L. Piso, though that depends on a restoration of the *Acts* of the Arval Brothers. Certainly Otho, something of an admirer of Nero, styled himself Imperator M. Otho Caesar Augustus. Vitellius at first eschewed both "Augustus" and "Caesar" in favor of "Germanicus"; he took "Augustus" when he entered Rome on 18 July, and "Caesar" only in the month before his downfall (Tac. *Hist.* 3.58.3). It evidently still had a pull, perhaps for the military, and Vitellius lacked military skills of his own. From that time on every Emperor was a Caesar, and Justin (41.6.8) was to use "Caesar" and "Augustus" as parallels to the Parthian royal designation "Arsaces."

Liberated from its role as a *cognomen* of the first dynasty, "Caesar" was free to move from one part of a Princeps' titulature to another. When in August 69 Vespasian began styling himself Imp. Caesar Vespasianus Augustus his elder son became T. Caesar Vespasianus (different orderings are found, but they are unofficial). The name had changed its position back to that of a *gentilicium*, giving a powerful echo of the first emperor's Imp. Caesar Augustus. As Emperor (79–81), Titus was Imp. T. Caesar Vespasianus. Caesar Domitianus substituted his personal *cognomen*, omitting the plebeian Vespasianus and becoming Imp. Caesar Domitianus Augustus on his accession in 81. "Caesar" was now sealed in the imperial titulature, shifting position only slightly with Imp. Nerva Caesar Augustus (96–8); a modest person may have thought it presumptuous to open his titulature with Flavian assertiveness and added "Caesar Augustus" to his name as a title. It reverted with Imp. Caesar Nerva Traianus Augustus (98–117), Imp. Caesar Traianus Hadrianus Augustus (117–38), and so on.

Under Antoninus Pius there was a novelty and further removal from the role of *cognomen*. The first son since Titus to become heir apparent to an Emperor, L. Ceionius Commodus, was adopted by Hadrian in 136 and became L. Aelius Caesar, taking the requisite *nomen* and significant *cognomen* of the incumbent emperor. Nerva had hastily "adopted" the absent Trajan in 97, rather perhaps as Galba had hastily "adopted" Piso in Rome; during the months before taking over sole power Trajan had not used the name of Caesar. But there is no reason why Hadrian should not have gone through the proper forms of adoption; indeed, the *Historia Augusta* notes the entry into Hadrian's family. It was as if another L. Domitius Ahenobarbus became Nero Claudius Caesar; but Ceionius did not have to change his original *praenomen*. Exactly the same was done, when the time came in 138, for T. Aurelius Fulvus Boionius Antoninus (later Pius). By 136 Hadrian was already in poor health. All that could be must be done for his heirs. When Antoninus came to power "Caesar" was moved into the original Augustan and now traditional position for the Princeps: he became Imp. Caesar T. Aelius Hadrianus. Another pair of adoptions had been carried out early in 138, when Hadrian was still alive, by Antoninus (Pius) himself: M. Annius Verus, the later Emperor M. Aurelius, became only M. Aurelius Aelius Verus, and was not "Caesar"; nor was his adoptive brother, born in 130 as L. Ceionius Commodus, who, as the son of L. Aelius Caesar, became L. Aelius Aurelius Commodus in 136. The title, evidently from these events now exclusively a mark of status, was conferred on the older brother only in 139 after the accession of Pius: M. Aurelius Caesar Augusti Pii filius (Aelius, going back to the unloved Hadrian, could be dropped). Significantly, the younger brother was not a Caesar until in 161 he also became Augustus at Marcus' behest as Imp. Caesar L. Aurelius Verus. The definitive change in the nature of "Caesar" is also shown by the nomenclature of two of M. Aurelius' sons: L. Aurelius Commodus and M. Annius Verus, born after the Emperor acceded, did not become Caesars until October 12, 166, when they were respectively five and three or four years old, with the title appended to their existing names (*HA Marc.* 12.7f., *Comm.* 11.13, cf. 1.10). When Commodus became his father's full colleague in 177 he metamorphosed from L. Aurelius Commodus Caesar to Imp. (Caesar) ... Augustus.

By now political color had been bleached out of the designation, and as a status indicator it was not only a pseudo-*praenomen* for the incumbent ruler but a pseudo-*cognomen* for an intended heir (*the* Caesar). When Marcus Aurelius admonished himself in his *Meditations* not to be "Caesarified" he did not have Julius in mind, but the conduct of a whole series of emperors (M. Aur. *Med.* 6.30.1). For the emperor the title Augustus should have made "Caesar" redundant but for the fact that it was entrenched and so seemed indispensable; for the heir it was essential. The idea was so thoroughly accepted by the end of the Antonine age and of the dynasty that gave it that name that, although the short-lived Imp. Caesar Helvius Pertinax Augustus refused the title for his son in 193, it nonetheless appeared on inscriptions and even coins. In this case the designation had been offered by the Senate (*HA Pert.* 6.9), translating it from the private domain into that of public and court protocol. Further confirmation followed: without even adopting him (for he had two sons of his own) Imp. Caesar Septimius Severus Pertinax raised D. Clodius Albinus, the governor of Britain, to the rank of Caesar (Dio 74.15.1); he was to be an heir, and Albinus hopefully assumed the name Septimius between his own *nomen* and *cognomen*. The *Historia Augusta* has it that Commodus had already granted him "the *imperium* of a Caesar" (*Caesareanum*) (*HA Sev.* 6.9; *Clod.* 2.2–5); this is surely a fiction, but the conception shows how the "Caesarship" developed, at any rate by the time of the *Historia Augusta*. When the time came to destroy Albinus in 195 Severus raised his elder son, (L.) Septimius Bassianus, to Caesar as M. Aurelius Antoninus, the name he had filched from the Antonine dynasty in a fictitious "adoption." Such elevations were performed with ceremony: that of the younger son P. Septimius Geta to Caesar in 197 was celebrated alongside that of his elder brother to Augustus. We catch another glimpse of one route to the title, by a senatorial decree made in this case in response to a popular and military demand, in the account of the life of Gordian III given by the *Historia Augusta*. When Maximus and Balbinus were declared Emperors in 238 and proceeded to the Rostra, the people of Rome, along with soldiers who had gathered, set up a cry of "We all ask for Gordian as Caesar!" The 14-year-old was hurried off and a decree was passed on the very same day; Gordian was brought into the House and hailed as Caesar (*HA Max. et Balb.* 3.3–5). Elsewhere, however, the language in which the appointments are couched suggests unilateral action by the incumbent emperor, who may have been away from Rome, that is, by edict; the Senate would of course show its acquiescence by using the term.

The ossification of the heir's title under Marcus Aurelius and Septimius Severus is clearly illustrated by the adjective that accompanied it, and which became standard: *nobilissimus* ("most noble"). It occurs again in 217 with Macrinus' son M. Opellius Diadumenianus and with Severus Alexander on his adoption by Elagabalus and before his elevation to the purple in 222. According to the *Historia Augusta* Caesar was now a designation that could be conferred on an emperor's father-in-law, specifically the "Macrinus" who was allegedly so honored by Alexander Severus (*HA Alex. Sev.* 49.3). The connection with a coming generation had been quite severed by the time this could happen (or be envisaged). The final development into tetrarchic practice, two senior Augusti seconded by two junior Caesars, was now quite natural. For the author of the *Historia Augusta* "Caesar" is the designation of men who are not regular emperors or usurpers; prematurely dead heirs, then (*HA Macr.* 1.1). The author's mini-history of the designation (*HA Aelius* 2.2–5) distinguishes three ways it could be acquired: by will; the (in fact not quite applicable) case of Trajan; and the way he thinks it was conferred on Aelius Verus, which was, the author claims, "in almost the same manner as in our time Maximian and Constantius were declared Caesars by your Clemency (Diocletian) as on true sons of the *Principes* and designated heirs of your August Majesty." This synopsis may be expanded. First came the Julian family *cognomen* (transferable to a cognate, Claudius); then its appropriation as a *gentilicium* by Octavian, preceded by "Imperator," and made available by the Flavians to more than one generation of the dynasty; next, resumption of the name as a pseudo-*cognomen* to be conferred at the ruler's will exclusively on immediate heirs, adopted or not, and normally men in the next generation; the connotation that they were not yet "Augusti" (*HA Ael.* 1.1f.) was precisely what constituted the Tetrarchic system. But this practice of using "Caesar" essentially for men who were *not* the Emperors of Rome or Constantinople did not prevent Emperors down to Arcadius and Honorius (*ILS* 797 of 401/2) from exhibiting it as part of the formulaic "Imp. Caes.," with diminishing frequency as more colorful titles took over, nor its derivatives "Tsar" and "Kaiser" from gracing the autocrats of Russia and Germany.

FURTHER READING

The evidence for imperial attitudes to Caesar is to be found in contemporary literature (Virgil, Horace, Ovid, and Livy) and architecture and art (see Zanker 1988), and in later accounts of the Augustan Principate, e.g. that of Cassius Dio. Scholars have come to diverse conclusions: see Syme 1939 for Augustus distancing himself from Caesar; he is followed by Ramage 1985 and Herbert-Brown 1994; Syme's view is attacked by White 1988. For Caesar's fate as a deity see Weinstock 1971 and Gradel 2002. For Claudius as an admirer of Caesar, see Levick 1978. As to the title "Caesar," the *Historia Augusta* is a useful source of information, though not always reliable; for a modern tabulation, see Kienast 1990. The ancient works mentioned here may be found translated in the Loeb edition (Harvard, MA).

CHAPTER SIXTEEN

Augustan and Tiberian Literature

Mark Toher

No consistent depiction of Caesar emerges from literature during the first three generations after his death. Much of the record is lacunose and how Caesar was viewed must be deduced from a collage of references in authors whose main theme was not Caesar but mention of whom served some purpose in their works. Such a procedure, while necessary, is also hazardous, as two examples illustrate. A passage expressing fulsome admiration of Caesar in Diodorus Siculus (32.27.3) exists only because it was excerpted in a Byzantine encyclopedia. Were we left to assess Diodorus' attitude toward Caesar solely on the basis of his manuscripts, our assessment would be very different. Elsewhere Diodorus betrays no such enthusiasm for Caesar, and on the basis of this evidence he would have been included with the Augustan authors who supposedly found Caesar awkward to address. Only one statement of judgment on Caesar has been preserved from all the work of Livy, but it illustrates the same point in a different way. Livy wondered whether it would have been better for the Republic had Caesar never been born (Sen. *QN* 5.18.4), and on the basis of this statement it has been assumed that the "Pompeian" Livy presented a subversive, even dark characterization of Augustus' adopted father (but see p. 232). In fact, one statement without context can be worse than none at all. In the substantial remains of his extremely adulatory biographical work on Augustus, the Greek writer Nicolaus of Damascus has two statements praising the assassin M. Brutus (Jacoby 1926: author no. 90, F 130.59, 100). Had we to judge Nicolaus' attitude toward Caesar and his assassins from the citation of just these lines, our understanding of the nature of his account would be the opposite of the truth.

The inconsistent image of Caesar in the literature of the first principates is not due solely to the chance preservation of texts or fragments. The full significance of Caesar's career for Roman history would not be apparent for a very long time. The Ides of March were followed by a dozen years of Triumviral turbulence and war, then to be followed by the achievement of the Augustan principate and its consolidation under his successor Tiberius. Except for the very beginning of these three eras, during the early part of the Triumvirate, Caesar and his memory did not have direct bearing on the actors and issues that made history. From their perspective Caesar did not have the historical significance that he would one hundred and fifty years on from 44 BC, and certainly not the significance of Caesar today.

In the absence of overarching themes around which to organize the analysis, the three eras mentioned provide a convenient arrangement for its presentation.

Triumviral Era

A number of contemporaries (G. Oppius, L. Calpurnius Bibulus, and M. Valerius Messalla Corvinus) wrote works on Caesar and his era, but these works are lost, as is their significance for the tradition on Caesar. Nevertheless, two contemporary judgments on Caesar after his assassination are extant, by an antagonist and by an ally.

Cicero was as vehement in his condemnation of Caesar as a tyrant when dead as he had been in absolving the Dictator of that same charge in a speech delivered in his presence just four months before his death (*Deiot.* 33–4). In personal correspondence with Atticus after the Ides, Cicero called Caesar a king (*rex* 14.11.1), a despot (*dominus* 15.4.3) and most frequently a tyrant (*tyrannus* 14.14.2, 4, 14.17.6, 16.14.1). In the more elevated context of Cicero's philosophical dialogue *De Officiis*, Caesar was the archetype of a tyrant who destroyed the orderly working of a free state to satisfy his lust for power, roused the hatred of the people and rightly paid with his life for his injustice (*De Off.* 2.23, 3.83–5). In the dialogue Cicero subverts Caesar's reputation for generosity and clemency towards his enemies (*liberalitas* and *clementia*) by showing how the misuse of both virtues can undermine the community (Duxbury 1988, 243–83). In the passionate rhetoric of the *Philippics*, Cicero could admit that Caesar had had positive qualities, but only in order to demean Marcus Antonius by comparison. Antonius strove for the position and power of Caesar, although he lacked his character and intelligence. Antonius might fear his own followers even more than did Caesar, who had considerable intellect and political skill. Caesar had won over the people by his building program, banquets, and largesse, his supporters by rewards, and his adversaries by clemency. And he had done the city one last benefit by showing how beautiful was the act, how grateful was the benefit, and how glorious was the fame in slaying a tyrant (*Phil.* 2.116–17).

Cicero's correspondence also affords some sense of how the Caesarians presented their case in the months after Caesar's assassination. Caesar was of illustrious character, and his death only served to plunge the state into chaos. His famed clemency had been his undoing: but for that there would have been no conspiracy and assassination (*Att.* 14.22.1). Among these Caesarians might be counted the historian Sallust, for he owed his career and fortune to the Dictator. The climax of his account of the Catilinarian conspiracy (*Bellum Catilinae*) presents a pair of speeches by Caesar and M. Porcius Cato arguing against and for the execution of the conspirators held in Rome. Sallust observed that Rome had been made great due to the *virtus* (manly spirit and excellence of character) of only a few men in her history, and that in his time only two men, Caesar and M. Porcius Cato, possessed *virtus*. Therefore the historian was moved to provide an account of their contrasting but complementary characters (*Bell.Cat.* 53.4–6; cf. Christ 1994: 88).

Sallust's Caesar is a Republican senator engaged in traditional debate with his colleagues. In his speech, he anticipates his famed clemency by arguing against the execution of the Catilinarians, and it is his generosity (*liberalitas*) that is stressed (49.3, 54.2–4). Caesar is much concerned with *dignitas* (honor), but it is the *dignitas* of the senatorial class that he asserts to justify his argument against executing the conspirators (51.7–8). In Sallust's judgment Caesar was great by virtue of his mildness and compassion (*mansuetudo et misericordia* 54.2) and he gained glory for his generosity and forgiveness. Sallust praises his indulgence (*facilitas*) and notes that he was so intent on helping others in need (*perfugium miseris*) that he neglected his own affairs (54.3–4).

It is obvious that this characterization of a genial and generous Caesar serves as antithesis to the inflexible morality (*severitas* and *constantia* 54.2–3) of Cato. But there is evident in Sallust's presentation of Caesar contrast of a different sort: Caesar the senator against Caesar the dictator and victor in civil war (Vogt 1938: 66). One loaded Caesarian term, *dignitas*, occurs in Caesar's speech, but in a context and attitude that is utterly opposite to Caesar's personal use of it to justify civil war. Another term closely (and sometimes infamously) associated with Caesar the Dictator, *clementia* (pardon for defeated opponents), is carefully avoided even as Sallust uses a series of synonyms to illustrate generosity and forgiveness as characteristic of Caesar's nature. Caesar himself did not use the term, which may explain its absence in Sallust, but it could be simply for stylistic reasons. *Clementia Caesaris* was made notorious by Cicero, a rhetorical artist whose style and vocabulary Sallust studiously avoided (Griffin 2003: 159–63).

Sallust's representation of Caesar has been the subject of much discussion and varied judgment. Because of his career with Caesar, partisan defense of his patron has been alleged to explain Sallust's prominent role for Caesar in his account of Catiline. An old theory has Sallust motivated to write his monograph by the publication or circulation of Cicero's "secret history" (*De Consiliis Suis*) in the months after the orator's death in December of 43. That work is supposed to have presented a tendentious account of Catiline, one detrimental to the memory of Caesar, and so Sallust was moved to defend Caesar, especially against the charge that he might have been an ally of Catiline in those years (Besser 1880: 2; John 1876: 725; Last 1948; Schwartz 1897: 580–1). At the other extreme, Sallust's portrait has been interpreted as ambiguous. His emphasis on Caesar's generous and kind nature must have seemed ironic to an audience who knew a more arrogant and uncongenial Caesar after his proconsulship in Gaul. The fact that only Cato is credited with *dignitas* in Sallust, and the assertion that Cato preferred to be good rather than simply have the reputation (*esse quam videri bonus malebat*, 54.6), seem to imply criticism of Caesar's character (*contra* Duxbury 1988: 315). Scholarly consensus has Sallust writing his account of Catiline between 42 and 40 BC, and his stress on Caesar's munificence seems to highlight by contrast the murder and rapacity of the recent proscriptions instituted by those competing to inherit Caesar's mantle.

It is a characterization of Caesar that is "pervaded by doubts and ambiguity" (Syme 1964: 117–18).

Positive or negative, Sallust's depiction of Caesar is subtle and complex. Along with the characterization of Caesar found in the work of Nicolaus of Damascus, it is the fullest and best in the extant literature until the work of Velleius Paterculus. It may have been remarkable in its own time simply because of its complexity. To judge from the evidence of coins and limited literary evidence, any presentation of Caesar in the Triumviral era was likely to have been one-dimensional and biased in the extreme. By pairing Caesar with Cato, Sallust seems to be striving for a balanced assessment of both men (Duxbury 1988: 293–334). "Caesar and Cato were divergent in conduct, principles and allegiance. Their qualities could be regarded as complementary no less than antithetic. In alliance the two had what was needed to save the Republic. That may be what the historian is gently suggesting" (Syme 1964: 120).

The Greek Diodorus Siculus, writing his universal history in the last years of the Triumviral era, provides the only other significant assessment of Caesar in this period and he is effusive in his praise. In describing the destruction of Corinth in 146 BC, Diodorus (32.27.3) takes the opportunity to note that the city was rebuilt a century later by Caesar, "he who has been called a god for his deeds" and who deserves the highest praise for his kindness (ἐπιείκεια):

> He exceeded all who came before him in the magnitude of his achievements and he justly earned his title [*divus*] for his virtue. In short, this man by his high birth and his talent as an orator, and by his generalship in war and freedom from avarice has earned the right to be held in high esteem and to be accorded praise in our history for his goodness (χρηστότης). In the magnitude of his accomplishments he exceeded all other Romans.

In light of his fulsome judgment on Caesar, it is notable that Diodorus ended his history with the year 60 BC (1.4.7), just before Caesar's rise to power. This is even more notable because in the next chapter (1.5.1), Diodorus says his history will end with the 730th year after the first Olympiad, i.e. 46 BC, the year Caesar celebrated his victory in the civil war. If this is not simply an error on Diodorus' part, it seems that he originally planned to give an account of Caesar's career, a man whom he admired more than any other, but then changed his mind. It is possible that as the Triumviral era unfolded and Diodorus composed his history at Rome, the idea of providing an account of Caesar's accomplishments and generosity became daunting for a Greek émigré who lacked the protection and prestige of a senatorial network and career (Sacks 1990: 169–91). It may have been that for Diodorus the Horatian embers of civil conflict were still flames (*Carm.* 2.1.6–8) and he was no Asinius Pollio.

Some allusions or references to Caesar in the poetry of the Triumviral era are more easily detected than explained. Contemporaneous with Sallust's depiction of Caesar was Vergil's description of the apotheosis of Daphnis in *Eclogue* 5.56–80. While it would be too crude to equate the figure of Daphnis with Caesar himself, the poet's description must have reminded his audience of Caesar's recent apotheosis, but to what purpose is unclear. In *Satire* 1.7.32–5, written in the mid-30s, Horace presents a quarrel between characters named Persius and Rupilius Rex before the praetor Brutus in Asia. The poem closes with Persius beseeching Brutus to live up to his family duty and slay the "king" (*rex*). Despite its jocular tone and the fact that the "voice" is that of a character in the poem rather than the poet's own, the audacity of Horace, who had fought at Philippi in the army of the assassins, is evident here and is in contrast to his attitude toward Augustus in his later poetry. A quatrain of an elegy of Gallus published in 1979 raises another aspect of the problem of interpreting allusion or reference to Caesar in poetry. It contains an address to "Caesar" in which the poet celebrates his return from some campaign and the temples that will be decorated with the spoils won (Anderson, Parsons, & Nisbet 1979: 140). Since the heir of Caesar called himself Gaius Iulius Caesar from the time he accepted his inheritance, such references to "Caesar," without a context that clarifies which Caesar is meant, remain ambiguous as to identity and significance. Occasionally this can lead to problems of real consequence, as in the case of the "Caesar" celebrated in the famous passage of Vergil's *Aeneid* 1.286–96. On the other hand, it has also been maintained that such passages were deliberately ambiguous. It was for the ancient reader to choose his Caesar (Kenney 1968: 106; Zarrow 2007: 34–7).

Principate of Augustus

Discussion of Caesar in Augustan literature has been dominated by a theory that Augustus tried to disassociate himself from the figure of Caesar after 27 BC, when Augustus claimed to have transferred control of politics and government to the senate and people of Rome (*RG* 34.1). This theory had its origins in the mid-nineteenth century with the Swiss scholar Johann Kaspar von Orelli, who observed that Horace, Vergil, and Ovid avoided praise of Caesar that might obscure the glory of Augustus (White 1988: 334). Orelli's observation, accepted readily by scholars after him, was developed into a more elaborate thesis by Sir Ronald Syme, who repeatedly asserted that Caesar and his memory presented problems for the Princeps and his program. As Orelli suggested, there was the issue of comparison with Caesar's personal military accomplishments and the meager record of Augustus in that field. Furthermore, Caesar's civil wars of 49 to 45 BC and his unprecedented exercise of the dictatorship recalled the illegal acts and violence of Octavian's Triumviral career rather than Augustus' revived Republic. Caesar better served Augustus as an abstracted divinity. "For all else, Caesar the proconsul and Dictator was better forgotten" (Syme 1950: 13–14). According to Syme, Anchises' exhortation to Caesar in the *Aeneid* (6.834–5) to disarm before his conflict with Pompeius is a "veiled rebuke," while Horace condemns the Dictator by his silence. Syme detected defamation of Caesar in the poets. In Vergil "the shield of Aeneas allows a brief glimpse of the future life, on the one side Catilina in hell, tormented by furies for ever, on the other an ideal Cato, usefully legislating among the blessed dead ... Virgil did not need to say where Caesar belonged. ... The picture is consistent. Livy, Virgil and Horace of all the Augustan writers stand closest to the government. On the whole, better to say nothing of Caesar, or for that matter of Antonius, save as criminal types" (Syme

1939: 317–18). Despite criticism (White 1988; Kienast 2001; Zarrow 2007), Syme's idea of a deliberate disassociation and even disparagement of Caesar in the Augustan writers has received wide acceptance, and it has remained very influential on scholars who consider Caesar's treatment in the literature of the era (e.g. Herbert-Brown 1994: 109–29; Donié 1996: 3–75). His theory has now been extended to explain the overall development of Augustus' ideology and political program (Hahn 1985) and has even been applied to evidence (coins of the Triumviral era in Ramage 1985: 224–6) which Syme himself acknowledged did not support his thesis.

Nevertheless, Syme's idea that Augustus disassociated himself from (and even defamed) aspects of Caesar's memory except for his divinity entails a significant problem and a number of doubtful premises. Syme based his theory almost exclusively on the evidence of Horace and Vergil; much of the rest of the literature of the Augustan age does not obviously support his claim. Asserting that Caesar does not appear as frequently or in the way he should in the poets assumes that we know how often he ought to have been addressed and in what appropriate manner. Furthermore, asserting that Augustus somehow disassociated himself from Caesar through the poets involves another premise that has become increasingly open to question, i.e. that Augustus controlled or even significantly influenced what the poets wrote. Finally, this theory of disassociation presupposes that the poets speak in their own "voice" and that the poetry directly reflects the views that the poets held (Zarrow 2007: 12).

In fact, after Augustus himself, Caesar is the most frequently cited individual in Augustan poetry (White 1988: 346–48). Only in comparison to Augustus can it be maintained that Caesar is somehow neglected or disparaged by the poets, and this brings up a significant if obvious point. The Augustan era was about Augustus and his family. If Drusus or Tiberius or other individuals seem to be treated more fulsomely than Caesar, that is because they were associated with Augustus and his regime. People and events of the past are frequently referred to only in passing, usually to illustrate a motif of the poem that related directly to Augustus or his ideology. Syme asserts a change in attitude toward Caesar after 27 BC, but there is no discernible difference between the treatment of Caesar in Horace's *Satires* or in the *Eclogues* and *Georgics* of Vergil and his depiction in the poetry after that date. The poets refer to Caesar most frequently in connection with the themes of divinity, civil war, and Augustus himself (Zarrow 2007: 44), in order to justify and glorify the regime of Augustus. Beyond this, however, there is no obvious pattern or characteristic governing Caesar's appearance in Augustan poetry.

The rebuke that Syme senses in Vergil's plea for Caesar to disarm (*Aen.* 6.834–5) can be interpreted differently. Horace (*Carm.* 2.1.3–4) betrays a similar attitude with his reference to the "grievous friendships" (*graves amicitiae*) of the civil war. In Tibullus (2.5.71–8), the star of the deified Caesar, a symbol of the gods' approval of Augustus in most authors, portends the disaster of civil war. Rather than indirect personal criticism of Caesar, such statements of lament have their origin in the poets' own experience and suffering in the terrible events of the Triumviral era. Syme's thesis becomes invalid if the Caesar praised by Jupiter in the first book of the *Aeneid* (286–96) is taken to be Julius Caesar and not Augustus. Plausible arguments have been presented for both identifications and this is not the place to review the issue (see Zarrow 2007: 62–71). Nevertheless, the simple fact that the identity of the Caesar so fulsomely lauded there is ambiguous (possibly intentionally so; cf. R. G. Austin 1971 on *Aen.* 1.286ff. and O'Hara 1990: 159–63) would seem to indicate that Vergil did not intend to disassociate Caesar from the glory of Augustus. The Augustan poet who most often refers to Caesar is Ovid, and there is no evidence of disassociation or reserve in his remarks. He praises Caesar for his military victories and for his reform of the calendar (*Fasti* 1.599–604, 3.155–66), and to mark a date he has an old soldier of Caesar proudly recall fighting under his command at Thapsus in 46 BC (*Fasti* 4.377–84). The goddess Vesta bids the poet not to omit mention of Caesar's assassination, since it was she who protected him; what fell by the assassins' weapons on the Ides of March was but the shade (*umbra*) of Caesar (*Fasti* 3.697–702).

Even if published in the time of Tiberius, in tone and perspective the astrological poem (*Astronomica*) of Manilius is an Augustan creation, and it may well have been composed entirely under Augustus (Bowersock 1990: 386–7). Like Ovid, Manilius refers only to aspects of Caesar that are significant to the Augustan program, i.e. his divine ancestry and the divinity accorded him by Augustus (1.798–802, 926, 4.934), his role as the father of Augustus (1.9, 913) and his assassination (2.593–4, 4.57–62). On this last issue Manilius is of interest as the first of many authors who resort to the iron will of fate to explain the riddle of how such a great soldier and statesman could fall victim to a conspiracy by those closest to him.

It is obvious that Caesar, like most figures mentioned in Augustan poetry, is subordinate to Augustus himself. The victory of Augustus at Actium is fought under the sign of Caesar's star (Verg. *Aen.* 8.681), and Caesar looks on proudly as that victory unfolds (Prop. 4.6.59–60) and he contemplates the other benefactions of Augustus (Ovid *Met.* 15.850–1). Despite his many accomplishments, Caesar's greatest deed and gift to Rome was his son (Ovid *Met.* 15.746–59). Frequently the poets referred to Caesar "to advance an argument concerning an aspect of Roman history, religion or power or to define another figure present in the passage. … The poets include Caesar in order to characterize a motif such as civil war or figures both human and divine" (Zarrow 2007: 44). In Augustan poetry Caesar became "a conventional point of reference to a discourse that unfolded elsewhere" (White 1988: 348). Therefore it is not surprising that Caesar appears most frequently in Ovid's *Fasti*, where Roman history, religion, and tradition are prevailing themes.

Syme's observation that aspects of Caesar's career presented problems for Augustus is correct, but it does not necessarily entail the conclusion that there was a concerted program of disassociation of Caesar in the literature of the era. Too often, especially among those who attempt to extend Syme's theory, the argument becomes circular, and ostensibly neutral or complimentary references become sinister by assuming as a premise the point (that there was a program of disassociation) to be proved. Rather than being suppressed, disassociated, or disparaged, the figure of Caesar is shown by the evidence to be a frequent, variegated tile in the mosaic of Augustan poetry.

When the evidence of Augustan prose is considered, the literary depiction of Caesar becomes even more varied and complicated. We are missing what would have been the two fullest treatments of Caesar by Augustan historians because of the loss of the history of Asinius Pollio and the relevant books of Livy. Pollio fought at Pharsalus with Caesar and was serving in Spain against the Pompeians at the time of Caesar's murder. He chose to side with Antonius in his rivalry with Octavian but had declared his neutrality in their conflict by the final battle at Actium. Pollio wrote his history, which covered events from 60 to probably 42 BC, not long after Actium, when the treatment of those inflammatory events was full of hazard for the author (Hor. *Carm.* 2.1.6–8). It is not possible to assess how Pollio presented Caesar in his history, but the proconsul and Dictator must have been a focal point of his account. Pollio professed to love and esteem Caesar (*Caesarem vero ... dilexi summa cum pietate et fide*, Cic. *Fam.* 10.31.3), but there is significant evidence that Pollio did not hesitate to criticize Caesar severely. When one of Caesar's henchmen, the quaestor L. Cornelius Balbus in Spain, elevated an actor to the equestrian order and then conducted local elections in an unconstitutional way, Pollio wrote that he was emulating the conduct of the Dictator Caesar in Rome (Cic. *Fam.* 10.32.1–2). Despite his professed love for Caesar, Pollio resented the compromise of personal ethics that his association with Caesar imposed on him (Cic. *Fam.* 10.31.3), and Pollio is unique in his critical assessment of Caesar's much admired autobiographical accounts (*commentarii*) of his campaigns in Gaul and his civil war with Pompeius (see Raaflaub, chapter 13 in this volume, pp. 179, 181). Pollio claimed (probably in his history) that either through design or defect of memory Caesar had been careless and had little regard for the truth in his *commentarii*. Nevertheless, Pollio did concede the possibility that Caesar intended new, corrected editions (Suet. *Iul.* 56.4). Pollio's criticism here, so contrary to the ancient and modern judgment on Caesar the author, may stem from the simple fact that Caesar's *commentarii* on the civil war were probably the main competition for Pollio's own account of that conflict. The contrast with Hirtius' self-effacing preface to the continuation of Caesar's *commentarii* could not be greater, and Pollio's insistence on autopsy in his narrative corresponds to the autopsy inherent in Caesar's autobiographical account (Morgan 2000: 58–9). The evidence suggests that Pollio would have been critical and quite likely tendentious in his treatment of Caesar in his history: he is said to have provided a flattering account (*egregia memoria*) of the assassins in his work (Tac. *Ann.* 4.34.4). However, Pollio's character was such that it is unlikely that he did so with the intent of pleasing Augustus.

The situation is equally vague with the evidence of Livy. Since books 103–16 of his history that dealt with Caesar are lost and the statements in the summaries (*periochae*) of those books provide no significant evidence regarding his presentation of Caesar, assessment of Livy's attitude depends on two statements in later authors, both of them difficult to interpret and one defective. During the reign of Tiberius, the historian Cremutius Cordus was brought to trial for statements in his history in which he eulogized the assassin Brutus and called his fellow conspirator Cassius the last of the Romans (Tac. *Ann.* 4.34.1). Tacitus then presents Cordus' speech in his own defense before Tiberius and the senate, in which Cordus says of Livy (*Ann.* 4.34.3):

> Titus Livius, eloquentiae ac fidei praeclarus in primis, Cn. Pompeium tantis laudibus tulit, ut Pompeianum eum Augustus appellaret; neque id amicitiae eorum offecit. Scipionem, Afranium, hunc ipsum Cassium, hunc Brutum nusquam latrones et parricidas, quae nunc vocabula imponuntur, saepe ut insignis viros nominat.

> Titius Livius, quite brilliant as he is for eloquence and credibility, first of all elevated Cn. Pompeius with such praises that Augustus called him "a Pompeian"; and that was no obstacle to their friendship. Scipio, Afranius, this very Cassius himself, this very Brutus – nowhere did he name them as "bandits" and "parricides" (the designations which are now imposed) but often as distinguished men. (trans. A. J. Woodman)

The significance of this statement for understanding Livy's treatment of Caesar depends on the interpretation of "Pompeianus." Some have taken it broadly with the names of other prominent opponents of Caesar mentioned by Cordus to mean that Livy gave an account of the civil wars that favored Pompeius and the Republican cause (Strasburger 1983: 268–9; Donié 1996: 48–9). Syme (1979: 75) thought there was no rebuke to the historian in this statement. The figure of Pompeius was useful to the Augustan ideology of the refounded state as the champion of the Republican cause against Caesar, "and Caesar was a 'bad man', suppressed by the heir to his name and power." The broad interpretation of "Pompeianus" has Livy writing his whole account of Caesar from a Republican perspective, but it may be that Augustus called Livy a Pompeian because of the way he treated Pompeius specifically. Depending on how one interprets Livy's last sentence, it may imply that the assassins did not receive the fulsome treatment accorded to Pompeius (Manuwald 1979: 191–2).

But there is another passage that has been taken to support the view that Livy's account was critical of Caesar. In his treatise on *Natural Questions*, Seneca the Younger used Caesar in an analogy to describe the effect of the winds: *quod de Caesare maiore* [MS *Maiori*] *uulgo dictatum est et a Tito Liuio positum, in incerto esse utrum illum magis nasci an non nasci reipublicae profuerit, dici etiam de uentis potest* (5.18.4: "it can also be said of the winds what has frequently been said about the elder Caesar and was posed as a question by Livy, that it is uncertain whether it was to the advantage of the republic that Caesar was born rather than not born"). This statement does seem to support the idea that Livy's account might have been anti-Caesarian, if in fact this is what Livy said in his history. The corrected reading *de Caesare maiore* is by no means sure: probably better is *de C. Mario* (Hine 1978; Badian 1993: 36, n. 51) based on *de C. Marior* of the two descent groups of the MSS. In this case, Seneca's statement has no relevance to Caesar.

Despite the tenuous and vague nature of these two statements, they have been used to argue that Livy's presentation of Caesar was hostile. This having been established, the nature of his presentation is elaborated through imaginative use of the evidence of the summaries of Livy's lost books (Donié 1996: 47–53) or a later author (Lucan) who supposedly used Livy in his characterization of Caesar (Strasburger 1983). In fact, given the lack of a context for either statement, they reveal very little about Livy's attitude toward Caesar. The appellation "Pompeianus," originating in Tacitus' re-creation of Cordus' speech, if accurate, can at most tell us something about Livy's attitude toward Pompeius. It does not necessarily entail a hostile or critical attitude toward Caesar. In a similar way, if the statement in Seneca is in fact about Caesar, it only shows that Livy could ask a quite reasonable question that might occur to anyone writing the history of the later Roman Republic; it does not necessarily entail a negative judgment of Caesar. Even if it is granted that both statements are negative in their attitude toward Caesar, do they together provide us with a sense of the full depiction of Caesar that presumably unfolded over the course of 14 books in Livy? There is clear evidence that complimentary or favorable assessments of the Republican heroes circulated and were tolerated in the Augustan era. In addition to Augustus' assessment of Livy as a "Pompeianus," the Princeps conceded Cato Uticensis his positive qualities: any man who resisted change to the constitution was a good citizen (Macrob. 2.4.18). But such anecdotal evidence does not mean that the memories of Cato and Pompeius were rehabilitated at the expense of Caesar's. In fact, such statements are preserved in the tradition because they were so singular and unexpected in the ideological context of the Augustan era.

By contrast with the lost accounts of Pollio and Livy, the Greek prose writers of the Augustan era are well represented by the complete works or substantial remains of the *Roman Antiquities* of Dionysius of Halicarnassus, Strabo's *Geography* and the biographical work on Augustus by Nicolaus of Damascus. However, neither Dionysius nor Strabo has much to say about Caesar. Dionysius' work on early Rome ended with the first Punic war and so he does not deal directly with Caesar and his era. He had a high estimate of the Julian clan, which had produced very distinguished commanders whose virtues did not fall short of their noble birth (*AR* 1.70.4), and he twice alludes to Caesar. In his discussion of a long-standing Roman law that punishment of a father could not be imposed on his son, he notes that this prohibition was ignored during and after the Sullan proscriptions, until it was restored to its original status by the man [Caesar] who brought about the destruction of the successors of Sulla (*AR* 8.80.2–3). In explaining why in 483 BC the consuls moved their levy for the army outside the city when the tribune Gaius Maenius threatened to prevent it, Dionysius notes that the tribunes possessed no authority outside the city. He then says that this issue was the cause of the civil war in his time since Caesar, claiming that he was justly protecting the rights of tribunes who had been driven from the city (ὁ δὲ τῇ προφάσει ταύτῃ χρησάμενος, ὡς ἀρχῇ δήμου ... αὐτὸς ὁσίως καὶ σὺν δίκῃ βοηθῶν), entered the city in arms and restored the men to their offices (*AR* 8.87.7–8). Donié (1996: 70) detects an incriminating tone in Dionysius here since he seems to imply that Caesar simply used the tribunes as a pretext to start a civil war. But this may be a misreading of Dionysius' Greek. The clause προφάσει ταύτῃ χρησάμενος, ὡς ... does not necessarily imply a falsely alleged motive; it can simply mean the justification that Caesar himself gave, without implication as to its truth or falsity. That is, in this passage Dionysius is simply repeating (and seemingly accepting) what Caesar himself said at three different points (*BC* 1.7, 22.5, 32.6) to justify his march on Rome. On the basis of what little evidence he presents, there is no reason to think that Dionysius had an unfavorable view of Caesar.

Strabo mentions Caesar frequently in his *Geography* in relation to a wide range of places in the Mediterranean where Caesar campaigned or which were affected by his political program. While Strabo is not critical of Caesar, and may even be said to be favorable to him (Donié 1996: 70–1; Clarke 1999: 286), he does report the truth about Caesar's failure in Britain (4.5.3), in contrast to the misleading description of Velleius Paterculus, for example (see below), and it is notable that Pompeius is even more prominent in Strabo's work than Caesar. Strabo's subject and the course of Pompeius' career may explain this, but Strabo does seem to equate the murder of Pompeius with the assassination of Caesar when he uses the same verb (δολοφόνεω at 14.1.37 and 17.1.11) to describe their deaths. On the other hand, when Strabo comes to discuss affairs in Alexandria, he says that Caesar established Cleopatra as the Queen of Egypt and that after the death of Caesar Antonius honored Cleopatra exceedingly, chose her as his wife, and had children by her (17.1.11). Strabo's discreet silence here about Caesar's own relationship with Cleopatra and the paternity of the son she called "little Caesar" (*Caesarion*) may be due as much to the sensitivities of Augustus as to concern for the reputation of Caesar.

The only substantial characterization of Caesar in the literature of these eras is in the excerpts of the so-called *Bios Kaisaros* by Nicolaus of Damascus (Jacoby 1926: author no. 90, FF125–30). The incomplete state of the text defeats any sure statement about the date of composition, original form or purpose of the *Bios*. The extant remains show it to be an extremely adulatory account of the life of Octavian down to 43 BC, and internal references indicate that the original work dealt with the Triumviral era and probably beyond.

The first third of the text presents Caesar as the admiring and protective mentor of the adolescent Octavian. He tests Octavian's intelligence and judgment (F 127.24), personally oversees his care when he is ill (F 127.20), and grants Octavian's requests on behalf of friends and suppliants for favors and pardon (F 127.16, 18, 27). More than a third of the extant text is devoted to an account of the conspiracy against Caesar and his murder. Nicolaus presents a remarkably dispassionate description of the conspirators and their motives and even more remarkably, a singular explanation for why Caesar became the victim of his enemies: he was by nature guileless and due to his many years away from Rome on campaign he had become politically naive (F 130.67: ὁ δὲ ἅτε ἁπλοῦς ὢν τὸ ἦθος καὶ ἄπειρος πολιτικῆς τέχνης διὰ τὰς ἐκδήμους στρατείας). This unheroic, imperceptive Caesar has been included in the evidence for a deliberate program to demean the memory of Caesar under Augustus (e.g. Donié 1996: 61–2, 68), and it is true that Nicolaus' characterization of Caesar is quite different from that in the later biographies and histories. But his singular characterization serves a more subtle purpose. In the last part of the *Bios*, Octavian is depicted as gradually coming to realize the true nature of Antonius' character. The rumor of a conspiracy by Octavian to assassinate Antonius becomes in Nicolaus a conspiracy *against* Octavian by Antonius. The young heir realizes the danger he is in only just in time and he acts to avoid the fate of his adopted father (F 130.124–31). The reason for Nicolaus' peculiar characterization of Caesar has to do with his depiction of a heroic Octavian, who was able to survive and succeed in just the circumstances in which Caesar had become a victim. While Nicolaus' presentation of Caesar may cast him in an unheroic guise, it is not necessarily the product of a program to demean Caesar. It is clear that the figure of Caesar in Nicolaus serves the purpose he does in most of the Augustan writers, as a complement or contrast to the glory of Augustus.

Augustus' own writings betray little about his attitude toward Caesar. Augustus composed an autobiographical work (*De Vita Sua*) that covered his life up to the end of his campaigns in Spain in 25 BC (Suet. *Aug.* 85.1), and it is supposed that it was published by the late 20s. The evidence of two fragments (Malcovati 1967: FF 6–7) indicates that Augustus in the second book of his work dealt with the comet which Octavian advertised as a sign of the apotheosis of Caesar. On the strength of this evidence, it has been suggested that the whole of Augustus' first book would have provided a fulsome account of the last years of Caesar's career as a preface to Octavian's entrance into public life (Donié 1996: 23). But if this were so, it would be difficult to resolve the paradox of Augustus encouraging a program of disassociation from Caesar through other writers while he himself was praising Caesar in his own work. Another (strange) possibility is that the naive and imperceptive Caesar in the work of Nicolaus, who is often thought to have followed closely the autobiography of Augustus, is actually derived from Augustus' own presentation of Caesar. Beyond this vague evidence and conjecture, there is no basis to judge how Augustus treated Caesar in this work. At the end of his life Augustus composed his famous précis of his achievements, his *Res Gestae*. Caesar is nowhere mentioned by name in this work and is only alluded to four times in contexts where Augustus writes of his treatment of his parent's assassins (2), his refusal to take Caesar's office of chief priest (Pontifex Maximus) while the incumbent was still alive (10.2), his paying out the legacy of Caesar's will (15.1), and his completion of projects begun by Caesar (20.3). Again, this seemingly spare, indirect presentation of Caesar, along with Augustus' explicit refusal in the *Res Gestae* to accept the office of Dictator when it was pressed on him (5.1) and his proclamation that he had transferred control of politics and government to the senate and people of Rome (34.1), suggests that even after half a century the Princeps was careful to distance himself from the Dictator (Ramage 1987: 66, 69, 142–3; Donié 1996: 24–5). In all other aspects, this last document of the Augustan era follows the pattern that is clear throughout much of Augustan literature in which Caesar served as a point of reference for the immediate (and in this case, self-referential) needs of the author in his primary purpose of praising himself and his lifelong program.

Principate of Tiberius

With the accession of Tiberius came a new era and a new perspective: Tiberius embodied the proof that the principate was an enduring system, not a peculiar novelty. Among the writers of the period there was no ambiguity in their praise of Caesar, who ceases to serve as a foil for Augustus and appears in his own right as the divine founder of the line of Caesars, the ultimate victor over his assassins and a heroic figure amid the death throes of the republic.

This being so, it should occasion no surprise that Caesar appears far more frequently than either Augustus or Tiberius in the nine books of memorable deeds and sayings composed by Valerius Maximus in the middle of Tiberius' principate. As with the Augustan authors, Valerius characterizes Caesar in relation to prominent aspects of his career (Wardle 1997). The adopted father of Augustus now becomes the divine founder of the line of Caesars (1, praef., 2.1.10 and 8.15 praef.; Donié 1996: 95; Wardle 1997: 345), and it may be that Valerius was the first author (and the last for some time) who understood Caesar to be the first *Princeps* (Wickert, *RE* 22.2 (1954), s.v. "princeps," 2025; Donié 1996: 101; cf. Ovid's reference to Caesar as *princeps* at *Fasti* 3.697). Caesar's murder, which provided the justification for the early career of Octavian in the Augustan ideology, becomes in Valerius an act of parricide against the State but one that ends not with the death of Caesar but with his divinity (1.5.7, 6.13, 8.8, 4.5.6, 6.8.4; Bloomer 1992: 210–11). Valerius does not avoid incidents in the career of Caesar that reflected unfavorably on him. He describes how Cato was escorted to jail by the whole senate after his arrest by the consul Caesar in 59 BC (2.10.7), and Valerius is unique in recounting a story of Caesar's demand that the father of Caesetius, a tribune Caesar had exiled, disown his son and the father's courageous refusal (5.7.2). But Caesar is only a secondary character in these exempla, the main purposes of which are to illustrate the prestige of Cato and the love of a father. More significant are converse examples where the assassin Brutus or Cassius is credited with some positive act or quality but then is excoriated by Valerius for having raised his hand against Caesar (3.1.3, 6.4.5). Caesar's famed and now divine clemency Valerius celebrates in relation to his dictatorial power, for it was only the *summa clementia* of Caesar that kept Caesetius' father from coming to harm (5.7.2). In a similar way, it was only due to Caesar's heart, "milder than gentleness itself" (*ipsa mansuetudine mitius pectus*, 6.2.11) that Servius Galba was not ejected from court after he objected to Caesar's auction of Pompeius' property.

Caesar is presented in a very different but no less adulatory way in the summary universal history of Velleius Paterculus. Writing at just about the same time as Valerius Maximus, the historian never refers to Caesar's divinity or *divus Iulius.* As in Nicolaus, Velleius' Caesar is a mortal Roman, but one whose accomplishments and virtue exceed all who came before. In Velleius there appears the first extant portrait of the heroic and tragic Caesar so familiar from later authors: a charismatic conqueror and eminent statesman forced to civil war by the intransigence of his opponents and who, when he had vanquished and pardoned them, became the victim of his own clemency. Velleius seems deliberately to avoid the approach of Sallust by not pairing Cato and Caesar in his account of the debate over the Catilinarian conspirators where the character and role of Cato are presented without mention of Caesar (2.35.1–4). But from the year 59, Caesar is the dominant figure in Velleius' narrative down to his assassination (2.41–57). Ever concerned about pace and space (*festinatio et brevitas)*, Velleius pauses to praise Caesar's ancestry, beauty, keen mind, superhuman courage, and generosity – as a military leader he was only to be compared with Alexander himself, but only in the latter's sober moments (2.41.1). Velleius even takes time to provide a detailed account of Caesar's kidnapping by pirates and his punishment of them to demonstrate that the courage and decisiveness of Caesar the general and statesman were already present in the young adult (2.41.3–42.3). Caesar's campaigns in Gaul were great achievements (*immanes res*) and in undertaking his invasion of Britain it was as though Caesar was "seeking to add another world to our empire"

(2.56.1), although Velleius tactfully avoids mentioning that his two invasions of that island failed. Velleius (2.44.1) admits that the pact of Caesar, Pompeius, and Crassus was destructive for the state (*societas potentiae exitiabilis*), but by Velleius' time this may have become a standard view that implied no great criticism of Caesar (cf. Woodman: 1983 ad loc.). Velleius follows the line of Caesar himself in his *commentarii* that the Dictator did all in his power to avoid conflict with Pompeius (2.48.5, 49.3, 50.2). But when it came, despite the fact that Pompeius, supported by the senate, seemed to have the better cause, which a person of old Roman values (*vir antiquus et gravis*) could laud, the pragmatist (*prudens*) would follow Caesar, who had the full support of his soldiers (2.49.2–3). This judgment of Velleius betrays an ambivalent attitude that both admired the lost republic even as it conceded its inevitable decline and so absolved Caesar of direct responsibility for it. Velleius' explanation of Caesar's assassination contains the elements found in later biographers and historians. His famed *clementia* toward defeated opponents, while a marvelous practice in itself, sowed the seeds of his own murder since those who were forgiven formed the conspiracy against him (2.52.4–6, 56.1, 3). In contrast to Nicolaus' characterization of Caesar as an imperceptive victim, Velleius (as Manilius) presents what would become the standard explanation of the murder of Caesar. In light of so many signs that portended the event, it was the power of destiny (*vis fatorum*) that confounded the judgment of so keen-minded and successful a statesman (2.57.2–3). Caesar would better have followed the advice of old friends, to hold with arms the position he had won by arms (2.57.1).

Writing at the end of Tiberius' principate, Seneca the Elder in his collection of material for declamation demonstrates that Caesar had already become a fixture in the rhetorical schools. Like Valerius Maximus (5.1.10), Seneca found in Caesar's weeping at the sight of the severed head of his son-in-law Pompeius an exemplum of the effect of family ties even on the most bitter of enemies (*Cont.* 10.3.1). And Caesar could play his role in what would become a favorite rhetorical topos, the death of Cicero. In contrast to the intolerable behavior of Antonius toward Cicero during the proscriptions, Caesar's pardon of Cicero after the battle of Pharsalus was acceptable. At least the crumbling republic had fallen into the hands of a good master (*bonus princeps*, *Suas.* 7.1).

Under Tiberius, facets of Caesar – his divinity, *clementia*, and victory over his assassins – that were prominent in the literature of the Augustan era became codified as beneficent aspects of the transition from failing republic to tranquil principate. At the same time, Velleius already presents many of the themes that would become standard by the early second century AD in the biographies and historical accounts of Caesar.

FURTHER READING

Donié 1996: 1–101 provides a comprehensive discussion of Caesar's treatment in the literature in the first century after his death in an analysis that extends widely Syme's theory of a disassociation of Caesar under Augustus. White 1988 is an important corrective to Syme's argument. Despite its title, Duxbury 1988 has an epilogue with much of value on Caesar's treatment in early imperial authors. The recent dissertation of Zarrow 2007 deals with Caesar's representation in all media (literature, inscriptions, coins, and architecture) of the Augustan age and shows that there is no consistent pattern to his representation.

CHAPTER SEVENTEEN

Neronian Literature: Seneca and Lucan

Matthew Leigh

Introduction

Julius Caesar features prominently in the prose works of the Stoic philosopher and tragedian L. Annaeus Seneca and is the dominant personality of the epic *Civil War* or *Pharsalia* of Seneca's nephew M. Annaeus Lucanus. To read of Caesar in the one is often to recall a parallel passage in the works of the other, and it is striking and informative to compare how the two writers engage with specific ethical issues: Should the wise man participate in civil war? What is the moral and political meaning of Julius Caesar's famous clemency towards his defeated foes? Yet Lucan's Caesar is far more than just the subject of a series of ethical commonplaces. He is the extraordinary product of Lucan's engagement with prose history and with the ancient biographical tradition regarding Caesar, and of his attempt to reimagine the features that Caesar there displays in truly epic terms. Where his great opponent Pompey is consistently characterized by fatigue, stasis, and decline, Caesar's dynamism and energy propel the *Civil War* forward and make inevitable the emergence of the imperial system that Lucan is so often at pains to deplore. If he is a villain, he is of that peculiarly charismatic cast of villain that Seneca himself perfects in the Atreus of his tragic *Thyestes*.

History to Epic: Swift-footed Caesar

Lucan introduces Caesar as a man constantly on the heels of the older Pompey. Rivalry in excellence is identified as a fundamental motive for civil war (Luc. 1.120); Caesar's Gallic campaigns are a challenge to the kudos of Pompey's eastern triumphs and his victory over the pirates (Luc. 1.121–4); Pompey can bear no equal and Caesar no superior (Luc. 1.125–6). Seneca likewise accuses Pompey of an insane love of false greatness and asserts that glory and ambition drove Caesar forwards; he adds that Caesar could bear no one man ahead of himself when the state bore two men ahead of it (Sen. *Ep.* 94.65).

Here then we see a first instance of how much the Caesars of Seneca and Lucan can have in common. The same cannot be said for what follows. Lucan begins with the acidic assertion that it is impossible to judge which of the two sides fought with greater justice, for each can bring forth a great judge in his defense: the gods favored the cause of the victor, Cato that of the defeated (Luc. 1.126–8). He then offers pen-portraits of the two contestants and accompanies each with an important simile. Pompey comes first, a man declining into senility, long unused to war and forgetful of his generalship, charmed by the personality cult of his own theatre, disinclined to rebuild his strength and happy to trust in his former fortune (Luc. 1.129–35). He is likened to an ancient oak tree, decorated with the spoils of ancient foes, but tottering on infirm roots and doomed to be sent crashing by the next storm to strike. Many a tree rises around it secure and strong, but it alone is worshiped (Luc. 1.135–43). So much for Pompey. I quote in full Lucan's account of his great rival:

> Contrast Caesar: he had not only
> a general's name and reputation, but never-resting
> energy; his only shame was conquering without war;
> fierce, indomitable, wherever hope and indignation called
> he moved to action, never shrank from defiling his sword,
> he followed up his own successes, pressed hard upon the deity's
> favour, driving back all obstacles to his high
> ambitions and rejoicing to create his path by destruction.
> Just so flashes out the thunderbolt shot forth by the winds through clouds,
> accompanied by the crashing of the heavens and sound of shattered ether;
> it splits the sky and terrifies the panicked
> people, searing eyes with slanting flame;
> against its own precincts it rages, and with nothing solid stopping
> its course, both as it falls and then returns great is the devastation
> dealt far and wide before it gathers again its scattered fires.
> (Luc. 1.143–57, trans. S. H. Braund)

The dynamism and boundless energy here attributed to Caesar is essential to his representation throughout the poem. Whenever and wherever he is met, he is already ahead of expectation and pressing ever forward: before he even enters the poem as an agent, he has *already* rushed over the Alps (Luc. 1.183–5); he puts an end to delay and heads across the Rubicon (Luc. 1.204–5); safely landed on the opposite bank, he moves forward faster than a Balearic sling-shot or a Parthian arrow (Luc. 1.229–30); the speech of the venal tribune Curio spurs him to action as does the cry of the spectators an eager racehorse at Olympia (Luc. 1.293–5); when an anxious senate chooses to take the omens for the coming war, it is a mark of what they face that the haruspex gazing into the liver of the slaughtered beast finds its head sick and flaccid, but on it growing the substance of another head, this one twitching and restlessly stirring the veins with the swiftness of its pulse (Luc. 1.626–9). If the former brings to mind Lucan's earlier reference to Pompey's incipient senility, and perhaps more specifically to the illness that nearly took him to his grave in the summer of 50 BC (Cic. *Tusc.* 1.86; Plut. *Pomp.* 57.1; Luc. 7.352–5; Juv. 10.283–6), the latter has a distinctively Caesarian character. What that character is we will now do well to consider in somewhat greater depth.

When Lucan's pen-portrait of Caesar emphasizes the general's determination ever to follow up his own successes (Luc. 1.148), there is a palpable overlap with the biographical tradition and particularly with Plutarch's assertion that Caesar treated those successes he had achieved as the spark to future, greater action, and lived in a state of constant rivalry with himself as if with another (Plut. *Caes.* 58.4–5). The same may also be said of the poet's insistence on speed. When, in particular, he states that the second head growing on the liver stirs the veins with swift pulse (Luc. 1.629 *celeri ... pulsu*), the image gains point by allusion to that quality of swiftness (*celeritas*) that historians and biographers alike identify as one of Caesar's most remarkable characteristics. Swift and decisive action is first attested by Caesar's biographers in the vengeance he takes against the pirates who take him prisoner in the East (Plut. *Caes.* 2.3; Suet. *Iul.* 7). The same quality then recurs in accounts of his propraetorship in Spain (Plut. *Caes.* 12.1; Suet. *Iul.* 18.1), throughout his Gallic campaigns (Plut. *Caes.* 20.3, 24.2, 26.2–3), and in the civil wars (Plut. *Caes.* 32.1). It is typical of such accounts also to specify the length of time that it took Caesar to complete a journey or a campaign: eight days to march from Rome to the Rhône (Plut. *Caes.* 17.4; cf. Suet. *Iul.* 57); ten days to bridge the Rhine (Plut. *Caes.* 22.5); 60 days to become master of all of Italy (Plut. *Caes.* 35.2); three camps captured in but one day (Plut. *Caes.* 53.2). And what is true of the military man is also true of the man of culture: Hirtius expresses his wonder at how quickly Caesar composed his *commentarii* (Caes. *BG* 8 pref. 5–6; cf. Suet. *Iul.* 56.3); Plutarch reproduces Oppius' account of how Caesar could ride and dictate multiple letters at the same time (Plut. *Caes.* 17.4); Pliny the Elder speaks of Caesar's vigor and swiftness winged with a certain fire (*vigorem celeritatemque quodam igne volucrem*), then illustrates this not by reference to warfare but rather with the claim that he was accustomed to write or read, dictate and listen to four or even seven letters at once (Plin. *HN* 7.91).

So Caesar is the man of speed and in Pliny, at least, that speed has a fiery aspect to it. We may bear this in mind as we consider perhaps the most famous example of this quality at work. Chapters 34–5 of Suetonius' *Life of Caesar* trace his headlong progress through the civil wars and follow him from Corfinium to Brundisium and on to Rome, Gaul, Spain, Macedonia, Pharsalus, Alexandria, Syria, the Pontus, Africa and Spain once more. Suetonius, as in his account of the Gallic campaigns, can defer to Caesar's own works for any longer narrative, but there is also a strong sense here that the biographer's prose is struggling to match the pace set by his subject. Speed is certainly at issue when Suetonius records Caesar's Pontic campaign: Pharnaces son of Mithridates is defeated within five days of Caesar's arrival and but four hours after he has come into Caesar's view. Or, as Caesar himself put it on the tablets borne in his later triumph: VENI VIDI VICI (Suet. *Iul.* 37.2). To Plutarch the very compression of Caesar's phrase mimes the instantaneous character of his victory (Plut. *Caes.* 50.3–4; cf. App. *B Civ.* 2.91.383; Dio 44.46). And to Florus, who essays the unfortunate variant "he came, he struck, he left" (Flor. 2.13.63 *venit, percussit, abscessit*), Caesar conducts the campaign in the manner of a thunderbolt (*more fulminis*). The overlap with Lucan's programmatic simile will not be missed.

Lucan, it has been argued, identifies the defining features of the Caesar of history and biography and reconceives them in properly epic terms. And if *celeritas* is indeed the mark of Caesar in almost all of our prose sources, then it is perhaps no surprise that one epic role that he plays throughout the *Civil War* is that of the swift-footed Achilles of Homer. That Lucan's epic provides an intense and sustained negation of the patriotic foundation myth of Vergil's *Aeneid* is so obvious as almost to overshadow the importance to his work of a number of other epic models. Yet it has been demonstrated that the combination in Lucan's proem of a seven-line introductory period followed by a single line asking the origins of the quarrel recalls most closely the structure of the proem to the *Iliad*, and when, at the outset of civil war, Caesar turns to his men and observes that this is now the tenth year that they have been fighting with him (Luc. 1.283, 300), there is a felicitous parallelism between the historical timescale of Caesar's Gallic command and the mythic paradigm of Homer's Trojan war (Hom. *Il.* 2.134, 295). The Pompey of history had long figured himself as Agamemnon conqueror of the East (Cic. *Att.* 7.1.2; Suet. *Iul.* 50.1; Dio 42.5.3–5; Ptolemaeus Hephaestion ap. Phot. *Bibl.* 190, 151a) and had had this title thrown in his face by allies impatient to fight at Pharsalus (Plut. *Pomp.* 67.3, *Caes.* 41.1; App. *B Civ.* 2.67.278). He had even reacted to Caesar's alleged adultery with his wife Mucia by dubbing him an Aegisthus (Suet. *Iul.* 50.1). Yet now in Lucan he faces in Caesar not an Aegisthus but rather an Achilles: the younger man, the warrior impatient and insubordinate.

The figuration is suggestive but it is not entirely sustained: the *Civil War* can become an *Iliad* only in so far as the basic historical facts of the civil war permit. Pompey beheaded on the sands of Egypt in book 8 of the poem bears a significant resemblance to Agamemnon murdered in the tragic *Agamemnon* of Seneca, but he is also very much Vergil's headless Priam cast out on the beach (Verg. *Aen.* 2.554–8). Caesar in turn plays Achilles to the Hector of the dying Domitius, and receives the same reminder of his own imminent mortality (Luc. 7.610–15; cf. Hom. *Il.* 22.356–60); in his vaunted clemency he may seek to emulate the attitude shown by Achilles to Priam in the final book of the *Iliad*. If, as seems likely, Lucan had planned to close his poem with the suicide of Cato after Thapsus, then the Republican hero's bitter scorn for his rival's forgiveness would have offered a mordantly antiphrastic rereading of Homer's coda.

It should finally be noted that, if Lucan figures Caesar as Achilles, he often does so across the intermediary figure of Alexander the Great. Plutarch and Cicero both record the visit of Alexander to the tomb of Achilles at Sigeum and his jealous observation of Achilles' good fortune in having Homer as herald of his fame (Cic. *Arch.* 24; Plut. *Alex.* 15.4). It is likewise a commonplace of the ancient lives of Caesar that, serving in Spain in 69 BC, he visited the statue of Alexander in the temple of Hercules at Gades and wept jealous tears over how much Alexander, and how little he himself, had achieved at the same age (Suet. *Iul.* 7.1; Dio 37.52.2; Plut. *Caes.* 11.3). Lucan in turn creates his own fiction of heroic emulation: Caesar, hot on the heels of the vanquished Pompey, makes an unscheduled and otherwise unwitnessed visit to the site of Troy (Luc. 9.950–99). All now is but a scene of destruction and Lucan quips that even the ruins have been ruined (Luc. 9.969 *etiam periere ruinae*). Caesar has a consistent tendency in the poem to trample on anything that stands in his way (for the verb *calcare*, see Luc. 7.294, 749, 9.1043–6), and here too a local tour-guide has to remind him that he is trampling on the shades of Hector (Luc. 9.976–7 *Phryx incola manes | Hectoreos calcare vetat*). Precisely at this moment, and even before Caesar has any chance to express any jealousy for his epic predecessors, Lucan leaps in to assure him of their mutual immortality:

> O how sacred and immense the task of bards! You snatch everything
> from death and to mortals you give immortality.
> Caesar, do not be touched by envy of their sacred fame;
> since, if for Latian Muses it is right to promise anything,
> as long as honours of the Smyrnaean bard endure,
> the future ages will read me and you; our Pharsalia
> shall live and we shall be condemned to darkness by no era.
> (Luc 9.980–6, trans. S. H. Braund)

Where Achilles had his Homer, and Alexander but the feeble Choerilus, Caesar will now have Lucan. The hero hastens on to Alexandria, pausing only to weep crocodile tears over the head of the fallen Pompey, and, ever the tourist, heads straight for the tomb of Alexander. Lucan launches into a vitriolic condemnation of Alexander (Luc. 10.20–44). Among the many insults heaped upon the Macedonian is the term "a star hostile to the peoples" (Luc. 10.35–6 *sidus iniquum | gentibus*). This is a clear allusion to the dog-star simile with which Homer evokes Achilles' approach to the walls of Troy and, in particular, the star's description as an evil sign and a bringer of fever to wretched mortals (Hom. *Il.* 22.25–32). But a few lines on in book 10, Cleopatra will flatter Caesar by calling him "a star favorable to our peoples" (Luc. 10.89–90 *tu gentibus aequum | sidus ades nostris*). Homeric allusion is but another weapon in her armory of seduction.

History to Epic: Caesar and his Subalterns

Caesar's biographers and the historians of his campaigns repeatedly emphasize the mutual devotion of the general and his troops. To Caesar those fighting for him are not soldiers (*milites*) but comrades (*commilitones*), and the worst name he can call them is citizens (*quirites*; Suet. *Iul.* 67.2, 70.2; App. *B Civ.* 2.93.392; Luc. 5.358). The material rewards for valor are lavish and are more than effective in binding the soldiers to their leader (Plut. *Caes.* 17.1, 55.2; Suet. *Iul.* 67.2). Caesar even recruits new legions from his own resources and grants citizenship to those he favors (Suet. *Iul.* 24.2). All this benevolence is repaid in full, and our sources pullulate with instances of valor and devotion to the general, particularly among the junior officer class: C. Acilius, who emulates the Athenian Cynegirus in the sea-battle at Massilia

(Val. Max. 3.2.22; Plut. *Caes.* 16.1; Suet. *Iul.* 68.4); the collective suicide of C. Vulteius and his Opitergian crew when trapped in the sea off Illyria (Livy *Per.* 110; Flor. 2.13.32–3; Comm. Bern. at Luc. 4.462); the centurion Scaeva and his lone stand at Dyrrachium (*Caes. BC* 3.53.3–5; Val. Max. 3.2.23; Suet. *Iul.* 68.3–4; Flor. 2.13.40; Plut. *Caes.* 16.2; App. *B Civ.* 2.60.247–50); C. Crastinus, the centurion who leads the charge at Pharsalus (*Caes. BC* 3.91, 99; Livy ap. Comm. Bern. at Luc. 7.470 and 471; Plut. *Pomp.* 71.1–3, *Caes.* 44.5–6, App. *B Civ.* 2.82.347–8); Granius Petro the quaestor or centurion who defies his Pompeian captors off Africa (Plut. *Caes.* 16.4; cf. [Caes.] *B Afr.* 44–6). Lucan in turn finds in these figures and their relationship to their leader a constant source of fascination. As in his handling of the speed of Caesar, he reaches back to the prose tradition and reconceives an essential feature of Caesar's representation in strikingly epic terms.

Among the embassy sent by Caesar in 51 BC to seek an extension of his Gallic command was an unnamed centurion. Learning that the senate had refused to grant this, he grasped his sword in his hand and exclaimed "But this will grant it!" (Plut. *Caes.* 29.5, *Pomp.* 58.2; cf. App. *B Civ.* 2.25.97 attributing these words to Caesar himself). This story appears to underlie the first of Caesar's centurions to appear in the *Civil War* – Laelius – and the speech he delivers at Luc. 1.359–86 asserting his absolute loyalty to Caesar's cause. Note how he is in effect but a hand to be put to the service of his master:

> "Come, lead us through the Scythian peoples, through Syrtis'
> inhospitable shores, through parched Libya's burning sands:
> to leave a conquered world behind as it marched on, this hand
> subdued with oar the Ocean's swollen waves
> and curbed the northern whirlpools of the foaming Rhine:
> to carry out your orders the necessary power and will I have."
> (Luc. 1.367–72, trans. S. H. Braund [slightly adjusted])

Laelius goes on to promise that with a right hand, however reluctant, he will plunge his sword, if so ordered, into his brother's breast, his father's throat, even the womb of his pregnant wife (Luc. 1.374–8). The men around him cry out in assent and promise their hands for whatsoever war Caesar should require (Luc. 1.387–9).

The collective suicide of Vulteius and his crew is not mentioned in Caesar's *Civil War*, but the detailed note of the *Commenta Bernensia* at Luc. 4.462 makes clear his appreciation for their deeds: to console the people of Opitergium for their loss, he granted 20 years' dispensation from military service and enlarged their boundaries by 300 centuries. And what is perhaps most striking in all Lucan's narrative is the speech of Vulteius himself urging his men to suicide, the claim that they have no better way to demonstrate their devotion to Caesar (Luc. 1.501–2), and the exhortation to ensure by deeds of great valor that, few though they are among the many thousands of casualties that he endures, Caesar should regard their fall as a loss and a disaster (Luc. 4.512–24, esp. 524 *damnum cladenque*). Here too Lucan appears to engage with a key feature of Caesar's generalship, for Suetonius reports that he so cherished his men that, on hearing of the 54 BC disaster of Titurius at the hands of Ambiorix (*audita clade Tituriana*), Caesar grew long his hair and beard in token of mourning and did not cut them short until vengeance had been achieved (Suet. *Iul.* 67.2). Yet now Lucan also locates this episode within the realm of myth. The shipmates who stab each other to death rather than fight on or surrender are compared to the sown men of Cadmus and Medea (Luc. 4.549–58), and Fama, the embodiment of rumor but also of epic fame, is said to have spoken of no ship with louder mouth as she runs through the world (Luc. 4.573–4). The implication is clear: Apollonius, Varro of Atax, and the rest can now fall silent; the Argo and its crew must content themselves with second place.

Two further examples may be cited of the reinvention of Caesar's loyal subalterns as figures of epic. Caesar himself lavishes praise on the centurion Crastinus who led the charge at Pharsalus and was found dead amidst the foe with a sword thrust full in his face (Caes. *BC* 3.91 and 99). Lucan in turn curses him for shattering the momentary hesitation that envelops both sides as they get ready to strike their own kin (Luc. 7.466–75). Yet where the Crastinus of the historians leads his men forward and strikes with the sword, in Lucan's epic he takes on the dimensions of the Homeric archer Pandarus (Hom. *Il.* 4.86–140) and particularly of the Tolumnius of Vergil (Verg. *Aen.* 12.266–8), and casts his spear into the foe. The centurion Scaeva is already a somewhat hyperbolic figure even in the dry narrative of Caesar's *commentarii*, and we are told that his shield, when brought to Caesar, was found to have been pierced in 120 places (Caes. *BC* 3.53.4). Lucan goes even further, has him strip off his armor lest he be deemed to have survived through it, and describes the forest of spears he now bears in his guts (Luc. 6.202–6). At one stage towards the end of his heroic stand, Scaeva in fact feigns incapacity and represents himself as an example of Caesar abandoned rather than of an honorable death (Luc. 6.233–5). This though is but a ruse by which he gains the chance to slay one more foe and mock the enemy for the frailty of their devotion to Pompey compared to his devotion to death (Luc. 6.236–45). Death apart, it is Caesar that Scaeva loves; he yearns to die before the eyes of his leader (Luc. 6.158–60) and is certain that vengeance will be at hand as soon as the sound of his struggle reaches the ears of the general (Luc. 6.162–5). Nor is he wrong (Luc. 6.246–7). This then is a mighty warrior and a devoted follower, but he is also an example of the perversion of martial valor (*virtus*) in civil war (Luc. 6.147–8). As Scaeva quits the scene, Lucan observes the fair fame he might have won had he but fought a foreign foe (Luc. 6.257–9), makes him an example of wars that can enjoy no triumph (Luc. 6.260–1, cf. 1.12), and finally exclaims "Wretch, with how great valor did you gain a master!" (Luc. 6.262 *infelix, quanta dominum virtute parasti!*).

When Lucan talks of the fame that Scaeva might have won had he fought in the national cause (Luc. 6.257 *felix hoc nomine famae*), he again reflects implicitly on his capacity to enter the annals of epic heroism. And indeed Lucan has every reason to meditate on this possibility, for through allusion he has located Scaeva in a long pattern of lone epic resistance that links the Homeric Ajax struggling to hold back the Trojans in *Iliad* 16 (Hom. *Il.* 16.102–11) and Turnus at bay in the Trojan camp in *Aeneid* 9 (Verg. *Aen.* 9.803–11). Yet perhaps the most important link in this chain is represented by the 15th book of the *Annals* of Ennius, where the Republican epic poet transfers key features of the resistance of Ajax not to another figure from the age of heroes but rather to the military tribune C. Aelius standing his ground in the Istrian war of 178–177 BC (Enn. *Ann.* 391–8 Sk.). Here indeed is the foreign war that guarantees heroic valor its meed of fame. Scaeva needs no such validation; to him it is enough that Caesar should approve.

History to Epic: Caesar and the Gods

The Caesar of the biographical tradition shows little respect for conventional religion in general and for omens in particular. This is most famously true of his mockery of the seer Spurinna and refusal to beware the Ides of March (Cic. *Div.* 1.119, 2.36–7; Suet. *Iul.* 81.4; App. *B Civ.* 2.153.645), but further examples abound (Suet. *Iul.* 59, 77). This places him in an interesting relationship to Lucan himself, for one of the most significant features of the *Civil War* is its elimination of the traditional epic gods as agents (if not of portents and other phenomena conventionally indicative of divine anger), and indeed perhaps the greatest proof of the absence or total indifference of the gods is precisely the fact of Caesar's victory (see esp. Luc. 7.445–59). This aspect of Lucan's Caesar is perhaps best exemplified by the famous episode of the desecration of the sacred grove of Massilia perpetrated in book 3 of the *Civil War* (Luc. 3.399–452). Caesar here finds himself in urgent need of timber in order to construct siege machinery (Luc. 3.398–4), but he and he alone is willing to seek that timber in the grove that Lucan so ghoulishly describes (Luc. 3.399–425). His men hesitate to touch it (Luc. 3.426–30); both the Gauls who groan outside and the Phocaean Greeks who rejoice within the walls do so because they presume that Caesar must now be subject to the vengeance of the gods (Luc. 3.445–8). As Caesar marches on unscathed, Lucan quips that fortune preserves many a guilty man and the divine forces know how to be angry only at the wretched (Luc. 3.458–9).

The Caesar of the historians and the biographers would never allow himself to be deterred from undertaking a hazardous voyage (Cic. *Div.* 2.52; Min. Fel. *Oct.* 26.4; Plut. *Caes.* 52.2–3; Dio 42.58.2). Plutarch and Suetonius both record one such sea journey undertaken in the course of the civil wars though Suetonius claims that he sailed across the Adriatic from Brundisium to Dyrrachium while Plutarch suggests that he endeavored to follow the opposite trajectory from Apollonia to Brundisium (Plut. *Caes.* 38; Suet. *Iul.* 58.2). In both instances Caesar boards a small boat (Plut. *Caes.* 38.1 specifies one of 12 oars) and does so by night, in disguise, and unknown to all; he then obliges the helmsman to sail on in the face of the storm and is as good as drowned before finally being obliged to put back to land. In Plutarch the helmsman's anxiety at the conditions leads Caesar to reveal himself, take him by the hand, and utter the exhortation: "Go on, good man, be brave and fear nothing: you carry Caesar and Caesar's fortune sailing with you" (Plut. *Caes.* 38.3). Lucan in turn addresses this episode in book 5 of the *Civil War* and entangles Caesar in perhaps the most notoriously hyperbolic storm of the famously stormy epic genre (Luc. 5.597–677). Here too Caesar embraces the challenge of Fortune (Luc. 5.592–3) and even addresses her, addresses the gods at the moment of his greatest peril

(Luc. 5.655–71). When finally Caesar is blown ashore, back where his great voyage began, Lucan comments: "And together, touching land, he recovered so many kingdoms, so many cities, and his fortune" (Luc. 5.676–7).

If Caesar in a storm is at once the Odysseus of *Odyssey* 5 and the Aeneas of *Aeneid* 1, in the opening stages of this episode he plays a rather different role. For Lucan has found a name for the otherwise anonymous helmsman – Amyclas – and has chosen to describe his humble hut in such a way as to recall that of the aged but hospitable Baucis and Philemon of Ovid, *Metamorphoses* 8 (Luc. 5.517 *cannaque intexta palustri*; cf. Ov. *Met.* 8.630 *et canna tecta palustri*). There is a point here, for Baucis and Philemon play host to Jupiter and Mercury in disguise, and it is only after they have demonstrated their complete benevolence and generosity towards previously unknown guests that the gods reveal themselves and offer them whatever reward they choose. Lucan's Caesar, however, is rather too impatient for all of this. Dressed though he is in plebeian garb, he is unable to speak in the manner of a private citizen (Luc. 5.537–8), and the first thing that he does when Amyclas opens the door is to instruct him to expect rewards greater than his modest prayers (Luc. 5.532), then order him not to delay to submit his destiny to a god who wishes to fill his humble home with sudden wealth (Luc. 5.536–7). It is perhaps a reflection of Caesar's *celeritas* that he has no time for the process of test and reward, that he reveals his 'divinity' from the first and short-circuits the time-honored structure of the theoxeny motif.

Moral Judgments and the Problem of Clemency

The sheer dynamism of Lucan's Caesar, like that of Seneca's tragic Atreus, undercuts any secure sense of disapproval at the moral or political character of their actions. For in both the *Civil War* and the *Thyestes*, there would be no epic, there would be no tragedy, but for the determination of the work's ostensible villain to drive the plot forward. Modern scholarship has paid particular attention to this aspect of both works and has founded metapoetic analyses on the tendency of the respective villains to describe their actions in terms otherwise applied by poets to their work: when Caesar launching the civil war bids Rome to "favor my undertakings" (Luc. 1.200 *Roma, fave coeptis*), his words are not far from those of Propertius launching a new poetic program (Prop. 4.1.67 *Roma, fave: tibi surgit opus*); when Atreus resolves to outdo the crime of Procne and Philomela, he uses the language of a playwright pitting himself against the works of a noted predecessor (Sen. *Thy.* 267–77). All this matters, for we do indeed gain far greater aesthetic pleasure from the energy of Caesar or the machinations of Atreus than ever we do from the inertia of Pompey or the empty pieties of Thyestes, but there is some way to go between asserting that Lucan's role in poetry is analogous to that of Caesar in politics and then concluding that for that reason Lucan is also in sympathy with Caesar's political program.

That any account of Lucan's politics cannot simply be founded on the identification of an aesthetic affinity with his Caesar is implicit in the works of one of the most important proponents of the metapoetic analysis of the *Civil War*. For Jamie Masters's *Poetry and Civil War in Lucan's Bellum Civile* (1992) follows up a pioneering analysis of Caesar as surrogate for the poet with an attempt to demonstrate at least one instance of explicit sympathy with his politics. This he finds in book 4 and the clemency shown by Caesar to the Republican forces he has defeated in Spain (Luc. 4.337–401). In a previous contribution to this topic, I argued against this position by asserting that the very lines that Masters identifies as most favorable to Caesar (Luc. 4.363–4), by allusion to key lines of Vergil and Ennius, also give him a Jovian aspect and remind the reader that any state that can do no better than appeal to the benevolence of an all-powerful ruler is one that has accepted that it is made up not of citizens but of subjects. In the short term, any act of clemency may seem preferable to a massacre, but in the longer term it will be realized that the man who arrogates to himself the right to spare or to forgive those who were once his fellow citizens has successfully subverted a crucial constitutional principle.

The point that I make is essential to our understanding of Caesar in Seneca, Lucan, and elsewhere. That Caesar chose not to persecute his defeated foes in the aftermath of civil war is something for which he is widely praised (Plut. *Caes.* 46.2, 57.3; Suet. *Iul.*75; Dio 41.62.1–63.6); his tears shed over the head and ring of Pompey are more often taken as proof of humanity (Val. Max. 5.1.10; Plut. *Caes.* 48.2) than of skill as an actor (Luc. 9.1055–6; Dio 42.8.2–3); and he gains credit for his refusal to examine the latter's correspondence and thus discover who had opposed him, who had stayed neutral in the war (Sen. *Ira* 2.23.4; Dio 41.63.5). Yet simply to launch the civil war was a crime against the state and, however dubious the motives of his principal opponent Pompey, it is possible to look to Cato for the unflinching defense of constitutional principle. This is as true of Seneca (Sen. *Prov.* 3.14, *Constant.* 1.3, *Ep.* 94.65, 95.70, 104.29–33) as it is of Lucan (e.g. 9.190–214), and the debate between Brutus and Cato in book 2 of the *Civil War* effectively replays and resolves one first staged by Seneca in his 14th *Epistle* (Luc. 2.234–325; cf. Sen. *Ep.* 14.12–13).

When Seneca addresses himself to the young king Nero, he commends to him a policy of moderation (Sen. *Clem.*, *passim*). Yet his model for the clement monarch is never Julius Caesar himself but rather the emperor Augustus (Sen. *Clem.* 1.9–11). It is one thing to praise clemency at a time when there is no practical alternative to monarchy, quite another to celebrate a man whose claim to spare his enemies was part and parcel of his subversion of the constitution they had been fighting to defend. It is for this reason that book 2 of the *De Beneficiis*, in a passage characterized by its bracing political realism and acceptance of the death of the Republic, can still admit that it was by injurious means that Caesar acquired the power to grant Brutus his life, and observe that the man does not save a fellow citizen who omits to kill him (Sen. *Ben.* 2.20.1–3). Likewise the recognition in the 24th *Epistle* that Cato had to die lest any man be able either to slay or to spare him (Sen. *Ep.* 24.6 *ne cui Catonem aut occidere liceret aut servare contingeret*).

It has been observed that *clementia* itself was very likely not part of the historical Caesar's political vocabulary. The same cannot be said of the verb *servare* and its often contradictory senses of "to save" and "to spare" (often represented in Greek sources by the verb σῴζειν). Plutarch, for instance, quotes Caesar's dictum that the greatest and sweetest reward he gained for victory in civil war was the chance to spare some of those who had fought against him (Plut. *Caes.* 48.2, cf. Luc. 9.1066–8) and records his reaction to the suicide of Cato: "O Cato, I begrudge you your death just as you begrudged me the chance to spare you" (Plut. *Caes.* 54.1, *Cat. Min.* 72.2). Cato himself, meanwhile, is made to give voice to the fundamental critique of clemency: "For if I were willing to be spared by grace of Caesar, I ought to go to him in person and see him alone; but I am unwilling to be under obligations to the tyrant for his illegal acts. And he acts illegally in sparing, as if their master, those over whom he has no right at all to be the lord" (Plut. *Cat. Min.* 66.2).

When therefore scholars find an endorsement of Caesar in the clemency scene in book 4 of the *Civil War*, they should not just consider the potential tensions internal to it, but also examine the rest of the poem and acknowledge the persistent tendency of Caesar's Republican foes to express distaste at any prospect of being spared by him. Domitius the commander of Corfinium is both humiliated and spared by Caesar in book 2 and resolves immediately to seek death and shun Caesar's gift (Luc. 2.512–15; cf. 524–5); this he finally achieves at Pharsalus where he dies rejoicing to have escaped a second pardon (Luc. 7.603–4). Pompey twice expresses distaste at the prospect of Caesar's clemency (Luc. 8.133–7, 314–16), while Cato merely hopes that the African king Juba will do to him what the Egyptian Ptolemy did to Pompey: he does not deprecate being spared by his enemy as long as he is spared with his head chopped off (Luc. 9.212–14). Yet perhaps the key scene is precisely Caesar's response to being presented with the head of Pompey in the closing lines of book 9. He repeats the adage, also quoted by Plutarch, that the greatest reward of civil war is the chance to spare his fellow citizens (Luc. 9.1066–8) and he betrays the true meaning of his clemency when he complains that he has in vain convulsed the world in civil war if any other power exists than his or if he has to share any land with another: by killing Pompey Ptolemy has usurped part of that absolute power over life and death that Caesar wanted for his own (Luc. 9.1075–8). Lucan himself thanks fortune for denying Caesar the chance to decide on Pompey's fate and for sparing Rome the shame of allowing Caesar to take pity on Pompey while he lived (9.1058–62).

When Lucan dedicates his poem to the future divinity Nero, then later lambasts the deification of dead emperors as a pernicious fiction (Luc. 1.33–66, cf. 6.807–9, 7.454–9), it is fashionable to speak of him "recontextualizing" his initial statement or deliberately injecting inconsistency into his poem. This I find a dubious alternative to the straightforward statement that the later passages unmask the emptiness of the former, for I cannot see how the claim can be inverted and the dedication to Nero be said seriously to recontextualize the later denunciations of emperor-cult. There is a similar problem with the interpretation of Caesar's pardon to the defeated Republicans in Spain. We will not pretend that clemency here is the less desirable alternative to a massacre or that the common troops whose relief at escaping civil war Lucan so lyrically evokes (Luc. 4.382–401) will feel the sting of accepting Caesar's right to forgive as strongly as do the traditionally empowered members of the senatorial oligarchy. Yet throughout the rest of the poem it is precisely the perspective of that oligarchy, that is to say of those who had effective rights to lose, that Lucan so consistently evokes. This, moreover, is a poem moving inexorably towards a climactic narrative of the African campaign. Lucan did not live to give voice to the defeated Cato's rejection of clemency but this he could not possibly have omitted. Lucan in book 4 of the *Civil War* presents the Republican general Petreius as ready to be spared, but how would the same man's suicide in the wake of Thapsus have recontextualized this act ([Caes.] *B Afr.* 94.1–2; Livy *Epit.* 114; Flor. 2.13.69; App. *B Civ.* 2.100.415)?

Conclusion

It is not possible in a contribution of this length to give a complete survey of the Caesar presented by Seneca and by Lucan. I hope instead, by concentrating in particular on Lucan's epic reinvention of key features of the Caesar of history and biography, to have given some idea of this figure's dynamism and excess. These same qualities also underpin his status as the active embodiment of Lucan's own aesthetic and complicate responses to his agency in the poem. Yet for all the poetic and metapoetic fascination that he exerts, Caesar is also the overthrower of the Republic and but the first of many Caesars ceaselessly pitted against the liberty of Rome (Luc. 7.691–7). Any artistic affinity that Lucan feels with his Caesar exists in productive tension with a clear-sighted and courageous assessment of his politics and what they bring.

FURTHER READING

The Latin text of Lucan cited here is that of the edition of A. E. Housman (Oxford, 1927). The translation is that of S. H. Braund (Lucan 1992). There are valuable general discussions of Lucan's Caesar in F. M. Ahl, *Lucan: An Introduction* ((Ithaca/London, 1976), pp. 189–230; W. R. Johnson, *Momentary Monsters: Lucan and his Heroes* (Ithaca/London, 1987), pp. 101–34; E. Narducci, *Lucano. Un'epica contro l'impero* (Rome/Bari, 2002), pp. 187–278; L. Nosarti, "Quale Cesare in Lucano?" *AClass* 38–9 (2002–3), 169–203. For Caesarian dynamism and Pompeian decline as represented by the programmatic first similes of the poem, see J. A. Rosner-Siegel, "The oak and the lightning: Lucan, *Bellum Civile* 1.135–57," *Athenaeum* 61 (1983), 165–77. For Lucan and Homer, see G. B. Conte, "Il proemio della *Pharsalia*," *Maia* 18 (1966), 42–53; M. Lausberg, "Lucan und Homer," *ANRW* 2.32.3 (1985), 1565–1622; and C. M. C. Green, "Stimulos dedit aemula virtus. Lucan and Homer reconsidered," *Phoenix* 45 (1991), 230–54. For Pompey and Agamemnon, see F. R. Berno, "Un truncus, molti re: Priamo, Agamemnone, Lucano (Virgilio, Seneca, Lucano)," *Maia* 56 (2004), 79–84. For Caesar and Alexander in Lucan and elsewhere, see P. Green, "Caesar and Alexander: aemulatio, imitatio, comparatio" in id., *Classical Bearings: Interpreting Ancient History and Culture* (Berkeley/Los Angeles/London, 1989), pp. 193–209. For Caesar and his subalterns, see M. Leigh, *Lucan: Spectacle and Engagement* (Oxford, 1997), pp. 158–233. For Caesar and the sacred grove, see M. Leigh, "Lucan's Caesar and the sacred grove: deforestation and enlightenment in antiquity," in P. Esposito and L. Nicastri (eds.), *Interpretare Lucano. Miscellanea di studi* (Naples, 1999), pp. 167–205. For Caesar and Amyclas, see E. Narducci,

"Pauper Amyclas. Modelli etici e poetici in un episodio della *Pharsalia*," *Maia* 35 (1983), 183–94. For the aesthetic affinities between Caesar and Lucan, see J. Masters, *Poetry and Civil War in Lucan's Bellum Civile* (Cambridge, 1992). For a similar approach to the role of Atreus in Seneca's *Thyestes*, see A. Schiesaro, *The Passions in Play: Thyestes and the Dynamics of Senecan Drama* (Cambridge, 2003). For Caesar's *clementia* in Lucan, see F. M. Ahl, *Lucan: An Introduction* ((Ithaca/London, 1976), pp. 192–7; J. Masters, *Poetry and Civil War in Lucan's Bellum Civile* (Cambridge, 1992), pp. 78–90; M. Leigh, *Lucan: Spectacle and Engagement* (Oxford, 1997), pp. 53–68. My comments here draw out the salient features of an overly convoluted argument and respond to the objections of J. J. O'Hara, *Inconsistency in Roman Epic: Studies in Catullus, Lucretius, Vergil, Ovid and Lucan* (Cambridge, 2007), pp. 131–42. For Seneca's verdict on Caesar, see M. T. Griffin, *Seneca: A Philosopher in Politics* (Oxford, 1976), pp. 184–8.

CHAPTER EIGHTEEN

The First Biographers: Plutarch and Suetonius

Christopher Pelling

How can you make Caesar intelligible? What features in his motivation, his success, or his failure need to be explained? What *sort* of explanation could possibly be adequate for so extraordinary a phenomenon?

Those were already good questions when, some century and a half after Caesar's death, Plutarch and Suetonius faced them within ten years or so of one another, Plutarch writing his *Caesar* under Trajan around 110 AD and Suetonius his *Divus Iulius* under Hadrian around 120.[1] The two men may even have met one another, for Plutarch had visited Rome several times; they may certainly have had acquaintances in common, for some of Plutarch's friends seem close to the circle of the younger Pliny (Jones 1971: 23–4, 51, 61), and Pliny exchanged letters with Suetonius and helped him in various ways (*Ep.* 1.18, 24, 3.8, 5.10, 9.34, 10.94–5; Wallace-Hadrill 1983: 4–6). But there is no sign that either knew the other's work, and the two biographies can be seen as independent ways of looking at the figure whose life, death, and legacy had done so much to shape the world in which they lived.

Not, of course, that these were the first to write Caesar-centered narratives. The first to do that was Caesar himself, though his *commentarii* covered only the last 15 years of his life and only their military aspects. One of Caesar's friends, C. Oppius, also wrote about him, and if we knew more about his work's scope and form we might well call him, rather than Plutarch or Suetonius, "the first biographer." It did contain anecdotal material which both Plutarch and Suetonius found valuable – the story, for instance, of how Caesar passed off an awkward social situation when he was served perfumed oil as a dressing (*Iul.* 53). Both biographers also tell how once, when Oppius fell sick, Caesar yielded to him the one bed in a cottage where they were billeting (*Caesar* 17.11; *Iul.* 72): it was presumably Oppius himself who told the tale. Particularly in the early parts of each biography Plutarch and Suetonius often seem to be drawing on the same source (Strasburger 1938: 72–3), and Oppius is probably the origin of at least the greater part of that shared material. But Plutarch knew that Oppius was not to be trusted when talking about Caesar's friends or enemies

(*Pomp.* 10.7–9), and both he and Suetonius read widely in other sources, including the mainline historical writers who had so much to say about Caesar. Asinius Pollio's narrative proved particularly useful to Plutarch, and it is normal to regard the extensive parallels between Plutarch and Appian as derived from a shared use of Pollio (Kornemann 1896; cf. Pitcher, chapter 19, p. 269). Suetonius too knew Pollio (*Iul.* 30.4, below, pp. 259–60; 55.4, 56.4); the two authors treat the crossing of the Rubicon in similar terms (*Iul.* 31–2 ~ *Caesar* 32), and Pollio, an eyewitness of the crossing, is probably the source.

Both Suetonius and Plutarch used other sources as well. Suetonius burrowed in archives and minutes: as a high member of the emperor's secretariat he had access to the imperial archives, though it is unclear that he derived anything of value for this Life (as he did for *Divus Augustus*). But he shows knowledge of the pamphleteering exchanges of the last Republic, and can deploy the accusations launched by Tanusius Geminus, the elder Curio, Caesar's fellow consul Bibulus, and M. Actorius Naso when paddling in the murky waters of the first Catilinarian conspiracy (*Iul.* 9; Naso is also quoted at 52.1, again for a scurrilous item). Another follower of Caesar, L. Cornelius Balbus, wrote about Caesar's end (we do not know in what form), and Suetonius quotes him at 81.1–2; a little earlier he quotes another work, apparently an unfriendly one, of T. Ampius (77.1). In Plutarch there are traces of the use of Cicero's memoir on his consulship, Livy, Strabo, and possibly Caesar himself (8.4, 47.3, 63.3, 3.4, 44.8). Surviving oral traditions may also play a part: the Arverni "point to" a sword that they captured from Caesar in the early stages of his final battle with Vercingetorix (26.8), and that part of Plutarch's narrative looks as if it is tailored to create a context where that sword, and the story the Gauls still tell about it, can find a place.

Wherever their material came from, both Plutarch and Suetonius knew how to impose their own shape upon it. Both, too, were writing their *Lives* in a series, and each series imposed its own perspective. For Suetonius Caesar looked forward: he was the first of the twelve Caesars that were his theme, ending with Domitian. Plutarch too had written a series of *Lives of the Caesars* some years earlier, but he had begun with Augustus, not Caesar, and ended with Vitellius. Now in the *Parallel Lives* he was comparing the great men of Rome with Greek counterparts: this Caesar is therefore not seen here as the first step towards the future, but as one of the last figures of the Republican past who can be compared with the great men of the Greek world, and Caesar is paired with the most spectacular conqueror of them all, Alexander the Great.

There are various ways that the different perspectives might be explained. Bowersock (1969) pointed to the way that Trajan revived the memory of Caesar, for instance by issuing commemorative Caesar coins in 107. Does that explain why Suetonius wished to include him in his series? Geiger (1975) elaborated this to a broader thesis about the principate's shifting ideology: the Flavian view held Augustus to be the founder, and this explained why Caesar did not figure in Plutarch's own *Lives of the Caesars.*[2] But a different view set in with Trajan's enthusiasm for Caesar, who – Geiger thinks – now began to count as the institutor of the regime, and thus in another passage of the *Parallel Lives* Plutarch himself now speaks of

Augustus as "the second ruler," *Numa* 19.6. Geiger may be right in thinking of an ideological shift, though if so it may not be a matter of imperial behest but a more bottom-up popular phenomenon in an epoch that "felt the attraction of a Caesar who was also a conqueror" (Syme 1958b: 434; cf. Pelling 2002: 253); but Levick and Barnes (chapters 15 and 20 in this volume) have good reasons for arguing that any change was less clear-cut (pp. 215–17, 278–80). The more significant fact about the coin-issues is that Caesar figured both in the series celebrating the emperors and in the separate one of Republican heroes, Brutus, Metellus Scipio, Sextus Pompeius, and others (*BMC* Imp. III^2 141 nos. 30–1, 142 nos. 696–8 ; cf. Levick, p. 218). That itself suggests Caesar's Janus-like qualities, as a figure who could look both forward and back.

Whatever the explanation for the two biographers' different perspectives, the choices they made are significant. First, that interest of Trajan and his age shows how much Caesar *mattered*; whatever one said about the man, there were readers who would care, and might find the presentation coming surprisingly close to home. Whether a writer wanted a contemporary implication or not, he would have to tread carefully – otherwise readers might find the wrong sort of contemporary implication. Secondly, the authors' choice of perspective also affects those questions of interpretation with which we began. Suetonius' Caesar set patterns for the future: patterns of the categories that would be appropriate for presenting later emperors; patterns for what he, and some of them, got right, and also – particularly in his actions as dictator – what he, and some of them, got wrong. Most of those explanations will rest on Caesar himself, the sort of person he was, the way he behaved, his skill or lack of skill in reading others. Suetonius chose a presentational strategy that suited those themes: there would be some linear narrative, particularly at the beginning and end of a Life, but much of his space would be given to analyzing the man's characteristics under separate headings or "categories" (*per species*) – his life-style, his sexual habits, his military and administrative skills, his attitude to the gods.

Plutarch's Caesar, set against that broader background of the Roman Republic, raises different questions. Of course Caesar's characteristics – his drive, his ambition, his charisma – matter here as well: they provide reasons for the pairing with Alexander. But there are also questions that center on the world in which he is moving, not just on the person himself. There had been brilliant Romans before, and threats to the established order before: Coriolanus, the Gracchi, Marius, Sulla, Pompey. What explained why Caesar was more successful, and why the consequences of his success were so much more lasting? Was it simply that he was abler? Or was it more a point about the history of the period? And Caesar's final failure, as much as his spectacular success, raised questions too. Did that suggest that, though the time for one-man rule might be coming, it had not come yet?

Those sorts of question go beyond Caesar's own personality. It is a feature of Caesar-narratives that biography and history often come close to one another, as Caesar turns Rome's story into a version of his own (Pelling 2006a; cf. Pitcher, p. 270); Plutarch's *Caesar* is no exception. That generic boundary is never quite crossed, but it is no coincidence that Plutarch's firmest statement of biographical principle comes in the proem to *Alexander and Caesar*, for it is in this pair that the difficulty of discriminating the two genres is at its most acute.

> It is not histories that we are writing, but Lives. Nor is it always his most famous actions that reveal a man's good or bad qualities; a clearer insight into a character is often given by a small matter, a word or a jest, than by engagements where thousands die, or by the greatest of pitched battles, or by the sieges of cities. (*Alex.* 1.1–2)

Notice that "often": often, not always. Plutarch does economize on some of the details of battles where thousands die and the sieges of cities, but those great events will also be unavoidably relevant for judging the man's "character." Little things do matter, and Plutarch will give us those as well. But Caesar, like Alexander, was above all a big-thing person. That, after all, was why Plutarch and Suetonius were writing about him.

That taste for the big things comes out early in Plutarch's Life, discussing Caesar's gifts as an orator:

> Caesar, they say, had a remarkable gift for political oratory, and he trained and developed this talent with great enthusiasm. The second place was unquestionably his, but he allowed the first to escape him: his attention was devoted to becoming first in power and in armed strength. His campaigns and his politics won him dominion in the state, but robbed him of that first prize in eloquence for which he was naturally fitted. Later, in his reply to Cicero's essay on Cato, he himself begged his readers not to compare his style with Cicero's: he was the military man, Cicero the skilled orator, with natural talent and the time to cultivate it. (*Caesar* 3.2–4)

One notices the barb in that last remark, as Plutarch looks forward to that "dominion" that Caesar will exercise: Cicero, Caesar implies, has had nothing more constructive to do with his time, while he himself has been the man of action. The main point however is to stress Caesar's direction. He is, from that early stage in the Life, a man who has made the biggest choice of all, to focus on power at all costs. That is reflected in anecdotes a little later:

> There is a story told of his journey across the Alps. He came to a tiny barbarian village, with just a handful of wretched people living there. Caesar's companions started to laugh and joke: "Do you think that here too there are rivalries for office, and struggles for top place, and jealousies of one mighty man against another?" Caesar replied in all seriousness: "I should prefer to be first man here than second in Rome." And there is another story too, relating to his time in Spain. He had some time to himself, and was reading a book about Alexander. He fell quiet for a long time, then he began to weep. His friends did not know what to make of this, and asked him why. "Don't you agree that it is a matter for tears?" he said. "When Alexander was my age, he was already master of so many nations – and I have not yet done anything distinguished at all." (*Caesar* 11.3–6)

So we always know where Plutarch's Caesar is going: to power, indeed to one-man power.

Plutarch's characterizing technique helps that impression. He favors "integrated" characters – not exactly stereotypes, but cases where a person's different characteristics go closely together, so that Coriolanus (for instance) is blustery, imperious, and no-nonsense not merely on the battlefield but also in politics, where the same traits are more disastrous; or Antony is warm-hearted, loose-living, jocular, and impetuous – qualities that endear him to his men but are more catastrophic when he shares his excesses with Cleopatra. When Caesar's characteristics are introduced – his devotion to friends, his relentless energy, his capacity to inspire devotion in his troops, even his capacity to keep a shorthand writer busy on horseback (*Caes.* 15–17) – they similarly hang together naturally, at least in the sense that they always help to explain his success. Suetonius' categories allow for different, unreconciled points to emerge under different headings: Caesar was thin; he suffered from epilepsy; he was physically unimpressive; he was very good at fighting; and in Suetonius those points are separated under different categories (*Iul.* 45.1, 45.2, 57–66); Plutarch brings them together, stressing that Caesar used campaigning as a way of building up his heath and struggling against his sickness (*Caes.* 17.1–3). So Plutarch takes even something that does not seem to fit, the physical frailty, and makes it suit the dominant characterization of the effective, determined man of success. Things that do not fit – Caesar's active sex-life, for instance, a theme in which Suetonius shows considerable interest – tend to be ignored by Plutarch; there is very little even on Cleopatra, with the famous scene with the carpet dismissed perfunctorily (49.1–3), and one famous episode, his affair with Servilia, figures not in this Life at all but in others (*Brutus* 5, *Cato minor* 24.1–3). The Caesar of this Life, unlike Suetonius' equivalent, has "no time for love" (Beneker 2002–3). And the narrative technique and the character go together. Caesar controls his world, subjects it to fit his own single-minded purpose: Plutarch controls the narrative with similar firmness and direction. Suetonius gives us the beads; Plutarch makes of them a necklace.

A large part of the explanation for the success of Plutarch's Caesar, then, rests in his own personality; but that is not enough. Historical factors matter too. Some of them Plutarch has treated in other Lives, and they can be taken as read here: the immense influence on politics exercised by Roman armies, for instance, especially if their generals offered big financial rewards (*Sulla* 12.12–14). Within *Caesar* itself the focus rests more on the power exercised by the Roman people, and Plutarch insistently applies a picture of politics influenced by Greek stereotypes, with the "few" systematically opposed to the "many" (de Blois 1992; Pelling 2002: 207–36). From early in his career Caesar plays for the support of "the many," spending profusely to win their good will (*Caesar* 4.4–8, 5.1–3): "people thought he was paying a fortune for some brief and fleeting acclaim; in fact he was buying the greatest thing of all, and it was cheap" (5.8). And "the impact on the people was so great that everyone sought new offices and new honors to repay him" (5.9; cf. 6.7). Even when Caesar is absent in Gaul, he is "playing the demagogue" through his agents (20.2), and when he wins a victory it "seemed more brilliant because it was Caesar who had won it. The affection of the ordinary people made sure of that" (21.2).

Still, that analysis too only takes us so far. Especially in Plutarch's polarized analysis, ambitious men had relied on "the people" for support before, and yet the experiences of the Gracchi and Marius and even Pompey had shown how determined and effective the opposition of "the few" could be. More is required to explain why

Caesar could achieve so much more, could indeed break the system. As Caesar comes to the end of his Gallic campaigns, Plutarch explains further.

> Caesar had long ago taken the decision to destroy Pompey, just as Pompey had decided to destroy Caesar. . . . There were pretexts at hand. Pompey himself afforded some, and others were furnished by the crisis and the sorry state of politics (*kakopoliteia*) at Rome. It had reached the stage where candidates for office would set out their banking-tables in public and offer bribes shamelessly to the common people; the voters had been purchased before they came down to the elections, and they gave their support not with their votes, but with their arrows and swords and slings. When the two sides separated they often left the rostra defiled with blood and corpses; they left the city in anarchy, like a ship drifting without a helmsman. Where would all this crazy turbulence end? Sensible people would be thankful if the outcome were monarchy, and nothing worse. Indeed, by now there were many who were ready to say in public that the state could only be cured by a monarchy, and the right thing to do was to take the remedy from the gentlest of the doctors who were offering it – meaning Pompey. (*Caesar* 28.1, 3–6)

Such people were only half-right, for the gentlest doctor was in fact to be Caesar, and Plutarch makes that explicit in another pair (*Comparison of Dion and Brutus* 2.2). Caesar's own ambitions are not altruistic: he is not applying a "remedy" for the state's sake but for his own, and for him these are only "pretexts." But, in explanatory power, they go beyond mere excuses. That "sorry state of politics at Rome," that *kakopoliteia*, does suggest that the time for monarchy was nigh.

Why, then, did Caesar, with all that ability and all that drive, not turn out to be the man to impose it? In Plutarch the qualities that make a person great are often the ones that also bring him down: we saw something of that with his Coriolanus and his Antony (above, pp. 255–6). The same is true here, though these decisive factors tend to be external ones. The factors that built Caesar up were the people, the army, and his friends, and he had always repaid the devotion of each group in kind. But after his victory these strengths started to turn against him. When he returned to Rome in 47 BC

> he was met by disapproval. That was partly because some of his soldiers had mutinied and killed two former praetors, Cosconius and Galba, but Caesar had ventured no harsher punishment than to call the men "citizens" instead of "soldiers": he had then given each of them a thousand drachmas, as well as parceling out a large part of the Italian countryside in land-grants. Dolabella's madness also started tongues wagging against Caesar, and so did Matius' avarice; so too did Antony's drunken excesses, and Corfinius' ransacking and rebuilding of Pompey's private house, as if it was not big enough already. The Romans did not like all this. Caesar himself knew what was going on, and it was against his will. But he had no choice. The political conditions forced him to make use of the men who were willing to be his agents. (*Caesar* 51.2–4)

So friends and army are both coming to be liabilities rather than assets, and to cost him the popular good will that had always been his strength; and there is nothing he can do about it. People were offended too by the triumph that he celebrated over fellow citizens (56.7–9), and his enemies made particular capital out of the vast honors that he was voted. Still, this too was not, in the main, his own fault. True, he "lusted for kingship" (60.1), taking further that ambition for domination that had governed his whole life; but the bigger mistakes are made by his friends, for instance the antics of Antony at the Lupercalia (61). They even spoilt a moment when Caesar himself was commenting that the honors needed to be cut back, not enhanced (60.4). The trouble was that he had just failed to rise to his feet to greet the consuls and praetors as they approached, followed by the whole senate, to offer him these honors.

> That distressed the people as much as the senate: they thought that an insult to the senate meant an insult to the whole state. Immediately those who could do so left the meeting, their eyes downcast in intense disapproval. (*Caesar* 60.5)

Caesar himself realized what a mistake he had made, and excused himself on the grounds of his epilepsy, for that condition tends to bring on dizzy fits.

> But this was not the explanation. Indeed, people say that Caesar was very willing to stand up to receive the senators, but was restrained by one of his friends, or rather his flatterers, Cornelius Balbus. "Remember you are Caesar," said Balbus. "You should expect them to show you the respect a superior deserves." (*Caesar* 60.8)

Alexander was destroyed by his own flaws, but Caesar himself is destroyed by others (Mossman 1988: 92): those others – friends, army, people – to whom he owed so much, and to whom he now owed his demise.

"The few" had always found ways of crushing those who threatened them (above, p. 256). The climate was now such that they could put down even their vanquisher, and Plutarch sounds the hollowness of all that driving ambition:

> Caesar died at the age of 56, outliving Pompey by a little more than four years. He had sought dominion and power all his days, and after facing so many dangers he had finally achieved them. And the only benefit he reaped was its empty name, and the perils of fame amid his envious fellow citizens. (*Caes.* 69.1)

Was all that single-mindedness indeed worthwhile? Had Caesar given up too much in that choice to pursue dominion "all his days"?

Whatever answer we give, this by now is not just Caesar's story. At the end there are echoes of Romulus, who similarly offended public opinion by his haughty spirit, by the clothes he wore, by his golden throne, by playing the tyrant; one version had Romulus too torn apart by angry senators; and Romulus' death, like Caesar's, was followed by the appearance of a man – in that case Proculus Iulius, in this Cinna the poet – announcing an ominous dream (*Rom.* 26–8; cf. Pelling 2002: 184–5). There are echoes of the Gracchi too: the way for instance that Tiberius felt that he had to risk coming to the Senate in order to defuse the accusations of wanting tyranny (*Ti.Gr.* 17 ~ *Caes.* 63–4); or Gaius' failure to restrain his more reckless friends, and the disaster they consequently bring (*C.Gr.* 13 ~ *Caes.* 51, above, p. 257); or the way the people's enthusiasm wavered but then burst out with new fervor after their champion's death (*Ti.Gr.* 21, *C.Gr.* 11, 18 ~ *Caes.* 67–8). Romulus at the beginning of the city, and the Gracchi at the beginning of the Republic's last phase, had revealed divisions and features of political life that were going to recur time and again, until the Republic could withstand them no more and Caesar, the man who had exploited those divisions most dynamically of all, himself fell their victim at the end. For Plutarch, it was Rome itself that explained most.

Suetonius' manner is different. To a much fuller extent than Plutarch, he is writing "not-history" (Wallace-Hadrill 1983: 8–10), emphatically avoiding the manner of historical narrative. An outline knowledge of politics is simply taken for granted: in the first chapter the teenage Caesar is aligned with "the opposite faction" (*partes*) to Sulla, and when Sulla then warns his followers that this boy will "one day destroy the *partes* of the optimates, which he and they had defended together," the passage assumes a similar two-party analysis to the one developed by Plutarch. From then on such a picture is taken as read (e.g. 5, 11, 15, 16.2, 19, 20.5). The violence and corruption of the late Republic is again simply assumed: 10.2, 12.1, 13, 14.2, 16.1, 17.2, 19, 20.1, 20.4–5, 23.2, 27.1–2, 54.3. Caesar intimidates and bribes more ruthlessly and effectively than anyone else, but that is where the explanatory train stops; there is no suggestion, as there was in Plutarch, that this also explains why the time for monarchy was near.

So the focus rests on Caesar's own personality, in itself not so different from Plutarch's version. This Caesar too is vastly ambitious (here too he groans at the way he has not yet rivaled Alexander's exploits, 7.1),[3] free-spending (10, 13, 18.1, 19.1, 26.2, 27), decisive and peremptory (as in an expressive sequence where he leaves Spain for Rome, then Rome for Spain, then again Spain for Rome, in each case before the proper time, 8, 18.1), eager to cause or exploit disruption (8, 9.1, 10.2, 11, 16.1, 20) but also shrewd enough to know when to draw back (3, 15.1, 16.2), intemperate in words and in action against his enemies (20.3–5, 22.2, cf. below, p. 263). Most of Caesar's actions – and Suetonius' manner is to detail many more individual actions than Plutarch – are felt to require no further explanation: Caesar was simply like that. But when it comes to the decision to go to civil war, this does require discussion.

> This [the defense of tribunes' rights] was the pretext for civil war, but people think the real causes were different. Gnaeus Pompey used to say that it was because Caesar's private wealth was not enough for him to finish the works he had started nor satisfy the popular expectations which he had generated of his return: he had therefore chosen to throw everything into confusion and tumult. Others think he feared that he might be called to account for the measures he had taken in his first consulship contrary to auspices, laws, and vetoes: Cato continually gave notice, even indeed swore, that he would prosecute Caesar as soon as he had dismissed his army, and it was commonly predicted that if Caesar returned a private citizen he would have to defend himself in a court surrounded by armed men, just as had happened with Milo. Asinius Pollio adds credibility to that view: he says that, on the battlefield of Pharsalus, Caesar looked at the dead enemy bodies lying before him and said (Pollio quotes the exact words): "they brought it on

themselves: I, Gaius Caesar, after such great achievements would have been found guilty, had I not sought help from my army." Some think that he was captivated by the thought of rule, weighed up his own power and that of his enemies, and took the chance for seizing the absolute power he had desired from his first youth. That seems to have been Cicero's view too: in the third book of *de Officiis* he writes that Caesar was always quoting the lines of Euripides which he translates as follows:

If wrong must be done, do it for a throne;
Be righteous in all else.
(Suet. *Iul.* 30, quoting Cic. *Off.* 3.82 and Eur. *Phoen.* 524–5)

The first of the suggested explanations, that mooted by Pompey, seems to be the one that Suetonius' own narrative suggests is least likely: from 26.2 on Caesar has been preparing for war (notice esp. 27.2, where Caesar has told the most disreputable of his followers that "they needed a civil war"), and Pompey's suggestion does not suit the sequence of 26.2, which made it clear that the big promises and populism are subsequent to his original decision to aim for something big. But Suetonius does not give any indication which of the other two explanations is more credible. Instead he leaves the question hanging in the air, rejoining the main stream of his narrative rather abruptly ("Thus, once news arrived that the tribunicial veto had been overridden and the tribunes themselves had left the city, he secretly sent on some cohorts in advance...," 31.1). There is not even any discussion of how well each explanation would sit with what we have seen of Caesar's personality: any or all of them would fit. This is not the first time that we have heard of the danger of prosecution: that was one explanation for his precipitate departure to Spain in 62 BC (18.1), and the danger was again in the air after his consulship (23.1). That final notion that Caesar might have aimed for tyranny from his youth is also consistent with the earlier narrative, for instance with the pronouncement of a dream-interpreter that "he will conquer the world," 7.2; but Caesar was then in his thirties, not in "his first youth," and the narrative has not developed the theme insistently enough for us to be sure that this explanation is right. The clearest earlier mention of "kingship," *regnum*, was in 9.2, where a letter of Cicero was quoted as saying that "Caesar as consul had established the kingship of which he had been thinking as an aedile": but that was a piece of malice, placed among other slanders (cf. 49.2), and the reader was left uncertain whether to believe it.

So, however elaborate this discussion of Caesar's reasons, not much seems at stake here, and whichever explanation we choose is unlikely to affect the way we read anything else in the Life. Perhaps it is better to think of it as pointing forwards rather than back, highlighting themes that are important for Suetonius' whole series. First, the narrative pause emphasizes the importance of the moment, and of this theme of one-man rule. The various explanations suggest other aspects of monarchy as well, its desirability, the sort of outrage its attractions can stimulate, the wild expenses it incurs that go beyond the resources of a private citizen. It also suggests the uncertainties and the wild accusations that were circulating, with the vindictiveness of Cato and the slanders of Pompey. Some of all this will change with later emperors: it will not be "prosecution" that they will have to face, and they will have a good deal more than "private wealth." Some of it will not, for malicious critics will continue to be a feature of the principate – the lampoons, for instance, against Augustus, Tiberius, Nero, Otho, and Domitian (*Div. Aug.* 2–4, 68–70, *Tib.* 59, *Nero* 39.2, *Otho* 3.2, *Dom.* 14, cf. *Iul.* 73; Wallace-Hadrill 1983: 63), or the nastiness with which people talked of the origins of the Flavians (*Div. Vesp.* 1, cf. *Vit.* 1–2) or of Vespasian's fiscal restraint (*Div. Vesp.* 16). But no-one will then have to worry whether ambition for the throne is lifelong or not; and, whatever be the truth about Caesar himself, we will see others who are all too ready to "do wrong for a throne."

This is not the only way in which *Divus Iulius* looks forward. The various categories that Suetonius uses to organize his characterization will often recur in later *Lives*: the public "works" (*opera*) an emperor sponsored, the spectacles and games he put on, the way he looked and dressed, his literary pursuits, his tastes in food and drink, where he lived, his sex-life, his marriages, the way he treated his soldiers or governed his provinces or delivered his legal judgments. In Caesar's case many of these are still embedded in Republican practice, so that the games and spectacles are for him part of the way he built his power (10, 26, 39), for his successors the way they exercised it. The categories can also suggest further patterns of historical change. Take the way Caesar treated his troops:

> When they did anything wrong, he made it his practice not to notice everything nor always to give appropriate punishments: in cases of desertion or mutiny he would investigate thoroughly and punish severely, but would turn a blind eye to other things. After a great battle and victory he would sometimes suspend duties and allow his men full license to celebrate riotously everywhere; he would boast that his soldiers could fight well even if they were smelling of perfume. When he addressed them publicly he would not call them his "soldiers," but by the more flattering title of "comrades." He kept them so smartly turned out that he gave them arms faced with gold and silver, both to make them look better and to make the men keener to hold on to them in battle through fear of losing them. He loved them so much that when he heard of Titurius' disaster he let his beard and hair grow, and would not cut them before he exacted vengeance. (*Divus Iulius* 67.1)

Compare and contrast Augustus, in a passage which at several points echoes this:

> [After the Varus disaster in 8 AD] they say he was so upset that for several months he grew his beard and hair and sometimes dashed his head against the door, shouting out "Quintilius Varus, give me back the legions," and he marked the day of the disaster every year as one of sadness and mourning.
>
> In military matters he made many changes and innovations, and reinstituted some ancient practices. He applied discipline most strictly. ...
>
> After the civil war he never, either in public address or in any edict, called any soldiers "comrades," but "soldiers," and he would not allow even his sons or stepsons to address them differently when they held military commands, thinking the word more suited to self-seeking than was required by military considerations or by the peaceful state of the times or by his own dignity or that of his house. (*Divus Augustus* 23.1–25.1)

Augustus loves his men just as much as Julius, but the times have changed, and a comparison of the two Lives makes the point. When a later emperor starts relaxing discipline, that too is a sign of the times (*Vit.* 8); or if an emperor tries to be a disciplinarian, he may or may not succeed, and that too will be a comment both on his authority and on the changing rhythm of events (*Tib.* 19.1, *Galba* 6, *Divus Vesp.* 4.6).

Other categories too are to be recurrently important. Under some headings Caesar is unmistakably good, a model for his successors: "he showed admirable moderation and clemency both in administration and as victor in the civil war" (*Iul.* 75.1); for Augustus too "there are many and great indications of his clemency and civility" (*Div. Aug.* 51.1), and later, at least in many respects, Vespasian "from beginning to end of his reign showed civility and clemency" (*Div. Vesp.* 12.1). Under others Caesar is just as clearly bad, and others will do better: in Gaul "he did not pass by any opportunity for war, however unjust or dangerous, offering provocation even to allied nations as much as to those who were hostile or uncivilised" (*Iul.* 24.3, cf. 54); contrast Augustus, who "never waged war on any nation without just and necessary reasons" (*Div. Aug.* 21.2). In some cases a theme is not specially marked for Caesar, but will become more significant for one or other of his successors: food and drink, for instance, where Caesar shows an abstinence markedly at odds with his lack of restraint in other areas (*Iul.* 53): among the various styles shown by his successors that theme becomes especially important for the glutton Vitellius (*Vit.* 13). Marriages (cf. *Iul.* 50–1) will become a leading theme for Claudius (*Div. Claud.* 26–7), and spectacles (*Iul.* 10, 26, 39) for Nero (*Nero* 11–3, 22–5, 53). Caesar's sex-life is uninhibited and notorious, but does not stand in the way of his success (*Iul.* 49–52); it will also be a keynote with several of his successors, especially Tiberius, and sometimes more damaging (*Tib.* 42–5, cf. *Div. Aug.* 68–9, *Cal.* 36, *Nero* 28–9, *Div. Titus* 7, *Dom.* 1, 22).

So *Divus Iulius* offers a repertoire of ways for gauging an emperor, not just Caesar himself (Lambrecht 1984: 35–6, 78–9, 147); and that gauging becomes particularly important at the end of the Life. Despite all Caesar's good qualities, especially that "clemency and moderation," the verdict is a negative one.

> The balance is tilted by his other actions and words, so that he is thought to have abused his power and to have been justly killed. (*Divus Iulius* 76.1)

Those are strong words, and redolent of the Republican past, for "justly killed," *iure caesus*, is the legal term used in cases of justifiable homicide: this was the language in which the lynching of the Gracchi had been excused (Pelling 2006b: 22–3 n. 15). But this too looks forward as well as back, as a similar judgment can sometimes be given when later emperors are assassinated.

> It can be agreed that Domitian paid the just penalty for his greed and his cruelty. (*Divus Vespasianus* 1.1)

So: what did Caesar get wrong?

> Not merely did he accept excessive honors – a continuing consulship, a permanent dictatorship, and the oversight of moral conduct, and also the first name "Imperator"

> and the additional name "Father of his Country," a statue among those of the kings, a dais in the orchestra; but he also allowed things to be voted to him that were too great for the pinnacle of human achievement (*ampliora humano fastigio*), a golden throne in the senate house and before the tribunal, a wagon and car for circus processions, temples, altars, images next to the gods, a couch, a priest, a college of Luperci, a month named after him; and he took and bestowed all honors at whim. (*Divus Iulius* 76.1)

He would not hold elections; he imposed magistrates for several years in advance; he vaunted his power, saying "the Republic was nothing, just a word without substance; Sulla did not know his ABC to discard his dictatorship; people should now be more careful what they said, and accept his words as having the force of law"; he neglected portents (76–7).

> But the following act was what stirred up particularly intense and deadly unpopularity. The whole senate was approaching him with a large number of particularly honorific decrees, and he received them while remaining seated in front of the temple of Venus the Mother. Some think he tried to stand up but was held back by Cornelius Balbus; others that he did not even try, and even scowled at C. Trebatius when he suggested that he should rise. (*Divus Iulius* 78.1)

It is the same episode as treated by Plutarch (above, p. 258), but for Plutarch it mattered a great deal that it was Caesar's friends who were at fault, not Caesar himself; for Suetonius it does not matter much. It would not be surprising if Caesar was himself at fault, and we would recognize the same person who had earlier been so intemperate (above, p. 259) – "he had gained what he wanted against his enemies' opposition and to their pain, and now he would dance on everyone's heads" (22.2). But nothing much turns on the choice between the two versions. Whatever the reason, it was fatal. Once again the accumulation of variants simply emphasizes the momentousness, marking it as something important enough to require explanation; but which explanation one prefers matters less.

Not merely is this an impressive catalogue of what Caesar got wrong, it also becomes a catalogue of what Augustus got right: no temples, no silver statues, and "when the people vehemently offered a dictatorship, he fell to his knees, tore the toga down from his shoulder, and bare-breasted begged them not to insist" (*Div. Aug.* 52). That last scene even re-enacts some details of Caesar's assassination itself (*Iul.* 82.1–2), as if to emphasize the perils that Augustus is pre-empting by going through the moves in the right way, in histrionic gesture rather than in bloody reality.[4] Augustus practices civility at elections too (56), and encourages free speech and debate (54–5) – none of that Caesarian style of "people should be more careful what they said." And Augustus makes a point of greeting and bidding farewell to the senate when *they* are the ones who are seated (53.3).

Later emperors too sometimes get things right, sometimes wrong, and either way the verbal similarities suggest that the template established by *Divus Iulius* is firmly in the reader's mind. Tiberius too knew that he, not the consuls, should be the one to stand (*Tib.* 31.2). He initially refused all but a few honors,

> and would not allow temples, *flamines*, and priests to be voted to him, nor statues and pictures except with his permission; and he would only grant that permission if they were to be placed not among representations of the gods but simply amid the temple decorations. (*Tib.* 26.1)

Gaius by contrast allowed all sorts of excessive honors, and "when warned that he had gone beyond the pinnacle (*se excessisse fastigium*; cf. *ampliora . . . humano fastigio* at *Iul.* 76.1 above) of *principes* and kings, began to claim divinity for himself" (*Cal.* 22.2). It is no coincidence that the narrative of his assassination follows the rhythm of Caesar's particularly closely: the threatening omens, the ruler's hesitation, the pressure from his friends to come into public, the sinking to the floor, the number of wounds (*Cal.* 56–8 ~ *Iul.* 81–2; cf. Mouchova 1968: 53–4). Claudius then got things right: in his case too that included knowing when to stand, in his case to respect magistrates who were presiding at the games, and he apologized to the tribunes for being unable to hear what they said unless they stood (*Div. Claud.* 12.2; cf. Levick, chapter 15 in this volume, p. 213). Nero at the end tries to learn from Caesar's lesson, becoming consul on the grounds that "the fates decreed that the Gauls could only be subdued by a consul" (*Nero* 43.2), whereas in Caesar's case the word "in the books of fate" was that "the Parthians could only be conquered by a king" (*Iul.* 79.3); but Nero sets about it the wrong way, throwing the current consuls out of office. It was the wrong lesson to learn, and it was anyway too late. Then Domitian judged things worst of all. He liked being addressed as "lord and god," *dominus et deus* (*Dom.* 13.2); he too was assassinated. Caesar's pattern had come back again; and if Suetonius chooses to end his work with a flattering remark about the "restraint" (*abstinentia*, a quality that Caesar generally lacked, 54.1) "and moderation of Domitian's successors" (*Dom.* 23.2), that may hint at the further pattern of these new Augustus-counterparts who knew how to avoid those archetypal mistakes.

So the different perspectives of our two writers affect what they choose to explain. Of course some of what we have just seen explains things about the fall of Suetonius' Caesar: if he had not made those mistakes, he would not have fallen. But Suetonius is much less concerned than Plutarch to explain *why* he made those mistakes. There is a sense in which Suetonius' Life, through providing this grid for describing and evaluating imperial rule, explains more about the history of the next century and a half than it does about Caesar's own rise and fall.

And moralism? After Trajan, Caesar might indeed seem more relevant a figure for the imperial present than he had before, and that may be one reason why Suetonius can regard the same headings as appropriate both for the first Caesar and for his eleven successors. Should we go further, and regard Suetonius as providing a template not just for understanding how past Caesars went right or wrong, but also for current Caesars to learn from those past errors and successes? Is this a narrative equivalent of the "On kingship" literature so frequent in the Greek world, where the knowledgeable thought fit to lecture the men of power? Or even perhaps a bold work criticizing the current Caesar under the mask of talking about his forerunners (Carney 1968)?

Probably not. There is nothing very remarkable in Suetonius' suite of imperial values. What counts as good and as bad government for Suetonius is by now conventional wisdom, and his virtues and vices are similar to those emphasized in Pliny's *Panegyricus*, on imperial coinage, in honorific inscriptions, and in Tacitus (Wallace-Hadrill 1983: 24, 142–74). Hadrian would not learn much from Suetonius that he did not know already, and we should think of the imperial present casting light on the imperial past more than the other way round. Readers who knew what to feel, or at least to say, about the delights of the glorious present would not be primed to struggle against the explanatory categories that Suetonius favored, to ask for instance whether Caesar or Caligula or Domitian might not have been so silly to think of formulating their power in divine terms, or to insist that the senate show them deference rather than the other way round. The current consensus on imperial values would lead a reader, even an imperial reader, to recognize immediately where Caesar went wrong.

Trajan might seem even more immediate a factor for Plutarch: the great Dacian conquests had come just a few years before he wrote the Life. Yet, when Plutarch has a chance to hint at these, he goes out of his way not to take it. When describing Caesar's unfulfilled last plans, he uses an extraordinary circumlocution – "to overrun Germany's neighbors and then Germany herself" – to avoid using the word "Dacia" (*Caes.* 58.6–7). Such language would have suggested *too* immediate and pointed a relevance: Plutarch painstakingly avoids those suggestions, and – this is where their contemporary resonance does become relevant – he has to be so elaborately roundabout in doing so because otherwise they might be felt. Plutarch's taste is for more timeless morals: of course contemporaries would still find thought-provoking the questions raised by so driven a life and the emptiness of its success; but they were, and are, issues for us all, not just for the superpowerful.

Even those differences in characterizing technique may seem no coincidence. To be focused enough to win power requires a personality where every aspect hangs together, where there is indeed no time for love, or to be pre-eminent in letters, or to draw back when the great moment arrives. To exercise that power, to be one of a series of Caesars, one needs to develop many skills and to be accomplished in many categories, not all of them necessarily related to one another. Plutarch presents the figure who carried all before him, for good and for ill (including perhaps his own ill); Suetonius presents a man whose model included prescriptions not just for triumph, but also for catastrophe.

FURTHER READING

Suetonius' intellectual context and aspirations are best treated by Wallace-Hadrill (1983), his literary skill by Steidle (1951), and the links of *Divus Iulius* with later imperial practice by Lambrecht (1984). The best general treatments of Plutarch are Jones (1971), Russell (1973), and Duff (1999). In my collection of Plutarch papers (Pelling 2002) the Roman Lives figure prominently; I also discuss questions of Caesar's literary presentation in Pelling 1997, 2006a, and 2006b. I shall be publishing a commentary on Plutarch's *Caesar* in the Clarendon Ancient History series.

NOTES

1 Not all the Lives in Suetonius' series need have appeared while their dedicatee Septicius Clarus was praetorian prefect (119–22), but presumably the first one did. Plutarch began his *Parallel Lives* after Domitian's death (Jones 1966), and the series was unfinished at the time of his own death some time after 120: *Caesar* was written sometime close to the *Brutus* (Pelling 2002: 2–11), and *Dion–Brutus* was the twelfth pair (*Dion* 2.7), about halfway through the series.

2 Geiger dates Plutarch's *Lives of the Caesars* to the reign of Nerva, when he assumes the Flavian perspective still prevailed; a date under Domitian is more likely (Jones 1971: 72–3, Bowersock 1998), but that need not affect this part of his argument.

3 The stories vary in detail, and it is probably Plutarch who has made the alterations: Pelling 2002: 257.

4 It even more closely mirrors a scene which Plutarch records (*Caes.* 60.6, *Ant.* 12.6) but Suetonius omits, when Caesar responded to popular murmurings by drawing the toga from his neck and offering his throat to anyone who wished to strike. Plutarch too doubtless suggests a similar contrast between the gesture and the approaching murderous reality. Suetonius probably knew the item; but if so, he does not complicate the Caesar/Augustus contrast by including it.

CHAPTER NINETEEN

The Roman Historians after Livy

Luke Pitcher

> "... and he [Tiberius] admonished the people with an edict, lest they should want Augustus to be cremated in the forum rather than the Campus Martius, the place that had been decided upon, in the same way that they had once thrown the funeral of the Divine Julius into chaos with excessive emotions. On the day of the funeral soldiers stood as a guard, to the accompaniment of much mirth amongst those who had themselves seen or had heard from their parents about that day of servitude still fresh and freedom fruitlessly demanded, when the murder of Caesar the dictator seemed to some the worst, to others the loveliest of deeds, whereas now an elderly leader, long established in power, who had provided his heirs in advance with resources for the state, apparently had to be guarded with military assistance so that his burial would be undisturbed."
>
> Tacitus *Annals* 1.8.6–7

The above passage, discussing the funeral arrangements for Augustus in AD 14, is taken from near the beginning of the *Annals* of Tacitus. This work chronicles the reigns of the emperors from Tiberius to Nero. One might assume that such an ambit would preclude any interest in a man killed more than half a century before Tiberius took on the mantle of emperor. As the extract above shows, such an assumption would be mistaken.

It is worth paying attention to exactly what Tacitus is doing here. This is not simply a passage about Julius Caesar. Rather, it is a passage about the use and perception of Caesar. Tiberius (according to Tacitus) wants to head off trouble at Augustus's funeral, trouble he anticipates on the basis of a historical analogy which those with long memories understand to be quite invalid. In forestalling what he sees as a similarity, the Emperor succeeds only in underlining a contrast.

A like complexity informs other Tacitean glances back at the Dictator. In the *Histories*, he is the focus of a very cynical nostalgia; his bloodshed was preferable to the contemporary sort. Otho and Vitellius are contrasted with Caesar, a power-hungry general who at least knew what he was doing. The historian paints the people of Rome in the aftermath of Galba's death "discussing the destruction of Italy, the ransackings of the provinces, Pharsalus, Philippi, Perusia and Mutina ... the world had almost been destroyed even when men of merit were contending for primacy, but the empire had remained when Gaius Julius and Augustus conquered ... would they now go into temples for Otho or Vitellius?" (Tac. *Hist.* 1.50). The olden days had a better class of warlord.

One notes, too, the treatment in this passage of Julius Caesar and Augustus as parallel cases – Pharsalus melts into Philippi and Perusia. The two are likewise casually conjoined at the end of the book, where Otho's hangers-on behave as "if they were following the dictator Caesar or the emperor Augustus" (Tac. *Hist.* 1.90). The Tiberius of Tacitus may have erred in likening the *end* of Caesar's career to that of Augustus, but the author discreetly indicates an unwillingness to see what they *did* as fundamentally dissimilar.

Caesar in Tacitus, then, is more than just a possible precedent for the Principate. He is an object lesson for the complexities and hazards inherent in using the past – a topic of special interest to the reflective historian. It is no coincidence that Tacitus' most celebrated passages concerning the character of his own enterprise (Tac. *Ann.* 4.32–3) and the capacity of historical memory to outlast repression (Tac. *Ann.* 4.35) flank his description of the trial of Cremutius Cordus, prosecuted under Tiberius because his histories praised Brutus and called Cassius "the last of the Romans" (Tac. *Ann.* 4.34–5). Caesar, to use a term lately coined (Grethlein and Krebs: forthcoming), constitutes for Tacitus an important "plupast" – the further past back to which the individuals and groups within his texts look and, in doing so, shed light on the historian's own conceptions of historical process and historiographical methodology.

Nor is Tacitus alone in finding Caesar a ghost at the feast even for literary endeavors far removed, at first sight, from the Dictator's temporal career. How Caesar might or might not have figured in retrospect in the lost histories of the elder Pliny is not readily retrievable. In the *Natural History*, however, he is a potent and unsettling presence. Book 7 of that work is devoted to man, the highest of living things (Plin. *NH* 7.1). Within this section, Caesar represents the pinnacle of mental power (Plin. *NH* 7.91), and tribute is paid to his magnanimity and sublimity of spirit (Plin. *NH* 7.93–4). Yet he is also, within Pliny's textual world, a disturbing figure, one who perverts the encyclopedist's love of large and precise numbers (cf. Plin. *Pref.* 17) into an arithmetic of carnage – the one million, one hundred and ninety-two thousand casualties that constituted the necessary evil of his conquests (Plin. *NH* 7.92). His profligate expenditure (Plin. *NH* 7.93) likewise draws the disapproval of parsimonious Pliny. The Caesar of the *Natural History* reveals the tension in the author's enterprise between the cataloguing of marvels and the censure of wonders which tip over into transgression or hubris, as seen when he joins the list of celebrity victims of the ill-omened urge to dig a canal through the Isthmus of Corinth (Plin. *NH* 4.10).

Even for those who had not made it their business to chronicle his career, then, Caesar remained a figure with whom the historically minded might find it interesting to engage, into the Flavian period and beyond. Still more thought-provoking, therefore, are the ways in which he was treated by those later historians who did make it part of their business to examine his deeds in detail. It is to these that we now turn.

Two of the longest extant treatments of Caesar from the period of the high Roman Empire are those written in Greek by Appian of Alexandria and Cassius Dio. Appian, writing around the middle of the second century, narrates Caesar's career in book 2 of his *Civil Wars*, a five-book section within the author's larger *Roman History*. Dio's history, which covered the period from the foundation of Rome to AD 229 in 80 books, was composed in the first half of the third century. It addressed Caesar's rise and ascendancy in books 37 to 44.

These two accounts show much similarity. This sometimes extends even to the level of verbal expression. For example, Appian and Dio make almost identical jibes at the expense of the men who hurried to associate themselves with the Liberators once Caesar was already dead: their plan backfired, and instead of acquiring a good reputation for something they had not done, they shared in the peril but not the glory (App. *B Civ.* 2.119.500; Dio 44.21.4). It is exceedingly probable that an important ultimate source for this period in both histories, as for Plutarch (cf. Pelling, chapter 18, p. 253), was the work of Asinius Pollio, whose tally of Pompeian casualties at Pharsalus Appian explicitly quotes (App. *B Civ.* 2.82.346).

Beyond the expression and analysis of particular episodes, there are also common elements to the broader presentations of Caesar that we find in the two historians. Both, like their predecessors in writing about the Dictator, accentuate the elements of speed, unexpectedness, and pre-emptive action in their accounts. Dio explicitly remarks on celerity as a Caesarian hallmark: "on all occasions, indeed, he did a great deal by his celerity and by the unexpectedness of his movements, so that if anyone should try to discover what it was that made him so superior in the art of war to his contemporaries, he would find by diligent comparison that there was nothing more notable than this very characteristic" (Dio 42.56.21). The surrounding narrative shows many examples of this technique in action (e.g. Dio 38.32.4, 38.34.6, 38.47.3, 39.2.1, 41.22.2, 41.44.2, 42.40.3). In similar vein, Appian vividly characterizes Caesar as "exulting always in the astonishment caused by his speed and the fear caused by his daring" (App. *B Civ.* 2.34.136), and has the general himself open a speech to his seditious men with an acknowledgment that celerity is his personal hallmark: "You are witnesses to how much speed I bring to everything I do" (App. *B Civ.* 2.47.192; in the Greek, "speed" is the first word of the whole speech).

Similarities in the portrayal of Caesar's *blitzkrieg* are accompanied by similarities in their handling of some aspects of his behavior, and in their attitude to the Ides of March. Caesarian *clementia* (or *philanthrōpia*, as both authors tend to render it in the Greek) is a recurrent feature of Appian's account (App. *B Civ.* 2.17.62, 2.35.141, 2.41.163, 2.43.171, 2.93.391, 2.133.556, 2.150.631). Dio openly describes him as the "kindliest of men" (Dio 42.55.3) and sees his merciful character as instantiated through his refusal to inspect Pompeius' records in the aftermath of Pharsalus (Dio 41.63.5; cf. also Plin. *NH* 7.94).

If *clementia* characterizes the accounts of Caesar himself in Dio and Appian, the theme of betrayal is prominent in the depictions of the Liberators. Appian's characterization of the deed in his later obituary for Cassius and Brutus is particularly damning – "an action inconceivable against a friend, ungrateful against the benefactor who had preserved them from war, illegal against a commander ... and a priest ...

and a dynast without parallel who had been more useful than any other to Rome and its supremacy" (App. *B Civ.* 4.134.562) – though he does leave it open whether the motivation was envy of Caesar's power or a genuine desire to avoid tyranny (App. *B Civ.* 2.111.462, 2.120.503). For Dio "a baleful frenzy which fell upon certain men through jealousy of his advancement and hatred of his preferment to themselves caused his death unlawfully, while it added a new name to the annals of infamy" (Dio 44.1.1) – although, again, the historian's actual subsequent picture of the drives compelling Brutus gives due weight to the pressures of tyrannicide (Dio 41.12–13).

In many respects, therefore, Appian and Dio show themselves much in line with earlier writing about Caesar. Their coverage, however, is by no means simply a case of putting old wine in new bottles. Their accounts of the dictator are conditioned to a very considerable extent by the demands and constraints of the sort of history that they are writing, as well as by their individual historiographical visions. What problems, then, faced these high imperial historians in narrating the Republican Dictator?

The authors themselves explicitly highlight some of the challenges. For Dio, selectivity is a pressing concern. He comments at a number of points that he relates only the most important and relevant of data concerning Caesar: the details of the Dictator's spectacles are mostly omitted as being an area where truth is hard to discern from exaggeration (Dio 43.22.4); he includes only the most notable of Caesar's laws (Dio 43.25.1); and is likewise selective in recording the measures passed and honors voted for his victories (Dio 42.19.3–4, 43.46.1). Such authorial interventions, to be sure, are a rhetorical gesture in themselves; they bring out the almost unexampled scale of all that is associated with Caesar through their very avowed unwillingness to go through everything. Nonetheless, Dio's comments point to a very real problem.

Appian and Dio were not setting out to write histories *of* Caesar, but histories that *included* him. Still less was it their aim to compose a biography. As we have already noted, Appian's coverage of Caesar is merely a part, albeit a substantial one, of his account of Rome's civil wars, which is itself a part (again, a substantial one) of a general survey of Roman history. Dio's structural organization of his grand work is less complex and thematic, but the fact remains that Caesar's career is a comparatively brief space of time for a narrative that encompasses almost a millennium of history.

Yet Caesar is a subject that might well seem to demand an intensity and scale of coverage that strains at the constraints of an annalistic history. It is instructive to see (Toher, chapter 16, p. 236) how the earlier imperial historian Velleius Paterculus explicitly acknowledges this conflict between the Dictator's inherent interest and the demands of the writer's larger work: "he lays his hand on me as I write and for all my hurry compels me to linger on him" (Vell. Pat. 2.41.1). Velleius's two books of history, of course, face this problem in a much more acute form than their successors. Appian's 24 books and Dio's 80 have less need to "hurry." The conundrum, however, remains. How can the singularity of a Caesar be accommodated within narratives that cannot afford to let him hog all of the limelight?

Close attention to the textual twists and turns of Appian and Dio illuminates how the two historians, in different ways, make room for Caesarian uniqueness within their larger attempts to make sense of Roman history. Both go to pains to signal the

Dictator's prominent position within this long narrative. The first and most condensed summary of Rome's development which Appian offers, in the general preface to his whole history (App. *Proem* 6.19–7.28), is as follows: five hundred years were spent conquering Italy, half under the kings and half without them; two hundred years were spent expanding the empire; then "Gaius Caesar, having obtained rule over the men of his time and strengthened Roman supremacy and thoroughly safeguarded it, retained the semblance and name of the republic but made himself monarch over all" (App. *Proem* 6.22).

Some, to be sure, have seen the "Gaius Caesar" of Appian's *Proem* as Augustus under his adoptive name (Bowie 1985: 889; cf. Bucher 2000: 416 n. 18). Appian certainly does speak of Augustus as the one who "strengthened the dominion which obtains even now" in his account of Caesar's funeral (App. *B Civ.* 2.148.617), but the very same sentence states that this "dominion" (which the subsequent passage makes clear means the Principate) was established by Julius. In Appian's terms, it was certainly Julius Caesar, and not his heir, who established the monarchy and strengthened Roman supremacy (cf. App. *B Civ.* 2.150.631, and, especially, *B Civ.* 4.134.562, quoted above). It is Julius to whom he refers in his initial whirlwind tour of Roman history – the only individual named, one notes, in the whole passage. From the first, Appian presents the Dictator as a turning point.

Dio is not quite so stark. He is, however, equally insistent about the character of Caesar's reign, even if he is disinclined to see it as marking the foundation of the Principate proper. The motivation of the Liberators draws from him the comment that "democracy, indeed, has a fair-sounding name ... but its results are seen not to agree at all with its title. Monarchy, on the contrary, has an unpleasant sound, but is a most practical form of government to live under" (Dio 44.2.1). This comment makes no sense in the context, of course, if Dio did not consider Caesar's reign monarchic. At the beginning of the succeeding book, moreover, Dio figures the (intended) relationship between Caesar and Octavian explicitly as a monarchic succession: "For Caesar, being childless and basing great hopes upon him [Octavian], loved and cherished him, intending to leave him as successor to his name, authority, and sovereignty" (Dio 45.1.2). This intention is not immediately fulfilled, of course, and Dio does not regard Caesar as the founder of the present Principate: as has been demonstrated elsewhere in this volume, the structure of his account makes it clear that he considers that accolade to belong to Augustus (cf. Barnes, chapter 20 in this volume, pp. 278–9). Nonetheless, the monarchic character of his domination is strongly marked.

Dio and Appian are alike inclined, then, to see Caesar as a turning point. He remains, however, a part (albeit a fascinating and sometimes frustrating one) of a greater whole. Both historians work to assimilate him into their own, somewhat different, conceptions of history.

How this works is perhaps best illustrated by observing certain divergences in the way the two authors structure their narratives of Caesar's rise to ascendancy. It is instructive to compare Appian's and Dio's accounts not of Caesar himself, but of the figures around him – in particular, the exact point at which they are noted as becoming alarmed by his ambition. In Appian, no sign of a rift with Pompeius is recorded before the death of Caesar's daughter Julia in 54 (App. *B Civ.* 2.19.68). In Dio, by contrast, the formation of the original compact between Caesar, Pompeius, and Crassus itself is partly motivated by fear of Caesar's growing power on the part of the other two: "Pompeius ... seeing that Crassus was in power and that Caesar's influence was increasing, feared that he should be totally overthrown by them. ... Crassus ... since he was far inferior to Pompeius, and thought that Caesar was going to rise to great heights, desired to set them against each other" (Dio 37.56.3–4). What explains the difference of emphasis?

It is tempting to write this off as a consideration of scale. Dio devotes eight books of his history to Caesar in comparison to Appian's one. It is not surprising, therefore, that the latter's account is sometimes less expansive. Nor can recourse to different sources be ruled out. Nonetheless, it is more profitable, perhaps, to look at how these varying treatments play into the individual themes which the two authors are intent on exploring.

Dio's account of the formation of the "First Triumvirate" foregrounds mutual suspicion and selfishness in a manner not at all surprising for an author relentlessly cynical about the self-interested basis of much human motivation. Caesar is in no sense divorced from this game. Rather, Dio emphasizes almost from the first the fact that the future Dictator understands how to play it better than almost anyone else. The calculations which lead Caesar to court Pompeius and Crassus in the first place are set out in loving detail: "if he made a friend of either of them alone, he would by that very fact have the other as his enemy and would meet with more failures through him than successes through the other's support. For on the one hand, it seemed to him that all men work more energetically against their enemies than they work with their friends ... on the other hand, he reflected that it was easier to stand in people's way and stop them reaching any eminence ... because he who stops another from becoming great gratifies others as well as himself" (Dio 37.55.1–3).

This sort of sententiousness is common from Cassius' narrative voice. It is more unusual to see it applied to their profit by the individuals *within* his text. Cicero, for example, whom Dio interestingly sets up almost as Caesar's unsuccessful foil in these books, notably fails to take on board the self-interestedness which Caesar recognizes: "most men are more inclined to feel annoyance at what irks them than to feel grateful to anyone for kindnesses" (Dio 38.12.5).

Caesar, by contrast, knows the rules of Dio's world, and behaves accordingly. Thus, the historian's lengthy disquisition on the mental states of Pompeius and Crassus as they formed the First Triumvirate is in fact a confirmation of Caesar's superior planning. He is *exploiting* the inevitable self-interest of others, and the desire of the other two men to aggrandize themselves in fact only plays into the master-manipulator's hands. Indeed, the hallmark of Dio's Caesar is his absolute readiness to subordinate anything, even his own native tendencies, to what is necessary for the achievement of his goals and the preservation of his unique status: "although Caesar possessed in reality a rather equable nature, and was not at all easily stirred to anger, he nevertheless punished many ... For he was not so much concerned about what had already happened as he was to forestall future attacks" (Dio 38.11.3–5). In similar vein, he loses his former fondness for Labienus when the latter starts deluding himself that he is Caesar's equal (Dio 41.4.4), and, in contrast to Pompeius, is happy to put up with unpopularity as long as he is the one on top (Dio 41.54.1). Dio's ongoing preoccupation with the minutiae of the political rat-race leads him to shape an account of Caesar's times which is therefore dense with plot and counter-plot, in which the motives and preoccupations of the other players in the drama of the late Republic are made explicit from the outset.

Appian's goals are somewhat different. It would not be accurate to say that he altogether lacks Dio's focus on the motivations of individuals and the agenda they pursue. Caesar as a personality is a palpable force in book 2 of the *Civil Wars*, the more so because of the very interesting formal exercise with which the historian chooses to end it (see pp. 274–5 below). It is also true that the downplaying of certain aspects of the Dictator in the *Civil Wars* may be explained in terms of his usual historiographical practices. For example, Appian's lack of interest in the perennially popular topic of Caesar's sexual incontinence (cf. Paterson, chapter 10, pp. 133–8), which stands in sharp opposition to the attitude of Dio (contrast Dio 42.34.3, 43.20.4, 43.27.2, 44.7.3), becomes less surprising when one notes the almost total absence of erotic elements from the rest of the extant *Roman History* (the married life of the younger Africanus (App. *B Civ.* 1.20.83), the story of Syphax (App. *Pun.* 10.38), and two sentences on Antonius and Cleopatra (App. *B Civ.* 5.1.1–2) are the most obvious of the very rare exceptions, although there was no doubt more about the last topic in the lost books on Egypt).

There is also, however, a more specific explanation for the way in which Appian chooses to handle the burgeoning of trouble between Caesar and Pompeius. Appian's history, as has already been noted, is not simply chronological in its arrangement; it is also topological and thematic. His declared interest during the *Civil Wars* section of his narrative is plotting the internal dissensions that racked the late Roman Republic through the various leaders who oversaw them: Marius and Sulla; Pompeius and Caesar; Marcus Antonius and Octavian (App. *Proem* 14.59). Appian's delay in addressing the tensions between Caesar and Pompeius has the effect of putting his reader in the same position, according to the historian, as the Roman people, who are thrown into fear by the very public event of Julia's death and the inferences they draw from it (App. *B Civ.* 2.19.68). Whereas Dio's account stays most focused on the plotting of the dynasts, Appian here focalizes through the people at large to give a vivid picture that accords with his personal view of the *Civil Wars* narrative: "men's boundless ambition and terrible love of power and unfailing endurance and the forms of countless woes" (App. *B Civ.* 1.6.24). It is not surprising, then, that the fear of the people concerning a rift between Caesar and Pompeius segues smoothly into a picture of the general anarchy then prevailing at Rome (App. *B Civ.* 2.19.69–71).

It is important not to be too reductive here. Nonetheless, the different textures which Dio and Appian bring to their account of the same period owe much to the former's interest in depicting Caesar as an individual supremely aware of the actions necessary to achieve his goals, and the latter's desire to depict the collateral damage of dynastic ambition. This difference of approach is not confined to events at Rome itself. Indeed, the way in which the historians handle the fate of Gomphi –a small town in Thessaly sacked and destroyed just before Pharsalus – is an excellent example of the two approaches in action. Dio (Dio 41.51.4–5) makes the destruction of this town a calculated act of public relations on Caesar's part aimed at securing the compliance of the surrounding area, "in order that by this act he might inspire the rest with terror," and immediately contrasts it with the fate of Metropolis, which stays intact because it capitulates without a struggle. Caesar, again, applies the exact amount of punishment necessary for his goals.

In Appian, by contrast, Metropolis is entirely unmentioned. Simple anger motivates Caesar's decision to sack Gomphi, and Appian's account lingers on the "noble sufferings" of the unfortunate town and the mass suicide of its leading men (App. *B Civ.* 2.64.269). Where Dio paints a picture of Caesarian efficiency, the historian of the *Civil Wars* finds another exemplum of endurance in the face of ambition.

The portraits of Caesar we find in Appian and Dio, then, are to a certain extent determined by the larger agenda of the two authors concerned, as much as by the historical traditions they inherited. Nonetheless, the *irreducibility* of Caesar, the extent to which he *does* tend to run away with a narrative into which he is placed, is something which both writers bring out. In Dio, Caesar's conquests push back the bounds not merely of Roman power, but also of knowledge.

The conceit that Caesar, through his explorations of Britannia, added a new world to the familiar Roman one, is by no means original to Dio. Lucan already makes much play with it (Luc. 5.356, 10.456); Velleius and Florus likewise exploit it (Vell. Pat. 2.46.1; Flor. 1.45.16). Dio, however, makes the increase of knowledge about the world a part of Caesar's achievement. While his portrait of the reaction to the British expedition is undeniably satirical – the people of Rome behave as if they had conquered Britannia just because they have now heard of it – the reasons he gives for this behavior are still worth noticing: "the previously unknown had become certain and the once unheard-of accessible" (Dio 39.53.2). In similar vein, he has Caesar boast that "countries whose very names we did not accurately know in former times we now rule" (Dio 38.38.4) in the course of an exhortation in the middle of the Gallic wars. When the general conquers, the narrator is once again insistent that the conceptual world of those he has left behind is broadened: "The Romans at home, when they learned of these deeds, were amazed that he had seized so many nations, whose names they had known but imperfectly before" (Dio 39.5.1). Dio's Caesar makes the world explicable as he conquers it: the general as historian.

Appian advertises Caesar's unusual stature in a somewhat different fashion. In his case, the uniqueness of Caesar generates an element of formal uniqueness within Appian's own text. It is by no means unusual for Appian to send off important figures in his text with an "obituary." Mithridates of Pontus is given an ample one (App. *Mith.* 112.541–50), for example, and we have already seen (pp. 269–70) some of the treatment which the historian gives Cassius and Brutus after Philippi (App. *B Civ.* 4.132.553–134.567). Caesar, however, is uniquely allotted not just an "obituary," but an extended point-by-point comparison of his career with that of Alexander the Great (App. *B Civ.* 2.149.621–154.649), which concludes book 2 of the *Civil Wars.* It is possible to view this as simply a rhetorical *tour de force*, yet Appian is on the whole sparing with such exercises. It makes more sense, perhaps, to suggest that Appian, by aping the characteristic moves of a *biography* rather than a history, is suggesting the ways in which an individual such as Caesar can force the story of political events to turn itself into the story of a life.

It is just this sort of interplay, the narrowing of a world to the fate of a man, that the summary history of Florus, the last text with which this chapter engages, delights to explore. This two-book condensation of Roman history, dating from not before the middle of the second century, plots Caesar as a supremely competent general. He is also, however, a representative of the disasters brought upon the Republic by an excess of success: "the cause of so great a disaster was the same as for all disasters, too much good fortune" (Flor. 2.13.8). For Florus, the compact between Caesar and Pompeius is sustained until the death of Julia only by mutual fear (Flor. 2.13.13). The civil war is a straightforward and lamentable contest for supremacy between two men, who "strove for the first place as though the fortune of so great an empire could not contain two" (Flor. 2.13.14), and it is figured as a duel between them: "Pompeius" and "the Senate" are regarded as simple synonyms (Flor. 2.13.15). The narrative strategy reprises that used in Florus's earlier account of the Gallic wars, where the conflict narrows at the conclusion of the story, in a somewhat Kipling-esque move, to the personal confrontation of Caesar and Vercingetorix: " 'You have defeated a strong man, strongest of men" (Flor. 1.45.26). It is at Caesar's end, however, that Florus contrives his neatest play upon the fusion of the world's fate with that of the Dictator. His Caesar dies "thinking of the Parthian expedition," and the death brings it about that "he who had filled the whole world with the blood of his fellow citizens at last filled the senate-house with his own" (Flor. 2.13.95).

In conclusion, then, Caesar presents himself to the writers of the high Roman Empire as a multifarious figure. For Tacitus, he is a locus of historical and historiographical self-reflexion, in response to whom the characters within his work themselves try to make sense of the past, as well as a document of the continuity of monarchic power at Rome. Pliny's Caesar is a troubling figure, who expands the world of the encyclopedist by his deeds, his discoveries, and his very nature, but, for all his testimony to the sublimity of the human spirit, bears witness at the same time to darker possibilities. In Florus, he presents a double aspect as the hammer of Rome's foes in the first book, and Pompeius's rival, driven by rage to fill the state with slaughter, in the second. But in this period, it is perhaps the lengthy treatments of Appian and Cassius Dio that give him his most intriguing expression. In them we see the challenges of interpretation and composition which an individual of Caesar's stature present to the writer of a large-scale history, and the intriguing ways in which such a writer can choose to react to him.

FURTHER READING

A thought-provoking study of Tacitus and the trial of Cremutius Cordus is J. Moles (1998) "Cry freedom: Tacitus Annals 4.32–35'. *Histos* 2:1–54 (www.dur.ac.uk/Classics/histos/

1998/moles.html). For Cassius Dio, the classic study-in-the-round remains F. Millar (1964), *A Study of Cassius Dio* (Oxford). Students of Appian and his response to this period will find much of interest in A. M. Gowing (1992) *The Triumviral Narratives of Appian and Cassius Dio* (Ann Arbor), D. Magnino (1993) "Le 'Guerre Civili' di Appiano," *ANRW* 2.34.1, 523–54 (Berlin), G. S. Bucher (1997) *Prolegomena to a Commentary on Appian's* Bellum Civile *book two* (diss. Brown University), and the same author's (2000) "The origins, program, and composition of Appian's *Roman History*," *TAPA* 130: 411–58.

CHAPTER TWENTY

The First Emperor: The View of Late Antiquity

Timothy Barnes

How was Julius Caesar remembered in Late Antiquity and after? Two surveys of Caesar's reputation over two millennia were published in the twentieth century. The earlier was produced by Friedrich Gundolf (1880–1931), a historian of literature, especially German literature, who translated Shakespeare into German (Schmitz 1987). Gundolf had a lifelong interest in and admiration for Caesar, whom he revered as a great man and on whose representation in German literature he had written his dissertation (Gundelfinger 1904). Writing under the Weimar Republic, Gundolf, who was both a Jew and a member of the circle of Stefan George, began by evoking the longing which he saw around him for a "future lord or savior" who might rescue bourgeois Germany from her post-war trauma, and he drew a contrast with "the great statesman" Caesar, for whose posthumous reputation he devised a rigid schema, according to which Caesar was first a mythical figure, then a magical name, and only became a historical person with John of Salisbury in the twelfth century (Gundolf 1924: 1, 93–9; cf. 1926: 14, 38).[1] Seventy years later Karl Christ published a more scholarly and systematic survey under the programmatic title "Caesar: Approaches to a Dictator," which began with the image of Caesar in the ancient world and concluded with late twentieth-century historians of Rome. Neither Gundolf nor Christ provided a satisfactory treatment of Caesar in Late Antiquity. Gundolf went astray by assuming that Caesar's image never changed in the ancient world after Lucan, Suetonius, and Plutarch (Gundolf 1924: 37), while Christ allotted Late Antiquity a mere four and a half pages out of three hundred (Christ 1994: 108–13), and he almost totally ignored Greek authors later than Cassius Dio, with the sole exception of Julian the Apostate.

The present essay documents the fact, which might at first sight seem surprising, that in Late Antiquity and in the Byzantine period Julius Caesar was generally regarded as the first Roman emperor. It then asks which writers remembered Caesar in any significant way and for precisely what they remembered him. For the most striking fact about the memory of Caesar in Late Antiquity is his almost complete absence as a historical exemplar, model, or ideal.

Neither the ancient inhabitants of the Roman world nor moderns who have written about the late Roman Republic and the early Roman Empire have returned a unanimous verdict on the question of who should be regarded as the first Roman emperor. Should the accolade be bestowed on Augustus, who permanently established an imperial system of government and administration, or on Julius Caesar, who became a monarchical ruler *de facto* after he defeated both Pompey and those who took up the banner of the Roman Republic after Pompey's death? Modern historians of Rome from Edward Gibbon to Michael Rostovtzeff, Ronald Syme, and Fergus Millar, reference manuals, and repositories of received wisdom such as the *Cambridge Ancient History* (both editions) have shown a marked preference for Augustus; indeed so marked is the preference for Augustus that a popular author has recently chosen "the first emperor" as the main title of his biography of Augustus (Everitt 2006).[2] On the other hand, Theodor Mommsen regarded Caesar not only as a monarch from 46 BC onwards, but as the creative genius who set Rome on the path which it followed until its decline and fall centuries later (Mommsen 1904: 3.461 = 1984: 5.127): in Mommsen's considered view, the monarchy came into existence with the Battle of Thapsus, and Augustus merely consolidated what Caesar had already created (Mommsen 1996: 57–64).

The predominant modern view owes more to the opinions of three respected ancient writers than is commonly admitted, even if it does not wholly derive from them. The young Plutarch wrote a series of lives of the Roman emperors, probably before the death of Domitian (Jones 1971: 72–80; Bowersock 1998: 195–205) rather than after 96 (as argued by Syme 1980a: 104–11). Although only one life survives in the combined *Galba and Otho*, the so-called Lamprias-catalogue indicates that Plutarch began with Augustus (Irigoin 1987: ccxxviii–ccxxix, ccciii–cccxviii, cf. Giannattasio Andria 2000), and in his later *Parallel Lives* Plutarch presents Caesar as a tyrant who was justly assassinated when he became dictator for life (*Caesar* 57.1; cf. *Numa* 19.1, *Alexander* 1.1). The historian Tacitus, writing in the early second century, explicitly presents Augustus as the first emperor of Rome and the creator of the imperial system under which he lived. Tacitus begins his *Annals* with the proposition that monarchy was the natural state of affairs at Rome, though interrupted for a period by the Republic until Augustus consolidated power in his own hands (1.1.1). Moreover, in a subsequent digression Tacitus characterizes the 20 years following the defeat and death of Pompey as a period of disorder and illegality which only ended when, in his sixth consulate (28 BC), Augustus, now securely in power after his victories in civil war, established the imperial system under which the historian and his contemporaries lived (3.28.1–2). In a later passage of the *Annals*, however, Tacitus observes that Nero was the first of those who had held supreme power at Rome not to write his own speeches: he then surveys Nero's predecessors in order, beginning with Caesar the dictator, who vied with the best orators (13.3.2).

A century later, Cassius Dio, who held a second consulate with the emperor Severus Alexander in 229, composed an enormous history of Rome from its mythical foundation down to his own day in 80 books. Julius Caesar is first mentioned in the surviving text of Dio in book 36 as aedile in 64 BC (36.37.8), though Dio had recorded his support of the *Lex Manilia* in 66 (36.43.2–4). Caesar inevitably bulks very large in Dio's narrative from 63 to 44 and he is often mentioned in Dio's narrative of the civil wars of 44–31 BC down to the interview between Octavian and Cleopatra in which the Queen of Egypt evokes her liaison with the great-uncle of the victor of Actium (51.12). But, like Tacitus a century earlier, Dio regarded Augustus as the one who firmly established monarchical rule in Rome (53.17.1) and he too presents Augustus as the man who created the political system under which the inhabitants of the Roman Empire still lived in his own day. Dio's account of the year 27 in book 53 is structured to reflect this belief:

3–10	Speech in which the victor in the civil wars offers to lay aside his powers
11–12	Reception of the speech: the Senate doubles the pay of his bodyguard and assigns him almost all the provinces with troops stationed in them for ten years
13–18	Digression explaining to Dio's Greek readers how the imperial system of administration instituted at this time worked and still works in the historian's own day
19	Writing imperial history is more difficult than writing Republican history because decisions now began to be taken in secret session rather than after public debate
20–2	Augustus' actions after receiving the title and some general features of his rule
22.5	Augustus goes to Gaul, then to Spain.

There are very few references to Caesar of any significance in the two and a half centuries of Roman history which Dio's narrative, admittedly not preserved in full, covers after the Battle of Actium (Smilda 1926: 321–340). They predictably concern his conquests (53.7.1) and his clemency (52.52.17, 56.38.4, 76[75].8.1, p. 344 Boissevain).

Two late Latin epitomators and an aggressively pagan historian writing around 500 repeat the view of Tacitus and Dio. Writing in 360, at the end of the reign of Constantius and with at least half an eye on the recent proclamation of Julian as Augustus in Gaul, about which he is conspicuously silent, Aurelius Victor revealed his pagan religious sympathies by praising Diocletian as a wise and great man while criticizing Constantine for admitting "unworthy men" (that is, Christians) to high public office (39.1, 41.20). In the opening sentence of his *Caesares*, Victor equates the beginning of monarchy and of the Roman Empire with the victory of the future Augustus at the Battle of Actium in 31 BC (*Caes.* 1.1: *mos Romae incessit uni prorsus parendi*), and both the sentiment and almost his exact words were repeated shortly after 395 in the opening sentence of the *Epitome de Caesaribus* (1.1), which subsequently notes in passing that the emperor Aurelian "was not dissimilar to Alexander the Great or Caesar the dictator" (78.9). Similarly, Zosimus, who was writing c. 500 and propounded an anti-Christian interpretation of the fourth century taken over from Eunapius of Sardis, breezily dismissed the claims of Caesar: according to Zosimus, the Romans chose Octavian to be monarch over them after their Republican polity had been completely ruined by the civil wars between Sulla and Marius, then between Caesar and Pompey (1.5.2).

The majority of both writers and the ordinary population of the Roman Empire, however, had taken a different view from the start. They believed that Julius Caesar, not Augustus, was the first emperor. The first extant writer to say so clearly is Josephus, who in both his major historical works states that Caesar was assassinated after ruling for three years and six or seven months (*BJ* 1.218 ≈ *AJ* 14.270), which implies that Caesar became a monarch when he defeated Pompey at the Battle of Pharsalus on August 9, 48.[3] The next is Pliny the Younger. Writing to Titius Aristo in defence of his habit of composing verses, Pliny appeals to a large number of precedents, among whom are five emperors explicitly designated as not being *exempla privata* – Julius Caesar, Augustus, Tiberius, Nero, and Nerva (*Ep.* 5.3.3–6) A few years later, Plutarch referred to Augustus as "the second who ruled" when explaining the origin of the name of the Roman month August (*Numa* 19.6). Since that contradicts what Plutarch says elsewhere in his *Parallel Lives*, he must here be reflecting the current opinion of others or following a written source rather than delivering a considered verdict of his own. Plutarch's younger contemporary Suetonius wrote a series of imperial biographies, mostly or entirely in the reign of the emperor Hadrian (117–38), which began with Julius Caesar. Unfortunately, the beginning of the *Divus Iulius* and the author's preface to the *Vitae Caesarum* as a whole have been lost in transmission, even though both survived long enough for a sixth-century writer to quote Suetonius' dedication to the praetorian prefect Septicius Clarus, who held that office from 199 to 122 (John the Lydian, *De magistratibus* 2.6, conveniently reprinted before the Latin text by Ihm 1908 = 1964: xix; cf. Birley 1997: 96, 114–15, 138–9). Hence it is not known how Suetonius explained or justified taking Julius Caesar as the first of a series of *Vitae Caesarum*, in which title *Caesares* appears to mean "emperors."[4] In the Antonine age, Appian stated emphatically that Caesar founded the monarchy (*Proem.* 6), and Fronto stated that the Republic ended with the victory of Caesar (*Ad L. Verum* 2.1.5–6: *postquam respublica a magistratibus ad C. Caesarem et mox ad Augustum translata est*, etc.). Similarly, in the fourth century, the emperor Julian wrote a polemical piece which he entitled *Symposion or Kronia* (better known under the inauthentic title *Caesars*), in which he reviewed the virtues and vices of all the emperors down to Constantine, whose conversion to Christianity he ridicules: Julius Caesar is the first to enter the banquet of the gods, and he is followed by Augustus, Tiberius, and the rest in chronological sequence.[5] Ammianus Marcellinus too regarded Julius Caesar as the first emperor, since he includes Caesar, along with the third-century emperor Claudius (268–70) and Diocletian's successor Galerius (293–311), as one of three *veteres principes* whom the cowardly Constantius conspicuously did not emulate (16.10.3).

On a priori grounds it might have been expected that Christian writers would agree with Tacitus and Dio, and some indeed do. For, whatever uncertainty there may be about the exact date at which Jesus was born, it certainly fell during the reign of Augustus. The gospel of Luke states so explicitly (2.1) and the other three gospels assume it. Hence those who wrote to defend Christianity against the hostility of the adherents of the traditional religions of the Roman Empire were able to gain debating points (and perhaps more) by linking the birth of the new religion to the establishment of the Roman Empire. The first to do so was Melito of Sardis, who addressed an apology to Marcus Aurelius in which he informed the emperor that "our way of thought" flowered among "your peoples" during the reign of Augustus and became a "portent of good" because "from then on the power of Rome grew great and splendid." The success of the Roman Empire, Melito suggests, was due entirely to Christianity (quoted by Eusebius, *HE* 4.26.7–8). Since the same conjunction recurs in Tertullian's *Ad Nationes* (1.7.8: "this name came into existence when Augustus was emperor"), it had probably been repeated by other Greek apologists of the late second century whose works are lost but who were known to Tertullian and probably used by him. Several Christian writers of the first half of the third century shared the perspective of Melito and Tertullian. Clement of Alexandria began his preferred list of emperors with Augustus, in the 28th year of whose reign the Savior was born (*Stromata* 1.144–5, quoting Luke 3.1: Jesus began his ministry in the fifteenth year of Tiberius), and both Hippolytus in his *Commentary on Daniel* (4.9) and Origen in his *Contra Celsum* (2.30) link the success and prosperity of the Roman Empire to the birth of Christ in the reign of Augustus.

The fullest extant exposition of the theme comes from the pen of Eusebius of Caesarea, who starts his *Ecclesiastical History* with the Incarnation during the reign of Augustus (*HE* 1.5–6, quoting Genesis 49.10). It is in his apologetical works, however, that Eusebius developed most fully his somewhat idiosyncratic theory that Christianity was the true, original religion of mankind, the religion of the Jewish patriarchs, which had been temporarily eclipsed by the Mosaic dispensation that was abolished by the coming of Christ. Eusebius elaborated this theory at great length in his enormous double treatise *The Preparation for the Gospel* and *The Demonstration of the Gospel*, in which he argued that it was no accident that Jesus was born in the reign of Augustus; for it was the establishment of monarchy by Augustus and his ending of all wars that created the necessary preconditions under which the most ancient of all religions could be reintroduced into the world (*PE* 1.4.3–5.10; *DE* 8.4.13). In the surviving books of the *Demonstration of the Gospel* Eusebius states emphatically that Augustus was the first emperor in at least four separate passages (*DE* 3.2.37, 3.7.31, 7.2.22, 8.1.19). A century later the Spanish priest Orosius repeated and enhanced Eusebius' historical claims: his seven books of *Historiae adversus Paganos* assume a divinely ordained intrinsic connection between the rule of the first emperor and the Incarnation, and Orosius devotes six books to disasters which occurred before the birth of Jesus and a seventh to the successes of the Roman Empire between the Incarnation and the time of writing in 417, when the barbarian invaders, so Orosius optimistically believed, had been permanently overcome and subdued. It is significant, however, that although Orosius held that Christ was born on 25 December in the 42nd year of Augustus, who was the first emperor, he was aware of the claim that the first emperor was in fact Julius Caesar (7.2.14: "Augustus Caesar, the first of all the emperors – though his father Julius Caesar showed himself the founder of the empire (*metator imperii*) rather than an emperor himself").

In the Christian chronographical tradition, on the other hand, it was Julius Caesar who led off the sequence of Roman emperors stretching down to a writer's own day. Theophilus of Antioch quotes a list of emperors and the lengths of their reigns from the otherwise unknown Chryseros, a freedman and *nomenclator* of Marcus Aurelius: Chryseros compiled chronological tables from the foundation of Rome to the death of Marcus, and he counted Julius Caesar as the first emperor with a reign of three years, seven months and six days (*Ad Autolycum* 3.27 = *FGrH* 96 F 1). The circulation of either Chryseros' list or another list also starting with Caesar was noted a few years later by Clement of Alexandria, who himself counted Augustus as the first emperor, but noted that others thought that it was Julius Caesar and that he reigned for three years, four months and six days (*Stromata* 1.144–5, according to the manuscripts). Clement's younger contemporary Julius Africanus agreed that Caesar was a monarch and thus the first emperor (frags. 53, 65.304 Wallraff, Roberto, & Pinggéra 2007). Eusebius of Caesarea too, in his *Chronicle* as opposed to his apologetical works, reckoned Julius Caesar as the first Roman emperor in a numbered series going as far as Constantine, whom Eusebius counted as the 34th Roman emperor and with whose *vicennalia* in 325–6 he ended. For this there was a good technical reason. In the chronological tables which form the second part of the bipartite *Chronicle*, it is the correlation of the start of Caesar's rule that links Christian chronology to Jewish chronology and to the *fila regnorum* of Greek and Hellenistic history. The *Chronicle* equated the first year of Julius Caesar with year 20 of the Jewish high priest Hyrcanus and year 3 of the Egyptian Queen Cleopatra (*Chronicle*, pp. 142–3, 154, 208–9 Karst; Jerome, *Chronicle* 156–7 Helm). The correlation 3 Cleopatra = 20 Hyrcanus = 1 Caesar enabled Eusebius to tie the chronology of the Roman emperors both to the secular chronology of the Hellenistic, Greek, and Ancient Oriental monarchies and to the sacred history of Israel and the Jews stretching back to Abraham. Furthermore, the equation of the first year of Caesar with the era of Antioch, which was the era of Caesar's victory over Pompey at Pharsalus, gave Eusebius a yardstick by which to ensure that the overlapping regnal years of emperors did not produce extra years in his overall chronology: he noted that the second year of Probus was year 324 in the Antiochene calendar and that the first year of the "Great Persecution" (19 Diocletian) coincided with year 350 of the era of Antioch (Jerome, *Chronicle* 223[k], 228[c]). The chronological framework of Eusebius' *Chronicle*, and hence its designation of Caesar as the first Roman emperor, became canonical not only for Latin writers who compiled continuations of Jerome's version of the *Chronicle*, but also in the Byzantine chronographical tradition – although John Malalas contrived to assert both that Augustus was the first to reign as monarch in Rome since the kings (7.13–14) and that Julius Caesar was the first to attain to sole rule over the Romans (9.1, 3). John the Lydian went much further: not only did he regard Caesar as the first emperor, but he credited him with creating the whole system of imperial administration devised by Augustus including imperial legates as provincial governors (*De Magistratibus* 1.37, 53, 3.6).

Besides his status as the first emperor, how and for what was Julius Caesar remembered by others than historians of Rome who wrote about the period when he lived? Polyaenus composed eight books of *Stratagems*, which he dedicated to Marcus Aurelius and Lucius Verus in 162 as the latter prepared to set off to fight the Parthians: Julius Caesar contributes 33 of the 900 examples which Polyaenus culled from the whole range of mythology, literature, and history known to him (8.23, cf. Melber 1885). Polyaenus is exceptional in having a professional interest in Caesar as a military commander. Several miscellaneous items concerning Caesar and his exploits appear elsewhere. A speaker in Athenaeus' *Deipnosophistae* found it remarkable that

Caesar crossed to Britain with one thousand ships, but only three personal slaves (6, 273b), and Aelian noted that "Caesar was not too proud to attend the school of Ariston, and Pompey that of Cratippus" (*Varia Historia* 7.21). But Caesar was far from being a familiar figure or historical example in Late Antiquity. He is named rather less frequently than might have been expected in the eleven speeches by orators from Gaul preserved with Pliny's speech of AD 100 in the corpus of Latin panegyrics (*Pan. Lat.* 2–10). The orator from Autun who thanked Constantine in 311 for alleviating the tax burden imposed on his city digressed to discuss the loyalty that the Aedui had always shown to Rome: a leader of the Aedui had been instrumental in inviting a Roman army and Caesar to cross the Rhône to repel Germans from Gaul (*Pan. Lat.* 5[8].3.3). Constantine is twice compared to Caesar. In the speech of 310 his siege of Massilia after it had been seized by Maximian is compared to Caesar's siege of the same city (*Pan. Lat.* 6[7].19.3). In the speech of 313 Constantine's capture of the Alpine town of Segusio is contrasted with Caesar's capture of Gomphi in Thessaly: whereas Caesar took and destroyed in a day an undefended town of feeble Greeks, Constantine captured a town defended by hardy inhabitants of the Alps and, unlike Caesar, he ordered his victorious soldiers to show clemency (*Pan. Lat.* 12[9].5.4–6.2). Subsequently, as he advanced on Rome, Constantine emulated the swiftness in action of both Scipio and Caesar (*Pan. Lat.* 12[9].15.3: *celeritatem illam in re gerenda Scipionis et Caesaris ... repraesentans*). Strangely, that is the sum of the references to Caesar in the eight speeches delivered between 289 and 313, and there are none at all in the speeches of 321 and 362. The latest speech, which Pacatus delivered in Rome in 389, names Caesar twice, in both cases together with other prominent figures of the Late Republic. Theodosius possessed a perfect memory, with a power of recall superior to Hortensius, Lucullus, and Caesar. After his victory in civil war, Rome had welcomed Theodosius without fear – a city which had suffered Cinna in his fury, Marius cruel after his exile, Sulla called "happy" because of her ruin, and Caesar who showed mercy only to the dead, a city which had lamented the heads of consuls on pikes, Cato who was compelled to kill himself, Cicero who was beheaded, and Pompey who was left unburied (*Pan. Lat.* 2[12].18.3, 46.1). In order to praise the clemency of Theodosius, therefore, Pacatus denies Caesar the moral quality of *clementia* for which he was most renowned. Pacatus' contemporary, the author of the *De viris illustribus*, had recently reiterated the conventional belief that Caesar put aside hatred after his victory and that the only enemies whom he executed were Lentulus, Afranius, and Faustus Sulla (78.9, from Suet. *Iul.* 75.3, who names the three as Afranius, Faustus, and Lucius Caesar).

Julius Caesar was not a standard measure of comparison for Greek orators of Late Antiquity either. For them the great conqueror of the past was Alexander the Great of Macedon. Thus, while Libanius never names or refers to Julius Caesar, he names Alexander seven times in his joint panegyric of the imperial brothers Constantius and Constans (*Orat.* 59.12, 24, 53–5), in at least 14 passages of the various speeches which he delivered before or about the emperor Julian (*Orat.* 11.73–7, 88, 250, 14.34, 15.2, 42, 74, 79, 17.17, 32, 18.260, 297, 19.13, 14, 20.22, 30, 32, 42), and more than 50 times in all (Richtsteig 1923: 8–9). Similarly, while Themistius invokes Alexander well over 30 times in his speeches in praise of emperors from Constantius to Theodosius (Downey and Norman 1974: 146), he names Caesar twice only: once he adduces Caesar as an example of clemency together with Pompey, Augustus, and Marcus Aurelius (*Orat.* 7, 96a), and once he compares victories of Theodosius over the Sarmatians before his proclamation as emperor to those of Lucullus over Tigranes, Pompey over Mithridates, and Caesar over the Gauls (*Orat.* 15, 198a; cf. Hansen 1967). Hence it is no surprise that historians such as Herodian in the third century, and Procopius and Agathias in the sixth, who wrote the history of their own times, never found any occasion to mention Caesar at all in retrospective reflections.

Ammianus Marcellinus, who, though Greek by origin and intellectual formation, soaked himself in Latin literature before writing his enormous history of Rome from the accession of Nerva to the death of Valens (Barnes 1998a: 192–5), names Caesar seven times in the surviving 18 books of history, and once invokes him anonymously. Ammianus' digression on Gaul naturally notes Caesar's Gallic campaigns and his subjugation of Gaul (15.11.6, 12.6); his digression on Egypt records that two libraries containing 70,000 volumes assembled by the Ptolemies were burnt during the Bellum Alexandrinum "under Caesar the dictator" (22.16.13; cf. den Boeft, den Hengst, Teitler, & Drijvers 1995: 299–300; Raven 2004: 12–21); and his second digression on the city of Rome alleges that degenerate Roman nobles consider a trip to Spoleto equal to the journeys of Alexander the Great or Caesar (28.4.18). Among Ammianus' emperors, one laudably imitated Caesar while another conspicuously failed to do so. When on campaign, Ammianus' hero Julian used to read and write in his tent at night as Caesar had (25.2.3), whereas Constantius was unaware that "some of the emperors of old" showed supreme courage in military emergencies and that one of them (he clearly alludes to Caesar's attempt to cross the Adriatic, which is written up by several Latin authors) "had entrusted himself to a small fishing-boat at the height of a raging storm" (16.10.3: *ignorans fortasse … alium anhelante rabido flatu ventorum lenunculo se commisisse piscantis*). None of this ought to occasion great surprise. But Ammianus also drew on his reading of Latin literature to reproduce two items which appear nowhere else. First, he quotes a letter of Cicero to Nepos scolding Caesar for cruelty (21.16.13; cf. den Boeft, den Hengst, & Teitler 1991: 263): this must come from the lost collection of Cicero's letters to Cornelius Nepos, which comprised three or more books (Macrobius, *Saturnalia* 2.1.4) and to which Ammianus refers in a passage defending his way of writing history (26.1.2). Second, he scolds Valens for failing to realize that "as the dictator Caesar used to say, the recollection of past cruelty is a wretched provision for old age" (29.2.18: *ut Caesar dictator aiebat, miserum esse instrumentum senectuti recordationem crudelitatis*).

Eusebius transmitted to later chronographers no more than a few basic facts about Caesar. The relevant entries in his chronological tables are reproduced by Jerome, in his translation and continuation (*Chronicle* 154[f], 155[a, g, h], 156[a, f], 157[a, c, d] Helm):

60 BC Caesar takes Lusitania and some islands in the Ocean
56 Caesar crosses the Rhine and ravages the Germans
51 Caesar takes the Germans and Gauls
50 The start of the civil war between Caesar and Pompey

49 Caius Julius Caesar was the first to acquire sole rule among the Romans, from whom the leaders of the Romans are called Caesars
47 Caesar in Egypt confirms the rule of Cleopatra in gratitude for sexual favors
45 Antonius proposes that the month Quintilis should be called July because Julius was born during it
44 On the ides of March C. Iulius Caesar is killed in the senate house

Some of this material was included in the popular chronicle composed by John Malalas in Antioch in the sixth century, which combined genuine erudition with a mishmash of invention, error, and confused information (Schenk von Stauffenberg 1931: 79–123[6]).[7] Although Malalas names Lucan, Livy, and Virgil, and refers to many buildings constructed by Caesar in Antioch and elsewhere, yet he makes Caesar the son-in-law (not father-in-law) of Pompey and states that when he captured Rome, he killed all the senators and ruled as an arrogant tyrant for 18 years (9.2–3).

For several centuries there were still serious historians who knew about the historical Caesar from the *Roman History* of Cassius Dio. In the early sixth century, Dio was one of many sources used by John of Antioch, who, through the *Excerpta Constantiniana* of the tenth century, provided much material for the anonymous lexicon known as the Suda in the eleventh century (Roberto 2005: lxxix–ci); and a full text of Cassius Dio was still available for Johannes Xiphilinus to make an epitome of books 38–53 in the 1070s and to be used by Johannes Zonaras for his history in the twelfth century. But all these three Johns were scholars, as was George Syncellus, who died shortly after 810 and whose *Ecloga Chronographica* contains accurate information relating to Caesar from Josephus and Eutropius. Moreover, anyone who wrote about the calendar, like John the Lydian, could not avoid recording Caesar's reform and the naming of the month Quintilis in his honor (Wünsch 1898: 186, 198). But what did the less educated know about Caesar?

The chronicle of George the Monk (George Hamartolos), who was writing c. 865 or slightly later, closes its seventh book and opens its eighth with the following two paragraphs (1.293.1–18 de Boor):

> The affairs of the Romans were formerly administered by consuls for 464 years until Julius Caesar, who was not born in the normal way. For, when his mother died in the ninth month, they cut her open and extracted him, from which "Caesar" comes. From him the emperors of the Romans were called Caesars, which is "cutting" in the Latin tongue.
>
> Ruling after this, Julius Caesar was the first to gain sole control of rule over the Romans. He ruled with great arrogance and boastfulness, whence he was called "dictator," which means monarch. Having controlled everything with rashness and tyranny for 18 years he was killed in the Senate. He gave the laws of the Romans, invented indictions and the leap-year, and called the month formerly called Quintilis "July." Under him was Judas the Galilean who is mentioned in the Acts of the Apostles, and Antipater the father of Herod became king of the Jews.

Much of this comes virtually word for word from Malalas (9.1, 3) and much reappears in later chronicles. The strange idea that Caesar invented the system of indictions, the 15-year cycle of taxation which officially began in AD 312, is first found in the Paschal Chronicle in the early seventh century, which also records the start of "Constantinian indictions" under the correct date (355, 522 Bonn).

As the centuries passed, Caesar gradually receded from the history that was remembered. When the Suda uses the name "Caesar," it usually means Augustus (e.g. *A* 4603, quoting Dio 53.26.1), and references to Julius Caesar usually comprise the bare name in a quotation illustrating a linguistic usage (e.g. *Δ* 367; *E* 1636, 1805, 3918; *H* 34), although one brings in the civil war against Pompey (*Π* 2165). Most of the substantive statements about Caesar in the Suda are familiar from Byzantine writers. Thus the entry for the word "Caesar" explains that Roman emperors are called Caesar "from Julius Caesar who was not born" in the normal way, but cut out of his dead mother because "in the language of the Romans 'Caesar' means 'cutting out,'" then goes on to state that Caesar was the first to be a monarch and rule over the Romans (*K* 1199). Two entries add to the familiar refrain that Caesar was "the first to rule as emperor" that he composed a translation of Aratus' *Phaenomena* and an *Art of Grammar* in Latin (*Γ* 10; *K* 1196). The *Art of Grammar* is presumably Caesar's lost work *De Analogia*, but the Latin version of Aratus survives: although the text indicates that its author is Germanicus Caesar, or conceivably Germanicus' adoptive father, the emperor Tiberius (Gain 1976: 16–20), while Lactantius, who quoted from the extant poem at the beginning of the fourth century, had identified its author as Germanicus Caesar (*Div. Inst.* 1.21.28, 5.5.4), the misattribution to Julius Caesar was already circulating in the reign of Constantine (Firmicus Maternus, *Mathesis* 2 pr. 2). The lexicon appears to derive its notice that Augustus was the nephew of Julius Caesar from John of Antioch (*A* 4413 = John of Antioch, frag. 73 Müller / 150.2 Roberto), and the story that Cleopatra used on the victor of Actium exactly the same spells or charms which she had used successfully to seduce both Julius Caesar and Mark Antony from Aelian (*I* 761 = Aelian, frag. 57 Hercher / 60a Domingo-Foresté). The Suda also alleges that Caesar fathered Selene, the daughter of Cleopatra (I 399).

Julius Caesar was not an important symbol or influential figure in Late Antiquity or for the Byzantines, except as a chronological marker of the transition from Republic to Empire. While Late Antique writers and Byzantine scholars retained some knowledge of the historical importance and actual achievements of Julius Caesar, he meant nothing to the majority of the populace, whose knowledge of and interest in him hardly went beyond gossip. For the Christian inhabitants of the Byzantine Empire the important transition was not from Roman Republic to Roman Empire, but from paganism to Christianity: at most levels, therefore, Caesar disappeared behind the imposing figure of Constantine.

FURTHER READING

On Caesar's reputation and influence in Western Europe, see now Maria Wyke, *Caesar: A Life in Western Culture* (Granta, 2007), which appeared after the present chapter had been completed. There is nothing comparable for the Greek East.

NOTES

1 On the place of these two works and two supplementary essays published in 1930 on Gundolf's scholarly œuvre as a whole, see Pöschl 1981.

2 My title alludes deliberately to the first emperor of China, Qin Shi Huang Di.

3 The absence of Julius Caesar from Pliny, *NH* 11.143–4 does not show that "Augustus counted as the first of the Caesars for the elder Pliny" (as asserted by Pelling 2002: 213), only that Pliny did not consider Caesar's "dark and lively eyes" (Suetonius, *Iul.* 45.1) as remarkable as those of the emperors Tiberius, Augustus, Claudius, Caligula, and Nero – whose eyes and eyesight he discusses in this order. Nor again does the younger Pliny's comparison of Trajan's consecration of Nerva as a god to the consecrations of Augustus by Tiberius, of Claudius by Nero, and of Vespasian and Titus by Domitian show that either he or Trajan considered Augustus the first emperor: Pliny cites these precedents in order to praise Trajan for not imitating predecessors who did the same as Trajan, but with different motives, Tiberius in order to introduce trials for *maiestas*, Nero to ridicule a recently dead emperor, and Domitian to glorify himself (*Panegyric* 11.1–2).

4 Geiger (1975, 2002: 93–5) dates Plutarch's imperial lives to the reign of Nerva and argues that Augustus headed the official list of good emperors for nearly a century after his death until Trajan introduced the name of Julius Caesar. But official celebration of Caesar's birthday began in 42 BC and its annual celebration on 12 July is attested during the reign of Tiberius (Degrassi 1963: 185–99, 208; cf. Barnes 1998: 144–1), in the *Feriale Duranum*, which is datable between 225 and 227 (*P. Dura*, col. ii.21), and perhaps at Theveste in Africa at about the same date (*CIL* 8.1858–9 = *ILAlg* 1.3040, 3041), and it is still registered, even if on the wrong day, in the fifth century calendar of Polemius Silvius (*CIL* 1^2, p. 261 = Degrassi 1963: 270). Admittedly, Caesar's birthday is absent from both the calendar for July and the list of imperial birthdays in the so-called Chronographer of the Year 354 (*CIL* 1^2, pp. 260, 255 = Degrassi 1963: 250–1). But that does not necessarily mean that Constantine removed Caesar from the list of imperial *divi* whose birthdays were officially celebrated, as argued by Zecchini (1990; cf. Degrassi 1963: 482). It should be noted that the fact that the Arval Brothers did not celebrate Caesar's birthday during the first century does not prove that it was not officially celebrated by others, since the only birthdays which the Arval confraternity ever celebrated were those of reigning emperors and their close relatives (Scheid 1998). It seems probable, therefore, that Caesar's birthday was officially celebrated in Rome continuously for several centuries.

5 Long (2006: 65–6) finds Caesar "a somewhat surprising guest" on the assumption that in 362 "contemporary habits of thought" regarded Augustus as the first emperor.

6 It should be noted that the apparently earlier work often cited as A. Schenk von Stauffenberg, *Caesar bei Malalas*, diss. Halle, 1930, is not the author's dissertation, which was examined and accepted by the University of Halle-Wittenberg in 1928, but merely a preprint of pages 79–123 of his book of 1931 issued separately, but with identical pagination.

7 Compare Symeon the Logothete (pseudo-Leo Grammaticus), p. 53.22–54.17 Bonn and George Cedrenus, p. 299.20–300.21 Bonn: both make Caesar an emperor, both report that a horse was born on his estates with cloven hooves that no-one else could ride, and both have some (though not the same) genuine snippets of information about Caesar's assassination.

CHAPTER TWENTY-ONE

The Irritating Statues and Contradictory Portraits of Julius Caesar

Paul Zanker

Once Caesar had attained the supreme position, he was heaped with honors on a scale which had never been accorded to any of the great men of the Republic before him. Among these honors a special role was played by the honorific statues, which were set up "in all the cities and temples of Rome" (Dio 44.4.4–5). Suetonius lists the most important of these *honores modo nimios* (*Iul.* 76.1) and mentions among them specific statues: a statue in ivory, which was to be carried into the Circus along with the images of the gods on a special stand, and *simulacra iuxta deos*, which were to be set up in the temples with the statues of the gods (compare Appian *B Civ.* 2.106).

The erection of numerous statues in honor of a single politician was not unusual in the late phase of the Republic (Vessberg 41–79; Lahusen 1984). But never had the statues played such an important and various role in political struggles as they did in the late period of Caesar's dictatorship. As with some other honors, it is often not clear, in the case of these statues, whether those who erected them were engaged in competing with each other, and so lost all sense of proportion, or whether they were deliberately aiming to discredit Caesar. After the further decision of the Senate, at the beginning of 44 BC, that Caesar's image should appear on the coinage – an honor never before granted to any magistrate in his lifetime – his image was ubiquitous in the Empire (Dio 44.4).

It is a characteristic feature of Roman honorific statues, that head and body are conceived separately. For the body, use was made generally of definite schemata, whose canonical shape had been gradually established since the late fourth century. These schemata express, in a propagandist fashion, specific basic values and virtues, civilian and military. The body of the statue was then provided with the individual head of the honorand, irrespective of the schema. Again, these portraits were not designed anew every time: types, once created, were copied repeatedly and placed on statues of the most various schemata. That makes it natural to treat statues and portraits separately.

The Ambitious Statues of the Dictator: Aims and Effects

The effect of a statue often depended less on the traditional schema for the body than on the place of its erection and on its inscription. Caesar's statues were placed in all the most conspicuous and significant sites in Rome: on the Rostra, or nearby; in the Forum Iulium; on the Capitol, in the immediate neighborhood of the temple of Jupiter; in the temple of Venus Genetrix. The proximity to other monuments was often especially significant; most significant of all, however, was their exploitation by politicians and the response of contemporaries. People experienced the presence of these works of art in a much more direct way, at that time, than we can imagine nowadays. Statues of gods, and human portraits, could encourage, warn, appear in dreams, announce events, form the center of religious ceremonies (Boschung 2002: 168–79). It was just this vital relationship that also made them available as an effective resource in political confrontations. Caesar's honorific statues offer impressive examples, when they are considered in their contemporary political context. We shall consider them in chronological order.

The statue of the "demigod" with the globe

The first controversial statue was set up to Caesar on the Capitol, at his return from Africa, in April 46 (Dio 43.14; Cic. *Deiot.* 34). Its position seems to have been a prominent one, outside the temple of Jupiter Optimus Maximus. The special feature of this honor was the schema selected for the statue, and also its inscription. The question of the statue's appearance has been much discussed (Cadario 2006: 27–32; Klöckner 1997: 55–7; Weinstock 1971: 40–50). Most probable, in my view, is a schema similar to that of the statue of Octavian on his denarii of 31 BC (Giard 1976: 66 pl. 1, 13–15; Zanker 1988: 41, fig. 31a [figure 21.1]). That schema depicted Caesar in the Hellenistic tradition, naked, and with one foot placed on the terrestrial globe. This schema (without the globe) is well attested for gods, kings, and Republican commanders, so that it was not something new. The globe was used as a symbol for power and extensive rule, both for the Genius Romanus and for the Dea Roma. Pompeius had already employed the globe for his victories in the different areas of the world, though not in direct connection with a statue.

The combination of statue and globe may be an innovation with Caesar; understood in the sense of universal personal rule, it may well have caused irritation. But the particular occasion for annoyance in Caesar's opponents probably lay in the inscription – or, rather, in the combination of the statue and the inscription: for in it Caesar was called "Demigod." Cassius Dio (42.21.2) uses the Greek word "Hemitheos": one would dearly like to know the wording of the Latin inscription.

Figure 21.1 Denarius with statue of Octavian, 31 BC or earlier. From Zanker 1988, fig. 31.

It was only the inscription that gave the explosive force, turning the pose with the globe, with its heroic or divine associations, into a statement that corresponded to the image. It is clear that Caesar still took the criticism to heart. At any rate, he had the inscription changed (Dio 42.21.1). That the connection with the globe did in fact correspond to Caesar's own image of himself is evidenced by his coinage in the opening months of the year 44 BC. On the reverse appears Venus Genetrix, the goddess who brought Caesar military success: she holds Caesar's Victoria in her hand and rests her shield on the globe (Hölscher 1967: 151 plates 2, 3).

Caesar enters the Forum Iulium as autocratic Imperator

A few months later, on September 26, 46 BC, Caesar dedicated his new Forum. It was the crowning completion of his fourfold Triumph. The Forum Iulium lay immediately next to the Comitium and was intended to contribute to the urgent need for courtrooms and for trading emporia (*LTUR*: II 299–306, Gros). In terms of Republican tradition, the building could be understood as a gift by the victorious general to Senate and People, from the booty of war. But at the same time the construction offered an unprecedented piece of self-glorification, which could compete on equal terms with the Theatre of Pompeius on the Campus Martius. The site was dominated by the temple of Venus Genetrix, standing on a lofty base: the goddess was claimed by Caesar and his family as their ancestress. The Curia, recently rebuilt by Sulla, was on Caesar's orders demolished and replaced by a new construction, the future Curia Iulia, which was to be fitted into the Forum Iulium: that, too, was a symbolic gesture that cocked a snook at all Republican traditions. Neither the Forum nor the temple, of course, was completed by 46 BC; both were completed by Octavian and rededicated in 29 BC. The statues erected on the Forum are especially interesting for us, because here we can be certain that they were erected with Caesar's consent, or at his suggestion.

Most frequently mentioned is a *statua loricata*; Pliny the Elder informs us that it was the first statue in Rome of a man in armor (*NH* 34.18). The passage has vexed the commentators, because older statues in armor are known to have existed in Rome. On the other hand, there does seem to have been something unusual about it, as Pliny adds that Caesar "permitted," *passus est*, the erection of the statue, which had been voted to him by the Senate (Stemmer 1978: 145). Perhaps this was the first armored statue inside the *pomerium*, within which, by ancient custom, no commander might enter in military uniform (Cadario 2006: 32–7). In that case, we are dealing with a breach of the rules by the Senate, accepted by Caesar. The *statua loricata Divi Iulii* must have been an impressive monument, as it soon became a well-known meeting point: at it, or near it, important public notices were displayed (Pliny *Ep.* 8.6.13; Suet. *Claud.* 28.1–2). It also served as the indicator for one of the seats of the financial administration (Corbier 1997: 11–40).

The second statue in the Forum Iulium, the *equus Caesaris*, also celebrated the Dictator as a great general, even comparing him (admittedly, in a very unusual way) with Alexander the Great. Unfortunately, this *equus Caesaris* is only mentioned by Statius (*Silv.* 1.85). The poet glorifies the newly erected colossal equestrian statue of Domitian in the Forum Romanum and compares it – in hyperbolic panegyric – with the equestrian statue of Caesar in the Forum Iulium, in front of the temple of Venus Genetrix (in his view, it is much less impressive, and in fact not worth looking at) (Cadario 2006: 36; Bergemann 1990: 160 L22; Kreikenbom 1992: 56–8). In this connection, Statius also mentions that Caesar's monument was a work of Lysippus, which originally represented Alexander – the head of Alexander was replaced only later on by the head of Caesar.

The display of masterpieces of Greek art as war booty had a long tradition in the endowing of the shrines of triumphators on the Campus Martius (Pape 1975). Even the rededication of a work by a change of portrait was nothing unusual (Blanck 1969: *passim*). Caesar had placed himself crudely in the place of Alexander, if we are to believe Statius. When we reflect on the way Pompeius and other Republican grandees stylized themselves as Alexander, and on the reworking of the head of Alexander, so as to depict Augustus, in celebrated paintings by Apelles which were set up in the Forum of Augustus, then we shall have to admit that Statius was right, and to start by accepting that Caesar took over a famous monument of the Macedonian for himself. In the light of the universal admiration for Alexander, we may assume that this represents, not a slighting of Alexander by Caesar, but rather a measuring of himself against him (Michel 1967: 102–4).

Both Suetonius (*Iul.* 61) and Pliny (*NH* 8.155) speak of a statue of Caesar's favorite horse, which stood, similarly, in the Forum Iulium – actually in front of the temple of Venus – and which, in the archaeological literature, is often identified with the *equus Caesaris* described by Statius. Like Alexander's celebrated Bucephalus, he would not bear any other rider, and he was distinguished by hooves which resembled human feet. Many scholars think in terms of confusion or inexactness on the part of the ancient authors. But why should we imagine that we know better than they did? If we take the ancient authors at their word, we should imagine a statue of his favorite horse, quite independent of the *equus Caesaris*, erected by Caesar himself

(Blanck 1969: 14, 107; Lahusen 1983: 22). That would be an emphatically extravagant gesture by Caesar – one which would thoroughly suit the Dictator's style.

Accordingly, Caesar represents himself, in the statues erected in his new Forum, as a great commander and a great conqueror: like Alexander, he can indulge his own inclinations to the full, by giving greater honors to his horse than to his generals, and by setting up a gilded statue of his mistress, Queen Cleopatra, in the temple of Venus Genetrix (App. *B Civ.* 2.102).[1] This autocratic behavior fits the picture very well when we think about his public appearances, and especially of that famous scene which was played out – not, perhaps, by chance – in the Forum Iulium. As the steps that led up to the temple of Venus were not, as was usual, at the front, but at the side, the vestibule offered an unequaled setting for ceremonial state actions. It was here that Caesar, seated on a golden chair and wearing the robe of a triumphator, received – without rising to his feet – the senators who came to offer him fresh honors (Dio 44.8; Suet. *Iul.* 78). This last, calculated, demonstration of his omnipotence was one of the last incentives that led to his assassination.

The statue "beside the kings" – and beside the tyrannicide

After the Battle of Munda (March 17, 45 BC), the Senate voted the setting up of new statues, which, along with the numerous other honors voted at the same time, were to surround the Dictator with an aura of the supernatural. By many, however, they were apparently greeted with disapproval (Suet. *Iul.* 76.1). That applies in particular to the ivory statue, which was carried into the Circus Maximus, probably as early as the Games at the Parilia (April 21, 45 BC), in the procession of the gods. It was, however, only by a later decision of the Senate, at the beginning of the year 44 BC, that Caesar received his own *ferculum* (litter) and also his own *tensa* (wagon with his clothing and cult objects).

The negative public reaction to the carrying of his statue in the Circus, as Matteo Cadario (2006: 37–51) has shown, is to be seen in the context of Caesar's second honoring with a statue, now that he was promoted to be *Dictator perpetuus*, in the temple of Quirinus. The erection of a portrait statue in a temple was not, in itself, anything extraordinary; in fact, Suetonius (*Iul.* 76.1) speaks, even in the context of the honors to Caesar, of *simulacra iuxta deos* – in the plural. What did make the dedication of the statue in the temple of Quirinus into something exceptional was that, in the case of Quirinus, it was the deified founder of the city, Romulus, who was in question. Above all, however, it was – as with the globe – the inscription which gave offense. It addressed Caesar, not just as a "demigod," but as "invincible god" (*theos aniketos*; Dio 43.45; Cic. *Att.* 12.53.2; 13.4.2, ed. H. Kasten).

While both the ivory statue in the Circus procession and the statue to the "invincible god" in the temple of Quirinus promoted the status of the Dictator, unabashedly, to the superhuman and very close to the divine, it was the third of the statues voted after Munda which attracted the most attention. This was the "statue among the kings" (Suet. *Iul.* 76.1; Dio 43.45). It stood with, or near, a group of statues representing the kings of Rome, either in the Area Capitolina or at its entrance (*LTUR*: IV, 368; most recently, Papini 2004: 155–66). This group was, in all probability, a historicizing dedication of the Hellenistic period, intended to recall the age of the famous kings. In that case, the choice of the place to erect the statue of Caesar played the deciding role; Cassius Dio is still conscious of that (43.45); here – quite contrary to his regular way of proceeding – he goes into detail, because he is obviously surprised by the place in which it was set up. "There eight statues stood together, seven for the kings and an eighth for the Brutus who overthrew the Tarquins. The statue to Caesar was erected near the last-mentioned (that of Brutus). It was, in fact, the deciding impulse which determined Marcus Brutus to conspire against Caesar." We can assume that the first of the set of kings was Romulus.

That was a more than ambiguous compliment to Caesar, who was accused, rightly or wrongly, of aiming at the kingship. The fact that, in addition to all that, the new statue of Caesar was erected next to that of Brutus, which held a drawn sword (Plut. *Brut.* 1.1), acquired (at least for Caesar's opponents) an unambiguous significance. It can hardly be imagined that the idea of giving the statue a position next to that of Brutus came from Caesar's friends; one asks oneself why Caesar allowed it to happen. The choice of position did, on the one hand, bring him close to the position of king, as indeed, did actually come to pass; but, at the same time, the statue of Brutus, the *conditor Libertatis*, was an unambiguous invitation to murder him. A possible explanation is that Caesar's opponents succeeded, by skillful positioning of the statue near that of Brutus, in counteracting the original honorific intention. Be that as it may, under the statue of Brutus were written graffiti such as "Would that you were alive!" – openly inciting the descendants of the regicide to commit the deed. At the same time, the Senate was praising Caesar as *liberator*, and Caesar himself vowed a temple to Libertas (it was, in fact, never built). Thus both parties were operating with the same slogans.

Cardario suspects, behind the setting up of the three statues after the Battle of Munda, the existence of an unified "Romulan program" (Cadario 2006: 31): it was to celebrate Caesar as the refounder of the state. But how, in concrete terms, are we to imagine that? I think it more likely that things developed spontaneously. One party sought to give a positive account of Caesar's claim to unlimited regal power by pointing to the kings, to Romulus and his superhuman qualities; the other party incited to opposition, relying on precisely this comparison, which so far exceeded all reasonable measure.

Instead of the Dictator, his statue is crowned

Nevertheless, in Caesar's last months came the dedication to Caesar of more statues: they were intended to play a role in political conflicts. Together with the reconstruction of the Curia Iulia as a kind of annexe to the Forum Iulium, Caesar planned to move the Rostra (orators' platform) – and indeed to the center of the Forum Romanum. That meant giving up the old unity of the Comitium, the Curia, and the Rostra: the traditional political center of Rome (*LTUR*: IV 212–14, Coarelli). It seems that a start was made on carrying this through soon after Caesar's return from Spain, late in 45 BC. Completion, of course, was reserved – here, too – for Octavian. The rebuilding made necessary the interchanging or the removal of the honorific statues which had been erected in past times on and around the Rostra. That was a ticklish business, since the Rostra were the most conspicuous and desirable site for such erections in the public space of Rome; consequently, that was where there stood some celebrated and historic monuments. Caesar used the moment for an action which won general attention. He had the equestrian statues of Sulla and Pompeius, his great opponents, which had been torn down by the populace after the Battle of Pharsalus, restored (Suet. *Iul.* 57.4; Dio 43.49). This gesture, which was generally very well received, did not spring from a spontaneous impulse: rather, it was connected with a policy of reconciliation, which he was consciously practicing at this time. The slogan attached to it was "the Clemency of Caesar." The Senate went so far as to decree a temple to the Clemency of Caesar (Suet. *Iul.* 57.4), and Appian even tells us of a group of cult images, which consisted of statues of Caesar and Clemency, reaching out their hands to each other. It is, however, unclear whether the statue, which was also depicted on coins, ever came to completion (*LTUR*: I 279; Cadario 2006: 55; Weinstock 1971: 233–42).

At the beginning of 44 BC the Senate voted two more statues for Caesar. This time, they were to be erected on the orators' platform. They were related to each other programmatically and were, therefore, probably set up as pendants (Dio 44.43). One, we are told, carried a wreath of oak leaves (the *corona civica*), the other a wreath of grass (the *corona obsidionalis*). Both these wreaths were venerable decorations, which in former times had been awarded to individuals, respectively for saving the lives of citizens and for delivering a town from siege. These wreaths acquired, by being awarded to Caesar in the absence of any specific occasion, a new and more general significance – as would happen, soon after, to Augustus' *corona civica*. They became the expression of the delivery and liberation of the state *simpliciter*. What was meant, of course, in Caesarian propaganda, was the delivery of the state from the captivity of the Optimates. This is also the significance of the bestowal on Caesar, at this time, of the honorific title of *pater patriae*.

To these throwbacks to the honors conferred in ancient Republican Rome corresponded the place in which they were erected: a place so full of significance for the Republic. The same is true for the statue which M. Antonius had put up after Caesar's death, and which by its inscription *parenti optime merito* ('to our most well-deserving father') so enraged Cicero (Cic. *Fam.* 12.3). One would like to know what dress was worn by the various statues on the tribunal: was it the simple toga, or the *toga triumphalis*, which Caesar was privileged to wear at all times – and which, evidently, he did wear?

One of these statues on the Rostra was the focus, not long after, of what appears to have been a deliberate provocation. Before, or at, the Feriae Latinae (January 26, 44 BC), one of the new statues was furtively decorated with a regal diadem. Again it is not clear who was behind it. Cassius Dio makes Caesar's enemies responsible (44.9), while Suetonius (*Iul.* 79.1) speaks of "someone from the crowd" (*quidam e turba*), who is said to have placed on the statue a laurel wreath with a white band tied to it (*statuae eius coronam lauream candida fascia praeligata imposuit*). When the popular tribunes had the crown removed, Caesar is said to have been angry with them: that suggests that the action was in fact taken by Caesar's friends (unless, as I suspect, the allegation itself originated with his enemies).

As in the former instance of the dedications on the Capitol, so here the statues serve as substitutes for the man represented: he was the real target of the action. The action was, in any case, a rehearsal for the public offering of the kingly title by M. Antonius at the Lupercalia (February 15, 44 BC). Suetonius calls the object *fascia candida*, a white band, such as the Hellenistic kings wore in token of their rank. Whether they were supporters or agents provocateurs, their action brought together an ancient Roman mark of rank with the Greek diadem. That seems to me symptomatic of the unprogrammatic groping to find a symbol and a name for what already existed *de facto*: the absolute autocracy of the Dictator.

Caesar's rather conventional self-representation

As in this case, it is often not easy, with many of the honorific statues of his last two years, to make out how far they were based on Caesar's support, or even on his own suggestion, and how far he simply allowed these exaggerated honors, including those meant as provocations, to take their course. How, in fact, did Caesar himself wish to be seen, in these last years? Our only archaeological evidence, apart from the decoration of the Forum Iulium, is, at the end, the statues erected on the Rostra and the coin bearing his own name, of which we must assume (*RRC*; Alföldi 1974) that they were issued with his consent.

In that context, the immediately surprising thing is the sober realism of the portraits, with their almost ostentatious representation of the marks of old age (figure 21.2). There were, after all, alternative possibilities. In the light of the debates over the kingly title, for instance, one might have expected a portrait which was more emotional, or even explicitly superhuman, such as was familiar with Hellenistic kings,

Figure 21.2 Denarius of M. Mettius, 44 BC showing Caesar as Dictator for the fourth time. From J. P. Kent, B. Overbeck, and A. Stylow, *Die römische Münze*, Munich 1973, Pl. 25 = *BMCRR* Rome 4135 = *RRC* 480/2a.

and such as had been employed in Rome by other political figures, including Pompey (Megow 2005: plates 4, 21, 23). That, however, was evidently not what Caesar wanted. On most of the coins he is wearing a wreath of strikingly large size. The significance of the wreath is disputed, but evidently it was an important attribute for Caesar's self-presentation. It cannot be explained simply as a cover for his baldness. There is good reason to suppose that it was intended as the gold wreath of the triumphator. Undoubtedly, we are dealing with the same wreath as Caesar wore in public together with the *toga triumphalis* (Dio 43.43; discussion, *RRC*: I, p. 488), and which young Octavian, after the death of Caesar, attempted to set up on the golden sella curulis (App. *B Civ.* 3.28), and placed on his coins as an emotional token of remembrance (*RRC*: no. 497, 2a; Schäfer 1989: 114ff.).

If this headdress, so surprising in itself, really is the wreath of a triumphator, that would provide an intelligible connection with the commonest representation on the reverse of his coins: that of Venus Genetrix. She holds out to Caesar the figure of Victoria, and – on some mintages – actually places her shield on the globe on which Caesar's statue on the Capitol had set its foot. Seen in this light, the coins confirm the self-interpretation already displayed in the Forum Iulium. It is above all his victories, and the protection of the divine ancestress of his family, that legitimate his rule. There is thus nothing new: his predecessors Sulla and Pompey had invoked their closeness to gods in their propaganda.

In this context it is striking how much emphasis is laid on the importance of *pietas* (see Wardle, chapter 8 in this volume). In the context of Caesar's portrait there appear, almost exclusively, objects of sacral significance, above all the *lituus* (staff) of an augur. The covered head on the later coins is another indication of priestly station and of his position as Pontifex Maximus. Admittedly, there is on the reverse a significant allusion to Venus Genetrix. But all this emphasis on *pietas* and on the priestly offices was not something new: in the case of Pompeius, and (later on) of M. Antonius and Octavian, emphasis had been laid on their piety and on their priestly positions.

The evidence is flimsy, but we get the impression that Caesar's own public display of his portrait was essentially different from the use made of it by his followers – or, in some cases, by hostile provocateurs. His supporters meant to place Caesar close to the gods; his own self-presentation was rather more conventional – as a great triumphator, whose claim to rule rested on his military achievements, assured to him by the divine ancestress of his house. Yet even this last point did not go further than the claims to divine patronage made by Sulla, Pompey, and other generals – except in their scale. Above all, neither in the Forum Iulium nor on the coinage do we find any trace of a claim to the kingship, or to divine honors. As for the latter, it appears that, as far as statues went, in the overheated atmosphere of the last months, they were set up by ill-advised partisans and (still more) by ill-intentioned opponents, working for his overthrow. In any case, the impulse to their erection did not come from Caesar. Seen in this light, it may well be that the last two statues erected on the orators' platform, with their wreaths of "Roman" type, corresponded more closely with Caesar's own intentions, if he was really concerned about his own depiction at all.

Octavian crowns Caesar's statues with a star

The story of Caesar's statues does not end with his death. It is true that, immediately after his murder, statues of him in various places in Rome were demolished. Appian (*B Civ.* 3.3) even speaks of a workshop in which they were collected and melted down. Those, however, seem to have been isolated actions; the partisans of the dead dictator soon put a stop to them. The famous monuments remained in existence, and some more – not very many – were added to the number. Above all, the young Octavian, of whom Mark Antony said that "he owed everything to his name," exploited them in the cleverest way imaginable (Donié 1996: 3ff.). The immediate task was the elimination of the Republicans; for that, the political slogan was "Revenge on Caesar's murderers!"

As early as Caesar's funeral, a wax image of the murdered man was put on the bier, in turning so as continually to exhibit all of his 23 wounds (App. *B Civ.* 2.147). In front of his bier, to reinforce the effect, there was carried his purple toga, soaked in his blood. Octavian pursued revenge, as *ultio paterna*, with extraordinary energy. He went unshaven, as a mark of mourning, for a whole year and had himself represented with that sign of mourning on his coins (*RRC*: 490, 493, 497). In addition, he carried his intention of revenge into practical and drastic effect. After the defeat and death of Brutus, Caesar's murderer, he had his head sent to Rome and laid at the foot of a statue of Caesar, in token of his revenge (Suet. *Aug.* 13.1). Another truly archaic scene was played out after the capture of Perugia, when Octavian had the whole of the upper class of the city slaughtered at an altar of Divus Iulius (Suet. *Aug.* 15; Dio 43.14).

From the beginning, Octavian saw in the figure of Caesar the key to his own political future. The decisive point was that not only should the memory of the murdered man be kept alive, but the figure of Caesar should be translated into a sphere above mere party struggles. The point was to establish the apotheosis, the path to which had already been prepared by the conferral of superhuman honors, as a cult of the Roman state. In this, heaven quite literally came to Octavian's assistance. Only a few months after Caesar's death, Octavian had put on, despite all opposition – on his own initiative and at his own expense – the Ludi Victoriae Caesaris. During this celebration, every evening for seven consecutive days, there appeared a brilliant comet in the northern sky! Among "the people," we are told, the story spread, spontaneously or not, that this was the mark of Caesar's acceptance among the gods. Octavian seized the extraordinary opportunity without hesitation and arranged for the *sidus Iulium* to shine for ever, by adorning Caesar with it. Cassius Dio (45.7) speaks of a new statue, with the star on its head, dedicated by Octavian in the temple of Venus Genetrix. The elder Pliny adds to this report, and quotes Octavian's *Memoirs* in support, that Octavian rejoiced in the sign and took it that the star had appeared for nobody but himself, and that he was to grow under its influence (*interiore gaudio sibi illum natum seque in eo nasci interpretatus est*). Pliny, for his part, strengthens this claim a century later, adding "and, in truth, it was for the health of the world" (*et, si verum fatemur, salutare id terris fuit*)!

The completion of the temple in honor of the new official god was long delayed – it was not consecrated until 29 BC – but a place for his cult, with an altar, was in

Figure 21.3 Aureus of Octavian, 36 BC. From Zanker 1988, fig. 26 = p. 81, Fig. 6.2.

existence much earlier in the Forum Romanum, at the place where Caesar's body had been burned (*LTUR*: III 116–19, Gros). Octavian, in any case, had the plan of the building, with the altar, shown on coins as early as 36 BC; he set the *sidus Iulium* shining on the top of the temple (*RRC*: 540,1 Pl.LIV [figure 21.3]). The cult statue of Caesar can be seen on the coins. Different coin dies represent it, sometimes with undraped upper torso, sometimes with the garment drawn over his head as he offers sacrifice. This seems to have been the most acceptable version; in addition, the deified one held in his right hand the *lituus* of an augur (Spannagel 1999: 311–13). The statue thus drew on the *pietas* theme of the portraits of Caesar on coins. Accordingly, the cult statue of Caesar as Divus did not need to differ from the honorific statues erected in his lifetime. Even the type showing him with his mantle round his hips, the upper part of his body bare, which on a coin of Augustus of 12 BC is crowned with a star, corresponds to a type which was used for emperors, for princes, and for private persons, both in their lifetime and after their death (Giard 1976: nos. 555–9).

Reference to Caesar as the guarantor of Octavian's claims to monarchy reached a climax in the years before his decisive defeat of his rivals. In the 30s he repeatedly depicts himself as Divi Filius, along with the Divus himself. The marks of age on Caesar's features are effectively juxtaposed with the portrait – sometimes positively boyish – of his youthful heir: Octavian was thus enabled to appear as the embodiment of renewal and of a new beginning (*RRC* nos.490.2, 534.2). The best portrait is to be found on an *aes* issue (*RRC* n.535.1 [figure 21.4]), where the features of the Divi Filius are obviously assimilated to those of his father.

The figure of Caesar becomes problematic, after the "restoration of the Republic"

Octavian did not emerge fully from the shadow of Caesar until after the Battle of Actium. In Augustus' *res publica restituta* the figure of Caesar went into eclipse. How

Figure 21.4 Sestertius, c. 36 BC. From J. P. Kent, B. Overbeck, and A. Stylow, *Die römische Münze*, Munich 1973, Pl. 30.

to deal with the memory of the *Dictator perpetuus*, who gave the Republic its death blow and aspired to the title of king? The portrait of the Divus vanishes from the coinage for many years, and so does the title DIVI FILIUS. When Agrippa set up a statue of Divus Iulius in the Pantheon, which he was erecting, really, in honor of Augustus, Dio Cassius makes that sound like a substitute: in fact, in keeping with the program of the 30s, what Agrippa really wanted was to erect a statue of Augustus among the gods. It was only when Augustus declined this honor that Agrippa set up the statue of Divus Iulius beside the statues of Venus and Mars. In the end, Augustus was set up with Agrippa in the vestibule (Dio 53.27).

Later, Augustus only twice renewed the commemoration of Caesar. The first time was on the coinage struck to mark the official opening of the Ludi Saeculares in 17 BC. On the obverse of the aurei and the denarii we see the herald of the games, in old-fashioned costume, his shield adorned with a star (Giard 1976: 273–6; *RIC*² I. Aug. 339–40). The reverse explains the star. On the head of Divus Iulius Caesar, depicted as rejuvenated, blazes a star (figure 21.5). It is the *sidus Iulium*, which had appeared on cue for the Secular Games. That is to call to mind, we should observe, not Caesar's deeds but his deification, and therewith the origins of Augustus. To make the whole business quite unambiguous, the Master of the Mint had the herald of the celebrations replaced, on another series of coins, by the head of Augustus, with that addition to his name – once so regularly employed, now repeated after a long absence – DIVI F (Giard 1976: 278–80; *RIC*² I. Aug.: p. 66). When we compare the two portraits, the significance of the rejuvenation of Caesar's head is easy to understand. Earlier on, Octavian's portrait had been assimilated to Caesar's; now it was the other way round!

It is less easy to understand why coins were minted in 12 BC on which Augustus himself places the star on Caesar's statue (Giard 1976: nos. 555–9; *RIC*² I.Aug. 415 [figure 21.6]). They appear after a number of issues honoring Agrippa. Agrippa had died in this same year. Donié thought there might be a connection with his Gaius and Lucius Caesar, the sons of Agrippa and Julia, who were marked out as his heirs. Their

Figure 21.5 Denarius of M. Sanguinius, Rome 17 BC. From Zanker 1988, fig. 132.

Figure 21.6 Denarius of L. Lentulus, 12 BC. From Zanker 1988, fig. 25.

portraits do in fact appear, with their mother Julia, on one of the portrait coins in the series (Giard 1976: nr 526; Donié 1996: 8). The presentation of his grandsons as his successors could only be based on their membership of the Julian family, and in that connection it was impossible to omit Divus Iulius. At the same time, the portrait itself shows how far the position had changed. Augustus towers high above the statue of the Divus Iulius; he wears the simple toga and holds the *clipeus virtutis*, which had been given to him long ago for saving the *res publica*, and which is shown much larger than Caesar's star (Zanker 1987: 43, ill.25a).

It is a pity that we do not know in what form Divus Iulius was represented in the Forum Augustum. He must have appeared there: that is beyond question. The idea that he formed a group of three with Mars and Venus in the Temple of Mars Ultor has been called into doubt recently by several scholars, in part with good arguments. In the gallery of statues in the porticus to the left of the temple, he cannot possibly, as Divus, have been represented on the same level as his ancestors, while the central position was occupied, we know, by Aeneas. Recently, Martin Spannagel has proposed, on good grounds, that the colossal statue of which fragments remain in the so-called Aula which closes off the end of the Porticus of the Iulii should be identified as Divus Iulius. In that case, he was given an outstanding position in the context of the family, while at the same time a certain distance was maintained from the old gods. It is a pity that the surviving fragments do not permit an unambiguous resolution of the problem (Spannagel 1999: 300–58; *contra*, M. Papini, *Bonner Jahrb.* 20 (2001): 576ff.).

The Many Faces of Caesar

An honorific statue could be looked at only from below and at a distance of at least 2.5–3 meters, as the base must be added to the height of the statue. The onlooker could thus take in only the general impression, not the details of head and face. Portrait busts, on the other hand, were intended to be seen from close range. It was only by observation from close up that anything could be discerned of the looks and the stance, or even of the self-conception, of the person represented – or, better, of the subject as a person, independently of his rank and his services to the public. It was only the close-up portrait that could awaken in the observer any memories and emotions. We have an extreme example in Cleopatra's unsuccessful attempt to soften her conqueror, Octavian. She received him seated on a couch in simple mourning costume. "Beside her," we are told, "she had many different portraits of his father [Iulius Caesar] and in her costume she had concealed all the letters he had written her. ... At moments she burst into lamentations; at others she threw herself to the ground before his portraits and adored them" (Dio 51.12).

What did Caesar really look like? The Tusculum portrait

The earliest portraits of Caesar which we have, and the only ones which were certainly made in his lifetime, are the images on coins, discussed above (pp. 295–6). At the opening of the year 44 BC, the Senate had extended to Caesar the right to strike his portrait on coins (Dio 44.4). In consequence, the mint masters struck Caesar's image on the denarii until the Ides of March and sometimes thereafter. Andreas Alföldi collected and published a great number of illustrations of these denarii (Alföldi 1974). While all these coin likenesses go back ultimately to the same original, the separate mintings vary enormously (Vessberg 138–48). That is not surprising: the dies must have been in need of constant renewal and improvement, as the work went on, and a number of die cutters must have been employed.

It often happened that recourse was had, not to an original, but only to a copy, itself already considerably altered. That meant that new variants were constantly arising, which exaggerate characteristic features, such as the folds in Caesar's neck or his angular features: the results often border on caricature. Among the highest-quality versions are the early coinages of M. Mettius (figure 21.2). They present Caesar, at the time

56 years old, with a thin face, regular features, and a long and wrinkled neck, with prominent Adam's apple (Alföldi 1959, ill.16). The forehead, high and bald, is covered – on almost all mintings – with a massive wreath, already discussed (p. 296). This portrait type, the basis of the coinage of 44 BC, was certainly not the first. There must have been earlier honorific statues with portraits of the younger Caesar. We know, though, of no corresponding representations in three-dimensional sculpture, although a coin from Nikea in Mysia may give us an idea of an earlier portrait (Johansen 1967: 8).

Fortunately, the portrait of Caesar which underlies the coin series of 44 BC is extant in several repetitions. The most faithful seems to be a portrait in Turin (figures 21.7, 21.8), found in the Forum of Tusculum as early as 1825, but only recognized as a portrait of Caesar by Maurizio Borda in 1940 (Borda 1943–4: 347–82; Johansen 1967: 34; ill.16; Johansen 1987: 28ff.). In general it agrees well with the best coinages of M. Mettius; to judge by the style, it could have been produced in the last years of Caesar. The surface, unfortunately, is heavily corroded. The bronze original which lies behind the Turin head (Tusculum type) is repeated in a total of six further replicas, which are of different dates and varying quality (see, most recently, Weiss, Osanna, & Schäfer 2004: 12). Two of these versions, one in Woburn Abbey (Angelicoussis 1992: 54 no. 22 [figure 21.9]) and the other in a private collection in Florence (Johansen 1967: 36 fig. 18), confirm all the significant features of the Turin head; the other copies present us with deliberate remodelings.

The artist to whom we are indebted for the original of the head in Turin was concerned, like the best portraitists of his time, to give a detailed reproduction of the physical appearance of the aging Dictator. We see a long neck with folds, an extremely projecting back to the head, a hollow and partly bald forehead, the sparse hair combed forward over it. In contrast with this portrait, the literary descriptions of Caesar's appearance, in Suetonius and other authors (Bernoulli 1882: 147–8) do not go beyond very general formulae. Caesar does seem to have been an extremely imposing figure. Even Cicero (*Brut.* 75) speaks appreciatively of his *forma magnifica*

Figure 21.7–8 Portrait of Caesar, Turin, Museo Archeologico. Photo Deutsches Archäologisches Institut, Rome.

Figure 21.9 Portrait of Caesar, Woburn Abbey. Forschungsarchiv für römische Plastik, Cologne.

et generosa. Velleius (2. 41) even thinks he was *forma omnium civium excellentissimus*. Elsewhere we hear of his lively black eyes, his full mouth, but most especially of his baldness, which he is said to have liked to conceal with a wreath. His normal manner was marked by a certain langor (Dio 43.43; Plut. *Caes.* 4).

"Psychological realism"?

The master who produced the Tusculum portrait was not only concerned to express Caesar's external appearance but also to capture something of his character in his expression. The almost imperceptible movement of the slightly lifted head, and the momentary contraction of the forehead and the mouth, tell of a watchful and superior presence. In the look of the eyes, slightly converging, one has the impression of discerning a certain aristocratic reserve or irony. The depiction of the highly individual expression brings out the superiority of the Turin head to the replica in Woburn Abbey, which is better preserved only in appearance: the surface of the face has undergone a fundamental modern scouring, in the course of which the special look of the eyes has been lost. While the posthumous portraits will not be treated here until later, the portrait of Caesar which was recently found on Pantelleria may be considered in brief here (Weiss, Osanna, & Schäfer 2004: 6), as it is possible to illustrate the peculiar expression of the Turin head by contrast (figure 21.10). To judge by the context of the discovery, the new find derives originally from a gallery of statues of the Julio-Claudian house, from the time of Claudius. Undoubtedly, the

Figure 21.10 Portrait of Caesar, Pantelleria. From Weiss, Osanna, & Schäfer 2004.

portrait rests on the same basic type as the Tusculum type; but here the features have been completely expunged and replaced by abstract, classicizing formulae, which lend the head an empty and masklike appearance.

The Tusculum-type portrait of Caesar belongs to a small group of very high-quality portraits, which have in common the wish to depict something of the individuality and character of the sitter, something transcending the realistic presentation of the physiognomy. Never before, and never again in the study of Roman portraits, do we come across psychological studies of comparable directness and penetration as in the first century BC. Such skill in portraiture presupposes the existence of a highly developed "realistic" style, not one smothered in emotional formulae, like most of the portraits in the directly Hellenistic tradition. An objective analysis and description of these studies in character is, of course, not possible; but comparison with some portraits from roughly the same time brings out more clearly what is unique to the particular portrait. I take my examples from the small group of portraits of which several copies are known. That means, in all probability, that the persons portrayed are men who have played a significant role in public life: that is to say, men active in politics.

Let us begin with the well-known later portrait of Pompeius, as it is represented by an excellently preserved head in Copenhagen (Megow 2005: ill. 29 [figure 21.11]). We are surprised at once, in contrast with the portraits of Caesar, by the almost

Figure 21.11 Portrait of Pompeius, Copenhagen, Ny Carlsberg Glyptotek. From Cat. Roman Portraits, Ny Carlsberg Glyptotek 1994, p. 25.

commonplace expression and the strained features. People have wanted to see the expression of a citizen among fellow citizens, which does not sit well with the allusion to Alexander in the hair springing up from the forehead (Giuliani 1986: *passim*). Chance will have it that we also recognize, in all probability, a portrait of M. Crassus, the third member of the First Triumvirate, extant in numerous versions (Megow 2005: ill. 34, 35 [figure 21.12]). It depicts the face, thin and bony, of a thoroughly prosaic man, his expression utterly dominated by hardness and the will to prevail. Again, a very different character is presented by a portrait, extant in two versions, in which people have attempted to see the orator Hortensius (Megow 2005: 42–3). It is arresting in its momentary look of attention, directed skeptically at an opponent. Further examples could be given, such as the traditional portrait of Cicero, unfortunately not well preserved, or the so-called pseudo-Cicero (Megow 2005: ill.57–9, 47–56). Again and again we see the same unvarying individual, with – each time – an unique expression. That changes fundamentally in the Augustan period, when even portraits of nobly born senators are made to resemble, in the dignified poise of the head and in their expression, the portraits of the Imperial family. A good example is the portrait, perhaps of Calpurnius Piso the Pontifex, which is preserved in an excellent bronze bust from

Figure 21.12 Portrait of M. Crassus, Paris Louvre. From a cast in the Museum für Abgüsse römischer Bildwerke, Munich.

Figure 21.13 Portrait of Calpurnius Piso Pontifex, Naples, Museo Archeologico Nazionale. Photo Deutsches Archäologisches Institut, Rome.

Herculaneum (Syme 1986: frontispiece; Vessberg, ill. 73; Fittschen & Zanker 1985: I, 21 A.7 [figure 21.13]).

One may well ask why, in the last phase of the Republic, there arose such accurate and perceptive studies, such penetrating presentations of the character of the sitters. And why did such a very different style of portraiture prevail under Augustus? Doubtless, there is a connection with the unprecedented culture of competition, which had developed in the late Republic and permeated every aspect of life. In the dominant class, especially, the desire was no longer merely to achieve and maintain power and influence, but to display it at every opportunity. At any rate, the portraits of this period show the desire in their subjects to appear as unique figures and unique personalities, with their own expressions and their own gestures, and to be recognized as such.

We have mentioned that portraits of Caesar were omnipresent, that statues of him stood in every town and in all the shrines (Dio 44.4; App. *B Civ.* 2.106). Most of them will have been made of bronze and have gone into the melting pot. That may explain why the number of surviving portraits is relatively small. But that Caesar's face was not only generally familiar but also found very attractive is proved by the phenomenon, so characteristic of the time, of the Period Face (Zeitgesicht). We observe it for the first time with Caesar. Many portraits from the period, which their style shows to have been created in the Caesarian period or immediately after it, are more or less reminiscent of the features of Caesar (Zanker 1981). Not a few were, until very recently, treated as authentic copies of portraits of Caesar. Among them are such celebrated heads as the Luxburg Caesar or that of Acireale (Boehringer 1933: ill. 44.1). Even the celebrated bust in Berlin, made of the hard green schist mined only in Egypt, represents, in all probability, not Caesar but one of his admirers from the Nile (Johansen 1987: 37 [figure 21.14]). If photographs of these pseudo-Caesars are compared with one another, it is easily seen that the portraits must be of different people; at any rate, they neither exhibit resemblances, in the sense of a fixed type, nor can they be arranged typologically. It is no less true that in the cut of the face, in the pronounced lines round the mouth, or in other details, they resemble, more or less, the authentic type of portrait of Caesar. Although Johansen (1967, 1987) exposed most of these pseudo-Caesars for what they are, there are constant attempts to discover new representations of Caesar. Interestingly, these portraits that resemble Caesar are often found on the grave reliefs of members of the Roman middle class and among the people of rank in Italian towns, not in those few portraits of aristocrats of which several copies are known. On gems and on ring-stones, too, we find portraits of Caesar and portraits which could resemble Caesar, but the attributions of

Figure 21.14 Portrait bust, Berlin, Staatliche Museen Antikensammlung. From Boehringer 1933.

M. L. Vollenweider are not without their problems, because the typological connections have not been demonstrated (Vollenweider 1974: 120–35, esp. ill. 75).

The phenomenon of a specific period of history being dominated by portraits of Caesar reflects the fascination exerted by Caesar as a historic figure. Later, one can see corresponding instances of the assimilation of particular, especially popular, emperors: above all, of Nero and Trajan (Zanker 1982). The fact that we can recognize, for the first time in the age of Caesar, what we may call an aesthetic focus on a leading figure of power is symptomatic of the way in which willingness to acknowledge a common model develops in the heart of a society, of the way in which psychological processes correspond to external political processes.

As Divus Iulius, Caesar becomes young and beautiful

When we speak of certainly identified types, we mean portraits which can be traced to a common model by means of unambiguous correspondences in detail (Boschung 1993b, with literature). Beside the Tusculum type, best represented by the head in Turin which we have discussed, there is another, more widespread type of Caesar portrait. This second type arose, very probably, only after Caesar's death; at any rate, it does not appear either on the coins minted in 44 BC or on those minted in the 30s. The tradition, consisting of a total of 11 copies, divides into two separate strands, the prototypes of which arose, probably, at some distance in time. It is rewarding to go through the complex material, as it permits some interesting historical consequences to be drawn (the matter is dealt with at greater length in Fittschen & Zanker forthcoming: II nos. 12, 13).

The original of the strand of the tradition that we call "Pisa" came into existence, probably, soon after the death of Caesar, in the late 40s or the early 30s. To reconstruct it, two substantially different portraits can be invoked. One is a head, completed as a bust, in the Pitti Palace in Florence (Boehringer 1933: ill. 22, 23; Johansen 1967: 29, ill.7; Johansen 1987: 22 ill.7); the other, an insertable head intended for a statue, is in the Museo dell'Opera del Duomo in Pisa (Faedo 1984: 133; Johansen 1967: 28, ill. 6; Johansen 1987: 22, ill. 6 [figure 21.15]). Unfortunately, both heads misrepresent the original on which they are based. A mistaken positioning on the base gives the head in the Pitti Palace a markedly sentimental character, not present in the original. In contrast to this, the Pisa head shows an energetic turn to the left and upwards; this is confirmed by two further replicas, in Turin and Leiden. It is true that the replica in Pisa also misrepresents the original, as the features of the face, having undergone profound alteration as a result of a reworking in modern times, have taken on a sharp, or even – thanks to the protruding eyes – fanatical expression, which is of interest only as an interpretation of the piece in modern times.

The original that is the basis for the copies of this first version represents a version of the Tusculum type (Turin portrait), which has been corrected both aesthetically and in expression. The most striking innovation is the lively and mobile locks of hair, which have replaced the bald forehead. The long hair on the neck, too, serves to make the likeness younger. On the other hand, the angular facial features

Figure 21.15 Portrait of Caesar, Pisa, Museo del Primaziale. Photo Deutsches Archäologisches Institut, Rome.

have been taken over, almost literally, from the Tusculum type – but without carrying over the expression. In place of the ironic and withdrawn expression, and the apparently chance movement of the head, there have come in an energetic movement of the head and an expression of determination. The rejuvenated image, which emphasizes energy and resolution, suits very well the situation after Caesar's death and deification (42 BC), when the memory of his person was being used by Octavian as a figurehead. In stylistic terms the portrait, with its realistic features – the long neck with wrinkles, the sunken features of the face – fits neatly into the tradition of late-Republican portraiture. The portraits of Octavian and Agrippa, from about or after 40 BC, offer a very good comparison (Boschung 1993a, ill. 1–14; Johansen 1971: 27; de Kersauson 1986: no. 22). In all these cases the classicizing marks, which will be so characteristic of the Augustan period, are still not present. The same goes for the majority of the reproductions which seem to have been produced in such numbers in the 30s or in the early Augustan period.

The second strand of the tradition, on the other hand, represents an unambiguously classicizing remodeling. Fortunately, we possess an excellent copy in the well-known portrait in the Vatican (Boehringer 1933: ill. 2, 25; Johansen

1967: 25, fig. 1; Johansen 1987: 17, ill.1, 2 [figure 21.16]), which is confirmed, in the main respects, by copies in Vienna and Parma (Johansen 1967: ill. 3, 4; Johansen 1987: 17, ill.1, 2). The hair on the forehead forms a solid row, as in the portraits of the princes Gaius and Lucius, and even of Tiberius; the curls and partings are now neatly arranged and give no impression of spontaneity. In the case of the hair on the neck, too, the long strands leading to the neck are shortened and arranged in classical order. The feature which does most, however, to produce the different effect of the whole is the regularizing of the proportions of the face. The sharp formulation of the protruding cheek bones and of the sunken cheeks, so prominent in the Pisa head, has given place to smooth transitions. Like the Prima Porta portrait (Zanker 1987: 105, ill. 83), the turn of the head aims at an impressive representation. The portrait in the Vatican, to judge by the characteristic way in which it is worked out, may have originated in the middle of the Augustan period, the period when the figure of Caesar was being allowed to emerge from the shadows, in the context of the Secular Games and of the presentation of the grandsons as Augustus' successors (see pp. 299–300 above). This rejuvenated and transfigured portrait would, at any rate, be in place in a portrait gallery of the Julio-Claudian house.

Figure 21.16 Portrait of Caesar, Musei Vaticani. Photo Deutsches Archäologisches Institut, Rome.

Caesar's portrait becomes a timeless monument

Despite this renewal of the portrait of Caesar in the style of the court portraits of the Julio-Claudians, it is probable that statues of Caesar were not often erected. Most portraits of Caesar are dated by their style to no later than the Augustan period. The lack of interest in statues of Caesar is clear from the fact that, with few exceptions, they are absent from the numerous statue groups of the Julio-Claudian period. To the three examples named by Rose and Boschung we can add the new replica of the Tusculum type, which was discovered recently on the remote island of Pantelleria, together with portraits of Antonia Minor and of Titus (Weiss, Osanna, & Schäfer 2004). As already remarked, this portrait, created in the time of Caligula or Claudius, has lost all the lively features which speak to us so vividly in the Turin head (above, p. 303).

The preservation of works in marble may be a matter of chance, but this striking absence of Caesar from the groups of statues, which in other respects have come down to us in such numbers, confirms that his memory, despite his deification, was but little cultivated in the period of the Julio-Claudian dynasty. The same seems to be true of the Flavian period. The absence of archaeological evidence is confirmed by a critical survey of the literary texts, which consistently maintain a rather distant attitude towards Caesar, and which do not conceal the ambiguity of his political image (Donié 1996: *passim*). Doubtless, it was the ideology of the Principate, and the mighty shadow of Augustus, that drove the figure of Caesar into the background. That did not change until Trajan. Admittedly, we are confronted here, not so much by the Divus Iulius and the *Dictator perpetuus*, as by the great general and the great conqueror. Trajan, renewing his policy of conquest, seems to have seen a model in him. That is connected particularly, in all probability, with Caesar's plans for his last expeditions: those against the Dacians in the north and the Parthians in the east. Those were the identical opponents which Trajan had singled out for conquest and definitive subjection. At the same time, we have evidence in Arrian, Plutarch, and Suetonius of a new interest in Caesar's biography. Suetonius goes so far as to present him as the first Princeps (Donié 1996: 158–230). Caesar appears on the restoration coins of Trajan, but it is disputed what this allusion to him was supposed to mean (Mattingly III: 142, nos. 696–8 pl. 23, 17–19; see Levick, chapter 15 in this volume, p. 218).

It is probably no accident that two portraits of Caesar from the Trajanic period, greater than life-size, have been found in Rome. That of him in armor, more than three meters in height (the arms and legs are restorations, the head original), has been known since 1550 AD; today, it stands – by the will of Mussolini – in the Chamber of the Parliament of the city of Rome, in the Palazzo Senatorio on the Capitol (Stemmer 1978: 74, ill. 48,1; Kreikenbom 1992: 154–5; Boehringer 1933: ill. 27–9; Cadario 2006: 35 [figure 21.17]). Its style corresponds extensively with a torso of Trajan found in Trajan's Forum; that allows us to infer a date about 110 AD. Perhaps the statue of Caesar, too, was set up in the Forum of Trajan. The portrait is based on the Tusculum type, but what we have is not a copy but a free

Figure 21.17 Statue of Caesar, Rome Palazzo Senatorio. Photo Deutsches Archäologisches Institut, Rome.

interpretation, in the style of the later portraits of Trajan. The hair on the forehead is arranged in neat rows, turning the baldness into a lofty brow. The face, ageless, reminds us by the style of its cutting of the Turin head; but it lacks an unambiguous expression.

More impressive in its effect is the second Trajanic portrait, coming from the Farnese collection (Boehringer 1933: ill. 30–1; Johansen 1987: fig. 20; Kreikenbom 1992: 56–9, 151–4 [figure 21.18]). The sculptor has been guided here rather more by the physiognomy of the Tusculum type, while at the same time the proportions and the details have been largely translated into the style of the time of Trajan. The sharply angled strands of hair, which give a metallic effect, are no less characteristic of formulas used by the Trajanic sculptors than the eyelids and the brows. Only the area round the mouth, and the folds of the nose, are still reminiscent of the physiognomy of Caesar. The decided turn of the head, together with the expression of the face, expresses sovereign command. From the lively first sketch, which the portrait in Turin permits us to imagine, there has come to birth a timeless image of a ruler, fixed in its representational stance.

Figure 21.18 Portrait of Caesar, Naples, Museo Archeologico Nazionale. Photo Deutsches Archäologisches Institut, Rome.

There is in the history of Roman portraiture no other figure whose likeness continued so constantly, over such a period of time, to be corrected and to be generally subject to such a profound process of change.

FURTHER READING

The possible ways of using images in politics are set out by P. Zanker in *The Power of Images in the Age of Augustus* (1988). Most studies of Roman portraiture are written for specialists. A solid introduction to the problems of research on portraits is offered by P. Stewart in *Roman Art* (2004). L. Giuliani's fundamental posing of the question and his original interpretations mark out his book *Bildnis und Botschaft. Hermeneutische Untersuchungen zur Bildniskunst der römischen Republik* [Portrait and message: hermeneutic investigations on the art of portraiture in the Roman Republic] (Frankfurt, 1986), unfortunately not translated into English. The second portrait of Pompey is a major focus of attention in the book.

The honorific statues of Caesar recorded in the literary tradition have been treated at length by M. Cadario, "Le statue di Cesare a Roma tra il 46 e il 44 a. C." (2006). Still highly suggestive are the relevant sections in Stefan Weinstock's famous work *Divus Julius* (1971).

The most recent comprehensive study devoted to the surviving portraits of Caesar is by F. S. Johanson (1987). His results are, in the most important respects, still valid today. Most of the portraits are reproduced in this study. Though out of date in scholarly terms, Erich Boehringer's *Der Caesar von Acireale* (Stuttgart, 1933) is still useful because of its numerous illustrations.

NOTE

1 Cassius Dio 51.22.3, contradicting Appian, names Augustus as the proposer of the statue; in connection with his triumph over Egypt, however, that makes little sense.

PART V

Caesar's Place in History

CHAPTER TWENTY-TWO

The Middle Ages

Almut Suerbaum

Introduction

As an author, Caesar has left few traces in medieval culture, although his œuvre was transcribed and transmitted in monasteries from the ninth century onwards. Yet as a person, he was widely known across medieval Europe, and he figures as an exemplary ruler and military leader in a wide range of texts from different genres and social contexts. He plays an important role in both Latin and vernacular discourse – it needs to be remembered that unlike classical civilization, medieval culture is inherently bilingual, using Latin as the medium of learned discourse, but simultaneously developing the vernacular language as a means of mediating and transmitting learned culture to lay people at the aristocratic courts. This interplay between the spheres of Latin and the vernacular is complex, and within the confines of this short survey the focus will be on German material, because it may serve as an example to illustrate tendencies which are observable, with variations, in the other vernaculars as well.

Concepts of Authorship: Manuscript Transmission and Commentary Tradition

There are more than two hundred extant manuscripts of the *commentarii*, yet it has been suggested (Brunhölzl 1983: 1353) that all of these can be traced back directly or indirectly to a single copy transcribed from papyrus to parchment. This derivation from a single manuscript suggests that Caesar's œuvre as a writer was not widely known in the Middle Ages, and this is confirmed by the fact that he does not feature in the elementary reading programs of the cathedral schools, where Statius and Theodul as well as Avianus convey a first acquaintance with Latin language and literature, or indeed in the reading canon for the *trivium*, the introduction to grammar, rhetoric, and dialectics as the first three of the seven liberal arts (Minnis 1988: 9–33). The events of the war in Gaul appear to have been familiar mostly through Lucan rather than Caesar himself, and even where the *commentarii* were known, they were often attributed to different authors: Orosius (fifth century) believed them to be the work of Suetonius, and Petrarch followed medieval commentary practice in attributing them to the grammarian Iulius Celsus Constantinus. Thus, the adaptor of the thirteenth-century *Faits des Romains*, for whom Caesar plays a prominent role in his account of Roman history from Caesar to Domitian, clearly had access to Caesar's *De bello Gallico*, yet he not only uses this alongside Lucan, Suetonius, and Sallust, but also attributes the majority of such passages to "Julien" or "Juliens," which in his context means Julius Celsus, the grammarian (Beer 1976: 29–30).

The transmission of Lucan provides an interesting insight into medieval notions of Caesar's significance. Like many works read as part of an elementary introduction to Latin language and literature, medieval copies of Lucan are often accompanied by commentaries, and it is the opening section of these medieval commentaries which is most important in this context. The *accessus*, an introduction guiding the student, usually offers a summary of the subject matter dealt with in the book and follows this with brief information about the author, his intention in writing the book, and an indication of where in the curriculum the study of a particular book might be most appropriate (grammar, or ethics). These *accessus ad auctores* are sometimes transmitted independently of the text and become brief handbooks of literary information and literary theory (Suerbaum 2000: 393–404). Characteristically, there appears to be no *accessus* to Caesar, since his *commentarii* were not part of the normal canon of reading, either at elementary level or within the curriculum for the *trivium*. Instead, students appear to have read Lucan's account, and as a result, much of what we might expect in a commentary on Caesar's work can in fact be gleaned from the commentaries to Lucan, since the *accessus* to Lucan not only gives us details about Lucan the author, but offers us insight into his subject matter and therefore serves as a compendium of those aspects of Caesar's biography most significant to medieval students and readers.

The *accessus* in its most common form (Huygens 1970: 39–40) sets out the major stages of Caesar's political career: consulship, alliance with Pompeius and Crassus, wars in Gaul, success in Germany – at which stage he is ordered back to Rome:

> Hac gemina elatus victoria imperare simul toti Germaniae parat cum Gallia, et quia Romani suis viribus diffidebant Parthosque timebant, Cesarem ut rediret iusserunt. Is vero, quia nihil memoria dignum gesserat, aliud quinquennium usurpavit victisque omnibus Gallis triumphum sibi a Romanis expostulat. Quo negato, conlectis undique presidiis quae in urbibus posuerat, armata manu patriam hostiliter invasit.
>
> Elated by this double victory he prepared to rule over all of Germany and Gaul, and because the Romans mistrusted their own strength and feared the Parthians, they ordered Caesar's return. He, however, since he had done nothing memorable, usurped another quinquennial period of office and, having defeated all of Gaul, demanded a triumph from the Romans. When this was denied, he collected the garrisons he had placed in the cities and attacked his country with force as an enemy.

The view of Caesar portrayed here is ambivalent: what the introductory remarks highlight is his wisdom (*sapientia*), yet his exploits as politician and general are described as ruthless and oppressive.

Conrad of Hirsau, drawing on the anonymous *accessus* to Lucan, retains this line in his didactic dialogue between master and pupil on the most important school authors:

> Describit igitur bellum quod erat inter Cesarem et Pompeium nobilissimum ducem Romanorum. (*Dialogus super auctores*, 1205–7)
>
> He [Lucan] describes the war between Caesar and Pompeius, the noble leader of the Romans.

When the pupil confesses to not knowing the subject matter of Lucan's book, he is chided: *Si nosti civilis belli historiam, libri huius habes materiam* (1223; If you know the history of the civil war, you know the subject matter of this book) and reminded that the war is called *bellum plus quam civile* (more than a civil war), because it set brother against brother, father against son, inciting the Roman people to bloody warfare. The ultimate cause of this war, according to the master's summary, was Caesar's unwillingness to tolerate anyone as his equal: *Maxima vera causa belli huius erat, quod Cesar nullum habere voluit equalem* (1242; The most important cause of this war was that Caesar refused to have anyone as his equal). Although Pompeius is accused of the same desire for power, this episode leaves a rather ambivalent picture of Caesar as usurping rulership on his own.

Within the *accessus* tradition, Caesar's life is therefore firmly the subject matter of another author's writing; Caesar's own literary work is not even mentioned or alluded to. Where Caesar does feature as an author, it is conversely in an apocryphal attribution: Boethius in his treatise *De geometria*, an introduction to geometry as one of the four liberal arts forming the *quadrivium*, the second cycle for advanced students, refers to Caesar as the author of a letter setting out the principles of geometry:

> Nunc ad epistolam Julii Caesaris veniamus, quod ad huius artis originem pertinet, ut nec ipsius auctoris [1354] gloria pereat, ut nobis plenissime rei veritas ad notitiam veniat; quisquis ille tamen hanc epistolam studiose legere voluerit quibusdam compendiis introductus, lucidius majorum dicta in brevi percipiet. (*De geometria*, PL 63, 1353–4)
>
> Now we reach Julius Caesar's letter, which is relevant to the origins of this art [i.e. geometry], so that the fame of this author may never perish, and so that we gain knowledge of the true nature of this matter; whoever has been willing to read this letter carefully, guided by certain summaries, will grasp the sayings of the great more clearly in summary.

The reason for claiming Caesar as an expert in geometry, especially trigonometry, appears to lie not so much in his writing, but in an aspect of his life that will become familiar to us in the vernacular historiographical narratives: Caesar, it seems, knew all about surveying terrain and towns in his capacity as a founder of cities:

> Divus Julius Caesar, vir acerrimus et multarum gentium dominator, frequentia belli militem exercuit, ... et postquam hostilem terram obtinuit, denuo novas urbes constituit, dato iterum coloniae nomine cives ampliavit.

> Milites colonos fecit, alios in Italia, alios in provinciis quibusdam. ... non solum eas civitates demum cingere muris, verum etiam loca aspera et confragosa satis alligari ... et ab agrorum nova dedicatione culturae colonias appellavit. (*De geometria* 1354)
>
> Julius Caesar, a hard man and the conqueror of many peoples, kept the soldiers in training by frequent wars, ... once he had conquered a region, he founded new cities and enlarged the settlements having given them the title "colonia." He turned soldiers into peasants, some in Italy, some in various provinces. ... He not only ordered the defeated cities to be surrounded by walls, but also caused inaccessible and uneven places to be leveled. ... Because of their use for agriculture, these places were named "colonia."

Medieval Historiography: Caesar the Politician and General

While Caesar as an author of literary works may not have been a known quantity for medieval writers and readers, Caesar the politician and general was very much a concept for them. The *accessus* to Lucan appears to have been one of the most influential sources of information on the life of Caesar, although assessment of his qualities and shortcomings differs markedly, depending on the political and social context of the individual historiographer.

Otto, bishop of Freising, appears to rely on material from such *accessus* as well as the histories of Orosius in his *Chronica sive historia de duabus civitatibus* (Chronicle of Two Cities, c. 1143–6). Caesar's life forms the concluding section of Otto's second book, marking the transition from the pagan to the Christian world. Orosius and Frutolf of Michelsberg are clearly important sources for Otto, yet the fact that he includes a reference to Caesar's five years of absence as the reason for the hostile reception received in Rome points to the use of other sources as well, since neither Orosius nor Frutolf mentions this detail:

> Porro cum in dominandis eiusmodi gentibus ultra statutum terminum, id est quinquennium, moram faceret Iulius, Romam revertenti a senatu consilio Pompeio et auctoritate consulis Marcelli debitus ei triumphus ac denuo consulatus negatur. (2.48)
>
> Furthermore, when Julius tarried beyond the appointed period, namely five years, in reducing these tribes to subjection, upon his return to Rome the triumph and the second consulship that were his due were refused him by the senate, through the advice of Pompey and the influence of Marcellus, then consul. (trans. Charles C. Mierow, p. 212)

The most likely source for such knowledge is the *accessus* to Lucan, but it is possible that Otto also drew on vernacular traditions, since this detail is found in two near-contemporary chronicles using the German language, the *Annolied* and the *Kaiserchronik*. Dependence on vernacular traditions suggests both that medieval commentaries such as the *accessus* may play an important role in transmitting cultural knowledge, and that there are quite clearly regional modes of reception.

For Otto of Freising, Caesar's political triumph and the resulting civil war are an occasion to reflect on the vicissitudes of human rule in general. Oscillating between domination over other nations and subjugation when they in turn rise, human life to Otto seems ever unstable, like the sea. Rome, which at the death of Caesar is torn apart by civil war, therefore marks the fitting point of transition at which Otto now harmonizes secular world history (the history of the world as the one city) with Christian history (the second city, the city of God): Caesar's death, which concludes the first part of Otto's work, heralds the birth of Christ and with it, a new era.

Honorius Augustodunensis, the German-born author who probably spent most of his career at French cathedrals, is another example of the ways in which knowledge about the ancient world is fitted into a framework which suited contemporary Christian society. In his encyclopedic *Imago Mundi*, world history is divided into six ages. The fifth of these is characterized by the transitions between the four great empires: from Babylon to Alexander the Great to Assyria and finally to Rome. Here, Caesar marks the end of the republic:

> Julius Caesar dictator et consul Galliam vicit. Pompeium consulem cum omni populo Orientis devicit. Hic primus monarchus quinque annos regnavit.
> Hic bissextum imo cyclum magnum composuit.
> Hic a senatu occiditur.
> Ab hoc Caesares sunt dicti. (*Imago mundi*, PL 172, 155)

> Julius Caesar, dictator and consul, defeated Gaul. He achieved complete victory over Pompeius the consul and the people of the East. He ruled for five years as the first single ruler. He composed the great twelve-month cycle [of his calendar]. He was killed by the senate.
> The title for emperors is derived from his name.

Vernacular Literature

Simultaneously with the Latin chronicles discussed in the previous section, Caesar becomes a feature in vernacular texts which, from different perspectives, address the historical transition from Roman past to the present day of the writers. Examples of this can be found in almost all Western European literatures, so that, here, examples from a few need to be seen as representative of more general trends. Across Europe, four different strands of reception are discernible, though it would be necessary to study in more detail how these are interrelated.

Chronicle: Caesar the exemplary ruler

German writers in the eleventh and twelfth centuries experiment with transposing Latin historiographical traditions into the vernacular. Perhaps the earliest example of this is the eleventh-century *Annolied* (c. 1080), a life of Anno, archbishop of Cologne, composed shortly after his death, probably as part of a campaign to speed his canonization. It draws on Lucan's *De bello civili*, or perhaps a Lucan *accessus*, for an outline of Caesar's life and represents him as a successful ruler whose name gave rise to the new term *keisere* (emperor) for kings. His success in battle is as much the result of political skill as of military force: the defeated tribes accept his rule by treaty. Caesar is seen as a force of civilization: he not only provides a new term for and model of rulership, but civilizes Germania by founding cities, and by introducing the Germans to the polite mode of address introduced in Rome in his honor:

Rômere, dů sin infinngin,
einin nûwin sidde aneviengin:
si begondin igizin den heirrin.
Daz vundin simi cêrin,
wanter eini dů habite alliu gewalt,
der é gideilit was in manigvalt.
Den sidde hîz er dů cêrin
diutschi liuti lêrin.
(*Annolied* 28.5–12)

When the Romans welcomed him, they started a new custom of addressing their lord in the polite plural form. They did this in Caesar's honor, for he alone now held all power which had previously been shared between many different hands. As a form of honor, he taught the Germans this custom as well.

In this way, Caesar the bringer of civilization and founder of German cities can provide a historical type for Anno, the bishop and architect of Cologne. For almost a third of the poem, therefore, Caesar takes center stage – he is the precursor, pointing backwards in a link to Alexander, mirroring his achievements yet transposing them onto territory which, unlike exotic India at the very margins of the known world, relates directly to the present of the eleventh-century readership, while at the same time referring forwards to Anno, whose achievements will not only emulate him but indeed surpass him. For this reason, the central section of the poem has been referred to as a "lay of Caesar" (*Caesarlied*; cf. Herweg 2002: 282), although to use that term would obscure the literary strategy behind the overt praise of Caesar: ultimately, he is not a figure of interest in his own right, but a means of conveying glory and authority to Anno by means of the established analogy with Caesar's qualities as ruler and architect.

The poet's view of Caesar has been the source of controversy in interpretations of the *Annolied*. Unlike other chroniclers who simply present Caesar as the first emperor, the poet is clearly aware of the republican past; his Caesar is first dispatched on his missions in Germany at the request of the senate (*Annolied* 18.1–9). The episode has a bearing on the author's position in the most important of political debates of the eleventh century, the relationship between emperor and pope. Some critics take it to suggest that the author aligns himself with the anti-imperial camp (Thurlow 1980), others have read it as evidence for the fact that Caesar triumphs against unreasonable opposition, hence foreshadowing the claims of the emperor (Thomas 1991). Convincing evidence from the text for either of these extremes is difficult to sustain (Herweg 2002), and it may be that the episode highlights the literary skill of the anonymous author in dealing with a problematic protagonist. Not unlike Caesar, bishop Anno clearly evoked mixed feelings: a local politician disliked for his ruthlessness – and yet a contender for sainthood, whose cause the author supports through carefully constructed historical analogy.

Where the *Annolied* uses world history as a frame for very specific local events, the twelfth-century *Kaiserchronik*, which draws on the *Annolied* as one of its sources, aims at providing universal history, and the thread running through world history is provided by recounting the lives of the emperors and rulers from the foundation of Rome to the present day of the German chronicler. The first seven hundred years of Roman history here receive short shrift, and the narrative moves swiftly, within a hundred lines, from Romulus and Remus to Caesar, who is presented as the first Roman ruler of note. The reason for this becomes apparent if we consider the underlying ordering principle of the *Kaiserchronik*: it is not so much an encyclopedic history of the world as a narrative of events leading up to the establishment of the Holy Roman Empire which unites the role of Roman emperor with that of the German king.

Caesar's first mission in the narrative of the *Kaiserchronik* is therefore the conquest of Germania. When a miraculous set of bells, which announce war in any of the dependent territories, begins to sound in Rome, Julius Caesar (Julius in the nomenclature of the German text) is dispatched to quell the uprising with 30,000 soldiers. The narrator sees him as *den helt jungen* (the young hero; *KChr* 252) and praises his justice: *vil sciere was er gerecht* (he was just through and through; *KChr* 268). Caesar in turn attacks and defeats the Swabians, Bavarians, Saxons, and finally the Franconians whom the narrator portrays as "sine alten mâgen" (his relatives of old; *KChr* 344), because like him they are descended from the Trojans. In subduing the Franconians, Caesar founds a series of cities along the Rhine – Deutz, Andernach, Ingelhaim, Mainz, Oppenheim – and builds a bridge across it at Mainz. Finally, after a siege of four years he conquers Trier. Here, he displays not just his bravery, but also his nobility by sparing the nobles of Trier, handing them back their castle as a fief, and rewarding both the brave in battle and the poor people with largesse. He stays in Trier until all German lords recognize him as their overlord (*unz im alle Dûtiske hêrren / willic wâren ze sînen êren*; *KChr* 453–4) His success, however, is a cause of envy back at home: on his eventual return to Rome, he is criticized for having lost part of his army, and for having stayed away from Rome for too long without leave (*ân ir urloup*; *KChr* 460) – this latter a central concern of twelfth-century knighthood, which is based around a concept of mutual and reciprocal responsibility between lord and vassals, or between ruler and people. His German allies, to whom he conveys news of this treatment, rally to his support and travel to Rome with a large army, which terrifies the Romans:

> do Juljus mit Tûtiscer riterscephte sô hérlichen chom
> und si sâhen scînen
> die braiten scar sîne,
> fan unte borten;
> ir lîbes si harte vorhten. (*KChr* 480–4)

When Caesar arrived there with the German knights in such splendor, and when they saw the huge crowd and its banners and flags, they were afraid for their lives.

Caesar's return to Rome in triumph is the occasion for the narrator to insert a long excursus: he interprets Caesar as the incarnation of the wild boar, the third beast of the apocalyptic vision seen by King Nebuchadnezzar in the book of Daniel.

Daz dritte ein fraislich eber was
den tiurlichen Juljum bezaichenet daz.
Der selbe eber zehen horn truoc,
dâ mite er sîne vîande alle nider slouc.
Juljus bedwanch elliu lant,
di dienten elliu sîner hant.
Wol bezaichenet uns daz wilde swîn
daz daz rîche ze Rôme sol iemer frî sîn.
(*KChr* 571–8)

The third beast was a terrifying wild boar, who signifies the excellent Julius Caesar. That same wild boar had ten horns, with which it felled all its enemies. Julius Caesar conquered all countries; they all served under him. Thus the wild boar signifies to us that the Roman Empire shall always be free.

Thus Caesar becomes not just the first in a series of Roman rulers, but the embodiment of Roman rule par excellence, extending the events of a historical and distant period into the present of twelfth-century readers, who would have seen themselves as still living in the third, namely Roman, empire. As a result, the further events of Caesar's life are relegated to the background: two couplets scantily summarize that he ruled for another five years, was killed by Romans in an act of disloyalty (*ungetrûwecl̂iche*), and buried near a column (*irminsûl*). It is in these details that the difference of focus between the Latin and the vernacular chronicles becomes most apparent even where they probably depend on common sources: for Otto of Freising's Latin chronicle, the death of Caesar still explicitly marks the closing phase of the Roman republic. In the vernacular narratives, this detail of Roman political history has been obliterated in an attempt to stress the analogies between the narrated story of Caesar and the experience of the twelfth-century readers, and Caesar himself is therefore presented as that which his name came to signify: an emperor.

While the treatment of the *Kaiserchronik* reveals knowledge of the events of Caesar's life as contained in Isidore or the *accessus* tradition, the focus of the vernacular narrative is German, not Roman, history: Caesar is transformed into the archetype of an ideal contemporary ruler, and use of Daniel's vision stresses the continuity between Roman and contemporary history while simultaneously stressing the inherently positive nature of Caesar's powerful rule. Thus, Roman secular history can be assigned a place in the history of salvation, fulfilling Old Testament prophecy about the transition of empire from one kingdom to the next until the end of the world in the coming of the Antichrist. Caesar the despot of the *accessus* has here been transformed into Caesar the model ruler, who embodies the ideal of twelfth-century kingship in combining physical bravery with respect for his opponents' honor (*êre*), liberality of gifts (*milte*), and the ability to forge alliances as a feudal lord.

Later versions, for example Jans Enikel's Viennese *Weltchronik* (late thirteenth century), largely abandon the framework of universal world history and instead emphasize the exotic, often conflating the story of Caesar with elements otherwise associated with the figure of Alexander the Great. Jans Enikel embellishes Caesar's conquests with accounts of his travels to the end of the earth, where he encounters creatures such as the One-eyed or Flatfooted Creatures, and Cyclopes, and drives them into exile in India.

> Zuo den kam her Julius
> und betwanc die liut sus
> daz si im muosten entwichen
> vil gar lesterlîchen.
> zwâr die mit den breiten füezen
> von im fliehen müezen
> und die einougen liut,
> die fluhen sam si üz der hiut
> her Julius wolt scheiden.
> si wârn waerlîch heiden.
> er jagt die selben liut dâ
> in daz verr Indiâ.
> (Enikel, *Weltchronik* 21135–21146)

Julius Caesar reached these people and defeated them, so that to their shame they had to flee. It is quite true: those with the flat feet and the one-eyed people fled as if Caesar were about to cut them out of their skins. They were heathens. He drove these people into faraway India.

These marvels at the margins of the world are otherwise known from the "Prester John" tradition, where such creatures are associated with India. It is unclear whether Jans Enikel based his excursus on one of the existing versions of Prester John's journey, or whether stories of these creatures were part of general oral knowledge. They underline, however, that for Enikel, Caesar is no longer associated with the ordering of world history according to the four kingdoms of Daniel's prophecy, but serves instead as a representative of aristocratic dominance who rather anachronistically expels Plato, Rigidus, and Pompeius from Rome in much the same way as he had driven the mythical creatures to India. What he achieves is not so much civilization, as in the *Annolied*, or world order, as in the *Kaiserchronik*, but forceful rule. This is highlighted by what appears to be an invented addition to Caesar's catalogue of achievements: Enikel makes him responsible for the legal custom according to which any man born in Germany, whether knight or servant, cannot be judged according to books (i.e. Roman law). All three texts exemplify the appropriation of a historical figure as justification for specific regional customs and ideals of civilization.

Romance: Caesar and King Arthur

As the German examples of the preceding section have demonstrated, local differences influence the reception of classical material and result in quite different images of Caesar. Britain is another interesting example of such localized appropriation. The term "Britain" here refers to a territory which spans modern northern France as well as the British Isles, an area where the predominant language, apart from Latin, is Norman French, despite the fact that Anglo-Saxon culture and its literary language retain a certain presence, revived by such authors as Lazamon in the thirteenth century. As with the German reception, the inherently bilingual nature of medieval culture is apparent, and the point of departure for Anglo-Norman courtly romance is again Latin historiography. Caesar's invasion of Britain and his defeat of Cassivellaunus is recounted at length in Orosius (hist. VI, cap. VIII–IX; PL 31, c.1011–15), and although neither Otto of Freising nor Honorius Augustodunenis makes any use of these sections except where they concern the province of Germania, they form the basis for Anglo-Norman chronicles. In Geoffrey of Monmouth's *Historia Regum Britanniae* (c. 1138), Caesar features as the Roman antagonist of Cassivellaunus, king of the Britons, and it is this chronicle, with its focus on British history, which becomes the source for a series of Anglo-Norman adaptations.

In composing his *Roman de Brut* (c. 1155) "for a Norman public which had a strong interest in the history and legends of their adopted country" (Weiss in Wace 1999: xiii), the Anglo-Norman poet Wace draws extensively on Geoffrey of Monmouth. Unlike the earlier German chronicles, the focus of interest is the local rulers, so that Rome itself no longer even features as a location. Also, the historical framework of the earlier chronicles is largely abandoned in favor of locations which still evoke historical resonances but do not use chronology as their organizing principle. Nevertheless, the Roman invasion of the British Isles is retained, and Caesar serves an important function for the presentation of the narrative: his successful invasion of Britain is presented as the result of his superior force, but is possible ultimately only because of divisions amongst the Britons.

Wace recounts Caesar's journey across France and Germany, where he is reputed to have founded many castles and cities (3853–4), but the focus of his narrative is Caesar's journey to Britain. Caesar first encounters it from across the sea, and when he asks about its name, he is told that the island is named after its first ruler, Brutus, who brought the Trojans there to settle. Caesar claims kinship and common descent with Brutus, but also asserts his own dominance. As a representative of Rome, which had in the past been besieged and sacked by the descendants of Brutus but has now regained its strength, he demands tribute from Cassivellaunus, the leader of the Britons, yet offers to negotiate peacefully about this by letter rather than by crossing the sea (3861–3894).

Such letter-diplomacy, not surprisingly, does not meet with the approval of Cassivellaunus, who accuses Rome in general, and Caesar, in particular, of greed and arrogance:

Si savies huem, so gentil sire
Come tu es, com osas dire
Que nus deion sers devenir
Ki n'avom apris a servir
Ne ja, so Deu plais n'aprendrum,
Ço saces tu, que nus puissom?

> How dare you say, a wise man, a noble lord like you, that we should become slaves, when we have not learned to serve, nor ever will learn, God willing. Do you think we could? (trans. Weiss)

This letter, challenging Caesar to fight, is reported verbatim in the text, and its emotionally charged rhetoric stands in stark contrast to the panegyric of Caesar with which the narrator had introduced the section. Wace's narrator differs quite markedly in his assessment of Caesar from that of the figures within the narrative: where Cassivellaunus berates Caesar's request for surrender and payment of tribute as evidence of Roman arrogance, the narrator goes out of his way to stress Caesar's qualities:

Julius Cesar li vaillanz,
Li forz, li pruz, le conquerantz,
Ki tant fist et tant faire pout,
Ki tut le mund conquist e out.

> Julius Caesar the noble, the strong, the brave, the conqueror who did, and could do, so much and who conquered and possessed the whole world. (trans. Weiss)

Yet even the letter by Cassivellaunus, for all that it suggests a contrast between free Britain and tyrannical Rome, does not attack Caesar personally; indeed, the force of the rhetorical appeal to him relies on the assumption that, as a wise man, he ought to have known better than to treat the Britons as slaves.

The function of such idealization becomes clearer as the narrative progresses: Caesar sees the futility of further diplomatic efforts and proceeds to invade Britain. The two armies confront each other, yet at the heart of Wace's description lies the detailed account of single combat between Caesar and Nennius, the younger brother of King Cassivellaunus, in which Caesar defeats Nennius and throws him to the ground. Despite this, Caesar fails to extract his sword from Nennius' shield and has to flee when supporters for Nennius arrive, leaving behind his sword called "Crocea Mors" (Yellow Death). This motif of the named and revered sword, taken away by the opponent as a trophy and buried with Nennius when he dies of his wounds shortly after the battle, bears all the hallmarks of the contemporary "chanson de geste" tradition, in which the swords of the great heroes Charlemagne, Roland, and King Arthur have distinctive names and are a metonymical extension of their carriers' prowess. Yet in this case, for all Caesar's strength in overpowering Nennius, the loss of his sword also becomes the symbol of general weakness, since the Romans are forced to flee from Britain, which in turn causes the French to rebel against Roman rule:

Mult haeient lur seinurie
E cremeient lur felonie. (4158–9)

They hated their domination and feared their cruelty. (trans. Weiss)

Such rebellion is short-lived, however, since

Caesar sout bien felun danter
E orguillus amesurer,
Bien sout coveitus apaier
E suntalent faire changier
E bien se sout humilier
La u force nen out mestier. (4163–70)

Caesar was good at taming malefactors and keeping the arrogant in check; he knew how to satisfy the greedy and make them change their mind and he knew how to lower his sights when force was unnecessary. (trans. Weiss)

Another attempt at invasion is equally unsuccessful, and Caesar again retreats to Gaul, defeated by the ferocity of Cassivellaunus and his allies. Whereas the description of the lighthouse built in France appears to be medieval invention, the details of Cassivellaunus' defences here at first sight bear a resemblance to *De bello Gallico* (5.18), in that Wace expands on Geoffrey's description of the Thames being planted *palis ferreis atque plumbatis et ad modum humani grossis subter amnem* (with stakes shod with iron and lead and as thick as a man's thigh below the surface). On closer inspection, though, it is probable that Geoffrey of Monmouth added this episode not with any direct knowledge of Caesar's text but from Bede's *Historia ecclesiastica* (1.2). Wace retains the description and elaborates on the scene, but ultimately, his narrative is more interested in political detail than military strategy, and his aim is to demonstrate how this second British victory is itself the cause of their final defeat: during the celebrations, a quarrel breaks out in which one of the Britons is killed, causing dissent between Cassivellaunus and his nephew Androgeus. Outraged at his uncle's hubris in usurping jurisdiction, Androgeus appeals to Caesar and offers his support for the Roman cause. Caesar duly defeats Cassivellaunus and leaves Britain in the hands of Androgeus and his heirs, having received symbolic tribute from him.

The narrator depicts Caesar as a perfect ruler who embodies many of the traits which tyrannical rulers like Cassivellaunus lack. Wace considerably extends the panegyric found in Geoffrey of Monmouth, turning Caesar from a successful general into the embodiment of contemporary ideals of rulership:

Cesar fu de Rome emperere,
Savies huem fu e bon donere,
lettrez fu, de grant clergie. (3839–41)

Caesar was emperor of Rome, a wise man and a generous giver; he was renowned for great chivalry and he was educated and very learned. (trans. Weiss)

Nevertheless, the narrative focus has shifted appreciably, so that the Roman victory is no longer the result of Caesar's superior and unquestioned political skills, but rather the outcome of a divided opposition, hence serving as a warning example against the political infighting that is so much part of the story of Wace's sequence of British rulers from Brut to King Arthur.

When Wace's Anglo-Norman chronicle in turn became the source of a Middle English adaptation, Lazamon's *Brut* (c. 1200), the shift in focus is immediately obvious in the poetic form of the work, because Lazamon uses an alliterative long line with sporadic internal rhyme, which appears to point to familiarity with, or at least some knowledge of, both the Old English or Celtic heroic traditions, and Latin epic forms, whether twelfth-century or classical. Lazamon's narrator is very prominent, often commenting on the story he is telling and on its protagonists. His presentation of Caesar is notable for its ambivalence from the start: Caesar is a formidable opponent to the British (*þe feond wes iwraððed* 3589), he is wise and very shrewd (*he wes wis and swiðe iwar* 3619), extricating the Romans after their second defeat by cunning in pretending to set up camp and thus allowing them to withdraw secretly to their boats during the night (3969–88). Yet the narrator also laments that he will have to go to hell despite his accomplishments (*wale þat eæuere ei sucche mon into helle sculde gan!* 3601). Lazamon's reservations here are concerned not with issues of Roman history, such as the politics of the late republic or the loss of senatorial control, as in some of the chronicles, but are conditioned by an awareness that Caesar represents the pagan world, which was about to be supplanted by Christian rule.

Ambivalence about Caesar is evident not just in narratorial comment, but also in authorial handling of the figure. Lazamon often expands and elaborates scenes narrated in Geoffrey and Wace, even if he faithfully retains their narrative sequence. In his account of the exchange of letters between Cassivellaunus and Caesar, Lazamon's Caesar acts in the same way as Wace's, ordering his fleet to be prepared. The main difference between the accounts lies not in factual details (80 ships in Wace, 60 in Lazamon), but in the inclusion of an extended description of Caesar's response:

> Cezar iseh þis writ   and he hit wraðliche biheold
> abholzen he as on mode,   je weorp hit to his foten. (3678–9)

> Caesar beheld this letter and he looked upon it angrily; enraged at heart, he threw it to the ground. (trans. Barron & Weinberg, in Layamon 1995)

Caesar's wrath is notable because it may signal an association of Caesar with Germanic heroic traditions. Wrath and anger are what heroic epic often associates with the great warriors, so we should not perhaps read such statements as equivalent to modern emotional responses. Yet in the world of Lazamon's *Brut*, the swiftness of Caesar's anger, although marking him as a formidable opponent, may also suggest distance on the part of the narrator, for whom *mesure*, the ability to behave with moderation and control, becomes a hallmark of ideal rulership (Hay 2002). In this respect, the figure of Caesar turns from a protagonist in his own right into a precursor of King Arthur: not yet the perfect embodiment of kingship, but a figure pointing towards events to come.

The power of such images and models in structuring contemporary medieval discourse may be illustrated by a final, rather idiosyncratic, example from thirteenth-century German literature. The anonymous verse narrative *Moriz von Craun* tells the story of an unfortunate knight who, despite his chivalric perfection, fails to win the love of his beloved lady, because she faces the dilemma of either committing adultery in rewarding Moriz, or breaking her promise of honoring chivalric virtue. The text appears to construct a concise and almost casuistic illustration of the inherent paradox of courtly love. Neither King Arthur nor indeed Roman history features directly, yet the interest of the enigmatic text lies in its prologue, which prefaces the exemplary story with an account of the history of knighthood. The author traces its origin back to the Greeks and from there constructs a chain of antecedents, adapting the traditional model of the *translatio imperii* as seen in the dream of Daniel (Worstbrock 1965: 20–2). Instead of the four kingdoms, he presents four stages of chivalry, which are passed on from the Greeks to the Romans, notably Julius Caesar:

ze Rôme ritterschaft beleip
dô mans von Kriechen vertreip.
Zehant dô sie was komen dar,
Julius Cesar
der emphienc sie ritterlîche
und twanc alliu rîche,
daz im dienten diu lant. (*Moriz von Craûn*, 113–19)

Chivalry stayed in Rome when it had been expelled from Greece. As soon as it had arrived in Rome, Julius Caesar received it in chivalric manner and conquered all countries so that they served him.

The image of Caesar as the conqueror of the known world is of course traditional, yet it is here not associated with his rulership, but seen as a mark of his education and chivalry. Caesar thus becomes a role model, not just for the rulers and generals, but for perfect male conduct more generally. As in the rest of the poem, it is likely that the author drew on French as well as German sources, and his image of Caesar here may be a conflation of the traditional historiographical image of Caesar the great ruler with the figure of Caesar in the Anglo-Norman romances, in which he is indirectly associated with the rise of Arthurian chivalry.

Contemporary politics: Caesar as a founder of nations

Even in the earliest vernacular adaptations, such as the *Annolied*, it is evident that the historiographical account of Caesar's life is set in analogy to contemporaneous events and political structures. This trend becomes even more pronounced in thirteenth-century French prose adaptations such as the *Faits des Romains* (c. 1213–14). Here, Roman history begins with Caesar, and the figure of Caesar himself and his "threat to the Republican ideals of senatorial authority" (Spiegel 1993: 119) becomes the foil for the work's patron, Philip Auguste. The analogy is made explicit in a parallel which is less than flattering to the king:

> Quant ge lis de Juilles Cesar que Luces Silla l'apeloit le valet mau ceint, si me membre de monseignor Phelipe le roi de France, que l'en pooit bien apeler le valet mau pignié quant il estoit joenes, car il estoit torjors hericiez. Ne il n'a pas mains de sens en lui que li ot en Juilles Cesar, fors seulement de letres, ne n'a pas meins eü affere que Juilles ot; et encontre ce que Juilles fu letrez, est li rois sanz malice, car la letreüre aguisa Juilles a meint malice.

> When I read that Lucius Sulla called Julius Caesar "the boy badly belted," I am reminded of my lord Philip the king of France, whom one might well have called "the boy ill combed" when he was young, because he was always disheveled. Nor did he possess less sense in him than there was in Julius Caesar, with the exception of [learning in] letters, nor did he accomplish less than Julius; and in contrast to Julius, who was literate, the king was without malice, for literacy goaded Julius to a great deal of malice. (trans. Spiegel 1993: 123)

Here, Caesar, "the boy badly belted," and King Philip Auguste, "the boy ill combed," are explicitly related to one another, although the function of such analogy has been a point of critical dissent, in that it can be seen either as a means of legitimizing the territorial ambitions of the Capetians (Beer 1976: 72–4), or, conversely, as a "pejorative analogue of the French king, who, like his Roman predecessor, weakened advisement and made the monarchy less a consultative and more an absolutist form of rulership" (Spiegel 1993: 120).

What the text constructs for its readers is an image of Gaul which allows them to reflect on contemporary realities without necessarily mirroring them. Gaul in the *Faits des Romains* is neither Roman nor directly contemporary France (Spiegel 1993: 130), although it often identifies elements of Caesar's Roman geography with political structures familiar to the thirteenth century: thus, Aquitania becomes Poitou, the Allobroges are rendered as the Burgundians, and Caesar's *Germani* are turned into the villains of the account – they are the *gens forsené* (1,117), the ferocious barbarians, a judgment which reflects thirteenth-century political allegiances and rivalries rather than Caesar's text. Where the focus of the German historiographical accounts and, to a lesser degree, the Anglo-Norman romances, is still prominently on models of kingship and on the style and legitimacy of imperial rule, the interest in the French adaptation appears to shift even further towards presenting a prehistory of contemporary social structures by rooting them in the classical past. Nevertheless, they are not translations of Caesar in a modern sense, because even recent studies (Schmidt-Chazan 1980) often perhaps underestimate the use made of glosses and commentaries to Lucan rather than direct reference to the texts. Nor are they examples of modern "national" history, since the shift of focus away from Rome and towards the reality of the contemporary readership is one discernible in the German *Annolied* and its polemic against the Bavarians as much as in the *Faits des Romains.*

The most prominent use of Caesar's reputation for contemporary politics is perhaps a forged document of 1359. Duke Rudolf IV of Habsburg, in an attempt to support his own cause against that of the Emperor, had his chancery produce a forged document, ostensibly made out by Caesar himself in the first year of the Roman empire. Here, Caesar's fame was used to support the claim of the electoral princes to sovereignty and independence. Petrarch, on behalf of the Emperor Charles IV, revealed the whole as a forgery – yet the forged letter remains a vivid illustration of the fact that Caesar's authority was considered to carry sufficient conviction to support a pressing political case. Here, as in earlier examples, the elements of his life that serve to support the argument are familiar: his role as leader and first emperor makes him a suitable precedent for an ever-changing series of contemporary claims.

Didactic discourse: Caesar as a wise man

Medieval ways of structuring history, as we have seen in the *Annolied* and the *Kaiserchronik*, moved towards a way of incorporating world history, and the events associated with ancient Greece and Rome, into salvation history, i.e. the events of the Old and New Testament, and as a result developed a tripartite model in which pagan, Jewish, and Christian history can be seen in relation to one another. Jacques de Longuyon's romance *Les Voeux du Paon* (1312–3) was the first to give this abstract model a concrete shape by attributing to each stage of history a triad of three heroes, each embodying the virtues of their age. Thus, Hector, Alexander and Caesar represent the pagan era, and Joshua, David, and Judas Maccabaeus the age of the Old Testament, whereas Arthur, Charlemagne, and Godfrey of Bouillon are the heroes of the Christian era (Ott 1993: 1104). This motif of the "Nine Worthies" spread quickly across fourteenth-century Europe and became a way of reflecting on aristocratic and chivalric life in general. What had started as a conceit usually embedded in larger narratives, often as a way of contrasting the defective present with the virtuous ideals of the past, acquires narrative independence in the course of the fifteenth century, when the motif turns into a topos in its own right, as in the *Histoire des Neuf Preux*, the *Triumphe des Neuf Preux* (translated into Portuguese and Spanish in the course of the sixteenth century), or the poems of Gower and Lydgate. This is manifest also in the fact that the series of the Nine Worthies is most prominent in contemporary imagination not as a text, but as a visual motif: representations of the Nine Worthies proliferate across Europe and appear to have been a popular motif for decorative art, from textiles, playing cards, and stained-glass windows to extended cycles of frescoes. Even the German-speaking area, for which there is no evidence of texts about the Nine Worthies, has numerous examples of visual representation, amongst which the frescoes at Schloss Runckelstein in northern Italy are perhaps the most spectacular (Haug 1982: 37). They are eloquent testimony to the fact that, in late-medieval culture, the figure of Caesar is part of a cultural knowledge that is transmitted not solely through texts, but also through visual shorthand, and anecdotal presence (Curschmann 1997: 30–3). The frescoes and murals thus give an indication of ways in which historical figures become part of general cultural knowledge, which may no longer be tied to the reception of specific texts. Overall, the way in which learned knowledge of Caesar's life, through specific classical source texts, interacts with popular cultural knowledge of a great man, not based on such textual evidence, is an issue that would merit more detailed examination in future.

Caesar in Early Modern Germany

With the first humanist translations of Caesar's works, Caesar the author re-enters the collective consciousness in the German-speaking world. The first complete translation of Caesar's works into French by Jean du Chesne (also Quesne) was published in 1473–4, though he still embeds the translation into a mirror for princes, employing classical history as a model for his own patron, Charles the Bold. The first translation following more exacting humanist standards was produced shortly afterwards in 1485 by Robert Gaugin. The first German translation, produced in 1507 by Matthias Ringmann (Philesius) and published in Strasbourg under the title *Julius der erst Römisch Kaiser von seinen kriegen* (Julius the first Roman emperor: about his wars), combines Caesar's *De bello Gallico* and *De bello civile* with Plutarch's life of Caesar. Like the earlier French translations, it associates philological interest with contemporary politics: Ringmann, from Strasbourg, was a friend of Jakob Wimpheling, who in his political tract *Germania* (1501) had used evidence from Caesar's life to argue that Alsace, the bilingual region at the borders between French- and German-speaking territories and home of many of the early humanists, had been part of the German empire since Caesar's times. This highlights how, despite the new philological engagement with Caesar's texts, the image of Caesar the military leader and conqueror remains dominant even in a period when copies of his literary works are more readily available. Two prominent German figures may serve to illustrate this point at least briefly: Albrecht Dürer and Martin Luther.

Dürer's *Triumph of Caesar*, showing him in the company of Pompeius and Crassus, does not survive; we know of it only through a description by Jacob Balde (Gundolf 1904: 148).

Luther, on the other hand, is evidence for an increasingly ambivalent attitude towards Caesar the politician, whereas he seems unconcerned with Caesar the author. In his *Tischreden* (Werke, vol. 62, Gespräch 2731, p. 185), Luther refers to Caesar as an exemplary ruler, and he uses Caesar, like Alexander, as the model of worldly success, but the critical overtones are unmistakable in other writings. A report on the organization of schools in Saxony associates Caesar with Nero:

> Es sagen etliche / wie kan o(e)brickeit von gott sein / und doch viel mit vnrechtem gewalt zuhirschen kommen sind / Als Julius. ...
> Also missbraucht auch ein tyrann Gottes ordenung / Als Julius odder Nero / Dennoch ist die ordenunge / dadurch recht vnd Fride erhalten wird / ein Go(e)tlich gescho(e)pffe / Ob schon die person / so sich der ordenung missbraucht / vnrecht thut.

> Many people say: how can order be divinely instituted, and yet many come to rule by unlawful force, as, for example, Julius [Caesar]? ... Therefore, a tyrant like Caesar or Nero abuses the order created by God. And yet the order itself, by which justice and peace are upheld, is divinely created, even if the person who abuses it does wrong.

The differentiation in this last statement is striking: Caesar, like Nero, is adduced as an example of tyrannical abuse of power – yet the occurrence of such abuse does not, so the theological argument runs, deny the existence of a divinely created order, but is simply evidence of human frailty. Caesar, the powerful ruler, has become an example of all-too-human sinfulness.

FURTHER READING

There are no comprehensive studies covering the reception of Caesar in medieval Europe, although, for those able to read German, the *Lexikon des Mittelalters* provides a useful survey of the material in the major European literatures. There are a number of studies with a focus on either French, or Anglo-Norman, or German literature: for French literature, the studies by Jeanette Beer (*A Medieval Caesar*, 1976) and Gabrielle Spiegel (*Romancing the Past: The Rise of Vernacular Prose Historiography in Thirteenth-Century France*, 1993), despite their comprehensive titles, mostly treat individual texts, especially the *Fait des Romains*. For the German material, Gundolf's original 1904 thesis (in German), unlike the later English reworking of his book ("Caesar") offers a wealth of detail, even if the framework of interpretation is outdated.

We still have to rely on Migne and the Monumenta Germaniae for editions of some of the Latin chronicles; and glosses and *accessus* have been only partially edited. Minnis (1988) provides an introduction to medieval concepts of authorship and ways in which scholastic learning influenced reading habits and manuscript transmission. The vernacular texts are mostly now available in critical editions, often with translation into a modern European vernacular.

CHAPTER TWENTY-THREE

Empire, Eloquence, and Military Genius: Renaissance Italy

Martin McLaughlin

> postquam bellatum apud Actium atque omnem potentiam ad unum conferri pacis interfuit, magna illa ingenia cessere.
>
> Tacitus, *Histories*, 1.1

> Eloquentia militarique re aut aequauit praestantissimorum gloriam aut excessit.
>
> Suetonius, *Divus Julius*, 55

The figure of Julius Caesar enjoys a predictably prominent role in Italy in the period between 1300 and 1600. With the advent of the humanist movement, spearheaded by Petrarch (1304–74), knowledge of the ancient world reached levels of accuracy unknown to previous centuries. Petrarch himself in his final years became fascinated by the figure of the dictator and composed what was then the longest Latin biography of Caesar, the *De gestis Cesaris.* Later humanists admired Caesar not only as the brilliant general and founder of the Roman Empire, but also as the author of the historical accounts of his Gallic and other campaigns: something like 250 humanist manuscripts of the *Commentaries* were made in this period, 26 of them containing portraits (Brown 1981), so his works and his image were extremely familiar to Italian intellectuals of the time. If one surveys the many allusions to Julius Caesar in Italy in these 300 years, two main trends stand out. The most striking feature is that for the first time since the end of antiquity Caesar is not just lauded as the founder of a divinely ordained Roman Empire (a "medieval" attitude enshrined in Dante's political views), or condemned as a violent usurper of power (the anti-Caesar tradition, slightly less prominent in the Middle Ages, but stemming ultimately from classical authors such as Cicero and Lucan), but instead provokes an unparalleled ideological debate about the values of monarchical versus republican forms of government, particularly in Florentine republican circles. A key role in this anti-Caesarian polemic was played by the discovery of Tacitus and his critique of the imperial style of government, epitomized by the opening sentence from the *Histories* cited above.

Although the sentence refers to the concentration of power in Augustus's hands, and the resulting decline in historical writing, Florentine republicans quoted it claiming that the dearth of *ingenia* began with Julius Caesar's usurpation of power and elimination of virtuous men. However, once the Florentine republic finally succumbs permanently to Medici rule after 1530, this ideological dimension recedes and attitudes in Italy revolve around the positive side of Caesar's achievements, encapsulated in the phrase from Suetonius cited above: the brilliant orator and writer on the one hand, and the military genius on the other. In what follows, I examine these two strands in turn, Caesar the founder of the Empire, and Caesar the historian of his own military exploits.

The Trecento: Dante, Petrarch, Boccaccio, Salutati

Dante's attitude to the founder of the Empire epitomizes one of the main attitudes to Caesar in the Christian Middle Ages. For the poet of the *Comedy*, as for other medieval thinkers, the single most important event in history was the Incarnation, and since Christ's birth as a man was willed by God, so his place of birth – a province of the Roman Empire – had divine sanction; therefore, the Roman Empire was the one earthly regime that had divine approval, as Dante argues in the fourth book of his philosophical work, the *Convivio* (1303–7), and in his political treatise, the *Monarchia* (1317–18). Caesar is thus placed by Dante amongst the virtuous heathens in Limbo in his *Comedy*, where he is described as "Caesar in arms with hawk-like eyes" (*Inferno* 4.123), the adjective *armato* evoking his military prowess, and the description of his eyes either deriving indirectly from Suetonius's description of them as *nigris vegetisque oculis* ("black and lively eyes," *Divus Julius* 45.1), though Dante had not read the Roman biographer, or simply symbolizing his acute mental powers or his pride. However, after this positive portrait, something of the ambivalence of Caesar's reputation emerges in the *Purgatorio*: on the one hand, on the terrace of slothful sinners, his military exploits are praised as models of commendable speed (18.101–2), while on the other, the lustful see him as an example of their own sin, since his sexual promiscuity led to his famously being addressed as "queen" by his troops during his triumphs (26.77). The positive view of Julius returns in the *Paradiso*, where the Emperor Justinian gives a lengthy, laudatory account of Caesar's speedy conquests before and during the civil war: here Julius' conquests are seen as willed by God in order to prepare the world for the universal peace of Augustus' reign in which Christ would be born (*Paradiso* 6.55–72). However, what was to prove the most controversial aspect of Dante's belief in the divine approval of the Roman Empire was that he placed at the very bottom of Hell those whom he considered the two worst political traitors in history, Brutus and Cassius, alongside the ultimate religious traitor Judas (*Inferno* 34.61–7).

It was also because of this privileged position as instigator of the divinely sanctioned Roman Empire that Julius was so often portrayed as the founder of famous

Figure 23.1 Julius Caesar founding Florence (detail). An exotic-looking Julius Caesar (his "oriental" headgear perhaps suggests his status as Emperor) beside the city he "founded." From *A Florentine Picture-Chronicle, being a series of 99 drawings representing scenes and personages of ancient history, sacred and profane, by Maso Finiguerra*, ed. Sidney Colvin (London: B. Quaritch, 1898), plate XCII.

cities throughout Europe. This tradition extended to Florence, where Dante's near-contemporary, the chronicler Giovanni Villani, draws on "il grande dottore Salustio" (Villani 1990–1: 48) to recycle the common view that Julius had founded Florence shortly after the suppression of the Catilinarian conspiracy, in order to spite the neighboring town of Fiesole, which had notoriously supported the conspirators (Villani 1990–1: 63–4). Although this view would be contested by Florentine humanists at the start of the next century, the myth had a powerful hold over the popular imagination and still appears in the *Florentine Picture Chronicle*, attributed to Maso Finiguerra or Baccio Baldini and dating from the 1470s (figure 23.1).

Nevertheless, opposition to Caesar ran almost as deeply throughout the Middle Ages. John of Salisbury, Thomas Aquinas, and Ptolemy of Lucca, who continued Aquinas's *De regimine principum* (c. 1267), denounced Caesar for violently seizing the republic and becoming a tyrant (Witt 1969; Skinner 1978: I, 55). However, this tradition, though also ultimately derived from Cicero and Lucan, was not dictated by any ideological critique of Empire, as would later be the case in republican Florence, but rather by a religious and philosophical condemnation of illegal usurpation of power.

Petrarch too was initially critical of the great general. It was probably his early reading of Lucan and parts of Suetonius that caused his early hostility to Caesar. His Latin epic, *Africa* (1338–64), has as its hero Scipio Africanus, and when in a dream vision Scipio's father prophesies to his son the future of Rome, he warns that Julius Caesar will conquer Gaul, Britain, and Germany, but adds that he would have been even greater had he only possessed a sense of moderation (*Africa* 2.219–28 in Petrarca 1926). Instead Julius will turn his victorious hands on the state in a civil war, and here Scipio senior condemns the ambition which leads one man to seize complete power for himself, to raid the treasury, enslave the senate, and drench the Capitol in blood (2.229–39). Such anti-Caesarian views were consistent with Petrarch's enthusiasm for Scipio and with his support in mid-century for Cola di Rienzo's ill-fated attempt to revive a Roman republic (1347–54), the poet at one stage even hailing Cola as a new Brutus, as well as a new Romulus and a new Camillus (Petrarca 1994: 64; Ferraù 2006b). However, despite his interest in Scipio and initially in Cola, the great humanist never explicitly states his support for a republican form of government (Ferraù 2006b), and in the end his reading of Suetonius (in his most heavily annotated copy of the Roman biographer Petrarch writes most annotations on the lives of Julius and Augustus: Billanovich 1960), of Caesar's *Commentaries* (which he attributed to Julius Celsus), and of the text he himself discovered in Verona in 1345, Cicero's *Letters to Atticus*, led to a revaluation of Caesar's achievements (Fenzi 2003). Political factors too, such as the poet's disillusionment with Cola's failure, and the humanist's subsequent patronage by single rulers such as the Visconti in Milan and the Carrara in Padua, account for his later pro-Caesar attitudes: in fact for Petrarch Caesar is a prototype more of a contemporary Signore than of a Roman Emperor, a private citizen who takes power to resolve a situation of civic discord. In his declining years, the humanist knew that it was local rulers such as the Visconti and Carrara families rather than the superpowers of the Church and the Empire that offered a valid model for political recovery in Italy at the end of the Trecento (Ferraù 2006c: 98–101).

Petrarch perhaps started the *De gestis Cesaris* as just another in the series of lives he had written for his *De viris illustribus* (1338–43), amongst which he had included an extended *Vita Scipionis* (c. 1357), but the length of his biography of Caesar outstripped even that of his life of Scipio, and it was in the end intended to be a free-standing biography. It circulated anonymously in rare editions of Caesar and was only reattributed to Petrarch in 1827 (Blanc 1985). Its medieval title at first glance seems to place it close to vernacular compilations such as the anonymous *I fatti di Cesare*, a farrago of legends based on Sallust, Lucan, and Suetonius, but translated from a French original; however, in reality Petrarch's work stands at the beginning of a new source-based historiography. In chapter 20, which comes after the account of the Gallic wars and before the civil war, the author interrupts the narrative to quote letters by Caesar in Cicero's *Letters to Atticus* (discovered by Petrarch himself, as we saw) to prove his real desire for peace, and to show that even Cicero, although anti-Caesar, was also highly critical of Pompey. Petrarch was proud of the novelty of his approach here, in eliciting evidence from the protagonist's own letters and from "a rather remote source," namely Cicero's letters (Petrarca 1827: 211; 2003: 209 Ferraù 2006d: 199).

The *Letters to Atticus* (esp. 9.7c, 9.13a, 10.8b) are exploited elsewhere by Petrarch (*Seniles* 16.5; Petrarch 1992: II, 622–3) to show that, contrary to medieval lore, Caesar did not introduce the royal plural (*nos* instead of *ego*): once again the humanist is concerned to produce the most accurate version even of linguistic history. The final chapter of the *De gestis*, before dealing with the assassination, offers a description of Caesar's appearance and *mores*, largely based on Suetonius, concluding that although Caesar had been at times rather impetuous and keen to seize power, as well as being adulterous, nevertheless no victor ever showed more clemency or munificence, and for this Petrarch can cite the evidence of "maximi auctores" (Petrarca 1827: 314–17; 2003: 302–4).

Petrarch's vernacular poetry evinces a similar movement from an anti- to a pro-Caesar stance: in two early sonnets from the 1330s, he says that Caesar's hands were more than ready to turn Thessaly vermilion with blood (Petrarca 2004: 44), and he recalls Julius's simulated tears on seeing the severed head of Pompey (Petrarca 2004: 102; Hainsworth 1988: 24–9). Yet the poet praises Julius as slaughterer of the barbarians in the great political canzone "Italia mia" (Petrarca 2004: 128.49–51) of 1345. This oscillation between his two heroes, Scipio and Caesar, continues in the *Triumphs*, though in the *Triumph of Fame* the movement appears to be in the opposite direction. In his first redaction of this text (c. 1351), he places as the front marchers in Fame's cohorts first Julius Caesar then Augustus and Drusus, and only after these Caesars come the two Scipios (*Triumph of Fame* Ia. 23–7: Petrarca 1996). However, in the later redaction (c. 1364), he places Scipio side by side with Caesar and is unable to say which is nearer the goddess Fame, though he does add that Scipio was a slave only to virtue, not to Love, whereas Caesar was in thrall to both, thus suggesting Scipio's superiority (Petrarca, *Triumph of Fame* 1. 22–4: Petrarca 1996; Martellotti 1947, 1975, 1976; Baron 1962).

Despite these oscillations Petrarch's mature views are to be found in the *De gestis* and in a late letter-treatise on the wise ruler (*Seniles* 14.1), written about the same time (1373) and dedicated to his patron, Francesco da Carrara, ruler of Padua. There he puts Caesar forward several times as a model for rulers to follow, including a whole page which claims that he epitomizes all the princely virtues: even Cicero said Julius forgot nothing except past injuries (Petrarch 1992: II, 527). However much he had admired Scipio and Cola in his earlier years, the mature Petrarch saw in Julius Caesar the prototype of the great general, the model ruler, and a complex human being.

Petrarch's disciple Giovanni Boccaccio wrote one of the first commentaries on Dante's *Inferno* (c. 1373–4), though the commentary only reached as far as canto 17 before Boccaccio's death. Despite Dante's placing of Julius Caesar amongst the virtuous heathens in canto 4, Boccaccio's commentary on the passage (Boccaccio 1965: 217–21) provides a mini-biography largely based on Suetonius, in which he condemns Caesar for lust and avarice as well as for his violent and tyrannical seizure of the state. Clearly the anti-Caesar tradition was still influential in Boccaccio's time, primarily because of Lucan's status as a canonical poet; but Boccaccio's attitude may also have stemmed from the fact that he possessed the manuscript of Tacitus's *Histories* (which he appears to have stolen from the monastery at Montecassino), and his anti-Caesarian critique seems to have been influenced here by the great historian's views. However, the most learned complete Dante commentary of the century, written 1375–83 by Benvenuto da Imola, is more ambiguous: in his commentary on *Inferno* 34 he says Caesar deserved assassination, but on *Paradiso* 6 he offers a more balanced account of his vices and virtues. Benvenuto was also more cautious on the question of whether Julius founded Florence (in his commentary on *Inferno* 15), rightly observing that the great general would never have had time to found all those cities whose foundation was attributed to him; for Benvenuto Caesar could not have founded Florence at the time of the Catilinarian conspiracy, as Sallust shows, and the commentator simply admits he does not know who founded Florence.

This ambivalent note is characteristic of the approach to the dictator in Florentine circles towards the end of the fourteenth century. Another of Petrarch's disciples, Coluccio Salutati (1331–1406), was a formidable humanist and Chancellor of the Florentine republic at the turn of the century (1375–1406). He was the first to realize that it was Caesar himself and not Julius Celsus who wrote the commentaries on the Gallic and other wars (Salutati 1891–1911: II, 299–300; Gilson 2005: 66–9), and just as Petrarch had found Cicero's *Letters to Atticus*, so Salutati discovered Cicero's *Letters to his Friends* (1392). But whereas Petrarch's discovery led him to criticize Cicero's abandonment of philosophical *otium* for political dealings that brought about his death, and to reassess Julius Caesar as a man of peace, Salutati's reading of the *Familiares* turned him against Caesar and enhanced his republican sympathies, causing him to declare that Julius turned the people's freedom into monarchical enslavement ("monarchie servitutem", Salutati 1891–1911: II, 389; Witt 1969: 462–4), and even to go so far as to quote Lactantius's phrase for Caesar, "patricida patriae" (Salutati 1891–1911: II, 409). These sentiments were most strongly expressed in Salutati's official writings for the Florentine republic: in a letter of 1394 to the rulers of Genoa he writes that Caesar's and Augustus' rule was simply the beginning of perpetual slavery (Viti 1992: 45, n. 139). However, the most famous defense of the Florentine republican tradition was his invective against Antonio Loschi, the Milanese humanist, who had attacked Florence's republican constitution and claimed that the city had not been founded by Romans. Salutati's *Invectiva* (1403) cites Sallust (*Catiline* 28.4) to show that the city was founded by Sulla's soldiers; hence it descended from the Roman republic, and he champions the achievements of republican *libertas* (Garin 1952: 16–21; Witt 1983: 246–52; Baldassarri 2007: 47–51). Yet Salutati too felt ambiguous about the figure of Caesar himself: despite his pro-republican stance, he also wrote a political treatise, *De tyranno* (c. 1400), in which he defended Dante's decision to place the great republican heroes Brutus and Cassius at the bottom of the *Inferno* (Witt 1983: 368–91). So by the end of the fourteenth century in Italy the widespread medieval adulation of Julius Caesar becomes in Petrarch and his disciples an admiration based on human criteria, thanks also to their knowledge of a wider range of historical sources. However, the increased knowledge of ancient texts also fostered a corresponding contestation of the founder of the Empire's status, particularly in ideological terms in Florentine circles, a trend that would reach new peaks in the following century.

The Quattrocento: Bruni and Poggio

The ambiguity concerning Caesar continues in the early Quattrocento in the works of Salutati's most famous pupil, and a later successor as Chancellor of Florence, Leonardo Bruni (1370–1444, Chancellor from 1427). This is very obvious in his most substantial early work, the *Dialogi ad Petrum Paulum Histrum* (1406), modeled on Cicero's *De oratore*: in the first book he portrays Niccolò Niccoli, the most anti-vernacular humanist of the time, criticizing the achievements of Dante, Petrarch, and Boccaccio as inferior to those of classical writers, but in the second he has Niccoli recant and praise their substantial contribution to Florentine culture. The attack on Dante in book 1 cites as his greatest mistake that of placing the republican heroes Brutus and Cassius in the pit of Hell. Dante was wrong to condemn Brutus and Cassius, says Niccoli, because "Caesar had taken possession of the commonwealth by force of arms, and when the good citizens had been slain he had taken away his country's liberty" (Bruni 1996: 110; Griffiths, Hankins, & Thompson 1987: 73). However, the accusation against Dante is retracted by Niccoli in book 2 (Bruni 1996: 128–34; Griffiths, Hankins, & Thompson 1987: 79–81). In addition, at the start of the second book Bruni also has Salutati explain that he could never share the view put forward by Lactantius and echoed by Bruni in his earlier *Laudatio Florentinae urbis* (1403–4) that Caesar was "patricida patriae" (Bruni 1996: 120; Griffiths, Hankins, & Thompson 1987: 76): the elderly Chancellor points out that he had defended Caesar in his *De tyranno* and will never cease to praise him to the heavens for his achievements. Nevertheless, Salutati adds that he would prefer his sons to look to Marcellus or Camillus rather than to Caesar as a model of virtue (Bruni 1996: 120–2; Griffiths, Hankins, & Thompson 1987: 77). The two-book structure of the *Dialogi* thus reflects the clearly ambivalent views held by Bruni at this stage, both about vernacular culture and about Caesar.

In his *Laudatio*, the panegyric in praise of Florence, Bruni observes that Rome flourished most before the Caesars destroyed the republic (Bruni 1996: 600; Gilson 2005: 83–8; Baldassarri 2007: 51–6), and he denounces Julius whose "facinora" had overthrown the Roman state (Bruni 1996: 604). However, immediately after this denunciation, he concedes that some have objected to the harsh "truths" told by Lucan because Caesar's serious vices were overshadowed ("obumbrabantur") by his many great virtues (ibid.): so Bruni decides it is safer not to say any more about him. In the *Laudatio* Bruni thus remains ambivalent about Caesar himself, but he is severely critical of the Empire as a regime. Claiming that Florence was founded when Rome was still a republic and at its peak in terms of power, freedom, and genius, he explicitly cites the opening of Tacitus's *Histories*, noting that "after the republic had been subjected to the power of one ruler, all those great talents ('preclara illa ingenia', Bruni's variant on Tacitus's 'magna illa ingenia') disappeared, as Tacitus says" (Bruni 1996: 606). It is important to note what Bruni does here: he takes Tacitus's remark about the dearth of historians and extends it to apply to all writers and indeed artists ("ingenia"), suggesting that only a strong republic will allow the arts to flourish, a point that Bruni makes again in the opening pages of his *History of the Florentine People* (1415–44). This work begins with the blunt statement of the city's republican origins: "The founders of Florence were Romans sent by Lucius Sulla to Faesulae" (Bruni 2001: 8), and cites Cicero's (*In Cat.* 2.9.20) and Sallust's (*Cat.* 24.2, 27.1, 30.1) mention of these colonizers. Bruni dates the decline of the Roman state to the moment when it lost its liberty and began to be ruled by emperors, saying that first Julius Caesar's civil wars then the "wicked triumvirate" of Octavian, Antony, and Lepidus caused the cruel slaughter of the best men (Bruni 2001: 49–51). In both the *Laudatio* and the *History*, then, Bruni goes further than Salutati in arguing the superiority of a republican over a monarchical regime, and one reason for his less hesitant approach was that the younger humanist had read and been influenced by Tacitus's major historical works (Witt 1969: 473–4). It is probable that Boccaccio's manuscript of Tacitus from Montecassino ended up in circles close to Bruni at the start of the Quattrocento: it was certainly owned by his one-time friend Niccolò Niccoli by 1427 (Reynolds and Wilson 1991: 133; Reynolds 1986: 407–8). Once more the discovery of new texts is put to ideological use.

On the other hand, when it comes to non-ideological aspects of Caesar, Bruni is more positive: in his *Life of Cicero* (1415), he applauds Caesar's clemency as evinced in his speech to the Senate against the execution of the Catilinarian conspirators (Bruni 1996: 442); and in the treatise on female education (*De Studiis et Litteris*, 1422–9), he ranks Caesar as a historian alongside Livy, Sallust, Tacitus, and Quintus Curtius, praising his *commentarii* for their supreme fluency and elegance ("summa facilitate venustateque"; Bruni 1996: 264). Bruni's commendation of Caesar the writer here is part of a widespread enthusiasm for the author of the *Commentaries* in Italy in the 1420s, because in 1421 the Lodi manuscript containing the full texts of Cicero's *Orator*, *De oratore*, and (for the first time since antiquity) the *Brutus* had been discovered and disseminated amongst leading humanists (Sabbadini 1905: 100–1; Reynolds 1986: 102, 107–8). The *Brutus* in particular had been fulsome in its praise of Caesar's *Commentaries*: Cicero praises them as "bare" (*nudi*), devoid of all ornament, with their "limpid and brilliant brevity" ("pura et inlustri brevitate," *Brutus* 262). The key terms, *nudi* and *pura*, would become the standard qualities ascribed to Caesar's pure Latin by humanists of the fifteenth and sixteenth centuries. In addition Cicero's remarks here on the difference between historical *commentarii* and *historia* were quoted time and again throughout the rest of the century, and they helped popularize the commentary genre in fifteenth-century Italy. Bruni himself wrote several works with this title: *Commentarii de primo bello Punico* (1418–21), a condensation of Polybius; *Commentarii rerum Graecarum*, a digest of Xenophon's *Hellenica*; and *Rerum suo tempore gestarum commentarius* (1440–1), a kind of autobiography of the years 1378–1440; but clearly it is only this last work that looks back to Caesar rather than to the ancient and medieval commentary tradition (Ramminger 2005: 77–80). Later, other humanists favored this Caesarian genre, and wrote their own autobiographical or biographical *commentarii*, such as Pius II (who owned his own copy of Caesar), Bartolomeo Facio, Giovanni Simonetta and others (Ianziti 1988, 1990, 1992).

Bruni, as we have seen, still retains a certain ambivalence about Caesar, if not about republican ideology. But his successor as Florentine Chancellor, Poggio Bracciolini

(1380–1459), went much further in a fierce polemic which he waged against humanists from the Este court in Ferrara. In April 1435 Poggio wrote to Scipione Mainenti, a Ferrarese humanist in the papal court, claiming that Scipio and the Roman republic were superior to Caesar and the Roman empire (Canfora 2001: 111–18). But a lengthy reply defending Caesar came from the pre-eminent Ferrarese humanist, Guarino da Verona (1374–1460), who had translated Plutarch's life of Caesar into Latin by 1414, and who here was clearly speaking on behalf of another single ruler, his patron, Leonello d'Este (Canfora 2001: 119–40). In reply to Guarino's letter, Bracciolini wrote a second, longer *Defensiuncula* to the Veronese humanist (Canfora 2001: 141–67).

What emerges most clearly in Poggio's initial letter is that he is prepared to criticize Caesar more harshly than any of his predecessors. Where Bruni had hesitated or counterbalanced Caesar's faults with his virtues, Poggio denies that there was any virtue in the man, and reverses Bruni's formula in the *Laudatio* – Caesar's faults were overshadowed ("obumbrabantur") by his virtues – to state that "his military virtues were magnificent but pernicious to the citizens and the state, and they must be obscured ('obscurentur') by the treachery and cruelty he showed against the republic" (Canfora 2001: 114). Similarly whereas Bruni had portrayed Salutati rejecting his earlier quotation of Lactantius's tag of "patriae patricida", Poggio actually uses this formula to write off even Caesar's military victories, saying he used his victories to attack, take over and destroy his fatherland "tamquam nefarius parricida" (Canfora 2001: 112). In fact Poggio actually distorts his sources, applying Sallust's description of Catiline to Caesar himself: Caesar is ambitious for power, surrounded by corrupt followers, prone to lust and greed (Canfora 2001: 113; Crevatin 1982: 292, 333), all vices attributed by Sallust to Catiline (Sall. *Cat.* 5). Poggio's final criticism of Caesar is that he is hated by all learned men as the parricide not only of his own fatherland, but also of Latin letters and the fine arts ("latinae linguae et bonarum artium parricida," Canfora 2001: 118). Like Bruni, he talks of the disappearance under the empire of *praeclara ingenia*, Bruni's variant on Tacitus's phrase *magna ingenia* at the opening of the *Histories*, and again expands the ancient writer's remarks about the dearth of historians into a general statement on the lack of all intellectual talent under the Empire. For Poggio what disappears are eloquence and literature, the fine arts and philosophy, all of which were at their peak in the republic: the good men who practiced such arts would be hated by the "monsters" who succeeded as Emperors. Again Poggio expands on Bruni's theory of the connection between republican freedom and the flourishing of culture, specifically mentioning philosophy, the liberal arts, and literature (Canfora 2001: 118).

Guarino in his reply to Poggio starts with his last point, and he is able to marshall a whole range of weighty authorities against the idea that Caesar had killed culture: Cicero's *Brutus*, Quintilian, Suetonius, and especially Plutarch, whose life of Caesar Guarino had translated. Guarino deliberately takes his first quotation from Caesar himself (Canfora 2001: 120) and cites from several Greek sources since he is aware that Poggio knows less Greek than himself. Nor does he have a problem in listing the many famous writers that flourished under Caesar and the Empire: poets from Catullus to Silius Italicus, historians from Sallust to Livy and Tacitus, philosophers from Seneca to Boethius. For Guarino, Scipio's achievements were limited to the military sphere, as even Livy acknowledged, whereas Caesar was "civis magnanimus, princeps prudentissimus, imperator excellentissimus" (Canfora 2001: 139). Poggio's final say on the matter, in his *Defensiuncula*, is equally lengthy but simply reiterates the points made in his first letter to Mainenti, though he makes intelligent use of source criticism to counter Guarino's many quotations from Greek. Scholars have debated whether the Scipio–Caesar debate between Poggio and Guarino was merely a rhetorical exercise or had a genuinely political dimension. From the vehemence with which the Tuscan attacks Caesar, which is consistent with the approach of other republican theorists such as Bruni, it is likely that this was no mere rhetorical exercise, but rather a fierce ideological debate, seriously argued by the two protagonists. This is confirmed by the fact that a few years later, in 1440, Pietro del Monte, another humanist from the only other important republic in Italy, Venice, reopened the dispute and again took the "republican" side, agreeing with Poggio that Caesar was a "turbulentus civis" and a tyrant (Canfora 2001: 68), though – as has been pointed out – del Monte was not against monarchy *per se*: rather he saw Caesar as an anti-type for a king (Rundle 2002). The debate also attracted the interest of the antiquarian Ciriaco d'Ancona who in 1435 wrote a Latin letter praising Caesar to Leonardo Bruni, but Ciriaco's was more a poetic than an ideological defense of the dictator (Schadee 2008a). After 1440 the Scipio–Caesar polemics continued to be read but no major humanist intervened in the controversy in writing.

It was no accident that the defense of Caesar from republican attacks should spring from the court at Ferrara. In fact the Este court appears to have promoted a particular cult of the figure of Julius Caesar throughout the fifteenth and sixteenth centuries: Guarino had translated Plutarch's life of Caesar by 1414, and in 1435 began a new translation of it, probably in the context of the dispute with Poggio, though the retranslation has not survived (Pade 1990). In addition he mentions Julius as a princely model on many occasions to his pupil, Leonello d'Este, and by 1432 he prepared for Leonello an emended and finely illustrated manuscript of Caesar's works (now in Modena, Biblioteca Estense, α. W. 1.3: see Brown 1972: 46; Grafton 1997: 22, 47). Another humanist at Leonello's court, Angelo Decembrio, provided a fictional portrayal of the court's literary discussions in the 1440s in his *Politia litteraria* (c. 1463), and it is no surprise that Caesar surfaces often in these debates: not only do the discussants show a deep knowledge of Caesar's Latinity, but Leonello is portrayed as attacking Petrarch's sonnet on Caesar's false tears at seeing Pompey's head (Petrarca 2004: 102) and claiming that in fact the dictator, famous for his clemency, often wept genuine tears (Decembrio 2002: 192–3). Even as late as 1590 Tasso, also attached to the Ferrarese court, would write a defense of the superiority of Caesar over Alexander the Great, in his *Risposta di Roma a Plutarco* (Tasso 1875: II, 323–78).

The most spectacular visual example of this cult came from the nearby court of Mantua in the second half of the century: Andrea Mantegna painted what he considered his masterpiece, the nine canvases of the *Triumphs of Caesar* (now in the Royal Collection in Hampton Court) for Francesco Gonzaga II of Mantua between 1485 and 1492. Once more, Caesar represented an ideal image of the Mantuan ruler, who was a successful soldier as well; in addition the turn of the century was the period when Caesar's popularity in Italy had been further enhanced by the advent of printing, as we shall see. The sequence of canvases depicts one or more of Julius's triumphs, probably the Gallic and Pontic War triumphs (Lightbown 1986: 140–53; Beard 2007: 154), ending with the dictator himself being crowned beneath a triumphal arch: Mantegna, in touch with the leading humanists of the day, would have read descriptions of triumphs in either manuscript or printed editions of Livy, Suetonius, Plutarch, Josephus, and Appian, but these were probably filtered through the account of Roman triumphs based on these antique sources by Flavio Biondo in his *Roma Triumphans* (c. 1460). Besides textual sources, Mantegna's archaeological details draw on images from the Arch of Titus in Rome, particularly for the long "tubae" (trumpets) and the winged deity (Fortuna? Victoria?) placing the crown on Caesar's head. The painter's depiction of besieged cities and siege-engines anticipates the images that would accompany Caesar's text in the sixteenth century, and Julius's triumphal moment in the final canvas constitutes a fitting image of the hold Caesar exercised over the Italian imagination at the turn of the fifteenth and sixteenth centuries.

From Poliziano to Machiavelli

The force of the Florentine republican tradition is reflected iconographically in the portraits of Caesar in contemporary manuscripts of his works. As Virginia Brown points out, the Florentine codices rarely depict Caesar as a medieval universal ruler holding a globe, thus celebrating the world Empire, but rather as the author of the *Commentaries*, or as the military leader (figure 23.2). However, Poggio's anti-Caesarian tirade, which earned him the name of "Caesaromastix" from Guarino in his reply, marked the high-water mark of anti-monarchical feeling in the fifteenth century. The republican tradition in Florence gradually fell silent as first, in 1434, Cosimo de' Medici returned from exile, and then, in the second half of the Quattrocento the Medici family tightened its grip on the governance of Florence and its territories, notably in the figure of Lorenzo the Magnificent. Not surprisingly, the critique of single rulers goes underground during this time and only resurfaces with the collapse of Medici rule and the brief return of the republic (1494–1512) in the work of the most famous Florentine republican thinker, Niccolò Machiavelli (1469–1527). It is no surprise, either, that, under the rule of Lorenzo the Magnificent, his Chancellor Bartolomeo Scala in his *History of Florence* (c. 1490–7) offers both the Brunian view that Florence was founded under the Roman republic and a restatement of the earlier tradition that it had been founded by Julius Caesar, claiming that as he is unable to decide which is true, all he can say for certain is that the city was founded by Romans. Even the great humanist of Lorenzo's court, Angelo Poliziano (1454–94), seems to move from a republican to an imperial standpoint: he had originally in 1472 held to the Brunian view that the city was founded by Sulla's veterans, but later, when dedicating his Latin letters to Lorenzo's son Piero in 1494, he proclaims that it was

Figure 23.2 Caesar the military leader at the opening of *De Bello Gallico*. From a Florentine manuscript, c.1450–1475 (Bodleian Library, Canon. Class. Lat. 266, f. 1r).

founded not in republican times but by Augustus himself and the other two members of his triumvirate, Mark Antony and Lepidus (Poliziano 2006: 8–16). Poliziano derives his evidence from an old manuscript of the *Liber regionum* which he attributed to Frontinus, and therefore considered more authoritative than the vague allusions to Fiesole in Cicero's and Sallust's accounts of Catiline's conspiracy. Poliziano's view became the new orthodoxy throughout the next century and resurfaces in Machiavelli's, Guicciardini's and Varchi's vernacular histories of Florence (Rubinstein 1957). Like Scala, even Machiavelli, when he is commissioned by the Medici Pope Clement VII to write his *Florentine Histories* (1524), subscribes both to Bruni's republican theory of the founding of Florence and to Poliziano's "imperial" theory of the triumvirate of Augustus as founders, stating that, following the wars between Marius and Sulla, and Caesar and Pompey, and afterwards between Caesar's killers and his avengers, first Sulla and later the triumvirate of Octavian, Antony, and Lepidus sent colonists to settle Fiesole (Machiavelli 1988: *Istorie fiorentine* 2.2).

Machiavelli's more critical views of Caesar are to be found in his two most famous political treatises. In *The Prince* (1513), Julius Caesar receives just one significant mention, when Machiavelli notes that the dictator, who had gained power through his munificence, would never have been able to sustain that level of spending had he lasted in office (Machiavelli 2005: ch. 16). However, his critique of Caesar is much more explicit and wide-ranging in the more republican *Discourses on the First Decade of Livy* (1516–17). The longest chapter to deal with Caesar suggests that Machiavelli knew the polemic between Poggio and Guarino, for he says that all rulers would prefer their citizens to be more like Scipio than Caesar (Machiavelli 2003: *Discorsi* 1.10). He then adds that Caesar's fame is due to the fear of writers under all the emperors: if authors had been free they would have said of Julius what they said of Catiline (interestingly, that is what Poggio had done). That Machiavelli is working within the Florentine-Tacitean tradition is confirmed when he then translates almost verbatim the whole of the second paragraph from the *Histories* (1.2), about the emperors bringing destruction on Italy, the burning of Rome, the profanation of religion, and the rewarding of wickedness. After this long list of outrages, which Tacitus had balanced with a list of instances of virtuous behavior (*Histories* 1.3), Machiavelli ignores these positive examples, simply adding a sardonic sentence of his own: "[Anyone who considers all these outrages], will recognize clearly how much Rome, Italy and the world owe to Caesar" (1.10). Elsewhere he notes that Caesar blinded people so they could not see the yoke he put on them (1.17), that his favor turned into fear (1.33), that he was the first tyrant in Rome (1.37), and so on. Machiavelli's denunciation in this republican treatise finds a number of echoes in the works of like-minded contemporaries, such as Francesco Patrizi and Francesco Guicciardini. Patrizi's *Institution of a Republic* (published 1518) sees Caesar as the usurper of the republic and an architect of tyranny; while Guicciardini in the *Considerazioni* (c. 1528) saw him as "detestable and monstrous" in setting up a tyranny against the wishes of its people (Guicciardini 1984; Skinner 1978: I, 161). However, although the Florentine republic revived briefly just after Machiavelli's death in 1527, once Medici power was definitively restored in 1530 the family remained in power for two centuries, and the anti-imperial note that had characterized Florentine political writings for over a century fell completely silent.

We saw that Machiavelli embraced the Caesarian foundation of Florence in his Medici-inspired *Florentine Histories*, and in another work of the same time, *The Art of War* (1520), he is even more positive about Caesar. In this work there is only praise of Caesar the general and strategist. He praises the brilliant tactician, seeing him as a model to follow in the way he trusted the infantry more than the cavalry (book 2; Machiavelli 1965: 55–6), the way he followed up a victory with great speed, unlike Hannibal, or attacked his enemy while they were crossing a stream (book 4, p. 120), how he cleverly had a bridge constructed while distracting his enemy by marching up one side of a river (book 5, pp. 146–7), and how he avoided fighting German tribes when they were desperate (book 6, p. 278). In the last page, Caesar and Alexander are cited as models for contemporary rulers for their willingness to endure hardship, and to march and fight alongside their own soldiers (book 7, p. 211). Only at this last mention does Machiavelli insert a brief reminder of his earlier criticism of

Caesar: although the "inordinate thirst for dominion" in some rulers is criticized, they certainly cannot be accused of effeminacy or cowardice (p. 211) – though the former accusation may be ironic given Caesar's and Alexander's ambivalent sexual reputations. But on the whole, Julius is the hero of Machiavelli's dialogue on war as much as he had been the villain of his republican *Discourses*. This was a harbinger of things to come: once the Florentine republic collapsed definitively, there began two centuries of foreign rule, Italians forgot about the ideological question of republic versus monarchy, and were left to admire Caesar the author and military strategist. It is to this last strand that we now turn.

Humanist enthusiasm for Caesar the author

In a previous section it was noted that after the discovery of the *Brutus* in 1421, which included Cicero's superlative praise of the *commentarii*, the status of Caesar's historical works rose even higher (Billanovich 1990). The 1430s were a high point of scholarship on Caesar: shortly after the dispute involving Poggio and Guarino, in 1438 Pier Candido Decembrio, the Milanese humanist and brother of Angelo, even translated the *Gallic War* and *Civil War* into Italian, dedicating it to the ruler of Milan, Filippo Maria Visconti. This was one of very few Latin texts to be translated into the vernacular in a century when humanists wrote almost exclusively in Latin. Decembrio's dedication to his prince points out that not just Julius but also Augustus, Tiberius, Germanicus, Caligula, Claudius, and Nero combined military expertise with knowledge of literature. The mention of some of the "darker" emperors in this context shows how keen Decembrio was to praise all single rulers, when dedicating his translation to a Visconti. This is confirmed by his criticism of Lucan's "more poetical than truthful accounts" ("più poeticamente che vere"; Frati 1921: 77). Decembrio also wrote a comparison of Julius and Alexander, and a *Vita Caesaris* for his series of biographies of famous men, *Vitae Aliquot Virorum Illustrium* (Viti 1987). Clearly this cult of Caesar fits in with northern Italian courtly cultures where cities like Milan, Mantua, and Ferrara were governed by a single ruler, but elsewhere in the peninsula there was similar enthusiasm. Other famous humanists, such as the two Barzizzas and Pius II, owned their own copies of Caesar's *Commentaries*, and the works were much read by the Aragonese kings of Naples: Bartolomeo Facio tells us that Alfonso the Magnanimous, a great reader of Livy, also took a copy of the *Commentaries* with him on expeditions and read from them every day (Billanovich 1990). In fact the one surviving Quattrocento commentary on Caesar's works comes from Naples: Parrasio's unpublished 1499–1500 commentary on the Gallic and Civil War (Brown 1976).

Also in this Neapolitan ambience, Lorenzo Valla, in his *Antidotum in Facium* (1447), regularly quotes from Caesar to justify lexical and syntactic choices in his own historical works (Valla 1981: 90, 233–4, 238, etc.), especially as he says Caesar wrote "latinissime" (Valla 1981: 90), and agrees even with his opponent Bartolomeo Facio that Livy, Caesar, and Sallust constitute a supreme triad of historians (Valla 1981: 128). In particular he appreciates the wit and unadorned brevity of Caesar's works, and his use of *sententiae* (Valla 1981: 233, 241–2). However, by the end of the century an occasional critical note emerges: even though in Pontano's dialogue *Antonius* (1491) Caesar is repeatedly cited for good Latin usage (Pontano 1944: 89–91), in his major dialogue on historiography, the *Actius* (c. 1498), Caesar is considered not as valid a model as Livy and Sallust since he only wrote *commentarii*, which were merely shorthand historical notes for others to write up as a full-blown history (Pontano 1944: 231; see on the genre, Kraus, pp. 160–1 and Raaflaub, pp. 179–80, in this volume). On the other hand, the popularity of the *Gallic War* as a school text is illustrated by the fact that at the start of Pontano's humorous dialogue, *Charon* (1491), a pedant grammarian in the underworld claims he would like to know from Caesar himself whether Gaul is divided "in tris" or "in tres partes" (Pontano 1944: 34)!

Even if Caesar is not considered as canonical a historian as Livy and Sallust, his style is much admired, especially by the most expert Latin critics. The "purity" of Caesar's Latin was the key quality ascribed to it in Cicero's *Brutus*, and this finds several echoes around this time. In 1484 the great scholar, Pico della Mirandola, praised Lorenzo de' Medici's Italian prose in his *Commentary on his Sonnets* as the equivalent of Caesar's pure Latin, an apposite comparison since Lorenzo too was a political ruler who was at the same time a first-rate writer (Garin 1952: 804). Also within the Medici circle, the great Florentine humanist and stylist, Poliziano, has strong words of praise for Caesar's Latin. In his second *Miscellanea* (1493–4), he disputes St. Ambrose's claim in his *Hexameron* that elephants sleep on their feet, and suggests that the Church father had been influenced by the similar claim made regarding elks in the *Gallic War* (6.27); at this point Poliziano reproduces verbatim the full passage on elks from Caesar just so that his readers can sample the purity ("verba mundissima") and elegance of Caesar's Latin (Poliziano 1978: 83). Even in vernacular circles in the 1520s, in Castiglione's influential *Book of the Courtier* (1528), Caesar is considered to be as valid a model of style as Sallust, Varro, and "the other good writers," even though their usage differs from Cicero's (*Book of the Courtier* 1.39; Castiglione 1967: 85), and a few chapters later Caesar is portrayed as a model of how to combine the active and scholarly lives (1.43).

In the first decades of the sixteenth century Caesar remains a by-word for pure Latin writing: in a famous debate on literary imitation in 1512, both the Ciceronian Pietro Bembo and his more eclectic opponent, Gianfrancesco Pico della Mirandola, agree in praising Caesar as a writer who is a highly suitable model for imitation (Santangelo 1954: 46, 48, 68, 69), especially for his *candor*, his pure Latinity, though Bembo worries that the danger of this style is that it can slip into *sermo rudis* (Santangelo 1954: 46). Bembo finds in Caesar the greatest *candor* and *puritas*, and claims his comparative neglect of eloquence was caused by the fact of his living such an active life (Santangelo 1954: 48). Bembo's theoretical praise here of Caesar was later put into practice: he sees Julius and Augustus as epitomizing the Golden Age of Latin literature (against the republican viewpoint of Bruni and Poggio), and since in his own *History of Venice* (begun 1530) he uses only words from that age, Caesar becomes an indispensable model: in his description of a cannon, he solves the problem of technical nomenclature by closely imitating a passage from the *Bellum Gallicum* (5.43.1) (McLaughlin 1995: 271–2).

From Milan and Venice to Florence and Naples, Caesar is revered in humanist circles for his pure and elegant Latin.

Italian editions of Caesar

The history of early printed editions of the *Commentaries* provides clear evidence of the extraordinary growth in the popularity of Caesar as an author: the first Italian edition was printed in 1469, there were at least nine editions of his works before 1500, and of course many more in the sixteenth century. Peter Burke's important survey of editions and translations of the ancient historians has established that in the period 1450–1700 Caesar was the third most popular ancient historian, behind Sallust and Valerius Maximus, in terms of the number of editions and translations printed throughout Europe. More precisely, Burke charted his striking rise in popularity: in the period 1450–99 Caesar was fourth after Sallust, Valerius, and Livy; in the period 1500–49 he came third (ahead of Livy), while the second half of the sixteenth century marks the high point of Caesar's popularity: between 1550 and 1599 the *Commentaries* command the highest number of editions and translations in Europe. However, in the following half-century, 1600–49, Caesar falls to tenth place, as Tacitus becomes the most read ancient historian, and Quintus Curtius, Livy, and Suetonius all finish above him (Burke 1966).

From the first edition to the end of the sixteenth century, Italians gradually produced more and more accurate texts of the *Commentaries.* As for the scholarly apparatus surrounding the text, here Italian humanists had to invent their own commentary material, since – unlike with poets such as Horace and Vergil – there was no late antique or medieval commentary tradition to follow. The paratexts surrounding Caesar's works were initially concerned with the geography of the wars, with maps of Gaul and Spain, and often contained lists of Latin toponyms and their modern equivalents. Raimondo Marliano's geographical index to the *Gallic War* appeared in the Milan 1477 edition and from then on was regularly reprinted in later editions, so that students could learn the modern equivalents of place names mentioned in Caesar's account of his wars (e.g. *Bactavi hodie holandini populi inter Belgas*). Thanks to the new medium, Caesar becomes a popular school author in Italy after 1500, particularly useful for teaching geography (Grendler 1989: 259–60; Black 2001: 262 n. 395).

Another major step forward in the sophistication of the paratextual apparatus came with the 1513 Aldine edition; it contained Giovanni Giocondo's (1433–1515) improved text, the by now standard geographical index, maps of Gaul showing where any significant military action took place, but now followed by his helpful illustrations of the construction of the bridge over the Rhine, of various military engines, and of the sieges of a number of cities, and a map of Spain. Giocondo also adds that he needed to consult the architectural treatises by Vitruvius and by Giocondo's near-contemporary Alberti in order to interpret such technical passages. So while at a basic level the new medium of print added helpful illustrations to clarify Caesar's descriptions, these visualizations were also valuable for those interested in engineering and other technological and military innovations. The 1513 and 1517 editions are dedicated by Giocondo to Giuliano de' Medici, and the Latin word order in the dedication underlines the appropriateness of this text for this leader: "Julius' *Commentaries* seem a highly appropriate gift for you, Giuliano, for this purest Latin work is suited to your spotless character" (*Iuliano Iulii commentaria, quod candidissimi animi tui moribus candidissimum hoc opus maxime conveniens videtur munus*; Caesar 1517: a ii v). The key word *candor*, regularly applied to Caesar's Latin, is linked here to Giuliano's upright character, while this interest in the significance of names is paralleled in other encomia of the time: rhetoricians suggested an association between Leo X and Augustus, as patrons of literary and artistic culture, and also correspondingly a parallel between his father Lorenzo the Magnificent and Julius Caesar; this is illustrated, for instance, by Andrea del Sarto's *Triumph of Caesar* in the Medici villa at Poggio a Caiano, where a Caesar (or Augustus) who looks like Lorenzo is portrayed as receiving gifts of exotic animals (Cox-Rearick 1984). Similarly Pope Julius II possibly took his papal name from his ambition to be a successful military leader as well as pope, and was perhaps also inspired by the fact that his predecessor on St. Peter's throne, the notorious Borgia pope, Alexander VI, had taken his name from another great military leader (Alexander the Great) and named his illegitimate son Cesare (Borgia) (Shaw 1993; Temple 2006). Cesare Borgia in turn identified strongly with his namesake: he had a sword made on whose scabbard was the motto *cum numine Caesaris omen* ("with Caesar's divine will, good omen"), though *nomine* would also have been appropriate (in fact the motto may have been deliberately ambiguous), and he even attempted to imitate Caesar's triumphs in his triumphant entry into Rome in 1500 (Wyke 2007: 76–9, 143–4).

While the first printed commentary on Caesar had appeared outside of Italy – in the Swiss Henricus Glareanus's 1538 edition (Margolin 1985) – the Italians produced two important commentated editions in the second half of the century. Fulvio Orsini owned three different MSS of Caesar's works, including one he claimed was 600 years old, now Vat. Lat. 3324 (Brown 1972: 4), and in 1570 he published his emended text along with variant readings and the first ever collection of fragments from works by or attributed to Caesar, as well as the by now standard elements of the apparatus: indices of place names, maps, and illustrations of sieges and fortifications (Caesar 1570). Both Orsini's edition and the one produced the following year by Aldus Manutius the Younger, which incorporated Orsini's readings, contained Paolo Manuzio's dedication of the work to Paolo Rhamnusio: there Caesar is recommended as a model for Rhamnusio's own Latin history of Doge Enrico Dandolo's conquest of Constantinople in the Fourth Crusade. The role of both Caesar and Dandolo is that of reminding Italians that in the past Romans and Venetians had conquered the military threat from the East. Aldo's edition was reprinted several times, and to the maps and figures of military bridges, fortifications, and siege-towers he adds illustrations of military formations and weapons, plus some of the stranger animals mentioned in the *Commentaries*, such as the elk and the bison (Caesar 1571). Caesar's text, then, was seen as instructive on several fronts: it taught pure Latin, princely virtues, military tactics and engineering, European geography, and natural history.

Italian vernacular translations of Caesar

Another striking, almost unique, indication of Caesar's importance in Italy was the number of translations into the Italian vernacular. Peter Burke's survey (1966) estimates that in the Cinquecento there were 27 editions of French translations of Caesar and 26 Italian editions, but perhaps more significantly, as far as Italy itself is concerned, these 26 editions meant that there were more Italian vernacular translations of Caesar than of any other ancient historian (21 of Tacitus, 19 of Livy, 12 of Sallust). After the unusually early translation by Pier Candido Decembrio in 1438, there was another fifteenth-century *volgarizzamento* in 1467 by a translator in the Este court who signed himself Polismagna (Tanturli 1988: 223), but neither of these was ever printed. However, two *volgarizzamenti* were published in close proximity at the start of the sixteenth century, at a time when few vernacular translations of the classics were being made in Italy, and a third one in the 1550s. In 1512 Agostino Ortica della Porta's was the first Italian translation of the *Commentaries* to be printed and was popular enough to go through 17 editions by 1574. It too contained a list of ancient place names with their modern equivalents, but interestingly the translator apologizes for the list's brevity, which was caused, he claims, by the speed with which he had to work towards publication: all this suggests an urgent demand for an Italian version. Della Porta's letter of dedication to Ottaviano di Campofregoso, the Genoese Doge, underlines the fact that this *volgarizzamento* will allow those who do not know Latin to read this great work and thus benefit from a knowledge of history, "della vita humana maestra e guida" (Caesar 1547: A ii r). Later editions of this translation will also include the standard paratexts from the Latin editions: apart from the geographical index and maps, there are regularly diagrams of bridges, palisades, sieges, etc.

This demand for a vernacular Caesar is further confirmed by the fact that soon after, in 1518, a Florentine, Dante Popoleschi, also had his translation printed. Here too the introductory letter (by Carlo Aldobrandi to the reader) praises the translator for his service "ad commune utilità," but adds, perhaps criticizing Della Porta's version, that Popoleschi's translation contains no new or recondite words, or strange sentences, but straightforward vocabulary, harmonious, ordered sentences, and idioms used by the most refined men (Caesar 1518: 1r). Popoleschi's Italian is thus the appropriate equivalent of Caesar's "pure" Latin. Possibly in this period of intense debate in Italy about the language question, Popoleschi's Tuscan version was seen in some circles as preferable to Della Porta's Genoese idiom. But we also find other reasons for this *volgarizzamento*: in his dedication of the work to Iacopo Quinto de Aragone de Appiano, after the obligatory praise of history largely lifted from Cicero, the translator notes that Caesar's name is still revered today amongst those he defeated, the French and Germans. The letter also adds another significant reason for this translation, namely the vicinity of those countries whom Caesar defeated in just eight years, for now the French and Germans (presumably the translator means Swiss mercenaries) "have so filled this Italy of ours with tumult and war that it seemed to me to be appropriate, both for this reason and for the trade that we have with such nations, that our people should through this translation of ours gain knowledge of those places" (Caesar 1518: 3v). Caesar's *Commentaries* thus afforded Italians, depressed by their lack of military success against foreign powers in the Italian wars, a consolatory backward glance at a happier military past when these same countries had been defeated by Roman military genius. This is very much the period and the context in which Machiavelli wrote his political treatises with their nostalgia for the great Roman past.

Another major Tuscan translation followed in 1554 by Francesco Baldelli. This version too contains the by now standard indexes and illustrations, and was popular enough to be reprinted, 20 years later, in an edition illustrated by the great architect Andrea Palladio. This beautiful 1575 edition, reprinted in 1598 (Caesar 1598), contains the usual maps and diagrams of fortifications and bridges, but also for the first time 34 etchings of ancient battles, formations, and encampments, all executed by Palladio himself: his aim was to make Caesar's text visually intelligible as well, so that features such as camps and towers in each illustration are labeled with a series of letters (a, b, c, etc.), which are clearly picked up in Caesar's text (figure 23.3). The edition was dedicated to Jacopo Boncompagno, natural son of Pope Gregory XIII, who was appointed captain general of the papal armies in 1573. In his dedicatory letter, Palladio points out that although Italy has been "depressed" by military

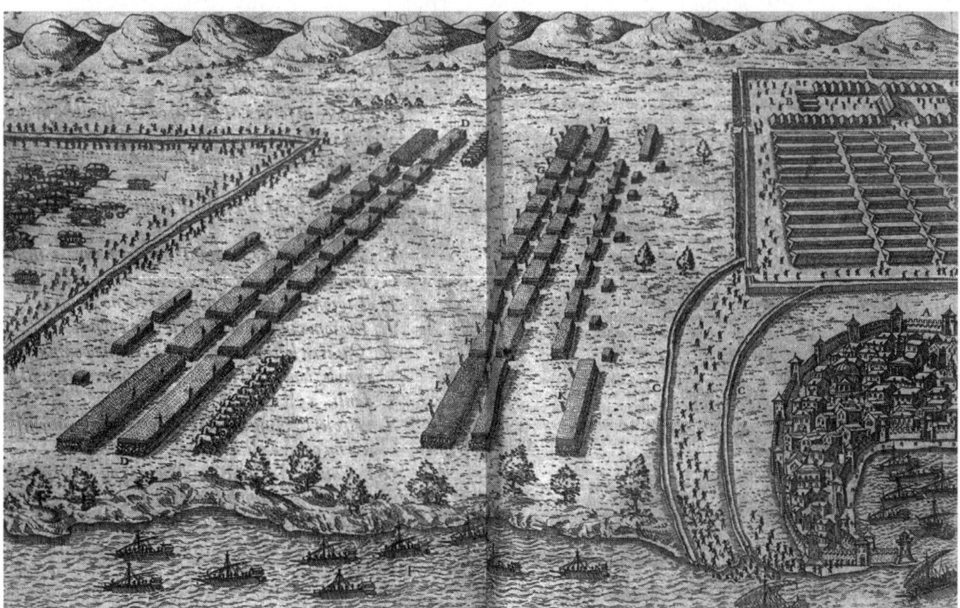

Figure 23.3 The Siege of Thapsus. Palladio's fine copper print of Caesar's Siege of Thapsus (46 BC) from *The African War* (attributed to Caesar). The print shows how Caesar placed the cohorts of his Fifth Legion (K) behind his three other lines of troops in order to withstand Metellus Scipio's elephants (E). From *Commentari di Giulio Cesare, con le figure in rame [. . .] fatte da Andrea Palladio per facilitare a chi legge, la cognition dell'Historia* (Venice: Girolamo Foglietti, 1598), pp. 380–1 (Magdalen College Old Library, E.9.4, pp. 380–1 by permission of the President and Fellows of Magdalen College, Oxford).

defeats in recent times, it is still worthwhile imitating the ancient Roman battle orders, despite recent radical changes such as the invention of firearms. After all, the Roman soldiers were mostly uneducated country folk, and their captains were not "Semidei," but humans whose clever actions can be imitated. In addition, Francesco Patrizi in his *Paralleli militari* (1594) noted that Palladio took such care over these visualizations because he saw them as valid exempla for contemporaries to follow against the Turkish threat (Patrizi 1594; Hale 1977), so once more the text and illustrations served a practical purpose, and the political-military context played a major role in Caesar's popularity in sixteenth-century Italy. In fact he will inspire other military theorists to compose their own tactical works: the significantly named Giulio Cesare Brancaccio (1515–86), a famous Neapolitan soldier, who fought in many important battles in the century, published in 1585 his eight books of *Della nuoua disciplina & vera arte militare*, based both on his military experience and on his study of Caesar's *Commentaries*. The subtitle informs the reader that in eight books he will explain "the art of war with brief rules for the convenience of soldiers, based on Julius Caesar, on how a prince can easily and cheaply defend himself in battle using only his own forces against however powerful an army, and how to attack and defeat all nations, again using his own forces" (Coldagelli 1971). These last phrases show that Brancaccio had read Machiavelli as well as Caesar. However, experience on the Italian battlefield showed that the ambitions of such works were unrealistic, and Julius Caesar remained only a distant ideal throughout the century to Italian military rulers unable to defend themselves against foreign domination.

Conclusion

In the period 1300 to 1600 the figure of Julius Caesar arouses an interest in the Italian peninsula that amounts almost to an obsession. Between the beginning and the end of the fourteenth century, from the age of Dante to that of Petrarch, humanist scholarship reveals the reality of Caesar as a human figure, no longer just a pawn in a providential plan for a divinely ordained empire, nor a mythical founder of cities, nor the inventor of the royal plural in Latin (and hence in the Romance vernaculars). Petrarch had even read some of his letters as well as his *Commentaries* (though he attributed the latter to Celsus). From 1400 onwards Caesar becomes a model for rulers and condottieri, particularly in Italian court culture, as far north as Milan and Ferrara and as far south as Naples, but at the same time in the strongest republic, Florence, he becomes a bitterly contested figure, notably in the works of Bruni, Poggio, and Machiavelli, in a wider ideological debate about republicanism and empire that has no parallel in other European countries of the time. When the last Florentine republic falls in 1530, anti-Caesarian animus gives way to admiration of the historian and military tactician, but these two aspects take on a particular inflection in Italy, where Caesar's *Commentaries* enjoy unparalleled popularity both in the original Latin and in the Italian vernacular.

In Renaissance Italy Julius Caesar was simply the most translated of all the ancient historians, suggesting that his appeal went far beyond those who could read Latin. As for his role as a Latin author, Erasmus's *De ratione studendi* (1512), which set the tone for many of the canonical ideas about ancient authors in the Cinquecento, ranked him as the fifth most important Latin writer overall and second only to Cicero as a model for Latin prose writing. As a model historian and writer of pure Latin, the author of the *Commentaries* evoked praise even from his ideological enemies such as Bruni and Poggio, but the Italian printed (and illustrated) editions throughout the sixteenth century show that his works were not just useful for learning sound Latin and ancient history: they also taught geography, military strategy and technology, architecture, and even natural history. The many editions of Italian translations of the *Commentaries* also testify to their wider relevance in the peninsula's military-political plight. The sixteenth century had begun with invasions by French, Swiss, and Spanish armies, culminating in the sack of Rome in 1527, and continued with the constant threat from the Turks and with the Spanish domination of the peninsula that was to last for over two centuries. No Italian state managed to field a consistently successful army against such forces, so Italians looked to Caesar's historical works both because they evoked an ideal past when Roman valor had reigned supreme against armies from the North and the East, and also because they sought in them practical rules for contemporaries, rules about military formations, tactics and the technology for launching and withstanding sieges: not for nothing are great architects such as Alberti and Palladio fascinated by Caesar's text, for it was in this period that Italian architects were called upon to design fortifications. In Italy competence in humanist scholarship as much as incompetence in military matters meant that Julius Caesar and his works were always in high demand.

FURTHER READING

The topic is a vast one, and one which has no overall treatment, but I am extremely grateful to the following scholars for expert advice in key areas: Vincenzo Fera, Nicola Gardini, David Rundle, Hester Schadee, and Lucy Whitaker. A good starting point on the textual tradition in the period is Brown 1976, and for a now slightly old-fashioned overview of the monarchical-republican debates Baron 1967. After that the most useful items are those dealing with the individual Italian authors: for Dante, Pastore Stocchi 1971; for Petrarch, Martellotti 1983 and Ferraù 2006a; for Salutati, Witt 1983; for Bruni, see Bruni 1996; for Poggio and Guarino, Canfora 2001; for Machiavelli, Skinner 1978. The recent edition of Petrarch's *De gestis Cesaris*, ed. G. Crevatin (Petrarca 2003) will facilitate further analysis of this important work, as will the forthcoming editions of all Petrarch's works in the series promoted by the Comitato Nazionale, headed by Michele Feo, to be published by Le Lettere, Florence. Some relevant volumes have already started to appear: *De viris illustribus II: Adam–Hercules*, ed. C. Malta (Florence: Le Lettere, 2007); *De viris illustribus IV: Compendium*, ed. P. de Capua (Florence: Le Lettere, 2007). See also Fera 2007. The catalogue of the 2008–09 Rome exhibition on Julius Caesar has two brief but useful chapters: Francesco Lo Monaco, 'Per la fortuna medievale di Cesare', in *Giulio Cesare: L'uomo, le imprese, il mito*, ed. Giovanni Gentili, Milan, Silvana Editoriale, 2008, pp. 88–93; and Claudio Strinati, 'Giulio Cesare, eroe rinascimentale', ibid., pp. 94–99. One other aspect that has received little attention so far, and where much more work needs to be done, is more detailed study of the many Italian translations, though here the essential starting point is Burke 1966.

CHAPTER TWENTY-FOUR

Some Renaissance Caesars

Carol Clark

Caesar's *Commentaries* were obviously extensively read in France in the sixteenth century. The Bibliothèque nationale de France holds editions published in Latin at Lyon in 1508, 1512, 1519, 1538, 1572, 1574, 1581, and 1588, and at Paris in 1522, 1528, 1534, 1543 and 1544, as well as translations by Robert Gaguin (1531), Étienne de L'Aigue (1545 and 1555), and Blaise de Vigenère (1576, 1589, and 1590), all Paris. Many readers, of course, would also have used the international scholarly editions published at Venice or Antwerp. They could have learned about Caesar's life from Suetonius, Sallust or Lucan, all available in Latin, and from Plutarch, available in Greek and in Latin translation, but also, from 1559, in Jacques Amyot's very successful translation into French. (It went through ten editions between 1559 and 1600, mostly at Paris but also at Lyon, Dijon, and Lausanne. North's *Lives*, an important source for Shakespeare's *Julius Caesar*, is based on Amyot's version.) Even to those whose Latin was rusty or non-existent, elements of Caesar's life-story would have been familiar from their appearance in school commonplace books and as exempla in public speeches. (We shall be discussing this point further apropos of Jean Bodin.)

If the medieval Caesar had become at times an almost mythical figure (in one version of his life, he marries Morgan le Fay and fathers Oberon), the more scientific approach to history which began to develop in the early modern period, with its greater concern for facts, chronology, and viewpoint, restored a Caesar more recognizable to those familiar with classical sources. Nevertheless, almost every account of his life or character offered at this period is colored to a greater or lesser extent by the social, political or intellectual position of the person (almost always a man) offering the account, or the person to whom it is offered.

The sixteenth-century Caesar was first and foremost the victorious general and founder of the empire, and, as such, a model for monarchs hoping to found or consolidate nations or groups of nations under their personal rule, and particularly for actual or aspiring Holy Roman Emperors. The emperor Charles V was not a man

Figure 24.1 François I, Julius Caesar, Aurora, and Diana in the forest of Fontainebleau. Bibliothèque nationale de France MS Fr. 13429.

of great learning, but he owned an Italian translation of Caesar's *Commentaries*, and commissioned from his court historian Pedro de Mexía a history of all the emperors from Julius Caesar to himself. (A similar work had been written for his predecessor Maximilian I by his historiographer Johann Spiessheimer, known as Cuspinianus. It was printed in 1540, after the deaths of both author and patron, under the title *De Caesaribus atque imperatoribus*.) Maximilian's patronage is gratefully recognized in the preface to the first translation of Caesar into German (*Julius, der erste römisch Keiser, von seinem Leben und Kriegen erstmals uss dem Latein in Tütsch gebracht*, Strasbourg, 1508), as is Charles's in that into Spanish (*Commentarios de Cayo Julio Cesar: dedicados ala S.C.C.M. del Emperador y Rey nuestro senor* (Alcalá, 1529). In his lifetime and for some time afterwards, Charles was believed to have written, or rather dictated to his secretary Willem Van Male, in 1550, a first-hand account of his own campaigns from 1515 to 1548: a kind of modern *Commentaries*. Van Male describes the composition sessions in a letter to a humanist friend. It was to have been Van Male's task to translate the text into Latin, and he modestly says that he had devised for it a style taking the best from those of Livy, Caesar, Suetonius, and Tacitus. But the work was never completed, and the manuscript, if it ever existed, was lost or suppressed in the sixteenth century.[1]

One of the great makers of history, Caesar was also revered as a writer of history and as an orator. Humanist educators in particular repeat how he excelled in both arms and letters, insisting on the importance of the latter to their princely pupils who no doubt were inclined to privilege the former.

The *Gallic War*, familiar to us all from our schooldays, was not in general use as a schoolbook in France until much later times: in the sixteenth century the preferred school authors were Cicero, Terence, and Virgil.[2] The earliest school edition of Caesar held in the Bibliothèque nationale de France dates from 1761 (printed for the École royale-militaire). But it appears to have been considered valuable reading for young monarchs and their heirs in our period. The first modern translation into French, made by Robert Gaguin in 1485 (first printed in 1531) is dedicated, with a prefatory letter, to the 15-year-old Charles VIII. Later, a remarkable treatment of Caesar's text was prepared for François I by François Demoulins (or De Moulins or Des Moulins: he latinized his name as Molinius), who had been the young king's tutor and was now his chaplain.[3] Ever since the victory of his troops over the Swiss at Marignan in 1515, François had been likened to Julius Caesar, conqueror of the Helvetii. His mother, the ambitious and managing Louise de Savoie, particularly encouraged this identification, and she encouraged Demoulins to compose for the king a version of the *Gallic Wars* in dialogue form, in which François should question Caesar about his campaigns and victories. The splendidly illustrated manuscript which resulted, begun in 1519, was completed in 1520 (when François's campaign to succeed Maximilian as Holy Roman Emperor was at its height) and remained in the royal collection until the partial dispersal of Henri III's books in 1589. Its three volumes are now held, one in London (BL MS Harley 6205), one in Paris (BnF MS Fr. 13429, fig. 24.1) and one at Chantilly (Musée Condé, MS 1139). It has never been printed, but a facsimile was made in 1894 for the Société des Bibliophiles français (BnF MS Facsim.144–6).

The text is given a frame-story in which François and Caesar meet three times, first in the forest of St-Germain-en-Laye, then in the forest of Fontainebleau, and in book 3 first in the maze at François's chateau at Cognac and then in the "forest de Crage." (No-one is quite sure where this is.) The occasion of their first meeting is unexplained: we are simply told that

> Francoys par la grace de Dieu Roy de France, secund Caesar victeur et domateur des Souyces, le dernier iour D'auril ung moys après la nativite de son secund filz en son parc de sainct Germain en Laye rancontra Iule Caesar, et l'interrogea subtilement du contenu en premier lyvre des commentaires.
>
> Caesar premier subjugateur des helveces luy fyt gracieuse response [. . .]
>
> (François by the grace of God King of France, second Caesar and victor over the Swiss, on the last day of April a month after the birth of his second son, in his park at St Germain-en-Laye, met Julius Caesar and subtly questioned him about the content of the first book of the *Commentaries*.
>
> Caesar, first subjugator of the Helvetii, graciously answered . . .)

There is, alas, nothing particularly subtle about the questions put in François's mouth: they are more like the prompts in a catechism. Caesar's original text is heavily cut, but lengthened again by being split up into question-and-answer form (with much scope for formal expressions of respect on both sides), and interspersed with "Additions" (titled as such and presumably by Demoulins himself, with more or less help from Pigghe), which can be anything from notes on place names or Roman military formations to reflections on kingship. We may sample Demoulins's rewriting method from the first page of Caesar's text:

> Le trescrestian Roy François
> Demande a Caesar
> En quantes parties est divisee toute la gaule qui vous a aultreffois tant donne de peine. Caesar dictez le moy ie vous prie.
>
> Caesar respond
> Roy liberal & pacifique vray heritier de ma gloire et fortune, ainsi que iay peu aultreffoys comprandre elle doyt estre divisee en troys parties habitees par troys peuples qui sont differans en troys manieres, en loix, institutions, & langages. Les troys peuples sont celtes, belges & aquitaniens.
>
> (The Most Christian King of France asks Caesar: Into how many parts is Gaul, which formerly cost you so much trouble, divided? Tell me, Caesar, I pray you.
>
> Caesar replies: Generous and peace-loving King, true inheritor of my glory and fortune, so far as I was able to understand long ago, it must be divided into three parts, inhabited by three peoples who differ from each other in three ways, in laws, institutions and languages. The three people are the Celts, the Belgians, and the Aquitanians.)

Figure 24.2 Title-page of Antoine de Bandole, *Les Paralleles de Cesar et de Henry IIII*, Paris, 1609. Bodleian Library, University of Oxford. Mason II 35.

In the second volume the meeting is much more circumstantially described, and takes on some of the attributes of romance. Caesar's arrival in the forest is preceded by that of two fair ladies: Aurora and Diana. In the illustrations François wears contemporary princely garb, but Caesar combines Roman military dress with a long beard like an enchanter of fable (see figure 24.1). In this volume the writer is at much greater pains than before to "bring the story home" to the young king. It begins with François hunting in the forest of Bièvre (near Fontainebleau). All his favorite dogs are listed by name, and Demoulins makes this the occasion for a disquisition on gaining the loyalty of dogs and men. François meets first Diana, who is also out hunting and is described and painted in fetching sixteenth-century hunting costume, showing a daring amount of calf in patterned close-fitting boots. The goddess wonders whether she should stay in this remote spot with the young huntsmen (François's reputation with women made this a very understandable worry), but Aurora reassures her and they settle down under a tree to observe François's meeting with Caesar, who appears as "ung ancien homme de venerable stature." François quickly recognizes him as "son amy Iule Caesar," and they proceed to have a discussion about the nature of empire, beginning:

> Le Roy demande.
> Invincible Caesar, dictes moy verite, que vous semble de nostre temps.
> Caesar respond.
> Il est Imperial.
> Le Roy demande.
> Quelles condicions sont requises a ung bon empereur.
> Caesar respond.
> Celles que iavoys.
>
> (The King asks: Invincible Caesar, tell me the truth. What do you think of our time? Caesar replies: It is Imperial. The King asks: What conditions are required in a good emperor? Caesar replies: Those that I had.)

Caesar goes on to describe his victory over Pompey. François asks if empire is a desirable thing (for the emperor); Caesar replies no, it is a painful duty, and gives a brief account of the lives and deaths of the Roman emperors who succeeded him. (In this version he is credited with knowledge of all important events from his own death to the time of writing.) François asks if Germans have the right always to elect the Holy Roman Emperor, and Caesar replies that they do not. François asks who does have the right, and Caesar replies Jesus Christ (the illustration to this page is a Crucifixion). Caesar expresses his regret that he lived too soon to have known Christ's message, and also contrives to hint that François himself would be the Lord's most likely choice.

The dialogue treatment of the *Gallic War* resumes on p. XXI *verso*, again with numerous "Additions" and 12 full-page illustrations of Roman siege engines. Interspersed in the text are also seven very fine medallion portraits labeled as those of Caesar's principal lieutenants. But the figures are in sixteenth-century dress and a contemporary hand has written by them the names of François's own closest comrades-in-arms.

The third volume has the most dramatic introduction. The meeting of François and Caesar takes place in a violent thunderstorm, when only the young king has dared to go out into the maze. Preceded by a "grande fulguration," Caesar appears, dressed in imperial robes, gathers François in his arms, kisses him, and calls him his son. There is talk of the Field of the Cloth of Gold, which is imminent, and François leaves for Ardres. Caesar appears to him again in the forest of Crage, and they resume their dialogue on the Gallic War.

We do not know, of course, with what attention François read these three volumes. They do smack somewhat too much of the schoolroom for a king of 25. He also owned a copy of Agostino Ortica della Porta's translation of the *Commentaries* into Italian (*Commentarii di Gaio Giulio Cesare,* Tusculum, s.d., BnF Res. J. 2326).

We have no idea, however, what effect the study of Caesar may have had on his political and military decisions.

But the *Gallic War* was often to be put before sixteenth-century readers as a manual of the military art. In 1558 Gabriel Symeoni, a Florentine humanist settled in Lyon, author of works on heraldry and a collection of emblems, produced a volume ambitiously titled *Cesar renouvellé par les observations militaires du S. Gabriel Symeon* (Paris, 1558) and dedicated to Monseigneur le Daulphin de France (the sickly 14-year-old future François II). Symeoni's method, like Machiavelli's treatment of Livy in the *Discorsi*, is to establish a series of military and political maxims and then to illustrate them from the *Commentaries.*

A similar but more systematic approach is followed by the much more historically important Peter Ramus, philosopher, rhetorician and deviser of the Ramist method, who published at Paris in 1559 a *Liber de moribus veterum Gallorum* and a *Liber de Caesaris militia.* Cl.-G. Dubois describes Ramus's method in these volumes as "cerner les concepts, les analyser et les regrouper" (grasping and defining ideas, analyzing them, and ordering them in groups). In the dedicatory letter to the first volume (both are dedicated to Charles, Cardinal de Lorraine) Ramus mentions that he has been giving daily lectures on the *Commentaries* (he held the chair of eloquence and philosophy, directly appointed by the King) and this, combined with careful private reading, has allowed him to present the fruit (*fructum*) of his studies in two small books. In the preface to the second, Ramus shows a more seemly modesty than Symeoni had done, acknowledging the incongruity of a work on the military art written by an arts don and dedicated to a cardinal:

> Quid Cardinali (inquies) cum istac arte? Ecquid (inquam) literarum professori cum clypeo et ense?
>
> (What has a cardinal, you will say, to do with this art? And what, I shall say, has a professor of letters to do with the sword and shield?)[4]

But he argues that while many Greeks, Romans, Italians, and Frenchmen have already written about Caesar, none have proposed a method of imitating his virtues (*virtutes*), and this is what he means to do. And while it is right for princes in time of war to seek peace, it is also appropriate for them in peacetime to study the arts of war (*magni principis proprium est et bello pacem quaerere, et in pace belli artes non contemnere*). This volume was translated into French by Pierre Poisson (*Traicté de l'art militaire)*, but not until 1583.

In the *Liber de moribus veterum Gallorum*, Ramus promises to record the way of life, customs, military discipline, and institutions of "our" ancestors (*maiorum patrumque nostrorum vitam, praelia, disciplinas, religiones, iura Rerumpublicarum et leges commemorabit*), showing the "sources from which we have drawn" (*fontes unde hausimus*). This work was translated immediately on its appearance by Michel de Castelnau (*Traicté des façons et coustumes des anciens Gauloys*, Paris, 1559): perhaps a sign of increasing interest among the educated French in their earliest recorded ancestors. Whereas Frenchmen had previously preferred to think of themselves as descended from the Franks, and through them (improbably enough) from the ancient Trojans, accounts of these legendary ancestors were now being replaced by studies of the historical Gauls, with Caesar as the principal source of information. Historians and jurists, particularly those opposed to the development of absolute royal power, increasingly wished to cast the Gauls in a heroic light and present their *iura* and *leges* as models of wise government. (Ramus, we note, refers to the Gaulish settlements as *respublicae*, a word which Caesar reserves for the Roman state.) A striking example is the *Franco-Gallia* (1573) of the Huguenot jurist Hotman, which attempted to show that monarchy should be elective and constitutional, by reference to the customs of ancient Gaul, before the Frankish invasion (*Franco-Gallia, libellus statum veteris reipublicae Gallicae, deinde a Francis occupatae, describens*). Translations of the *Gallic War* accordingly appear accompanied by increasingly detailed maps which attempt to relate territories and settlements of the Gauls to contemporary French provinces and towns, allowing local antiquarians to identify themselves more reliably with their Gaulish ancestors.

The first edition of the *Gallic War* accompanied by a map had appeared at Venice in 1513, but Demoulins warns against the use of it, and commissioned for his third volume two specially drawn maps, one of northwestern and one of southwestern and central France, labeled with an odd mixture of French and Latin place names. Many of his "Additions" identify tribe name used by Caesar with the inhabitants of present-day French towns. Indeed he encourages François to heed Caesar as the best source of information about the Gauls, his subjects, and also the "nature des Souyces & Alemans," his past and likely future enemies. Caesar is a sure and reliable witness, he says, speaking from experience and not hearsay. (Demoulins of course, in common with most of his contemporaries, takes it for granted that the "nature" of particular peoples, geographically defined, will still be the same as it was in Caesar's day.)

Identifying the peoples conquered by Caesar as the ancestors of contemporary Frenchmen lent the *Commentaries* an added interest, but of course could also compromise Caesar's hitherto unquestioned status as hero, making him appear instead as the cruel oppressor of the rude but noble Gauls.

Caesar's own nobility of character is increasingly questioned as the century progresses, and particularly after the outbreak of the Wars of Religion in 1562. To those who lived through these fratricidal conflicts, which raged intermittently for over 30 years, civil war seemed the worst of human misfortunes, and Caesar, the victor of the Roman civil wars, appears, especially in Protestant writing, as less a hero than a tyrant, willing to sacrifice the peace and lives of his countrymen to his personal ambition. In this version of the story, particularly as told by the "monarchomaques," the theorists of the right of resistance to tyrants, it is Brutus, not Caesar, who is the hero. A good example of their writings is the *Vindiciae contra tyrannos* (Vengeance against tyrants) published in 1578 under the pseudonym of Junius Brutus. (The reference is probably to the semi-legendary sixth-century tyrant-slayer. Caesar's assassin, however, believed himself to be descended from the man with whom he shared a forename.)

According to the author of the *Vindiciae* (once thought to be Philippe de Duplessis-Mornay, but now believed to be Hubert Languet), magistrates are the true representatives of the people's will. At this time France had a hereditary caste of lawyers, magistrates, and officials, known as the "gens de robe." This class, with its regard for tradition and customary law, provided most of the antiquaries and political thinkers that we shall be looking at in the second part of this chapter, and we regularly find in their writing an uneasy combination of admiration for Caesar as man and writer and hostility to him as the destroyer of Republican institutions.

When Henri III, the Huguenots' *bête noire*, died childless in 1589 the heir apparent was the Protestant Henri de Navarre. But he had to fight a four-year war against the Ligue, partisans of extreme Catholicism and an alliance with Spain, and to abjure the Protestant faith, before being formally accepted as Henri IV in 1594. (Popular history ascribes to him the saying "Paris vaut bien une messe," Paris is worth a mass.) His bravery, intelligence in military matters, and mild cynicism about the supernatural, his victory in civil war introducing a much longed-for period of stability, and finally his death by assassination all made the comparison with Caesar tempting, and at least two contemporary works are based on this analogy, one by Georges l'Apostre, a Catholic polemicist, published at Utrecht in 1598 (*La devise de Henry IV, où il est comparé à Cesar*) the other by Antoine de Bandole (*Les Paralleles de Cesar et de Henry IIII. Avec les Commentaires de Cesar, & les Annotations de Blaise de Viginere* [sic]. *De nouveau Illustrez de Maximes Politiques par ledit De Bandole* (Paris, 1600; further editions in 1609 and 1625), which is wholehearted in its praise of the king.

The first 40 pages of this sizable tome are occupied first in generalizations about war and the natures of men, and then by an account of the civil wars of the century just ended, for which the blame is firmly put on Spanish interference. The parallels proper between Caesar and Henri begin on page 44 and continue to page 122, which is a summary of Henri's life to date. The remainder of the book is a re-edition of Blaise de Vigenère's translation of the *Commentaries* with, in the margins, political maxims added by Bandole. The 1609 edition of the work is dedicated to Monseigneur le Daulphin, the future Louis XIII, then aged eight (see fig. 24.2), to whom Bandole promises "la fortune d'Alexandre, tant que vous suivrez la resolution de CESAR et la vaillance de HENRY" (the good fortune of Alexander, so long as you imitate the resolve of Caesar and the bravery of Henry).

Of members of the magistrate class applying their reading of Caesar to their own purposes in the latter half of the century, three stand out: Étienne Pasquier (1529–1615), Jean Bodin (1530–96), and Michel de Montaigne (1534–92).

A practicing lawyer and specialist in customary law, once a pupil of Hotman (though he remained a Catholic), Pasquier began while still young and continued throughout his life to collect information about French history and customs. This he published under the title *Recherches de la France*, of which book I appeared in 1560, book II in 1565, and the complete work, in ten books, in 1621, after his death.

Pasquier's debt to Caesar is the most obvious in the first five chapters of book I of the *Recherches*, which treat of the ancient Gauls. In the first chapter he argues that the Gauls were underestimated by posterity because they did not write down their own history (the chapter begins with a general discussion of the relative value of oral and written history). Pasquier means to correct this misjudgment, and to "reconnoistre au vray la grandeur de nos ancestres," their "coeur genereux" and "vertu" (to recognize the true greatness of our ancestors, their noble hearts and virtue). Julius Caesar did not consider them barbarians, says chapter 2: this was because of the good organization of their society (many examples given from the *Commentaries*). Chapters 3 and 4 discuss detailed points in Caesar's account of the Gauls, and chapter 5 concludes this section by examining the failings of the Gauls which allowed the Romans to overcome them. Again most illustrations are from the *Commentaries.* The main failing mentioned is their reliance on allies to help them face the Roman onslaught: Pasquier condemns this approach, and says that it is essential for each society to have sufficient native forces of its own for its defense (a position already taken by Machiavelli in the *Discorsi*).

An almost exact contemporary, and for some years a colleague, of Pasquier's was Jean Bodin, professor of law at Toulouse and later *procureur du roi*. He also seems to have had some diplomatic responsibilities, visiting England in 1581 in connection with the projected marriage of the duc d'Alençon to Queen Elizabeth. The work for which he is best known is *Les Six Livres de la Republique*, first published in French in 1576, then translated into Latin (by the author) in 1586 and into English in 1606, a pioneering if forbidding work of political theory. ("Republique" here means "state," not specifically "republic".) Julius Caesar plays a surprisingly small role in this work, but a larger one in Bodin's earlier *Methodus ad facilem historiarum cognitionem* (Method for the easy understanding of history), 1566 (and 1572, 1576, 1579, etc.), which puts forward ideas on the correct method but also the purpose of historical study.

Bodin argues (with much justification) that most reading of history undertaken in schools in his day had as its purpose rhetoric: the development of effective oratory. Schoolboys were required to keep commonplace books, in which they entered under topic headings famous deeds, but more often famous sayings (*apophthegmata)* from ancient history. The deeds might later be used as exempla in their compositions, the sayings as ornament. Bodin argues that students should not be content to collect words as a stimulus to eloquence, but should study the plans and deeds of great men as a stimulus to effective action. But this study must be systematic, as the rhetorical study was, and chapter III of the *Methodus* considers how to establish the appropriate topic headings (*loci communes*) for making extracts from history. He suggests that readers, rather than copying extracts, should mark in the margins of their texts, briefly if possible, passages that exemplify the chosen *loci communes,* e.g. U for *Utile*, useful and H for *Honestum*, honorable (he observes that the useful and the honorable often – though that implies not always – go hand in hand). We have seen that many printed versions of the *Commentaries* already do something similar, and in Bandole's later *Paralleles* the marginal notes will seem almost to overwhelm the text. Montaigne's marginal annotations to his copy of the *Commentaries* (Antwerp, 1570) are much more economical.

In Chapter IV, on the choice of the best historians, Bodin gives as his criteria for a good historian that he should have had personal knowledge of the period and events described (all sixteenth-century writers on Caesar mention this as his great strength), but also that he should have been praised by his contemporaries or near successors, who had themselves been involved in the same events. On these grounds he places Caesar among the seven best historians of all time, rivaled among the Romans only by Sallust.

In the long chapter VI (150 pages in Mesnard's modern translation) on the constitution of states (a first sketch for the *Republique)*, there are 20 references to Caesar, mostly on the customs of the Gauls, but also in the passage referring to factions in states, where Bodin observes how commonly men elected by the people to established offices in the state use this power to establish an unconstitutional tyranny. It was thus, he observes, that the Roman people fell under the yoke of Caesar (one of the few negative references to Caesar in this work). He also challenges Caesar's account of how faction works, though professing himself reluctant to disagree with the great historian about anything.

The much shorter chapter IX, on how to tell the origins of peoples, again draws heavily on Caesar (16 references to his account of the Gauls). In chapter V, on judging the value of histories, Bodin had already stressed the importance of taking into consideration the "nature" of peoples, and given some indication of how this might be determined. To him "nature" is a given that human institutions cannot change: new laws can have only temporary effects, and we presently see the peoples reverting to their original character. He attributes these characteristics to terrain, winds, etc. (an early example of the "climate theory" often attributed to Montesquieu but already found in Machiavelli and indeed Polybius). In chapter IX he returns to these ideas, and also suggests how languages, and particularly place and tribe names, may be used to determine the origins of peoples.

Montaigne knew both Pasquier and Bodin personally, and takes issue with Bodin on the subject of Cicero and Cato in book II, chapter 32 of his *Essais*. His background was similar to theirs: he had legal training and as a young man had held the office of magistrate as a member of the Parlements first of Perigueux and then of Bordeaux. He was elected Mayor of Bordeaux in 1581 and re-elected for a further two-year mandate in 1583 (his father had previously held this office), and is believed to have engaged in secret diplomacy between the crown and Henri of Navarre in the later 1580s. Like most of the magistrate class Montaigne was a moderate in politics, remaining a Catholic and loyal to the crown but horrified by the bloodshed and treachery of the religious wars, detesting the excesses of the Ligue and the interference of Spain. Many differences, however, set him apart from men even of his own apparent type.

For a start, his family was attempting to pursue its social ascent from the class of merchants, to which it had clearly belonged in his great-grandfather's day, to the landed, military aristocracy. Steps on the way were buying land (his grandfather had bought the estate of Montaigne), military service (his father had served in the Italian wars), and a period of "living nobly" – that is, without any visible means of support but the revenues of one's estate. The fact that Montaigne's father bought him the *charges* of magistrate at Perigueux and Bordeaux (inheritance or purchase from the previous incumbent were the normal methods of succession to such offices) suggests that he was envisaging a period in the *noblesse de robe* for his son before the family's final accession to the *noblesse d'épée*. But Montaigne obviously had other ideas, and since he was to die without male heirs the question of the family's status was never fully resolved.

Montaigne's upbringing, as he describes it in book I, chapter 26 of the *Essais*, had been most unusual. Wishing him to be a good Latinist, his father (who himself had little book-learning) entrusted him, as soon as he could leave his wet-nurse, to a German tutor who was instructed to speak to him in nothing but Latin. As a result, Montaigne says, he spoke Latin before French, and by the time he was seven or eight read the *Metamorphoses* as other children would read a fairy tale. At age six he was sent away to boarding-school, though accompanied by a private tutor (common practice for noble boys at that time). There, he says, "mon latin s'abastardit incontinent" (my Latin promptly became corrupt); nevertheless, one thing he enjoyed was taking leading parts in Latin plays written by the masters, Buchanan, Guerente, and Muret. He may, therefore, have acted in Muret's *Julius Caesar.* But he did not, so far as we know, read Caesar himself with any attention until he was 45.

Montaigne's encounter with Caesar is extremely well documented, since his copy of the *Commentaries* (Antwerp: Plantin, 1570) survives. It is held in the Musée Condé library at Chantilly, and contains more than six hundred marginal notes. (The books most heavily annotated are the *Gallic War* book VII and the *Civil War* book III.) Most of the notes are summaries in a few words of the passage in question ("Victoire de Cesar sur les Anglois"), sometimes with a word or two of judgment ("Paroles braves de Divico à Cesar," "Honteuse [shameful] supplication des Gaulois à Cesar"), but sometimes take the form of maxims ("Le soldat aux guerres civiles donne plus à la crainte qu'au devoir" – a soldier in civil war is driven more by fear than duty). Some of these maxims are directly translated from the text, in which case the Latin is underlined, others are of Montaigne's own devising, but it must be said that none are strikingly original. Much more interesting is the 350-word judgment of Caesar written on the flyleaf. Montaigne tells us in *Essais* II, 10 that since his memory began to deteriorate with age, he has formed the habit of writing a page or so of personal comment in his books as he finishes reading them. In this chapter of the *Essais* he reproduces his own comments on Guiccardini; those on Caesar do not appear verbatim, but elements of them are reused in this chapter and in II, 33.

Dates written in Montaigne's own hand show that he was reading and annotating the *Commentaries* between 25 February and 21 July 1578, probably about the same time as Bodin's *Methodus*, and he judges Caesar firstly and principally as a historian ("le plus disert, le plus net et le plus sincere historien qui fut iamais" – the most eloquent, the clearest and the most honest historian that ever was), praising his modesty and his impartial treatment of his enemies. This is the book, says Montaigne, that a general should constantly have before his eyes, as the Maréchal Strozzi did, studying him as Alexander did Homer, or Marcus Brutus Polybius.

Caesar is a constant presence in the *Essais* also, with about a hundred references to him by name and many others (usually the better-known stories) in which he is simply referred to as "the man who said," "the general who said," or even, in the context of the civil wars, "ce brigand," "cette ame desreiglee" (that disordered spirit).

Montaigne, like the other members of the magistrate class whom we have mentioned, regarded with horror the civil wars of his own times and attempts, by both Protestants and extreme Catholics, to overturn France's traditional institutions. Montaigne also had a reverence, which he himself recognized as beyond reason, for the institutions of republican Rome:

> Me trouvant inutile à ce siecle, je me rejecte à cet autre, et en suis si embabouyné que l'estat de cette vieille Romme, libre, juste et florissante ... m'interesse et me passionne.
>
> (Finding myself of no use to this century, I turn back towards that other time, and am so besotted by it that the state of that old Rome, free, just and flourishing, involves me and raises my passion).

At such moments, despite all his admiration for Caesar, he says, " ... j'ay attaqué cent querelles pour la defence de Pompeius et pour la cause de Brutus" (I have a hundred times taken sides in defense of Pompey and in the cause of Brutus) (*Essais* III, 9, 996). (The name Brutus occurs nineteen times in the *Essais*, but not all the references are to the assassin of Caesar.)

Even in the manuscript judgment of 1578, which begins by describing Caesar as "un des plus grands miracles de Nature," Montaigne refers to his "injuste et tres inique cause," meaning the civil and not the Gallic war: in the *Essais* he does not appear particularly interested in Caesar as a source for Gaulish history, nor in the project of rehabilitation of the Gauls. In the part of *Essais* II, 10 composed around the same time he uses even stronger language, referring to "sa mauvaise cause et l'ordure de sa pestilente ambition."

In the first of the three chapters largely devoted to Caesar, book II, chapter 33, "Histoire de Spurina" (none of Montaigne's chapters are devoted to a single subject and often their titles do not correspond to their content) he begins by considering the varied power of the human passions as motivators of our conduct, then focuses on "love" (in the context, sexual desire) and ambition, taking Caesar as the main example. As well as his well-documented sexual attraction, all Caesar's excellent qualities are listed and illustrated: learning, eloquence, vigilance, energy, tolerance of fatigue, clemency, self-confidence, supreme courage, kindness to his friends, and moderation in victory over his enemies. But, says Montaigne,

> ... toutes ces belles inclinations furent alterees et estouffees par cette furieuse passion ambitieuse ... ce seul vice, à mon advis, perdit en luy le plus beau et le plus riche naturel qui fut onques, et a rendu sa memoire abominable à tous les gens de bien, pour avoir

voulu chercher sa gloire de la ruyne de son pays et subversion de la plus puissante et fleurissante chose publique que le monde verra jamais.

(All these good inclinations were corrupted and stifled by that furious passion of ambition ... this one vice, in my opinion, destroyed in him the finest and richest nature that ever was, and made his memory hateful to all good men, for having sought his own glory through the ruin of his country and the overthrow of the most powerful and flourishing state that the world will ever see.)

If chapter 33 is a character study of Caesar, chapter 34 is an account of his military methods ("Observations sur les moyens de faire la guerre de Jules Cesar"), and chapter 36 ("Des plus excellens hommes") considers him, in competition with Alexander, for the place of one of the three greatest men in history. (The other two are Homer and Epaminondas.) The two were equal in many things, says Montaigne, and Caesar even greater in some (an addition after the first appearance of the chapter says that they were like two fires or two torrents ravaging the world), but in the end he gives the preference to Alexander because Caesar applied his great gifts to "la ruine de son pays et l'empirement (worsening) universel du monde."

The second edition of the *Essais* appeared in 1588, including a new book III, of thirteen longer chapters, and numerous additions to the first two books which had been published in 1580. A third, posthumous edition of 1595 again includes many, some long, additions and a few alterations to the text of 1588, made by Montaigne before his death in 1592 with a view to a new edition. Some of the most hostile mentions of Caesar (for example the reference at III, 1, 802 to the "enhortements enragez de cette ame desreglee," – the insane exhortations of that disordered soul) are found in this later material, as are at least half a dozen comparisons between Alexander and Caesar, perhaps the product of a rereading of Amyot's Plutarch. But though Montaigne's hostility to Caesar as the destroyer of republican institutions is undiminished, his chief interest in him now seems to be as a personality, and one who can be studied, not as a model for imitation (not, at any rate, for a private citizen like himself) but as another example of a human being. As he says in the final chapter (III, 13, "De l'experience," 1073):

La vie de Cesar n'a poinct plus d'exemple que la nostre pour nous; et emperiere et populaire, c'est tousjours une vie que tous accidents humains regardent.

(Caesar's life holds no more examples for us than our own; whether an emperor's or an ordinary man's, it is still a life subject to all the chances of human existence.)

Caesar and Alexander are now both praised for their ability to unbend and behave like ordinary human beings, even in moments when great demands are being made of them:

Quand je vois et Caesar et Alexandre, au plus espais de sa grande besogne, jouyr si plainement des plaisirs naturels, et par consequent necessaires et justes, je ne dicts pas que ce soit relascher son ame, je dicts que c'est la roidir, sousmetant par vigueur de courage a l'usage de la vie ordinaire ces violentes occupations et laborieuses pensees.

(When I see Caesar and Alexander, in the thick of their great tasks, enjoying so fully the pleasures which are natural, and therefore necessary and just, I do not call this relaxing one's soul but bracing it for effort, using one's strength of mind to submit those violent preoccupations and demanding thoughts to the requirements of everyday life.)

"Sages," he adds in 1592, "s'ils eussent creu que c'etait la leur ordinaire vacation, cette-cy l'extraordinaire." (If only they had been wise enough to think of the latter as their everyday concern, the former [war] as the extraordinary one.)

His ideal of human excellence is no longer Caesar or Alexander (nor, as it once briefly was, Cato the Younger), but Socrates:

Vrayment il est bien plus aisé de parler comme Aristote et vivre comme Caesar, qu'il n'est aisé de parler et vivre comme Socrate (III, 12, 1055).

(Truly, it is easier to speak like Aristotle and live like Caesar than it is to speak and live like Socrates.)

Awe has been replaced by respect, and the "miracle de Nature," the victorious general, brilliant strategist, tireless campaigner, eloquent orator, and incomparable historian, must now take second place to the man Montaigne came to regard as most fully human.

FURTHER READING

On late-medieval translations of Caesar, see M. Schmidt-Chazan, "Les traductions de la *Guerres des Gaules* et le sentiment national au Moyen Age," in *Annales de Bretagne et des pays de l'Ouest* 87 (1980), and Frédéric Duval, "Le *Livre des commentaires Cesar sur le fait des batailles de Gaule* par Robert Gaguin (1485)," *Cahiers de recherches médiévales*, 13 spécial, 2006 (http://crm.revues.org//index856.html).

On plays, J. Grevin, *César*, ed. J. Foster (Paris, 1974) includes the Latin text of Muret's *Julius Caesar.*

On sixteenth-century views of Gauls, see Cl.-G. Dubois, *Celtes et Gaulois au XVIe siècle: le développement d'un mythe nationaliste* (Paris, 1973), and C. Beaune, *Naissance de la nation France* (Paris, 1985), appendix to chapter 8: "Troyens et Gaulois aux 15e et 16e siècles" (available in English as *The Birth of an Ideology*, trans. S. Ross, 1991).

On François I see A.-M. Lecoq, *François Ier imaginaire* (Paris, 1987).

On sixteenth-century ideas of historiography, see G. Huppert, *L'Idee de l'histoire parfaite* (Paris, 1973).

On Bodin, the "monarchomaques", see J. W. Allen, *A History of Political Thought in the Sixteenth Century* (London, 1928, and many subsequent editions).

Montaigne's comments on Caesar are printed in the introduction to Pierre Villey's edition of the *Essais* (Paris: Presses Universitaires de France, 1965, 1983), p. xlv (and in many other places). Page references are to this edition. Many English translations of the *Essais* are available. The quickest way of locating passages in Montaigne's French text is with the help of R. E. Leake, *Concordance des* Essais *de Montaigne* (Geneva, 1981).

NOTES

1 A Belgian Baron, Kervyn de Lettenhove, published in 1862, under the title of *Commentaires de Charles-Quint*, a French translation by himself of a manuscript in Portuguese then held in the French Imperial Library. If this document is related to Charles's and Van Male's project, it can only be at several removes. Information in this paragraph is from de Lettenhove's introduction.

2 Caesar was, however, the subject of two dramas written for performance by schoolboys: Marc-Antoine Muret's *Julius Caesar* (1544) and Jacques Grevin's *La mort de Cesar*, discussed by Griffin, chapter 25, pp. 380–5, 391, 392, 396.

3 For the production of these volumes Demoulins enlisted the help of the better-known Flemish humanist Albert Pigghe (Pighius) and the painter Goffredus Batavus. The Bibliophiles français chose to attribute authorship of the text to Pigghe, so that their facsimile is catalogued under Pighius, A., *Les Commentaires de César*.

4 Montaigne made the same observation, again apropos of Caesar: "Que peut-on esperer d'un medecin traictant de la guerre, ou d'un escholier traictant des dessins des Princes?" (*Essais* II, 10, 418; What can we hope of a doctor writing about war, or a student discussing the plans of Princes?)

CHAPTER TWENTY-FIVE

Shakespeare's *Julius Caesar* and the Dramatic Tradition

Julia Griffin

No one from antiquity offered more possibilities for a playwright than Julius Caesar. The span of his life provided a range of potential dramatic topics, and also of reactions to his character. The classical authors regarded him with admiration (Sallust, Caesar himself), or abhorrence (Lucan), or, more often, a mixture of the two (Cicero, Plutarch). Every major event in which he was involved might be regarded in two ways: was he merciful or corrupt in his attitude to Catiline? Were his conquests in Gaul and Britain to be admired or abhorred? How far was he responsible for the Civil War? Was his assassination a murder or a tyrannicide? The classical basis of western school education ensured that, until quite recently, these questions were familiar to every schoolchild. In the Renaissance, they provided excellent topics for rhetorical training and Latin prose composition: ideas about Caesar were proposed by the educational reformer Erasmus for debate, a practice that may lie behind the soliloquy Shakespeare gives to the hesitating Brutus (Baldwin 1944: II 328; Altman 1978: 47). Unlike those characters on whom the sources were unanimous (Cato, always good; Catiline, always bad), Caesar allowed for disagreement, or a mixed response.

Caesar plays fall into three groups: plays about the Catiline conspiracy; plays about the Civil War, involving Pompey, sometimes Cato, and sometimes Cleopatra; and plays about the assassination, with Brutus and often Portia, and sometimes Caesar's ghost.[1] In this chapter, I shall attempt to combine two chronological orders, arranging the plays in three sections by historical sequence (conspiracy, Civil War, assassination), and, within each section, by the order in which they were written. The radiating central point is Shakespeare; I shall consider the dramatic Caesar from 1545 (the earliest play about him which might have been known to Shakespeare) to c. 1762, when Voltaire produced what he claimed was a literal translation of the first three acts of *Julius Caesar* – thus concluding his own ambivalent role in introducing this predecessor-rival to the international stage. Plays involving Caesar were written during these centuries in Latin, French, English, Italian, German, and Dutch – though not, it seems, in Spanish or Portuguese.[2] Many of the plays I shall mention are not well known; I provide a checklist of them in the appendix to this chapter, which might serve as a rudimentary bibliography of Caesar on stage from the beginnings to Voltaire.

Caesar and Catiline

> César était un grand homme, mais Cicéron était un homme vertueux
> (Voltaire, Preface to *Catiline, ou Rome Sauvée*)

The first of the three dramatized phases of Caesar's life, the events around the Catiline conspiracy (63 BC), offers the thinnest pickings: it is the least well represented in any time period, and much of what there was has not survived. We know of five English plays on the subject before Ben Jonson's *Catiline his Conspiracy* (1611): all of them are lost, as is the Latin play performed at St. Omer half a century later (1666) (Harbage and Schoenbaum 1964). Not all of these, perhaps, were relevant to this chapter, as playwrights who tackle the conspiracy often choose not to write about Caesar at all; much later, the young Ibsen saw no need to include him in his *Catiline*. Those who do so take one of two approaches. He is either an opponent of Catiline, or a seditious villain. (That Catiline might have had some right on his side is an idea that seems not to have occurred to any playwright before Ibsen.) Sallust, the chief narrative source for the story, is careful to exonerate Caesar from any part in the conspiracy (see on this Toher, chapter 16, 225–7); a playwright who follows Sallust will keep him for the last act, as in the Dutch *L. Catilina* (1669) by Lambert van der Bosch, who faithfully translates the long speech for clemency given to him by Sallust. Elsewhere among the classical sources, however, there are different suggestions – particularly in Plutarch's *Life of Crassus*, which asserts that Cicero clearly implicated both Crassus and Caesar (*Crass.* 13.3; the work to which Plutarch alludes is now lost); and in the work on the conspiracy by the Renaissance historiographer Constantinus Felicius Durantinus, which hints at Caesar's guilt (Duffy 1947: 25).

Ben Jonson seizes on this hint. Apparently a flop at its first performance, his *Catiline* comes across, at least on reading, as a work of terrific power, thrillingly cynical in its vision of the *ragione di Stato* – and the heart of it is the Machiavellian figure of Caesar, a secret supporter of Catiline. With his ally Crassus, he hovers behind the action, limiting himself in public to sarcastic asides on Cicero, the play's beleaguered hero – "Up glory!" he mutters, to Cicero's maiden speech in the Senate – while keeping his conspiring private and his options open. Jonson's Cicero delivers himself, later on, of verbatim translations of his own Latin orations; but for Caesar, Jonson invents a wholly original incident in which, under cover of night, he visits Catiline to encourage him in his evil course:

Caesar Come, there was never any great thing yet
Aspired, but by violence or fraud,
And he that sticks for folly of a conscience
To reach it –
Catiline – Is a good religious fool.
Caesar A superstitious fool, and will die beast.
Good night. [. . .]
What you do, do quickly, Sergius.
(III.iii.27–36)

And he leaves, declining Catiline's offer to light his way out. The wholly non-classical, blasphemous echo of that last line is shocking: Caesar uses Christ's words to Judas ("That thou doest, do quickly," John 13:27) as he incites his stooge to "violence or fraud" – the stooge he will soon abandon and betray. Having done so, he is disturbed, two acts later, to find that Cicero's spies have delated him to the Senate. This delation is reported by Sallust, among others; but Jonson, who has put Caesar's guilt beyond question, makes it into the kernel of another, brilliantly original scene, in which he and Cicero shadow-box with each other:

Flaccus Here is a libel too, accusing Caesar,
From Lucius Vectius, and confirm'd by Curius.
Cicero Away with all, throw it out o' the court.
Caesar A trick on me too?
Cicero It is some men's malice.
I said to Curius I did not believe him.
Caesar Was not that Curius your spy that had
Reward decreed upon him, the last Senate,
With Fulvia, upon your private motion?
Cicero Yes.
Caesar But has he not that reward yet?
Cicero No.
Let not this trouble you, Caesar, none believes it.
Caesar It shall not if that he have no reward;
But if he have, sure I shall think myself
Very untimely and unsafely honest
Where such as he is may have pay t'accuse me.
Cicero You shall have no wrong done you, noble Caesar,
But all contentment.
Caesar Consul, I am silent.
(V.iv.249–64)

Cicero knows Caesar is guilty, but does not want to accuse him because he fears "To stir too many serpents up at once" (IV.ii.470); Caesar knows that Cicero knows, and wants only to bluff him out of acknowledging it. The outcome of this little exchange is not certain, but it seems that Caesar has carried his point. He goes on to deliver his famous appeal for clemency, recorded by Sallust; in Jonson's play, the same words become shamelessly hypocritical. Nor does there seem to be any defensible reason for him to support Catiline, a self-proclaimed villain in the play (much worse than in Sallust's history), interested only in anarchy and destruction. But he gets away with it. "Caesar, be safe," are Cicero's last words to him (V.vi.163). Catiline is defeated, but this more formidable opponent remains at large. The happy ending withers into irony.

Later seventeenth-century drama does little with this part of Caesar's life. Van den Bosch's *L. Catilina* (1669) limits his participation to one act and his speech (more or less) to Sallust; M. F. Besteben, *De 'tsamenswering̃e Catalinae* (1647), gives him just one line. More than a hundred years separate Jonson's play from the next extended treatment: Voltaire's *Catiline, ou Rome Sauvée* (1749; first published 1752). As with his play on the assassination (discussed below, pp. 388–9), Voltaire claimed to be writing in response to an English precedent – in this case Jonson, to whom he refers, in his Preface, with the mixture of admiration and contempt that Renaissance English drama usually inspired in him. His comments on Jonson suggest that he either had not really read his play, or remembered it only vaguely: he complains that Cicero delivers his denunciation in prose, not verse, because Jonson thought he had to; one glance at the page would have put paid to this objection. Much more of an influence was the near-contemporary French *Catilina* (1749) by Prosper Jolyot de Crébillon, whose success Voltaire greatly resented (Lepape 1994: 194–7). Crébillon, however, had chosen not to include Caesar at all; Voltaire, inspired or not by Jonson, makes him central to the story. In this version, he is fascinating and dangerous – a potential threat, just kept under control by Cicero, who here, as in Jonson, is the hero of the story. Again, Caesar is the serious problem, while Catiline is hardly more than a frenetic buffoon. When the letter arrives denouncing Caesar, the latter responds by sweeping out of the Senate to take up arms against Catiline. As he says:

J'ai lu; je suis Romain, notre perte s'annonce.
Le danger croît, j'y vole, et voilà ma réponse.
(IV.vii.9–10)

(I have read it; I am a Roman; our defeat is imminent; the danger is growing; I am on my way; and there is my reply.)

Despite the misgivings of Cato, Cicero plays to his ambition and – in defiance of historical fact – gives him the military command against Catiline, reminding him:

Vous êtes dangéreux, vous êtes magnanime –
En me plaignant de vous, je vous dois mon estime ...
(V.iii.29–30)

(You are dangerous, you are great of heart – while I complain of you, I must respect you.)

Caesar repays Cicero's confidence, but it is clear that the danger he represents is not over. The play ends with Cicero praying, evidently anxious, that this "âme généreuse" will not be corrupted. Like Jonson, Voltaire read back something of Caesar's later life into this early episode: like everyone writing on Caesar, he found a character so richly represented in the writing of the past that his personality overflowed historical fact to create its own dramatic reality.

Caesar in the Civil War: Pompey, Cleopatra, and Cato

Caesar gods and men can witness
Themselves enforc'd it, much against the most
I could enforce on Pompey for our peace.
(Chapman, *The Tragedy of Caesar and Pompey* IV.iv.11–13)

Cornelia What noble Virtues am I doom'd to hate.
(Cibber, *Caesar in Ægypt* III, p. 46)[3]

The second of the three areas of Caesar's life to appear on the stage was the second in historical order: the Civil War, beginning with Caesar's crossing of the Rubicon and ending with his triumph over the forces of Pompey and the Senate. These events covered three years and many thousands of miles, and most plays focus on one (occasionally more than one) of three sub-areas: Caesar and Pompey; his adventures in Egypt; and the suicide of Cato. Several of Plutarch's *Lives* supply material for this story. The most extensive classical source for all of them, however, was Lucan's epic, which presents Caesar as a charismatic demon, distinguished by ruthlessness, hypocrisy, and appalling energy (see Leigh, chapter 17, pp. 240–3). This figure was to have his influence on Renaissance drama – ranting power-maniacs such as Marlowe's Tamburlaine owe much to Lucan's rhetoric (Blissett 1956); when presenting Lucan's own subject, however, playwrights offer a more complicated picture. On stage, the conqueror displays more vulnerability and compunction than might have been expected.

The earliest Civil War play to survive is Robert Garnier's *Cornélie* (1574), translated by Thomas Kyd in 1594. Cornélie, or Cornelia, is Pompey's widow, and most of the action of this rather scattered play is devoted, sympathetically, to the defeated side; the heroine, aided by Cicero, laments the tragedy of her life through most of Acts I, II, III, and V. She does not actually mention her victorious enemy until Act III, when she receives her husband's ashes from his faithful freedman, Philip (Phillippe). Then she curses Caesar: "Let me but see the murdrer murdered." (III.iii.78) Philip, however, responds that Caesar has mourned Pompey, and done so sincerely. This episode provides a test case in defining an author's attitude to Caesar. Lucan had presented the scene with dark brilliance: Caesar receives the head from the Egyptians and, after a quick check, *pretends* to grieve (*BC* 9.1035–43). Plutarch said simply that he turned away his head and wept (*Pomp.* 80.5, *Caes.* 48.1). A later reader might take it either way, or both at different times: Petrarch, in a famous sonnet, makes the supposed grief an image of hypocrisy; later, in his biography of Caesar, he gives a much more sympathetic report (Martellotti 1947: 155; see McLaughlin, chapter 23, pp. 338–9). By giving the denial here to Cornelia, clearly not an unbiased reporter, and providing an opposing voice, Garnier leaves the question open; the audience is invited to sympathize with the widow, but not necessarily to blame the conqueror.

Caesar himself makes no appearance until Act IV, by which time the subject is his own danger, rather than Pompey's. (We will return to this part of the play at p. 381 below.) He does not get to express his own feelings about the Civil War. This happens for the first time in a very different sort of play: *The Tragedie of Caesar and Pompey. Or Caesars Revenge* (anon.; published in 1607 but probably written in about 1593) – a straggling pageant, "privately acted by the Studentes of Trinity Colledge in Oxford," which runs right through from the Civil War (Acts I and II) to the deaths of Brutus and Cassius.[4] Here Caesar draws this regretful moral from his success over Pompey:

> O that ambition should such mischiefe worke
> Or meane Men die for great mens proud desire.
> (I.ii.230–1)

His behavior on stage is scrupulous: he regrets the Roman bloodshed and laments over Pompey; no one suggests that this is other than sincere. Given that Discord, at the beginning of the play, has gloated over his triumph, all this is perhaps a surprise. Less surprisingly, Discord gloats again later over his fall. The general effect is one of sequential moralizing, with no coherent political attitude – the same effect produced by *The Mirror for Magistrates* (first published 1559), a dismal series of poems highly popular in Tudor England.

Caesar looks much more like Lucan's villain at the beginning of George Chapman's *Caesar and Pompey*, speculatively dated to 1605. Chapman rearranges history to maximize Caesar's ruthlessness and opportunism (he pushes in the Senate a proposal to allow Pompey to bring his army into Italy, just so that he can justify doing the same himself: not something Caesar actually did);[5] later, however, he displays more attractive characteristics. He is brave when he entrusts himself "and his fortunes" (II.v.45) to a boat in a storm – and Chapman, tweaking history again, heightens his courage by making him do this after, rather than before, his calamitous defeat in one of the early battles of the war. He accepts responsibility for his own mistakes (unlike Pompey, who blames all of his on luck); and he is generous in victory, mourning both Pompey and Cato sincerely – at least, no sniping voice throws doubt on it. According to Plutarch, the people of Utica put up a statue of Cato, in a gesture of defiant loyalty, just as Caesar was advancing on the town; Chapman, in one last historical readjustment, gives the idea to Caesar himself:

> My lords and citizens of Utica,
> His much renown of you quit with your most;
> And by the sea, upon some eminent rock,
> Erect his sumptuous tomb, on which advance
> With all fit state his statue [. . .]
> (V.ii.218–22)

This noble behavior is more consistently on show in a rather later play, *Pompeius Magnus* (1621) by Pierre Mousson S.J., who emphasizes throughout Caesar's regret for the war. The play ends with his grief over Pompey – and his awareness of how later cynics may choose to take it:

Quas ipse lachrymas spargo? Simulatas mihi
Infensa, & istos ora qui fletus cavant
Dicet coactos Roma:
(V p. 101)

What are these tears I myself am shedding? Angry Rome will say I have faked them, and forced these tears that line my face.

To avoid any possible suspicion among readers of the published work, Mousson provides an "Argumentum" in which he explains that Caesar was acting out of clemency and gentleness of nature, "clementia & morum comitate" (p. 84). This is perhaps the most straightforwardly positive dramatization of the Civil War Caesar.

After chasing Pompey to Egypt, Caesar spent some months there himself, thus providing playwrights with an opportunity to introduce some love interest in the reliably exotic form of Cleopatra. *Caesars Revenge* includes her, but has little room in its crowded itinerary (she appears in two scenes, and by Act III Caesar is explaining that his feelings for her are over); she reaches star status in *The False One* (?1620), a collaborative effort by John Fletcher and Philip Massinger. The Prologue describes the play's Caesar simply as "amorous," but he turns out also to be self-critical, blaming himself at length for the War:

What have I done, that speakes an antient *Roman*?
A good, great Man? I have enterd *Rome* by force,
And on her tender wombe, (that gave me life)
Let my insulting Souldiers rudely trample [. . .]
(II.iii.36–9)

As a hero in love, he is treated with some irony: the instant fancy he takes to Cleopatra is undercut by a caustic commentary from his faithful follower, Sceva, who remains on stage throughout, and the romance is further downgraded when Caesar forgets Cleopatra, briefly but entirely, at the sight of the Egyptian treasury. He appears to be wholly dismayed by the news of his ex-rival's murder, but Sceva's asides raise the possibility that this is a cynical performance, as in Lucan:

now do I wonder
How he would looke if *Pompey* were alive againe,
But how he would set his face?
(II.i.163–5)

He redeems himself, however, by his dashing escape in the last act from a treacherous Egyptian ambush – as does Cleopatra, whose superb courage here offsets her earlier willingness to sleep with him in return for political support.

He has no need for redemption in Corneille's glittering tragicomedy *La Mort de Pompée* (1644), which downplays the political situation to focus on the hero's private qualities. Corneille manages to present him as both gallant and astute, behaving irreproachably with the play's two women: young, love-smitten Cleopatra (Cléopâtre), and Cornelia (Cornélie), just widowed and superbly grand. In defiance of historical fact, this Cornelia has followed her dead husband to Egypt, where she is impressed in spite of herself by the conqueror's magnanimity towards her: "O ciel, que de vertus vous me faites haïr!" ("O Heaven, what virtues you make me hate!" III.iv.72), she exclaims – torn, like so many of her creator's characters, between conflicting duties. Like Garnier, Corneille includes a scene *à deux* between Cornelia and Philip (Philippe), the freedman responsible for Pompey's cremation; Philip praises Caesar's behavior, to which she responds not with curses but only sardonic reservations, rather like those of Sceva in Fletcher and Massinger's play:

> César est généreux, j'en veux d'être en accord,
> Mais [. . .]
> Sa vertu laisse lieu de douter à l'envie
> De ce qu'elle ferait s'il le voyait en vie.
> (V.i.1543–6)

(Caesar is generous, against my will I acknowledge it, but [. . .] his virtue leaves envy room to wonder what [he] would do if he saw Pompey alive.)

Yet these acknowledgements of his virtue, coming from such an enemy, do much to soften that suggestion. Cornelia goes so far as to save Caesar's life by warning him of the Egyptian plot against him; otherwise, as she says, Rome would lose "ses deux plus nobles têtes," his and Pompey's, at the hands of ignoble foreigners. Caesar's relationship with Cleopatra is correspondingly elevated. Gone is any suggestion of an affair; she tells her *confidante* early on that she is hoping he will divorce his wife for her sake, but the play ends with his crowning her, not proposing.

This play, popular enough to have been translated into English twice in two years, has a dramatic *Nachleben* of its own. It is the ultimate inspiration for Handel's opera, *Giulio Cesare in Egitto* (1724), which takes the final step in exonerating Caesar from hypocrisy: he actually makes an offer of truce to Pompey before learning that he is dead, thus avoiding the usual suspicion that he would have found him very embarrassing alive. Corneille also provides the basis for a final English play, *Caesar in Ægypt* (1725) by Colley Cibber (best known as the King of the Dunces in Pope's *Dunciad*). Whereas the opera, with its ludicrous invented love-intrigues, reduces only the seriousness of the original, Cibber reduces its courtliness. His presentation of Caesar has an ironic cast that seems sometimes closer to an anticipation of Shaw's *Caesar and Cleopatra* than to Corneille. Caesar and Cleopatra have their affair again, and on rather casual terms: Caesar, to Cleopatra's pique, refuses to feel jealous of Antony's obvious interest, and indeed tells him coolly that he is welcome to her afterwards. Less courtly, he becomes more introspective, and the political situation comes back into view. Shown Pompey's head ("at some distance," as the stage direction puts it; Corneille had omitted it altogether), he responds with vigorous disgust; but, left on stage with a confidant, he reflects that Cato would not have been convinced by his behavior:

Cato would term it but a specious Bribe
For Power: That *Pompey*'s Blood was, in Regard
To *Rome*, reveng'd, to court her Senate's Favor
(II, p. 36)

He ends the play by sending a message of his own to the Senate:

Tell them, this!
The laws they fight for, *Caesar* will maintain;
Nor are they safer, in their hands, than his!
(V, p. 74)

This would certainly not have suited Cato, but it is a long way from Lucanian villainy.

As a final subsection of this second phase of Caesar's story, we have a handful of plays centered on the death of that other great Republican opponent, Cato himself. Chapman's play gives much room to this, but an equal amount to the rise of Caesar and the defeat of Pompey. (This gives an unusual sort of structure, as many have pointed out: see Kistler 1979.) Chapman, following history, made Caesar arrive in Utica after Cato's death; the first playwright to focus on Cato alone was Jacques Auger, whose tragedy *La Mort de Caton* (1648) began the tradition of bringing his enemy in earlier, in time for a conversation between the two. Auger's Caesar tries to argue Cato out of suicide, succeeding only in establishing himself as a blustering anti-hero. (In fine contrast to his courtly appearance in Corneille's play, he here brusquely silences Cornelia's denunciations: "Taisez-vous, Cornélie," V p. 75.) Auger's Caesar is unusually unattractive; in none of the Cato plays, however, does he have a more than secondary role. It was never possible in ancient works for anyone to upstage Cato, and the same remains true in seventeenth to eighteenth-century drama – with predictably limited results. Non-musical plays rarely give Caesar much time on stage. In the best-known of them, Joseph Addison's *Cato* (1713), he never appears at all; in those by François-Michel Deschamps (1715) and Johann Gottsched (1732), he appears halfway through and blusters away, further disadvantaged by absurd unhistorical plot-twists by which he is in love with Cato's daughter, Porcia, and she, for complicated reasons, is living under a false name as Queen of Parthia. In the world of opera, this romantic situation (minus the Parthian twist) is an inevitable part of the Cato story. One libretto, amazingly, uses it to reconcile the two great antagonists – Matteo Noris's *Catone Uticense* (1701), which ends with Cato falling on Caesar's neck and handing over his daughter, "Flaminia," with whom Caesar is in love; this is unusual, but the love affair (here unhappy) provides the basis for Pietro Metastasio's very popular libretto, *Catone in Utica* (1728), set to music more than 20 times before 1800.

Thus, between the various operas on "Catone in Utica" and "Giulio Cesare in Egitto" (this topic still more popular than the first),[6] the operatic Caesar was established primarily, by the late eighteenth century, as a lover – either of Cato's daughter or of Egypt's queen. Both roles showed him at the height of his political success. In non-musical drama, however, this part of his story was never the favorite. The majority of plays were always concerned with the events of the Ides of March.

The Death of Julius Caesar

Shakespeare's forerunners

Polonius I did enact Julius Caesar. I was kill'd i'th' Capitol. Brutus killed me.
(*Hamlet* III.ii)

And so we move to the most popular of the three acts of Caesar's story: his death, subject of both the earliest and the latest of our plays. The challenges presented by this part of the story are different and, as regards the character of Caesar, greater. Plays on Catiline make him either a supporter of the status quo or a villain; in the Civil War plays, he appears as an overturner of the state, with whatever degree of honorable reluctance. But for this final phase, he is both the revolutionary and the established head of state. Writers throughout our time-period struggled to translate the Roman situation into their own, non-republican terms: as we have seen in previous chapters, Caesar was often seen as a proto-king, a predecessor of the monarchs of Europe. On the other hand, some argued that in Rome the Senate is equivalent to the king, and thus Caesar is, in modern terms, an anti-monarchist. (This ploy is used in Sir William Alexander's play, discussed below, where Brutus has a speech to the effect that the Senate is their rightful ruler and so Caesar is a usurper; see Kewes 2002: 158.) Dying at the hands of his fellow senators, Caesar might appear as a tyrant or as a victim (see, for a full treatment of the debate, Miola 1985). Either attitude may be found in the drama, and sometimes both.

Caesar first appears on stage in a Latin tragedy, *Julius Caesar*, by the French scholar Marc Antoine Muret (also known by the Latin form of his name, Muretus) c. 1544 – a play in which the young Montaigne, his pupil, possibly performed (see Clark, chapter 24, p. 366).[7] The play was translated, rather freely, into French by another of his pupils, Jacques Grévin, as *César* (1561). The two establish a general pattern for plays on the subject by setting up two irreconcilable viewpoints and giving time to each: scenes alternate between Caesar, restless and still ambitious, and the conspirators Brutus and Cassius, determined to restore republican liberty. Both plays include the assassination in their scope, but do not show it on stage: they establish the solution most of their successors will follow by locating it between acts (Acts IV and V in Muret, III and IV in Grévin). Muret ends with the ghost of Caesar announcing his translation to the heavens; Grévin ends with Mark Antony threatening revenge. Though both authors give the last word to Caesar's side, they show some sympathy for both parties. Muret takes the unusual step of making the outcome satisfactory to everyone: Brutus and Cassius congratulate themselves for liberating Rome, and the ghost gloats over the retribution that awaits them. Both attitudes were available.

The earliest fragment of an English dramatist's work on Caesar is the epilogue (all that survives) of Richard Eedes's *Caesar Interfectus* (1582), a deft specimen of the Renaissance educational technique of argument *in utramque partem*, on both sides: Caesar was wrong to seize power, right to wield it with clemency; Brutus was right to restore liberty, wrong to kill Caesar. Orlando Pescetti's assassination tragedy, *Il Cesare* (1594), ends with three choruses, one of male citizens celebrating liberty, one of women deploring war, and a third of soldiers praising Caesar and demanding vengeance. The first play to side unequivocally with the killers seems to be *Brutus* (1596), an early Latin work by the German scholar Michael Wirdung (Virdungus). Here Caesar, assassinated, begins the play as a revenging Senecan ghost, up from the Underworld to bring chaos to the world; bereft of Cassius, who has killed himself before the play begins, Brutus quotes from his own letters to Cicero and kills himself without repenting the assassination.

All of these plays are academic in nature – the work of scholars, most of them young, none of them professional playwrights, and all scrupulous in their adherence to the neoclassical unities of time, place, and action. Two plays already mentioned, both baggier in their structure, also find room for the assassination – at least by anticipation. Act IV of Garnier's *Cornélie* is divided between the two sides, the first scene a dialogue between Cassius and Decimus Brutus, working each other up on the subject of Caesar's tyranny, the second between Caesar and Antony, Caesar rejecting Antony's advice to kill all his potential enemies and declaring that he is ready to die instead. *Caesars Revenge*, in Acts III–V, condemns Caesar for ambition but comes down harder against Brutus, who ends the play bound for Hell.

Shakespeare

At least some of these dramas were probably known to Shakespeare when he came to write his own play, first performed in 1599. Approaching the play from the perspective of Caesar in drama reveals how far Shakespeare recognized the same patterns and decisions as other dramatists of the assassination, and where his particular originality lay. Like almost everyone who includes women in the cast (many do not), he limits them to Portia and Calpurnia. There were other possibilities: Cleopatra herself was in Rome at the time, as Cicero makes clear (*Att.* 14.6): not one playwright includes her, though it might have made for some interesting scenes. Like others, Shakespeare includes dialogues between Brutus and Cassius, Brutus and Portia. Later playwrights often included a scene between Caesar and Brutus, of one sort or another (the first, it seems, was Marie Anne Barbier, in 1710): Shakespeare's predecessors did not, and neither did he. Sometimes we can see something like a residue of an earlier dramatic idea in *Julius Caesar*, for example in the relations of Caesar and Antony. Many playwrights, from Grévin onwards, chose to pair them as a rival alliance to Brutus and Cassius, inventing for them (with no explicit classical precedent) their own scene *à deux*; Shakespeare does not use this idea, but there is a glimpse of it in the short exchange between the two men at the end of the Lupercalia scene in Act I.

There is a difference, however. In most plays which show Caesar in private conference with Antony, he is urged to act more sternly against trouble-makers like Brutus (so, for example, in Grévin and Garnier, and the later Scudéry, Barbier, and Conti); Shakespeare's Antony, by contrast, reassures Caesar about Cassius. Shakespeare takes remarks by Caesar quoted by Plutarch as isolated aphorisms and puts them into a dialogue; the result produces an impression of Caesar's ability (he detects the danger), and also his self-deception, as he immediately insists he does not fear it. Other choices made by his predecessors find no place at all in Shakespeare's play. Most dramatists give Caesar at least one soliloquy; Shakespeare does not – he is only ever on stage alone for long enough to speak three lines (II.ii.1–3). This is a significant decision. The soliloquizing Caesar may display a range of moods – restless (in Muret), or nervous (in Grévin), or anxious (as in the just-post-Shakespeare play by Sir William Alexander); whatever his mood, he will sound confiding, giving the audience a glimpse of his private self. The act of soliloquizing produces a certain sense of intimacy for the audience; the nature of the soliloquy also provides one simple way of indicating whether Caesar does or does not have right on his side. As we shall see, the Duke of Buckingham, rewriting Shakespeare's play at the end of the seventeenth century, availed himself of both advantages when he made his insomniac Dictator soliloquize in private on the tyranny of his own ambition. But Shakespeare's Caesar is never private. Even with the people in whom he comes closest to confiding, his wife and Antony, he refers to himself in the third person, using his name like a title; Shakespeare was inspired, perhaps, by Caesar's own writing in his *commentarii*, but the effect, on stage, is rather different:

> Caesar should be a beast without a heart
> If he should stay at home today for fear.
> No, Caesar shall not.
> (II.ii.42–4)

> I rather tell thee what is to be feared
> Than what I fear: for always I am Caesar.
> Come on my right hand, for this ear is deaf [. . .]
> (I.ii.211–13)

Shakespeare invented this deafness for him. An impression results not of a virtuous ruler or of a ruthless tyrant, the traditional choice, but of a powerful presence with a blank behind it. This Caesar is monumental, a Colossus; but he is also a hollow man, an unintegrated sum of fixed image and aging matter. By showing him unaware of his own vulnerability, Shakespeare increases the audience's awareness of it. He might have had in mind for the character the famous passage from Seneca's *Thyestes*, beloved in the Renaissance, on the dangers of such a life – here in the splendid translation by Sir Thomas Wyatt, from the generation before Shakespeare:

> For him death grip'th right hard by the crop [*throat*]
> That is much known of other, and of himself, alas!
> Doth die unknown, dazed, with dreadful face.
> (Wyatt 1978: 94)[8]

Caesar dies declaiming his own name.

Brutus, by contrast, does soliloquize. At the beginning of Act II, he reveals his uncertainty in a long soliloquy about the killing, and how to justify it: the argument he reaches is that Caesar, though no tyrant at present, might later become one. However unsatisfactory this argument might appear – in the eighteenth century, one "T. Killigrew" pointed out that it "will Iustefie my killing any man" (Blakemore Evans 1958: 231) – Shakespeare's concept of a brooding, hesitant Brutus was a dramatic innovation. In most assassination dramas, Brutus delivers a soliloquy at some point before the killing; Shakespeare's predecessors, however, make these soliloquies quite straightforward in nature. In Muret's play, as in Grévin's, Brutus berates himself at length for not living up to his ancestors and ridding Rome of a tyrant:

Quousque tandem, Brute, virtutem tuam
Dormire pateris otiosam degener?
(II.98–9)

(How long then, degenerate Brutus, will you allow your virtue to slumber in idleness?)

In most of the pre-Shakespearean tragedies, Brutus takes the lead, proclaiming his outrage and determination before Cassius can get a word in. In Pescetti's play, indeed, he tries to stir up Cassius against Caesar:

O Cassio, credi
Tu, ch'io non sappia, ch'in cotesto tuo
Petto non meno ardir si chiude, e serra,
Ch'in quel di Giulio? E che cotesto braccio
Non è del suo men nerboruto, e forte?
Di me nulla diro [. . .].
(I, p. 24)

(O Cassius, do you think I do not know that there is no less ardor closed and confined in this breast of yours than in that of Julius? That your arm is no less sinewy or strong than his? I say nothing of myself . . . .)

Plutarch, however, insists that the initiative for the killing came from Cassius. I quote here from the translation by Sir Thomas North, used by Shakespeare: "Cassius being a choleric man and hating Caesar privately, more than he did the tyranny openly, he incensed Brutus against him" (*Caesar* 8.3; Spencer 1964: 91). Shakespeare follows Plutarch: Brutus' soliloquy follows a prolonged persuasion scene from Cassius – in which Cassius sounds rather as Pescetti's Brutus did in the passage above. Adding to this impression of a manipulated Brutus, Shakespeare invents the detail that the anonymous "writings" he finds, apparently from unknown citizens, urging him to kill Caesar (writings mentioned by Plutarch), are all secretly written by Cassius himself (I.ii.314ff.). Most later tragedies will take the Plutarchan line: Cassius is the instigator, Brutus the follower – increasingly tormented, as the tradition develops, by the whole prospect of killing.

Shakespeare's Brutus, however, is a more complex creation than either his robust forebears or his squeamish successors. His anxiety before the killing is not matched by any remorse after it; he delivers no soliloquies after the event. And he takes the lead in an extraordinary scene where the conspirators ritually wash their hands in Caesar's wounds:

> Stoop, Romans, stoop,
> And let us bathe our hands in Caesar's blood
> Up to the elbows and besmear our swords.
> (III.i.105–7)

There seems to be no classical source for this. A few years after Shakespeare, a messenger in Sir William Alexander's play describes the conspirators bloodying their hands: it is shocking even in a messenger's speech, much more so on stage, and this speech from Shakespeare's Brutus appalled some readers in the eighteenth century. The Duke of Buckingham, rewriting the play, removed it; Alexander Pope, editing, reassigned it, with no textual authority, to Casca: "In all the editions this speech is ascribed to Brutus, than which nothing is more inconsistent with his mild and philosophical character" (quoted in Furness 1913: 145 n. 122).

Pope's editorial nemesis, Lewis Theobald, laughed at him for this, but most of the eighteenth-century translators would follow him, though indirectly (they used the Shakespeare edition by Pope's friend Warburton) – La Place, LeTourneur, and Voltaire (see below) in French; Wieland in German. LeTourneur, in a stage direction, actually exempts Brutus from the action: "Tous, excepté Brutus, trempent leurs épées dans le sang de César" ("All, except Brutus, soak their swords in Caesar's blood") (LeTourneur 1836: 113). But Shakespeare's Brutus takes the lead in bloodthirstiness. Then, once out of Rome, he assumes a disquietingly Caesarian habit of referring to himself magniloquently, as a model:

> There is no terror, Cassius, in your threats:
> For I am armed so strong in honesty
> That they pass by me as the idle wind,
> Which I regard not.
> (IV.iii.66–9; compare Caesar on his own star-like constancy, III.i.60ff.)

> think not, thou noble Roman,
> That ever Brutus will go bound to Rome.
> He bears too great a mind.
> (V.i.110–12)

Shakespeare does not shrink from the hard logic of the revenge plot, by which the perpetrator takes on the role of the victim. Brutus, like Caesar, falls for and by his own reputation.

Other unusual features of Shakespeare's assassination play emerge from reading it as one of many. One is the way it begins. Other playwrights offer a range of possibilities for this: a soliloquy by Caesar (Muret and Grévin); an allegorical figure, Senecan-style (*Caesars Revenge* begins with the figure of Discord, gloating); a debate among the gods (Pescetti and Alexander); a dialogue between Brutus and Cassius (Scudéry and Conti's *Giulio Cesare*); or between Caesar and Antony (Voltaire). Other dialogue arrangements also occur: the Dutch playwright Someren begins with Calpurnia and the Soothsayers. But no other play begins remotely like Shakespeare's *Julius Caesar*: with a crowd scene, minus either gods or any major characters, setting out the political situation not by describing but by showing it – the popularity of Caesar with the plebeians, the resentment he inspires in the political class. The next scene is again unique. Most of our plays begin on the morning of the assassination; Shakespeare begins at the annual festival of the Lupercalia, one month before (combined, in a telescopic movement, with the triumph over the Pompeians, actually five months earlier than that). Thanks to this decision, Antony makes his first appearance not, as in most plays, privately conferring with Caesar, but in public and "for the course" (so the stage direction in the First Folio) – that is, in some version of near-nakedness, ready to strike at the crowd with strips of goatskin as he runs the sacred fertility race. Caesar, with his first words in the play, commands his wife, Calpurnia, to stand in Antony's way, and Antony to be sure to touch her. Shakespeare took the idea of the scene from Plutarch, but used it with a difference: Antony is not asked to touch Calpurnia in any of the classical sources. All he does is to offer Caesar the crown. Caesar's concern with Calpurnia's barrenness is Shakespeare's idea; it provides a very discreet introduction to the theme of Caesar's Heir – a theme which will recur in the last two acts, where the newcomer Octavian quietly establishes his claim.

A second feature to note is the bloodiness of the killing itself. On Brutus' directions, quoted above, the conspirators ritually blood themselves, as after a hunt, "wash [ing]" in Caesar's wounds. Immediately after this, Brutus and Cassius imagine the assassination scene taking place on the stages of the future:

Cassius How many ages hence
Shall this our lofty scene be acted over
In states unborn and accents yet unknown?
Brutus How many times shall Caesar bleed in sport
That now on Pompey's basis lies along,
No worthier than the dust?
(III.i.111–16)

In fact, however, the scene is unusual. Few of the plays that cover the assassination actually show it: Caspar Brülow in German; Georges de Scudéry in French; Roeland van Leuve in Dutch; and in English, just Shakespeare and the anonymous author of *Caesars Revenge*.

Including the scene made it necessary to decide on a historically debatable topic: whether Caesar had or had not spoken at the point of death. The classical authors were divided on this. Plutarch gives him no words; Appian has him cry out "like a wild beast" (*B Civ.* 2.117); in Suetonius, he expresses himself in Greek: "Kai su, teknon" – "You too, my child" (*Div. Iul.* 82.3). (Dio reports this story but comments that the best authorities say he was silent: 44.19.) Muret, Grévin, and Pescetti had followed Plutarch; playwrights after Shakespeare generally follow Suetonius, incorporating Caesar's exclamation into the Messenger's Speech that describes the killing. Shakespeare himself takes a third course. He had already used, or devised, a non-classical Latin tag for the occasion: in *The True Tragedy of Richard Duke of York* (1595; the first published version of *3 Henry VI*), King Edward uses it to his brother Clarence, who has declared his support for the King's opponents: "*Et tu, Brute*? Wilt thou stab Caesar too?" In *Caesars Revenge*, too, the dying Dictator says "Brutus" rather than "son": this play may have influenced Shakespeare, though uncertainty about the date complicates the question. It may be that both playwrights independently wished to avoid any suggestion of patricide. Plutarch mentions an old rumor that Brutus might have been Caesar's son (*Brutus* 5.2), and Shakespeare alludes to it in another early play, *2 Henry VI* (1594), where a character remembers how "Brutus' bastard hand / Stabbed Julius Caesar." But whatever his reasons for departing from Suetonius' wording, Shakespeare followed him, as critics have often pointed out, in one curious and unique way: the bilingualism (see, for example, Garber 1987: 54). Suetonius' Caesar speaks Greek, in the midst of a Latin text; Shakespeare's speaks Latin, in the middle of the play's English. The effect is to set the quotation off, to highlight it as a quotation. In *The True Tragedy*, it really was a quotation, in an obvious sense: the King was using it as such, quoting or pretending to quote Caesar. But Caesar, in *Julius Caesar*, can only be quoting himself. In no other play on the subject are the characters so self-conscious, so aware of their place not only in Roman history but in the history of drama.

Later versions

Shakespeare's was to be the most influential play ever published on Caesar. For the next 150 years, however, plays on the assassination continued to be written – sometimes even performed – with no knowledge of it. First came *The Tragedy of Julius Caesar* (1607), by William Alexander, a soporific neoclassical piece written in dreary cross-rhyming: the "Argument" suggests an anti-Caesarian position, but little sense of it comes through from the play itself (it ends with a long Chorus on the unknowability of destiny). Caspar Brülow's *Caius Julius Caesar Tragoedia* (1616), by contrast, sprawls from pre-assassination to the Battle of Actium – a longer span than any other play except *Caesars Revenge* and Shakespeare: it presents Caesar sympathetically, devoting a whole scene to Cicero's praise of him (see, for a summary, Gundelfinger 1904: 52–6). *La Mort de César* (1635) by Georges de Scudéry is an unambiguously pro-Caesar play, featuring an unusually treacherous and unappealing Brutus. Marie Anne Barbier's play of the same name (1710) is a romantic extravaganza, closer in content to a *précieuse* novel or an opera libretto than to any of the other plays; in it, Brutus, Portia, Antony, and Octavia (Caesar's niece) dance out an elaborate combination of love intrigues, ending in the assassination of the kindly and benign Dictator. Two Dutch plays, by Johann Someren (1670) and Roeland van Leuve (1723) seem to divide their sympathy: Someren's play is called "the revenge for conquered freedom," but ends with Caesar's ghost urging on a revenge of its own; van Leuve's Caesar dies on stage with a uniquely long and emotional speech, but the play ends with the mutual farewells of Brutus and Cassius, still exclaiming about liberty. Dutch interest in the subject also led to translations of both Scudéry and Barbier: in the second case, the anonymous translator changed the play completely by rewriting the last scene, replacing a lamentation by the Caesarians with a celebration by the conspirators. The two endings together seem to restore the usual ambivalence the subject inspires.

Meanwhile, Shakespeare's *Julius Caesar*, popular in more or less unaltered form – unlike many of Shakespeare's plays – throughout the seventeenth century (Ripley 1980: 13–22), had begun to generate a new tradition of its own. John Sheffield, third Duke of Buckingham, produced two plays on the assassination, *The Tragedy of Julius Caesar, Altered* and *The Tragedy of Marcus Brutus* (both c. 1716), by rewriting Shakespeare's play and dividing it in half at the point of Antony's funeral oration. Shakespeare provides the basis of the first play (whole scenes are preserved almost unchanged), but the tone of the revision is more consistently stately. Gone are Caesar's deafness, Brutus' bathing in his blood. Expanding the scale, Buckingham has room to increase the roles of both his leading men: the Dictator gets to soliloquize (as we have seen) on the tyrannical burden of his own ambition; Brutus gets more time with Portia. Unlike Shakespeare's Caesar, this one decides, honorably, to make Brutus praetor, though recognizing that he is (in a direct lift from Shakespeare) "very dangerous"; Brutus responds with an additional fit of anguish. Buckingham also provides a Prologue, in which he explains his attitude to Caesar. The imagery (very disagreeable to a modern taste) is characteristic of the period:

> At distance now of sev'nteen hundred Years,
> Methinks a lovely Ravisher appears,
> Whom, tho' forbid by Virtue to excuse,
> A Nymph might pardon, and could scarce refuse.
> (fol. E2)[9]

If Caesar is a lovely rapist, Brutus' morality is also left ambiguous – more explicitly so than in Shakespeare. "Here lies the Greatest Man that e'er was Good" comments his friend Lucilius, in the last scene of *Marcus Brutus*, but the Caesarian side has the last word: "He lov'd his Country, but he kill'd his Friend" (V.vi, p. 453). Everyone has gained in dignity; ambivalence remains.

Through Buckingham, Shakespeare began, though at a remove, to have an influence on the Continent. Antonio Conti, a Venetian aristocrat, read Buckingham's work, and was inspired by it to write on the subject himself (Fletcher 1981: 442). Like Buckingham, he eventually wrote two plays, one named after Caesar and one after Brutus; unlike him, he wrote both of them on the same part of the story: the assassination. In the first play, *Giulio Cesare* (1718), Caesar receives the usual mixed treatment. In a long letter published with it, Conti explains that he has made the character great in mind and magnificent in action, but also cunning and ambitious; Brutus, with all his merits, deserves censure for his ingratitude and his unrealistic idealism. This even-handedness, apparently, Conti came to regret. He explains in the Preface to the second play, *Marco Bruto* (1744), that critics had complained that they did not know which side they were supposed to take; here he will make it clear that Brutus, and Brutus alone, is the hero. To do this, he plays up the character's hesitation to the absolute maximum: Cassius and Portia spend most of the play pressuring him and complaining to each other. To direct audience sympathy still further, Conti also takes the extraordinary and probably unique step of removing Caesar himself altogether from a play about his own assassination. In so far as the subject allows, his Brutus performs a heroic act that has no victim – an indication of the difficulty of presenting the story unequivocally.

Conti's *Giulio Cesare* and Buckingham's two plays were all known to Voltaire. But he also experienced Shakespeare's play at first hand on his visit to London in 1726; and, on his own account, he was overwhelmed – despite all the faults that he perceived in it. In his *Discours sur la Tragédie* (1730), addressed to Lord Bolingbroke, he recalls his excitement:

> Avec quel plaisir n'ai-je point vu à Londres votre tragédie de Jules-César, qui, depuis cent cinquante années, fait les délices de votre nation! Je ne prétends pas assurément approuver les irrégularités barbares dont elle est remplie. [. . .] Mais, au milieu de tant de fautes grossières, avec quel ravissement je voyais Brutus, tenant encore un poignard teint du sang de César, assembler le peuple romain, et lui parler ainsi du haut de la tribune aux harangues [. . .]. (Voltaire 1964: 106–7)
>
> (With what pleasure did I see in London that Julius Caesar tragedy which has been the delight of your nation for a hundred and fifty years! Certainly I do not pretend to approve of those barbarous irregularities of which it is full [. . .]. But, in the middle of so many gross faults, with what delight did I see Brutus, still holding a dagger stained with Caesar's blood, summoning the Roman people and addressing them thus from the height of the rostra [. . .].

– and he proceeds to translate the whole of Brutus' speech. It was the beginning of a long, tempestuous relationship with Shakespeare.

His choice of an episode for praise might seem surprising. Brutus with bloodstained hands is, as we have seen, a troubling image in the early eighteenth century: this might seem an obvious example of an "irrégularité barbare." But Voltaire responded to the energy of the scene – the merit, as he put it, of "action." He set out to compose a play on the same subject himself, paying Shakespeare the complicated compliment of writing it in the "English taste" (by which he meant austere and without love interest). For his later Catiline play, as we saw, he claimed, unconvincingly, the influence of Ben Jonson; Shakespeare's play, by contrast, he clearly knew very well. Still, however English he might have thought it, *La Mort de César* (first performed in 1733) comes much closer to the older French plays on the subject than to Shakespeare, built up as it is of soliloquies and dialogue, with a tight time-line and a small cast list. It begins with a dialogue between Caesar and Antony: Grévin's *César*, the first French Caesar play, includes one in the first act; it ends with Antony's oration, which is how Grévin's also ends. Voltaire's innovation was to take up Plutarch's rumor and make Caesar not just Brutus' friend, but his father – an idea which Shakespeare had chosen to ignore. It provides Voltaire with opportunities for extended agonizing for Brutus, plus a neat way of barring him from bloodshed without removing him from the conspiracy; he also – coincidentally? – provides a twist of his own on Shakespeare's theme of Caesar's Heir. As Brutus' father, Caesar spends some time revealing his softer side; when off this topic, he expresses himself as a political cynic, turning the rhetoric Shakespeare's Cassius had used of him (Caesar the Colossus) against Rome itself, to justify his seizure of power:

> Nos moeurs changent, Brutus; il faut changer nos lois.
> La liberté n'est plus que le droit de se nuire:
> Rome, qui détruit tout, semble enfin se détruire.
> Ce colosse effrayant, dont le monde est foulé,
> En pressant l'univers est lui-même ébranlé [. . .]
> (III.iv.184–8)

(Our customs change, Brutus; we must change our laws. Liberty is now no more than the right to harm oneself; Rome, the destroyer of all, seems at last to be destroying itself. This alarming Colossus, which treads down the world, in pressing on the universe is shaken itself.)

Nevertheless, he recognizes his affinity with his son:

> Si je n'étais César, j'aurais été Brutus
> (I.i.120)

(If I were not Caesar, I would have been Brutus.)

Both take extreme positions: the inflexible power-seeker; who disowns his own son when he refuses to take his side; the rigid idealist, who will defend his ideals even against his own father. In the last scene, Antony makes public the secret of Brutus' birth, and the paternal Caesar triumphs posthumously, the outraged people mourning him as Brutus' father and their own.

Voltaire claimed the credit for introducing Shakespeare to France; there would also be a smaller reciprocal movement. In 1758, Voltaire's Shakespearean play was translated into English, and altered in the process to Caesar's advantage. Aaron Hill, man of letters and friend (sometimes) of Pope, published an article in his own periodical, *The Prompter* (1736), complaining that no one did Caesar justice:

> while the lowest, and most virulent, of Writers can expatiate on Those Arts of His, most liable to Censure, the very choicest, and most able Wits fall short, when they attempt his Virtues. [. . .] Even our Great Shakespeare has shot wide: and after This Confession, Monsieur de Voltaire must look upon it as no Injury, that I cannot like the Picture, He has lately given us [. . .]. (quoted in Fletcher 1975: 75)

Rising to his own challenge, Hill adapted Voltaire's *La Mort* to produce a Caesarian drama of his own. With Hill, Caesar finds a voice as rationalist thinker in the

Enlightenment mode – an ancient Roman version, in fact, of Lord Bolingbroke, to whom Hill dedicated his play:

> *Caesar* [*kneeling*] Hear me, *thou!* Self-producing, dark, first cause!
> All ruling! All-pervading! Aweful Power,
> Whom, under various names, blind worship seeks!
> If, till compell'd, I draw the public sword,
> Sheath'd, in my bosom, let me guilty fall! [*Rises*]
> (I.iii; p. 266)

And yet even Hill, as dramatist, felt the force of the other side. Antony ends the play – not, this time, with a rabble-rousing eulogy, but an unexpectedly low-key reflection on the nature of ambition:

> All fruit of power is *pain*: and what is *fame*?
> When ev'n a Caesar's glory stains his name.
> (V.vii; p. 327)

The story of Shakespeare, Caesar, and Voltaire ends with its own anticlimax. In the thirty years after *La Mort*, French interest in and enthusiasm for Shakespeare exploded, and the first translation appeared. Voltaire became increasingly restive; his protégé was becoming a rival. In this darkened mood, he returned to *Julius Caesar*. This time, he set about producing a literal translation of the first three acts: the point, as he made clear in his *Avertissement*, was to show his fellow countrymen that they had no idea what Shakespeare was really like, and would be appalled if they had.[10] The undignified nature of some parts of the play become, in Voltaire's footnotes, the focus of sarcastic attack – in particular the representation of Caesar himself. Beneath Caesar's boastful descriptions of himself as danger's older brother, more constant than the northern star, Voltaire notes: "Traduit mot à mot," "Traduit avec la plus grande exactitude" ("translated word for word"; "translated with the greatest exactitude," pp. 170, 183). The last note concerns the action of the conspirators immediately after Caesar's death. Voltaire translates literally the speech of Brutus that Pope had reassigned to Casca: "Baignons tous dans son sang nos mains jusques au coude" ("Let us all bathe our hands to the elbow in his blood"), and comments:

> C'est ici qu'on voit principalement l'esprit différent des nations. Cette horrible barbarie de Casca ne serait jamais tombée dans l'idée d'un auteur français. (p. 187)
>
> (It is here that one principally sees the different spirit of the two nations. This horrible barbarity of Casca's would never have entered the mind of a French author.)

Gone is the admiration of Brutus waving his bloody dagger; even from Casca, this bloodthirsty suggestion now fills Voltaire with contemptuous cultural superiority. Leaving the play at this point, though, makes an extra-intentional impact. In taking it on himself to put an end to the false reign of Shakespeare, he had cast himself, inevitably, in the role of Brutus. His righteous indignation was not enough to stop the tide: some 15 years later, the second French translation of Shakespeare appeared;

a very grand production, dedicated to the King. As Brutus himself found out, Caesar was a hard ghost to exorcise.[11]

Conclusion

> *Enter a Spirit in the Shape of* Caesar, *full of Wounds.*
>
> (Buckingham, *The Tragedy of Marcus Brutus* III.v – stage direction)

I shall try here to draw some general conclusions from the wide range of representations touched on in this chapter. First, there are surprises. The most straightforwardly negative depiction appears in a play about Catiline, where Caesar's role is marginal; the Civil War plays never present him as darkly as does Lucan, their principal source. The tears over Pompey's head, in Lucan an emblem of perfect hypocrisy, become, on stage, something harder to condemn. Second, less surprisingly, the plays reveal a shift of interest. The earliest are divided among the three areas of Caesar's life; by the end of the eighteenth century, the assassination is much the most common. The exception is opera, where Cleopatra dominates (followed, at some distance, by the dying Cato), but even this was about to change, with G. Sertor's very popular libretto *La Morte di Cesare* (1791). Third, the assassination plays, as a group, present the subject as a dilemma, not demonizing either side. More sympathetic portrayals of Brutus become fashionable in the eighteenth century, but Caesar continues to evoke a mixed response. Inheriting a long tradition of debate, playwrights, from Muret to Voltaire, bring the controversy onto the stage: even writers who take, in prose, a simple line on the story (Buckingham, for example, and Aaron Hill) seem unable to present it dramatically without some ambivalence.

From the mid-eighteenth century onwards, Shakespeare's play was established as a classic in Europe. Many translations appeared before 1800, more or less faithful: von Borck and Wieland in German, La Place and LeTourneur (and Voltaire) in French, Valentini in Italian. Beyond the span of this essay is the fascinating and undervalued dramatic work of J. J. Bodmer, Swiss scholar and poet, who engaged in a sort of imaginative dialogue with Shakespeare's play, and J. G. Herder, who based a libretto on it, set to music by J. C. F. Bach (the music, sadly, has not survived). Sometimes negotiating with Shakespeare was a thornier experience. Voltaire ended by attacking him; so, at the very end of the eighteenth century, did the Revolutionary playwright Marie-Joseph Chénier, who criticized the play for much the same sort of reason as Voltaire. The most famous example of this difficult relationship, much later, is Bernard Shaw, who thought that Caesar might have regarded Shakespeare as Shakespeare's Brutus regards the buffoon "poet" who bursts into his camp (quoted in Ure 1969: 41). Despite periodic denigrators, though, the play has continued to fulfill its own characters' prediction. Thanks to Shakespeare, Caesar bleeds worldwide in sport; nothing in his life is as famous as his death. Thanks to Shakespeare, we are all haunted by Caesar's ghost.

APPENDIX

This is a chronological checklist of European plays that include the character of Caesar, up to and including Voltaire. The earliest translations of Shakespeare are also included. The list makes no claim to be comprehensive, but includes all the plays mentioned in the chapter. I have omitted all plays in which Caesar hovers in the background but does not appear, for example Joseph Addison's *Cato* (1711). The only exception is Antonio Conti's *Marco Bruto*: Caesar does not actually appear in it, but the whole play centers on his assassination; hence its inclusion.

Cat = Catiline play; *CW* = Civil War play (includes one or more of: death of Pompey, death of Cato, Caesar in Egypt); *A* = Assassination play; *G* = Caesar's ghost only; * = translation or adaptation

1542–5 Marc Antoine Muret (Muretus), *Julius Caesar* (trans. into Dutch by J. Michaelius, 1545) [*A*]
1561 Jacques Grévin, *César* [*A*]
1574 Robert Garnier, *Cornélie* (trans. into English by Thomas Kyd, 1594) [*CW*]
1582 Richard Eedes, *Caesar Interfectus* (only the epilogue survives) [*A*]
1585 Nikodemus Frischlin, *Julius Redivivus* [comic play in which Caesar and Cicero return to earth in order to admire sixteenth-century Germany]
1594 Orlando Pescetti, *Il Cesare* [*A*]
c. 1507 Anon., *Caesar and Pompey; or, Caesars Revenge* (published 1607) [*CW/A*]
1596 Michael Wirdung (Virdungus), *Brutus* (1596) [*G*]
1599 William Shakespeare, *Julius Caesar* (see below for translations)[*A*]
?1605 George Chapman, *Caesar and Pompey* (published 1631) [*CW*]
1607 William Alexander, *The Tragedy of Julius Caesar* [*A*]
1611 Ben Jonson, *Catiline his Conspiracy* [*Cat*]
1616 M. Caspar Brülow, *Caius Julius Caesar Tragoedia* (1616) [*A*]
?1620 John Fletcher and Philip Massinger, *The False One* [*CW*]
1621 Pierre Mousson (Mussonius), *Pompeius Magnus* [*CW*]
1633 Jasper Fisher, *Fuimus Troes* [Caesar in Britain]
1635 Georges de Scudéry, *La Mort de César* (trans. into Dutch by H. Verbiest, 1650) [*A*]
1644 Pierre Corneille, *La Mort de Pompée* (trans. 1663–4 into English twice: by Katherine Philips and by a collaborative group of poets including Edmund Waller.) [*CW*]
1648 Jacques Auger, *La Mort de Caton, ou L'Illustre Desesperé* [*CW*]
1647 M. F. Besteben, *De 'tsamenswerínge Catalinae* [*sic*] [*Cat*]
1651 Anon., *Marcus Tullius Cicero* [*G*]
1669 Lambert van den Bosch *L. Catilina* [*Cat*]
1670 J. van Someren, *C. Iulius Caesar, ofte wraeck van vermande vryheydt* [*A*]
1677 G. F. Bussani, *Giulio Cesare in Egitto* (opera libretto) [*CW*]

1701 Matteo Noris, *Catone Uticense* (opera libretto) [*CW*]
1710 Barthold Feind, *Der durch den Fall des grossen Pompeius erhöhte Julius Caesar* (opera libretto) [*CW*]
1710 Marie Anne Barbier, *La Mort de César* (trans. into Dutch by ?R. van Leuve, 1728; last scene changed) [*A*]
1715 François-Michel-Chrétien Deschamps, *Caton d'Utique* (1715) (trans. into English, 1716) [*CW*]
c. 1716 John Sheffield, Duke of Buckingham, *The Tragedy of Julius Caesar* (first published 1722) (adapted from Shakespeare)[*A*]
The Death of Marcus Brutus (first published 1722) [*G*]
1718 Antonio Conti, *Giulio Cesare* (published 1726) [*A*]
1719 Shakespeare, rev. "Dryden/Davenant" *Julius Caesar* (1719) (with extra ghost scene) [*A*]
1723 Roeland van Leuve,[1] *Cezars Dood* [*A*]
1724 Nicola Haym, *Giulio Cesare in Egitto* (opera libretto; adaptation of Bussani) [*CW*]
1725 Colley Cibber, *Caesar in Ægypt* (adaptation of Corneille) [*CW*]
1728 Pietro Metastasio, *Catone in Utica* (opera libretto) [*CW*]
1732 Johann C. Gottsched, *Der Sterbende Cato* [*CW*]
1733 François Marie Arouet de Voltaire, *La Mort de César* (first published 1736) (trans. into Dutch by I. Voordaagh, 1737; revised by Louis–Gérôme Gohier 1794) [*A*]
1741 *Kaspar Wilhelm von Borck, *Der Tod von Julius Caesar* (first German trans. of Shakespeare's play; rhyming alexandrines. A new act added) [*A*]
1744 Conti, *Marco Bruto* [*A*]
1746 *Pierre-Antoine de la Place, *Jules César* (first French trans. of Shakespeare; part prose trans., part summary)
1749 Voltaire, *Catiline, ou Rome Sauvée* (first published 1752) [*Cat*]
1756 *Domenico Valentini, *Giulio Cesare* (first Italian trans. of Shakespeare; prose)
1758 *Aaron Hill, *The Roman Revenge* (adaptation of Voltaire, *La Mort de César*)
1762 *Voltaire, *Jules César* (first published 1764) – "literal" trans. of Shakespeare Acts I–III; blank verse)

1 Roeland van Leuve is sometimes credited with the translation of Barbier's play, in Dutch *Der Doodt van Julius Cezar*, published anonymously in 1728. The British Library copy of this translation is credited, wrongly, to "H. Verbiest," who in fact published, in 1650, a translation not of Barbier but of Scudéry. Verbiest's translation is also called *Der Doodt van Julius Cezar*, but it is quite different from either van Leuve's *Cezars Dood* or the 1728 *Der Doodt van Julius Cezar*, themselves quite different from each other. The unfortunate near-identity of title for all three of the originals (Scudéry, Barbier, and van Leuve) has led to a grand complication in the library records. All these Dutch plays are different again from I. Voordagh, *Der Dood van Cesar* (1737) – a translation of Voltaire, *La Mort de César*.

The earliest surviving Dutch translation of Shakespeare's *Julius Caesar* dates from the late nineteenth century. German translations are recorded (traveling players) from 1626, six of them by 1660; but there are no survivals.

Between Voltaire and the end of the eighteenth century the following appeared:

1763 J. J. Bodmer, *Julius Caesar* [*A*]
1768 J. J. Bodmer, *Marcus Brutus* (1768). [*G*]
1774 J. G. Herder and J. C. F. Bach, *Brutus* (cantata; music lost) [*A*]
1776 *Pierre LeTourneur, trans. of Shakespeare into French (prose)
1785 *Christoph Martin Wieland, trans. of Shakespeare into German (prose)
1786–7 Vittorio Alfieri, *Bruto Secondo* (first published 1789) [*A*]
1789 Poinsinet de Sivry, *Caton d'Utique* [*CW*]
1790 Marie-Joseph Chénier, *Brutus et Cassius, ou Les Derniers Romains* (influenced by Shakespeare) [post-*A*]
1791 G. Sertor, *La Morte di Giulio Cesare* (opera libretto, influenced by but not based on Voltaire) [*A*]
1793 Revision of Voltaire, *La Mort de César*, by Louis-Jérôme Gohier (end of play changed) [*A*]

The website CESAR (= Calendrier électronique des spectacles sous l'ancien régime et sous la révolution) lists a further eight plays in French, published between 1621 and 1796 – two on Cato and six on Caesar's death – which I have not been able to trace. The following list shows editions of the plays I have cited in the chapter.

Alexander, Sir William, *The Tragedy of Julius Caesar* (London, 1607)

Anon., *Caesars Revenge* (?1590s; first published 1607), ed. F. S. Boas (Malone Society, 1911)

Auger, Jacques, *La Mort de Caton, ou L'Illustre Desesperé* (Paris, 1648)

Barbier, Marie Anne, *La Mort de César* (Paris, 1710)

Besteben, M. F., *De 'tsamensweringe Catalinae* [sic] (1647) first published and ed. G. van Eemeren (Leuven/Amersfoort: Centrum Renaissancedrama handschriftencahier, 1988)

Borck, Casper Wilhelm von *Der Tod von Julius Caesar* (Berlin, 1741)

Bosch, Lambert van den, *L. Catilina* (Dordrecht, 1669)

Brülow, M. Caspar, *Caius Julius Caesar Tragoedia* (Strasbourg, 1616)

Buckingham, John Sheffield, Duke of, *The Tragedy of Julius Caesar, Altered* (London, ?c. 1716) (first published 1722) in *The Tragedy of Julius Caesar, Altered and The Tragedy of Marcus Brutus*, facsimile reprint with introduction by Michael Wilding (Oxford: Cornmarket Press, 1970)

Buckingham, John Sheffield, Duke of, *The Tragedy of Marcus Brutus* (c. 1716; first published 1722), reprinted as above

Bussani, G. F., *Giulio Cesare in Egitto* (1677), ed. Craig Monson, Collegium Musicum (Yale University), 2nd ser., vol. 12 (Madison, WI: A-R editions, 1991)

Chapman, George, *Caesar and Pompey* (London, ?1612; published 1631), ed. Thomas Marc Parrott in *The Plays of George Chapman: The Tragedies* (New York: Russell and Russell, 1961)

Cibber, Colley, *Caesar in Ægypt* (London, 1725)
Conti, Antonio, *Il Cesare* (1718; published Faenza, 1726); published as *Giulio Cesare* in *Le Quattro Tragedie* (Florence, 1751)
Marco Bruto (1744) in *Le Quattro Tragedie*
Corneille, Pierre, *La Mort de Pompée* (Paris, 1644), ed. André Stegmann in *Corneille: Oeuvres Complètes* (Paris: Éditions du Seuil, 1963) (trans. 1663–4 both by Katherine Philips and by a collaborative group of poets including Edmund Waller)
Deschamps, François-Michel, *Caton d'Utique* (Paris, 1715)
Eedes, Richard, *Caesar Interfectus* (written c. 1582) (only epilogue survives); first pub in Geoffrey Bullough (ed.), *Narrative and Dramatic Sources of Shakespeare*, vol. 5 (London: Routledge and Kegan Paul, 1964)
Fletcher, John and Philip Massinger, *The False One* (London, ?1620), ed. Robert Kean Turner in *The Dramatic Works in the Beaumont and Fletcher Canon* gen. ed. F.S. Boas vol. VIII (Cambridge: Cambridge University Press, 1992)
Garnier, Robert, *Cornélie* (Paris, 1574), ed. Jean-Claude Ternaux, in *Cornélie. Tragédie.* (Paris: Champion, 2002). Translated by Thomas Kyd as *Pompey the Great, his faire Corneliaes Tragedie* (1595), ed. F. S. Boas in *The Works of Thomas Kyd* (Oxford: Clarendon Press, rev. edn 1955).
Gottsched, Johann C., *Der Sterbende Cato* (?Leipzig, 1732)
Grévin, Jacques, *César* (Paris, 1561); ed. Jeffrey Foster, *César de Jacques Grévin* (Paris: A. G. Nizet, 1974)
Haym, Nicola, *Giulio Cesare in Egitto* (Audivis, 1995)
Hill, Aaron, *The Roman Revenge* (London, 1758), in *The Dramatic Works of Aaron Hill, Esq.*, vol. 2 (London, 1760)
Jonson, Ben, *Catiline his Conspiracy* (London, 1611), ed. W. F. Bolton and Jane F. Gardner (Lincoln: University of Nebraska Press, 1973)
La Place, Pierre-Antoine de, *Le Theatre Anglois*, vol. 3; includes *Jules César* (London, 1746)
Leuve, Roeland van, *Cezars Dood* (?Amsterdam, 1723; 2nd edn, Amsterdam, 1775, is the only one to survive)
Metastasio, Pietro, *Catone in Utica* (1729) in *Italian Opera 1640–1770* (London and New York: Garland Publishing, 1983)
Mousson, Pierre [Petrus Mussonius], *Pompeius Magnus* (1621); in *Tragoediae seu Diversarum Gentium et Imperiorum Magni Principes* (La Flèche, 1621)
Muret, Marc Antoine [M. A. Muretus], *Julius Caesar* (1542–5); ed. Jeffrey Foster, *César de Jacques Grévin* (see above under "Grévin")
Pescetti, Orlando, *Il Cesare* (Verona, 1594)
Scudéry, Georges de, *La Mort de César* (Paris, 1636), ed. Harold L. Cook (New York: Publications of the Institute of French Studies, 1930)
Shakespeare, William, *Julius Caesar* (first perf. 1599; first published London, 1623), ed. David Daniell (London: Arden Shakespeare, 3rd series, 1998)
Someren, J. van, *C. Iulius Caesar, ofte wraeck van vermande vryheydt* (Dordrecht, 1670)
Valentini, Domenico, *Giulio Cesare* (Sienna, 1756)
Voltaire, François Marie Arouet de, *La Mort de César* (first performed 1733; first published Paris, 1736), in André M. Rousseau (ed.), *Voltaire: La Mort de César* (Paris: Société d'Édition d'enseignement Supérieur, 1964)

Voltaire, François Marie Arouet de, *Jules César* (partial translation of Shakespeare) (c.1762; first published in *Commentaires sur Corneille* (Paris, 1764), in André M. Rousseau (ed.), *Voltaire: La Mort de César* (Paris: Société d'Édition Supérieur, 1964)

Voltaire, François Marie Arouet de, *Catiline, ou Rome Sauvée* (1749; first published Paris, 1758); in *The Complete Works of Voltaire*, gen. eds. W. H. Barber and Ulla Kölving, vol. 31A, ed. Paul LeClerc (Oxford: Alden Press, 1992)

Wirdung, Michael [Michael Virdungus], *Brutus* (Jena, 1596)

FURTHER READING

Some of the plays discussed in this chapter are available in modern English editions: Chapman, Jonson, and Fletcher and Massinger (see Appendix). Bullough 1964 includes the epilogue (all that survives) from *Caesar Interfectus* plus selections from *Caesars Revenge* and Pescetti's *Il Cesare*, all translated into English. In French, there are modern editions of Grévin, Scudéry, Corneille, and Voltaire (see Appendix); no modern translations into English. Old texts of all of these are available through GALLICA, the electronic respository of the Bibliothèque Nationale, which also offers Deschamps. Muret is conveniently included in the 1974 edition of Grévin. A few of the plays in other languages are available in the original on the Internet: Gottsched's *Der Sterbende Cato* (German), Wirdung's *Brutus* (Latin), and the plays on Catiline by Besteben and van den Bosch (Dutch). Of the operas, Handel's *Giulio Cesare in Egitto* is easily available, often complete with Haym's libretto (for example, in the Astrée recording with James Bowman and Lynn Dawson: Audivis 1995). The Metastasio and Bussani libretti are available in modern editions (see Appendix).

Except for Jonson's and Chapman's, non-Shakespearean Caesar plays of the sixteenth to early seventeenth centuries have attracted little criticism. H. M. Ayres 1910 covers six plays. Muret and Grévin are the subjects of essays by La Penna and Pineaux in Chevallier 1985; Pineaux also discusses Garnier. Kewes 2002 discusses Alexander's play and *The False One*, with reference to their historical context; Waith 1989 compares *The False One* with Corneille. For Chapman, Kistler 1979 discusses the character of Caesar in relation to Renaissance training in debate; Tricomi 1992 compares Chapman with Shakespeare. For Jonson, Boehrer 1997 discusses the Humanist background to the play's treatment of Caesar.

Shakespeare's *Julius Caesar* is, of course, a hugely popular subject. Baldwin 1944 provides an extensive account of Shakespeare's classical education; Martindale 2004 includes essays on that and other related topics. Spencer 1964 prints four of Plutarch's *Lives* in North's translation, used by Shakespeare; Bullough 1964 prints selections. The many fine essays and book-length studies of *Julius Caesar* and Shakespeare's Rome include MacCallum 1910, Wilson Knight 1931, Schanzer 1963, Hunter 1977, Miola 1985 (on the tyrannicide debate), Garber 1987, Gary B. Miles 1989, and Kahn 1997. Shapiro 2005 discusses the play in the context of its year of performance. Two recent collections of essays are Richard Wilson 2002 and Zander 2006.

For operas on Caesar in Egypt, see Monson 1985. For a quaint account of Noris's Cato opera, and a comparison between it and Addison's *Cato*, see Walker 1799, available on the Internet through Google Books. The On-Line Grove Dictionary of Opera is a wonderful resource.

For revisions of Shakespeare in the seventeenth and eighteenth centuries, see Ripley 1980 and Dobson 1991; for the first translations into Italian and German, see Sestito 1978 and

Theisen 2006. A website, in progress, by Professor Markus Marti of the University of Basel, lists all known European translations of Shakespeare almost up to the present day. Buckingham, Conti, and Voltaire are considered together by Fletcher 1981; Voltaire's use of Shakespeare is discussed, to very different effect, in Lounsbury 1902 and Besterman 1967. Jusserand 1899 gives a fascinating account of the fortunes of Shakespeare in eighteenth-century France. For eighteenth-century Caesar plays beyond the orbit (or the immediate orbit) of Shakespeare, Montoya in Enenkel 2002 has an essay on Barbier; Fletcher 1975 considers Hill and Voltaire.

NOTES

1 There is also another category, for which there is no room for discussion here: plays in which Caesar appears in order to make a patriotic point about the author's own country. Nikodemus Frischlin's *Julius Redivivus* (1585), a comedy, has Caesar and Cicero return to earth in order to admire sixteenth-century Germany; Jasper Fisher's *Fuimus Troes* (1633) shows Caesar in Britain, behaving chivalrously but not besting the natives. (This play derives, to some degree, from Shakespeare's *Cymbeline.*)

2 Although the Roman Republic is a popular topic in Spanish lyric poetry, there seem, oddly, to be no dramatic treatments – at least in our time period.

3 When plays are not divided into scenes, I shall refer to them by act and page number, to make them easier to find. The texts are all listed in the Appendix.

4 Even on the earliest dating, this is not the next play on the subject to be written. By the mid-1590s, three or four plays had appeared, all anonymous and all lost: *The History of Caesar and Pompey* – possibly two plays (1581), *I Caesar and Pompey* (1594), *II Caesar and Pompey* (1595); in addition, there were two more called "Ptolomy"/"Telome," which may have been relevant (see Harbage & Schoenbaum 1964). None survives.

5 In 62, Pompey's supporter Metellus urged that Pompey should be allowed to bring his army into Italy in order to keep order in the Catiline crisis (Plut., *Cat. Min.* 26.2; see Gruen, chapter 3, p. 29); Caesar seems to have supported this, but did not propose it. In 49, Caesar's supporters argued that he should be allowed to keep his command if Pompey kept his; Caesar himself was responsible for this proposal, but did not make it in person as he was out of Rome at the time. Chapman conflates these two scenes, creating a manipulative and ruthless picture of Caesar.

6 The first *Giulio Cesare in Egitto* libretto was written by G. F. Bussani; first set to music by Antonio Sartorio in 1676, it was employed by several other composers and adapted by other librettists in the course of the eighteenth century. Nicola Haym, who adapted Bussani's libretto for the famous Handel opera, reduced the original's boisterousness considerably: in Bussani, Achillas (Pompey's killer), Ptolemy, and the Roman Curio all fall in love with the widowed Cornelia, and Curio is successful; Haym eliminates Curio as suitor, and also most of the manifold disguises Bussani had devised. See Monson 1985 for a full discussion.

7 The date of the play is not certain: Bloemendal 2002: 304–5 argues for 1547; Ginsberg 1973: 247 dates it to "c. 1543."

8 Shakespeare would have known this poem in the slightly different version published in a collection known as *Tottel's Miscellany*, 1557.

9 This imagery also appears in Buckingham's "Ode on Brutus" (first published in *Poems on Affairs of State* III (1704), pp. 10–14): Rome is the "violated Dame" who "walk'd smilingly along," happy to have been made an honest woman by the rapist Caesar, whose Dictatorship apparently counts as a marriage.

10 Twentieth-century critics have been divided on the merits of this work: Thomas Lounsbury castigated it in the strongest terms for its viciousness and bad faith, but Theodore Bestermann and André Rousseau have taken it seriously as a contribution to Shakespeare translation. The *Avertissement* includes a strictly literal translation of part of *Othello* I.i, in which Iago shouts abusively about Othello and the "beast with two backs"; the effect, in the context of Voltaire's French, is outrageously comical.

11 As a final irony, Voltaire's own original play, *La Mort de César*, would be used twice before the century was out as the basis for plays sympathetic to Brutus. In 1786–7, Vittorio Alfieri would write a play on the subject, *Bruto Secondo*, which follows Voltaire's lead in making Brutus Caesar's son, but ends differently, cutting off before Antony turns the crowd against Brutus. A few years later, in 1793–4, *La Mort* was radically revised by Louis-Jérôme Gohier, Minister of Justice in the new revolutionary order, who rewrote the final scenes to show the conspirators, in defiance of historical fact, turning the crowd against Antony. Gohier himself ended up in the employ of Napoleon – the new Caesar (see Biskup, Canfora, and Nicolet, chapters 26, 29, and 27 in this volume).

CHAPTER TWENTY-SIX

The Enlightenment

Thomas Biskup

The eighteenth century was, as Immanuel Kant famously stated, the age of Enlightenment but not an enlightened age (Schröder 2002). This chapter will thus not limit itself to examining the role the historical Caesar played in the works of a select band of enlightened writers, such as Voltaire and Rousseau; it will also consider the wider role Caesar was given in historiography and literature from the mid-seventeenth century on, between the conclusion of the Peace of Westphalia (1648) and the dissolution of the Holy Roman Empire (1806), or – to take the corresponding changes in French politics – between the accession of Louis XIV (1643) and the rise of Napoleon. The latter's career opened up the new phase of nineteenth-century Caesarism, which will be considered in another chapter. Such a view will also allow the consideration of America and England, countries not usually associated with Enlightenment thought, although France and Germany will be at the center of this chapter.

Although much was written on Caesar in the seventeenth and eighteenth centuries, we know little about the reception of the historical figure Caesar in political thought during that period. Friedrich Gundolf's *Caesar: Geschichte seines Ruhms* [Caesar: a history of his fame], first published in 1924, is still the only overview of the reception of Caesar in the "high literature" of the time, such as the works of Corneille and Schiller, Voltaire and Goethe (Gundolf 1924). Like Ernst Kantorowicz's biography of the medieval Emperor Frederick II, it emerged from the right-wing intellectual circle of the German poet Stefan George (1868–1933) (Stahlmann 1989). In its apodictic style, lack of footnotes, and aesthetic pretensions, Gundolf's *Caesar* is a celebration of human "greatness" as such, rather than a scholarly analysis of its literary construction. Kantorowicz, following emigration during the Nazi period, was able to follow up his monumental Frederick biography with his seminal *The king's two bodies*, which carefully dissected the mythology of medieval kingship that he had still fêted uncritically as the birth of modern man in his earlier work (Benson & Fried 1997). Gundolf died as early as 1931, and it is idle to speculate whether he would have chosen a similar path (had the Jew, originally Gundelfinger, survived the Nazi period at all). Certain, however, is that nobody else took up the baton.

Although this gap in scholarship is more easily spotted than accounted for, it is no mere coincidence. Caesar may have been omnipresent as both author and historical figure throughout the early modern period, but in the seventeenth and eighteenth centuries he was not the exemplary model of "greatness" that he had been in the Renaissance, and which he was again to become in nineteenth-century literature. Authors of the age of Enlightenment had, it seems, issues with Caesar: for that period he was too problematic a figure to be appreciated in straightforwardly positive terms. Throughout the period, authors tended to highlight the problematic aspects of his character, career, and death, rather than his achievements. Authors found it difficult to reconcile his military genius and literary skills with the establishment of his dictatorship, and the circumstances of his murder. Analyzing the way authors confronted these problems, however, can offer us a particular insight into the distinct intellectual strands and political culture of Old Regime Europe.

Caesar in Old Regime Political Culture

Throughout the seventeenth and eighteenth centuries, Caesar the author of the *Commentaries* remained central to the education of those groomed for public life. Even writers critical of his character and career, such as Rousseau, praised the "candor and truth with which the greatest man on earth spoke of himself" as a lesson worth teaching to young men (Rousseau 1969: 29–30).

Caesar the politician, in contrast, was a much more contested figure in an age when theories of resistance were at the heart of political debate (Friedeburg 2001). The regimes that were established around and after the middle of the seventeenth century, when the wars that had torn apart England (the Civil War), France (Wars of Religion and Fronde) and Germany (the Thirty Years War) had ended, remained in power until the French Revolution and Napoleon transformed Europe's political and social landscape yet again (Woolrych 2002; Bercé 1996; Asch 1997; Parker 1997). Anxious to put the terrifying experiences of the previous decades behind them, the political culture of these regimes was characterized by corporate privileges, social distinctions, and the aristocratic notion of glory, which determined the place of Caesar in political debate, literature and the arts. Caesar the conqueror thus remained an important point of reference; some authors justified Caesar's usurpation of power as the only way out of the turmoils of the late Roman Republic, and most authors agreed that the Republic could not have continued even without Caesar. However, the transformation of Rome into a dictatorship remained deeply problematic for an age in which political legitimacy was conveyed by right of birth (even electoral monarchies such as the Holy Roman Empire and the Netherlands usually remained in the hands of one dynasty), or by highly ritualized election from a circle of patrician families.

Hereditary monarchs from the old dynasties that dominated European politics during this period found it difficult to identify with a usurper murdered by aristocrats in his own capital. Panegyric literature made numerous references to Caesar-like courage or military genius throughout the early modern period, and military authors up to and including Napoleon regularly compared the abilities of contemporary commanders to Caesar's exploits: for instance, the German translation of Henri de Rohan's *Le parfaict Capitaine: Kriegs-Regeln des perfecten Capitains uber den Julium Caesar, ersten römischen Kayser*, was first published in 1609, and reprinted several times throughout the seventeenth and eighteenth centuries. However, Caesar was rarely put at the center of royal iconography, and figured much less prominently in history painting or sculpture than other figures of Greek and Roman history, such as Alexander the Great, Augustus, or the younger Cato (Pigler 1974: vol. 2, 374–5). Louis XIV (1643–1715), who is usually considered the epitome of absolutism but whose reign had started with the aristocratic revolt of the Fronde, may have translated Caesar's *Commentaries* in his teens, but he chose Alexander the Great (in addition to Apollo) as his symbol in his early years, and the Emperor Augustus in his maturity (Burke 1992). Having pacified post-civil war Rome, supported the arts, and established a dynasty ruling over the greatest empire on earth, Augustus was one of the two great models for seventeenth- and eighteenth-century monarchs. After 1660, propagandists of the Stuart dynasty, which had returned to Britain following the demise of Cromwell's Commonwealth, also built on the parallels between Caesar's death and the execution of Charles I (1625–49). They claimed that Charles II (1660–85) and, later, Queen Anne (1702–14) had brought peace to the British Isles after the upheavals of the civil war, quite as the first *princeps* had done in Rome (Weinbrot 1978: 49–50).

Caesar as a Republican Anti-model

In the city states that had survived the rise of the princely territorial state, such as Venice, Geneva, and Germany's free Imperial cities, the entire constitutional framework was designed to keep rule by one person at bay. They accordingly chose their ancient heroes from among staunchly republican figures who had never abused their military command to threaten the collective rule of the Senatorial elite (Gottdank 1999: 55–63). Scipio Africanus was thus *the* hero of seventeenth- and eighteenth-century Venice but he was in general popular with republicans and writers opposing absolute monarchy from a corporatist position. For the Abbé Castel de Saint-Pierre, whose writings attacked Louis XIV and everything he stood for, Scipio was the greatest hero in Roman history, while Caesar ranks scarcely better than Catiline, the only difference being that Caesar succeeded where Catiline failed (Grell 1995: 1088). Later in the eighteenth century, this view of Caesar as the great republican anti-model was reinforced on the other side of the Atlantic by the American colonists fighting for independence from Britain. They were convinced that "the purpose of history was the prevention of tyranny" (Richard 1994: 85), and took as their models Cato of Utica, Brutus, Cassius, and Cicero, who had died fighting for the survival of the republic. Detesting all leaders who had destroyed the republic for their own gain, they reserved their particular wrath for Caesar, whose corruption had supposedly destroyed Roman freedom and virtue, quite, as in their view, the corrupt George III (1760–1820) was bent on suppressing the colonists (Schild 2007).

The anti-monarchical fervor aside, the Americans were, however, only following models provided by the British themselves. Distancing themselves from Stuart Augustanism, the elites of Hanoverian Britain, where power was concentrated in the aristocracy and Parliament, considered the Roman Republic a model rather than the Roman Empire. Appropriating the Roman discourse of *amicitia, libertas* and *virtus* for the purposes of the Whig oligarchy, Britain's landed classes identified with Rome's senatorial elite, highlighting the republic's liberty and domestic peace safeguarded by patrician rule while denouncing both rebellious populism epitomized by the Gracchi or Caesar, and Imperial slavery established by Caesar (again), recently reborn in Ludovican France, and averted in 1688 (P. Ayres 1997: 3–12). Joseph Addison's tragedy *Cato*, which closely followed Plutarch's lives of Caesar and Cato, and upheld the ideal of republican virtue rather than praising the messy reality of republican politics, was a prime example of this view, and the fact that it was also a favorite of the American "founding fathers" is testimony to the similarities of political language on either side of the Atlantic (Richard 1994: 57). Taking its inspiration from Italian republican writings of the sixteenth century, this Atlantic Republicanism identified with pre-Caesarian Rome and the ancient city states of Greece, and abhorred the egalitarianism of the French Revolution (E. Burke 1987). The demonization of Caesar by Britain's ruling Whig elite, however, made him attractive for opponents of the *status quo* when the Whig oligarchy itself was beginning to look frail around 1740. More radical Tories such as the historian Nathaniel Hooke then unmasked Cicero and Cato as hypocrites defending the rule of the privileged few behind a rhetorical façade of civic virtues, and reassessed Tiberius Gracchus and Julius Caesar as the true standard-bearers of the real people, thus attacking Walpole's oligarchy in the shape of the Roman senatorial oligarchy (P. Ayres 1997: 20–1).

Caesar in Enlightenment France

Although operating in a very different political context, the Swiss-republican dramatist Johann Jakob Bodmer, author of *Julius Caesar: Ein Trauerspiel* (Bodmer 1763), and the radical author of the *Social Contract*, Rousseau, were similar to British and American writers in considering Caesar as a villain displaying lust for power over men and women in public as well as in private (Paulin 2003). In general, however, Continental writers were less severe on Caesar than the English-speaking world. In part this has to do with the particular place Caesar held in the "national" historiographies of both Germany and France, as heroic conqueror of ancient Gaul and importer of civilization there, and as the first Roman Emperor in the Holy Roman Empire of the German Nation. In addition, Caesar played a comparatively marginal role in absolutist propaganda during this period. This meant that he was less exposed to the wrath of absolutism's fiercest opponents than Alexander and Augustus, who were upheld by one side and attacked by the other as the prime examples of princely virtue or vice. Instead, writers criticizing the existing monarchical regimes from a non-corporatist point of view and setting their hopes on "enlightened" monarchy used the figure of Caesar to promote a model of change that (apart from his death) might appeal to rulers willing to forge an alliance with enlightened reformers.

It was only in the nineteenth century that French historians discovered the figure of Vercingetorix as an early proponent of "Gallic" independence; eighteenth-century French writers, in contrast, integrated Caesar's conquest of Gaul into a narrative of French cultural superiority, as it had supposedly brought Roman culture to peoples that may have been exceptionally ferocious fighters but had, until Caesar's arrival, lived in ignorance and barbarism (as the Germans on the far side of the Rhine still did) (Grell 1995: 1129–32).

To be sure, Caesar's usurpation of power remained a problem, and the legitimacy of his assassination was discussed in both drama and historiography – a highly delicate question in the context of the various assassination attempts on French kings from the sixteenth to eighteenth centuries (Van Kley 1984). Fénélon defended Brutus and Cassius as freedom-loving virtuous citizens, whereas Voltaire was fascinated by the combination of greed and clemency – "*tyran et père de patrie*" – which in his view characterized Caesar (Flamarion 2003: 65). Always critical of regicide, Voltaire had a more ambivalent view of tyrannicide, which he discussed in three dramas, most importantly his *La mort de César*. In this first French adaptation of Shakespeare's Caesar, Voltaire carefully weighed the assassins' love of liberty and the efficiency of Caesar's dictatorial system of government (Couvreur 2003). After all, for French *philosophes* attacking the injustices and inefficiencies of eighteenth-century absolutism, Caesar was not only a usurper but also an early example of "enlightened despotism," an energetic ruler who had the power, the insight and the will to carry through far-reaching reforms, such as introducing the new, Julian calendar, against the corporatist interests of the conservative elite. It was no coincidence that Voltaire wrote his Caesar drama in England, and in close succession to his *Lettres philosophiques* (1733, English 1734), in which he introduced English political thought from Bacon to Locke and Newton to the French, as well as attacking the French government and Catholic (state) Church for religious intolerance. Voltaire consequently thought of his sometime friend Frederick II "the Great" of Prussia (1740–86) as a "great man" in Caesar's comprehensive mold while Charles XII of Sweden (1697–1718) fell off in comparison as a mere soldierly "hero"; it was a distinction Labruyère had already exemplified through the comparison of Caesar and Alexander (Voltaire 1978b: 1396; Peyrefitte 1992: 149).

This highlights the fact that enlightened writers, taking their inspiration from Plato's concept of the philosopher king described in the *Republic* and taken up again by Hobbes, had raised the standards for true royal greatness (Beales 2005b: 28–9): legal reforms and even philosophical reflection were now a necessary complement to military success and cultural patronage, which improved Caesar's standing in comparison to Alexander or Augustus as well as Frederick the Great's vis-à-vis Louis XIV. In his *Observations on the Romans*, the republican-spirited Mably denounced Alexander as a power-hungry conqueror who "left nothing behind him but ruins," while admitting that Caesar at least displayed "heroic courage and elevation of the soul," and in their influential *Roman History*, Crevier and Rollin gave Caesar the accolade of a "model sovereign" – had he only been put onto the throne by birth or by election (Mably 1751: vol. 1, 152–3, 165–71; Crevier & Rollin 1755: 427–9; Wright 1997). For Voltaire, it was clear that the most enlightened periods of human history, among which he counts Caesar's reign, depended on the mutual advancement of enlightened ruler and civilized people (Voltaire 1978a), and the most famous *philosophe* stated: "The best thing that can happen to mankind is to have a philosopher-prince." Here, Caesar as a man of power who reflected upon his own deeds in his *Commentaries* is an example as well as Marcus Aurelius and the Prussian *roi-philosophe*. This gave "despotism," a term which for long had only had negative associations in political theory, a novel positive meaning. It may not be so surprising that a monarch, such as the Habsburg Emperor Joseph II (1765/80–90), advocated the concentration of all power in a despot for a limited time to modernize the state and abolish ancient laws, but even in the greatest work of the Enlightenment, Diderot's *Encyclopédie*, despotism now received a more balanced discussion; Montesquieu and his followers, however, continued to see Caesar as an illegitimate usurper responsible for the abolition of all liberty (Beales 2005b: 48; Diderot 1765: 154–8 "République romain," 333–8 "Romain empire").

Caesar in the Holy Roman Empire

In Germany, the idea of monarchs supporting enlightened thought and carrying through reforms had closer connections to political activity than elsewhere (Scott 1990). Caesar was compared to Frederick the Great as a benevolent ruler and scholarly writer fighting superstition and as an insurmountable hero, and both rulers were held up as appropriate examples to the great and the good for all times (Butenschoen 1789: 443–54; Zimmermann 1790: vol. 3, 199). However, with a newly found sense of proportion, and in contrast to the sixteenth century, none of the small-state representatives of "enlightened absolutism," such as Carl Friedrich of Baden (1738–1811) and Carl Wilhelm Ferdinand of Brunswick (1780–1806), was compared to Caesar anymore. In general, the idea of "despotism" as a means of pushing through radical reforms never really took hold in Germany, where the entire constitution of the Holy Roman Empire was based on "mixed government" with participation of Emperor, princes, and estates, a source of pride for most German publicists right up to the end of the Empire in 1806 (P. H. Wilson 2004).

In German historiography, Caesar had, however, long been awarded a particular place as "the first Roman Emperor," a title all heads of the Holy Roman Empire of the German Nation, as it was officially known, held until its dissolution in 1806 under Napoleonic pressure. They, indeed, held the title of "Caesar" as well, as in "Ferdinandus Tertius Caesar" for Emperor Ferdinand III (1637–57), and in explicit reference to the title used by the ancient Roman emperors. In an engraved portrait of Emperor Leopold I (1658–1705), decorated with symbolic and allegorical ornaments, the emperor's head is surrounded by the inscription "Quod in coelis sol, hoc in terra Caesar," likening the Emperor both to the sun and to Caesar. Here, again, "Caesar" signifies the title, but the historical figure remained inscribed in the title (Hanemann 1685).

This was of particular importance as the entire history of the Holy Roman Empire was also closely linked up with salvation history: according to an influential interpretation of the Bible's Book of Daniel, the Roman Empire was the last of the four great monarchies that would exist before the end of the world, and Caesar as its "founder," as well as the Germans as his heirs, thus had a crucial role in a *Heilsgeschichte* culminating in the Last Judgment. This view had been particularly strongly advocated in the Middle Ages but it maintained a position in some circles of eighteenth-century historiography, which were particularly close to the (Catholic) institutions of the Empire (Uhse 1716: preface). In general, however, historiography, dictionaries, and the tables of Roman emperors added to eighteenth-century legal handbooks invariably continued to list Caesar as "No. 1" in a continuous line stretching up to "No. 147," i.e. the contemporary Habsburg Emperor Charles VI (1711–40) (*Historischer Entwurff* 1741; similar: Bornmeister 1678). Joseph II uniquely combined the roles of Caesar as founder of the Roman Empire and as "enlightened despot" (Beales 2005c), but in all other cases the figure of Caesar legitimized Imperial rule in a more traditional way. In Germany's courtly literature, Caesar consequently appears as a virtuous monarch rather than as a faction leader in the civil war, and in this context his assassination is usually strongly condemned as regicide: in a play staged at the court of Elector Frederick Augustus "the Strong" of Saxony (1694–1733), the spirit of a very royal Caesar (note the *pluralis maiestatis*!) thus maintains that "although Brutus's murderous band has robbed our life, the fame of our royal weapons will never wane" (*Cartel* 1695). If Caesar was put at the center of a play, he usually appeared in the familiar shape of a German prince, and it was his love life which was at the center rather than the moral issues connected with the usurpation of power or his assassination (Feind 1705). Like other early modern rulers, Caesar thus appeared locked in a web of dynastic marriages, where the forging of political alliances was articulated in the language of love and affection (Higemone 1698; for the role of such printed plays in the media of the Holy Roman Empire, see Bauer 2003).

In contrast to the series of French Caesar dramas from Corneille and Voltaire on, however, Caesar remained a relatively marginal figure on the German stage even in the wake of the Shakespeare cult that gripped German literature in the second half of the eighteenth century (Paulin 2003). The protagonists of Weimar classicism, Schiller and Goethe, were fascinated by Caesar in their later years as they saw Napoleon's career mirrored in his, but in general they were interested in ancient Greece rather than Rome – testimony to a wider aesthetic change occurring throughout Europe at the end of the eighteenth century. Goethe used the figure of Caesar for the last part of his *Faust* drama, but he never got round to writing the Caesar tragedy he had envisaged as a young man (Seel 1967: 92–136). This is not to say that German literature of the time shied away from political topics: rather, debates centered on other questions, such as freedom of expression in a court-dominated political culture (Redekop 2000; Klippel 1990). In England and France, the popularity of the themes of regicide, tyrannicide, and parricide, which were put on stage in the various Caesar tragedies, mirrored the experiences of civil war and regicide. German *Aufklärer* such as Christoph Martin Wieland, straining to maintain moral integrity and independence at court while helping rulers along the path of enlightened virtue, were more interested in analyzing the patronage system of Imperial Rome, for instance Emperor Augustus's relationship with Horace (Lefèvre 1989).

However, a series of dramas discussing the problem of violent regime change by focusing on Cato and the younger Brutus was put on stage particularly in times of political conflict, for instance in seventeenth-century Strasbourg and early 1700s Hamburg (Feind 1711). Also, the poet and Leipzig professor Johann Christoph Gottsched wrote a Cato drama modeled on Addison's by then classic tragedy, whose original also circulated in several German translations. Most of these dramas appear to have been written in free Imperial cities or trading centers with a strong republican tradition, such as Leipzig, but even there, baroque German theatre preferred the elder Brutus over the Caesar-murdering younger one: in Germany as well as in pre-revolutionary France, it was in particular the story of Brutus having his own sons executed for high treason that made the creator of the Roman republic stand out as a model of unselfish patriotism. Even this arch-republican, however, did not necessarily stand for anti-absolutist sentiment but could also be integrated into the princely canon of virtues, as the German translation of Cathérine Bernard's *Brutus* demonstrates (Bernard 1699). Staged as an example of princely "Großmuth" (magnanimity) at the court of Duke Anton Ulrich of Brunswick-Wolfenbüttel (1685/1704–14) by members of the ducal family, it is a poignant reminder that in continental Old Regime Europe, where political activity was almost always restricted to those of high birth, no figure of classical antiquity was unconditionally tied to one particular political cause or system.

Caesar in Enlightenment Historiography

With Montesquieu and Voltaire and the emergence of a self-consciously enlightened historiography in Germany, the religious aspects of historiography became less prominent in the course of the eighteenth century. But so did the role of the great individual in history. For the anti-absolutist Montesquieu, history was not the battlefield of exceptional men (read: monarchs), virtuous or not, but a chain of causes and effects, the higher rationality of which is intelligible only with hindsight. The end of the Roman Republic was thus a necessary event, and had not Caesar brought it about, somebody else would have done so. Caesar's hunger for power was not a sign of his individual moral deficits but rather a problem he shared with all men of his time: it was not Caesar who was corrupt but Rome as a whole (Montesquieu 2000: 166–75; Volpilhac-Auger, Andrivet, Weil, & Courtney 2000). Frederick the Great, although admiring Montesquieu as one of the few modern historians who held a rank in historiography similar to Thucydides, did not accept the legitimation of Caesar's assassination as the just killing of a usurper. The Prussian king rather insisted that "the state of the republic was dominated and agitated by brute force to such a degree that it could not be saved from the domestic wars tearing it apart in any other way than by falling under the rule of a single leader" (Montesquieu 1957: 96, 217; Merten 1987).

Voltaire elegantly dismissed the theological four-monarchies model of world history by dividing history into four periods of human achievement culminating in Louis XIV's France. Together with Augustus, Caesar is allowed to preside over one of these great "siècles," but it is the civilizations and peoples, rather than the individuals and events, that constitute Voltaire's history (Muhlack 1991: 118–19). Voltaire's concept of a "transfer" of high civilization from ancient Greece and Rome down to Ludovican France mirrored, of course, the traditional German claim that the Roman Empire had been "transferred" to the Germans via Charlemagne and the Ottonian emperors. However, eighteenth-century German historians, whether Protestant and North German like Johann David Köhler or Catholic and in Imperial service like Johann Christoph Schmidt, also turned their back on this teleological model of human history, and rather wrote the history of the peoples, and their states, that had lived on the Empire's territory (Köhler 1767; Schmidt 1780). The Göttingen professor August Ludwig Schlözer was not the only historian to expand his fold to "all peoples and states of the world"; for him, Caesar became a figure not more important than "Attila, the Inkas and Timur" (Schlözer, quoted in Muhlack 1991: 156).

If the role of "great men" was considerably reduced in this new model of history, Caesar was given a newly important role within it beyond the classic discussion of *virtus* and *libertas*. Building on Montesquieu's interest in a higher rationality of history, Herder demanded that the history of mankind must not be written as the history of chance but should, like natural history, consider the "exact interlinking of all circumstances" (Herder 1989: 651–4). Even the Protestant theologian Herder shunned the view that history had an intended divine purpose; neither could he see any reason to prefer one period or region over another, putting an end to the old preference for Greco-Roman antiquity as well as to the use of history as a repository of moral exempla. Rather, he identified in the "benevolent, animated, comprehending spirit of Caesar" one of those great individuals in world history (a novel concept in itself) who allow insight into the workings of humanity and reason, an expression of "the one soul of the world, the one human reason, the one human truth" through which past and present are connected over all differences of space and time (Herder 1989: 611). Here, Herder went further than other enlightened historians of civilization and opened up a novel way of thinking about the philosophy of history, which would later be taken up by Hegel's concept of the "Weltgeist."

Conclusion: Caesar, Frederick, and Napoleon

For the nineteenth-century philosopher Hegel as well as for the eighteenth-century philosopher Kant, Napoleon and Frederick the Great were the greatest men of their respective times. Commenting on the role Napoleon played in world history, Hegel famously spoke of the "*Weltgeist* on horseback" he had seen riding to the battle of Jena; for Kant, the eighteenth century had been "the age of Enlightenment, the century of Frederick" (Kant 1970: 58). Putting the "greatness" of Napoleon and Frederick, and thus also the particularities of their own age, into historical perspective, contemporaries of both turned to Caesar yet again (Lefèvre 1989; one example is the comparison between revolutionary France and Rome in Liebenroth 1797). The way this comparison was articulated, however, rather highlights the break represented by the French Revolution, which separates the two rulers more fundamentally than the mere 13 years separating their reigns might suggest. As a successful general bringing a revolutionary period to an end by establishing a military monarchy ruling over a huge empire, Napoleon was considered a new Caesar: his world-shaking rise to power fundamentally transformed the political structures of France and the European continent.

Such a career had been hardly imaginable at all in the pre-revolutionary monarchies of continental Europe, and it had been abhorred in the "post-revolutionary" regimes of eighteenth-century Britain and America, where, following the Glorious Revolution and the War of Independence, Caesar had become a symbol of everything threatening the oligarchical rule of the land-owning elites. As radical Tory pamphlets attacking the Whig oligarchy as well as Voltaire's writings highlight, it was throughout Europe (with the partial exception of Germany) rather opponents of the *status quo*, who appropriated the historical figure of Caesar to break up what they considered to be ossified political and social structures. It was to a large degree the implicit provocation that mattered here, while the actual aims of these Caesar-admirers, or perhaps rather "users," could be quite different, ranging from another version of oligarchy in the case of Britain's Tories to the enlightened despotism favored by some *philosophes*. As always when early modern writers used the panoply of figures from ancient history and mythology, it just depended on what aspect of Caesar's character and career was chosen: his close relationship with the Roman people; his conquests; his emergence as sole victor from the civil war; or the *clementia* he displayed vis-à-vis his defeated opponents.

Before the French Revolution, however, such a use of Caesar as a proponent of change was always qualified and limited. When likening the hereditary monarch Frederick II to Caesar, even Voltaire only ever fully praised Caesar's military and intellectual achievements, while discussing the issue of forceful regime change and his dictatorship much more cautiously. For *Aufklärer* and *philosophes*, who were all still writing within the context of early modern confessional states, the religious tolerance of the Prussian *roi-philosophe* alone seemed to open the way for mankind to proceed to a new age; this after all is what earned him Kant's epithet. The political culture of eighteenth-century Europe was shaped by the memory of the previous two centuries of regicides and civil wars, which had been wars of religion as well as struggles for political hegemony. In Caesar's praise or condemnation, the shadow of Caesar's assassination as a usurper thus remained ever present; it was left to the nineteenth century to think of Caesar primarily in terms of Napoleon's rise to power in an age of revolution.

FURTHER READING

A good starting point is provided by the works on "Atlantic republicanism" in Britain and North America by Weinbrot 1978, Richard 1994, and P. Ayres 1997, which all provide ample material on Caesar. Gummere 1963 is interesting for the reception of antiquity in American literature before 1800 whereas Ripley 1980 only concentrates on the production aspects of Shakespeare's Caesar. In French political thought, the republican Mably's critique of the Bourbon monarchy is put at the center of Wright 1997 while easy access to different aspects of Voltaire's work is now provided by Trousson and Vercruysse, *Dictionnaire général de Voltaire* (Paris: Éditions Champion, 2003). A good introduction to the political thought of the German Enlightenment is provided by Klippel 1990, who emphasizes that it was neither as unpolitical nor authoritarian as often maintained. For the work of the greatest philosopher of the time, see *Kant: Political Writings*, ed. H. Reiss (Cambridge: Cambridge University Press, 1970).

The use of ancient models of rulership by Louis XIV of France is analyzed in P. Burke 1992, which is, however, best read in conjunction with other works, such as the excellent survey of French history by Bercé 1996. The most comprehensive work on the institutional channels and modes of the reception of antiquity in seventeenth- and eighteenth century France is Grell 1995 in two volumes, which also dedicate various sections to Caesar. Almost exactly the same period in Italian art history is covered by Gottdank 1999, who however focuses on Venetian painting. More comprehensive is the painstaking survey of Pigler 1974.

Although the centrality of antiquity for seventeenth- and eighteenth-century German literature, philosophy, and art is recognized in a plethora of scholarly works, there is no survey dedicated to the reception of Caesar. Here, Paulin 2003 provides an indirect approach by analyzing the reception of Shakespeare, and also his Caesar, in Germany. The best survey of early modern German history is Wilson 2004, which rightly puts the devastating experiences of the Thirty Years War at the center while highlighting the German (or, officially, still Roman) Empire's durability right up to its enforced dissolution in1806. For the discussion of philosophical kingship, Beales 2005a is essential, while the changing models of monarchical rule throughout Europe are considered by Scott 1990.

CHAPTER TWENTY-SEVEN

Caesar and the Two Napoleons

Claude Nicolet

The name of Caesar resounded frequently in the course of the French Revolution, though not all that much more often than those of the Gracchi, of the Scipios, of Augustus, or of Catiline. In fact it was Rome itself, in its entirety, that served as an arsenal in those political conflicts. This was obviously a cultural phenomenon, for the majority of the participants – the delegates to the Estates General of 1789, to the Legislative, and to the Convention, the journalists, and soon even the soldiers – had had the same sort of education, based on rhetoric or law, for which classical antiquity was a decoration and adornment, indispensable, though present purely for effect. It is Rome that has a particular role to play in this: first, because her language and her history were better known, in general, than those of Greece; but especially because the memory of Rome was more immediate and more vivid. In a certain sense, there was still, in the eighteenth century, a political continuity, an almost uninterrupted legitimacy, between the Roman Empire and the majority of the European states, not least in France. The Revolution, however, seems to slip out of control, to escape from the hands of its agents, with the fall of the monarchy, the war, then the revolutionary government and the Terror. Much more than the Greek ideas of "tyranny" or "democracy," then, it is Rome and the terrible image of her "dictatorship" that haunts men's minds – at the same time, and often at the same moment, an object of longing and aspiration and, on the contrary, of dread and denunciation. Two heroes of Roman history lend themselves, in unequal measure, to this tradition of "the toga of power,"[1] Sulla and, of course, Caesar: both generals (but we know that at Rome every politician is also a general). The first (whether or not he gave his dictatorship the title *constituendae reipublicae*, which one must be careful not to interpret as "establishing a constitution") abdicated and died as a private citizen. The second had perhaps more ambition, and could in any case pass for the first of the Emperors, but he was assassinated while Permanent Dictator. Be that as it may, there is ascribed to Catherine II – an enlightened despot, perhaps, but ambitious to extend her power over Poland – the famous remark, à propos of a French Revolution that she detested,

"There will come a Caesar." With greater accuracy, Burke, also an irreconcilable enemy of the Revolution, predicted that "This Revolution will end in absolute military power."

These prophecies – or rather Catherine's – were they fulfilled? In other words, was Napoleon Bonaparte, installed in power by the *coup d'état* of the 19 Brumaire, a new Caesar in fact and in intention? There is no point in looking for the answer to this question in the *Précis des guerres de Jules César* that he dictated to Marchand towards the end of his stay on St. Helena, and which was published in 1836. To find distraction from the boredom that was becoming more and more oppressive, he formed the plan of studying the campaigns of the greatest generals in history – Condé, Vauban, Turenne, Hannibal, Frederick II, and naturally Alexander and Caesar. So, Caesar was just one among others. The books were acquired for him, except for Polybius, which could not be found on St. Helena. The work (90 octavo pages) is a continuous account, rather uncritical, of the life and campaigns of Caesar. In fact, its principal interest consists in the ongoing analysis that Napoleon makes of the practical conditions of war and of the ancient military campaigns as compared with what modern armies would have been able to achieve under the same conditions, equipped with firearms, artillery, baggage trains, telescopes, and engineering units. On all these points, the exposition of Napoleon is immediately very relevant and very convincing, but its real subject is modern warfare and his own campaigns: Roman history, in short, serves only as a point of comparison. As for politics (and therefore the central question of Caesarism), that is almost entirely absent, except in the last five or six pages. Caesar, by virtue of being sole Dictator, had in 45 BC complete power: he was the leader of and the heir to the popular party. But "the deliberative assemblies could no longer govern"; so he was accused of wanting to make himself king; nothing could be more absurd. "If he had wanted that, he could have achieved it by the acclamations of his army and of the senate before bringing in the faction of Pompey. . . . Caesar did not want to be king, because he could not have wanted it; he could not have wanted it, since, after him, for six hundred years, none of his successors wanted it. It would have been a strange idea to replace the curule chair of the conquerors of the world with the decayed and despised throne of the conquered." It is obvious that the Emperor was well placed to find there some analogy with his own position: he himself had in fact also avoided the title of king. But that was a completely negative resemblance.

"First Consul," at first for a period, then for life, confirmed by plebiscites with overwhelming majorities, Bonaparte exercised a power that was in fact monarchical. But everyone can see the precarious and incomplete character of his power – the numerous assassination attempts or plots of which he was the victim prove that there was a secret expectation of the "Ides of March." There was a need to escape the provisional. That was what is suggested by a curious pamphlet, in the guise of a historical analysis with transparent allusions, that was published anonymously in the autumn of 1799, under the title *Parallèle entre César, Cromwell, Monk et Bonaparte. Fragment traduit de l'anglais* [Analogy between Caesar, Cromwell, Monk and Bonaparte. A fragment translated from the English]. Attributed to Lucien Bonaparte, then Minister of the Interior, but composed perhaps by Fontanes, and undoubtedly with the consent of the First Consul himself, this pamphlet concerns us here only for what it says about Caesar. He is certainly better than Cromwell, who was only a civil war soldier, or Monk, who only knew how to betray: "Caesar alone is comparable to the conqueror of Italy and of Egypt in talent and glory, but he was a demagogue." Like Bonaparte, he did indeed finish the civil wars, but "by crushing the party that had more justice on its side," while the former "rallied the citizens against the party of brigands"; Caesar "reached supreme power by stifling the voice of the good citizens by the frenzied cries of the mob, and the acclamations of his soldiers were the only votes cast for the 'Dictator'; while the power of the First Consul received the sanction of three million citizens voting individually and in secret, exercising their liberty to its fullest extent." In brief, "Caesar was a usurper and a tribune of the people, Bonaparte is a legitimate consul." If Lucien Bonaparte was indeed the instigator of this pamphlet, which seemed to be content with the consular solution, i.e. the republican one, he nonetheless raised by implication the question of the sequel: in order to ensure the future, was it necessary to find a dynastic solution? This was without doubt too soon: Bonaparte had the text suppressed and soon removed Lucien from his ministry.

And yet, the decisive step was taken in 1804: on a motion, officially inspired, of the Senate, Bonaparte took the title "Empereur des Français." This was a hereditary monarchy with rules of succession in precise alignment with salic law (male primogeniture): no question here of dictatorship. The titulature (empire, emperor), the symbolism (the bees, derived from the Merovingians), the ceremonial of the new regime (sacred) were carefully thought out and chosen to achieve the intended goal – power that was hereditary but legitimate, authoritarian but not despotic – by retracing the course of time to the moment when the "principles" of the Revolution were recognized. No divine right: the basis of power is clearly popular consent; no title of king, but precisely that of Emperor. There is no need to believe that it was continuity with the Roman empire that was particularly implied; at this time, the title evokes only the "Roman empire of the German nation," still possessed by the Habsburgs. That is clearly confirmed by the petitions that Berthier was charged with circulating to the army (which was to vote): "The moment has come when the Nation, proud of its leader, needs to invest him with a brilliance that reflects back on itself. It is time to confer on him a title more appropriate to his deeds, to the extent of the French empire, to the status he holds in Europe. Does not the title of Emperor, borne by Charlemagne, belong of right to the man who recalls him before your eyes, as legislator and as warrior?"

Napoleon as late as 1814 would always insist on this point, explained in part by his reading of Mably. For example, in 1810 he wrote to his brother Louis, whom he had made King of Holland, to exhort him always to remember "that he has returned, after a thousand years, the Empire to the French": that was again to invoke Charlemagne. In 1809, he replied to a request from the Institute, proposing to him the titles of Augustus and Germanicus, "that he could not see anything to envy in what we know of the Roman Emperors. It ought to be the chief task of the Institute to show what a difference there is between their history and ours: how terrible for future generations are the memories left by Tiberius, Caligula, Nero, Domitian and all the princes who ruled without laws to legitimate them, and without rules of succession,

Figure 27.1 Jean Auguste Dominique Ingres, Napoleon on His Imperial Throne, 1806. A mixture of Roman, Merovingian, and Carolingian imagery is apparent. Musée de L'Armée, Paris. Photo © Erich Lessing / akg-images.

and who committed so many crimes. The only man who distinguished himself by his character and by glorious actions – was Caesar, and he was not Emperor .... But his name has been dishonored by so many pathetic princes that it is no longer associated with the memory of the great Caesar, but with that of a mob of German princelings, no less weak than ignorant. ... The title of the Emperor is 'Emperor of the French.' "

For this Carolingian conception of his power Napoleon had reasons of foreign policy more than of internal politics. It was the framework in which to insert his European system: Napoleon had himself crowned at Milan as "King of Italy"; and, after obtaining from Francis of Hapsburg the renunciation of his German imperial title (he was from 1806 only "Emperor of Austria"), he made himself Protector of a German Confederation; neither the precedent of the French monarchy nor the precedent of ancient Rome would have been of any use for such an intention.

It is only in the writings from St. Helena, under the impact of his defeat, his ill luck, and his fall, that another interpretation saw the light. Napoleon realized that he had never exercised, up to 1812, more than actual power, a dictatorship rendered necessary by the continual campaigns that were forced on him. If, on the contrary, he had been victorious in Russia, "on returning to France, in the bosom of my great, brave, magnificent, tranquil and glorious country, I would have proclaimed her limits unalterable ... all new expansion, anti-national. I would have associated my son with the Empire; my 'dictatorship' would have finished and his constitutional reign would have begun" (Las Cases 1968: 328). "There they are: more of my dreams," he adds. Sulla rather than Caesar, in fact.

The Appearance of Caesarism

The word "Caesarism" (or its equivalents) appeared at almost the same moment in Europe, around 1845–50, at first for talking about the struggle between the Papacy and the Empire (J. F. Böhmer, or Proudhon, *Césarisme et christianisme,* 1863). In France, the word (and the concept) were articulated in a work that had a certain success, the *Ère des Césars* of Auguste Romieu, 1850, followed in 1851 by *Le Spectre rouge*. An elite graduate of the Polytechnic, and deputy prefect under the July Monarchy, Romieu claimed to have discovered the true nature of the power of the Roman Emperors: essentially that of generals created by the Praetorians, or, in time, by barbarian troops, in order to end the idle discussions of the Senate and the farce of popular election. Against the proletarian masses in Europe that constituted the "new barbarians," the parliamentary regimes offered only "disastrous errors" emanating from the reformers, from the philosophy of the eighteenth century, in short, from the spirit of the modern age. There was only one solution: military power, "the new Caesars," that he saw springing up almost everywhere in the world, from Russia to America. In France, he first placed his hopes in Bugeaud; but believed that the heir of Napoleon, the Prince-President, "seems to have understood that restoration of the power of the Emperor is an illusion." The Caesarism of Romieu thus belongs to the abundant literature that will extol (as late as 1940 in France) military dictatorships.

Louis-Napoléon Bonaparte

Much more important, by virtue of its protagonists, its form, and its content, was the Caesarism of Louis-Napoléon, who, to begin with, had himself made Caesar by the *coup d'état* of December 2, 1851, but who, even before seizing power and mounting a throne, had defended the *Idée Napoléonienne* (1840). It plagiarized quite closely the *Précis des guerres de Jules César*, but in terms that were even clearer: "the tutelary and democratic power of the plebeian hero who ensured the independence of peoples and was the true representative of our revolution." But the most original feature is certainly the fact that Napoleon III as Emperor signed, wrote (whatever was said about it in 1866), and published in 1865–6 a great *Histoire de Jules César*, of which the first two volumes stopped at the crossing of the Rubicon, but the sequel was of course intended. It was not, as Mérimée, "the friend of the family," believed and perhaps hoped, a question of reflections expressing the political program and philosophical credo of Louis Napoléon, but of a true work of history, complete and detailed, equipped with the apparatus of proofs and even of scholarly discussions. This book he had conceived and intended, indeed, to claim as his creation. But he needed collaborators, and he did not dream of concealing the fact. He collected, and had collected for him, a mass of dossiers (analyses of ancient texts, summaries of book or articles, etc.) with which friends and various specialists supplied him. Besides Mérimée, the Inspector of Historic Monuments and, despite his society successes, a respectable historian of Rome (*Essai sur la Guerre sociale*), the Emperor benefited from the advice (and the material) furnished by Louis Alfred-Maury (whose interest was in geography and Ancient Gaul), by Victor Duruy, whom he appointed Minister of Public Education, and above all by the learned epigraphist Léon Renier, Librarian of the Sorbonne, member of the Institute since 1856, who since 1852 had been engaged in collecting and publishing the Latin inscriptions of Algeria. After being put in touch with the Emperor by the latter's foster sister, Mme. Cornu, who was very familiar with academic circles, he was deputed to negotiate in Italy the purchase of the Campana collection. In 1861 Napoleon III created for Renier the first chair of Latin epigraphy in the Collège de France. In 1862, after meeting in Rome the architect and archaeologist Pietro Rosa, Renier suggested to the Emperor that he buy from the King of Naples the Farnese Gardens on the Palatine and there excavate "the Palace of the Caesars," schemes with which he would be occupied until 1870. Renier would also be behind the creation by Duruy in 1867 of the École Pratique des hautes Études, in order to introduce into France a "training in research" in the German style, based on seminars. He would become the first president of the fourth section of this École, which was called "the section of historical and philological sciences."

Two other collaborators would play an essential and creative role. A young archaeologist and epigraphist from Baden, Wilhelm Froehner, was recommended by the adoptive aunt of the Emperor, Stéphanie de Beauharnais. Arriving in Paris with a scholarship, he was warmly received and appointed as *lecteur* from 1863 to 1870 by the Emperor; he ended by being named in 1867 deputy conservationist at the Louvre. He remained faithful to the memory of the Emperor after 1870 and left to the Cabinet des Médailles his wonderful collection of small objects and ancient inscriptions. In his case, Napoleon III benefited from pure erudition. But even more important was the collaboration of Major, later Colonel, Eugène Stoffel. A graduate of the Polytechnic, this artillery officer had an interest in the questions of military history and topography that were posed by the identification of the site of Alesia. Napoleon III made him his aide-de-camp and entrusted to him in the end the coordination of the research, all of it original, that he inspired and ordered for the study of Caesar's operations and battlefields. From 1862 to 1865, he supervised the excavations of Alesia that were directed on the spot, with care and competence, by Victor Perret. Stoffel corrected on many points the map published (prematurely) in 1861 by the "Commission for the topography of Gaul." He personally extended research to the battlefields of Spain, Italy, Greece and the Balkans, Africa, and Asia. The Emperor, on his advice, had entrusted some projects to young archaeologists from the École d'Athènes, Léon Heuzey and Georges Perrot, who were charged, among other things, with transcribing the famous inscription of the *Res Gestae* of Augustus inscribed, in Latin and in Greek, on the walls of the Temple of Rome and

Augustus at Ancyra. This transcription was communicated to Mommsen and served as a basis for his first edition of 1865. This enterprise of Stoffel and the Emperor extended well beyond Gaul: into Spain, where it inspired the collection of modern ordnance survey maps (of which two plates were offered to the Emperor in 1865); into Egypt, where he obtained from the Khedive Ismael, and entrusted to Mahmoud Bey "el Falaki" (the astronomer), multiple soundings and the diagrams that issued, in 1872, in the celebrated map of ancient Alexandria. Military attaché at Berlin from 1866 to 1870, Stoffel would analyze the causes of the Austrian defeat at Sadowa and issue warnings that proved vain. After the war, he remained faithful to the memory of Napoleon III and decided to use the documents and maps already collected for the sequel to *Histoire de Jules César*, which appeared in two volumes in 1887.

The novelty of the work of Napoleon III and Stoffel consisted in the precision of the chronology, the distances, the stages, the geographical and topographical reports, as opposed to a purely philological military history written by armchair strategists. These books still deserve to be consulted for themselves. But their historiographical legacy, especially for France, is also essential. To start with, the sums dispensed by the Emperor on the civil list, essentially for excavations in France and abroad and for the reports, were estimated (in 1868) at 8 million gold francs. But to that must be added the foundation of museums (that of National Antiquities at Saint-Germain among others), and the purchase or publication of books (for example, the *Oeuvres complètes* of Borghesi). There was also the founding of new chairs or posts. It is considerable and almost without equal.

But all that was far from being neutral, epistemologically or politically. The Caesar of Napoleon III and of Stoffel is certainly that of Napoleon I and the *Idée napoléonienne*. But with a notable twist: starting from their research on Caesar, they both encountered Vercingetorix, that is, the man who was, in their eyes, not only the *preux* that Mommsen glimpsed, but the true hero of the independence of a Gaul already ready to form itself into a true nation. Stoffel wanted to establish the *Commentaries* as the set text for all French schools. Now if, for the French of 1870, Rome was to blame for having slowed down this flowering, she had on the other hand succeeded in making the Gauls, spiritually and politically, into Latins, thereby assuring them a thousand years' head start on the Germans.

As we have seen (p. 6–7, cf. 429, 433, 438), in Europe generally the historiography of Caesar started its development with Mommsen's *History of Rome*. From Rostovtzeff and Max Weber to Zvi Yavetz or Peter Baehr, by way of Marx or Gramsci, it was principally the social problems of capitalist or socialist Europe that were expressed in this historical literature. France is a completely different case. Despite the repugnance felt by the Republicans for Bonapartism, the *César* of Napoleon III (and of Stoffel), endorsed by the founders of the University during the years 1875–85, remained the standard work of reference. But in the twentieth century another book, magisterial yet controversial, would capture the attention of the French: the two large volumes of J. Carcopino's *Des Gracques à Sulla* and his *César* (1935). Written for a collection of "Great Manuals" of higher education, these books, which were constantly republished up to 1968, made use of all the techniques and all the discoveries of modern scientific history, along with the data provided by ancillary sciences such as philology, epigraphy, numismatics, and papyrology. But, unlike Napoleon III, Carcopino made of Caesar the conscious creator of the imperial monarchy, who wanted to add the title of "King" to that of *dictator perpetuus*, and who had foreseen, but not desired, the orientalization of the Empire. The senseless assassination on the Ides of March, which prolonged by twenty years the horrors of civil war, did not stop this process. Naturally, the inspiration for this vigorous portrait has been sought in Carcopino's political ideas, as well as in the European context of the time. Yet Carcopino was an admirer neither of Mussolini nor of Hitler, not even of Maurras. He shared with most of the French bourgeoisie a contempt for parliamentary government, of which he would give, after the Liberation, a savage portrayal in the figure of Cicero. All in all, the France of the twenty-first century is the only country in Europe which has not recovered from having two Caesars as its rulers.

FURTHER READING

Z. Yavetz, 1983. *Julius Caesar and His Public Image*. London: Thames & Hudson.

P. Baehr, *Caesar and the Fading of the Roman World: a Study in Republicanism and Caesarism* (New Brunswick, NJ: Transaction Publishers, 1998).

C. Nicolet, *La Fabrique d'une nation. La France entre Rome et les Germains* (Paris: Perrin, 2003).

NOTE

1 An allusion to the title of the book by J. Bouineau, *Les toges du pouvoir, ou la Révolution de droit antique* (Toulouse, 1986).

CHAPTER TWENTY-EIGHT

Republicanism, Caesarism, and Political Change

Nicholas Cole

"Well Doctor, what have we got, a republic or a monarchy?" Benjamin Franklin is supposed to have been asked as he left the Constitutional Convention in 1787. Franklin's reply is reported as "A republic if you can keep it." Whatever the veracity of the anecdote, recorded by James McHenry (McHenry 1906: 85), the story reveals two important truths about the Founding period. Despite slanders later put about by opponents of the Federal system (Washington to Hamilton, July 29, 1792; see also Freeman 1995), no one at the Convention had seriously entertained the possibility of monarchy in the United States. Nevertheless, as the question supposedly put by "Mrs Powel of Philada" indicated, there seemed only two basic models for government in the modern world. The monarchies of Europe based their authority on "ancestral" constitutions and divine right (Pocock 1987: 30–55). whereas the republics of post-Independence America offered a different model that was variously called "republican" or "free" government, or, borrowing a phrase from Livy, an empire or government "of laws, and not of men" (J. Adams 2000b: 288; the 1780 Constitution of Massachusetts used the phrase "government of laws"). Despite variations, and notwithstanding all the important details that would be the subject of controversy for months and years to come, the basic form of such a government seemed clear: a popularly elected legislature, an executive, and a separate judicial branch (W. P. Adams 2001: 156–7, 53ff.). Franklin's answer points to the second truth – that there was uncertainty about whether a republic could be sustained. By the time McHenry's journal was published, some of the early fears of American republicans appeared to have been realized – not in America but in Europe, where "Caesarism" seemed to offer a third alternative: popularly mandated dictatorship. This essay charts the relationship between the republicanism of the eighteenth and nineteenth centuries and an enduring discussion in America and Europe about the career of Caesar and its implications for modern republics. It was a discussion that was a cipher for a broader debate about the nature of popular sovereignty and the authority of popularly elected politicians.

The word "Caesarism" itself would not be in common use until the middle of the nineteenth century (Yavetz 1971: 189; Baehr 1998: 102–6), but many of the intellectual challenges posed by what would become known as "Caesarism" were first addressed by thinkers in America's new republic at the end of the eighteenth. "No popular Government," Alexander Hamilton warned President Washington in 1792, "was ever without its Catilines and its Caesars. These are its true enemies" (Alexander Hamilton to George Washington, August 18, 1792). Fear of Caesars and Catilines was linked to apprehension that a republican government was inherently vulnerable. American thinkers and politicians were very much aware that a popular government had never been attempted on the scale of even a single American state,[1] let alone the scale of the Federal Government. Perhaps, indeed, it had never been attempted successfully. "It is not easy to bring home to men of the present day," Henry Sumner Maine observed in his nineteenth-century essays on *Popular Government*, "how low the credit of Republics had sunk before the establishment of the United States" (Maine 1976: 201). As Gordon Wood has put it, "everyone" in America knew that a republic "was a fragile beauty indeed" (Wood 1998: 65–6).

In a famous passage near the start of the essays written in support of America's Federal Constitution, known as the *Federalist Papers*, Hamilton wrote, "It has frequently been remarked, that it seems to have been reserved for the people of this country … to decide the important question, whether societies of men are really capable or not of establishing good government by reflection and choice, or whether they are forever destined to depend for their political constitutions on accident and force" (*Federalist* 1). With the important exception of men like Paine who urged their countrymen not to look to the past but only to reason (Paine 1989: 3–5),[2] American revolutionaries and state-builders saw themselves as the heirs of the defeated champions of the Roman Republic. During the Revolutionary War, George Washington had Addison's *Cato* performed for his men to boost morale (Litto 1966: 447). Thomas Jefferson, though suspicious of too close an association of the American experiment with that of Rome (Jefferson 1954: 129), was responsible for the neoclassical design of the new Virginian Capitol building, which in turn helped to set the pattern for American government building (Wood 1988: 17; for detail about the Virginia State Capitol, see Kimball 2002).

The doctrines of popular sovereignty and majority rule were at the heart of American republicanism. Expressing the sentiment of the day, the Declaration of Independence proclaimed that governments only drew their "just powers from the consent of the governed" and that each people had a right and a duty to establish government "laying its foundation on such principles and organizing its powers in such form, as to them shall seem most likely to effect their Safety and Happiness." It seemed equally self-evident that the rational choice of a free people would be some sort of representative republic (W. P. Adams 2001: 122–3). "Government" ought to be, John Adams had written long before the Revolution, "a plain, simple, intelligible thing, founded on nature and reason, and quite comprehensible by common sense" (J. Adams 2000a: 26). Popular commitment not only to the idea of popular sovereignty but to what we would now describe as "representative democracy" (the term did not yet exist) was extremely strong and the separation of powers was universally regarded as a fundamental of good government (see *Federalist* 42). Commenting on proposals to establish a Dictator on the Roman model to prosecute the War of Independence that had nearly been carried in the Virginia Assembly, Jefferson questioned whether the measure would have been accepted by the Virginian citizenry. It seemed more likely that they would have immediately overthrown the government and re-established the republic (Jefferson 1954: 128).

"The people can never wilfully betray their own interests," James Madison wrote in the *Federalist*, "but they may possibly be betrayed by the representatives of the people" (*Federalist* 63). American theorists hoped that a combination of carefully written constitutions, bicameral legislative chambers, frequent elections, and a veto-wielding executive would be adequate defense against a corrupt legislative assembly.[3] Yet theorists also feared the people themselves – not their fitness to govern over the long term, but their susceptibility, even if only for a time, to the persuasions of Caesar-like figures (for American fear of "democracy" see Palmer 1953 and Shalhope 1990: 97ff.).

This fear of demagogues, despite a strong commitment to popular government, led to a tension in their thinking. Writing in support of a Federal Senate in 1787, Madison argued that although in "all free governments" the "cool and deliberate sense of the community ought ... to prevail over the views of its rulers," there were also "particular moments when the people, stimulated by some irregular passion, or some illicit advantage, or misled by the artful representations of interested men, might call for measures which they themselves will afterwards be the most ready to lament and condemn." Of the ancient states that had attempted a republic, he noted, only those with a senate not under the direct control of the people had been at all "long-lived" and had avoided "the fugitive and turbulent existence of other ancient republics" (*Federalist* 63). Although Jefferson asserted the principle of majority rule as a fundamental principle of political theory,[4] many committed republicans feared the consequences of asserting that principle on all occasions. "On what principle does the voice of the majority bind the minority?" Madison cautioned him. "It does not result I conceive from the law of nature but from compact founded on conveniency. A greater proportion might be required by the fundamental constitution of a Society if it were judged eligible" (Madison to Jefferson, February 4, 1790). A similar argument was made by James Wilson, who conceded that the majority principle was indeed the normal model in civil society, but that it was a principle flowing from a universally agreed contract (J. Wilson 1967a: 304–6). Both men feared the constitutional instability that might result from holding that majority rule was itself a principle of natural law – for how then could constitutional law be safe from "irregular passion"? It was a fear that would be vindicated by the eventual product of the French Revolution, and the form of government it created: Caesarism.

Caesar was of interest to late eighteenth-century republicans not as a unique historical figure of exceptional abilities or ambitions, but as the consequence of institutional deficiencies in the Roman State, which the modern "science of politics"[5] could identify and explain. In this they were not being original. Montesquieu, for example, whose works were amongst those they most frequently cited (Lutz 1984: 193), had treated Caesar in a similar way in his *Considerations on the Causes of the*

Greatness of the Romans and their Decline (1734). Though he did think that Caesar had many exceptional qualities, so that it would have been "very difficult for him ... not to have governed the republic in which he was born" (Montesquieu 1965: 106), Montesquieu was interested in examining the failings of the Roman state over an extended period, and deducing more universal lessons about government or human nature. "Finally, the republic was crushed," he wrote, "and we must not blame it on the ambition of certain individuals; we must blame it on man – a being whose greed for power keeps increasing the more he has of it, and who desires all only because he possesses so much." If Caesar and Pompey had not been the cause of Rome's fall, others would have taken their place (Montesquieu 1965: 108). This sense, that Caesar was not exceptional, but rather an example of an inherent danger facing republics, is represented in one of the earliest symbols of republican government adopted in America, the state seal adopted by Virginia on Independence. The obverse of the seal shows Virtue standing over a figure representing Tyranny, with the motto "*Sic Semper Tyrannis.*" The scene is generic and yet it recalls, especially in conjunction with the other classical imagery on both sides of the seal, in particular the assassination of Caesar.

Discussion of the details of Caesar's career was rare. Adams offered an extended account of the history of Rome in his *Defence of the Constitutions of the United States of America*, but in the first volume disposed of Caesar's career in a single sentence: "Caesar followed, and completed the catastrophe" (J. Adams 1797: 361). Though he did offer a slightly more lengthy account of Caesar in his third volume, Caesar himself was of interest only because he stood at the end of a much longer period of failure and decline. Though they differed on much in their interpretation of ancient history, America's politicians were extremely consistent in their treatment of Caesar's significance. Earlier thinkers had debated whether his actions were right or not, and whether his assassins should be praised or blamed (Trenchard and Gordon 1995: 87ff.). Montesquieu, indeed, had offered a defense of Caesar's assassins and of the principle of assassinating a tyrant (Montesquieu 1965: 108–11). Yet the politicians of America's Revolutionary generation did not even debate the point for rhetorical effect. Only very rare glimpses of a more positive view of Caesar can be detected. There is, it is true, a contemporary engraving that appears to depict Washington as Caesar, but this was a European work, not an American one, and appears to misunderstand Washington's role (Wills 1984: 138–9). The choice of the pseudonyms "Brutus" and "Cato" by opponents of the new Federal Constitution proposed in late 1787 is unremarkable. More puzzling is the choice of "Caesar" by one of the earliest defenders of the Constitution to oppose them. The two letters published by the "Caesar" of 1787, direct replies to "Brutus" and "Cato," have frequently been ascribed to Hamilton, though there is more than enough cause to doubt that he authored them. The choice of name suggests a level of insensitivity to public sentiment that is out of character even for Hamilton, and the content of the two "Caesar" letters displays none of the flair and subtlety present in the much more famous and significant defense of the Constitution, the *Federalist Papers*, which he, Madison, and Jay published under the name "Publius" (Cooke 1960).

If there was little interest in discussing Caesar himself, either to condemn or to praise him, there was much interest in discussing the problems inherent in republican government that his career seemed to personify. Caesar was seen as a dangerous promoter of faction, and above all as a dangerous demagogue, who had used his ability to manipulate popular opinion in order to subvert the constitution. Fear of faction – and of the demagogues that would exploit it – was present at the very founding of the American state, and almost always associated with the experience of the ancient world. It was a danger to which all republics, America included, were thought to be vulnerable. "The instability, injustice and confusion," Madison warned, "introduced into the public councils, have, in truth, been the mortal diseases under which popular governments have everywhere perished" (*Federalist* 10), and they continued to be a threat in America. Or, as Hamilton put it, given the example of the "history of the petty republics of Greece and Italy," if "it had been found impracticable to have devised modes of a more perfect structure, the enlightened friends of liberty would have been obliged to abandon the cause of that species of government as indefensible" (*Federalist* 9).

Perhaps most insidious of all Caesar's characteristics had been his successful masquerade as a friend of the Republic. Discussing the "Caesars" of his own day, Hamilton saw this as one of the identifying features of a Caesar-like politician. His opponents were accusing him of harboring "monarchist" sentiments, and of championing economic policies that would undermine republican government (Washington to Hamilton, July 19, 1792. For an account of the disputes, see Dunn 2004: 35–73). Hamilton used the parallel of Caesar to turn this accusation on its head: "The truth unquestionably is, that the only path to a subversion of the republican system of the Country is, by flattering the prejudices of the people, and exciting their jealousies and apprehensions, to throw affairs into confusion, and bring on civil commotion." The danger to the republic did not come from those who favored a strong Federal government, he wrote, but from those who opposed it. He distrusted the motives of those who were mounting "the hobby horse of popularity," joining in "the cry of danger to liberty" and "taking every opportunity of embarrassing the General [Federal] Government & bringing it under suspicion." "It has been aptly observed," he wrote, making his parallel clear, "that *Cato* was the Tory – *Caesar* the Whig of his day. The former frequently resisted – the latter always flattered the follies of the people. Yet the former perished with the Republic[;] the latter destroyed it" (Hamilton to Washington, August 18, 1792).

Much of the fear of constitutional instability in a republic, or of forces working to overthrow it, was almost certainly groundless, as Hamilton himself observed: "Tis curious to observe the anticipations of the different parties. One side appears to believe that there is a serious plot to overturn the state Governments and substitute monarchy to the present republican system. The other side firmly believes that there is a serious plot to overturn the General Government. ... Both sides may be equally wrong, & their mutual jealousies may be materially causes of the appearances which mutually disturb them ..." (Hamilton to Washington, August 18, 1792). Nevertheless, the perception of an emerging "popular" party and an opposing party that favored commercial interests undoubtedly strengthened the notion that the emerging party system in America mirrored the factional fighting that Caesar had been able to use to his advantage. That "faction" or political parties were an evil that the architects of America's political system unsuccessfully hoped to avoid is often remarked upon.[6] Less frequently noted, but significant for assessing Caesar's influence in the history of republican thought, is the fact that eighteenth-century politicians expected the emergence of political parties to mirror the structure of the factions at Rome, the one representing the people, the other opposing it; the political rhetoric of the period recast the controversies of the day in those terms. The danger that politics might divide the people into a "popular" and an opposing faction is an important part of Madison's treatment of faction in *Federalist* 10 and Hamilton's in *Federalist* 35.

Figures, then, who deliberately courted the popular vote were regarded with suspicion. Of one of them, Hamilton wrote:

> Mr. Burr's integrity as an Individual is not unimpeached. As a public man he is one of the worst sort – a friend to nothing but as it suits his interest and ambition. Determined to climb to the highest honours of State, and as much higher as circumstances may permit – he cares nothing about the means of effecting his purpose. Tis evident he aims at putting himself at the head of what he calls the "popular party" as affording the best tools for an ambitious man to work with. Secretly turning Liberty into ridicule, he knows as well as most men how to make use of the name. In a word, if we have an embryo-Caesar in the United States 'tis Burr. (Hamilton to an unknown correspondent, September 26, 1792)

Hamilton made a similar charge against Jefferson, though – perhaps because both were serving in Washington's administration at the time – he stopped just short of calling a him a Catiline or a Caesar. Nevertheless, suspecting him of harboring desires to undo the whole Federal project (see his "Catullus" essays I and II, reprinted in Hamilton 1904b: 247ff.), he drew parallels between Jefferson and the two infamous Romans. Jefferson, he wrote in a public essay, "has hitherto been distinguished as the quiet, modest, retiring philosopher; as the plain, simple, unambitious republican. He shall not now, for the first time, be regarded as the intriguing incendiary, the aspiring turbulent competitor." He continued:

> I am not sufficiently acquainted with the history of his political life to determine; but there is always a first time when characters studious of artful disguises are unveiled; when the visor of stoicism is plucked from the brow of the epicurean; when the plain garb of Quaker simplicity is stripped from the concealed voluptuary; when Caesar coyly refusing the proffered diadem, is seen to be Caesar rejecting the trappings, but tenaciously grasping the substance of imperial domination. ("Catullus" III, in Hamilton 1904b: 271)

Though he certainly did not welcome the comparison with Caesar, Jefferson was more than happy to claim his place as the leader of the popular faction, presenting his political opponents as the enemies of republicanism and the people, and calling his 1800 election victory over John Adams a second "revolution" (Jefferson to Spencer Roane, September 6, 1819). The Constitution, with its complex process for the election of the President, went far beyond the mere weighting of votes for different states. Instead the popular choice of President was mediated through an electoral college, a device that was clearly intended to prevent the election of a "Caesar," and to deny an elected President a direct popular mandate. The electoral college was alleged to be superior to election "by the people in their collective capacity where the activity of party zeal, taking advantage of the supineness, the ignorance, and the hopes and fears of the unwary and interested, often places men in office by the votes of a small proportion of the electors" (*Federalist* 64). With the exception of Washington's election as President, this system never worked as intended. Instead, it was rapidly recognized that whatever the formal arrangements, choice of the President was effectively by popular vote, and party faction was very much associated with the election.[7]

Though the charge of being "a Caesar" had been leveled at Jefferson, it was Andrew Jackson, in many ways Jefferson's political heir, who was the first president to be widely associated with Caesar. He portrayed opponents as anti-republican, asking "Shall government or the people rule?" (Wilentz 2005: 302). More than ever before, Jackson's election in 1828 was won through the use of a well-organized party machine. While it is and was possible to overemphasize the extent to which Jackson represented a break with the past, his opponents attacked him for a number of things that seemed to subvert the more traditional role of the president: his consolidation of the "spoils system" whereby government posts were given to members of his party (estimated by those who condemned the system in the late nineteenth century to amount to more than 90,000 jobs in the Federal government: Lecky 1981: 69); an expanded use of the veto, based on a claim that he was the only national politician with a direct mandate from the American people (a claim, in fact, that Jefferson had also made, at least in his correspondence); and selection of his own successor.[8] These all seemed to his opponents to be dangerous innovations, and certainly worthy of comparison with Caesar; Jackson's background as a military hero made it seem all the more apt (E. Miles 1968).

Some saw in Jackson the welcome rise of true "democracy" in America; others saw a dangerous principle asserting itself, and the debate continued even after he had left office. The inaugural issue of the *United States Magazine and Democratic Review* dedicated itself to advocating the "high and holy DEMOCRATIC PRINCIPLE which was designed to be the fundamental element of the new social and political system created by the 'American Experiment' " (*United States Magazine and Democratic Review*, October 1st, 1837, p. 1). Only a month earlier, the *American Quarterly Review* had attacked Jackson's administration for courting the votes of the poor by declaring itself "the friend of poverty and ignorance and the foe of all property and intelligence." It accused the administration of making "divisions in society – the most dangerous and most unnatural – a division between the poor and the rich," and of using "popularity to beat down the better reason of its opponents." It warned:

> This state of things will grow worse and worse, the more the idea spreads that this country was meant to be a democracy and not a republic – that all power was intended to be exercised directly by the people ... A representative republic is not a democracy; it was constructed to avoid the dangers on which Greece and Rome went to pieces – by the

> preponderance of the democratic elements. Polybius foretold that the republic of Rome would be destroyed when the people knew their power.[9]

It condemned the flattery of "the demagogue and the democrat" and warned of the upheaval and unrest that democratic government would bring, as "all legislation" was rendered "irregular and insecure." Unable to fully adjust to the changes that universal suffrage had brought to politics, Jackson's opponents, the Whig Party, continued to view the courting of the popular vote as akin to Caesar's populism, and just as dangerous.[10]

In America the biggest threat to the Constitution proved to be slavery, not the popular vote, but in Europe, and France in particular, republics seemed to suffer just the fate that American writers had hoped to avoid. Even in 1794, watching the progress of affairs in France, Hamilton worried that there seemed "nowhere any thing but principles and opinions so wild, so extreme, passions so turbulent, so tempestuous, as almost to forbid the hope of agreement in any rational or well-organized system of government ... that after wading through seas of blood, in a furious and sanguinary civil war, France may find herself at length the slave of some victorious Sylla, or Marius, or Caesar" ("Americanus" I in Hamilton 1904a: 77). In less than a decade, Napoleon I had seized power in France and, taking the title *Premier Consul*, had embraced the comparison with Caesar. Just as American thinkers had feared, this modern Caesar won his power through claiming to be a friend of the people, and used the concept of popular sovereignty to undo the constitution that would otherwise have been a bar to his position. His dictatorship was confirmed by plebiscite, an innovation that would be copied by his nephew later in the century. Remarking in a 1865 essay entitled "Caesarism as it now Exists" on Napoleon III's publication of his history of Julius Caesar, the English commentator Walter Bagehot wrote: "That the French Emperor should have the spare leisure and unoccupied reflection sufficient to write a biography is astonishing, but ... his choice of subject is very natural. Julius Caesar was the first who tried on an imperial scale the characteristic principles of the French Empire. ... On the big page of universal history, Julius Caesar is the first instance of a democratic despot" (Bagehot 1968a: 111).

The despotisms of Caesar and Napoleon III were similar, Bagehot argued and "No one will ever make an approach to understanding [the French Empire] who does not separate it altogether, and on principle, from the despotisms of feudal origin and legitimate pretensions." Monarchies appealed to duty and conscience, and claimed divine right; Napoleon claimed to be the "people's agent" (Bagehot 1968a: 111). The direct popular mandate given to a single figure by plebiscite was held to supersede any other claim to represent the people. Napoleon I had explained his position to a hostile legislature in 1813: "You call yourselves representatives of the nation. It is not true ... I alone am the representative of the people! Twice have twenty-four millions of French called me to the throne – which of you durst undertake such a burden?" (Burrienne 1836: 280).

The legitimacy of such a claim troubled thinkers throughout the century – indeed, the concept of "legitimacy" became a litigated question only after the French Revolution and Napoleon's seizure of power (M. Richter 1982; Holmes 1982; for the use of the word in Britain, see Semmel 2000: 146ff.). It was difficult to disentangle the authority claimed by a Caesarist regime from the doctrine of popular sovereignty advocated by supporters of republicanism. As Maine noted wryly, commenting on Napoleon III's ascension, "The arguments of the French Liberal party against the Plébiscite, during the twenty years of stern despotism which it entailed upon France, have always appeared to me to be arguments in reality against the very principle of democracy" (Maine 1976: 61). Writing in *The Economist* while Napoleon III still ruled, Bagehot struggled to balance his obvious disapproval for the political system adopted by the French with an assessment of why the regime was popular. "Louis Napoleon," he wrote, "is a Benthamite despot. He is for the 'greatest happiness of the greatest number.' He says, 'I am where I am, because I know better than any one else what is good for the French people, and they know that I know better' " (Bagehot 1968a: 111). He conceded that in the short term the system had the appearance of success: "the French Empire is really the *best finished* democracy that the world has ever seen ... An absolute government with a popular instinct has the unimpeded command of a people renowned for orderly dexterity." The French bureaucracy was "not only endurable but pleasant." The public perception, Bagehot reported, was that the government did serve the "welfare of the masses" (Bagehot 1968a: 112).

Ever since the accession of Napoleon, Bagehot had emphasized that while he understood the reasons for Napoleon's popularity, the form of government troubled him: "a government may be suitable for the tastes and predilections of a particular people at a particular time, and may confer great benefits ... and yet that government may not be intrinsically or generally desirable" (Bagehot 1968c: 90). He acknowledged the present stability and prosperity Napoleon had brought. As a ruler, Napoleon did not seem an awful choice, for the present: "The intelligence of the Emperor on economical subjects – on the bread and meat of the people," he wrote, "is really better than that of the classes opposed to him." Bagehot's criticism of the system was that its policy served the "*present happiness*" well enough, but he feared for the future; the suppression of political discourse in the state would injure its politics eventually; corruption within the huge apparatus of government that supported the Emperor was rife; and ultimately the regime was too dependent on popular faith in one man. "The democratic despot – the representative despot – must have the sagacity to divine the people's will and the sagacity to execute it" (Bagehot 1968a: 113–16).

After the regime collapsed he criticized the principle of Caesarism on a more fundamental level. Caesarism, as he defined it now, was:

> that peculiar system of which Louis Napoleon ... is the greatest exponent, which tries to win directly from a *plebiscite*, i.e. the vote of the people, a power for the throne to override the popular will as expressed in representative assemblies, and to place in the monarch an indefinite "responsibility" to the nation, by virtue of which he may hold in severe check the intellectual criticism of the more educated classes and even the votes of the people's own delegates. This is what we really mean by Caesarism, – the abuse of the confidence reposed by the most ignorant in a great name ... A virtually irresponsible power obtained by one man from the vague preference of the masses for a particular name. (Bagehot 1968b: 156)

Bagehot poured scorn on the claim of a Caesarist regime to be "the people's agent." He argued that the authority the Emperor claimed by virtue of the plebiscite was used to silence "the reasoned arguments of men who both know the popular wish and are sufficiently educated to discuss the best means of gratifying those wishes." Even in comparison with the "personal government" of the Prussian monarchy that had defeated it, Caesarist government in France had been overly dependent on the Emperor, and other organs of the state had been fatally weakened (Bagehot 1968b: 156–7).

Bagehot's definitions of Caesarism limited the term in practice to the French experience under Napoleon I and Napoleon III, and perhaps make it difficult to distinguish from "Bonapartism," but other writers analyzing the politics of the nineteenth century used the term more expansively. The definition advanced by the sociologist Max Weber after the First World War certainly covered Bonapartism, but also features of parliamentary democracy. "Caesarism" as he defined it was not a distinct form of government, as Bagehot had thought it to be, but present to some degree in every state with a wide suffrage. He argued that in democratic Germany and in all democracies a political leader no longer came to the fore selected by "a circle of notables" or because he had proved his abilities in parliament, "but rather because he uses the means of *mass* demagogy to gain the confidence of the masses and thereby gains power. Essentially this means that the selection of the leader has shifted in the direction of *Caesarism*." The "specifically Caesarist instrument," he acknowledged, was "the plebiscite," but the plebiscite shared important features with other types of election. If the plebiscite was "a confession of 'belief' in the vocation for leadership of the person who has laid claim to this acclamation," surely "every kind of *direct election by the people* of the bearer of supreme power, and beyond this every kind of position of political power which in fact rests upon the trust of the masses rather than that of parliament ... lies on the road towards ... 'pure' forms of Caesarist acclamation." He singled out the presidency of the United States as an example: the president's position was legitimated by "democratic" nomination and election, and "the president's superiority in relation to parliament [Congress] rests on this very fact" (Weber 1994a: 221).

Even where a political leader's position did not rest directly on popular election, Weber argued, there could be a Caesarist element to his authority. "The position of the English prime minister," he pointed out, "certainly does not rest de facto on the confidence of parliament and its parties but on the trust of the masses in the country and the army in the field." He argued that parliaments were not rendered useless, as enemies of republicanism suggested, but would have to accept that in mass democracies they would not be able to select their own political leader (Weber 1994a: 222). Elsewhere, he linked the rise of plebiscitary leadership in a mass democracy to the rise of political parties, which were the inevitable product of mass suffrage. In Britain after 1868, he wrote, "To win over the masses it was necessary to call into being an enormous apparatus of associations which were democratic in appearance" and to organize the vote in each locality. This "newly emerging machine, no longer directed from parliament," he argued, concentrated power into fewer hands, and ultimately into the hands of the single party leader.

Gladstone's victory over Disraeli, therefore, was a victory for Caesarist charisma (Weber 1994b: 341–2).

It is easy to accuse Weber of anachronism, or of misrepresenting British and American politics, but here is not the place to analyze in detail his view of foreign politics. His definition of "Caesarism," however, captures Caesar's place in the debates and fears of theorists and politicians since 1776. Mass democracy and the emergence of recognizably modern party systems had transformed the nature of politics, and the various stages of this transformation had often provoked fears of "a Caesar" or accusations of "Caesarism" from those opposing populist politicians. Echoes of these cries endure in modern American politics. It was not until 1951 that the Twenty-Second Amendment formalized what had until then been merely a strong tradition, underpinned by the example of George Washington, that presidents of the United States should not seek a third term in office. On November 7, 1874, *Harper's Weekly* published a cartoon about American fear of Caesarism by Thomas Nast (see figure 28.1). Entitled "Third Term Panic" and drawing on one of Aesop's fables, it showed a donkey dressed in a lion's skin marked "Caesarism" intimidating an elephant labeled "The Republican Vote." Nast's cartoon attacked the *New York Herald* for putting about the suggestions that Grant would seek a third term and that doing so would amount to Caesarism. The images stuck, and the Donkey and Elephant remain to this day the symbols of the Democratic and Republican parties in America.

Historical writing reacted to, but did not fully engage with, the challenges for political theory posed by Caesarism. Caesar's historical reputation experienced

Figure 28.1 *Harper's Weekly*, November 7, 1874.

something of a renaissance in the nineteenth century, reaching its zenith with J. A. Froude's *Caesar: a Sketch* (1879), in which Caesar is presented as the only politician to perceive the problems of Rome, whose every act of mercy is emphasized, and every execution or grasp of power excused. Cicero, not Caesar, is presented as the villain of the work. A favorable account of Caesar was also presented by Mommsen, who praised Caesar as a "monarch ... never seized with the giddiness of the tyrant. He is perhaps the only one among the mighty ones of the earth, who in great matters and little never acted according to inclination or caprice, but always without exception according to his duty as ruler" and who "made no false step of passion to regret" (Mommsen 1894: 312). His Caesar was indeed a "democratic" dictator, whose "monarchy was so little at variance with democracy, that democracy on the contrary only attained its completion and fulfilment by means of that monarchy. For this monarchy ... [was] the representation of the nation in the man in whom it puts supreme and unlimited confidence" (Mommsen 1894: 325). Mommsen was aware that his praise of Caesar might be seized upon by advocates of Caesarism in Europe, and did his best to forestall such use of his work. The very perfection of Caesar he attempted to use as an argument against modern Caesarism. "According to that same law of nature in virtue of which the smallest organism infinitely surpasses the most artistic machine, every constitution however defective which gives play to the free self-determination of a majority of its citizens infinitely surpasses the most brilliant and humane absolutism," he argued. Caesar's dictatorship established monarchy under the most ideal of all conditions, but it only represented the "least of evils" and replaced not a free republic but "oligarchic absolutism" (Mommsen 1894: 326–7).

Is the election of a dictator a legitimate democratic choice, or do charismatic leaders who seek to clothe themselves with a popular mandate subvert democracies and republics? It was a controversy that the figure of Caesar had been used to address since the founding of the American republic, and one which would be settled by experience rather than by intellectuals. Totalitarian dictatorship in the twentieth century would discredit the very question. There are echoes of Caesarism in every "presidential" style of government, but if the shadow of Caesar is no longer cast over political debate, it is ultimately because the experience of modern democracies has been that strong constitutional arrangements can indeed contain charismatic leaders.

FURTHER READING

An influential account of the power of the name of Caesar in later ages is Gundolf 1928. An excellent discussion of the relationship of Caesarism to historical writing is contained in Yavetz 1983: 10–57. The collection of essays in Baehr and Richter 2004 provides a good introduction to the theoretical problems posed by Caesarism and by dictatorship more broadly.

For further discussion of Caesar in early America, a good starting point is Malamud 2006. The literature on republicanism is vast, but the standard account of American republicanism remains Wood 1998.

For an introduction to American Constitutionalism, see Lutz 1988 and the extensive work on the subject by John Philip Reid in his series, *The Constitutional History of the American Revolution*. An older treatment of the subject, interesting because the lectures it contains date from the eve of the Second World War and discuss these issues with an eye to challenging American exceptionalism and isolationism, is McIlwain 1947.

The legacy of Caesar was not the only basis on which the Bonapartes justified their power and authority. For an introduction to broader issues see Mansel 1988, Lyons 1994, and W. H. C. Smith 2005.

NOTES

1 "Brutus" I, reprinted in Storing and Dry 1985: 113. For the Federalist justification see *Federalist* 9.
2 For Paine's view of the classics, see the discussion in Aldridge 1968.
3 For constitutional law see Jefferson 1954: 123–5. For bicameral assemblies see *Federalist* 62 and 63, and J. Wilson 1967a: 290–2; for frequent elections see *Federalist* 53; for veto power see *Federalist* 73.
4 Jefferson to Madison, September 6, 1789; also his "Opinion on the Residence Bill," reprinted in Jefferson 1999: 159.
5 For use of the term see, for example, Jefferson 1954: 119; *Federalist* 9; Wilson 1967a: 303; J. Wilson 1967b: 762.
6 See Wood 1998: 58–60. Perhaps the two most commented-upon papers in the *Federalist* are 10 and 35, both of which deal with the problem of faction.
7 The tension of the non-partisan ideal and the political reality was the theme of Ketcham 1984. See especially pp. 104, 128–9, 141ff.
8 Cf. M. Wilson 1988: 426–7; Jefferson to Spencer Roane, September 6, 1819.
9 *American Quarterly Review*, September 1837: 67–8. Cf. Madison's comments about the danger of a majority faction that knew its power in *Federalist* 10.
10 For the inability of the Whig party to adjust to the challenge of Jackson, see Formisano 1969; Marshall 1967. For Jackson's populism compared to Caesar, see M. L. Wilson 1995: 632–5; Miles 1968.

CHAPTER TWENTY-NINE

Caesar for Communists and Fascists

Luciano Canfora

Caesarism: what Caesar adopted at the end of his political trajectory was an incomplete and provisional solution, as if he had renounced the making of a choice. In proclaiming himself emperor, Napoleon Bonaparte drew his inspiration from the development of the Roman constitution after Caesar – namely the Empire – but he too avoided the word "monarchy." He went further than Caesar and carried the Caesarian model to its extreme; nonetheless, although eventually defeated, he perpetuated the "myth" of Caesar. Besides, on St. Helena he dictated a literary work, *Précis des guerres de Jules César*, that represents a sort of "settlement of accounts" between the Emperor and his Roman archetype, a discussion that is not only military, but historiographical and political as well. For Napoleon does not simply reconsider the great military campaigns of his model, as the title would lead us to think, mixing together praise and criticism: he also talks about politics and the regime established by Caesar. He pays particular attention to the characterization of a "third way" that Caesarism embodied, between oligarchy on the one side and a popular regime on the other. There is one aspect in particular in which Bonaparte feels that he is on the same wavelength as Caesar: his decision to seek a reconciliation, an agreement, with the nobility that had fought against him. In this respect, Bonaparte even arrives at a formulation that seems to anticipate Robert Michels's "iron law of oligarchy":

> Chez les peuples et dans les révolutions l'aristocratie existe toujours: la détruisez-vous dans la noblesse, elle se place aussitôt dans les maisons riches et puissantes du tiers état: la détruisez-vous dans celles-ci, elle surnage et se réfugie dans les chefs d'atelier et du peuple. (*Précis des guerres de Jules César*, XVI, § 1)

> An aristocracy always exists among all peoples and all revolutions: you eliminate it from the nobility, and immediately it places itself in the rich and powerful families of the third estate; you eliminate it from these, and it finds a refuge among the leaders of the working class.

Among other things, in these few lines there is a fairly clear reference to those pages of the *commentarii* on the civil war (3.20–1) in which Caesar writes about the crushing of Caelius Rufus' efforts to support the demands of debtors and about the very severe steps taken by Antony – Caesar's *magister equitum* – to repress the uprisings aimed at the cancellation of debts (Liv. *Per.* 113; Plut. *Ant.* 9–10). These revolts arose in Italy when the defeat of Pompey appeared certain.

It should not occasion surprise, therefore, that Alphonse de Beauchamp (1767–1832), who started as a Jacobin and finished his career writing the memoirs which Fouché circulated under his own name, should have released in 1823 – soon after Napoleon's death (5 May 1821) – the *Vie de Jules César.* This is, at least in its premises, a *roman à clef*, in which Bonaparte is also a target.

The fact that Napoleon tried to revive a form of charismatic military rule, for which Caesar was a source of inspiration, made it possible to understand that the rule of Caesar was not a monarchy *sic et simpliciter.* Napoleon "reads" and interprets that remote experience, he draws fundamental and peculiar elements from it, and he builds up a model, namely, Bonapartism. And his contemporaries saw how different it was from the "salutaires et protectrices monarchies modernes" ("salutary and protective modern monarchies"), to use the words of Alphonse de Beauchamp.

On the other hand, for the members of the ruling classes of late-republican Rome (who thought they had brought Caesarism to an end through the "tyrannicide" of the Ides of March) the Caesarian experiment could only be placed, in constitutional terms, on the side of "monarchy," which was utterly illegal in Rome. Moreover, it had the character of usurpation, and hence of "tyranny." While *regnum* – and, most of all, aspiring to it – is at Rome a crime and an attack on the constitution, the notion closest to it, if one looks to the Greek tradition of political thought, is tyranny. King-usurper and tyrant coincide, and, from the point of view of the Roman ruling classes, both are present in the figure of Caesar and in the kind of power which he established through the dictatorship for life. It is not irrelevant to add, in this respect, that, before becoming the antithesis and the opposite of *politeia*, and consequently of democracy, the tyrants had been the (pro-popular) mediators of the insoluble conflicts in Greece during the sixth century BC.

How far the Caesarian experiment appeared to be tipped towards monarchy, and consequently to be unsustainable, emerges clearly from the fact that Octavian distanced himself from it. He brought off a stroke of political genius when, even if at the heavy price of the long conflict against Antony (who was infatuated with the Hellenistic model), he managed to obtain, at the same time, the control and support both of the legions and of the Caesarian faction, and also to establish a form of rule that could be presented as the "restoration of the Republic." Moreover, by simplifying and taking away from the Caesarian experiment the peculiar character of a Bonapartist "third way," did not Eduard Meyer, in one of his most famous books (*Caesars Monarchie und das Principat des Pompejus*), classify the government of Caesar as a "monarchy," and the way in which Pompey behaved *in re publica* as a "principate" and thus as an anticipation of the form of government invented by Augustus?

Eduard Meyer wrote his book in 1917 (and published it in 1918), while in Russia – revolutionized by the war and by the succession of upheavals – the individual power of Lenin was establishing itself. This was a "left-wing Bonapartism," of which Meyer was an admirer, as he stated a few years later in the essay "Das neue Russland" (in *Deutsche Rundschau* 52 [1925], no. 205, pp. 101–18). Furthermore, the publication of the book preceded by a few years a "right-wing Bonapartism" in Italy – the dictatorship of Mussolini – which asserted itself thanks to the inability of the revolutionaries to "do as in Russia" and the inability of the bourgeois state to "overwhelm the revolution."

While reflecting in prison on the defeat suffered by the "revolution" in Italy and, in an almost transparent fashion, on the dictatorial forms assumed by the rule of the Bolsheviks in the USSR, Antonio Gramsci came to draw a distinction between a "progressive" Caesarism (Caesar and Napoleon I) and a "regressive" Caesarism (Napoleon III and Bismarck). However questionable this distinction may be considered, one should not lose sight of the underlying premise, which precedes the distinction itself and is common to both the Caesarisms, the premise that, in Gramsci's happy formulation:

> [il cesarismo] esprime sempre la soluzione arbitrale, affidata a una grande personalità, di una situazione caratterizzata da un equilibrio di forze a prospettiva catastrofica. (Gerratana 1975: 1619)
>
> [Caesarism] always expresses the arbitrary solution, entrusted to a great personality, of a historical and political situation characterized by a balance of forces, with a prospect of catastrophe.

And immediately before this:

> il cesarismo esprime una situazione in cui le forze in lotta si equilibrano in modo catastrofico, cioè si equilibrano in modo che la continuazione della lotta non può concludersi che con la distruzione reciproca. (ibid.)
>
> Caesarism expresses a condition in which the forces involved in a struggle are counterbalanced in a way which is disastrous, i.e. they are so evenly matched that the continuation of the struggle cannot conclude without mutual destruction.

Gramsci then continues:

> Si tratta di vedere se nella dialettica "rivoluzione/restaurazione" è l'elemento rivoluzione o quello restaurazione che prevale, poiché è certo che nel movimento storico non si torna mai indietro *e non esistono restaurazioni "in toto."* (ibid.)
>
> The question is whether, in the dialectical pair "revolution/restoration," it is the side of revolution or of restoration that prevails. That is because it is certain that, in the movement of history, the direction is never reversed, and there is no such thing as a restoration "*in toto.*"

Indeed, Caesar is the character around whom these patterns connect. It is indeed bizarre to see how enthusiastically Marx talks about Caesar, in a famous letter to Engels, written during the months in which Marx is certainly reading Mommsen's *Römische Geschichte*, as can be deduced from other letters. The letter in question, dated February 27, 1861, is well known for its judgment – recalled many times – on

Spartacus ("grosser General, kein Garibaldi!", which means "a great general, but no Garibaldi he!") and on Appian, the Greek-Egyptian historian from Alexandria. Further on in the letter, Marx shows very emphatically his appreciation of Caesar's "military" daring, which was proof of his unquestioned superiority over his enemies:

> Pompejus reiner Scheißkerl; erst durch Escamotage ... als "young man" v. Sulla u.s.w. in falschen Ruf gekommen. ... Sobald er Caesar gegenüber zeigen soll was an ihm – Lauskerl. Caesar machte die allergrößten militärischen Fehler, absichtlich toll, um den Philister, der ihm gegenüber stand, zu decontenanciren. Ein ordinärer röm. General, etwa Crassus, würde ihn sechsmal während des Kampfes in Epirus vernichtet haben. (Marx and Engels 2005: 380)

> Pompey, a real shit; acquired spurious fame only, by confiscations, as Sulla's "young man," ... As soon as he was brought face to face with Caesar and had to show what stuff he was made of – a mere louse. Caesar perpetrated the most stupendous military blunders, deliberately crazy ones, to discountenance the Philistine opposing him. Any ordinary Roman general – Crassus, say – would have annihilated him six times over during the fighting in Epirus. (Marx 1987: 264)

This page exudes sympathetic exaltation of Caesar, which goes even beyond the admiring tone adopted by Bonaparte. The latter, at least in this respect, does not hesitate to denounce the tactical mistakes made by Caesar, especially during the civil war. His risky military conduct in Epirus stands out among these: "Les manœuvres de César à Dyrrachium sont extrêmement téméraires: aussi en fut-il puni"; *Précis des guerres de Jules César*, XI, § 4. ("Caesar's maneuvers at Dyrrachium" – Bonaparte writes here – "are extremely rash: therefore he was punished.")

Mommsen's enthusiasm for Caesar is well known, and there is no need to recall it here except incidentally, in order to point out that in Mommsen it coexists with his liberal *forma mentis* (especially when he was writing the *Römische Geschichte*). It is even possible that Marx was influenced by reading Mommsen's *Römische Geschichte*, but there is undoubtedly something else in the wholehearted appreciation shown by Marx for Caesar's pre-eminence and for his boldness: a relationship that has no complex about "dictatorship."

The attempts to write a Roman history from a Marxist perspective also had to reckon with Caesar. Quite often, there was attributed to Caesar the historical role of beginning a new era, by putting an end to the unbearable contradictions of the oligarchic city state, which could no longer rule such a huge empire. Francesco De Martino, in the third volume of his *Storia della costituzione romana*, made the fullest and best-balanced attempt at interpretation in that sense. For De Martino, too, it was just as certain that "a political class, the senatorial nobility, which had become unable to guarantee a correct administration of the State and was only determined not to waive any of its privileges" ("Una classe politica, la nobiltà senatoria, divenuta incapace di assicurare la retta direzione dello Stato, decisa soltanto a non rinunciare ad alcuno dei suoi privilegi," AA.VV. (1956), *Cesare nel bimillenario della morte*, Rome/Turin, Edizioni Radio italiana, p. 194) rose against Caesar.

References to Caesar recur in the writings of some exponents of communism in Italy (Gramsci, Togliatti), but not in France or Russia. Similarly, Caesar is present, with varying fortunes, in the ideology and the language of Italian Fascism, but not in that of Germany or Spain (the latter, if anything, celebrated the Augustan bimillenary, somewhat late, and only to please Mussolini). An interesting instance of this is the complete absence of the name of Caesar in the six very rich volumes of the *Selected Works* (a wide selection) of Lenin, printed in Moscow in all the most important languages of the world. The name of Caesar appears only once, in an extract from Hegel's book *Lectures on the Philosophy of History*, an extract that Lenin made during the first half of 1915. Here, as in the other parts of the work, Hegel's words alternate with Lenin's summaries: "He [Caesar] removed the eternal contradiction [by abolishing the republic, which had already become a 'shadow'] and created a new one" (Lenin 1961: 312). Lenin's words in brackets summarize the wider Hegelian context. In the margin Lenin merely derives from his reading this gist of the argument: "Hegel and 'contradiction' in history," but nothing with reference to Caesar. The reason for this absence is clear: for the men of the twentieth century, Caesarism already has a different name: "Bonapartism" (both the face of it presented by Napoleon I and that by Napoleon III). For, when the communist movement splits because of Trotsky's dramatic "schism," the latter will accuse Stalin of "Bonapartist" aspirations, not of "Caesarism."

On the other hand, in the political and cultural situation in Italy during the Fascist epoch, there is a revival of Caesar. By presenting itself as a "revolution," though centered on the dominant figure of a "leader," Fascism found it useful, especially at the beginning, to turn to the "model" represented by Caesar. Caesar is viewed as the one who best combined, in himself and in his career, two elements: the revolution against the old order and the pursuit of unbounded personal power.

In the famous *Colloqui* with Emil Ludwig, printed and bound by Mondadori on June 23, 1932, and translated into English by Eden and Cedar Paul with the title *Talks with Mussolini* (Paul 1932), Mussolini expresses "in thrilling tones" (Paul 1932: 210; "Con tono cupo e interiormente eccitato," p. 208 in the Italian critical edition published by Mondadori, Milan in 1950), as the interviewer says, this "ultra-Mommsenian" judgment on Caesar: "Caesar, after Christ the greatest figure that ever lived" ("Cesare, il più grande dopo Cristo fra quanti siano mai vissuti"), with the marginal variant "the greatest man, after Christ, etc." ("il più grande uomo, dopo Cristo, etc.") which reveals the anti-Christian streak that Mussolini sometimes allowed to appear. This evaluation appears in the chapter entitled *Sull'arte* (On Art). In the chapter *Pericoli della dittatura* (The dangers of dictatorship), Mussolini defends, against the objections of the interviewer, Caesar's decision to liquidate Vercingetorix (Paul 1932: 137), then a prisoner. The way he altered his own words, when already in proof, is revealing: he had said "one must not pass a harsh judgment upon Julius Caesar for having had Vercingetorix tortured" ("non si dovrebbe giudicare Cesare dal fatto che egli ha torturato Vercingetorige," p. 134 of the Italian critical edition), but then in his own handwriting he changed "torturato" (tortured) – which was the truth – to "incarcerato" (imprisoned)! Once more, in the chapter *Agire e pensare* (Action and reflection) at page 193 (of Paul 1932), when Mussolini characterizes *Julius Caesar* by Shakespeare as "A great school for rulers" ("Una grande scuola per governanti," p. 190 of the Italian critical edition), Ludwig asks him "Do you take this Roman as a model?" ("Sente questo romano come un modello?"; ibid.). Mussolini thinks about the answer and then replies:

> Not exactly, but the code of the Roman virtues is always in my mind. . . . The material I have to shape is still the same; and, beyond it, there is still Rome. (Paul 1932: 193–4)
>
> Non precisamente, ma tutta la pratica delle virtù latine mi sta dinanzi. . . . Il materiale è lo stesso. E là, fuori, è sempre ancora Roma.

These words, spoken by Mussolini near the tenth anniversary of the "March on Rome," contrast with the entry *Cesare* in the *Enciclopedia italiana*, written by the Jewish fascist Mario Attilio Levi, which culminates, albeit admiringly, in the theory that, by dreaming of a Hellenistic monarchy, Caesar went "against tradition and against History" ("Contro la tradizione e contro la Storia"). The entry seriously irritated Mussolini (*Enciclopedia italiana*, vol. 11, 1931).[1]

1932 was an important year for Fascism, inasmuch as it was the tenth anniversary of the "March on Rome," and the regime received countless marks of international recognition from the United Kingdom, France, the USA, and Greece, where Metaxas would try to emulate Mussolini. There is a significant example of this undisputed prestige, which ensured that the European and North American establishment took for the most part a not entirely favorable view of the anti-Fascist exiles. Even important representatives of the French government – the place of exile for Italian anti-Fascism – spoke of Mussolini with admiration, and in November 1932 a number of *Europäische Review*, entirely devoted to the decennial of Fascism, was published in Berlin and included a wide-ranging chapter written by Pierre Cot, a high-ranking representative of the left wing of the French Radical Party. In this essay, despite his clarification of the unambiguous distance from Fascism of his own political views, the author repeatedly expresses his admiration for Mussolini as a "great statesman" and the "regenerator" of the Italian people (p. 744). It is, therefore, noteworthy that in 1932 many books came out on Caesar: they indicated the widespread perception that it was legitimate to associate Fascism with the Caesarian experiment ("Caesarism"). The first of these books that is worth mentioning is *Jules César* by Auguste Bailly (1878–1967), who was a highly successful French academic, novelist, and literary critic. It was published by Fayard and, immediately after, was published in Italy by Bemporad (Florence) with a long preface by the translator Giuseppe Morelli (who regularly contributed to the journal *Critica fascista*). The most significant section is chapter 16, entitled *Un fascismo democratico* (A democratic Fascism), which is entirely focused on the problem of defining the kind of rule instituted by Caesar. It is neither a monarchy nor a tyranny – Bailly writes – and, in order to understand it, we must turn to modern experience: "Modern politics allows us to define it in one word: it is a fascism" ("La politique moderne nous permet de le désigner d'un mot: c'était un fascisme"). For – he continues – under Caesar, the State submitted to "the intelligence and the ability of one man" ("à l'intelligence et à l'énergie d'un homme"), and what was, in Bailly's opinion, the peculiar characteristic of Fascism came about: "the effort to organize, in which nothing remains from the past except what can be adapted to the present needs" ("effort d'organisation, où ne subsiste du passé que ce qui peut s'ajuster aux nécessités présentes"), as well as the renaissance "of the national sentiment after so many disagreements and conflicts" ("du sentiment national après tant de dissensions et de déchirement") (p. 240). Caesar's fascism – Bailly adds – was doubly detested by the aristocracy, inasmuch as the aristocracy was deprived of its privileges while Caesar "was imposed on them by democracy" ("lui était imposé par la démocratie").

This chapter did not go unnoticed. The word "democratic" could irritate Fascists, since it was completely opposite to the self-portrayal of Fascism. This is the reason why the translator Morelli devotes more than seven pages, out of the 25 of his entire preface, to demonstrating that that definition is not appropriate. There was a fear that, by using the image of Caesar, he wanted

> to try to contrast a democratic fascism with the fascism, pure and simple, that was a truly Italian creation of the twentieth century, making one believe that the latter had a character that was anti-democratic.
>
> cercare di contrapporre un fascismo democratico al fascismo senza aggettivi, creazione prettamente italiana del secolo ventesimo, facendo credere che questo abbia un carattere antidemocratico. (Morelli, p. xvi)

Bailly was asked for clarification, before the translation was put on the market, and he hastened to reassure the Italian public that such was not his intention. The translator acknowledged this, although, in an attempt to show off, he explained to him that Caesar, like Mussolini, had assumed "total" power (the dictatorship) in order to "reconstruct the State" "ricostruire lo Stato" (p. xvii); moreover, he provides the example of Garibaldi (who "was for utterly unlimited dictatorships and governed only through dictatorship"; "era per le dittature illimitatissime e non governò se non attraverso la dittatura," p. xxi); then he concludes:

> Se si volesse parlare di *democrazia organizzata*, *centralizzata*, *autoritaria*, che è quella del fascismo italiano secondo la definizione del suo Capo, allora potrebbe qualificarsi democratico anche il fascismo di Cesare [*sic*]. (p. xix)
>
> If we want to talk about "organized, centralized, and authoritarian democracy," which is that of Italian fascism according to the definition of its leader, then Caesar's fascism [*sic*] could be defined as democratic too.

In the same year (1932), the Milanese publishing house Treves-Treccani-Tumminelli (afterwards taken over by Garzanti) put out two biographies: *Caesar* by Friedrich Gundolf, which had appeared in Germany in 1924 (the author died in 1931), in the accurate and faithful translation of Eugenio Giovannetti, and *Stalin* by Essad Bey (pseudonym of the rich Jewish-Georgian Lev Nussimbaum, who converted to Islam). When Essad Bey offered this biography to Mussolini in 1937, he asked the "Duce" for "the honor" of writing his biography. Mussolini, though, let the proposal drop when he learned that, in the meantime, Nussimbaum, because of his Jewish origins, had been banned in Germany (on Essad Bey there is now the excellent study by Tom Reiss, *The Orientalist*, 2005). The biography of Stalin was intended to be very hostile towards the Bolshevik leader – and indeed it was so – but at the same time it ended up exalting his political greatness, presenting him as the omnipotent leader of all Asia, which was ready to launch the "revolution" in Europe. However, when the volume was presented to the Italian public, the Milanese publisher tried to attenuate its Manichean pattern and presented Stalin as the author of an enormous transformation: "the Russia of the Soviets, so overflowing with anonymous strength, so full of collective sacrifice, so resolute in its historic will" ("la Russia dei soviet così traboccante di anonima forza, così ricca di sacrificio collettivo, così decisa nella sua volontà di storia"). Besides, in the same period (1932) the USSR and Italy were making progress towards a transitory détente and starting to negotiate treaties of cooperation and friendship (non-aggression).

On the other hand, the translation of Gundolf's *Caesar* (again published by Treves) resulted in an embarrassing failure. First of all, this is not a biography but a "history of Caesar's reputation," as the subtitle says. Moreover, Gundolf might have been truly appreciated by Giovannetti's restless mind, with its mystical tendencies, but he was not the "right author" for the political climate in Italy. Gundolf, Stefan George's favorite student, was the embodiment of one strain of the German right which was not at all interested in Fascism, and which, in the following years, was in fact completely left aside by Nazism. Certainly, Gundolf liked Mommsen's almost "idolatrous" exaltation of Caesar, but in Gundolf's book the emphasis was not on the Caesar who combines the left and right wings (democratic fascism!) but on the conflict between the East and the West. Gundolf approves of a Caesar rethought through the categories of Bachofen. In order to understand what this means, it is sufficient to read this passage:

> The mission of Rome consists in subjecting the sensually material nature that dominates in Oriental cults to the virile spirit of the West through the foundation of the patriarchal State. What the sensual Greeks claimed, the Romans accomplished: the control of nature through moral action, the ordering of the world in accordance with a manly spirit, the spiritual victory over the East. What began in the Persian Wars, what had succeeded fleetingly in the march of Alexander, was completed by the destruction of Carthage and Jerusalem.
>
> La missione di Roma è la sottomissione della natura sensualmente materiale, che domina nei culti orientali, allo spirito virile dell'Occidente, con la fondazione dello Stato patriarcale. Quello che i sensuali Elleni vantavano compirono i Romani: il controllo della natura attraverso l'azione morale, l'ordinamento spiritualmente virile del mondo, la spirituale vittoria sull'Oriente. Quello que era incominciato nelle guerre greco-persiane, che era riuscito fuggevolmente nella marcia di Alessandro, fu compiuto dalla distruzione di Cartagine e di Gerusalemme. (F. Gundolf, *Caesar in neunzehnten Jahrhundert*, Berlin: Georg Bondi, 1926, p. 79; in the Italian translation by Giovannetti, p. 332).

All this mass of nonsense flew in the face of the facts, starting from the special protection extended to the Jews both by Alexander and, most of all, by Caesar. Indeed, the salvation of the latter during the difficult "Alexandrian war" (48–7 BC) was due to the Jewish troops that came to his support in the battle of the Nile Delta. That is to say nothing of Caesar's decision to restore strength and importance to Egypt, the last Hellenistic monarchy. This "Bachofenian-Gundolfian" occidentalist model, clumsily relaunched by Giovannetti in his translation, might be appropriate, if at all, to Octavian Augustus. And it is towards that sort of model that the regime will direct itself, through an imperceptible but clear shift from Caesar towards Augustus, culminating in the widespread celebrations in 1937.

With the foundation of the "Empire" (May, 1935) and the bimillenary of Augustus, Fascism definitely shifted its symbolical preference to Augustus, the great commander who stabilized "Italy" and avenged it against "the East." Caesar was overshadowed, but he became fashionable again – as the conqueror of Gaul – during the growing dispute with France. Just after the beginning of the war Goffredo Coppola, a leading Fascist intellectual who, later on, would be shot along with Mussolini in Dongo, wrote a challenging but unsatisfactory biography of Caesar for UTET (Turin), in the series *I grandi Italiani* directed by Luigi Federzoni, the president of the "Camera dei Fasci" (the organ instituted by the Fascist regime to replace the "Chamber of Deputies," one of the two houses of the Italian Parliament). Shortly after, however, the tune would completely change, and in September 1943 Fascism would reinvent itself as republican, and the icons of Caesar and Augustus would be replaced by that of Mazzini.

The revaluation of Caesar by the Communists, for instance in the Gramscian distinction between "negative" and "positive" Caesarism, can be explained not only by the desire to save Caesar from appropriation by the Fascists, but above all by a more political reason. For, from the very first moment it appeared on stage in the twentieth century by taking power in Russia (November 7, 1917), the Communist movement, too, combined revolutionary radicalism with the radical dominance of a "leader," i.e. the power of one individual. Even though *a posteriori* (especially after the XXth Congress of the CPSU, February 1956) the "collegial" nature of Lenin's leadership has been often emphasized, in fact his pre-eminence was from the beginning beyond question, accepted even by another leader like Trotsky, who had a strong inclination to assert his own "Bonapartism." In short, the positive regard of the Communists for the phenomenon of "Caesar" derives from both these factors.

While "Bonapartism" is an unpleasant word in the Communist lexicon, even if one simply thinks about the constant aversion to this kind of "rule" expressed in his day by Marx, still Caesar, who was more distant in time and who for a long period was himself leader of the faction of the *populares*, became a more useful model. In a note dating to December 1942, but only published posthumously in August 1965, Palmiro Togliatti – the acknowledged leader of Italian Communism for 35 years and a man of international prestige – writes: "The greatest man of Roman history: Caesar" ("l'uomo più grande della storia di Roma, che fu Cesare"). This judgment seems to follow almost literally that made by Concetto Marchesi, another important member of the central committee of the Italian Communist Party and a Latinist at the University of Padua. In his famous book *Storia della letteratura latina* (Milan: Principato, 1924, 4th edn 1936), the chapter on Caesar begins in this way: "In Rome in 100 BC Julius Caesar was born, the greatest man that the City has ever given to the world" ("In Roma nacque nell'anno 100 a.C. Giulio Cesare, l'uomo più grande che l'urbe abbia dato al mondo", Marchesi 1936: vol. I, p. 314).

However, the judgment expressed by Togliatti in that note from the end of 1942 was not simply an explosion of enthusiasm in the wake of the authoritative book by the most influential intellectual among the Communists during the Fascist years. Togliatti arrived at that judgment while preparing an outline for a study of history, addressed to the Italian and Spanish militants of the Communist party in exile in Moscow; the title was: *Principali falsificazioni nell'insegnamento della storia di Roma nelle scuole fasciste* (Principal falsifications in the teaching of Roman history in the Fascist schools; annotated text in *Quaderni di storia* 3 [1976], pp. 183–95). In that context, the line of reasoning developed by Togliatti limited his praise. The creation of an empire with pretensions to universality – Togliatti observes – such as that to whose foundation Caesar made an outstanding contribution by obliterating the old oligarchic Republic, produced adverse effects. For it promoted the "cosmopolitanism" of the Italian intellectual classes (a defect that continued for centuries, according to Gramsci and Togliatti). At this point, Togliatti makes this judgment: "We could say that Caesar, the greatest man in the history of Rome, was also the one who caused the most serious damage to the Italian people as a nation" ("Si potrebbe dire che l'uomo più grande della storia di Roma, che fu Cesare, fu quello che arrecò maggiori danni agli italiani come nazione"). A strange conclusion, indeed, that may imply even a critical allusion to the choice made by Stalin – by origin a Georgian – to merge the Russian national identity into the more general framework of the USSR. Or perhaps this is just an over-subtle interpretation.

FURTHER READING

On "Caesarism," including its inextricable relationship with "Bonapartism," the studies of I. Cervelli, collected in the two volumes *Rivoluzione e cesarismo nell'Ottocento*, Turin: Aragno, 2003, offer an excellent introduction.

See also T. R. S. Broughton, *The Magistrates of the Roman Republic*, vol. II: anni 81–44 a.C. (Cleveland: American Philological Association, 1952); and vol. III, *Supplement* (Atlanta: Scholars Press, 1986), pp. 105–8.

NOTE

1 On this episode see Cagnetta 1990: 160–74.

CHAPTER THIRTY

A Twenty-First-Century Caesar*

Maria Wyke

On March 27, 2003, only days after the invasion of Iraq (and on the eve of a conference in Rome on the reception of Julius Caesar), the Italian newspaper *Il Messaggero* asked: "Is the President of the United States of America the Caesar of the twenty-first century?"[1] On that same Thursday, the magazine of the Italian newspaper *Corriere della Sera* carried a similar question on its front cover: "But is the American empire like that of Rome?"[2] Within the magazine, in the course of an extensive interview, the classical scholar Luca Canali was asked whether he saw any parallel between George W. Bush and Gaius Julius Caesar, given that they were both the supreme heads of two superpowers. The professor scornfully dismissed such historical analogies: Caesar was the greatest man in history ("il più grande uomo della Storia"), how could he be compared with Bush? Privately, Caesar was extremely cultivated, friend to the greatest intellectuals of his time (whereas, the interviewer concedes, Bush doesn't know his Slovenia from his Slovakia). Publicly, Caesar was a great political leader, who relied upon the justice of his efforts in both peace and war to win the goodwill of all the people. He was an unconquerable general, who had the courage to enter the field of battle, to fight on the front line. He was assassinated only because he preferred not to live guarded day and night. A great man indeed. At this point the interviewer gives up any further attempt at comparing Bush with Caesar, and tries out other Roman analogies for American empire until they are pushed playfully beyond the limits of credibility (Saddam Hussein as Hasdrubal, Osama Bin Laden as Mithridates, Dick Cheney as Agrippa, Donald Rumsfeld as Cato).

Classicists may question the validity of comparing the United States with ancient Rome and its president with Julius Caesar, but Canali's scathing rebuttal forms an

* This chapter was first published as the Afterword in M. Wyke (ed.), *Julius Caesar in Western Culture* (Malden, MA, Oxford, and Carlton, Victoria: Blackwell, 2006). It is reprinted here with a few minor changes.

obstacle to the examination of why, in recent years, such comparisons have been made so often, been taken so seriously, and become so influential in Anglo-American political debate. In the lead up to the invasion of Iraq in March 2003, and continuing on in its aftermath, one common rhetorical strategy which emerged in the popular media to criticize American foreign policy and its perceived aggression was to find multiple parallels between the empire of ancient Rome and modern American imperialism, and between Julius Caesar and this new "imperial presidency."[3] Newspaper articles and editorials, both in the United States and abroad, carried such resonant headlines as "All roads lead to D.C.," "Rome, AD ... Rome, DC?," "The Last Emperor," "Hail Caesar!"[4] The deployment of such historical analogy has by now become entrenched in popular political discourse and continues to emerge in book-length studies of contemporary American imperialism by those critical of it, such as Senator Robert C. Byrd's *Losing America: Confronting a Reckless and Arrogant Presidency* (2004) and Chalmers Johnson's *The Sorrows of Empire: Militarism, Secrecy, and the End of the Republic* (2004). In newspapers and books, on television and radio, and across the Internet, the last few years have witnessed a vigorous debate about the seemingly close correspondences between Roman and American empire: correspondences such as overwhelming military strength, the centrality of technology to power, strategic bases around the world, the vigorous pursuit of a policy of invasion and conquest (both militarily and culturally), the deployment of propaganda to demonstrate and sustain power, the rapid aggrandizement of executive authority, and demagogic leadership.[5]

While classical historians may well flinch at such attempts to make past events speak directly to the present, to make Rome and Caesar the prism through which to perceive contemporary global politics, the Director of the Center for Strategic Studies at Johns Hopkins University, Eliot A. Cohen, argues in pointed contrast that practitioners and pundits have the last word over scholars in this regard. Precisely because politicians and policymakers are frequently finding lessons in history, taking them to heart, and even acting upon them, academics have an *obligation* to examine how history is informing, and how it should inform, current understanding of the United States of America as a hyperpower.[6] In my chapter, therefore, rather than looking backward over the rich reception history of Julius Caesar, I propose to take a look around this new mode of reception which makes such an urgent claim on our attention. I am not here concerned with the workings of the general comparison between Roman and American empire (now almost a cliché of contemporary political discourse) but, in view of our collection's theme, with occasions where the parallel has touched on the exercise of presidential authority, and been pressed to shape the Bush administration as a form of Caesarian government. In both cases (American empire and the Caesarian presidency), I shall be concerned only tangentially with details of the historical accuracy or appropriateness of Roman analogies. My focus, rather, will be on their development and their rhetorical purpose: when, at the start of the new millennium, both politicians and commentators turn to Julius Caesar to talk of domestic and international crisis, *cui bono*?

The Coming Caesars

Claims that the United States of America is becoming an empire and its president a Caesar have long been intertwined. During his period of office in the 1830s, Andrew Jackson in particular was accused of both pursuing territorial expansion and augmenting the power of the president. As Margaret Malamud has elaborated in Wyke 2006 (ch. 9), to Jackson's opponents he was a Caesar, that is to say an arrogant general turned demagogue who was now leading the republic into domestic tyranny and a damaging imperialism.[7] But it was in the twentieth century and, specifically, after World War II – when it was recognized that the United States was becoming the heir to Europe's old colonial empires[8] – that this dual Roman analogy (of empire and, therefore, of emperor) was first deployed at length and in depth in order to envisage an apocalyptic future for the western world.

In 1957, the French critic Amaury de Riencourt published a book which received considerable attention in the United States because in it he maintained that Europe now stood in the same relation to America as Greece had once stood to Rome. Just as Roman civilization had been fated to overcome Greek culture and master the world, so American civilization was now destined to take over European culture and dominate the world of tomorrow. For de Riencourt, this was clearly an organic, biocyclical process which could only degenerate into a universal state under the sway of a Caesarian ruler. Hence he entitled his grim political prophecy *The Coming Caesars*. Among the vast array of elaborate classical parallels and similarities amassed in the book (lent some credibility in part because many had already been put to use by American politicians and their critics right from the time when the Founding Fathers were debating the relative merits of federalism), two in particular were decisive for the author: the adoption by both Rome and America of the course of democratic growth *and* imperial expansion. For both the consequence was (or now would be) loss of liberty, centralization, and the arrival of Caesarism: "Our Western world, America and Europe, is threatened with Caesarism on a scale unknown since the dawn of the Roman empire."[9]

After depicting Franklin D. Roosevelt as the first real "pre-Caesarist" president, that is, as the one who, during the era of the New Deal and in the later crisis of world war, most nearly established dictatorial rule, de Riencourt concluded:

> [T]he President of the United States is the most powerful single human being in the world today. Future crises will inevitably transform him into a full-fledged Caesar, if we do not beware. Today he wears ten hats – as Head of State, Chief Executive, Minister of Foreign Affairs, Chief Legislator, Head of Party, Tribune of the People, Ultimate Arbitrator of Social Justice, Guardian of Economic Prosperity, and World Leader of Western Civilization. Slowly and unobtrusively these hats are becoming crowns and this pyramid of hats is slowly metamorphosing itself into a tiara, the tiara of one man's world imperium. (330–1)

In this context, ancient Rome and Caesar are not trusty guides to follow but warning beacons that shed light on the bleak destiny of the world. Or, a little more optimistically, the step back into Roman history which de Riencourt takes is presented by him as an opportunity to wake up and see properly the road we have all been traveling along like somnambulists (6), and to adjust our path as best we can and before it is too late (356).

At the time, de Riencourt's thesis became the subject of considerable debate. Political conservatives rejected his Roman analogies as robustly as they denied his bold predictions for America's future place in the world. In the *National Review*, the libertarian conservative Frank Meyer objected firstly that the author's argument constituted a sinister European imposition on the United States, designed to depict the latter speciously as the dull and soulless Roman master of a Europe painted as a once sparkling Greece. Secondly, Meyer noted, it depended on an outmoded philosophy of history as cyclical, borrowed from Oswald Spengler's sensational, but long since discredited, two-volume study *The Decline of the West* (1926–8). Finally, it ignored an essential characteristic of American political life, namely, its Christian vision of the innate value of the person and of his freedom under God. Confident of Christian America's difference from pagan Rome, Meyer boldly concluded that Americans would indeed determine the fate of the West, but on their own terms: any future American era of western culture will be "not Caesarist, but free."[10] More recent (and more mundane) objections to *The Coming Caesars* have included de Riencourt's inability to count hats, as well as the extraordinary historical contortions, contradictions, and contentions practiced by the author in order to turn America into the new Rome and Caesarism into its destiny.[11]

In order to sustain a close and complex match over some 350 pages of text between the histories of Europe and ancient Greece, and between those of the United States and ancient Rome, de Riencourt is clearly constrained to twist and distort all four.[12] And the achieved match is reinforced by the constant traffic of historical terminology across the centuries and the sea: the New Deal starts with the Gracchi in Rome, Roosevelt is the first real tribune of the people, Julius Caesar establishes a permanent bureaucracy after the downfall of Roman Big Business and relies on Clodius against Milo's Tammany Hall. The whole argument is embedded in a contradictory philosophy of history which is simultaneously cyclical (civilizations overwhelm cultures and then ossify and degenerate into lethal tyrannies until the cycle begins again) and apocalyptic (expanding democracy leads to imperialism which in turn destroys republican institutions and concentrates absolute power in a single man, leading to nuclear holocaust and the end of history). Few critics since have been prepared to argue for such thoroughgoing historical coincidence, or to return to a biocyclical understanding of history (as rise and fall, ebb and flow, growth and decay). But at moments of political extremity or crisis, there has again been a turn to de Riencourt's highly original and flamboyantly dramatic use of ancient Rome and Julius Caesar – namely, to paint a monitory vision of the future of the presidency, of America, and of the world.[13]

Less than ten years later, for example, the front page of the issue of *National Review* for May 3, 1966 carried the legend: "Imperial America: A look into the future." Inside the journal, the philosopher Thomas Molnar, while acknowledging national resistance to the idea, accepted with little hesitation or need for sustained analysis that by now the United States had become an imperial power like Rome. Clearly, American diplomacy and its armed forces have become at least in part reluctant heirs to European conquests, garrisoning GIs from Saigon to Léopoldville in order not to colonize but to "protect" and provision with a *Pax Americana*, currently guarding oceans and sea-routes, air-routes, and space orbits from "a great Asian power." Molnar exploits the dual Roman analogy not to ponder America's growth to empire but to pick apart what he perceives to be the tremendous and troubling domestic consequences of such growth. Empire *needs* a single power center, imperial responsibility brings with it increased centralization. If the United States has grown like Rome from small agrarian republic to empire, then will the parallel hold and its Chief Executive also become an Imperial Caesar?[14]

Here Molnar catalogues what he perceives to be the extraordinary degree of community already perceptible between modern American presidents and Caesar (or, variously, the Caesars). They empty traditional institutions of their power (the Roman Senate, the American Congress). They are charismatic figures who promise but only partly deliver to the demands of the newly important masses. For their double role as chief administrator and commander-in-chief of the armed forces, they are compensated by considerable privileges (a crown for Julius, four mandates for Roosevelt). They curb the legislative arm of government, contain popular discontent (free grain distributions, anti-poverty funds), and acquire a large staff who duplicate all forms of government and whose political existence is tied to their leader alone. Molnar's conclusion demonstrates the predictive and apocalyptic functions the Roman equivalence is once again made to serve: "The end of the story? Caesar reaches for absolute power, and absolute power corrupts Caesar first, the public and its morality next. Priests or television screens divinize his Image. Eager, famished enemies appear at the gates."[15]

The author completes his analysis by reassuring his presumably somewhat alarmed readers that these thoughts on a Caesarian presidency are merely an intellectual exercise and that none of his predictions might come true. However, although he makes no direct reference to the current president of the United States (Lyndon B. Johnson), the date his article was published is not without significance. Only a year earlier Johnson had authorized open-ended military intervention in Vietnam at the same time as he undertook sweeping policy innovations at home.[16] Criticism of the secrecy with which the president came to his decisions was portrayed in a political cartoon linked to an editorial that appeared in the *Washington Post* on June 10, 1966, only a month after the publication of Molnar's Roman speculations. On the left, a bespectacled, short senator dressed in Roman tunic and boots holds a cigar in one hand and raises up a scroll in the other on which is written: "Dirksen accuses administration of lack of candor on Vietnam." On the right, a tall President Johnson dressed in toga and Roman sandals, and wearing a laurel wreath, finds himself backed against a pillar. The caption over the president's head reads: "EV [*sic*] TU?," identifying the confrontation as one between an American Brutus and his bemused Caesar.[17]

Throughout the 1960s and on into the mid-1970s and beyond, the Vietnamese conflict brought to prominence on the political left a critique of American imperialism and its association with an imperial presidency.[18] But as discussion moved from speculation and prediction to confirmation and description, the original need for the critique to be dressed in dramatic Roman tropes appears to fade, the necessity of examining the distinctiveness and the specifics of the United States' commitments overseas and the massive growth in presidential powers at home becomes more apparent. Even de Riencourt in his next book, *The American Empire* (1968), fails to sustain his previous use of ancient Rome and Caesar as historical analogy beyond some small mention in his introductory pages, at the same time as he asserts that his earlier predictions have all come true. While *The Imperial Presidency* (1973), Arthur Schlesinger's study of the gradual appropriation by the presidency of powers originally reserved by the Constitution to Congress, in particular the vital decision to go to war, manages without mention of ancient empire and the Roman dictator.[19] Widespread acknowledgment of military interventionism abroad and executive predominance at home now required much less in the way of historical analogy or even historical metaphor for their exploration. Until the end of the 1980s, apocalyptic anxieties about American expansion were assuaged for some by the assumption that US military growth and the creation of a colossal bureaucratic machinery at home were necessary, but merely temporary, departures from the nation's republican origins, part of a Cold War strategy of containment rather than conquest, and held in check by the opposition of the eastern empire of the USSR.[20] In the early years of the twenty-first century, however, Roman historical analogies have re-emerged and in the most unexpected quarters.

In Praise of Imperialism

The fall of the Berlin Wall in 1989 constituted a turning point for the United States with regard to its stature in the world. From that date, if not before, an influential neoconservative foreign policy group started to develop a coherent grand strategy for the United States now that it was understood to have emerged as the world's only superpower. Planning for a full-scale transformation of the international order included the publication of a manifesto and the establishment of a website in 1997, Project for the New American Century (PNAC: www.newamericancentury.org), through which it began to advocate aggressive intervention abroad, expressed as a doctrine of military might conjoined with moral leadership. Signatories included individuals who were to become key members of George W. Bush's administration, such as Paul Wolfowitz, Dick Cheney, and Donald Rumsfeld.[21] At first New Right circles were careful to dismiss the idea that such a doctrine constituted a call to empire (and thus an invitation to critical comparisons with a Roman past associated with domestic tyranny, imperial overstretch, and ultimate collapse that use of the term "empire" might justify). Empire was construed as an outmoded ideological accusation routinely wielded during the twentieth century by the left. Even a few years later, Donald Kagan, Professor of Classics and History at Yale University and co-chairman of a report produced for the PNAC in 2000 on "Rebuilding America's

Defenses," published an article in the *Atlantic Journal and Constitution* (which was then posted up on the PNAC website), in which he declared that:

> All comparisons between America's current place in the world and anything legitimately called an empire in the past reveal ignorance and confusion about any reasonable meaning of the concept empire, especially the comparison with the Roman empire ... The Romans acquired the greatest part of their empire by direct military conquest, subjected their people to Roman law, and imposed taxes and compulsory military service under Roman command. They deprived their subjects of freedom and autonomy ... To compare the United States with any such empire is ludicrous.[22]

Despite Kagan's comments, such reluctance to make comparison largely evaporated after September 11, 2001 and the terrorist attacks on the World Trade Center and the Pentagon. That day and its outcomes spurred more hawkish neoconservative intellectuals, political figures, and commentators to appropriate, even to revel in, both the concept of empire and historical comparison with ancient Rome. Now enthusiastic assertions about the second coming of the Roman Empire began to litter the prestigious print media, as well as being repeated and widely diffused in foreign policy journals, bulletins of think tanks, conferences, monographs, and across the Internet. For example, a comment to the *New York Times* in 2002 by the conservative columnist for the *Washington Post* Charles Krauthammer continues to this day to be endlessly recycled and analyzed both in print and on the web: "People are now coming out of the closet on the word 'empire.' ... The fact is no country has been as dominant culturally, economically, technologically and militarily in the history of the world since the Roman Empire."[23] In order, however, to secure for the United States the grandeur and the glory of Roman Empire, rather than its loss of liberties, its cruelties, and its fall, there are evident rules attached to this feverish embrace of ancient Rome in establishment discourse: such views are not to be expressed in the most official contexts (that is, those closest to the president), and careful attempts must always be made to disassociate the acceptance of empire from distasteful suggestions of economic dominance, racism, or tyranny, and to picture this imperium instead as a uniquely beneficial, civilizing mission.[24] As Michael Ignatieff, Professor of Human Rights Policy at Harvard University, noted: "the 21st century imperium is an invention in the annals of political science, an empire lite, a global hegemony whose grace notes are free markets, human rights and democracy, enforced by the most awesome military power the world has ever known."[25]

But it was a rare commentator who would be so bold as to take up the *dual* historical parallel with Rome and claim a positive similarity between George W. Bush and Julius Caesar. Such a rhetorical strategy was especially dangerous and required careful expression, however tentatively undertaken or momentarily mentioned, for in the political history of the United States of America Caesar had commenced his career as the quintessential enemy, symbolic of British tyranny against which a whole nation of American Brutuses had so bravely fought in the War of Independence.[26] Nonetheless, five months after the September 11 attacks, on February 2, 2002 (just after the president had delivered the State of the Union speech to Congress in which he notoriously attacked North Korea, Iraq, and Iran as an "axis of evil"), another columnist for the *Washington Post* observed that:

> George W. Bush delivered such a stunning State of the Union speech, during which he dazzled Congress with a mix of Julius Caesar and Billy Graham, that it left the opposition virtually speechless. Who is going to argue with the scourge of evil, the conqueror of Afghanistan? ... Richard Gephardt, House Democratic leader, was reduced, in his reply to the president, to complaining that Bush did not mention campaign reform. Can you imagine that Caesar, addressing the Senate, would be faced with the effrontery of a query about the state of Rome's sewers?[27]

In her brief reference to Caesar, the journalist Mary McGrory appears to bestow on Bush by association the character of an eloquent orator, a high-minded statesman above trivial questions of domestic reform, a popular and resolute decision-maker, and, most importantly of all in the heated context of the War on Terrorism and the invasion of Afghanistan, a triumphant war-time commander-in-chief and conqueror. Any possible hint of dictatorship or cruelty is seemingly offset by the additional association of Bush with Christian fundamentalism. Only later in the article does it emerge more clearly that historical analogy may here have an ironic purpose, that McGrory is twisting the Roman metaphor back against those now deploying it so pretentiously, perhaps even perniciously, as a cloak to cover domestic (and foreign) wrong-doings. For she goes on to argue that the gravity and high-mindedness of the president's oratory conveniently worked to render any questions about the Enron scandal vulgar. A commander-in-chief has no need to make mention of such matters: "when you are briefing the country on survival and revival, you have no time for such trifles."[28]

Twenty-First-Century Caesar

The New Right's appropriation soon after September 11, 2001 of the tropes of historical destiny, of glorious and beneficent empire resurgent, could be countered either by exposing it as a hollow sham (a matter of no substance, merely of rhetoric),[29] or by a return to the earlier twentieth-century critiques of American empire as leading to Caesarism and to apocalypse. Such critiques begin to gather momentum after the president's address to the United Nations on September 12, 2002 (the day after the first anniversary of 9/11), when George W. Bush declared that if the UN was not going to act against Iraq, the United States would do so alone.[30] A spate of articles, in both the British and the American press, subsequently compared the US president negatively with Julius Caesar, or with the Roman emperors more generally.

The day after the address, Robert Fisk, the Middle East correspondent for the British newspaper the *Independent*, observed that seated in the UN General Assembly, surrounded by green marble fittings and a backcloth of burnished gold, the president was able to enjoy the furnishings of an emperor, "albeit a diminutive one."

Indicating how Bush was selling his war against Iraq on the basis that such a regime supported terrorist attacks, the correspondent ended his piece dramatically: "What was the name of that river which Julius Caesar crossed? Was it not called the Rubicon? Yesterday, Mr Bush may have crossed the very same river."[31] The same day, another British newspaper, the *Guardian*, carried a lead comment by its columnist Polly Toynbee, in which she described Bush as "this unlikely emperor of the world," telling the UN in effect to pass a resolution on war or be bypassed. "What the US wants, the UN had better solemnise with a suitable resolution – very like the Roman senate and one of its lesser god-emperors."[32] The accompanying political cartoon by Jas showed a wreathed and togate emperor incongruously waving a small Stars and Stripes in his hand as he stands in an advancing armored personnel carrier. Similarly, a photomontage of Bush as a wreathed and breastplated Roman emperor, gesturing thumbs down for death (figure 30.1), appeared a few days later on the cover of the tabloid insert of the same newspaper above the legend: "Hail, Bush. Is America the new Rome?" Although the enclosed article by Jonathan Freedland (which it was designed to illustrate) was concerned with the historical analogy of empire rather than emperor, the image strongly suggests a critique of the presidency as an imperial, ruthless, and arbitrary mode of leadership.

Figure 30.1 "Hail, Bush." Cover of G2, *Guardian* (September 18, 2002). Photomontage by Steve Caplin. Reproduced by permission.

Toward the end of 2002, across the Atlantic, a similarly Caesarian condemnation of George W. Bush appeared in *Harper's Magazine* under the title: "Hail Caesar!" Referring back to the decision on October 11 by Congress to invest the president with the power to order an invasion of Iraq whenever it occurred to him to do so, the writer Lewis H. Lapham described it as "[a]kin to the ancient Roman practice of enthroning a dictator at moments of severe crisis." He continued, sardonically, both Senate and House of Representatives were much relieved to have escaped the chore of republican self-government and pass it over to Caesar's sword. Despite the absence of slaughtered goats, the subtext of their vote could still be understood as a submissive prayer to their great general:

> Our President is a Great General; he will blast Saddam Hussein and rescue us from doom. To achieve this extraordinary mission he needs extraordinary powers, so extraordinary that they don't exist in law ... Great is Caesar; God must be with him.[33]

Here, as in the British examples above, Caesar appears as a natural consequence of and counter to the neoconservative embrace of empire.[34] Comparison of Bush and Caesar works to create a striking and sensational narrative of the abrogation of power by traditional republican institutions, the usurpation of their authority by an untrustworthy leader, a turn in time of crisis to dictatorship, the illegitimate declaration of war, the march blindly across forbidden borders into an invasion which will bring with it historic, potentially disastrous, consequences.[35] And as the moment of invasion drew nearer, early in 2003, even libertarian advocates of empire such as Michael Ignatieff touched nervously again upon the apocalyptic visions of a Thomas Cole or an Amaury de Riencourt:

> The impending operation in Iraq is thus a defining moment in America's long debate with itself about whether its overseas role as an empire threatens or strengthens its existence as a republic. The American electorate, while still supporting the president, wonders whether his proclamation of a war without end against terrorists and tyrants may only increase its vulnerability while endangering its liberties and its economic health at home .... To call America the new Rome is at once to recall Rome's glory and its eventual fate at the hands of the barbarians.[36]

Across the Rubicon

Throughout this chapter, I have explored some of the causes and the purposes of what has been called the "analogico-historical method"[37] for interpreting American foreign policy and its recent transformations, a method which appeared in political debate in print and then online through the course of the twentieth century and which has taken on an extraordinary vigor in the early years of the twenty-first. Whereas the analogy with Roman Empire has come to belong both to the right as well as the left of the political spectrum (a boast as well as a condemnation), the twinned analogy with Julius Caesar has been deployed almost exclusively in critical key. This is not only as a result of what Caesar was (insofar as it can be discovered from his own writings and other ancient sources),[38] but also of what he has become in the political discourses of Europe and the United States.[39]

As foil for western traditions of republicanism, Julius Caesar has come to symbolize the moment of greatest danger to the Roman Republic. He was its ruin. His self-interested ambition led him to usurp senatorial authority by arms. His designs on monarchy led to the establishment of the rule of emperors. The expansion of empire and the centralization of power led ultimately to Rome's fall. Caesar has been index and embodiment of a devastating turning point in history.[40] Caesarian analogy thus generates, legitimates, and renders more plausible an especially vivid representation of American politics. It paints a portrait of its foreign policy in the bright reds of a bloody imperialism, its president in the deep purples of a ruthless tyranny. It constructs this moment in the early years of the twenty-first century as equal in historical significance to that when the Roman Republic collapsed. It ennobles those politicians and pundits who utilize it with the *gravitas* of a brave American Cicero or Cato, and links them back to their own nation's Founding Fathers (who had used the analogy before them) as new guardians of that republican legacy.[41]

Curiously, however, although the analogy with Roman Empire has been strongly predictive and bleakly apocalyptic on many occasions in its use, the Caesarian analogy has rarely been pressed for the particulars of Caesar's bloody end. Rarely, that is, until the months and years after the invasion of Iraq, until, that is, debate shifted toward the uncertain issue of a post-invasion settlement. First hints can be discerned in an article by Brad Warthen which was released on March 31, 2003 (only twelve days after the invasion) by *Knight Ridder/Tribune News Information Services*, a leading information provider to American print, television, and electronic media. He begins:

> George W. Bush has crossed his Rubicon, and he has taken us with him. Julius Caesar set world history on a new course when he took his legion into Italy in defiance of the Senate. President Bush has taken an equally irrevocable step by entering the Tigris and Euphrates basin to wage war in spite of UN objections.[42]

While the author goes on to claim that he welcomes this development – with great power comes the responsibility to act and only Bush is single-minded enough to pull it off – he acknowledges that this, perhaps even more than previous turning points in history, creates problems, not just opportunities: "This Rubicon is wider than the one Caesar crossed." Current problems are likely to last, but Bush could not. More explicitly, and aggressively, Denise Giardina argued in an editorial which featured in the *Charleston Gazette* on May 12, 2003 that Bush had "assumed the mantle of Julius Caesar. He is in the process of ruining the American republic and establishing an American/corporate empire." The president should be impeached and stand in the dock to be tried for war crimes.[43]

Perhaps only within the relative safety – the pastness, the theatricality, the tradition, the cultural authority – of performances of Shakespeare's *Julius Caesar* has it been possible to touch upon Caesar's assassination as a lesson about contemporary events, for fear of appearing literally to advocate the president's assassination.[44] In recent years, two notable modern-dress productions of the play were staged, coinciding roughly with the Ides of March and with the second anniversary of the invasion, in which an American flavor was injected into Roman (and, of course, Renaissance) politics rather than the other way around. One was directed by Deborah Warner at the Barbican Theatre in London. Audiences could observe that the *mise-en-scène* of the play's battle scenes closely mimicked on stage one of the photographs of the Iraq war that had been inserted in their programs in between details of the production. In the program, coordinated by the presence of the color purple on facing pages, a photograph of a smiling Bush in the combat uniform of the US airforce was also placed side by side with a quotation from Act 2.1 of the play: "Between the acting of a dreadful thing/And the first motion, all the interim is/Like a phantasma or a hideous dream." A few pages along, coordinated now in yellow, the photograph of a soldier at the ready in Iraq was placed facing a quotation from 4.3: "You have done that you should be sorry for." While in press interviews the director suggested in passing a possible connection between the excessive authority of Caesar and that of Bush, these other analogical strategies would seem instead to be indicating a lesson for Bush in Brutus, namely, the danger of failing to consider carefully and be well prepared for the aftermath of assassination, the dreadful consequences of tyrannicide.[45] The other production, directed by Daniel Sullivan at the Belasco Theatre, New York, achieved considerable press coverage for its casting of the Hollywood film star Denzel Washington as Brutus. Again the *mise-en-scène* was suggestive of modern-day battle, with explosive sound effects of gunfire and overhead helicopters, costumes of business suits and camouflage fatigues, props of assault rifles and photo ID security badges. The assassination, however, was located in a boardroom, and off stage. On at least one occasion, the star of the production attempted explicitly to fix a much more provocative analogy for the play's potential audiences. According to the *New York Times* for April 3, 2005, in interview Washington pulled out a photograph of the president surrounded by his inner circle and asked who would lead the rebellion "if he decided he wanted to make himself King, like Julius Caesar." Asked by the interviewer who would be Brutus, he replied: "the obvious one is Colin Powell."[46]

While the analogical strategies employed for these modern stagings of Shakespeare could well be regarded as merely superficial devices for the generation of publicity and good box office, they are nonetheless indicative of the continuing attraction of Caesar as a mechanism for reflecting upon American politics and its global repercussions in the twenty-first century. Toward the end of the twentieth century, in his study of the traditions of republicanism and Caesarism, Peter Baehr argued that Julius Caesar and the Roman world were now disappearing from political discourse, and fading from the social memory of the West.[47] Although his concern was largely with sustained discussion of Caesar in political theory, and mine has been with passing reference in popular political debate, I hope that this chapter has begun to demonstrate that in the early years of the twenty-first century Caesar has by no means vanished from the imagination of western culture.

FURTHER READING

In the edited collection M. Wyke, *Julius Caesar in Western Culture* (2006), you can find a number of chapters on modern receptions of Julius Caesar in Italian cinema and American schools (Wyke), British theatre and its restagings (Slater), Italian fascist theatre (Dunnett), French popular novels, children's histories and films (Pucci) and French political debate (Hemmerle). Wyke, *Caesar: A Life in Western Culture* (2007) includes brief discussions of modern detective fiction and historical novels, theatre, cartoons, television series, films, computer games, advertising, and the role of Caesar in modern politics. G. Woolf, *Et Tu, Brute? The Murder of Caesar and Political Assassination* (2006) touches engagingly on modern politics in its exploration of the impact of Caesar's assassination through the ages. In French, the old – but still useful – collection edited by R. Chevallier, *Présence de César* (1985) contains articles on Caesars Palace, Asterix, and other modern receptions. In German, there is K. Christ, *Caesar: Annäherungen an einen Diktator* (1994), which includes discussion of modern literature and scholarship. On contemporary American political discourse, the imperial presidency and "American empire," web searches can reveal the most up-to-date analogies being made in the electronic and print media between Julius Caesar and George Bush, American foreign policy and Roman imperialism. Recent book-length explorations of these analogies include C. Murphy, *Are We Rome? The Fall of an Empire and the Fate of America* (2007) and C. Johnson, *Nemesis: The Last Days of the American Republic* (2006).

NOTES

1 Roberto Livi, "Il presidente Usa sarà il Cesare del XXI secolo?" *Il Messaggero* (March 27, 2003), 9.
2 Edoardo Vigna, "Ma l'impero Americano è come quello Romano?" *Sette* (*Corriere della Sera*), n. 13 (2003), 33–43. I am most grateful to a participant at the conference, Jan Nelis, for drawing the magazine to my attention.
3 The term was originally coined by Arthur Schlesinger (1973), and applied to a presidency which, in his view, had gradually usurped some of the most crucial powers originally allocated by the Constitution to Congress.
4 These articles and others like them are discussed further below. Most were found through a ProQuest Newspaper database search for the combination of names "Caesar" and "Bush" undertaken at the Library of Congress in March 2004 that revealed a clustering of such critical comment during the course of 2002–3. Articles on America as a modern Roman Empire are now legion and some of the most important have been conveniently collated under the heading "Militarized Globalism and Empire – Advocates, Skeptics, and Critics" at www.comw.org/qdr/empire.html, a webpage sponsored by the Project on Defense Alternatives.
5 For the purposes of this chapter, I am restricting my analysis to newspaper and related electronic material.
6 Cohen 2004. Downloaded from www.foreignaffairs.org on March 14, 2005.
7 See also E. Miles 1968 and Miller 1990.
8 For this postwar recognition of an emerging American empire, see Liska 1978, Miller 1981: 123–41. Cf. C. Johnson 2004: 193.

9 Riencourt (1957), 5. Hereafter citations are given parenthetically in the text.
10 F. S. Meyer 1957, on which see Stromberg 2001. Cf. the critical review by Weaver 1957.
11 Miller (1981: 123–41) notes the problem about the number of hats but is otherwise fairly well disposed toward de Riencourt's thesis, believing the Caesars to have finally arrived in Washington. Baehr 1998: 257–65 provides further comment on and criticism of de Riencourt's use of Spengler.
12 With respect to the analogical strategies adopted by critics of Andrew Jackson, Miles 1968: 362 noted that Americans are inclined to attribute the loss of Roman liberty to causes they consider menacing to their own. Similar observations could be made about de Riencourt's contemporary take on Roman history.
13 As Baehr 1998: 264.
14 See, on Molnar, Stromberg 2001.
15 Molnar 1966: 411.
16 See, for example, Grantham 1998: 253–305; Greenstein 2001: 75–89; Chafe 2003: 266–93.
17 The political cartoon can be accessed from the Prints and Photographs Online Catalog of the Library of Congress, Washington, DC. Its identifying reproduction number is LC-USZ62-127072.
18 Foster 2002.
19 Compare also Liska: 1978, for whom the Roman is just one past empire which might illuminate that of modern America and one whose differences, as well as similarities, must be acknowledged.
20 See, for example, Stromberg 2001; Bacevich 2002, esp. vii–ix; Foster 2002.
21 On the significance of the fall of the Berlin Wall, see Bacevich 2002, esp. vii–ix; Ferguson 2004: 27; C. Johnson 2004: 18–21. On the development of the Project for the New American Century (PNAC), see e.g., Keller and Mills 2003; Johnson 2004: 227–30.
22 Kagan 2002. On neoconservative reluctance to use the term "empire," see Freedland 2002; Ferguson 2004: 4; Johnson 2004: 3. More favored terms include "hegemony," "liberal imperialism," "humanitarian intervention."
23 The comment is quoted in Eakin 2002, for example, and reappears in other articles and books and on numerous websites.
24 On the neocon embrace of America as genuine empire and a new Rome after September 11, 2001, see Eakin 2002; Foster 2002; Freedland 2002; Ignatieff 2003: 22; Keller and Mills 2003; Prestowitz 2003; N. Smith 2003: 252; Johnson 2004: 3–4, 67–95, 283–4; Ferguson 2004: 4–5.
25 Ignatieff 2003: 24. Cf. N. Smith 2003.
26 On the reception of Julius Caesar in the United States, see Wyke 1999b: 175–9 and 2004; Malamud (in Wyke 2006). E. A. Miles 1968: 373–4 notes that some supporters of Andrew Jackson attempted to describe him favorably as Caesarian, but more often rejected the comparison as too dangerous.
27 McGrory 2002.
28 My thanks to Tim Whitmarsh and his colleagues at the University of Exeter for first drawing my attention to the potential ironies in McGrory's Caesarian comparison.
29 See, for example, the Doonesbury cartoon strip by Garry Trudeau. Around the time of the invasion of Iraq, the cowboy hat which had been used to represent the president and to depict him as totally without substance was replaced by a Roman helmet. Those aspiring to a role as managers of the post-invasion peace were represented as ostentatiously attempting to take on some of the accouterments of Roman imperialism (the title

proconsul, the toga, the fasces, the Latin language) while failing totally to understand any consequent responsibilities. For this technique compare, for example, Martinez 2004.

30 On the significance of this moment, see Johnson 2004: 73, 90; Byrd 2004, 159–61.

31 Fisk 2002. The article clearly impressed Johnson, who begins a chapter of his book on *The Sorrows of Empire* (2004) quoting from it and then closes the chapter by employing for himself the same metaphor of crossing a Rubicon (15 and 37, respectively).

32 P. Toynbee 2002.

33 Lapham 2002: 9.

34 Holland 2003 notes how difficult it is for Bush's opponents to resist the image of him as a Roman emperor dressed in toga and laurel wreath.

35 For such criticisms of Bush, see for example the account by Senator Byrd (2004) of the president's persistent assault on the separation of powers after 9/11, and the acquiescence of Congress in handing over to him even their constitutional power to declare war. See also Johnson 2004, esp. 256, 284, 291–8.

36 Ignatieff 2003: 24, 25.

37 As Liska 1978: ix.

38 See, for example, the first four chapters in Wyke 2006.

39 In Wyke 2006, for example, see chapters 5 through 16.

40 On Caesar and the traditions of republicanism, see, for example, Miller 1990: 71–2; Baehr 1998, esp. 4–5; Johnson 2004: 15.

41 Compare Miles 1968 and Miller 1990 on the moral sheen cast on Andrew Jackson's opponents by their use of Roman analogy. In a review of Robert C. Byrd's recent condemnation of the president, quoted on the back cover of the book, Arthur Schlesinger says that the senator "speaks with the voice of a Founding Father defending the traditional ideals of the old republic against the ideological radicals who have seized Washington, today an occupied city."

42 Warthen 2003.

43 Giardina 2003.

44 Compare Miles 1968: 370–1, who argues that opponents of Andrew Jackson found scant consolation in reflecting on Caesar's bloody death for what that might imply, especially after an attempt was made on the president's life in 1835.

45 See, for example, the review in the *Observer* for April 10, 2005. Since the invasion of Iraq, there has been much discussion of a failure on the part of the Bush administration properly to plan a postwar settlement; see e.g., Ferguson 2004.

46 For details of the New York production, see the website www.caesaronbroadway.com and reviews such as those in the *New York Times* (April 4, 2005), the *Hollywood Reporter* (April 2, 2005), *Newsweek* (April 18, 2005), and *United Press International* (May 8, 2005).

47 Baehr 1998: 16–20, 285.

Bibliography

Adams, John. 1797. *A Defence of the Constitutions of Government of the United States of America*, vol. 1. Philadelphia: Printed by Budd and Bartram.

Adams, John. 2000a. "A dissertation on the canon and feudal law," in C. Bradley Thompson (ed.), *The Revolutionary Writings of John Adams.* Indianapolis: Liberty Fund, pp. 19–36.

Adams, John. 2000b. "Thoughts on government," in C. Bradley Thompson (ed.), *The Revolutionary Writings of John Adams.* Indianapolis: Liberty Fund, pp. 285–93.

Adams, W. P. 2001. *The First American Constitutions: Republican Ideology and the Making of the State Constitutions in the Revolutionary Era.* Lanham, MD: Rowman & Littlefield.

Adcock, F. E. 1956. *Caesar as Man of Letters.* Cambridge: Cambridge University Press.

Ahl, F. M. 1976. *Lucan: An Introduction.* Ithaca, NY/London: Cornell University Press.

Aigner Foresti, L. 2000. "Gli Etruschi e la politica di Cesare," in Gianpaolo Urso (ed.), *L'ultimo Cesare. Scritti, riforme, progetti, poteri, congiure.* Rome: "L'Erma" di Bretschneider, pp. 11–33.

Aili, H. 1995. "Caesar's elks and other mythical creatures of the Hercynian forest," in Monika Asztalos and Claes Gejrot (eds.), *Symbolae Septentrionales. Latin Studies Presented to Jan Öberg.* Stockholm: Stockholm University Press, pp. 15–37.

Aldridge, A. O. 1968. "Thomas Paine and the Classics," *Eighteenth Century Studies* 1.4, 370–80.

Alexander, M. C. 1990. *Trials in the Late Roman Republic, 149 BC to 50 BC.* Toronto: University of Toronto Press.

Alföldi, A. 1959. "Das wahre Gesicht Caesars," *Antike Kunst* 2, 27–31 Taf. 16.

Alföldi, A. 1974. *Caesar in 44 v.Chr.*, vol. 2. Bonn: R. Habelt.

Alföldi, A. 1975. "Review of Stefan Weinstock, *Divus Julius*," *Gnomon* 47, 154–79.

Allen, J. W. 1928. *A History of Political Thought in the Sixteenth Century.* London: Methuen.

Altman, J. B. 1978. *The Tudor Play of Mind: Rhetorical Inquiry and the Development of Elizabethan Drama.* Berkeley/Los Angeles: University of California Press.

Anderson, R. D., P. J. Parsons, and R. G. M. Nisbet. 1979. "Elegiacs of Gallus from Qasr Ibrîm," *JRS* 69, 125–55.

Andrieu, J. 1949. "La Division en livres et les mentions d'auteur dans le Corpus Césarien," *REL* 27, 138–49.

Angelicoussis, E. 1992. *The Woburn Abbey Collection of Classical Antiquities*, Monumenta Artis Romanae 20. Mainz am Rhein: P. von Zabern.

Annolied. 1996. Ed., trans., and comm. Eberhard Nellmann, 4th rev. edn. Stuttgart: Reclam.

Asch, R. G. 1997. *The Thirty Years War: the Holy Roman Empire and Europe, 1618–1648*. Basingstoke: Macmillan.

Austin, N. J. E. and N. B. Rankov. 1995. Exploratio. *Military and Political Intelligence in the Roman World from the Second Punic War to the Battle of Adrianople*. London/New York: Routledge.

Austin, R. G. 1971. *P. Vergili Maronis Aeneidos Liber Primus*. Oxford: Oxford University Press.

Ayres, H. M. 1910. "Shakespeare's *Julius Caesar* in the light of some other versions," *Publications of the Modern Language Association of America* n.s. 18.2, 183–227.

Ayres, P. 1997. *Classical Culture and the Idea of Rome in Eighteenth-Century England*. Cambridge: Cambridge University Press.

Bacevich, A. J. 2002. *American Empire: the Realities and Consequences of U.S. Diplomacy*. Cambridge, MA: Harvard University Press.

Badian, E. 1957. "Caepio and Norbanus," *Historia* 6, 318–46.

Badian, E. 1968. *Roman Imperialism in the Late Republic*, 2nd edn. Ithaca, NY: Cornell University Press.

Badian, E. 1969. "Two Roman non-entities," *Classical Quarterly* 19, 198–204.

Badian, E. 1990a. "The consuls, 179–49 BC," *Chiron* 20, 409–41.

Badian, E. 1990b. "Review of Ch. Meier, *Caesar* (1982)," *Gnomon* 62, 22–39.

Badian, E. 1993. "Livy and Augustus," in W. Schuller (ed.), *Livius. Aspekte seines Werkes*. Xenia 31. Konstanz: Universitätsverlag Konstanz, pp. 9–38.

Baehr, P. 1998. *Caesar and the Fading of the Roman World: A Study in Republicanism and Caesarism*. New Brunswick, NJ: Transaction Publishers.

Baehr, P. and M. Richter (eds.). 2004. *Dictatorship in History and Theory: Bonapartism, Caesarism, and Totalitarianism*. Cambridge: Cambridge University Press.

Bagehot, W. 1968a. "Caesarism as it now exists," in Norman St. John-Stevas (ed.), *Collected Works of Walter Bagehot, vol. 4: The Economist*, pp. 111–16.

Bagehot, W. 1968b. "The collapse of Caesarism," in Norman St. John-Stevas (ed.), *Collected Works of Walter Bagehot, vol. 4: The Economist*, pp. 155–9.

Bagehot, W. 1968c. "France or England," in Norman St. John-Stevas (ed.), *Collected Works of Walter Bagehot, vol. 4: The Economist*, pp. 89–94.

Bailly, A. 1932. *Jules César*. Paris: Fayard.

Baldassarri, S. U. 2007. "A tale of two cities: accounts of the origins of Fiesole and Florence from the anonymous *Chronica* to Leonardo Bruni," *Studi Rinascimentali* 5, 29–56.

Baldwin, T. W. 1944. *William Shakspere's Small Latine and Lesse Greeke*, 2 vols. Urbana: University of Illinois Press.

Balsdon, J. P. V. D. 1939. "Consular provinces under the Late Republic," *JRS* 29.1, 57–73.

Balsdon, J. P. V. D. 1962. "Roman History, 65–50 B.C.: five problems," *JRS* 52, 134–41.

Baltrusch, E. 2004. *Caesar und Pompeius*. Darmstadt: Wissenschaftliche Buchgesellschaft.

Barchiesi, A. 2001. "The crossing," in S. J. Harrison (ed.), *Texts, Ideas, and the Classics*. Oxford: Oxford University Press, pp. 142–63.

Barlow, J. 1998. "Noble Gauls and their Other in Caesar's propaganda," in K. Welch and A. Powell (eds.), *Julius Caesar as Artful Reporter: the War Commentaries as Political Instruments*. London: Duckworth, and Swansea: Classical Press of Wales, pp. 139–70.

Barnes, T. D. 1998a. *Ammianus Marcellinus and the Representation of Historical Reality*. Ithaca, NY/London: Cornell University Press.

Barnes, T. D. 1998b. "Tacitus and the *Senatus consultum de Cn. Pisone patre*," *Phoenix* 52, 125–48.

Baron, H. 1962. "The evolution of Petrarch's thought: reflections on the state of Petrarch studies," *Bibliothèque d'Humanisme et Renaissance*, 24, 7–41. Repr. in his *From Petrarch to Leonardo Bruni: Studies in Humanistic and Political Literature* (Chicago: Chicago University Press, 1968), pp. 7–50.

Baron, H. 1967. *The Crisis of the Early Italian Renaissance: Civic Humanism and Republican Values in an Age of Classicism and Tyranny*, rev. edn. Princeton, NJ: Princeton University Press.

Barroll, J. Leeds. 1958. "Shakespeare and Roman history," *Modern Language Review* 53, 327–43.

Barton, A. 1984. *Ben Jonson, Dramatist*. Cambridge: Cambridge University Press.

Barwick, K. 1951. *Caesars Bellum Civile. Tendenz, Abfassungszeit und Stil*. Berlin: Akademie-Verlag.

Batstone, W. W. and C. Damon. 2006. *Caesar's Civil War*. Oxford: Oxford University Press.

Bauer, V. 2003. "Höfische Gesellschaft und höfische Öffentlichkeit im Alten Reich: Überlegungen zur Mediengeschichte des Fürstenhofs im 17. und 18. Jahrhundert," *Jahrbuch für Kommunikationsgeschichte* 5, 29–68.

Beales, D. E. D. 2005a. *Enlightenment and Reform in Eighteenth-Century Europe*. London: Tauris.

Beales, D. E. D. 2005b. "Philosophical kingship and enlightened despotism," in his *Enlightenment and Reform in Eighteenth-Century Europe*. London: Tauris, pp. 28–59.

Beales, D. E. D. 2005c. "Was Joseph II an enlightened despot?" in his *Enlightenment and Reform in Eighteenth-Century Europe*. London: Tauris, pp. 262–86.

Beard, M. 1990. "Priesthood in the Roman Republic," in M. Beard and J. North, *Pagan Priests*. Ithaca, NY: Cornell University Press, pp. 17–48.

Beard, M. 2007. *The Roman Triumph*. Cambridge, MA: Harvard University Press.

Beard, M., J. North, and S. Price. 1998. *Religions of Rome*. Cambridge: Cambridge University Press.

Beare, R. 1979. "The imperial oath under Caesar," *Latomus* 38, 469–73.

Beaune, C. 1985. *Naissance de la nation France*. Paris: Gallimard.

Beer, J. M. A. 1976. *A Medieval Caesar*. Geneva: Librairie Droz.

Beneker, J. 2002–3. "No time for love: Plutarch's chaste Caesar," *GRBS* 43, 13–29.

Benson, R. L. and J. Fried (eds.). 1997. *Ernst Kantorowicz: Erträge der Doppeltagung Institute for Advanced Study, Princeton/Johann Wolfgang Goethe-Universität*. Stuttgart: Steiner.

Bentley, G. E. 1956. *The Jacobean and Caroline Stage*, 4 vols. Oxford: Clarendon Press.

Benvenuto da Imola. 1887. *Comentum super Dantis Aldigherij Comoediam*, ed. J. P. Lacaita, 5 vols. Florence: Barbera.

Bercé, Y.-M. 1996. *The Birth of Absolutism: a History of France, 1598–1661*. Basingstoke: Macmillan.

Bergemann, J. 1990. *Römische Reiterstatuen: Ehrendenkmäler im öffentlichen Bereich*. Mainz: Zabern.

Bernard, C. 1699. *Brutus: Trauer-Spiel/Dem Durchlauchtigsten Fürsten und Herrn/Herrn Anthon Ulrich/Hertzogen zu Braunschweig und Lüneburg/u. Zur Gemüths-Ergötzligkeit vorgestellet Auf dem kleinen THEATRO Des Fürstlichen Lust-Hauses Saltzdahlen*, trans. F. Bresson, C. Wolfenbüttel, and Christian Bartsch.

Berno, F. R. 2004. "Un truncus, molti re: Priamo, Agamennone, Lucano (Virgilio, Seneca, Lucano)," *Maia* 56, 79–84.

Bernoulli, J. J. 1882. *Römische Ikonographie*, vol. 1. Stuttgart: W. Spemann.

Besser, J. 1880. "De coniuratione Catilinaria dissertatio philologica." Dissertation, Leipzig.

Besterman, T. (ed.). 1967. *Voltaire on Shakespeare*. Studies on Voltaire and the Eighteenth Century 54. Geneva: Institut et musée Voltaire.

Bianchi Bandinelli, R. 1970. *Rome, the Centre of Power: Roman Art to AD 200* (trans. Peter Green). London: Thames & Hudson.

Bickerman, E. J. 1980. *Chronology of the Ancient World*, rev. edn. London: Thames and Hudson.

Biel, S. 1996. *Down with the Old Canoe: A Cultural History of the Titanic Disaster*. New York: W. W. Norton.

Billanovich, G. 1960. "Nella biblioteca del Petrarca. Un altro Svetonio del Petrarca (Oxford, Exeter College, 186)," *Italia medioevale e umanistica* 3, 28–58. Repr. in his *Petrarca e il primo Umanesimo* (Padua: Antenore, 1996), pp. 262–94.

Billanovich, G. 1990. "Nella tradizione dei *Commentarii* di Cesare. Roma, Petrarca, i Visconti," *Studi petrarcheschi*, n.s. 7, 263–318.

Birley, A. R. 1997. *Hadrian: The Restless Emperor*. London/New York: Routledge.

Black, R. 2001. *Humanism and Education in Medieval and Renaissance Italy: Tradition and Innovation in Latin Schools from the Twelfth to the Fifteenth Centuries*. Cambridge: Cambridge University Press.

Blakemore Evans, B. 1958. "The problem of Brutus: an 18th-century solution," in Don Cameron Allen (ed.), *Studies in Honor of T. W. Baldwin*. Urbana: University of Illinois Press.

Blanc, P. 1985. "De la transgression comme scandale à la transgression comme idéal: Le double image de César dans l'oeuvre et pensée de Pétrarque," in R. Chevallier (ed.), *Présence de César. Actes du colloque des 9–11 décembre 1983: Hommage au doyen Michel Rambaud*. Paris: Les Belles Lettres, pp. 35–55.

Blanck, H. 1969. *Wiederverwendung alter Statuen als Ehrendenkmäler bei Griechen und Römern*. Rome: "L'Erma" di Bretschneider.

Blissett, W. 1956. "Lucan's Caesar and the Elizabethan villain," *SP* 53, 553–75.

Bloemendal, J. 2002. "Tyrant or stoic hero? Marc-Antoine Muret's *Julius Caesar*," in Karl A. Enenkel, Jan L. De Jong, and Jeanine De Landtsheer (eds.), *Recreating Ancient History: Episodes from the Greek and Roman Past in the Arts and Literature of the Early Modern Period*. Leiden/Boston: Brill, pp. 303–18.

Bloomer, W. M. 1992. *Valerius Maximus and the Rhetoric of the New Nobility*. Chapel Hill: University of North Carolina Press.

Boatwright, M. T. 1988. "Caesar's second consulship and the completion and date of the *Bellum Civile*," *CJ* 84.1, 31–40.

Boccaccio, G. 1965. *Esposizioni sopra la Comedia di Dante*, in *Tutte le opere*, ed. Vittore Branca, vol. 6. Milan: Mursia.

Bodmer, J. J. 1763. *Julius Cäsar: Ein Trauerspiel*. Leipzig: Weidmann.

Boehrer, B. 1997. "Jonson's *Catiline* and anti-Sallustian trends in Renaissance humanist historiography," *SP* 94, 85–102.

Boehringer, E. 1933. *Der Caesar von Acireale*. Stuttgart: Kohlhammer.

Bömer, F. 1953. "Der Commentarius. Zur Vorgeschichte und literarischen Form der Schriften Caesars," *Hermes* 81, 210–50.

Booth, J. 2007. *Cicero on the Attack: Invective and Subversion in the Orations and Beyond*. Swansea: Classical Press of Wales.

Borda, M. 1943–4. "Il ritratto tuscolano di Giulio Cesare," in *Rendiconti della Pontificia Accademia Romana di Archeologia*, vol. 20, 347–82.

Borkowski, A. and P. du Plessis. 2005. *Textbook on Roman Law*, 3rd edn. Oxford: Oxford University Press.

Bornmeister, S. 1678. *Neu-eröffneter Schau-Platz/ Der/ von C. J. Caesare, bis auf jetzt regirenden Leopoldum, Römisch-Teutschen/ wie auch Morgenländischen Kaiser: Auf welchen/ nach der Jahr-hundert-Ordnung/ nebens allerhand Politisch/ und andern nothwendigen Discursen/ dero Lebens-Verrichtungen fürstellig gemacht; und dabey/ sowol vielfältig der alten Teutschen/ als auch andere merck-würdige Begebenheiten/ eingeführet werden*. Nuremberg: Johann Hofmann and Andreas Knorzen.

Boschung, D. 1993a. *Die Bildnisse des Augustus*. Berlin: Gebr. Mann.

Boschung, D. 1993b. "Die Bildnistypen der iulisch-claudischen Kaiserfamilie: ein kritischer Forschungsbericht," *Journal of Roman Archeology* 6, 39–79.

Boschung, D. 2002. *Gens Augusta. Untersuchungen zu Aufstellung, Wirkung und Bedeutung der Statuengruppen des julisch-claudischen Kaiserhauses*. Mainz: P. von Zabern.

Boulay, C. 1985. "L'Image de César sous le fascisme d'après *l'Enciclopedia Italiana Treccani*," in R. Chevallier (ed.), *Présence de César. Actes du Colloque des 9–11 décembre 1983: Hommage au doyen Michel Rambaud*. Paris: Les Belles Lettres, pp. 373–90.

Bourne, F. C. 1977. "Caesar the Epicurean," *CW* 70, 417–32.

Bowersock, G. W. 1969. "Suetonius and Trajan," in *Hommages à Marcel Renard*, vol. 1 (*Coll. Latomus* 101, Brussels), pp. 119–25.

Bowersock, G. W. 1990. "The pontificate of Augustus," in K. A. Raaflaub and M. Toher (eds.), *Between Republic and Empire: Interpretations of Augustus and his Principate*. Berkeley/Los Angeles/London: University of California Press, pp. 380–94.

Bowersock, G. W. 1998. "*Vita Caesarum*. Remembering and forgetting the past," in *La Biographie antique*, ed. W. W. Ehlers. Entretiens sur l'Antiquité classique 44. Geneva: Vandœuvres, 193–209.

Bowie, E. L. 1985. "Appian," in P. E. Easterling and B. W. Knox (eds.), *The Cambridge History of Classical Literature. Volume 1: Greek Literature*. Cambridge: Cambridge University Press.

Branam, G. C. 1956. *18th-Century Adaptations of Shakespearean Tragedy*. Berkeley/Los Angeles: University of California Press.

Brennan, T. Corey. 2000. *The Praetorship in the Roman Republic*, 2 vols. Oxford/New York: Oxford University Press.

Brind'Amour, P. 1983. *Le Calendrier romain*. Ottawa: Ottawa University Press.

Broughton, T. R. S. 1951–2, 1986. *The Magistrates of the Roman Republic*. 3 vols. Atlanta, GA: Scholars Press.

Broughton, T. R. S. 1991. *Candidates Defeated in Roman Elections: Some Ancient Roman "Also-Rans."* Transactions of the American Philosophical Society, vol. 81.4. Philadelphia: American Philosophical Society.

Brown, R. D. 1999. "Two Caesarian battle-descriptions: a study in contrast," *CJ* 94, 329–57.

Brown, R. D. 2004. "*Virtus consili expers*: an interpretation of the centurions' contest in Caesar, *De Bello Gallico* 5, 44," *Hermes* 132, 292–308.

Brown, V. 1972. *The Textual Transmission of Caesar's Civil War*. Leiden: Brill.

Brown, V. 1976. "Caesar," in F. E. Cranz and P. O. Kristeller (eds), *Catalogus Translationum et Commentariorum*, vol. 3. Washington, D.C.: Catholic University of America Press, pp. 87–139.

Brown, V. 1979. "Latin Manuscripts of Caesar's 'Gallic War,'" in *Palaeographica Diplomatica et Archivista. Studi in Onore di Giulio Battelli*. Rome: Edizione di Storia e Letteratura, pp. 104–57.

Brown, V. 1981. "Portraits of Julius Caesar in Latin MSS of the *Commentaries*," *Viator* 12, 319–60.

Brunhölzl, F. 1983. "Caesar im Mittelalter," in *Lexikon des Mittelalters*, vol. 2, c.1352f.

Bruni, L. 1996. *Opere letterarie e politiche*, ed. P. Viti. Turin: UTET.

Bruni, L. 2001. *History of the Florentine People*, ed. and trans. J. Hankins, vol. 1: Books I–IV. Cambridge, MA: Harvard University Press.

Brunt, P. A. 1971. *Italian Manpower*, 225 B.C.–A.D. 14. Oxford: Clarendon Press.

Brunt, P. A. 1986. "Cicero's *officium* in the Civil War," *JRS* 76, 12–31.

Brunt, P. A. 1988. "Amicitia in the late Roman Republic," in *The Fall of the Roman Republic*. Oxford: Clarendon Press, pp. 351–81.

Bryant, J. A., Jr. 1965. "*Catiline* and the nature of Jonson's tragic fable," in Jonas A. Barish (ed.), *Ben Jonson: a Collection of Critical Essays*. Englewood Cliffs, NJ: Prentice Hall, pp. 147–59.

Bucher, G. S. 1997. "Prolegomena to a commentary on Appian's *Bellum Civile* book two." Dissertation, Brown University.

Bucher, G. S. 2000. "The origins, program, and composition of Appian's *Roman History*," *TAPA* 130, 411–58.

Bullough, G. 1964. *Narrative and Dramatic Sources of Shakespeare* (8 vols), vol. 5. London: Routledge and Kegan Paul.

Burckhardt, L. A. 1988. *Politische Strategien der Optimaten in der späten römischen Republik*. Stuttgart: Franz Steiner Verlag.

Burke, E. 1987. *Reflections on the Revolution in France*, ed. J. G. A. Pocock. Indianapolis: Hackett.

Burke, P. 1966. "A survey of the popularity of ancient historians," *History and Theory* 5, 135–52.

Burke, P. 1992. *The Fabrication of Louis XIV*. New Haven, CT: Yale University Press.

Burrienne, Louis Antoine Fauvelet de. 1836. *Memoirs of Napoleon Bonaparte*, vol. 3. London: Richard Bentley.

Butenschoen, J. F. 1789. *Caesar, Cato und Friedrich von Preussen, ein historisches Lesebuch*. Heidelberg: Friedrich Ludwig Pfähler.

Byrd, R. C. 2004. *Losing America: Confronting a Reckless and Arrogant Presidency*. New York: W.W. Norton.

Cadario, M. 2006. "Le statue di Cesare a Roma tra il 46 e il 44 a. C.," *Annali della Facoltà di Lettere e Filosofia dell'Università degli Studi di Milano* 59.3, 25–70.

Caesar, J. 1517. *Commentaria Caesaris prius a Iucundo impressioni data posterius a nobis diligentissime revisa [...]*, ed. G. Giocondo. Venice: Agostino de Zanni.

Caesar, J. 1518. *Commentarii di Iulio Cesare tradotti di latino in lingua fiorentina per Dante Popoleschi*. Florence: Giovanni Stefano di Carlo da Pavia.

Caesar, J. 1547. *Commentarii di Gaio Giulio Cesare, tradotti di latino in volgar lingua per Agostino Ortica della Porta Genovese [...]*. Venice: Aldus.

Caesar, J. 1570. *C. Iulii Caesaris Commentarii novis emendationibus illustrati. Eiusdem librorum, qui desiderantur, fragmenta. Ex bibliotheca Fulvii Ursini Romani*. Antwerp: Christophe Plantin.

Caesar, J. 1571. *C. Iulii Caesaris Commentarii ab A. Manutio emendati et scholiis illustrati*. Venice: Aldus.

Caesar, J. 1598. *Commentari di Giulio Cesare, con le figure in rame [...] fatte da Andrea Palladio per facilitare a chi legge la cognition dell'Historia*. Venice: Girolamo Foglietti.

Caesar, J. 1982. *The Conquest of Gaul* (trans. S. A. Handford), rev. with a new introduction by Jane F. Gardner. Harmondsworth: Penguin.

Cagnetta, Mariella. 1990. *Antichità classiche nell'Enciclopedia italiana*. Rome/Bari: Laterza.

Cairns, F. 1979. *Tibullus: A Hellenistic Poet at Rome*. Cambridge: Cambridge University Press.

Canfora, D. (ed.). 2001. *La controversia di Poggio Bracciolini e Guarino Veronese su Cesare e Scipione*. Florence: Olschki.

Canfora, L. 1993. *Studi di storia della storiografia romana*. Bari: Edipuglia.

Canfora, L. 2007. *Julius Caesar: The People's Dictator* (trans. M. Hill and K. Windle). Edinburgh: Edinburgh University Press. Published in the US as *Julius Caesar: The Life and Times of the People's Dictator* (Berkeley: University of California Press).Originally published as *Giulio Cesare. Il dittatore democratico* (Rome/Bari: Laterza, 1999).

Carcopino, J. 1968. *Jules César*. Paris: Presses Universitaires de France. First published in 1935.

Carney, T. F. 1968. "How Suetonius' *Lives* reflect on Hadrian," *PACA* 11, 7–24.

Cartel So Julius Cæsar an die Drey vorhergegangenen Monarchen/ gehalten/ bey Eröffnung der Weltberühmten Renn-Bahn/ Des Durchleuchtigsten Beherrschers derer fruchtbaren Elben-Auen/ Den 5. Februarii, 1695, [S.1]. 1695. [2] Bl.

Carter, J. M. (ed., intro., trans., and comm.). 1991. *Julius Caesar: The Civil War, Books I & II*. Warminster: Aris & Phillips.

Carter, J. (ed., intro., trans., and comm.). 1993. *Julius Caesar: The Civil War, Book III*. Warminster: Aris & Phillips.

Castiglione, B. 1967. *The Book of the Courtier*, trans. G. Bull. Harmondsworth: Penguin.

Chafe, W. H. 2003. *The Unfinished Journey: America since World War II*, 5th edn. New York: Oxford University Press.

Chambers, E. K. 1951. *The Elizabethan Stage*, 4 vols., 2nd edn. Oxford: Oxford University Press. First published 1923.

Champeaux, J. 1987. *Fortuna. Recherches sur le culte de la fortune à Rome et dans le monde romain des origines à la mort de César*, vol. 2. Paris: de Boccard.

Champlin, E. 1991. *Final Judgments: Duty and Emotion in Roman Wills 200 B.C.–A.D. 250*. Berkeley/Los Angeles/Oxford: University of California Press.

Chang, J. S. M. J. 1970. "*Julius Caesar* in the light of Renaissance historiography," *Journal of English and Germanic Philology* 69, 63–71.

Chaplin, J. D. 2000. *Livy's Exemplary Rome*. Oxford: Oxford University Press.

Chênerie, M. 1974. "L'Architecture du *Bellum Civile* de César," *Pallas* 21, 13–31.

Chevallier, R. (ed.). 1985. *Présence de César. Actes du colloque des 9–11 décembre 1983: Hommage au doyen Michel Rambaud*. Paris: Les Belles Lettres.

Christ, K. 1974. "Caesar und Ariovist," *Chiron* 4, 251–92.

Christ, K. 1994. *Caesar. Annäherungen an einen Diktator*. Munich: Verlag C. H. Beck.

Clarke, K. 1999. *Between Geography and History: Hellenistic Constructions of the Ancient World*. Oxford: Oxford University Press.

Clarke, M. L. 1981. *The Noblest Roman: Marcus Brutus and his Reputation*. London: Thames & Hudson.

Cluett, R. 2003. "In Caesar's wake: the ideology of the Continuators," in F. Cairns and E. Fantham (eds.), *Caesar against Liberty: Perspectives on his Autocracy*. Cambridge: Francis Cairns, pp. 118–31.

Coarelli, F. 1969. "Le 'Tyrannoctone' du Capitole et la mort de Tiberius Gracchus," *Mélanges d'Archéologie et d'Histoire* 81, 137–60.

Cobley, E. 1993. *Representing War: Form and Ideology in First World War Narratives.* Toronto: University of Toronto Press.

Cohen, E. A. 2004. "History and the hyperpower," *Foreign Affairs*, July/August. Downloaded from www.foreignaffairs.org, March 14, 2005.

Coldagelli, U. 1971. "Giulio Cesare Brancaccio," *Dizionario biografico degli italiani* 13, 780–84.

Collins, J. H. 1959. "On the date and interpretation of the *Bellum Civile*," *AJP* 80, 113–32.

Collins, J. H. 1972. "Caesar as a political propagandist," in Hildegard Temporini (ed.), *ANRW* I.1. Berlin: De Gruyter, 922–66.

Colson, F. H. 1919. "The analogist and anomalist controversy," *Classical Quarterly* 13, 24–36.

Conte, G. B. 1966. "Il proemio della *Pharsalia*," *Maia* 18, 42–53.

Cooke, J. E. 1960. "Alexander Hamilton's authorship of the 'Caesar' letters," *William and Mary Quarterly* 17.1, 78–85.

Corbeill, A. 1996. *Controlling Laughter: Political Humor in the Late Roman Republic.* Princeton: Princeton University Press.

Corbier, M. 1997. "Pallas et la statue de César. Affichage et espace public à Rome," *Revue Numismatique* 152, 11–40.

Costantini, M. 1993. "Xénophon ou l'art de la bonne distance," in D. Poli (ed.), *Cultura in Cesare: Atti del convegno internazionale di studi, Macerata-Matelica, 30 aprile–4 maggio 1990*, 2 vols. Rome: Il Calamo, pp. 137–48.

Couvreur, M. 2003. "Mort de César," in R. Trousson and J. Vercruysse (eds.), *Dictionnaire général de Voltaire.* Paris: Éditions Champion, pp. 846–9.

Cox-Rearick, J. 1984. *Dynasty and Destiny in Medici Art: Pontormo, Leo X and the Two Cosimos.* Princeton, NJ: Princeton University Press.

Craig, C. 2004. "Audience expectations, invective, and proof," in J. Powell and J. Paterson (eds.), *Cicero the Advocate.* Oxford: Oxford University Press, pp. 187–213.

Cranston, P. E. 1975. "Rome en anglais se prononce 'Roum': Shakespeare versions by Voltaire," *Modern Language Notes* 90.6, 809–37.

Crawford, M. H. 1974.*Roman Republican Coinage.* Cambridge: Cambridge University Press.

Crawford, M. H. (ed.). 1996. *Roman Statutes*, vol. 1. London: Institute of Classical Studies.

Crevatin, G. 1982. "La politica e la retorica," in *Poggio Bracciolini 1380–1980.* Florence: Sansoni, pp. 281–342.

Crevatin, G. 1989. "L'edizione incompiuta del *De gestis Cesaris*," *Annali della Scuola Normale di Pisa*, s. 3, 19, 193–208.

Crevier, J. B. L. and C. Rollin. 1755. *Histoire romaine depuis la fondation de Rome jusqu'à la bataille d'Actium: c'est-à-dire jusqu'à la fin de la République*, vol. 15. Halle: Gebauer.

Croizy-Naquet, C. 1999. *Écrire l'histoire romaine au début du XIIIe siècle.* Nouvelle Bibliothèque du moyen âge 53. Paris: Honoré Champion.

Cupaiuolo, F. 1984. "Caso, fato e fortuna negli storici latini," *Bollettino di Studi Latini* 14, 3–38.

Curschmann, M. 1997. *Vom Wandel im bildlichen Umgang mit literarischen Gegenständen. Rodenegg, Wildenstein und das Flaarsche Haus in Stein am Rhein.* FreiburgSchweiz: Universitätsverlag Freiburg Schweiz.

Dante Alighieri. 1966–7. *La Divina Commedia secondo l'antica vulgate*, ed. G. Petrocchi, 3 vols. Milan: Mondadori.

de Blois, L. 1992. "The perception of politics in Plutarch's Roman *Lives*," *ANRW* II 33.6, 4568–615.

Decembrio, A. 2002. *De politia litteraria*, ed. N. Witten. Munich/Leipzig: Saur.

Degrassi, A. (ed.) 1963. *Inscriptiones Italiae* 13.2. Rome: Istituto Poligrafico dello Stato.
De Kersauson, K. 1986. *Musée du Louvre. Catalogue des portraits romains* I. Paris: Ministère de la culture et de la communication, Éditions de la Réunion des musées nationaux.
De Libero, L. 1992. *Obstruktion*. Stuttgart: Franz Steiner Verlag.
De Martino, F. 1973. *Storia della costituzione romana*, vol. 3. Naples: Jovene.
den Boeft, J., D. den Hengst, and H. C. Teitler. 1991. *Philological and Historical Commentary on Ammianus Marcellinus, XXI*. Groningen: Egbert Forsten.
den Boeft, J., D. den Hengst, H. C. Teitler, and J. W. Drijvers. 1995. *Philological and Historical Commentary on Ammianus Marcellinus, XXII*. Groningen: Egbert Forsten.
Diderot, D. (ed.). 1765. *Encyclopédie ou Dictionnaire raisonnée des sciences, des arts, et des métiers, par une société de gens de lettres*, vol. 14. Neufchatel: Samuel Faulche.
Dobson, M. 1991. "Accents yet unknown: canonisation and the claiming of *Julius Caesar*," in Jean I. Marsden (ed.), *The Appropriation of Shakespeare*. Hemel Hempstead: Harvester Wheatsheaf, pp. 11–28.
Dodington, P. M. 1980. "The function of the references to engineering in Caesar's 'Commentaries.'" Dissertation, University of Iowa.
Domaszewski, A. von. 1909. *Abhandlungen zur römischen Religion*. Leipzig/Berlin: Teubner.
Domenicucci, P. 1990. "Osservazioni sul *De Astris* attribuito a Giulio Cesare," in *La Cultura in Cesare. Università di Macerata Quaderni Linguistici e Filologici* 5. Rome: D. Poli, pp. 345–58.
Donié P., P. 1996. *Untersuchungen zum Caesarbild in der römischen Kaiserzeit*. Hamburg: Verlag Dr. Kovač.
Downey, G. and A. F. Norman. 1974. *Themistii Orationes* 3. Leipzig: Teubner.
Drumann, W. 1906. *Geschichte Roms in seinem Übergange von der republikanischen zur monarchischen Verfassung: oder Pompeius, Caesar, Cicero und ihre Zeitgenossen*, 2nd edn., ed. P. Groebe, vol. 3. Leipzig: Borntraeger, pp. 125–684, 696–827 (entries by P. Groebe).
Drummond, A. 1995. *Law, Politics, and Power: Sallust and the Execution of the Catilinarian Conspirators*. Stuttgart: Franz Steiner Verlag.
Dubois, Cl.-G. 1973. *Celtes et Gaulois au XVIe siècle: le développement littéraire d'un mythe nationaliste*. Paris: J. Vrin.
Duff, T. 1999. *Plutarch's Lives: Exploring Virtue and Vice*. Oxford: Clarendon Press.
Duffy, E. M. T. 1947. "Ben Jonson's debt to Renaissance scholarship in *Catiline* and *Sejanus*," *Modern Language Review* 42.1, 24–30.
Dugan, J. 2005. *Making a New Man: Ciceronian Self-Fashioning in the Rhetorical Works*. Oxford: Oxford University Press, pp. 177–89.
Dunn, S. 2004. *Jefferson's Second Revolution: the Election Crisis of 1800 and the Triumph of Republicanism*. Boston: Houghton Mifflin.
Duval, F. 2006. "Le *Livre des commentaires Cesar sur le fait des batailles de Gaule* par Robert Gaguin (1485)," *Cahiers de recherches médiévales* 13, 167–82.
Duxbury, L. C. 1988. "Some attitudes to Julius Caesar in the Roman Republic: Catullus, Cicero and Sallust." Dissertation, University of Oxford.
Dyck, A. R. 2001 "Dressing to kill: attire as a proof and means of characterization in Cicero's Speeches," *Arethusa* 34.1, 119–30.
Eakin, E. 2002. "All roads lead to DC," *New York Times*, March 31: section 4/4.
Eckstein, A. 1987. *Senate and Genera: Individual Decision Making and Roman Foreign Relations, 264–194 B.C.* Berkeley: University of California Press.
Eckstein, A. 2006a. "Conceptualizing Roman Imperial Expansion under the Republic," in N. Rosenstein and R. Morstein-Marx (eds.), *A Companion to the Roman Republic*. Oxford: Blackwell, pp. 567–589.

Eckstein, A. 2006b. *Mediterranean Anarchy, Interstate War, and the Rise of Rome.* Berkeley: University of California Press.

Eden, P. T. 1962. "Caesar's style: inheritance versus intelligence," *Glotta* 40, 74–117.

Edwards, C. 1993. *The Politics of Immorality in Ancient Rome.* Cambridge: Cambridge University Press.

Eilers, C. 2003. "Josephus' Caesarian *Acta*: history of a dossier." *SBL* Seminar Paper 42.

Erdkamp, P. 1998. *Hunger and the Sword: Warfare and Food Supply in Roman Republican Wars (264–30 B.C.).* Amsterdam: J. C. Gieben.

Erickson, B. 2002. "Falling masts, rising rivers: the ethnography of virtue in Caesar's account of the Veneti," *AJP* 123, 601–22.

Evans, E. C. 1935. "Roman descriptions of personal appearance in history and biography," Harvard Studies in Classical Philology 46, 43–85.

Evans, E. C. 1941. "The study of physiognomy in the second century A.D.," *TAPA* 72, 96–109.

Everitt, A. 2006. *The First Emperor: Caesar Augustus and the Triumph of Rome.* London: John Murray. (Published in the USA as *Augustus: The Life of Rome's First Emperor.* New York: Random House.)

Ezov, A. 1996. "The 'missing dimension' of C. Julius Caesar," *Historia* 45, 64–94.

Fabre, P. (ed. and trans.). 1936. *Julius Caesar, La guerre civile*, 2 vols. Paris: Les Belles Lettres.

Faedo, L. 1984. "Testa di Giulio Cesare," in S. Settis (ed.), *Camposanto Monumentale di Pisa. Le Antichità* II. Pisa: Pacini.

Fear, A. 2005. "A journey to the end of the world," in J. Elsner and I. Rutherford (eds.), *Pilgrimage in Graeco-Roman and Early Christian Antiquity.* Oxford: Oxford University Press, pp. 319–31.

Feeney, D. 2007. *Caesar's Calendar: Ancient Time and the Beginnings of History.* Berkeley: University of California Press.

Feind, B. 1705. *Die Römische Unruhe. Oder: Die edelmüthige Octavia. In einem Singspiel*, s.l.

Feind, B. 1711. *L'amore verso la patria = Die Liebe gegen das Vaterland. Oder: Der Sterbende Cato.* Hamburg: Greflinger.

Fenzi, E. 2003. "Grandi infelici: Alessandro e Cesare," in his *Saggi petrarcheschi.* Florence: Cadmo, pp. 469–92.

Fera, V. 2007. "I *Fragmenta de viris illustribus* di Francesco Petrarca," in *Caro Vittò: Essays in Memory of Vittore Branca*, ed. Jill Kraye and Laura Lepschy in collaboration with Nicola Jones (*The Italianist* 27, special supplement 2). Reading: The Italianist, pp. 101–32.

Ferguson, N. 2004. *Colossus: The Rise and Fall of the American Empire.* London: Allen Lane.

Ferraù, G. 2006a. *Petrarca, la politica, la storia.* Messina: Centro Interdipartimentale di Studi Umanistici.

Ferraù, G. 2006b. "Petrarca, Cola, l'Impero," in his *Petrarca, la politica, la storia.* Messina: Centro Interdipartimentale di Studi Umanistici, pp. 15–52.

Ferraù, G. 2006c. "Petrarca e la politica signorile," in his *Petrarca, la politica, la storia.* Messina: Centro Interdipartimentale di Studi Umanistici, pp. 53–101.

Ferraù, G. 2006d. "Tra storiografia e politica," in his *Petrarca, la politica, la storia.* Messina: Centro Interdipartimentale di Studi Umanistici, pp. 103–205.

Firpo, G. 2000. "Cesare e i Giudei," *Urso*: 125–41.

Fisher, Lizette Andrews. 1907. "Shakespere and the Capitol," *Modern Language Notes*, 177–82.

Fishwick, D. 1975. "The name of the demigod," *Historia* 24, 624–8.

Fisk, R. 2002. "The mantra that means this time it's serious," *Independent*, September 13: 1/4.

Fittschen, K. and P. Zanker. 1985–7. *Katalog der römischen Porträts in den capitolinischen Museen und den anderen kommunalen Sammlungen der Stadt Rom*, vols. 1 and 3 (vol. 2 not yet published). Mainz: Phillip von Zabern.

Fitzgerald, J. 1996. *Greco-Roman Perspectives on Friendship*. Atlanta, GA: Scholars Press.

Flamarion, É. 2003. "Antiquité latine," in R. Trousson and J. Vercruysse (eds.), *Dictionnaire général de Voltaire*. Paris: Éditions Champion, pp. 61–9.

Fletcher, D. 1975. "Aaron Hill, translator of *La Mort de César*," *Studies in Voltaire and the Eighteenth Century* 137, 73–9.

Fletcher, D. 1981. "Three authors in search of a character: Julius Caesar as seen by Buckingham, Conti and Voltaire," in *Mélanges à la mémoire de Franco Simone*, vol. 2. Geneva: Editions Slatkind, pp. 441–52.

Formisano, R. P. 1969. "Political character, antipartyism and the second party system," *American Quarterly* 21.4, 683–709.

Foster, J. B. 2002. "The rediscovery of imperialism," *Monthly Review* 54.6, 1–16.

Fraenkel, E. 1956. "Eine Form römischer Kriegsbulletin," *Eranos* 54, 189–94.

Frati, C. 1921. "Il volgarizzamento dei *Commentari* di Giulio Cesare fatto da P. C. Decembrio," *Archivum Romanicum* 5, 74–80.

Freedland, J. 2002. "Rome, AD ... Rome, DC?" *Guardian*, September 18: G2/2–4.

Freeman, J. B. 1995. "Slander, poison, whispers and fame: Jefferson's 'Anas' and political gossip in the Early Republic," *Journal of the Early Republic* 15.1, 25–57.

Friedeburg, R. von (ed.). 2001. *Widerstandsrecht in der frühen Neuzeit: Erträge und Perspektiven der Forschung im deutsch-britischen Vergleich*. Berlin: Duncker & Humblot.

Furness, H. H. 1913. *The Variorum Shakespeare:* Julius Caesar. Philadelphia, PA: J. B. Lippincott.

Gain, D. B. 1976. *The Aratus ascribed to Germanicus Caesar*. London: Athlone Press.

Garber, M. 1987. *Shakespeare's Ghost Writers: Literature as Uncanny Causality*. New York/London: Routledge.

Gardner, J. F. 1967. *Caesar, The Civil War, together with The Alexandrian War, The African War, and The Spanish War by other Hands*. Harmondsworth: Penguin.

Gardner, J. F. 1998. *Family and* Familia *in Roman Law and Life*. Oxford: Clarendon Press.

Garin, E. (ed.) 1952. *Prosatori latini del Quattrocento*. Milan/Naples: Ricciardi.

Geiger, J. 1975. "Zum Bild Julius Caesars in der römischen Kaiserzeit," *Historia* 24, 444–53.

Geiger, J. 2002. "*Felicitas Temporum* and Plutarch's Choice of Heroes," in Philip A. Stadter and Luc van der Stockt (eds.), *Sage and Emperor: Plutarch, Greek Intellectuals, and Roman Power in the Time of Trajan (98–117 A.D.)* (Leuven: Leuven University Press), pp. 93–102.

Gelzer, M. 1912. *Die Nobilität der römischen Republik*. Leipzig: Teubner.

Gelzer, M. 1968. *Caesar: Politician and Statesman*, trans. Peter Needham. Oxford: Blackwell. (Translated from *Caesar. Der Politiker und Staatsmann*, 6th edn. 1st edn. published 1921.)

Gelzer, M. 1969. *The Roman Nobility* (trans. and intro. Robin Seager). Oxford: Blackwell. (Translation of *Die Nobilität der römischen Republik* and *Die Nobilität der Kaiserzeit*.)

Gerratana, V. (ed.). 1975. *Antonio Gramsci. Quaderni del carcere*. Turin: Einaudi.

Gesche, H. 1976. *Caesar*. Darmstadt: Wissenschaftliche Buchgesellschaft.

Giannattasio A. R. 2000. "*Galba e Otone* tra biografia e storia," in I. Gallo and C. Moreschini (eds.), *I generi letterari in Plutarco. Atti del VIII Convegno plutarcheo, Pisa, 2–4 giugno 1999*. Naples: M. D'Auria., pp. 81–91.

Giard, J.-B. 1976. *Catalogue des monnaies de l'Empire romain*, vol. 1. Paris: Bibliothèque nationale.

Giardina, D. 2003. "Iraq: Bush should be impeached and tried for war crimes," *Charleston Gazette*, May 12: 5A.

Gilson, S. 2005. *Dante and Renaissance Florence.* Cambridge: Cambridge University Press.

Ginsberg, E. S. 1973. "The legacy of Marc-Antoine de Muret's *Julius Caesar*," in J. IJsewijn and E. Kessler (eds.), *Acta conventus Neo-Latini Lovaniensis.* Leuven: Leuven University Press, pp. 247–52.

Giovannini, A. 1983. *Consulare Imperium.* Basel: F. Reinhardt Verlag.

Girardet, K. M. 2000. "Caesars Konsulatsplan für das Jahr 49: Gründe und Scheitern," *Chiron* 30, 679–710.

Giuliani, L. 1986. *Bildnis und Botschaft. Hermeneutische Untersuchungen zur Bildniskunst der römischen Republik.* Frankfurt am Main : Suhrkamp.

Gleason, M. W. 1995. *Making Men: Sophists and Self-Presentation in Ancient Rome.* Princeton: Princeton University Press.

Goldberg, S. 2005: *Constructing Literature in the Roman Republic.* Cambridge: Cambridge University Press.

Goldstein, M. 1956. "Pope, Sheffield, and Shakespeare's *Julius Caesar*," *Modern Language Notes* 71, 8–10.

Goldsworthy, A. 1996. *The Roman Army at War 100 BC–AD 200.* Oxford: Oxford University Press.

Goldsworthy, A. 1998. " 'Instinctive genius': the depiction of Caesar as general," in Welch and Powell, pp. 193–219.

Goldsworthy, A. 2006. *Caesar: The Life of a Colossus.* New Haven, CT: Yale University Press.

Gomez, J. G., J. A. Kotler, and J. B. Long. 1995. "Was Julius Caesar's epilepsy due to a brain tumor?" *Journal of the Florida Medical Association* 82, 199–201.

González, J. 1986. "The *Lex Irnitana*: a new copy of the Flavian Municipal Law," *JRS* 76, 147–243.

Gotoff, H. C. 1984. "Towards a practical criticism of Caesar's prose style," *Illinois Classical Studies* 9, 1–18.

Gotoff, H. C. 1993. *Cicero's Caesarian Speeches: a Stylistic Commentary.* Chapel Hill: University of North Carolina Press.

Gottdank, A. 1999. *Venedigs antike Helden: Die Darstellung der antiken Geschichte in der venezianischen Malerei von 1680 bis 1760.* Munich: Deutscher Kunstverlag.

Gowing, A. M. 1992. *The Triumviral Narratives of Appian and Cassius Dio.* Ann Arbor: University of Michigan Press.

Gradel, I. 2002. *Emperor Worship and Roman Religion.* Oxford: Oxford University Press.

Grafton, A. 1997. *Commerce with the Classics: Ancient Books and Renaissance Readers.* Ann Arbor: University of Michigan Press.

Graf von Rothenberg, K.-H. 1996. *Caesaris Bellum Helveticum*: Lincolnwood, IL: NTC.

Grantham, D. W. 1998. *Recent America: The United States since 1945*, 2nd edn. Wheeling, IL: Harlan Davidson.

Graves, R. (trans.). 1957. *Gaius Suetonius Tranquillus: The Twelve Caesars.* Harmondsworth: Penguin.

Green, C. M. C. 1991. "Stimulos dedit aemula virtus: Lucan and Homer reconsidered," *Phoenix* 45, 230–54.

Green, P. 1989. "Caesar and Alexander: aemulatio, imitatio, comparatio," in his *Classical Bearings: Interpreting Ancient History and Culture.* London: Thames and Hudson, pp. 193–209.

Green, W. H. 1932. "Julius Caesar in the Augustan poets," *CJ* 27, 405–11.

Greenstein, F. I. 2001. *The Presidential Difference: Leadership Style from FDR to Clinton*, 2nd edn. Princeton: Princeton University Press.

Grell, C. 1995. *Le dix-huitième siècle e l'antiquité en France 1680–1789.* Oxford: Voltaire Foundation.

Grendler, P. 1989. *Schooling in Renaissance Italy: Literacy and Learning, 1300–1600.* Baltimore: Johns Hopkins University Press.

Grethlein, J. and C. Krebs. (forthcoming). *The Historian's Plupast.*

Grévin, J. 1974. *César*, ed. J. Foster. Paris: A. G. Nizet.

Griffin, M. T. 1976. *Seneca: A Philosopher in Politics.* Oxford: Clarendon Press (reprinted with Postscript 1992).

Griffin, M. T. 1994. "The intellectual developments of the Ciceronian age," in *Cambridge Ancient History, vol. 9: The Last Age of the Roman Republic, 146–43 B.C.* Cambridge: Cambridge University Press, pp. 689–728.

Griffin, M. T. 1997. "From Aristotle to Atticus: Cicero and Matius on friendship," in J. Barnes and M. Griffin (eds.), *Philosophia Togata II.* Oxford: Clarendon Press, pp. 86–109.

Griffin, M. T. 2003. "Clementia after Caesar: from politics to philosophy," in F. Cairns and E. Fantham (eds.), *Caesar against Liberty? Perspectives on his Autocracy.* Papers of the Langford Latin Seminar 11. Cambridge: Francis Cairns.

Griffin, M. T. 2008. "*Iure plectimur*: the Roman critique of Roman imperialism," in T. Corey Brennan and Harriet I. Flower (eds.), *East West: Papers in Ancient History Presented to Glen W. Bowersock.* Cambridge, MA: Loeb Classic, pp. 86–111.

Griffiths, G., J. Hankins, and D. Thompson (eds). 1987. *The Humanism of Leonardo Bruni: Selected Texts.* Binghamton, NY: Medieval and Renaissance Texts and Studies, in conjunction with the Renaissance Society of America.

Groebe, P. 1918. *RE*, vol. 10. Stuttgart, s.v. *C. Iulius Caesar*, nr. 131, coll. 186–259.

Gross, W. H. 1940. *Bildnisse Traians.* Berlin: Gebr. Mann.

Gruen, E. S. 1974. *The Last Generation of the Roman Republic.* Berkeley/Los Angeles/London: University of California Press.

Gruen, E. S. 1977. "M. Licinius Crassus: A Review Article," *American Journal of Ancient History*, 2, 117–28.

Gruen, E. S. 1992. *Culture and National Identity in Republican Rome.* Ithaca, NY: Cornell University Press.

Guicciardini, F. 1984. *Antimachiavelli*, ed. G. Berardi. Rome: Editori Riuniti.

Gummere, R. M. 1963. *The American Colonial Mind and the Classical Tradition: Essays in Comparative Literature.* Cambridge, MA: Harvard University Press.

Gundelfinger [Gundolf], F. 1904. "Caesar in der deutschen Literatur." Dissertation, Berlin (1903). Published as *Palaestra* 33 (Berlin: Mayer & Müller, 1904); reprinted New York, 1967.

Gundolf, F. 1924. *Caesar. Geschichte seines Ruhms.* Berlin: Georg Bondi. (Translated into English by J. W. Hartmann as *The Mantle of Caesar.*)

Gundolf, F. 1926. *Caesar im neunzehnten Jahrhundert.* Berlin: Georg Bondi.

Gundolf, F. 1928. *The Mantle of Caesar* (trans. Jacob Wittmer Hartmann). New York: Macy Masius, Vanguard Press.

Gundolf, F. 1929. *The Mantle of Caesar* (trans. Jacob Wittner Hartmann). London: Grant Richards and Humphrey Toulmin at the Cayme Press.

Gundolf, F. 1968. *Caesar. Geschichte seines Ruhms.* Darmstadt: Wissenschaftliche Buchgesellschaft. (This volume reprints Gundolf 1924, 1926, and two supplementary essays from 1930.)

Hahn, I. 1985. "Augustus und das politische Vermächtnis Caesars," *Klio* 67, 12–28.

Hainsworth, P. 1988. *Petrarch the Poet: An Introduction to the "Rerum Vulgarium Fragmenta."* London: Routledge.

Hale, J. 1977. "Andrea Palladio, Polybius and Julius Caesar," *Journal of the Warburg and Courtauld Institutes* 40, 240–55.

Hall, J. 2005. "Politeness and formality in Cicero's letter to Matius (Fam 11, 27)," *Museum Helveticum* 62, 193–213.

Hall, L. G. H. 1998. "*Ratio* and *romanitas* in the *Bellum Gallicum*," in K. Welch and A. Powell (eds.), *Julius Caesar as Artful Reporter: the War Commentaries as Political Instruments.* London: Duckworth, and Swansea: Classical Press of Wales, pp. 11–43.

Hamilton, Alexander. 1904a. *Works of Alexander Hamilton (Federal Edition)*, ed. Henry Cabot Lodge, vol. 5. New York: G. P. Putnam's Sons.

Hamilton, Alexander. 1904b. *Works of Alexander Hamilton (Federal Edition)*, ed.Henry Cabot Lodge, vol. 7. New York: G. P. Putnam's Sons.

Hammond, C. 1996. *Julius Caesar: Seven Commentaries on the Gallic War with an Eighth Commentary by Aulus Hirtius.* Oxford: Oxford University Press.

Hanemann, W. 1685. *Quod in coelis sol, hoc in terra Caesar. Die Sonn bestrahlt und ziert das gantze firmament*, engraved portrait, s.l and s.n.

Hansen, G. C. 1967. "Nachlese zu Themistios," *Philologus* 111, 110–18.

Harbage, A. and Schoenbaum, S. (eds.). 1964. *Annals of English Drama, 975–1700.* Philadelphia: University of Pennsylvania Press.

Harmand, J. 1973. "Une composante scientifique du Corpus Caesarianum : le portrait de la Gaule dans le De Bello Gallico I–VII, 523–95," in *ANRW* 1.3, 523–95.

Harris, W. V. 1979. *War and Imperialism in Republican Rome 327–70 B.C.* Oxford: Clarendon Press.

Haug, W. 1982. "Das Bildprogramm im Sommerhaus von Runkelstein," in W. Haug, J. Heinzle, D. Huschenbett, and N.Ott (ed.), *Runkelstein. Die Wandmalereien des Sommerhauses.* Wiesbaden: L. Reichert, pp. 15–62, repr. in W. Haug, *Strukturen als Schlüssel zur Welt. Kleine Schriften zur Erzählliteratur des Mittelalters.* Tübingen: Niemeyer, 1989, pp. 687–708.

Havens, G. R. 1944. "Voltaire and English critics of Shakespeare," *Franco-American Pamphlets* 2 ser.16. New York: American Society of the French Legion of Honor.

Hay, L. 2002. "Measures of kingship in Layamon's Brut," in Rosamund Allen, Lucy Perry, and Jane Roberts (eds.), *Layamon: Contexts, Language and Interpretation.* London: King's College London, Centre for Late Antique and Medieval Studies, pp. 299–312.

Henderson, J. 1996. "XPDNC/Writing Caesar (*Bellum Civile*)," *CA* 15.2, 261–88.

Hendrickson, G. L. 1906. "The *De Analogia* of Julius Caesar," *CP* 1, 97–210.

Hendrickson, G. L. (ed. and trans.). 1971. *Cicero, Brutus.* London: Heinemann, and Cambridge, MA: Harvard University Press.

Herbert-Brown, G. 1994. *Ovid and the* Fasti. Oxford: Oxford University Press.

Herder, J. G. 1989. *Johann Gottfried Herder: Werke in zehn Bänden, vol. 6: Ideen zur Philosophie der Geschichte der Menschheit*, ed. M. Bollacher, J. Brummack, U. Gaier, G. E. Grimm, H. D. Irmscher, R. Smend, and R. Wisbert. Frankfurt-am-Main: Deutscher Klassiker Verlag.

Hering, W. 1963. *Die Recensio der Caesarhandschriften*. Berlin: Akademie-Verlag.

Herweg, M. 2002. Ludwigslied, De Heinrico, Annolied. *Die deutschen Zeitdichtungen des frühen Mittelalters im Spiegel ihrer wissenschaftlichen Rezeption und Erforschung.* Imagines Medii Aevi 13. Wiesbaden: Reichert.

Heskel, J. 1994. "Cicero as evidence for attitudes to dress in the Late Republic," in J. L. Sebesta and L. Bonfante (eds.), *The World of Roman Costume.* Madison: University of Wisconsin Press, pp. 133–45.

Higemone. 1698. *Die Grosse Kayser-Liebe: Oder der liebende Caesar: Aus der frantzösischen Sprache übersetzet*. Leipzig: Hülse.

Hine, H. 1978. "Livy's judgement on Marius (Seneca, *Natural Questions* 5.18.4; Livy, *Periocha* 80)," *LCM* 3, 83–7.

Historischer Entwurff Der Deutschen Reichs-Verfassung vor- bey- und nach- Seiner Kayser-Wahl, alter- und jetziger Zeiten, Nebst: Einer TABELLE, aller des Reichs-Fürsten und Stände, und einer genauen Verzeichnis aller Römischen Kayser, so wohl Occidentalischer als Orientalischer, sambt deren Nahmen, Vaterlande, Jahren oder Monathen ihrer Regierung, auch Art, Ort, und Zeit ihres Todes und Alters. Aus bewehrten Geschicht-Schreibern zusammen getragen, und bis auff den Tod Ihro Kayserl. Majestät CAROLI VI. fortgesetzt. 1741. Freystadt (= Breslau).

Holland, T. 2003. "What Bush can learn from the Romans," *New Statesman*, August 25: 20.

Holmes, S. 1982. "Two concepts of legitimacy: France after the Revolution," *Political Theory* 10.2, 165–83.

Holmes, T. Rice 1911. *Caesar's Conquest of Gaul*. Oxford: Clarendon Press.

Holmes, T. Rice 1923. *The Roman Republic and the Founder of the Empire*, 3 vols. Oxford: Clarendon Press. Repr. New York: Russell & Russell, 1967.

Holmes, T. Rice 1936. *Ancient Britain and the Invasions of Julius Caesar*. Oxford: Oxford University Press.

Hölscher, T. 1967. *Victoria Romana*. Mainz: Phillip von Zabern.

Horsfall, N. 1983. "Some problems in the 'Laudatio Turiae,'" *BICS* 30, 85–98.

Horsfall, N. 1995. "Rome without Spectacles," *Greece and Rome* 42, 49–56.

Horsfall, N. 1999. "The legionary as his own historian," *Anc. Soc.* 29.2, 107–17.

Horsfall, N. 2000. "Virgil, Aeneid 7: a commentary," *Mnemosyne* Supplement. Leiden/Boston/Cologne: Brill.

Housman, A. E. (ed.). 1927. *M. Annaei Lucani Belli Civilis Libri Decem*. Oxford: Blackwell.

How, W. W. 1926. *Cicero Select Letters*, vol. 2 Notes. Oxford: Clarendon Press.

Hunter, G. K. 1977. "A Roman thought: Renaissance attitudes to history exemplified in Shakespeare and Jonson," in Brian S. Lee (ed.), *An English Miscellany: Presented to W. S. Mackie*. Cape Town: Oxford University Press, pp. 93–118.

Huppert, G. 1973. *L'Idee de l'histoire parfaite*. Paris: Flamarion.

Huygens, R. C. B. (ed.). 1970. *Accessus ad auctores. Bernard d'Utrecht. Conrad d'Hirsau, Dialogus super auctores*. Leiden: Brill.

Ianziti, G. 1988. *Humanistic Historiography under the Sforzas: Politics and Propaganda in Fifteenth-Century Milan*. Oxford: Oxford University Press.

Ianziti, G. 1990. "Storiografia e contemporaneità. A proposito del *Rerum suo Tempore Gestarum Commentarius* di Leonardo Bruni," *Rinascimento* 30, 3–28.

Ianziti, G. 1992. "I *Commentarii*: appunti per la storia di un genere quattrocentesco," *Archivio Storico Italiano*, 150, 1029–63.

Ignatieff, M. 2003. "The burden," *New York Times Magazine*, 5 January.

Ihm, M. 1908. *C. Suetonii Tranquilli Opera* 1. Leipzig: Teubner. Repr. 1964, Stuttgart: Teubner.

Irigoin, J. 1987. "Histoire du texte des 'Œuvres morales' de Plutarque," in *Plutarque: Œuvres morales* 1.1. Paris: Les Belles Lettres, pp. ccxvii–cccxviii.

Jacoby, F. 1926. *Die Fragmente der griechischen Historiker*, part 2A. Berlin: Weidmannische Buchhandlung.

Jefferson, Thomas. 1954. *Notes on the State of Virginia*, ed. William Peden. Chapel Hill: University of North Carolina Press for the Institute of Early American History and Culture, Williamsburg, Virginia.

Jefferson, Thomas. 1999. *Political Writings*, ed. Joyce Appleby and Terence Ball. Cambridge: Cambridge University Press.

Jehne, M. 2000. "Caesar und die Krise von 47 v. Chr.," in Gianpaolo Urso (ed.), *L'ultimo Cesare. Scritti, riforme, progetti, poteri, congiure.* Rome: "L'Erma" di Bretschneider, pp. 151–73.

Jervis, A. 2001. "Gallia scripta: images of Gauls and Romans in Caesar's 'Bellum Gallicum.'" Dissertation, University of Pennsylvania.

Johansen, F. S. 1967. "Antichi ritratti di Caio Giulio Cesare nella scultura," *Analecta Romana* 4, 7–68 Tav. I–XXVII.

Johansen, F. S. 1971. "Ritratti marmorei e bronzei di Marco Vipsanio Agrippa," *Analecta Romana* 6, 17–48.

Johansen, F. S. 1987. "The portraits of Gaius Caesar: a review," in *Ancient Portraits in the J. Paul Getty Museum*, vol. 1, pp. 17–40.

John, C. 1876. "Die Enstehungsgeschichte der catilinarischen Verschwörung," *Jahrbücher für classische Philologie*, Supplementband 8.701–819. Leipzig: B. G. Teubner.

Johnson, C. 2004. *The Sorrows of Empire: Militarism, Secrecy, and the End of the Republic.* New York: Metropolitan Books.

Johnson, C. 2006. *Nemesis: The Last Days of the American Republic.* New York: Metropolitan Books.

Johnson, W. R. 1987. *Momentary Monsters: Lucan and his Heroes.* Ithaca, NY/London: Cornell University Press.

Jones, A. H. M. 1960. *Studies in Roman Government and Law.* Oxford: Blackwell.

Jones, C. P. 1966. "Towards a chronology of Plutarch's work," *JRS* 56, 61–74. Repr. in B. Scardigli (ed.), *Essays on Plutarch's Lives* (Oxford: Clarendon Press), pp. 95–123.

Jones, C. P. 1971. *Plutarch and Rome.* Oxford: Clarendon Press.

Jones, E. 1971. *Scenic Form in Shakespeare.* Oxford: Clarendon Press.

Jones, E. 1977. *The Origins of Shakespeare.* Oxford: Clarendon Press.

Jusserand, J. J. 1899. *Shakespeare in France under the Ancien Régime.* London: Unwin. First published in French, 1898.

Kagan, D. 2002. "Reaction to 'Bush's real goal in Iraq': Comparing America to ancient empires is 'ludicrous,'" *Atlantic Journal and Constitution*, October 6. Downloaded from Project for the New American Century website, www.newamericancentury.org, March 30, 2004.

Kagan, K. 2006. *The Eye of Command.* Ann Arbor: University of Michigan Press.

Kahn, C. 1997. *Roman Shakespeare: Warriors, Wounds and Women.* London: Routledge.

Kaiserchronik. 1892. Ed. Eduard Schröder. Monumenta Germaniae Historica, Deutsche Chroniken 1, 1. Hanover: Hahn. Repr. Berlin/Zurich, 1964.

Kamm, A. 2006. *Julius Caesar: A Life.* London: Routledge.

Kant, I. 1970. "An answer to the question: 'What is Enlightenment?'" in H. Reiss (ed.), *Kant: Political Writings.* Cambridge: Cambridge University Press, pp. 54–60.

Kaser, M. 1971. *Das römische Privatrecht* I, 2nd edn. Munich: C. H. Beck.

Kaster, R. A. (ed., trans., intro., and comm.). 1995. *Suetonius: De Grammaticis et rhetoribus.* Oxford: Clarendon Press.

Kaster, R. A. 2006. *Cicero: the Speech on Behalf of Publius Sestius.* Oxford: Oxford University Press.

Keegan, J. 1991. *The Face of Battle.* London: Pimlico. (First published 1976.)

Keitel, E. 1987. "Homeric antecedents to the *cohortatio* in the ancient historians," *Classical World* 80, 153–72.

Keller, J. and M. Mills. 2003. "'Empire' losing evil associations," *Deseret News*, April 27: A.01.

Kenney, E. J. 1968. "Review of E. Norden, *Kleine Schriften*," *Classical Review* n.s. 18, 105–7.

Ketcham, R. L. 1984. *Presidents above Party: The First American Presidency, 1789–1829*. Chapel Hill: University of North Carolina Press.

Kewes, P. 2002. "Julius Caesar in Jacobean England," *The Seventeenth Century* 17.2, 155–86.

Kienast, D. 1990. *Römische Kaisertabelle. Grundzüge einer römischen Kaiserchronologie*. Darmstadt: Wissenschaftliche Buchgesellschaft.

Kienast, D. 2001. "Augustus und Caesar," *Chiron* 31, 1–26.

Kierdorf, W. 1980. *Oratio Funebris*. Meisenheim am Glan: Hain.

Kimball, F. 2002. *The Capitol of Virginia*, ed. Jon Kukla, assisted by Martha Vick and Sarah Shields Driggs. Richmond: Library of Virginia.

Kistler, S. F. 1979. "The significance of the missing hero in Chapman's *Caesar and Pompey*," *Modern Language Quarterly* 40, 339–57.

Klippel, D. 1990. "The true concept of liberty: political theory in Germany in the second half of the eighteenth century," in E. Hellmuth (ed.), *The Transformation of Political Culture: England and Germany in the Late Eighteenth Century*. Oxford: Oxford University Press, pp. 447–66.

Klöckner, A. 1997. *Poseidon und Neptun. Zur Rezeption griechischer Götterbilder in der römischen Kunst*. Saarbrücken: Saarbrücker Drückerei und Verlag.

Klotz, A. 1910. *Caesarstudien*. Leipzig: Teubner.

Klotz, A. 1918. "Caesar als Schriftsteller," in *RE*, 10. Stuttgart, coll. 259–75.

Klotz, A. (ed.). 1950. *C. Iuli Caesaris Commentarii*, vol. 2: *Commentarii Belli Civilis*, 2nd edn. Leipzig: Teubner. Repr. with *addenda et corrigenda* by W. Trillitzsch, 1969.

Knight, G. W. 1931. *The Imperial Theme*. London: Methuen.

Koestermann, E. 1963–8. *Cornelius Tacitus: Annalen*. Heidelberg: C. Winter.

Köhler, J. D. 1767. *Kurzgefaßte und gründliche Teutsche Reichs=Historie vom Anfang des Teutschen Reichs mit König Ludwigen dem Teutschen bis auf den Badenschen Frieden. Mit allen accurat im Kupfer vorgestellten Königlichen und Kaiserlichen Hand=Zeichen oder MONOGRAMMATIBUS. Nunmehr nach des sel. Verfassers Tod vermehret und bis auf die neuesten Zeiten fortgesetzt*. Frankfurt-on-Main: Christoph Niegels seel. Wittib.

Komnick, H. 2001. *Die Restitutionsmünzen der frühen Kaiserzeit: Aspekte der Kaiserlegitimation*. Berlin and New York: De Gruyter.

Konstan, D. 1997. *Friendship in the Classical World*. Cambridge: Cambridge University Press.

Kornemann, E. 1896. "Die historische Schriftstellerei des C. Asinius Pollio," *Jahrbücher für classische Philologie*, Supplementband 22, 555–691.

Kraner, F., W. Dittenberger, and H. Meusel (eds.). 1960. *C. Iulii Caesaris Commentarii de Bello Gallico*, with contributions by H. Kiepert and H. Opperman, 3 vols. Hildesheim: Weidmann.

Kraner, F., Hofmann F., and Meusel H. (comm.). 1963. *C. Iulii Caesaris Commentarii De Bello Civili*, 13th updated edn, with a new epilogue by Hans Oppermann. Berlin: Weidmann.

Kraus, C. S. 2007. "Caesar's account of the Battle of Massilia (*BC* 1.34–2.22): some historiographical and narratological approaches," in J. M. Marincola (ed.), *A Companion to Greek and Roman Historiography*. Malden, MA/Oxford: Blackwell, pp. 371–8.

Krebs, C. B. 2006. "'Imaginary geography' in Caesar's Bellum Gallicum," *AJP* 127, 111–36.

Kreikenbom, D. 1992. *Griechische und römische Kolossalporträts bis zum späten ersten Jahrhundert n. Chr*. Berlin: De Gruyter.

Kunkel, W. (trans. J. M. Kelly). 1973. *An Introduction to Roman Legal and Constitutional History*, 2nd edn. Oxford: Clarendon Press.

Lacey, W. K. 1961. "The tribunate of Curio," *Historia* 10, 318–29.
Lahusen, G. 1983. *Untersuchungen zur Ehrenstatue in Rom: literarische und epigraphische Zeugnisse*. Rome: G. Bretschneider.
Lahusen, G. 1984. *Schriftquellen zum römischen Bildnis*. Bremen: B. C. Heye.
Lambrecht, U. 1984. *Herrscherbild und Principatsidee in Suetons Kaiserbiographien: Untersuchungen zur Caesar- and zur Augustus-Vita*. Bonn: R. Habelt.
Lapham, L. H. 2002. "Hail Caesar!" *Harper's Magazine* 305.1831, 9–11.
Las Cases, Emmanuel De. 1968. *Le Mémorial de Sainte-Hélène*. Preface by Jean Tulard. Paris: Points.
Last, H. 1944. "Cinnae quater consulis," *CR* 58, 15–17.
Last, H. 1948. "Sallust and Caesar in the 'Bellum Catilinae,'" in *Mélanges de philologie, de littérature et d'histoire anciennes offerts à J. Marouzeau*, pp. 355–69. Paris: Belles Lettres.
Lateiner, D. 2005. "Signifying names and other ominous accidental utterances in classical historiography," *GRBS* 45, 35–57.
Laurence, R. and J. Paterson. 1999. "Power and laughter: Imperial dicta," *PBSR* 67, 183–97.
Lausberg, M. 1985. "Lucan und Homer," *ANRW* 2.32.3, 1565–1622.
Layamon. 1995. *Brut, or, Hystoria Brutonum* (ed., trans., and comm. W. R. J. Barron and S. C. Weinberg). Harlow: Longman.
Leake, R. E. 1981. *Concordance des* Essais *de Montaigne*. Geneva: Droz.
Le Boeuffle, A. 1972. Astronomical introduction and notes in H. le Bonniec (ed.), *Pline: Histoire Naturelle XVIII*. Paris: Les Belles Lettres.
Le Bohec, Y. 2003. "César et la religion," in C. Alonso del Real et al. (eds.), *Urbs aeterna. Actas y colaboraciones del coloquio internacional "Roma entre la literatura y la historia." Homenaje a la profesora Carmen Castillo*. Pamplona: Ediciones Universidad de Navarra, pp. 543–51.
Lecky, W. E. H. 1981. *Democracy and Liberty*, vol. 1. Indianapolis: Liberty Fund.
Lecoq, A.-M. 1987. *François Ier imaginaire*. Paris: Macula.
Lee, G. (ed., intro., trans., and notes). 1990. *The Poems of Catullus*. Oxford: Clarendon Press.
Lefèvre, E. 1989. "Wielands Augustusbild," in K. Christ and E. Gabba, E. (eds.), *Römische Geschichte und Zeitgeschichte in der deutschen und italienischen Altertumswissenschaft während des 19. und 20. Jahrhunderts I: Caesar und Augustus*. Como: Biblioteca di Athenaeum, pp. 71–87.
Le Gall, J. 1999. *La Bataille d'Alesia*. Paris: Publications de Sorbonne.
Leggatt, A. 1981. *Ben Jonson: his Vision and his Art*. London/New York: Methuen.
Leggatt, A. 1988. *Shakespeare's Political Drama: the History Plays and the Roman Plays*. London/NY: Routledge.
Leigh, M. 1997. *Lucan: Spectacle and Engagement*. Oxford: Clarendon Press, pp. 158–233.
Leigh, M. 1999. "Lucan's Caesar and the sacred grove: deforestation and enlightenment in antiquity," in P. Esposito and L. Nicastri (eds.), *Interpretare Lucano. Miscellanea di studi*. Naples: Arte tipografica, pp. 167–205.
Lendon, J. E. 1999. "The rhetoric of combat: Greek military theory and Roman culture in Julius Caesar's battle descriptions," *CA* 18: 273–329.
Lenin, V. I. 1961. *Collected Works, vol. 38: Philosophical Notebooks*. London: Lawrence-Wishart.
Lepape, P. 1994. *Voltaire le Conquérant*. Paris: Éditions du Seuil.
LeTourneur, P. 1836. *Oeuvres de Shakspeare*. Paris. First published Paris, 1776–83.
Levick, B. 1978. "Antiquarian or revolutionary? Claudius Caesar's view of his Principate," *AJP* 99, 79–105.
Liebenroth, F. E. F. von. 1797. *Julius Cäsar oder der Sturz der Römischen Republik: Ein Pendant zum Fall der Französischen Monarchie*. Magdeburg: Georg Christian Keil.

Lightbown, R. 1986. *Mantegna: With a Complete Catalogue of the Paintings, Drawings and Prints*. Oxford: Phaidon–Christie's.

Lincoln, A. B. 1993. "La politica di mito e rito nel funerale di Giulia: Cesare debutta nella sua carriera," in D. Poli (ed.), *Cultura in Cesare: Atti del convegno internazionale di studi, Macerata-Matelica, 30 aprile–4 maggio 1990*, 2 vols. Rome: Il Calamo, pp. 387–96.

Linderski, J. 1995. *Roman Questions*. Stuttgart: Steiner Verlag.

Linderski, J. 2007. *Roman Questions II*. Stuttgart: Steiner Verlag.

Lintott, A. 1993. *Imperium Romanum: Politics and Administration*. London: Routledge.

Lintott, A. 1999a. *The Constitution of the Roman Republic*. Oxford: Clarendon Press.

Lintott, A. 1999b. *Violence in Republican Rome*, 2nd edn. Oxford: Oxford University Press.

Lintott, A. 2008. *Cicero as Evidence: A Historian's Companion*. Oxford: Oxford University Press.

Liou-Gille, B. 1999. "César, *flamen dialis destinatus*," *REA* 101, 433–59.

Liska, G. 1978. *Career of Empire: America and Imperial Expansion over Land and Sea*. Baltimore: Johns Hopkins University Press.

Litto, F. M. 1966. "Addison's Cato in the Colonies," *William and Mary Quarterly* 23.3, 431–49.

Long, J. 2006. "Julian Augustus' Julius Caesar," in Maria Wyke (ed.), *Julius Caesar in Western Culture*. Oxford: Blackwell, pp. 62–82.

Lossmann, F. 1957. "Zur literarischen Kritik Suetons in den Kapiteln 55 und 56 der Caesar-vita," *Hermes* 85, 47–58.

Lounsbury, Thomas J. 1902. *Shakespeare and Voltaire*. New York/London: Benjamin Blom. Reissued 1968.

Lucan. 1992. *Civil War* (trans., intro., and notes S. H. Braund). Oxford: Clarendon Press.

Luther, M. 1982. *Studienausgabe*, ed. Hans-Ulrich Delius. Berlin: Evangelische Verlagsanstalt.

Lutz, D. S. 1984. "The relative influence of European writers on late eighteenth-century American political thought," *American Political Science Review*, 189–97.

Lutz, D. S. 1988. *The Origins of American Constitutionalism*. Baton Rouge/London: Louisiana State University Press.

Lyons, M. 1994. *Napoleon Bonaparte and the Legacy of the French Revolution*. Basingstoke : Macmillan.

Mably, G. B. de. 1751. *Observations sur les romains*. Geneva: Compagnies des Libraires.

MacCallum, M. W. 1910. *Shakespeare's Roman Plays and their Background*. London: Russell & Russell.

Macey, S. L. 1971–2. "The introduction of Shakespeare into Germany in the second half of the eighteenth century," *Eighteenth-Century Studies* 5.2, 261–9.

Macfarlane, R. T. 1996. "*Ab inimicis incitatus*: on dating the composition of Caesar's *Bellum Civile*," *Syllecta Classica* 7, 107–32.

Machiavelli, N. 1965. *The Art of War*, rev. trans. E. Farneworth: Indianapolis/New York/Kansas City: Bobbs-Merrill.

Machiavelli, N. 1988. *Florentine Histories*, trans. L. F. Banfield and H. C. Mansfield. Princeton, NJ: Princeton University Press.

Machiavelli, N. 2003. *Discourses on Livy*, trans. J. Conway Bondanella and P. Bondanella. Oxford: Oxford University Press.

Machiavelli, N. 2005. *The Prince*, trans. P. Bondanella, intro. M. Viroli. Oxford: Oxford University Press.

MacMullen, R. 1984. "The legion as society," *Historia* 33, 440–56.

Magnino, D. 1993. "Le 'Guerre Civili' di Appiano," *ANRW* 2.34.1, 523–54.

Maine, H. S. 1976. *Popular Government*. Indianapolis: Liberty Fund.

Malamud, M. 2006. "Manifest Destiny and the eclipse of Julius Caesar," in Maria Wyke (ed.), *Julius Caesar in Western Culture*. Oxford: Blackwell, pp. 148–69.

Malcovati, E. 1967. *Imperatoris Caesaris Augusti operum fragmenta*, 4th edn. Augusta Taurinorum: In aedibus Io. Bapt. Paraviae et sociorum.

Malitz, J. 1987. "Die Kalenderreform Caesars. Ein Beitrag zur Geschichte seiner Spätzeit," *Anc. Soc.* 18, 103–31.

Mansel, P. 1988. *The Court of France, 1789–1830*. Cambridge: Cambridge University Press.

Manuwald, B. 1979. *Cassius Dio und Augustus*. Palingenesia 14. Wiesbaden: Steiner.

Marchesi, C. 1936. *Storia della letteratura latina*, 4th edn. Milan: Principato. First published 1924.

Margolin, J.-C. 1985. "Glaréan, commentateur du *De bello gallico*," in R. Chevallier (ed.), *Présence de César. Actes du colloque des 9–11 décembre 1983: Hommage au doyen Michel Rambaud*. Paris: Les Belles Lettres, pp. 183–212.

Marincola, J. M. 1997. *Authority and Tradition in Ancient Historiography*. Cambridge: Cambridge University Press.

Marincola, J. M. (ed.). 2007. *A Companion to Greek and Roman Historiography*, 2 vols. London: Blackwell.

Marinoni, E. "Cesare al Rubicone. L'elemento soprannaturale," in Michelotto, P. G. (ed.), λόγιος ἀνήρ. *Studi di antichità in memoria di Mario Attilio Levi*. Milan: Cisalpino. 2002, pages 277–85.

Marshall, B. A. 1976. *Crassus: A Political Biography*. Amsterdam: Adolf M. Hakkert.

Marshall, L. L. 1967. "The strange stillbirth of the Whig party," *American Historical Review* 72.2, 445–68.

Martellotti, G. 1947. "Petrarca e Cesare," *Annali della Scuola normale superiore di Pisa*, s. 2, 16, 149–58. Repr. in G. Martellotti, *Scritti petrarcheschi*, ed. M. Feo and S. Rizzo (Padua: Antenore, 1983), pp. 77–89.

Martellotti, G. 1974a. "Alcuni aspetti della filologia del Petrarca," *Lettere italiane* 26, 288–96. Repr. in G. Martellotti, *Scritti petrarcheschi*, ed. M. Feo and S. Rizzo (Padua: Antenore, 1983), pp. 538–48.

Martellotti, G. 1974b. "Il *De gestis Cesaris* del Petrarca nel *Corpus Caesarianum*," *Italia Medioevale e Umanistica* 17, 281–311. Repr. in G. Martellotti, *Scritti petrarcheschi*, ed. M. Feo and S. Rizzo (Padua: Antenore, 1983), pp. 424–56.

Martellotti, G. 1975. "'Inter colles Euganeos': le ultime fatiche letterarie del Petrarca," in G. Billanovich and G. Frasso (eds), *Il Petrarca ad Arquà*. Padua: Antenore, pp. 165–75. Repr. in G. Martellotti, *Scritti petrarcheschi*, ed. M. Feo and S. Rizzo (Padua: Antenore, 1983), pp. 457–67.

Martellotti, G. 1976. "Storiografia del Petrarca," *Convegno internazionale Francesco Petrarca (Roma-Arezzo-Padova-Arquà, 24–27 aprile 1974)*. Rome: Accademia dei Lincei. Repr. in G. Martellotti, *Scritti petrarcheschi*, ed. M. Feo and S. Rizzo (Padua: Antenore, 1983), 475–86

Martellotti, G. 1983. *Scritti petrarcheschi*, ed. M. Feo and S. Rizzo. Padua: Antenore.

Martindale, C. and M. 1990. *Shakespeare and the Uses of Antiquity*. London/New York: Routledge.

Martindale, C. and Taylor A. B. (eds.). 2004. *Shakespeare and the Classics*. Cambridge: Cambridge University Press.

Martinez, A. 2004. "One speech trumps a whole state," *Los Angeles Times*, January 23: E/19.

Marx, K. 1987. *Collected Works*, vol. 41. London: Lawrence & Wishart.

Marx, K. and F. Engels. 2005. *Gesamtausgabe Band XI*. Amsterdam: Akademie Verlag.

Masters, J. 1992. *Poetry and Civil War in Lucan's Bellum Civile*. Cambridge: Cambridge University Press.

Mattern, S. P. 1999. *Rome and the Enemy: Imperial Strategy in the Principate.* Berkeley: University of California Press.

Mauricius von Craûn. 1999. Ed., trans., and comm. Dorothea Klein. Stuttgart: Reclam.

Maus, K. E. 1984. *Ben Jonson and the Roman Frame of Mind.* Princeton, NJ: Princeton University Press.

May, J. 1988. *Trials of Character: the Eloquence of Ciceronian Ethos.* Chapel Hill: University of North Carolina Press.

McCall, J. 2002. *Cavalry of the Roman Republic: Cavalry Combat and Elite Reputations in the Middle and Late Republic.* London/New York: Routledge.

McDermott, W. C. 1983. "Mamurra, *eques Formianus*," *Rh.Mus.* 126, 292–307.

McGrory, M. 2002. "That's presidential," *Pittsburgh Post-Gazette*, February 2: A/11.

McHenry, J. 1906. "Papers of Dr. James McHenry on the Federal Convention of 1787," *American Historical Review* 11.3, 595–624.

McIlwain, C. H. 1947. *Constitutionalism Ancient and Modern.* Ithaca, NY: Cornell University Press.

McLaughlin, M. L. 1995. *Literary Imitation in the Italian Renaissance: the Theory and Practice of Literary Imitation from Dante to Bembo.* Oxford: Clarendon Press.

McNamee, L. F. 1959. "The first production of *Julius Caesar* on the German stage," *Shakespeare Quarterly* 10, 409–21.

Megow, W. R. 2005. *Republikanische Bildnistypen.* Frankfurt am Main: P. Lang.

Meier, C. 1961. "Zur Chronologie und Politik in Caesars ersten Konsulat," *Historia*, 10, 68–98.

Meier, C. 1966. *Res Publica Amissa: Eine Studie zu Verfassung und Geschichte der späten römischen Republik.* Wiesbaden: Franz Steiner Verlag.

Meier, C. 1982. *Caesar.* Berlin: Severin und Siedler. (Translated into English by David McLintock.)

Meier, C. 1995. *Caesar* (trans. David McLintock). New York: Basic Books, and London: HarperCollins. Original published 1982.

Melber, J. 1885. "Über die Quellen und den Wert der Strategemensammlung Polyaens. Ein Beitrag zur griechischen Historiographie," *Jahrbücher der classischen Philologie*, Supplement-Band 14. Leipzig: Teubner, pp. 415–668 (also published separately as a monograph).

Melchior, A. A. 2004. "Compositions with blood: violence in Late Republican prose." Dissertation, University of Pennsylvania.

Méniel, B. and Ribémont B. (eds.). 2006. *La Figure de Jules César au Moyen Âge et à la Renaissance.* Cahiers de Recherches Médiévales 13.

Merten, D. 1987. "Friedrich der Große und Montesquieu – zu den Anfängen des Rechtsstaats im 18. Jahrhundert," in W. Blümel, D. Merten., and H. Quaritsch (eds.), *Verwaltung im Rechtsstaat, Festschrift für Carl Hermann Ule zum 80. Geburtstag.* Cologne: Heymanns Verlag, pp. 189–208.

Meyer, E. 1918. *Caesars Monarchie und das Principat des Pompejus: innere Geschichte Roms von 66 bis 44 v. Chr.* Stuttgart/Berlin: Cotta.

Meyer, E. 1922. *Caesars Monarchie und das Principat des Pompejus*, 3rd edn. Stuttgart: Cotta.

Meyer, F. S. 1957. "Principles and heresies. America: no Imperial Rome," *National Review* 4.10, 233.

Michel, D. 1967. *Alexander als Vorbild für Pompeius, Caesar und Marcus Antonius: Archäologische Untersuchungen.* Brussels: Latomus, Revue d'études latines.

Michels, A. K. 1967. *The Calendar of the Roman Republic.* Princeton, NJ: Princeton University Press.

Miles, E. A. 1968. "The Whig party and the menace of Caesar," *Tennessee Historical Quarterly* 27, 361–79.

Miles, G. B. 1989. "How Roman are Shakespeare's 'Romans'?" *Shakespeare Quarterly* 40, 257–83.

Millar, F. 1964. *A Study of Cassius Dio*. Oxford: Clarendon Press.

Millar, F. 1998. *The Crowd in Rome in the Late Republic*. Ann Arbor: University of Michigan Press.

Miller, A. 1990. "Thomas Cole and Jacksonian America: *The Course of Empire* as political allegory," *Prospects* 14, 65–92.

Miller, A. S. 1981. *Democratic Dictatorship: the Emergent Constitution of Control*. Westport, CT: Greenwood Press.

Miniconi, P.-J. 1951. *Étude des thèmes "guerriers" de la poésie épique gréco-romaine*. Paris: Presses Universitaires de France.

Minnis, A. 1988. *Medieval Theory of Authorship: Scholastic Literary Attitudes in the Later Middle Ages*, 2nd edn. Aldershot: Wildwood House.

Minyard, J.-D. 1971. "Critical notes on Catullus 29," *CP* 66, 174–81.

Miola, R. S. 1985. "*Julius Caesar* and the tyrannicide debate," *Renaissance Quarterly* 38, 271–89.

Mitchell, T. N. 1969. "Cicero before Luca (September 57–April 56 B.C.)," *TAPA* 100, 295–320.

Mitchell, T. N. 1979. *Cicero: The Ascending Years*. New Haven, CT: Yale University Press.

Mitchell, T. N. 1991. *Cicero: the Senior Statesman*. New Haven, CT: Yale University Press.

Moatti, C. 1997. *La Raison de Rome: Naissance de l'esprit critique à la fin de la République*. Paris: Éditions du Seuil.

Moles, J. 1998. "Cry freedom: Tacitus Annals 4.32–35," *Histos* 2, 1–54.

Molnar, T. 1966. "Imperial America," *National Review* 18.18, 409–11.

Mommsen, Theodor. 1894. *The History of Rome* (trans. William Purdie Dickson). London: Richard Bentley.

Mommsen, Theodor. 1904. *Römische Geschichte*, 9th edn. Berlin: Weidmannsche Buchhandlung. Originally published 1854–6.

Mommsen, T. 1996. *A History of Rome under the Emperors* (trans. C. Krojzl). London: Routledge. Original published as *Römische Kaisergeschichte. Nach den Vorlesungs-Mitschriften von Sebastian und Paul Hensel 1882/86*, ed. B. and A. Demandt. Munich: Beck, 1992.

Monson, C. 1985. "*Giulio Cesare in Egitto* from Sartorio (1677) to Handel (1724)," *Music and Letters* 66, 313–43.

Montaigne, M. de. 1965, 1983. *Essais*, ed. Pierre Villey. Paris: Presses Universitaires de France.

Montero, S. 2000. "Los prodigios en la vida del ultimo Cesar," in Gianpaolo Urso (ed.), *L'ultimo Cesare. Scritti, riforme, progetti, poteri, congiure*. Rome: "L'Erma" di Bretschneider, pp. 231–44.

Montesquieu, C. S. de. 1957. *Betrachtungen über die Ursachen von Größe und Niedergang der Römer. Mit den Randbemerkungen Friedrichs des Großen*. Bremen: Carl Schünemann.

Montesquieu, C. S. de. 1965. *Considerations on the Causes of the Greatness of the Romans and Their Decline*, trans. David Lowenthal. New York: The Free Press.

Montesquieu, C. S. de. 2000. "Considérations sur les causes de la grandeur des romains et de leur décadence," in C. S. de Montesquieu, *Oeuvres complètes de Montesquieu*, vol. 2. Oxford/ Naples: Voltaire Foundation/ istituto Italiano per gli studi filosofici, pp. 1–318.

Montoya, A. 2002. "Caesar the father in Marie-Anne Barbier's *La Mort de César* (1709)," in Karl A. Enenkel, J. L. de Jong, and J. de Landtheer (eds.), *Recreating Ancient History*. Boston/Leiden: Brill. pp. 319–37.

Morgan, L. 1997. "*Achilleae comae*: hair and heroism according to Domitian," *Classical Quarterly* 47, 209–14.
Morgan, L. 2000. "The autopsy of C. Asinius Pollio," *JRS* 90, 51–69.
Morstein-Marx, R. 2004. *Mass Oratory and Political Power in the Late Roman Republic.* Cambridge: Cambridge University Press.
Morstein-Marx, R. 2007. "Caesar's alleged fear of prosecution and his *ratio absentis* in the approach to the Civil War," *Historia* 56, 159–78.
Morstein-Marx, R. 2008. "*Dignitas* and *res publica*: Caesar and Republican legitimacy," in K.-J. Hölkeskamp (ed.), *Eine politische Kultur (in) der Krise? Die "letzte Generation" der römischen Republik.* Munich: Oldenbourg.
Morstein-Marx, R. and N. Rosenstein. 2006. "The transformation of the Republic," in Nathan Rosenstein and Robert Morstein-Marx (eds.), *A Companion to the Roman Republic.* Malden, MA/Oxford: Blackwell, pp. 625–37.
Mosci Sassi, M. G. 1983. *Il sermo castrensis.* Bologna: Patrón.
Mossman, J. M. 1988. "Tragedy and epic in Plutarch's *Alexander*," *JHS* 108, 83–93. Repr. in B. Scardigli (ed.), *Essays on Plutarch's Lives* (Oxford: Clarendon Press, 1995), pp. 209–28.
Mouchova, B. 1968. *Studie zu Kaiserbiographien Suetons.* Prague: Charles University.
Muhlack, U. 1991. *Geschichtswissenschaft im Humanismus und in der Aufklärung: Die Vorgeschichte des Humanismus.* Munich: Beck.
Mulgan, R. G. 1979. "Was Caesar an Epicurean?" *CW* 72, 337–9.
Münzer, F. 1920. *Römische Adelsparteien und Adelsfamilien.* Stuttgart: Metzler. Translated into English by T. Ridley as *Roman Aristocratic Parties and Families* (Baltimore: Johns Hopkins University Press: 1999).
Murphy, C. 2007. *Are we Rome? The Fall of an Empire and the Fate of America.* Boston: Houghton Mifflin Co.
Mutschler, F. H. 1975. *Erzählstil und Propaganda in Caesars Kommentarien.* Heidelberg: Winter.
Napoléon I. 1836. *Précis des guerres de Jules César*, écrit par M. Marchand à l'île Sainte-Hélène sous la dictée de l'empereur; suivi de plusieurs fragments inédits. Paris: Gosselin.
Napoléon III. 1865–6. *Histoire de Jules César*, 3 vols. Paris: Imprimerie impériale.
Narducci, E. 1983. "Pauper Amyclas. Modelli etici e poetici in un episodio della *Pharsalia*," *Maia* 35, 183–94.
Narducci, E. 2002. *Lucano. Un'epica contro l'impero.* Rome/Bari: GLF editori Laterza.
Németh, B. 1984. "Death of Cotta and date of Lucretius' De Rerum Natura," *Acta Classica Univ. Scient. Debrecen* 20, 39–41.
Nicolaus of Damascus. 1999. *Life of Caesar*, in F. Jacoby, *Die Fragmente der griechischen Historiker* IIA, no. 90, frr. 125–30.
Nicolet, C. 1991. *Space, Geography, and Politics in the Early Roman Empire* (trans. Hélène Leclerc). Ann Arbor: University of Michigan Press. Original published as *L'Inventaire du monde: geographie et politique aux origines de l'Empire romain* (Paris 1988).
Nicolet, C. 2003. *La Fabrique d'une nation. La France entre Rome et les Germains.* Paris: Perrin.
Nisbet, R. (ed.). 1961. Cicero, *In L. Calpurnium Pisonem oratio.* Oxford: Oxford University Press.
Noak, B. 2002. "The Dutch Republic between hauteur and greed: Lambert van den Bosch and his drama *L. Catilina*," in Karl A. Enenkel, Jan L. De Jong, and Jeanine De Landtsheer (eds.), *Recreating Ancient History.* Boston/Leiden: Brill, pp. 339–56.
North, J. A. 1975. "Praesens Divus," *JRS* 65, 171–7.
North, J. A. 2008. "Caesar at the Lupercalia," *JRS* 98, 144–60.
Nosarti, L. 2002–3. "Quale Cesare in Lucano?" *AClass* 38–9, 169–203.

Nousek, D. L. 2004. "Narrative style and genre in Caesar's *Bellum Gallicum.*" Dissertation, Rutgers University.

Oakley, S. P. 1997. *A Commentary on Livy Books VI–X. Vol. I: Introduction and Book VI.* Oxford: Oxford University Press.

Odelman, E. 1972. "Études sur quelques reflets du style administratif chez César." Dissertation, Stockholm University.

O'Hara, J. J. 1990. *Death and the Optimistic Prophecy in Vergil's* Aeneid. Princeton, NJ: Princeton University Press.

O'Hara, J. J. 2007. *Inconsistency in Roman Epic: Studies in Catullus, Lucretius, Vergil, Ovid and Lucan.* Cambridge: Cambridge University Press.

Oldfather, W. A. and G. Bloom. 1927. "Caesar's grammatical theories and his own practice," *AJP* 48, 584–602.

Oldsjö, F. 2001. *Tense and Aspect in Caesar's Narrative.* Uppsala: Uppsala University Library.

Oppermann, H. 1933. *Caesar, der Schriftsteller und sein Werk.* Leipzig: Teubner.

Osgood, J. 2006. *Caesar's Legacy: Civil War and the Emergence of the Roman Empire.* Cambridge: Cambridge University Press.

Ott, N. 1993. "Neun gute Helden," *Lexikon des Mittelalters*, VI, c. 1104–6.

Ottmer, H. M. 1979. *Die Rubikon-Legende: Untersuchungen zu Caesars und Pompeius' Strategie vor und nach Ausbruch des Bürgerkrieges.* Boppard: Harald Boldt.

Pade, M. 1990. "Guarino and Caesar at the court of the Este," in M. Pade, L. Waage Petersen, and D. Quarta (eds.), *La corte di Ferrara e il suo mecenatismo, 1441–1598. The Court of Ferrara and its Patronage.* Copenhagen/Modena: Museum Tusculanum/Panini, pp. 71–91.

Pailler, J. M. 1988. *Bacchanalia. La repression de 186 av. J.-C. à Rome et en Italie.* Paris: de Boccard.

Paine, Thomas. 1989. "Common sense," in Bruce Kuklick (ed.), *Political Writings.* Cambridge: Cambridge University Press, pp. 3–45.

Paladino, I. 1994. "Cesare e Iuppiter," in G. Sfameni (ed.), Ἀγαθὴ ἐλπίς: *Studi storico-religiosi in onore di Ugo Bianchi.* Rome: L'Erma di Bretschneider, pp. 187–95.

Palmer, R. R. 1953. "Notes on the use of the word 'democracy' 1789–1799," *Political Science Quarterly* 68.2, 203–26.

Pape, M. 1975. "Griechische Kunstwerke aus Kriegsbeute und ihre öffentliche Aufstellung in Rom" Dissertation, Hamburg University.

Papini, M. 2004. *Antichi volti della Repubblica: la ritrattistica in Italia centrale tra IV e II secolo A.C.* Rome: L'Erma di Bretschneider.

Parker, G. 1997. *The General Crisis of the Seventeenth Century*, 2nd edn. London: Routledge.

Pastore Stocchi, M. 1971. "Cesare, Giulio," in *Enciclopedia Dantesca*, vol. 3. Rome: Treccani, pp. 221–4.

Patrizi, F. 1594. *Paralleli militari.* Rome: Luigi Zannetti.

Paul, E. and C. (trans.). 1932. *Talks with Mussolini.* London: George Allen & Unwin. Original published as Emil Ludwig, *Colloqui con Mussolini* (Milan: Mondadori, 1932).

Paul, G. M. 1982. "*Urbs capta*: sketch of an ancient literary motif," *Phoenix* 36, 144–55.

Paulin, R. 2003. *The Critical Reception of Shakespeare in Germany 1682–1914: Native Literature and Foreign Genius.* Hildesheim: Olms.

Peachin, M. 2001. *Aspects of Friendship in the Graeco-Roman World.* Portsmouth, RI: Journal of Roman Archaeology.

Pellegrini, G. 1957. "The Roman plays of Shakespeare in Italy," *Italica* 34.4, 228–33.

Pelling, C. 1981. "Caesar's battle-descriptions and the defeat of Ariovistus," *Latomus* 40, 741–66.

Pelling, C. 1997. "Tragical dreamer: some dreams in Roman historians," *Greece and Rome* 44, 197–213.

Pelling, C. 1997. "Plutarch on Caesar's fall," in Judith M. Mossman (ed.), *Plutarch and his Intellectual World*. Swansea: Classical Press of Wales, pp. 215–31.

Pelling, C. 2002 "Plutarch's *Caesar*: A *Caesar* for the Caesars," in Philip A. Stadter and Luc van der Stockt, *Sage and Emperor: Plutarch, Greek Intellectuals, and Roman Power in the Time of Trajan (98–117 A.D.)*. Leuven: Leuven University Press.

Pelling, C. 2002. *Plutarch and History*. Classical Press of Wales.

Pelling, C. 2006a. "Breaking the bounds: writing about Caesar," in J. Mossman and B. C. McGing (eds.), *The Limits of Biography*. Swansea: Classical Press of Wales, pp. 255–79.

Pelling, C. 2006b. "Judging Julius Caesar," in M. Wyke (ed.), *Julius Caesar in Western Culture*. Oxford: Blackwell, pp. 3–26.

Petrarca, F. 1827. *Historia Iulii Caesaris*, ed. C. E. C. Schneider. Leipzig: Fleischer.

Petrarca, F. 1926. *Africa*, ed. N. Festa. Florence: Sansoni.

Petrarca, F. 1992. *Letters of Old Age. "Rerum Senilium Libri I–XVIII"* (trans. A. S. Bernardo, S. Levin, and R. A. Bernardo), 2 vols. Baltimore/London: Johns Hopkins University Press.

Petrarca, F. 1994. *Lettere disperse*, ed. A. Pancheri. Parma: Guanda.

Petrarca, F. 1996. *Trionfi, Rime estravaganti, Codice degli abbozzi*, ed. V. Pacca and L. Paolino. Milan: Mondadori.

Petrarca, F. 2003. *De gestis Cesaris*, ed. G. Crevatin. Pisa: Scuola normale superiore di Pisa.

Petrarca, F. 2004. *Canzoniere*, ed. M. Santagata, rev. edn. Milan: Mondadori.

Peyrefitte, R. 1992. *Voltaire et Frédéric II*. Paris: Albin Michel.

Picard, G. C. 1977. "César et les Druides," in *Hommage à la mémoire de Jérôme Carcopino*. Paris: Les Belles Lettres, pp. 227–33.

Pigler, A. 1994. *Barockthemen: Eine Auswahl von Verzeichnissen zur Ikonographie des 17. und 18. Jahrhunderts*. Budapest: Akadémiai Kiadó.

Pocock, J. G. A. 1987. *The Ancient Constitution and the Feudal Law: a Study of English Historical Thought in the Seventeenth Century*. Cambridge: Cambridge University Press. First published 1957.

Poli, D. 1993. *Cultura in Cesare: Atti del convegno internazionale di studi, Macerata-Matelica, 30 aprile–4 maggio 1990*, 2 vols. Rome: Il Calamo.

Poliziano, A. 1978. *Miscellaneorum Centuria Secunda. Editio Minor*, ed. V. Branca and M. Pastore Stocchi. Florence: Olschki.

Poliziano, A. 2006. *Letters*, ed. and trans. S. Butler, vol. 1: books I–IV. Cambridge, MA: Harvard University Press.

Pollini, J. 1990. "Man or God: Divine assimilation and interpretation in the late republic and early principate," in K. A. Raaflaub and M. Toher (eds.), *Between Republic and Empire: Interpretations of Augustus and his Principate*. Berkeley, CA: University of California Press, pp. 334–63.

Pontano, G. 1944. *Dialoghi*, ed. C. Previtera. Florence: Sansoni.

Pöschl, V. 1981. "Gundolf's Caesar," *Euphorion* 75.2, 204–16. (The whole issue is a commemoration volume for Gundolf.)

Potter, D. 1998. "Caesar and the Helvetians" in A. Powell and Kathryn Welch (eds), *Julius Caesar as Artful Reporter: the War Commentaries as Political Instruments*. London: Duckworth, and Swansea: Classical Press of Wales.

Powell, J. G. F. 1995. "Friendship and its problems in Greek and Roman thought," in D. Innes, H. Hine, and C. B. R. Pelling (eds.), *Ethics and Rhetoric: Classical Essays for Donald Russell on his Seventy-Fifth Birthday*. Oxford: Clarendon Press, pp. 31–45.

Prestowitz, D. 2003. "The new American empire?" *Knight Ridder Tribune News Service*, June 18: 1.

Price, S. R. F. 1986. "The future of dreams: from Freud to Artemidorus," *Past and Present* 113, 3–37.

Pucci Ben Zeev, M. 1998. *Jewish Rights in the Roman World*. Tübingen: Mohr.

Raaflaub, K. 1974a. *Dignitatis contentio. Studien zur Motivation und politischen Taktik im Bürgerkrieg zwischen Caesar und Pompeius*. Munich: Beck.

Raaflaub, K. 1974b. "Zum politischen Wirken der caesarfreundlichen Volkstribunen am Vorabend des Bürgerkrieges," *Chiron* 4, 293–326.

Raaflaub, K. 2003. "Caesar the liberator? Factional politics, civil war, and ideology," in Francis Cairns and Elaine Fantham (eds.), *Caesar against Liberty? Perspectives on His Autocracy*. Cambridge: Francis Cairns, pp. 35–67.

Raaflaub, K. 2007. "Caesar und Augustus als Retter römischer Freiheit?" in Ernst Baltrusch (ed.), *Caesar*. Darmstadt: Wissenschaftliche Buchgesellschaft, pp. 229–61.

Raaflaub, K. (forthcoming). "Creating a grand coalition of true Roman citizens: on Caesar's political strategy in the *Bellum civile*," in Brian W. Breed, Cynthia Damon, and Andreola Rossi (eds.), *"See How I Rip Myself!" Rome and Its Civil Wars*. New York/Oxford: Oxford University Press.

Radin, M. 1918. "The date of composition of Caesar's Gallic War," *CP* 13, 283–300.

Rajak, T. 1984. "Was there a Roman charter for the Jews?" *JRS* 74, 107–23.

Ramage, E. S. 1985. "Augustus' treatment of Julius Caesar," *Historia* 34, 223–45.

Ramage, E. S. 1987. *The Nature and Purpose of Augustus' "Res gestae."* Stuttgart: Franz Steiner Verlag Wiesbaden.

Ramage, E. S. 2006. "Funeral eulogy and propaganda in the Roman Republic," *Athenaeum* 94, 39–64.

Rambaud, M. 1966. *L'Art de la déformation historique dans les Commentaires de César*. Paris: Les Belles Lettres.

Rambaud, M. 1969. "César et l'epicurisme." In *Actes du VIIIe congrès de l'association G. Budé*, pp. 411–35. Paris: Les Belles Lettres.

Rambaud, M. 1974. "L'espace dans le récit césarien," in R. Chevallier (ed.), *Littérature gréco-romaine et géographie historique. Mélanges offerts à Roger Dion*. Caesarodunum 9 bis. Paris: Picard, pp. 111–29.

Ramminger, J. 2005. "A commentary? Ermolao Barbaro's supplement to Dioscorides," in M. Pade (ed.), *On Renaissance Commentaries*. Hildesheim/Zurich/New York: Olms, pp. 65–85.

Ramsey, J. T. and A. Licht. 1997. *The Comet of 44 B.C. and Caesar's Funeral Games*. American Classical Studies 39. Atlanta, GA: Scholars Press.

Rasmussen, D. 1963. *Caesars Commentarii. Stil und Stilwandel am Beispiel der direkten Rede*. Gottingen: Vandenhoeck & Ruprecht.

Raven, J. 2004. "The resonances of loss," in J. Raven (ed.), *Lost Libraries: The Destruction of Great Book Collections since Antiquity*. Basingstoke/New York: Palgrave Macmillan.

Rawson, E. D. 1975. "Architecture and sculpture: the activities of the Cossutii," *PBSR* 43, 36–47.

Rawson, E. D. 1978. "Caesar, Etruria and the *disciplina Etrusca*," *JRS* 68, 132–46.

Rawson, E. D. 1985. *Intellectual Life in the Late Roman Republic*. Baltimore: Johns Hopkins University Press.

Rawson, E. D. 1994. "Caesar: civil war and dictatorship," in *Cambridge Ancient History*, vol. 9, 2nd edn. Cambridge: Cambridge University Press, pp. 464–73.

Redekop, B. W. 2000. *Enlightenment and Community: Lessing, Abbt, Herder, and the Quest for a German Public.* Montreal: McGill-Queen's University Press.

Reggi, G. 2002. "Cesare, *De Bello Civili*, III 105, 3–6," *PP* 57, 216–26.

Reiss, T. 2005. *The Orientalist: In Search of a Man Caught between East and West.* London: Chatto & Windus.

Reynolds, L. D. (ed.). 1986. *Texts and Transmission: A Survey of the Latin Classics.* Oxford: Oxford University Press.

Reynolds, L. D. and N. G. Wilson. 1991. *Scribes and Scholars: a Guide to the Transmission of Greek and Latin Literature*, 3rd edn. Oxford: Clarendon Press.

Richard, C. J. 1994. *The Founders and the Classics: Greece, Rome, and the American Enlightenment.* Cambridge, MA: Harvard University Press.

Richards, E. G. 1998. *Mapping Time: the Calendar and its History.* Oxford: Oxford University Press.

Richter, M. 1982. "Toward a concept of political illegitimacy: Bonapartist dictatorship and democratic legitimacy," *Political Theory* 10.2, 185–214.

Richter, W. 1977. *Caesar als Darsteller seiner Taten.* Heidelberg: Winter.

Richtsteig, E. 1923. *Index Nominum Propriorum* = vol. 12 of *Libanii Opera*, ed. R. Förster. Leipzig: Teubner.

Ridley, R. T. 2000. "The Dictator's mistake: Caesar's escape from Sulla," *Historia*, 211–29.

Riencourt, A. de. 1957. *The Coming Caesars.* New York: Coward-McCann.

Riencourt, A. de (1968). *The American Empire.* New York: Dial Press.

Riggsby, A. 2004. "The rhetoric of character in the Roman courts," in J. Powell and J. Paterson (eds.), *Cicero the Advocate.* Oxford: Oxford University Press, pp. 165–85.

Riggsby, A. M. 2006. *Caesar in Gaul and Rome: War in Words.* Austin: University of Texas Press.

Ripley, J. 1980. *Julius Caesar on Stage in England and America, 1599–1973.* Cambridge: Cambridge University Press.

Rizzo, F. P. 2002. "Cesare 'hemitheos,'" *Annali della Facoltà di Lettere e Filosofia* 35, 613–20.

Robert, J. A. and Gaines J.F. 1979. "Kyd and Garnier: the art of amendment," *Comparative Literature* 31, 124–33.

Roberto, U. (ed., intro., and trans.) *Ioannis Antiocheni Fragmenta ex Historia chronica.* Texte und Untersuchungen 154. Berlin/New York: Walter de Gruyter, 2005.

Roller, M. 2004. "Exemplarity in Roman culture: the cases of Horatius Cocles and Cloelia," *CP* 99, 1–56.

Rose, C. B. 1997. *Dynastic Commemoration and Imperial Portraiture in the Julio-Claudian Period.* Cambridge: Cambridge University Press.

Rose, M. 1992. "Conjuring Caesar: ceremony, history, and authority in 1599," in Linda Woodbridge and Edward Berry (eds.), *True Rites and Maimed Rites.* Urbana/Chicago: University of Illinois Press.

Rosenstein, N. 1990. *Imperatores Victi: Military Defeat and Aristocratic Competition in the Middle and Late Republic.* Berkeley: University of California Press.

Rosenstein, N. 2004. *Rome at War: Farms, Families, and Death in the Middle Republic.* Chapel Hill: University of North Carolina Press.

Rosenstein, N. 2006a. "Aristocratic Values," in Nathan Rosenstein and Robert Morstein-Marx (eds.), *The Blackwell Companion to the Roman Republic.* Oxford: Blackwell, pp. 365–83.

Rosenstein, N. 2006b. "War and peace, fear and reconciliation at Rome," in Kurt Raaflaub (ed.), *War, Peace, and Reconciliation in the Ancient World.* Oxford: Blackwell, pp. 226–44.

Rosenstein, N. 2007. "The aristocracy and war," in Paul Erdkamp (ed.), *The Blackwell Companion to the Roman Army.* Oxford: Blackwell, pp. 132–47.

Rosenstein, N and Morstein-Marx R. (eds.). 2006c. *A Companion to the Roman Republic.* Malden, MA/Oxford: Blackwell.

Rosner-Siegel, J. A. 1983. "The oak and the lightning: Lucan, *Bellum Civile* 1. 135–57," *Athenaeum* 61, 165–77.

Rossi, A. 2003. *Contexts of War: Manipulation of Genre in Virgilian Battle Narrative.* Ann Arbor: University of Michigan Press.

Roth, J. P. 2006. "Siege narrative in Livy: representation and reality," in S. Dillon and K. E. Welch (eds.), *Representations of War in Ancient Rome.* New York: Cambridge University Press, pp. 49–67.

Rotondi, G. 1966. *Leges Publicae Populi Romani: elenco cronologico con una introduzione sull'attività legislativa dei comizi romani.* Hildesheim: Georg Olms.

Rousseau, J. J. 1969 "Mémoire présenté a M. de Mably sur l'éducation de M. son fils," in his *Oeuvres complètes*, vol. 4. Paris: Gallimard, pp. 1–32.

Rowe, G. O. 1967. "Dramatic structures in Caesar's *Bellum Civile*," *TAPA* 98, 399–414.

Rubinstein, N. 1957. "Il Poliziano e la questione delle origini di Firenze," in *Il Poliziano e il suo tempo.* Florence: Sansoni, pp. 101–10.

Ruebel, J. S. 1996. "Caesar's *Dignitas* and the outbreak of civil war," *Syllecta Classica* 7, 133–41.

Rundle, D. 2002. "Carneades' legacy: the morality of eloquence in the humanist and papalist writings of Pietro del Monte," *English Historical Review* 117, 284–305.

Rüpke, J. 1992. "Wer las Caesars *bella* als *commentarii*?" *Gymnasium* 99, 201–26.

Russell, D. A. 1973. *Plutarch.* London: Duckworth.

Sabbadini, R. 1905. *Le scoperte dei codici latini e greci ne' secoli XIV e XV*, 2 vols. Florence: Sansoni.

Sacks, K. S. 1990. *Diodorus Siculus and the First Century.* Princeton, NJ: Princeton University Press.

Salutati, C. 1891–1911. *Epistolario*, ed. F. Novati, 4 vols. Rome: Istituto Storico Italiano.

Santangelo, G. 1954. *Le epistole "De Imitatione" di Giovanfrancesco Pico della Mirandola e di Pietro Bembo.* Florence: Olschki.

Scardigli, B. (ed.). 1995. *Essays on Plutarch's Lives.* Oxford: Clarendon Press.

Scarola, M. 1987. "Il muro di Avaricum: lettura di Cesare, *B.G.* 7,23," *Materiali e discussioni per l'analisi dei testi classici* 18, 183–204.

Schadee, H. 2008a. "*Caesarea Laus*: Ciriaco d'Ancona praising Caesar to Leonardo Bruni," *Renaissance Studies*, 22, 435–49.

Schadee, H. 2008b. "Caesar's construction of Northern Europe: inquiry, contact, and corruption in *De Bello Gallico*," *Classical Quarterly* 58, 158–80.

Schäfer, T. 1989. *Imperii Insignia, Sella Curulis und Fasces.* Mainz: Von Zabern.

Schanzer, E. 1963. *The Problem Plays of Shakespeare.* London: Routledge and Kegan Paul.

Scheid J. 1998. *Commentarii fratrum Arvalium qui supersunt.* Rome: Ec. fr. de Rome.

Scheid, J. with P. Tassiani and J. Rüpke. 1998. *Recherches archéologiques à la Magliana. Commentarii Fratrum Arvalium qui supersunt. Les copies épigraphiques des protocoles annuels de la confrérie arvale (21 av.–304 ap. J.-C.).* Roma Antica 4. Rome: École française de Rome and Soprintendenza Archeologica di Roma.

Schenk von Stauffenberg, A. 1931. *Römische Kaisergeschichte bei Malalas. Griechischer Text der Bücher IX–XII und Untersuchungen.* Stuttgart: Kohlhammer.

Schiesaro, A. 2003. *The Passions in Play: Thyestes and the Dynamics of Senecan Drama.* Cambridge: Cambridge University Press.

Schild, G. 2007. "Res Publica Americana. Romrezeption und Verfassungsdenken zur Zeit der Amerikanischen Revolution," *Historische Zeitschrift* 284.1, 31–59.

Schmidt, J. D. 1780. *Kurzgefaßte teutsche Kaiser- und Reichshistorie aus bewährten Schriftstellern zusammengetragen, und seinen Zuhörern zu ihren Wiederhohlungen gewidmet*. Vienna: Johann Thomas Edler von Trattner.

Schmidt-Chazan, M. 1980. "Les traductions de la 'Guerre des Gaules' et le sentiment national au moyen âge," *Annales de Bretagne et des pays de l'ouest* 87, 387–407.

Schmitz, V. A. 1987. "Friedrich Leopold Gundolf," in *Badische Biographien*, n.s. 2. Stuttgart: Kohlhammer, pp. 111–13.

Schröder, C. 2002. *"Siècle de Frédéric II" und "Zeitalter der Aufklärung": Epochenbegriffe im geschichtlichen Selbstverständnis der Aufklärung*. Berlin: Duncker & Humblot.

Schwartz, E. 1897. "Die Berichte ueber die catilinarische Verschwoerung," *Hermes* 32, 554–608.

Scott, H. M. (ed.). 1990. *Enlightened Absolutism: Reform and Reformers in Later Eighteenth-Century Europe*. London: Macmillan.

Scouten, A. H. 1978. "*Julius Caesar* and Restoration Shakespeare," *Shakespeare Quarterly* 29, 423–7.

Seager, R. 1979. *Pompey: a Political Biography*. Berkeley: University of California Press.

Seager, R. 2002. *Pompey the Great: a Political Biography*, 2nd edn. Oxford: Blackwell.

Sebesta, J. L. and L. Bonfante (eds.). 1994. *The World of Roman Costume*. Madison: University of Wisconsin Press.

Sedley, D. 1997. "The Ethics of Brutus and Cassius," *JRS*, 87, 41–53.

Seel, O. 1967. *Caesar-Studien*. Stuttgart: Klett.

Semmel, S. 2000. "British radicals and 'Legitimacy': Napoleon in the mirror of history," *Past and Present* 167, 140–75.

Sestito, M. 1978. *"Julius Caesar" in Italia (1726–1974)*. Bari: Adriatica Editrice.

Shackleton Bailey, D. R. 1965. *Cicero's Letters to Atticus*, vol. 1. Cambridge: Cambridge University Press.

Shackleton Bailey, D. R. (trans.). 1978a. *Cicero's Letters to Atticus*. Harmondsworth: Penguin.

Shackleton Bailey, D. R. (trans.). 1978b. *Cicero's Letters to His Friends*, 2 vols. Harmondsworth: Penguin.

Shalhope, R. E. 1990. *The Roots of Democracy: American Thought and Culture, 1760–1800*. Boston: Twayne.

Shapiro, J. 2005. *1599: A Year in the Life of William Shakespeare*. London: Faber and Faber.

Shatzman, I. 1972. "Caesar: An economic biography and its political significance," *Scripta Hierosolymitana* 23, 28–51.

Shaw, C. 1993. *Julius II: The Warrior Pope*. Oxford: Blackwell.

Shifflett, A. 1997. "'How many virtues must I hate?' Katherine Philips and the politics of clemency," *Studies in Philology* 94.1, 103–35.

Simón, F. M. 1996. *Flamen Dialis. El sacerdote de Júpiter en la religion romana*. Madrid: Ediciones Clásicas.

Skinner, Q. 1978. *The Foundations of Modern Political Thought*, 2 vols. Cambridge: Cambridge University Press.

Smilda, H. 1926. *Cassii Dionis Cocceiani historiae Romanorum Index Historicus = Cassii Dionis Cocceiani historiae Romanorum quae supersunt*, ed. U. P. Boissevain, 4. Berlin: Weidemann.

Smith, N. 2003. "After the American *Lebensraum*: 'Empire,' empire and globalization," *Interventions* 5.2: 249–70.

Smith, W. H. C. 2005. *The Bonapartes: the History of a Dynasty.* London: Hambledon.

Sohmer, S. 1999. *Shakespeare's Mystery Play: the Opening of the Globe Theatre 1599.* Manchester/New York: Manchester University Press.

Spannagel, M. 1999. *Exemplaria Principis. Untersuchungen zu Entstehung und Ausstattung des Augustusforums.* Heidelberg: Archäologie und Geschichte.

Spencer, T. J. B. 1957. "Shakespeare and the Elizabethan Romans," *Shakespeare Survey* 10, 27–37.

Spencer, T. J. B. (ed.). 1964. *Shakespeare's Plutarch.* Harmondsworth: Penguin.

Spiegel, G. M. 1993. *Romancing the Past: the Rise of Vernacular Prose Historiography in Thirteenth-Century France.* Berkeley: University of California Press.

Spielvogel, J. 1993. *Amicitia und res publica.* Stuttgart: Franz Steiner.

Spilman, M. 1932. *Cumulative Sentence Building in Latin Historical Narrative.* Berkeley: University of California Press.

Stadter, P. A. 1993. "Caesarian tactics and Caesarian style: *Bell. Civ.* 1.66–70," *CJ* 88, 217–21.

Stadter, P. A. 2005. "Revisiting Plutarch's *Lives of the Caesars*," in A. Pérez Jiménez and F. Titchener (eds.), *Valori letterari delle opere di Plutarco. Studi offerti al Professore Italo Gallo dall' International Plutarch Society.* Málaga: Logan, pp. 419–35.

Stadter, P. A. and L. van der Stockt (eds.) 2002. *Sage and Emperor: Plutarch, Greek Intellectuals, and Roman Power in the Time of Trajan (98–117 A.D.).* Symbolae Facultatis Litterarum Lovaniensis, Series A / 29. Leuven: Leuven University Press.

Stahlmann, I. 1989. "Täter und Gestalter: Caesar und Augustus im Georgekreis," in K. Christ and E. Gabba (eds.), *Römische Geschichte und Zeitgeschichte in der deutschen und italienischen Altertumswissenschaft während des 19. und 20. Jahrhunderts I: Caesar und Augustus.* Como: Biblioteca di Athenaeum, pp. 107–28.

Stanton, G. R. 2003. "Why did Caesar cross the Rubicon?" *Historia* 52, 67–94.

Staveley, E. S. 1954–5 "The conduct of elections during an interregnum," *Historia* 3, 193–211.

Steel, C. 2001. *Cicero, Rhetoric and Empire.* Oxford: Oxford University Press.

Steidle, W. 1951. *Sueton und die antike Biographie.* Munich: Beck.

Stemmer, K. 1978. *Untersuchungen zur Typologie, Chronologie und Ikonographie der Panzerstatuen.* Berlin: Mann.

Stepper, R. 2003. *Augustus et sacerdos. Untersuchungen zum römischen Kaiser als Priester.* Wiesbaden: Franz Steiner.

Stevens, C. E. 1953. "Britain and the *Lex Pompeia Licinia*," *Latomus* 12, 14–21.

Stevenson, T. R. 1998. "The 'divinity' of Caesar and the title *Parens Patriae*," in T. W. Hillard et al. (eds.), *Ancient History in a Modern University*, vol. 1. Grand Rapids: Eerdmans, pp. 257–68.

Stewart, P. 2004. *Roman Art.* Oxford: Oxford University Press.

Stewart, R. 1997. "The jug and *lituus* on republican coin types: ritual symbols and political power," *Phoenix* 51, 170–89.

Stockton, D. 1962. "Cicero and the *Ager Campanus*," *TAPA* 93, 471–89.

Storch, R. H. 1977. "The author of *de Bello Hispaniensi*: a cavalry officer?" *AClass* 20, 201–04.

Storing. 1985. *The Anti-Federalist*, ed. Herbert J. Storing and Murray Dry. Chicago: University of Chicago Press.

Strasburger, H. 1938. *Caesars Eintritt in die Geschichte.* Munich: Neuer Filser.

Strasburger, H. 1953. "Caesar im Urteil der Zeitgenossen," *Historische Zeitschrift* 175, 225–64.

Strasburger, H. 1983. "Livius über Caesar. Unvollständige Überlegungen," in E. Lefèvre and E. Olshausen, *Livius. Werk und Rezeption. Festschrift für Erich Burck zum 80. Geburtstag.* Munich: C. H. Beck, pp. 265–91.

Stromberg, J. R. 2001. "Empire and reaction," *Middle East News Online* (March 14). Downloaded from www.MiddleEastWire.com, March 20, 2004.

Suerbaum, A. 2000. "'Litterae et mores.' Zur Textgeschichte der mittelalterlichen Avian--Kommentare," in Klaus Grubmüller (ed.), *Schulliteratur im späten Mittelalter.* Munich: Fink, pp. 383–434.

Syme, R. 1938a. "The allegiance of Labienus," *JRS* 28, 113–25. Reprinted in *Roman Papers*, vol. 1 (Oxford: Clarendon Press, 1979), pp. 62–75.

Syme, R. 1938b. "Caesar, the Senate and Italy," *PBSR* xiv, 1–31. Reprinted in *Roman Papers*, vol. 1 (Oxford: Clarendon Press, 1979), pp. 88–119.

Syme, R. 1939. *The Roman Revolution.* Oxford: Clarendon Press.

Syme, R. 1950. "A Roman post-mortem: an inquest on the fall of the Roman Republic." Todd Memorial Lecture 3. Sydney: Australasian Medical. Reprinted in *Roman Papers*, vol. 1 (Oxford: Clarendon Press, 1979), pp. 205–17).

Syme, R. 1958a. "Imperator Caesar: a study in imperial nomenclature," *Hist.* 7, 172–88. Reprinted in *Roman Papers*, vol. 1 (Oxford: Clarendon Press, 1979), pp. 361–77.

Syme, R. 1958b. *Tacitus.* Oxford: Oxford University Press.

Syme, R. 1964. *Sallust.* Berkeley/Los Angeles/London: University of California Press.

Syme, R. 1979–91. *Roman Papers*, ed. E. Badian and A. R. Birley, 7 vols. Oxford: Clarendon Press.

Syme, R. 1980a. "Biographers of the Caesars," *MH* 37, 104–28. Reprinted in *Roman Papers*, vol. 3, ed. A. R. Birley (Oxford: Clarendon Press, 1984), pp. 1251–75.

Syme, R. 1980b. "No Son for Caesar?" *Historia* 29, 422–37. Repr. in R. Syme, *Roman Papers*, vol. 3, Oxford 1984, pp. 1236–50.

Syme, R. 1985. "Caesar: drama, legend, history," *New York Review of Books* 32.3, 12–14. Reprinted in *Roman Papers*, vol. 5 (Oxford: Clarendon Press, 1988), pp. 702–7.

Syme, R. 1986. *The Augustan Aristocracy.* Oxford: Clarendon Press.

Syme, R. 1999. *The Provincial at Rome*, ed. A. Birley. Exeter: Exeter University Press.

Tanturli, G. 1988. "La cultura fiorentina volgare del Quattrocento davanti ai nuovi testi greci,". *Medioevo e Rinascimento* 2, 217–43.

Tarver, T. 1996. "Varro, Caesar and the Roman calendar: a study in Late Republican religion," in A. H. Sommerstein (ed.), *Religion and Superstition in Latin Literature*, pp. 39–57. Bari: Levante.

Tasso, T. 1875. *Le prose diverse*, ed. C. Guasti, 2 vols. Florence: Le Monnier.

Tatum, W. J. 1991. "The marriage of Pompey's son to the daughter of Ap. Claudius Pulcher," *Klio* 73, 122–9.

Tatum, W. J. 1999. *The Patrician Tribune: Publius Clodius Pulcher.* Chapel Hill: University of North Carolina Press.

Tatum, W. J. 2006. "The final crisis (69–44)," in Nathan Rosenstein and Robert Morstein-Marx (eds.), *A Companion to the Roman Republic.* Malden, MA/Oxford: Blackwell, pp. 190–211.

Taylor, L. R. 1949. *Party Politics in the Age of Caesar.* Berkeley: University of California Press.

Taylor, L. R. 1960. *The Voting Districts of the Roman Republic.* Papers and Monographs of the American Academy in Rome 20. Rome: American Academy in Rome.

Taylor, L. R. 1968. "The dating of major legislation and elections in Caesar's first consulship," *Historia,* 17, 173–93.

Temkin, O. 1971. *The Falling Sickness: A History of Epilepsy from the Greeks to the Beginnings of Modern Neurology*, 2nd edn, rev. Baltimore: Johns Hopkins University Press.

Temple, N. 2006. "Julius II as second Caesar," in M. Wyke (ed.), *Julius Caesar in Western Culture*. Oxford: Blackwell, pp. 110–27.

Theisen, B. 2006. "The drama in rags: Shakespeare reception in eighteenth-century Germany," *Modern Language Notes* 121.2, 505–13.

Thomas, H. 1991. "Julius Caesar und die Deutschen. Zu Ursprung und Gehalt eines deutschen Geschichtsbewußtseins in der Zeit Gregors VII. und Heinrichs IV.," in Stefan Weinfurter (ed.), *Die Salier und das Reich, vol. 3: Gesellschaftlicher und ideengeschichtlicher Wandel im Reich der Salier.* Sigmaringen: Thorbecke, pp. 245–77.

Thurlow, P. A. 1980. "Augustine's City of God, pagan history and the unity of the Annolied," in *Reading Medieval Studies: Annual Proceedings of the Graduate Centre for Medieval Studies in the University of Reading* VI. Reading: Graduate Centre for Medieval Studies, pp. 44–67.

Torrigian, C. 1998. "The *logos* of Caesar's *Bellum Gallicum*, especially as revealed in its first five chapters," in K. Welch and A. Powell (eds.), *Julius Caesar as Artful Reporter: the War Commentaries as Political Instruments.* London: Duckworth, and Swansea: Classical Press of Wales, pp. 45–60.

Townend, G. B. 1987. "C. Oppius on Julius Caesar," *AJP* 108, 325–42.

Toynbee, J. M. C. 1957. "Portraits of Julius Caesar," *Greece and Rome*, 2nd ser., 4.1, 2–9.

Toynbee, P. 2002. "The last emperor," *Guardian*, September 13: 17.

Treggiari, S. 1991. *Roman Marriage*. Oxford: Clarendon Press.

Trenchard, J. and T. Gordon. 1995. *Cato's Letters, or, Essays on Liberty, Civil and Religious, and Other Important Subjects*, vol. 1. Indianapolis: Liberty Fund.

Tricomi, A. H. 1982. "The dates of the plays of Chapman," *English Literary Renaissance* 12.2, 242–66.

Tricomi, A. H. 1992. "Shakespeare, Chapman, and the Julius Caesar play in Renaissance humanist drama," in Mario A. Di Cesare (ed.), *Reconsidering the Renaissance*. Mediaeval and Renaissance Texts and Studies 93. Binghamton, NY: Center for Medieval and Early Renaissance Studies, pp. 395–412.

Turcan, R. 1977. "César et Dionysos" in R. Tomasson (ed.), *Hommage à la mémoire de Jérome Carcopino*, pp. 317–25. Paris: Les Belles Lettres.

Tyrrell, W. B. 1978. *A Legal and Historical Commentary to Cicero's Oratio Pro C. Rabirio Perduellionis Reo*. Amsterdam: Adolf M. Hakkert.

Uhse, E. 1716. *Der Römisch-Orientalisch-Teutschen Kayser merckwürdiges Leben und Thaten von Julio Cesare an/biß auff ietzige Kayserl. Mjest. Carolum. VI. addurat, deutlich und ausführlich beschrieben, nebst deren beygefügten Portraits und Symbolis.* Leipzig: Friedrich Groschuff.

Ungern-Sternberg, J. 1970. *Untersuchungen zum spätrepublikanischen Notstandsrecht: Senatsconsultum ultimum und hostis-erklärung*. Munich: Verlag C. H. Beck.

Ure, P. (ed.). 1969. Julius Caesar*: A Casebook*. London: Macmillan.

Urso, G. (ed.). 2000. *L'ultimo Cesare. Scritti, riforme, progetti, poteri, congiure.* Rome: "L'Erma" di Bretschneider.

Valla, L. 1981. *Antidotum in Facium*, ed. M. Regoliosi. Padua: Antenore.

Vanggaard, J. H. 1988. *The Flamen*. Copenhagen: Museum Tusculanum Press.

van Hooff, A. J. L. 1974. "The Caesar of the *Bellum Hispaniense*," *Mnemosyne* 27, 123–38.

Van Kley, D. K. 1984. *The Damiens Affair and the Unraveling of the Ancien Régime, 1750–1770*. Princeton, NJ: Princeton University Press.

Velz, J. W. 1971. "Caesar's deafness," *Shakespeare Quarterly* 22, 400–1.

Vessberg, O. 1941. *Studien zur Kunstgeschichte der römischen Republik*. Leipzig: O. Harrassowitz.

Villani, G. 1990–1. *Nuova cronica*, ed. G. Porta, 3 vols. Parma: Guanda.

Viti, P. 1987. "Pier Candido Decembrio," *Dizionario Biografico degli Italiani*, vol. 33, 488–98.

Viti, P. 1992. *Leonardo Bruni e Firenze. Studi sulle lettere pubbliche e private*. Rome: Bulzoni.

Vogt, J. 1938. *Cicero und Sallust über die Catilinarische Verschwörung*. Frankfurt am Main: Verlag Moritz Diesterweg.

Vollenweider, M.-L. 1974. *Die Porträtgemmen der römischen Republik*. Mainz: P. von Zabern.

Volpilhac-Auger, C., P. Andrivet, F. Weil, and C. Courtney. 2000. "Introduction: Considérations sur les causes de la grandeur des romains et de leur décadence," in C. S. de Montesquieu, *Oeuvres complètes de Montesquieu*. Oxford/Naples: Voltaire Foundation/Istituto Italiano per gli studi filosofici, pp. 3–86.

Voltaire, F. M. A. de. 1978a. "Le siècle de Louis XIV," in his *Oeuvres historiques*. Paris: Gallimard, pp. 603–1274.

Voltaire, F. M. A. de. 1978b. "Précis du siècle de Louis XV," in his *Oeuvres historiques*. Paris: Gallimard, pp. 1293–1571.

von Freising, O. 1912. *Chronica, sive Historia de duabus civitatibus*, ed. A. Hofmeister. Hanover/Leipzig: Hahn. Translated and introduced by Charles C. Mierow, *The Two Cities: A Chronicle of Universal History to the Year 1146 A.D.* (New York: Columbia University Press, 1928).

Wace. 1999. *Roman de Brut: A History of the British*, ed., trans., and comm. J. Weiss. Exeter: University of Exeter Press.

Waith, E. M. 1989. "The death of Pompey: English style, French style," in W. R. Elton (ed.), *Shakespeare and Dramatic Tradition*. Newark: University of Delaware Press, pp. 276–85.

Walker, J. C. 1799. *Historical Memoir on Italian Tragedy, from the Earliest Period to the Present Time*. London.

Wallace-Hadrill, A. 1983. *Suetonius*. London: Duckworth.

Wallraff, M., with U. Roberto and K. Pinggéra (eds.). 2007. *Iulius Africanus, Chronographiae: The Extant Fragments*. Die griechischen christlichen Schriftsteller der ersten Jahrhunderte, n.s. 15. Berlin/New York: Walter de Gruyter.

Walsh, P. G. 1961. *Livy, his Historical Aims and Methods*. Cambridge: Cambridge University Press.

Ward, A. 1977. *Marcus Crassus and the Late Roman Republic*. Columbia: University of Missouri Press.

Warde Fowler, W. 1916. "An unnoticed trait in the character of Julius Caesar," *CR* 30.3, 68–71.

Wardle, D. 1997. "'The sainted Julius': Valerius Maximus and the Dictator," *CP* 92, 323–45.

Wardle, D. 2002. "*Deus* or *Divus*: The genesis of Roman terminology for deified emperors and a philosopher's contribution," in G. Clark and T. Rajak (eds.), *Philosophy and Power in the Graeco-Roman World*. Oxford: Oxford University Press, pp. 181–91.

Wardle, D. 2005. "Unimpeachable sponsors of imperial autocracy, or Augustus' dream team (Suetonius *Divus Augustus* 94.8–9 and Dio Cassius 45. 2. 2–4)," *Antichthon* 39, 29–47.

Wardman, A. E. 1967. "Description of personal appearance in Plutarch and Suetonius: the use of statues as evidence," *CQ* 17, 414–20.

Warthen, B. 2003. "The 'long haul' will last longer than Bush presidency; so then what?" *Knight Ridder Tribune News Service*, March 31: 1.

Watson, A. 1974. *Law Making in the Later Roman Republic*. Oxford: Clarendon Press.

Watson, A. 1975. *Rome of the XII Tables: Persons and Property*. Princeton, NJ: Princeton University Press.

Way, A. G. (trans.). 1955. *Caesar: Alexandrian War. African War. Spanish War*. Cambridge, MA: Loeb Classical Library.

Weaver, R. M. 1957. "Review of Amaury de Riencourt, *The Coming Caesars.*" *The Freeman* 7 (October), 61–3.

Weber, Max. 1994a. "Parliament and government in Germany," in Peter Lassman and Ronald Speirs (ed.), *Political Writings.* Cambridge: Cambridge University Press, pp. 130–271.

Weber, Max. 1994b. "The profession and vocation of politics," in Peter Lassman and Ronald Speirs (ed.), *Political Writings.* Cambridge: Cambridge University Press, pp. 309–69.

Weinbrot, H. D. 1978. *Augustus Caesar in "Augustan" England: the Decline of a Classical Norm.* Princeton, NJ: Princeton University Press.

Weinstock, S. 1971. *Divus Julius.* Oxford: Clarendon Press.

Weiss, R.-M., M. Osanna, and T. Schäfer. 2004. *Caesar ist in der Stadt. Die neu entdeckten Marmorbildnisse aus Pantelleria.* Hamburg: Helms-Museum.

Welch, K. 1998. "Caesar and his officers in the Gallic War Commentaries," in K. Welch and A. Powell (eds.), *Julius Caesar as Artful Reporter: The War Commentaries as Political Instruments.* London: Duckworth, and Swansea: Classical Press of Wales, pp. 85–110.

Welch, K. and A. Powell (eds). 1998. *Julius Caesar as Artful Reporter: The War Commentaries as Political Instruments.* London: Duckworth, and Swansea: Classical Press of Wales.

White, P. 1988. "Julius Caesar in Augustan Rome," *Phoenix* 42, 334–56.

Wilentz, S. 2005. *The Rise of American Democracy.* New York: Norton.

Will, W. 1992. *Julius Caesar: Eine Bilanz.* Stuttgart.

Williams, C. A. 1999. *Roman Homosexuality: Ideologies of Masculinity in Classical Antiquity.* Oxford: Oxford University Press.

Williams, J. H. C. 2001. *Beyond the Rubicon: Romans and Gauls in Republican Italy.* Oxford: Oxford University Press.

Wills, G. 1984. *Cincinnatus: George Washington and the Enlightenment.* London: Robert Hale.

Wilson, E. (ed.). 1961. *Shaw on Shakespeare.* London: Cassell and Co.

Wilson, J. 1967a. *The Works of James Wilson*, ed. Robert Green McCloskey, vol. 1. Cambridge: Belknap Press of Harvard University Press.

Wilson, J. 1967b. *The Works of James Wilson*, ed. Robert Green McCloskey, vol. 2. Cambridge: Belknap Press of Harvard University Press.

Wilson, M. 1988. "Republicanism and the idea of party in the Jacksonian period," *Journal of the Early Republic* 8.4, 419–42.

Wilson, M. L. 1995. "The 'country' versus the 'court': A republican consensus and party debate in the Bank War," *Journal of the Early Republic* 15.4, 619–47.

Wilson, P. H. 2004. *From Reich to Revolution: German History, 1558–1806.* Basingstoke: Palgrave Macmillan.

Wilson, R. (ed.). 2002. Julius Caesar*: A New Casebook.* Basingstoke: Palgrave.

Winterbottom, M. 1983. "Caesar," in L. D. Reynolds (ed.), *Texts and Transmission.* Oxford: Oxford University Press, pp. 35–6.

Wiseman, T. P. 1971. *New Men in the Roman Senate, 139 B.C.–A.D. 14.* Oxford: Oxford University Press.

Wiseman, T. P. 1974. "Legendary genealogies in Late Republican Rome," *Greece and Rome* 21, 153–64.

Wiseman, T. P. 1992. "Julius Caesar and the *Mappa Mundi*," in *Talking to Virgil: a Miscellany.* Exeter: University of Exeter Press, pp. 23–42.

Wiseman, T. P. 1993. "Rome and the resplendent Aemilii," in H. D. Jocelyn (ed.), *Tria Lustra: Essays and Notes Presented to John Pinsent.* Liverpool: Liverpool Classical Monthly, pp. 181–92. Repr. in T. P. Wiseman, *Roman Drama and Roman Historiography* (Exeter: University of Exeter Press, 1998), pp. 106–20.

Wiseman, T. P. 1994. "The Senate and the *populares*, 69–60 B.C." and "Caesar, Pompey, and Rome, 59–50 B.C.," in J. A. Crook, A. Lintott, and E. Rawson (eds.), *Cambridge Ancient History, vol. 9: The Last Age of the Roman Republic, 146–43 B.C.* Cambridge: Cambridge University Press, pp. 327–81, pp. 368–423.

Wiseman, T. P. 1998. "The Publication of *De Bello Gallico*," in K. Welch and A. Powell (eds.), *Julius Caesar as Artful Reporter: The War Commentaries as Political Instruments.* London: Duckworth, and Swansea: Classical Press of Wales, pp. 1–9.

Wissowa, G. 1902. *Religion und Kultus der Römer.* Munich: C. H. Beck.

Witt, R. G. 1969. "The *De tyranno* and Coluccio Salutati's view of politics and Roman history," *Nuova Rivista Storica*, 53, 434–74.

Witt, R. G. 1983. *Hercules at the Crossroads: The Life, Works, and Thought of Coluccio Salutati.* Durham, NC: Duke University Press.

Wood, G. S. 1988. "The significance of the Early Republic," *Journal of the Early Republic* 8.1, 1–20.

Wood, G. S. 1998. *The Creation of the American Republic 1776–1787.* Chapel Hill: University of North Carolina Press.

Woodman, A. J. 1977. *Velleius Paterculus: the Tiberian Narrative, 2.94-131.* Cambridge: Cambridge University Press.

Woodman, A. J. 1983. *Velleius Paterculus: the Caesarian and Augustan Narrative (2.41–93).* Cambridge: Cambridge University Press.

Woodman, A. J. 2004. *Tacitus: The Annals.* Indianopolis: Hackett.

Woolf, G. 1988. *Becoming Roman: The Origins of Provincial Civilization in Gaul.* Cambridge: Cambridge University Press.

Woolf, Greg. 2006. *Et tu, Brute? The Murder of Caesar and Political Assassination.* London: Profile Books.

Woolrych, A. 2002. *Britain in Revolution, 1625–1660.* Oxford: Oxford University Press.

Worstbrock, F. J. 1965. "Translatio artium. Über die Herkunft und Entwicklung einerkulturhistorischen Theorie," *Archiv für Kulturgeschichte* 4, 1–22.

Wright, J. K. 1997. *A Classical Republican in Eighteenth-Century France: the Political Thought of Mably.* Stanford, CA: Stanford University Press.

Wünsch, R. 1898. *Joannis Laurentii Lydi liber de mensibus.* Leipzig: Teubner.

Wyatt, Sir Thomas. 1978. *The Complete Poems*, ed. R. A. Rebholz. New Haven, CT/London: Yale University Press.

Wyke, M. 1999. "Sawdust Caesar: Mussolini, Julius Caesar, and the drama of dictatorship," in M. Wyke and M. Biddiss (eds.), *The Uses and Abuses of Antiquity.* Bern/New York: Peter Lang, pp. 167–86.

Wyke, M. 2004. "Film style and fascism: *Julius Caesar*," *Film Studies* 4, 58–74.

Wyke, M. (ed.). 2006. *Julius Caesar in Western Culture.* Malden, MA/Oxford/Carlton, Victoria: Blackwell.

Wyke, M. 2007. *Caesar: a Life in Western Culture.* London: Granta.

Yavetz, Z. 1971. "Caesar, Caesarism, and the historians." *Journal of Contemporary History* 6.2, 184–201.

Yavetz, Z. 1983. *Julius Caesar and his Public Image.* London: Thames & Hudson.

Zander, H. (ed.). 2006. *Julius Caesar: New Critical Essays.* New York/London: Routledge.

Zanker, P. 1968. *Forum Augustum. Das Bildprogramm.* Tübingen o. J.: Wasmuth.

Zanker, P. 1981. "Das Bildnis des Holconius Rufus," *Archäologischer Anzeigen*, 349–61.

Zanker, P. 1982. "Herrscherbild und Zeitgesicht," in *Römisches Porträt. Wege zur Erforschung eines gesellschaftlichen Phänomens. Wissenschaftliche Konferenz 12.-15. Mai 1981.*

Wissenschaftliche Zeitschrift der Humboldt-Universität zu Berlin. Gesellschafts- und Sprachwissenschaftliche Reihe 31, 2–3. Berlin: Humboldt-Universität, pp. 307–12.

Zanker, P. 1988. *The Power of Images in the Age of Augustus*, trans. A. Shapiro. Jerome Lectures 16. Ann Arbor: University of Michigan Press. Original published as *Augustus und die Macht der Bilder* (Munich: Beck, 1987).

Zarrow, E. M. 2007. "The image and memory of Julius Caesar between Triumvirate and Principate (44BCE–CE 14)." Dissertation, Yale University.

Zecchini, G. 1990. "Costantino e i 'Natales Caesarum,'" *Historia* 39, 349–60.

Zecchini, G. 2001. *Cesare e il mos maiorum*. Stuttgart: Steiner Verlag.

Zimmermann, J. G. von. 1790. *Fragmente über Friedrich den Grossen zur Geschichte seines Lebens, seiner Regierung, und seines Charakters*. Leipzig: Weidmannsche Buchhandlung.

Zumpt, A. W. 1874. *De Dictatoris Caesaris die et anno natali*. Berlin: Hayn.

Index

For 16th–18th c. plays and operas about Caesar, their authors and dates, see Appendix to chapter 25, pp. 392–396

For Roman names in 'J', see under 'I', except for Julian, Julius Celsus Constantinus, Jupiter, Juvenal